MICROPROCESSORS AND MICROCOMPUTER DEVELOPMENT SYSTEMS

MICROPROCESSORS AND MICROCOMPUTER DEVELOPMENT SYSTEMS

Designing Microprocessor-Based Systems

MOHAMED RAFIQUZZAMAN

California State Polytechnic University
Pomona

HARPER & ROW, PUBLISHERS, New York
Cambridge, Philadelphia, San Francisco,
London, Mexico City, São Paulo, Sydney

Sponsoring Editor: John Willig
Project Editor: David Nickol
Designer: T. R. Funderburk
Production: Delia Tedoff
Compositor: Science Press
Printer and Binder: R. R. Donnelley & Sons Company
Art Studio: Vantage Art, Inc.

MICROPROCESSORS AND MICROCOMPUTER DEVELOPMENT SYSTEMS:
DESIGNING MICROPROCESSOR-BASED SYSTEMS

Copyright © 1984 by Harper & Row, Publishers, Inc.

All rights reserved. Printed in the United States of America. No part of this book may be used or reproduced in any manner whatsoever without written permission, except in the case of brief quotations embodied in critical articles and reviews. For information address Harper & Row, Publishers, Inc., 10 East 53d Street, New York, NY 10022.

Library of Congress Cataloging in Publication Data

Rafiquzzaman, Mohamed.
   Microprocessors and microcomputer development systems.

  1. System design. 2. Microprocessors. 3. Microcomputers. I. Title.
QA76.9.S88R33   1984   001.64   83-12626
ISBN 0-06-045312-5

CONTENTS

Preface xiii

1. INTRODUCTION TO MICROCOMPUTER DEVELOPMENT SYSTEMS AND MICROPROCESSOR-BASED DESIGN 1

   1.1 Basic Features 1

   1.2 System Development Flowchart 7
       1.2.1 Software Development 7
       1.2.2 Hardware Development 9
       1.2.3 Diagnostic Design 10

   1.3 Designing Hardware and Software for a Specific Application 10
       1.3.1 Software Development 11
       1.3.2 Hardware 12
       1.3.3 Diagnostic 12

2. MICROCOMPUTER FUNDAMENTALS 13

   2.1 Introduction to Microprocessor Systems 13
       2.1.1 A Basic Microprocessor System 14
       2.1.2 Programs 15
       2.1.3 Input/Output 15
       2.1.4 Memories 18
       2.1.5 Minicomputers and Microcomputers 22

   2.2 Number Systems and Boolean Logic 22
       2.2.1 Decimal and Binary 22
       2.2.2 Octal 23
       2.2.3 Hexadecimal 23

2.2.4 Bit Position Terminology 24
2.2.5 Basic Boolean Operations 24
2.2.6 Arithmetic and Logic Operations 26
2.2.7 Number Representations 27

2.3 Software Fundamentals 33
2.3.1 The Microcomputer as a Logic Device 33
2.3.2 Flowcharts 34
2.3.3 Programming Languages 35

Problems and Questions 41

3. MICROCOMPUTER SYSTEM HARDWARE AND I/O TECHNIQUES 43

3.1 Basic Hardware Concepts 43
3.1.1 The Bus Concept 43
3.1.2 The Three-State Bus 44
3.1.3 The System Bus 47
3.1.4 Input and Output Ports 50
3.1.5 Address Decoding for Multiple Devices and Memories 51

3.2 Address Decoding 55
3.2.1 The Address Decoder 55
3.2.2 Linear Select Decoding 58
3.2.3 Logic Comparator Decoding 58
3.2.4 Combinational Logic Decoding 59
3.2.5 I/O Mapped Decoding 60

3.3 Memories and Peripherals 60
3.3.1 Types of Memories 60
3.3.2 ROMs and RAMs 61

3.4 Typical Microprocessor I/O Techniques 63

Problems and Questions 63

4. TYPICAL 8-BIT MICROPROCESSORS AND MICROCOMPUTERS 65

4.1 Intel 8085 66
4.1.1 Introduction 66
4.1.2 8085 Pins and Signals 68
4.1.3 The Instruction Cycle and Execution 70
4.1.4 Machine Cycles 72
4.1.5 Program Execution 72
4.1.6 Review of 8085 Instruction Set 72
4.1.7 Subroutines and Stack 83
4.1.8 Mathematical Algorithms 85

4.2 Intel 8048 Microcomputer   99
    4.2.1 Introduction   99
    4.2.2 Instruction Set   102
    4.2.3 Addressing Modes   105
    4.2.4 I/O Capability   105

4.3 Zilog Z80   109
    4.3.1 Introduction   109
    4.3.2 Addressing Modes   111
    4.3.3 Instruction Set   112
    4.3.4 Input/Output   125

4.4 Motorola 6800   127
    4.4.1 Introduction   127
    4.4.2 Addressing Modes   127
    4.4.3 Instruction Set   129
    4.4.4 I/O Capability   129

4.5 Motorola 6809   133
    4.5.1 Introduction   133
    4.5.2 Addressing Modes   135
    4.5.3 Instruction Set   136
    4.5.4 I/O Capability   139

Problems and Questions   141

5. 8085 INPUT/OUTPUT   145

5.1 8085 Programmed I/O   145
    5.1.1 8355/8755 I/O Ports   146
    5.1.2 8155 I/O Ports   146

5.2 8085 Interrupt System   150
    5.2.1 TRAP   150
    5.2.2 RST7.5   150
    5.2.3 RST6.5   151
    5.2.4 RST5.5   151
    5.2.5 INTR   151

5.3 8085 DMA   160

5.4 8085 SID and SOD Lines   161

Problems and Questions   162

6. INTEL 8086 AND ZILOG Z8000   165

6.1 Intel 8086   166
    6.1.1 8086 Architecture   168

        6.1.2 Addressing Modes   173
        6.1.3 Instruction Set   174
        6.1.4 Input/Output   180
        6.1.5 8086 CPU Pins and Signals   183

  6.2 Zilog Z8000   188
        6.2.1 Z8000 CPU Organization   188
        6.2.2 Register Architecture   190
        6.2.3 Addressing Modes   193
        6.2.4 Instruction Set   194
        6.2.5 Interrupts   206
        6.2.6 Z8000 Pins and Signals   206
        6.2.7 A Typical Z8000 System   209

  Problems and Questions   213

7. MOTOROLA 68000 AND INTEL 432   215

  7.1 Motorola 68000   215
        7.1.1 Processor Architecture   216
        7.1.2 Addressing Modes   219
        7.1.3 Instruction Set   223
        7.1.4 68000 Pins and Signals   227
        7.1.5 68000 System Diagram   232
        7.1.6 68000 Byte Addressing   232
        7.1.7 System Features   232
        7.1.8 Looping   244
        7.1.9 68000 Peripheral Circuits   245
        7.1.10 Interfacing the 68000 to the
                6846 ROM I/O Timer (RIOT)   246

  7.2 Intel 432   250
        7.2.1 General Data Processors (GDP)—
              iAPX43201 and iAPX43202   252
        7.2.2 Interface Processor (IP)—iAPX43203   268
        7.2.3 432 Operating System—iMAX   278
        7.2.4 432 Applications   278
        7.2.5 Conclusion   279

  Problems and Questions   279

8. TYPICAL MICROPROCESSOR INTERFACE CHIPS   281

  8.1 Typical ROM/EPROM, RAM, and I/O Chips   281
        8.1.1 Intel 2716 EPROM   282
        8.1.2 Intel 8355/8755 ROM/EPROM with I/O   284
        8.1.3 Intel 8155/8156 RAM with I/O and Timer   288

8.2 Typical Serial I/O Interface Chips 299
    8.2.1 Motorola 6850 Asynchronous Communications Interface Adapter (ACIA) 300

8.3 Keyboard/Display Controller Chips 309
    8.3.1 Intel 8279 Keyboard/Display Controller Chip 312

8.4 Direct Memory Access (DMA) Controller Chips 328
    8.4.1 Intel 8257 DMA Controller 331

Problems and Questions 339

9. FUNDAMENTALS OF MICROCOMPUTER DEVELOPMENT SYSTEMS 341

9.1 Basic Features 341
    9.1.1 Hardware 342
    9.1.2 Operating Systems and Debugging Techniques 345

9.2 Software Development Aids 350
    9.2.1 Editors 351
    9.2.2 Assemblers 354
    9.2.3 Disassembly 362
    9.2.4 Linkers 364
    9.2.5 Loaders 365
    9.2.6 Command Files 365
    9.2.7 High-Level Language Compilers 366
    9.2.8 Interpreters 366
    9.2.9 Monitors 366
    9.2.10 Operating Systems 367

9.3 Operator Consoles for Microcomputer Development Systems 367

9.4 Mass Storage for Microcomputer Development Systems 369
    9.4.1 No Storage 369
    9.4.2 Paper Tape 369
    9.4.3 Cassette Tape 369
    9.4.4 Flexible Disk 369
    9.4.5 Hard Disk 370

9.5 Development System Architectures 370
    9.5.1 Master/Slave System 370
    9.5.2 Single-Processor System 371

9.6. Debugging and Integration 372
    9.6.1 In-Circuit Emulators 372
    9.6.2 Debugger 373
    9.6.3 Debugging with Emulation 373
    9.6.4 Debugging in Real Time 375
    9.6.5 Getting It All Together 376

9.7 High-Level Languages with Microprocessors   377
    9.7.1 BASIC   378
    9.7.2 PL/M   379
    9.7.3 COBOL   380
    9.7.4 Pascal   380

Problems and Questions   385

10. POPULAR MICROCOMPUTER DEVELOPMENT SYSTEMS   387

10.1 Hewlett-Packard HP 64000   388

10.2 Intel Development Systems   388
    10.2.1 Intel Models 120 and 225   390
    10.2.2 Intel MDS Model 286   392
    10.2.3 Intel Network Development System I (NDS I)—Model 290   394
    10.2.4 The Intellec Mainframe Link (IML)   397

10.3 Tektronix Development Systems   414
    10.3.1 Tektronix 8001 Microprocessor Development Lab (MDL)   414
    10.3.2 Tektronix 8002A   417
    10.3.3 Tektronix 8500 Series MDL   420

10.4 GenRad Systems   439
    10.4.1 2300 Stand-Alone Software   440

Problems and Questions   456

11. THE HEWLETT-PACKARD (HP) 64000   457

11.1 System Description   457

11.2 Development Station Description   458

11.3 Getting Started   460
    11.3.1 Powering Up   460
    11.3.2 Loading System Software   460
    11.3.3 Soft Keys   461
    11.3.4 Special Functions Keys   462

11.4 Editor   462
    11.4.1 Using the Editor   464

11.5 The HP 64000 Assembler   466
    11.5.1 Assembler Commands   466
    11.5.2 64000 Macros   468

11.5.3 Using Assembler Pseudos   474
11.5.4 Examples of Some Common
        Errors and Their Results   477

11.6 HP 64000 Linker   484
    11.6.1 Linker Initialization   485

11.7 HP 64000 Emulator   486
    11.7.1 Emulation Equipment   486
    11.7.2 Analysis   486
    11.7.3 Symbolic Debug   487
    11.7.4 64000 Emulation Architecture   487
    11.7.5 Emulation with a Different Processor   487
    11.7.6 Beginning the Emulation Session   490

11.8 Command Files   493
    11.8.1 Simple Command File Example   494
    11.8.2 Another Command File Example   494
    11.8.3 Command File Example: Passing Parameters   495

11.9 Simulated I/O   495

11.10 64000 Examples Demonstrating the Software
                    and Hardware Development on Typical Systems   496
    11.10.1 64000 Boot Up   496

    Problems and Questions   542

12. DESIGN PROBLEMS   545

12.1 Design Problem No. 1   545
    12.1.1 Problem Statement   545
    12.1.2 Solution to Design Problem No. 1   546

12.2 Design Problem No. 2   560
    12.2.1 Problem Statement   560
    12.2.2 Solution to Design Problem No. 2   560
    12.2.3 Methodology   571
    12.2.4 Results   571
    12.2.5 Conclusion   572

12.3 Design Problem No. 3   575
    12.3.1 Problem Statement   575
    12.3.2 Solution to Design Problem No. 3   575
    12.3.3 System Hardware Description   576
    12.3.4 System Software Description   584

    Problems and Questions   592

APPENDIX A 8085 Instruction Set   597
APPENDIX B The Intel 8279   620
APPENDIX C 8085-Based Microcomputer—
            The HP 5036A Schematic   633
APPENDIX D HP64000   Miscellaneous Information   637
APPENDIX E Miscellaneous Program Listings   650

Bibliography   675
Index   677

PREFACE

Microprocessors are used extensively these days in a wide range of applications. These typically include process control, communication systems, digital instruments, electronic games, and home applications. Therefore, it is absolutely necessary for computer engineers and scientists to be able to design microprocessor-based systems for various applications at the chip level. A microcomputer development system is used as a tool for designing hardware and software for such microprocessor-based applications.

The aim of this book is to familiarize the readers with the basic concepts of typical 8-, 16-, and 32-bit microprocessors, interface chips, and microcomputer development systems necessary to design and develop hardware and software for microprocessor-based applications. A step-by-step procedure for designing applications using a typical development system is also covered. A number of examples that are derived from practical applications have been provided in simplified form.

The book is self-contained and includes such topics as microcomputer architecture and programming. The book assumes a background in basic digital logic. An elementary course in microprocessors would be helpful but not essential since the book contains a number of basic topics. These basic materials are included so that the book can be used for professional reference.

The author has chosen to emphasize the characteristics and principles common to all microcomputer development systems, relating them by means of laboratory exercises involving a specific system with a particular microprocessor. The Hewlett-Packard (HP) 64000 and Intel 8085 are used for this purpose. The HP 64000 is used in this book to demonstrate the characteristics of a typical development system for the following reasons:

1. The 64000 is the only system in the market which provides soft key features, hence it is easy to work with.
2. The 64000 is universal and multiterminal-based.
3. The 64000 provides the typical development system features such as editors, compilers, assemblers, linker, emulators, debuggers, and logic analyzers.

This book illustrates the microprocessor-based system design at the chip level using the Intel 8085 and its support chips, and provides a thorough step-by-step design procedure for designing a system for a specific application. The author feels that once the reader understands the development system concepts using the 64000, it will be quite easy to carry out microprocessor-based design using any other development system and any microprocessor.

The book is divided into twelve chapters. Chapter 1 provides, from an introductory point of view, the basic features of development systems and their role in designing hardware and software for microprocessor-based products. Chapters 2 through 4 include typical microcomputer architecture and programming, and hardware concepts that relate them to the Intel 8085. Chapter 5 contains 8085 I/O techniques. These I/O concepts are used extensively in developing the 8085-based systems in Chapters 10 and 11. Chapters 6 and 7 discuss typical 8-, 16-, and 32-bit microprocessors. Chapter 8 provides a thorough discussion on typical microprocessor interface chips. These include ROM, EPROM, RAM, I/O, keyboard, and DMA controller chips. Chapter 9 includes the fundamentals of microcomputer development systems. These include editors, compilers, assemblers, linkers, emulators, and logic analyzers. Chapter 10 provides an overview of the popular development systems. These include Intel, Tektronix, GenRad (formerly Futuredata), and Hewlett-Packard. A thorough coverage of the theory and operation of a specific development system such as the 64000 is given in Chapter 11. A systematic procedure for developing hardware and software for 8085-based systems using the HP 64000 is given in Chapter 12.

The book can be used in a number of ways. It can easily be adopted as a text for an undergraduate level one-quarter or one-semester course in microprocessor-based design in a two- or four-year engineering, computer science, or engineering technology program. The students are expected to have a background in digital logic and be familiar with Boolean algebra, K maps, basic transistor and MOS devices, and so on. The book can also be used by industrial personnel who wish to upgrade their knowledge of microprocessors, microcomputer development systems, and design techniques.

The author wishes to extend his sincere appreciation to Keith Guerrin and Scott Stuteville of Hewlett-Packard, Jim Holman of Disneyland, John McIntyre of Tektronix, Tom McKann of GenRad, Jeff Moritz of Beckman Instruments, and my students S. Kitagawa, Dave Johnson, Tom Pollard, and others for reviewing the manuscript and making valuable comments. The author would also like to thank Intel, Hewlett-Packard, Tektronix, GenRad, Advanced Micro Devices, Motorola, and Zilog for their kind permission to reprint the various diagrams, tables, and programs found throughout the text. My sponsoring Editor, John Willig, and Project Editor, David Nickol, of Harper & Row have done an outstanding job in bringing this book to publication.

I am indebted to Dr. W. C. Miller of the University of Windsor, Canada, and the Honorable Sam Bretzfield, Consul General of Bangladesh, for their support and inspiration throughout the writing effort.

The author would like to thank Christi Camp for typing this manuscript and its revisions.

I dedicate this book to three of my favorite relatives—my grandfather, the late Mr. Mir Ali, my father-in-law, the late Mr. Shamsul Huq, and my brother-in-law, the late Mr. Marghoob Hasan. I will always remember them for their continual inspiration during the preparation of this manuscript.

Finally, I am also grateful to my parents, my wife, Reba, my son, Tito, and my brothers and sisters for their infinite patience and support.

Mohamed Rafiquzzaman

MICROPROCESSORS AND MICROCOMPUTER DEVELOPMENT SYSTEMS

CHAPTER 1

INTRODUCTION TO MICROCOMPUTER DEVELOPMENT SYSTEMS AND MICROPROCESSOR-BASED DESIGN

The efficient development of microprocessor-based systems necessitates the use of a microcomputer development system. The microcomputer development system is used for the design, debugging, and sometimes the documentation of a microprocessor-based system. This introductory chapter will cover the attributes of typical microcomputer development systems as well as the methods used to design and debug some specific microprocessor applications.

1.1 Basic Features

When the first 4- and 8-bit microprocessors appeared on the market, the hardware costs associated with a microprocessor system were so high that the labor costs (logic design, software, debug, etc.) were of lesser impact on the total project cost. With the constant decreasing cost of new microprocessor components, the labor costs of developing new products have taken on a more significant role. The microcomputer development system's main function is to simplify the product development stage and therefore obtain the maximum efficiency from the design team, whether it be a single engineer or a large team.

Development systems allow the parallel design of hardware and software so that the design can be tested and debugged before any actual hardware simulations occur. Some development systems allow the simulation of software without any of the final hardware being available to the software engineer.

Development systems fall into one of two categories: systems supplied by the device manufacturer and systems built by after-market manufacturers. The main difference between the two categories is the range of microprocessors that a system will accommodate. Systems supplied by the device manufacturer (Intel, Motorola, RCA, etc.) are limited to use for the particular chip set manufactured by the supplier. In this manner, an Intel development system may not be used to develop a Motorola-based system. The other category contains systems that are more universal in usage. Software and emulation hardware is available for the universal systems (Tektronix, Hewlett-Packard, AMI, etc.) to develop most of the popular microprocessors.

Within both categories of development systems, there are basically three types available: single-user systems, time-shared systems, and networked systems. A single-user system consists of one development station that can be used by one user at a time. Single user systems are low in cost and may be sufficient for small systems development. Time-shared systems usually consist of a "dumb" type terminal connected by data lines to a centralized microcomputer-based system that controls all operations. A networked system usually consists of a number of smart Cathode Ray Tubes (CRTs) capable of performing most of the development work and can be connected over data lines to a larger central computer. The central computer in a network system usually is in charge of allocating disk storage space and will download some programs into the user's work station computer. The networked development systems are becoming more popular because they allow more throughput of data which allows the user to develop the programs faster and easier. The cost per station of networked systems is less than that of the single-user system as the number of stations increases.

A microcomputer development system is a combination of the hardware necessary for microprocessor design and the software to control the hardware. The basic components of the hardware are the central processor, the CRT terminal, mass storage device (floppy or hard disk), and usually an In-Circuit Emulator (ICE).

The central processor is the heart of the development system. Whether a microprocessor in a single-user system or a large processor in a time-shared multiuser system, the central processor is responsible for the overall control of the development system. In a single-user system, the central processor executes the operating system software, handles the Input/Output (I/O) facilities, executes the development programs (editor, assembler, linker, etc.), and allocates storage space for the programs in execution. In a large multiuser networked system the central processor may be responsible for mass storage allocation while a local processor may be responsible for the I/O facilities and execution of development programs.

The CRT terminal provides the interface between the user and the operating system or program under execution. The user enters commands or data via the CRT keyboard and the program under execution displays data to the user via the CRT screen. In early development systems, CRTs were not used and a mechanical teletype was used to communicate with the development system. The current CRTs communicate with the operating system at speeds in excess of ten times the speed of the old teletypes. The CRT of a single-user system may be connected directly to the central processor while CRTs in time-shared systems may be connected to remote computers via phone lines (using modems).

A disk drive of some kind is necessary for mass storage of user data. Some of the current complex operating systems and high-level development programs require large amounts of system Random Access Memory (RAM) to operate and little memory is left available for user data such as source code for the program under development. For this reason, the operating system must allocate the available memory and store unused portions of the program on a disk. A common technique for memory management is the use of *overlay* files. An overlay is a portion of a program that is not always needed and is therefore not kept in the limited RAM space. When the overlay is needed, it is read from the disk and overlays another program in memory that is no longer needed. The use of overlays and other memory management techniques allows the use of complex programs that would otherwise not be available for use on the smaller computers in popular use today. The user's files, such as source code, are also stored on the disk.

Most of the single-user systems use a flexible (floppy) disk for mass storage while the time-shared and networked systems tend to use a hard disk for mass storage. Cost and performance are directly related in the disk systems. The cost of flexible disk systems is low but the storage capability is also low. The access time of a flexible disk (the delay time before the data are available after they have been requested) is also slow compared with hard disks or standard memory. The access time of a hard disk is much shorter than a flexible disk and the storage capability is much greater, but the higher cost of a hard disk system may be prohibitive to a small user. If a hard disk system is purchased, the price can usually be returned in decreased development times.

The ICE is an invaluable tool that turns a general-purpose computer into a development system. The ICE is a hardware circuit that connects the development system to the microprocessor (target) system under development. The ICE plugs into the target system in place of the microprocessor and is electrically and functionally identical to the target microprocessor. By controlling the ICE, the development system may execute test programs for the microprocessor under development. While the ICE is operating the target system, the development system may display parameters (such as register contents). By using an ICE, the program may be debugged in the development system RAM rather than having to be programmed into a Read-Only Memory (ROM) and inserted into the target system. Breakpoints (program locations where the designer wishes to halt the program and examine the program status) may be set with an ICE and the user may examine the progress of a program and then restart the program from the same point if necessary. An error in a program may be changed in RAM in a matter of seconds while the process of programming a new Programmable Read-Only Memory (PROM) may take several minutes of expensive development time. As the target systems get more complex in their hardware configurations and software, the ICE becomes an indispensable tool for microprocessor development.

The equipment listed above comprises a basic development system but most systems have other devices such as printers and PROM programmers attached. A printer is needed to provide the user with a hard copy record of the program under development. Many simple programs may be developed completely on the CRT but a printer is needed to provide the documentation necessary for advanced program development. After a program has been fully debugged and tested, the PROM programmer is used to load the machine code into a PROM for final prototype testing. Figure 1.1 shows a typical development system.

The hardware for a development system is necessary, but would be useless without the proper development software. As the developments become more and more advanced, the operating systems remove many of the routine tasks from the user, making the user's time more productive. Many development systems are self-promoting, freeing the user from the responsibility of looking up commands and procedures in operating manuals.

The main programs necessary to microprocessor development are the operating system, editor, assembler, linker, compiler, and debugger.

The operating system is responsible for executing the user's commands. The operating system (such as CP/M, MP/M, UNIX, etc.) handles I/O functions, memory management, and loading of programs from mass

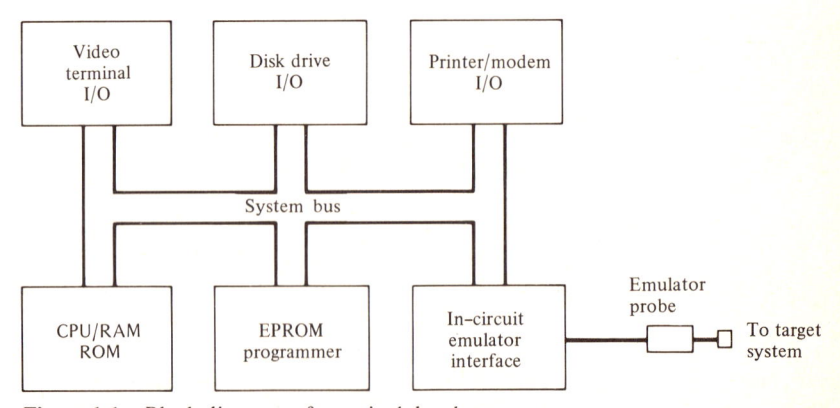

Figure 1.1 Block diagram of a typical development system.

storage into RAM for execution. The larger the development system, the larger and more capable the operating system.

The editor is used to develop the user's program. Whether the program is in assembly language or a high-level language such as PASCAL, the program must first be entered into the development system via an editor. The editor allows the user to enter and edit the source code; single characters or entire lines can be inserted or deleted from the source code.

Early editors allowed only one line at a time to be edited and were therefore called *line* editors. The line to be edited was first specified and then special commands used to alter the contents of the line.

Most current editors are *context* editors where a section of source code is shown on the CRT in real time. The source code is shown completely on the CRT and is therefore in context, which is how the name was coined. As an edit is made to the source code, the change is displayed immediately on the CRT. Instead of using complex command to edit the source code, simple cursor movement commands allow the user to point to the section of source code to be modified. When the cursor is positioned, the new text may be entered. Many editors allow *block* operations where many lines or even entire files may be moved to other locations or duplicated.

After the source code has been generated, it must be converted to hex (object) code that may be executed by the target processor. Assembly language source code is converted by an assembler while high-level language source code is converted by a compiler.

An assembler translates the ASCII character data that are entered under the editor into the object or hex code used by the target microprocessor. In addition to standard assembly language instructions, the assembler will recognize special commands called *pseudoinstructions*. A pseudoinstruction is a command that is entered along with the assembly language, but is recognized by the assembler to generate special formats or data during the assembly. For example, an ORG statement is used to set the starting address or origin of the program. Pseudoinstructions exist that allow the user to put titles on each page of the listing, format the listing for easier reading, insert data tables into a program, set program symbols, and so on.

Many current assemblers have *macro* capability. A macro is a set of assembly language instructions that is specially marked in the source code. The macro is given a name that is called whenever the user wishes to execute that same set of assembly language commands. The difference between a macro and a standard assembly language CALL command is that the macro is a function of the assembler only and when it is used, it is not a subroutine (which is a set of instructions with RET command), but is duplicate code actually inserted into the final object code. Macros can be used to save typing time because repetitious code does not have to be retyped over and over.

Most current assemblers used are *two-pass* assemblers. They operate by making two passes over the source code to generate the object code. The first pass will collect all the labels and symbols used by the program and assign addresses and values to them as needed and put them into a large table. The second pass generates the actual object code and refers to the table whenever a label is found to obtain the address or data to use in place of the label. Early generation assemblers were of a single-pass type and made the use of labels more difficult because a label had to be defined in the source code before it could be used, making jumps and references to code that would occur later in the source code very inconvenient.

The linker is used to combine separate programs (or even a single program if that is all that exists) into a final operating program. Linkers are commonly used when many different designers are working on a program and each designer is writing one section of the program. When each individual program is written and has been successfully assembled, the linker takes all the individual programs, makes any address changes necessary to make the programs fit together, and produces a final program that executes at the address specified during *linking*. In this manner a section of code may be written and debugged to operate at a particular address and then linked together with other programs to actually execute at a different address. The output of the linker is called absolute code and is the actual machine code for the target machine.

The debugger provides an invaluable method for interactive execution and testing of the user's program. After the user's program has been assembled and linked, the absolute code is loaded by the debugger.

On some smaller development systems where the central processor is the same as the target system, the absolute code may be loaded and executed on the central processor without the user's hardware. This method is satisfactory for checking out the logic of the program, but it cannot be used to check the program under real operating conditions in the user's hardware.

Most development systems use an emulator to actually debug the program. An emulator is a program written for one processor to execute the machine code of another processor. Emulators may be written for many different processors, allowing the designer to develop programs for many different processors on a single development system.

Once the emulator is in operation, the user may examine the operation of the program, halt it at particular locations to check program status, or dynamically display program operation (such as registers or memory locations) while the program is in operation.

Emulators also allow the user to modify the contents of the program without reediting and assembling. This allows minor changes to be made and tested before they are incorporated into the source code.

Some programmers prefer the convenience of writing programs in a high-level language and not dealing with the details of actual assembly language. Compilers are used to take a high-level program language such as PASCAL or PL/M and convert the high-level statements into machine language code for the target microprocessor. Compilers and high-level languages are convenient to use and save much programming time, but they do not generate very efficient machine code. For this reason, code generated by a compiler may be too large for the capacity of the target system and therefore cannot be used.

In conclusion it can be said that the constant advances in development systems will be a deciding factor in the final cost of microprocessor systems. The easier and faster a designer can develop a microprocessor program, the lower the end cost. As hardware costs drop and labor costs increase, the advanced development systems will become more and more critical to the economical production of microprocessor systems.

1.2 System Development Flowchart

The total development of a microprocessor-based system typically involves three phases: software design, hardware design, and program diagnostic design. A systems programmer will be assigned the task of writing the application software, a logic designer will be assigned the task of designing the hardware, and typically both designers will be assigned the task of developing diagnostics to test the system. For small systems, one engineer may do all three phases, while on large systems several engineers may be assigned to each phase. Figure 1.2 shows a flowchart for the total development of a system. Notice that software and hardware development may occur in parallel to save time.

1.2.1 Software Development

The first step in developing the software is to take the system specifications and write a flowchart to accomplish the desired tasks that will implement the specifications. The flowchart should be properly structured to ensure efficient program flow.

The assembly language or high-level source code may now be written from the system flowchart. Individual software designers may be given portions of the flowchart to develop individual modules that will be linked together after they are debugged. As much hardware information as possible should be made available at this point so that hardware dependent portions of the program may be entered with the proper data.

After the source code has been written, it may be entered into the editor. Labels should be used whenever possible and symbols should be used in place of direct data. For example, if the A register needs to be loaded with a

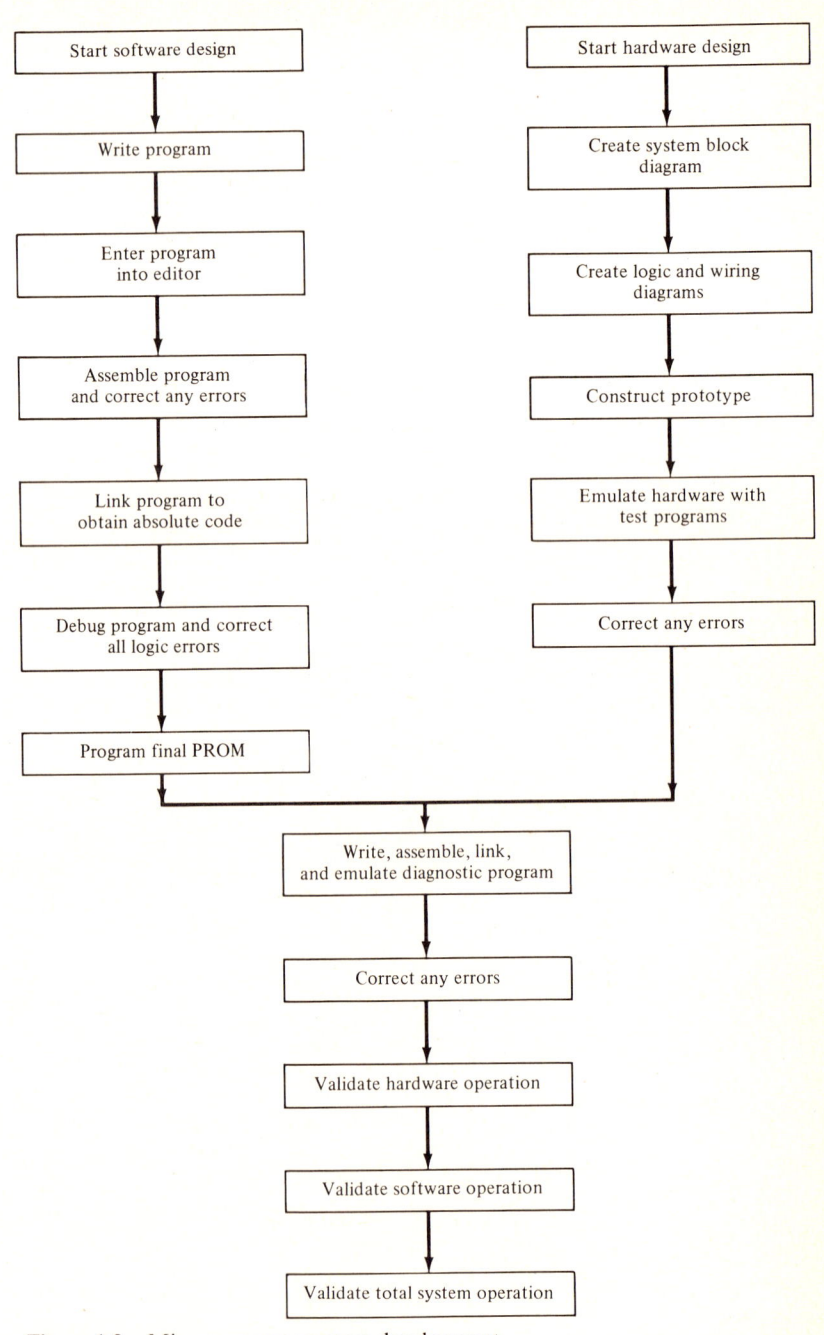

Figure 1.2 Microprocessor system development.

count of 26H, a self-documenting way of accomplishing it using an 8085 would be as follows:

```
         MVI   A,COUNT  ;PRESET COUNT VALUE
  COUNT EQU  26H
```

By using symbols and labels whenever possible, it is easy to go back and change a value (COUNT for example) at the location where it is defined rather than finding each occurrence in the source code.

Once the complete source code has been entered, it may be assembled. The assembler will check for syntax errors and print error messages to help in the correction of errors. Many advanced assemblers will assemble source code for many different microprocessors. In order to identify which microprocessor is to be used, a special command is entered in the source code to tell the assembler what microprocessor is in use.

The normal output of an assembler is the object code and a program listing. The object code will be used later by the linker. The program listing may be sent to a disk file for use later or it may be directed to the printer I/O if a printer is available.

The linker can now take the object code generated by the assembler and create the final absolute code that will be executed on the target system. The emulation phase will take the absolute code and load it into the development system RAM. From here, the program may be tested using breakpoints or single-stepping. Single-stepping allows the designer to watch the program execute one instruction at a time and monitor program status. During single-stepping, registers may be displayed to detect any program problems that may occur.

After all the bugs have been removed from the program, the final absolute code may be loaded into a PROM for use in the prototype hardware developed by the hardware design team.

1.2.2 Hardware Development

Working from the system specifications, a block diagram of the hardware must be developed. The block diagram will include all major hardware sections and show how they interconnect.

The logic diagram may now be drawn using the block diagram as a guide. Great care should be taken to design a system that uses the most efficient logic available. Minimum parts count may be important if space is limited. In a system where cost is a limiting factor, parts count may be increased if less expensive parts are available which will perform the same function.

A wiring list and parts layout diagram is then made from the logic diagram. Care should be taken to ensure that all pin connections are correct, for in most cases the design engineer will not be constructing the prototype and will therefore not be able to detect any errors during construction. A prototype may now be constructed and tested for wiring errors.

When the prototype has been constructed it may be debugged for correct operation using standard electronic testing equipment such as oscilloscopes, meters, logic probes, and logic analyzers.

After the prototype has been debugged electrically, the development system in-circuit emulator may be used to check it functionally. The ICE will verify addressing, correct I/O operation, and so on.

At this time, the prototype is finished and ready for final diagnostic testing.

1.2.3 Diagnostic Design

Both the software team and the hardware team may now focus their attention on diagnostic checkout of the system. Diagnostics must be developed which will fully test the system to make sure it will meet its design parameters. If the system is primarily I/O in nature, a program must be developed which will thoroughly test the I/O facilities of the system.

Some facilities of complex systems cannot be fully tested because to test for every possible permutation of input conditions may take more time than is available for testing. For this reason, it is important that the test data input to the system is carefully selected so that it is representative of the typical input data.

The diagnostic program is developed identically to other software on the development systems using the editor, assembler, and so on.

The final diagnostic program is then executed on the target system using an in-circuit emulator to verify the correct operation of all hardware in the system. Any hardware bugs are corrected at this stage and the diagnostic program is run until all bugs are corrected. After the hardware has been validated the diagnostic program can be used to check out the software program written for the prototype.

The final step in the system development is to validate the complete system by running operational checks on the prototype with the finalized system software installed. As with the diagnostic software, test data used during validation must be carefully selected to ensure that the test results are valid.

1.3 Designing Hardware and Software for a Specific Application

As an example of the techniques described in developing a microprocessor-based application, a simple controller will be designed. The function of the controller will be to control eight different lights in a house and simulate an occupied house by randomly turning lights on in one section of the house while turning them off in other portions of the house. This system could easily be designed using random logic but it serves as a good example of microprocessor development.

From the specifications, the designer decides that the Intel 8085 chip set would provide all capabilities while providing a compact circuit. An 8755 will be used for program storage (2K × 8 EPROM) and an 8155 for timing and RAM (one programmable timer and 256 × 8 RAM). The system block diagram is shown in Figure 1.3.

1.3.1 Software Development

It has been decided that port A of the 8755 will serve as the output port so all hardware dependent information is now known. Random timing is desired so a flowchart is written to use the 8155 timer to provide a time base and some random number generator to decide how much time should be used between on times and off times.

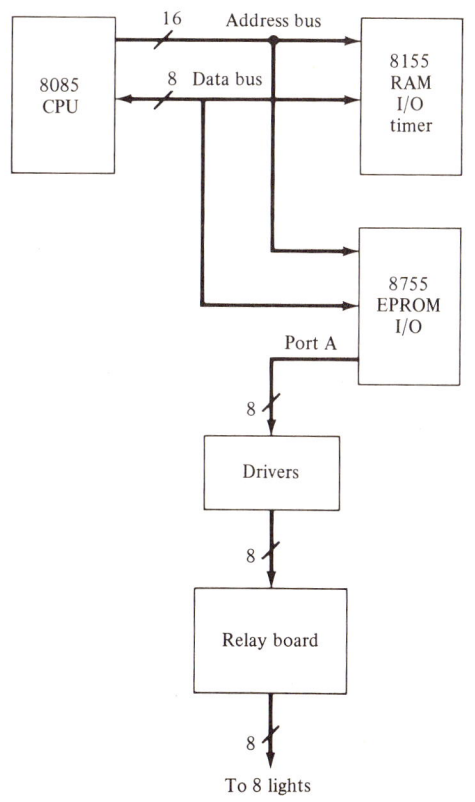

Figure 1.3 Light sequencer block diagram.

From the flowchart the 8085 assembly language is written and entered into the editor. Commenting the assembly language source code is important to debugging and comments are entered in a field reserved for them. The assembly language source code is now assembled, linked, and then emulated to test for correct operation. Any logic errors found in program flow should be corrected at this point.

1.3.2 Hardware

From the system block diagram (Figure 1.3) a logic and wiring diagram should be drawn. As specified, a typical Intel 8085 minimum chip set is being used. Relays are used to control the 110 V ac lights and a driving circuit is needed for the relays. A crystal should be specified which will provide a suitable time base for the 8155 timer.

After the wiring diagram is complete, the prototype can be built and then debugged. The first stage of debug will be to check for wiring errors and test power and ground connections to the IC sockets before the chips are installed. After the circuit has been powered up voltage levels to the relay drivers may be checked to verify their operation. After initial checkout, the hardware may be exercised using the ICE to verify I/O, timer, and RAM operation.

1.3.3 Diagnostics

The only program operation that needs to be tested is that the relays sequence on and off properly. To test this, a diagnostic program is needed that will sequence the data sent to port A of the 8755. Since in actual operation the time intervals are several hours, the diagnostic program should use shorter intervals so that the entire program sequence may be seen in a short time. When the diagnostic program has been designed, it may be edited, assembled, linked, and emulated as with previous software programs.

After the diagnostic program has been executed and the hardware validated, the finished program written for the final system may be loaded into PROM and installed in the prototype.

The light sequencer is now completely designed and tested and ready for installation.

CHAPTER 2

MICROCOMPUTER FUNDAMENTALS

This chapter first introduces the hardware that makes up a microprocessor system. Then software concepts and programming languages are discussed. Finally, an example of how hardware and software work together as a logic device is presented.

2.1 Introduction to Microprocessor Systems

The introduction of the microprocessor has caused a dramatic change in the design of logic systems. In the traditional approach, often called "random" or "hardwired" logic, systems are designed using individual logic blocks (such as flip-flops, gates, and counters) as required by the application. These blocks are interconnected to provide the needed data flow. Using random logic, each application requires a unique design, and there is little similarity among different systems. This approach is similar to analog circuits in that the structure of the circuit parallels the function being performed. Once constructed, the function of the circuit is difficult to change.

The microprocessor, on the other hand, provides a general-purpose control system which can be adapted to a wide variety of applications with little circuit modification. The individuality of different systems is provided by a list of instructions (called the program) that control the system's operation. There are therefore two different aspects of microprocessor systems: the actual components (called hardware) and the programs (called software).

This chapter contains material modified from *Practical Microprocessors—Hardware, Software and Troubleshooting,* copyright © 1979. Reprinted by permission of Hewlett-Packard.

2.1.1 A Basic Microprocessor System

Consider a system with a keyboard and a numeric display, as in a pocket calculator. When a key is pressed, the corresponding number should appear on the display. This system is a natural application for a microprocessor.

Figure 2.1 shows the block diagram of a system for doing this. The microprocessor (also called the processor) is the "brains" of the system. It contains all of the logic to recognize and execute the list of instructions (program). The memory stores the program, and may also store data.

The microprocessor needs to exchange information with the keyboard and display. The input port, from which the processor can read data, connects the processor to the keyboard. The output port, to which the processor can send data, connects the processor to the display.

The blocks within the microcomputer are interconnected by three buses. A bus is a group of wires which connect the devices in the system in parallel. The microprocessor uses the address bus to select memory locations or input and output ports. One can think of the addresses as post office box numbers; they identify which locations to put information into or to take information out of.

Once the microprocessor selects a particular location via the address bus, it transfers the data via the data bus. Information can travel from the processor to the memory or an output port, or from an input port or memory

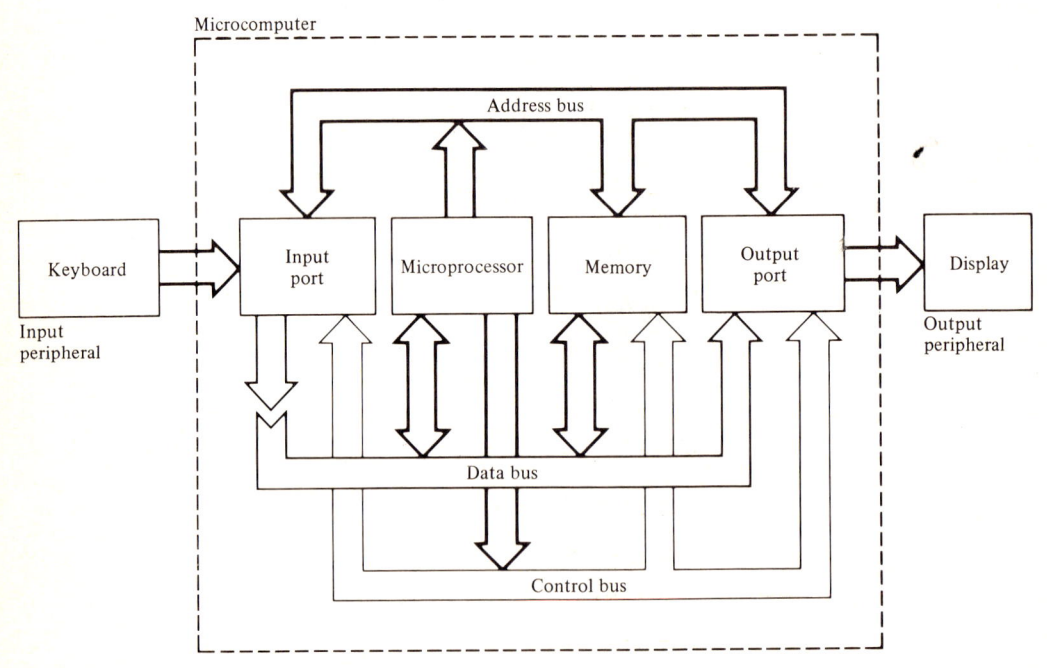

Figure 2.1 Basic microprocessor system.

to the processor. Note that the microprocessor is involved in all data transfers. Data usually does not go directly from one port to another, or from the memory to a port.

The third bus is called the control bus. It is a group of conductors carrying signals which are used by the microprocessor to notify memory and I/O devices that it is ready to perform a data transfer. Some signals in the control bus allow I/O or memory devices to make special requests to the processor.

A single digit of binary information (1 or 0) is called a bit (a contraction of binary digit). One digital signal (high or low) carries 1 bit of information. Microprocessors handle data not as individual bits, but as groups of bits called words. The most common microprocessors today use 8-bit words, which are called bytes. These microprocessors are called 8-bit processors. For an 8-bit processor, byte and word are often used interchangeably. Be aware, however, that word is also used to mean a group of 16 or more bits.

2.1.2 Programs

To direct the system to perform the desired task, an appropriate list of instructions is required. For example:

1. Read data from the keyboard.
2. Write data to the display.
3. Repeat (go to step 1).

For the microprocessor to perform a task from a list of instructions, the instructions must be translated into a code that the microprocessor can understand. These codes are then stored in the system's memory. The microprocessor begins by reading the first coded instruction from the memory. The microprocessor decodes the meaning of the instruction and performs the indicated operation. The processor then reads the instruction from the next location in memory and performs the corresponding operation. This process is repeated, one memory location after another.

Certain instructions cause the microprocessor to jump out of sequence to another memory location for the next instruction. The program can therefore direct the microprocessor to return to a previous instruction in the program, creating a loop which is repeatedly executed. This enables operations that must be repeated many times to be performed by a relatively short program.

2.1.3 Input/Output

A complete microprocessor system, including the microprocessor, memory, and input and output ports is called a microcomputer. The devices

16 Chapter 2 MICROCOMPUTER FUNDAMENTALS

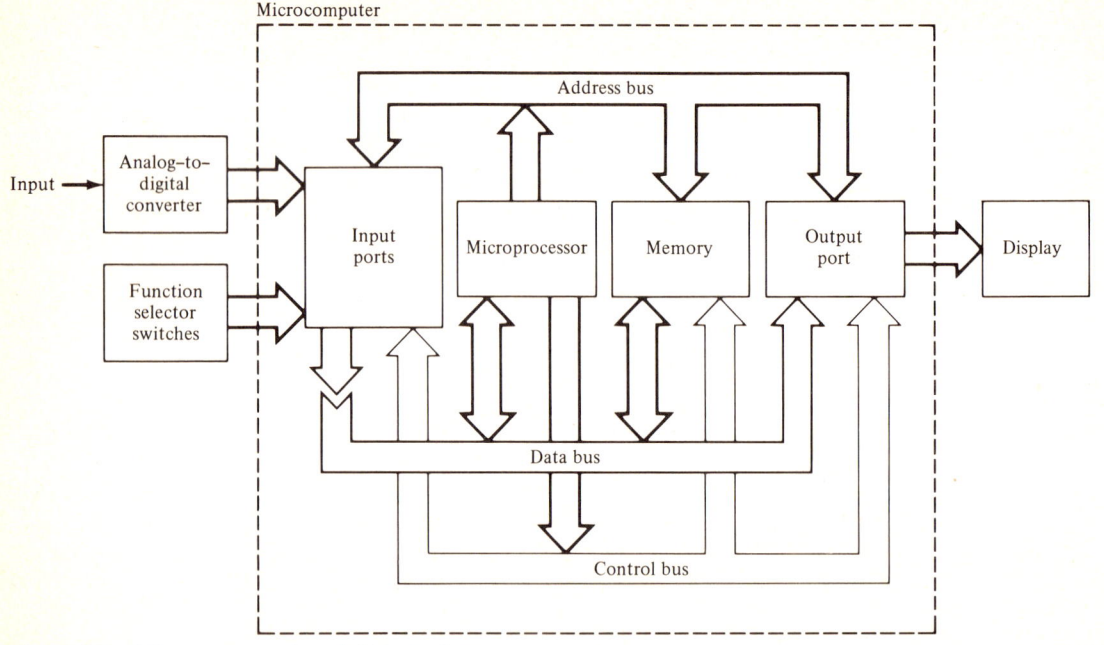

Figure 2.2 Microprocessor-based digital voltmeter.

connected to the input and output ports (the keyboard and display for example) are called peripherals, or Input/Output (I/O) devices. The peripherals are the system's interface with the user. They may also connect the microcomputer to other equipment. Storage devices such as tape or disk drives are also referred to as peripherals.

An example of a microprocessor application from the instrumentation field is the microprocessor-based digital voltmeter (see Figure 2.2). Its input peripherals are an analog-to-digital converter and the range and function selector switches. The output peripheral is a digital display. The basic microcomputer is the same, whether the application is a calculator or a voltmeter; the difference is in the peripherals and the program.

All devices in the microprocessor system exchange information with the

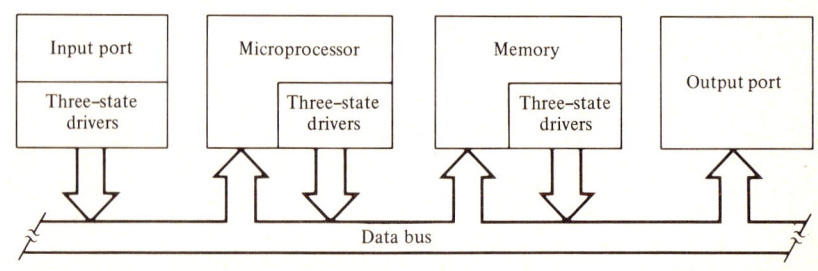

Figure 2.3 Three-state drivers in microprocessor system.

microprocessor over the same set of wires (the data bus). The microprocessor selects one device to place data on the data bus and disconnects the others. It is the three-state output capability of the devices on the bus that enables the processor to selectively turn devices on and off.

Figure 2.3 shows how three-state drivers are used in microprocessor systems. All devices that put data on the data bus have three-state drivers on their outputs. The microprocessor generates control signals (part of the

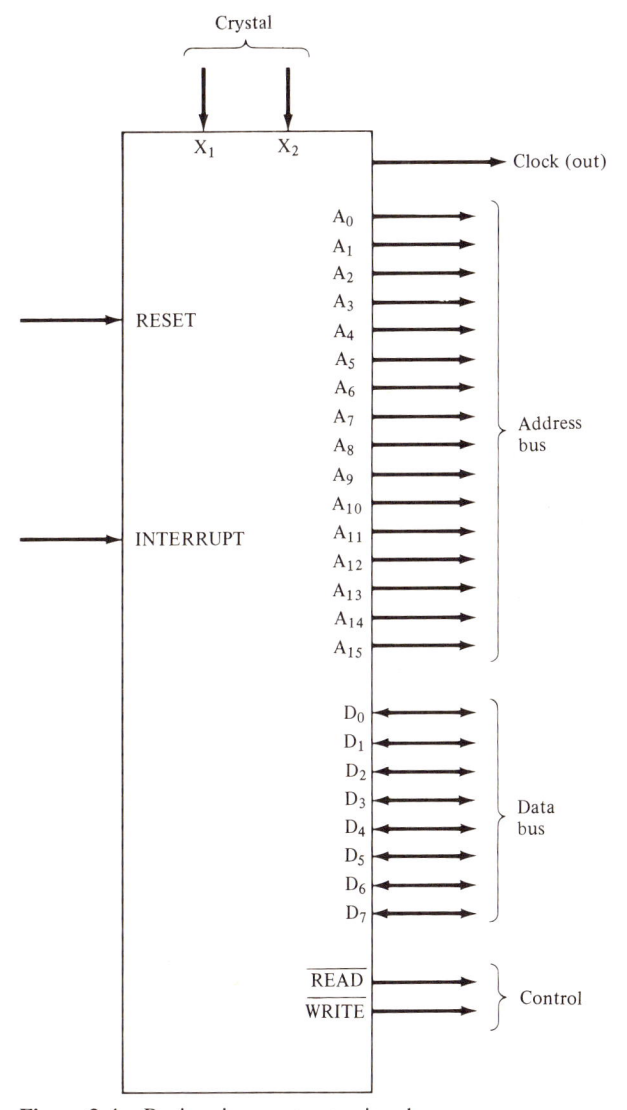

Figure 2.4 Basic microprocessor signals.

control bus) to enable the three-state drivers of the device from which it wants to read data. The three-state drivers of the other devices are disabled. Figure 2.4 shows the basic signals that connect to a typical microprocessor. There are 16 address outputs which drive the address bus, and eight data pins which connect to the data bus. The data pins are bidirectional, which means that data may go into or out of them. READ and WRITE are the control signals that coordinate the movement of data on the data bus.

The two signals shown on the left of the diagram provide additional control functions. The RESET input is used to initialize the microprocessor's internal circuitry. The INTERRUPT input allows the microprocessor to be diverted from its current task to another task that must be performed immediately. The use of these signals, plus others that have not been mentioned here, is described in Chapter 3.

The two connections at the top are for an external crystal, which is used to set the frequency of an oscillator in the microprocessor. The output of this oscillator is called the system clock. The clock synchronizes all devices in the system and sets the rate at which instructions are executed.

The microprocessor usually consists of three sections namely, the control unit, Arithmetic and Logic Unit (ALU), and register sections. The control unit controls and synchronizes all data transfers and transformations inside the microprocessor. The ALU performs all the arithmetic and logic functions. The register section contains four basic registers inside the microprocessor chip. These are: Program Counter (PC), Instruction Register (IR), Data Counter (DC), or Memory Address Register (MAR), and Accumulator (A). The program counter is used to store the address of the program. It usually points to the next instruction to be executed. The instruction register contains the next instruction to be executed. The data counter or memory address register stores the address of data. Finally, the accumulator typically contains data or results of an arithmetic or logic operation. For 8-bit microprocessors, the accumulator and instruction registers are typically 8-bits long and, the data counter and program counter are 16-bits long.

2.1.4 Memories

Microprocessor systems usually use integrated circuit memories to store programs and data. They can store many bits of data in a single IC. Currently, devices are available with capacities of over 65,000 bits on one chip. A 65,536-bit memory can store over 8,000 alphanumeric characters, or about three pages of this text on a piece of silicon about a third of an inch square.

The simplest memory device is the flip-flop, which stores one bit of information. Registers contain up to eight flip-flops on a single IC, each with its own data in and data out pins but with a common clock line.

Introduction to Microprocessor Systems   19

Large-Scale Integration (LSI) technology made it possible to put thousands of flip-flops on a single IC, but a new problem was created. With thousands of flip-flops on an IC, there cannot be a separate data pin for each. The solution to this problem is to use address inputs to select the particular memory location (flip-flop) of interest. A decoder on the memory chip decodes the address and connects the selected memory location to the data pins.

Figure 2.5 shows a conceptual diagram of an 8-bit memory (most memories are much larger). Only the data output circuits are shown for simplicity. The decoder converts the binary address inputs to eight separate outputs, one for each possible combination of the three address lines. These signals control the three-state drivers at the output of each memory cell (flip-flop). The data from the addressed cell is placed on the data output line. This technique allows a single data pin to be used for all locations on the memory chip.

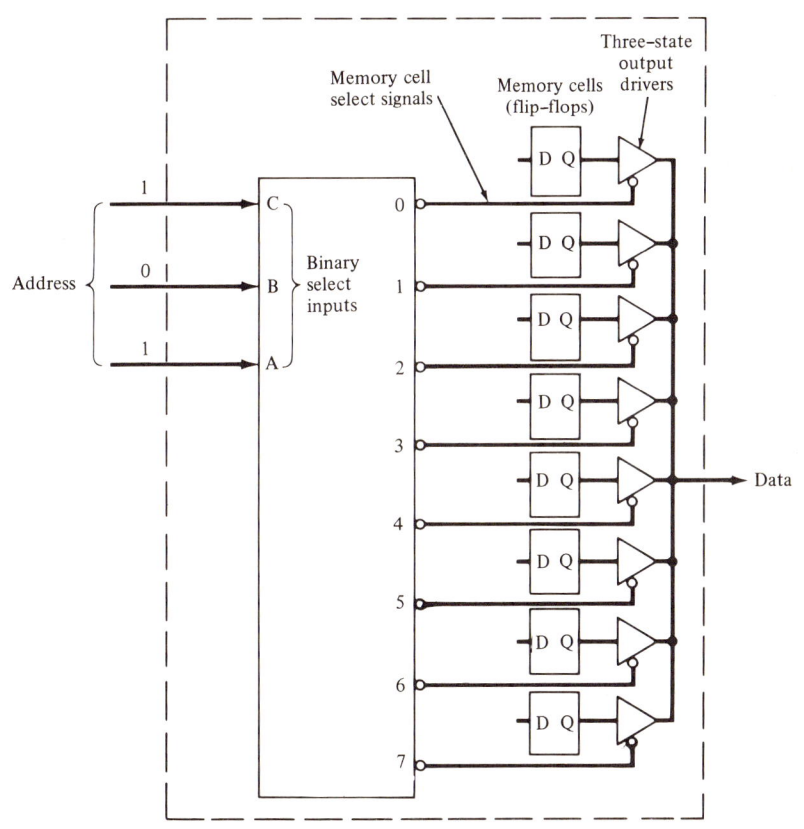

Figure 2.5 Conceptual diagram of 8-bit memory, showing how all memory cells share single data line. Location 5 (101 binary) is shown selected.

Each memory location can contain a group of bits rather than just one bit as in the example above. Each can hold 1, 4, or 8 bits, depending upon the particular IC. If the IC has eight data pins, then each memory location stores 8 bits of data. Note that while the memory may contain thousands of locations, only one may be accessed at a time.

The number of addressable locations depends upon the number of address lines. With one address line, two locations can be selected: address 0 and address 1. With two address lines, one of four locations can be selected: 00, 01, 10 and 11. The general rule is:

$$\text{number of locations} = 2^N$$

where N equals the number of address lines. The memory ICs used with microprocessors fall into two broad categories: ROMs and RAMs. A ROM (Read-Only Memory) is a memory that can only be read. The data is programmed into it at the time of manufacture, or by a special programming procedure prior to installation in the circuit. A program recorded into a ROM is often referred to as firmware.

A RAM (Random Access Memory) is a memory into which data can be stored and then retrieved. RAM is actually a misnomer; random access means that the time to access any memory location is the same, a characteristic also present in ROMs. Read/Write (R/W) memory is a more accurate term for what are usually called RAMs, but RAM is widely used to mean integrated circuit read/write memory. A digital tape recorder

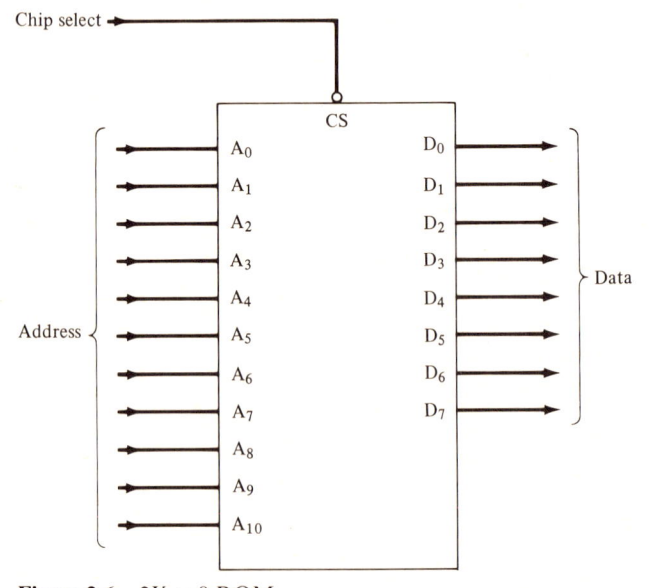

Figure 2.6 2K × 8 ROM.

is an example of a memory that is not random access, since the time to access a particular location depends upon the position of the tape.

An important characteristic of semiconductor RAMs is that they are volatile; they lose their data when power is turned off, and when turned back on, they contain unknown data. ROMs do not have this problem, so they are used for permanent program and data storage. Since the contents of a ROM cannot be modified, RAMs must be used for temporary program and data storage.

Figure 2.6 shows a ROM containing 2,048 words of 8 bits each, or 16,384 bits. When using large numbers that are powers of two, K is often used to mean 1,024 (2^{10}). Thus, this memory has 2K bytes or 16K bits. Since each location contains 8 bits, it is called a 2K × 8 ROM.

When the Chip Select ($\overline{CS}$) input is low, the ROM's output drivers are enabled. When $\overline{CS}$ is high, the data outputs are in the high impedance state. The three-state outputs allow the data lines of many memory devices to be connected together, with one device selected by bringing its $\overline{CS}$ input low.

Figure 2.7 shows a 1K × 8 RAM. This RAM contains 1,024 locations of 8 bits each. The data lines are bidirectional, since data can go into or out of the memory. RAMs have an additional control line called $\overline{WRITE}$. To store data in the RAM, an address is selected, the data is placed on the data lines, and the $\overline{WRITE}$ line is brought low. When the data and address are all set, the chip select is pulsed, and the data is stored in the memory.

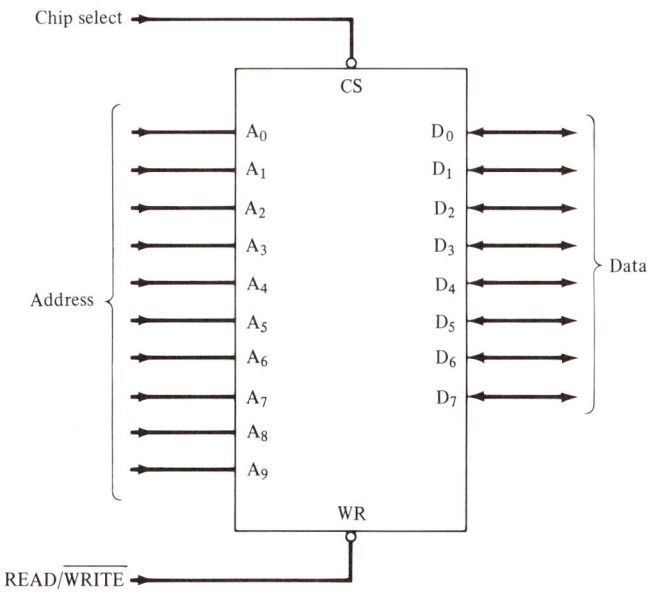

Figure 2.7 1K × 8 RAM.

The write line determines the direction of the data flow. The write line is usually active low, and is often called the RD/$\overline{\text{WR}}$ (or R/$\overline{\text{W}}$). This notation indicates that if the signal is high, a read is performed, and if it is low, a write is performed. Note that this input has no effect unless the chip select is true.

2.1.5 Minicomputers and Microcomputers

A microcomputer is functionally similar to a minicomputer, and, in fact, the distinction between the two is becoming less and less clear. A microcomputer's Central Processing Unit (CPU) is the microprocessor. A minicomputer's CPU is usually a PC board with dozens of less complex, but faster integrated circuits on it. The main functional difference is that minicomputers are usually faster. They are also larger and more expensive. As microprocessors have increased in speed and power to compete with the older minicomputers, new minicomputers have been developed which are even faster and more powerful. These new minicomputers often use microprocessors internally. Thus, while the basic distinctions of speed, power, and size remain, the exact boundary is becoming vague. Microcomputers are now finding applications in systems where a minicomputer would be far too bulky and expensive.

2.2 Number Systems and Boolean Logic

In this section, we will review the decimal, binary, octal and hexadecimal number systems. Examples involving arithmetic and Boolean logic are also included.

2.2.1 Decimal and Binary

The number system used by most people is the decimal or base ten system. With base ten, ten different numbers from 0 to 9 can be represented with one digit.

Microprocessors use the binary or base two system. In this system, with one digit two different numbers namely, 0 and 1 are represented.

Binary to decimal number conversion can be carried out as follows:

$$10011_2 = 1 \times 2^4 + 0 \times 2^3 + 0 \times 2^2 + 1 \times 2^1 + 1 \times 2^0$$
$$= 16 + 0 + 0 + 2 + 1$$
$$= 19_{10}$$

Number Systems and Boolean Logic 23

The reverse process, that is, converting from decimal to binary is carried out by continuously dividing the number to be converted by 2 and keeping track of the remainders. For example, consider the following:

$$9 \div 2 = 4 \text{ Remainder } 1$$
$$4 \div 2 = 2 \text{ Remainder } 0$$
$$2 \div 2 = 1 \text{ Remainder } 0$$
$$1 \div 2 = 0 \text{ Remainder } 1$$
$$9_{10} = 1\ 0\ 0\ 1_2$$

2.2.2 Octal

Binary numbers are more difficult to work with than decimal numbers for humans. The reason for this is that binary numbers contain so many 1's and 0's.

In order to minimize this problem, a more compact form of binary number representation called the octal or base eight is used. In this system, the binary number is grouped into 3 bits starting at the right. For example, the binary number $100\ 010_2$ can be converted to octal as follows:

$$\underbrace{100}_{4}\ \underbrace{010}_{2_8}$$

2.2.3 Hexadecimal

Another compact form representation of binary numbers is the hexadecimal or base sixteen, number system. The binary number is represented in groups of four starting at the right. Since 4 bits can have decimal values from 0 to 15, a way is needed to represent the decimal values 10 through 15 with a single character. The letters A through F are used for this purpose.

As an example of hexadecimal number, consider the following:

$$\underbrace{0101}_{5}\ \underbrace{1111}_{F} \rightarrow 0101\ 1111_2 = 5F_{16}$$

Table 2.1 shows the relationship between decimal, binary and hexadecimal numbers.

Hexadecimal numbers are preferred over octal because an 8-bit number can be represented by two hexadecimal digits where three octal digits are required for the same thing.

Table 2.1. Hexadecimal Number Representation

Decimal	Hexadecimal	Binary
0	0	0000
1	1	0001
2	2	0010
3	3	0011
4	4	0100
5	5	0101
6	6	0110
7	7	0111
8	8	1000
9	9	1001
10	A	1010
11	B	1011
12	C	1100
13	D	1101
14	E	1110
15	F	1111

2.2.4 Bit Position Terminology

When referring to binary numbers, it is often necessary to refer to a particular bit or group of bits. The right-most bit is called the Least Significant Bit (LSB), and the left-most bit is called the Most Significant Bit (MSB).

When referring to a group of bits at one end of a word, the left-hand bits are called the high-order (or most significant) bits, and the right-hand bits are called the low-order (or least significant) bits.

2.2.5 Basic Boolean Operations

There are four basic Boolean operations. These are OR, AND, exclusive OR and NOT. Microprocessors typically have instructions to perform these Boolean operations. All the Boolean operations (OR, AND, and exclusive OR) except NOT are performed on two input variables. In each case, one output is provided. The NOT operation is performed on one input to provide one output.

Table 2.2. OR Gate Truth Table

Inputs A	Inputs B	Output = A V B
0	0	0
0	1	1
1	0	1
1	1	1

OR Operation

If two input variables A or B to an OR gate are both 0, then the output is zero. Otherwise the output is 1. Typically, the symbols + or ∨ are used. Table 2.2 gives the truth table for an OR gate.

AND Operation

If two input variables to an AND gate A AND B are both 1, then the output is 1. Otherwise the output is 0. Typically the symbols dot · or ∧ are used. Table 2.3 provides the truth table for the AND gate.

Table 2.3. AND Gate Truth Table

Inputs		Output = A ∧ B
A	B	
0	0	0
0	1	0
1	0	0
1	1	1

Exclusive OR Operation

If two input variables A and B to an exclusive OR gate are the same, the output is 0. Otherwise, the output is 1. Typically, the symbols ⊕ or ∀ are used. Table 2.4 gives the truth table for an exclusive OR gate.

Table 2.4. Exclusive OR Gate Truth Table

Inputs		Output = A ⊕ B
A	B	
0	0	0
0	1	1
1	0	1
1	1	0

NOT Operation

NOT inverts any binary digit or a group of digits. That is,

$$\text{NOT } 1 = 0$$
$$\text{NOT } 0 = 1$$

Using these four basic logic operations, other logic functions can be performed. For example, combining AND with NOT generates NAND and combining OR with NOT generates NOR.

2.2.6 Arithmetic and Logic Operations

Binary Addition

The four possible combinations for adding two binary digits are:

$$Augend + Addend = Result + Carry$$

$$0 + 0 = 0$$
$$0 + 1 = 1$$
$$1 + 0 = 1$$
$$1 + 1 = 0 + 1$$

Consider adding two 8-bit numbers as follows:

```
Intermediate carry     1 1
                   0 1 0 1  0 0 1 1   (83₁₀)
                 + 0 0 1 1  1 0 0 0   (56₁₀)
                   ─────────────────
                   1 0 0 0  1 0 1 1₂  139₁₀
```

Binary Subtraction

Binary subtraction can be carried out via the twos complement arithmetic.

The twos complement of a binary number can be obtained by replacing 0's with 1's and 1's with 0's in the number and then adding 1. The first step generates a "one complement of the number."

The binary subtraction can be performed by adding the twos complement of the subtrahend to the minuend. As an example, consider the following binary subtraction:

```
Minuend      0 0 1 0  0 1 1 1    (39₁₀)
Subtrahend   0 0 0 1  1 0 1 0   -(26₁₀)
             ─────────────────
             0 0 0 0  1 1 0 1₂  = 13₁₀
```

The above can be performed using the twos complement as follows:

Twos complement of the subtrahend = 0 0 0 1 1 0 1 0 = 1 1 1 0 0 1 0 1
$$+ \ 1$$
$$\overline{1\ 1\ 1\ 0\ \ 0\ 1\ 1\ 0}$$

```
                 Minuend = 0 0 1 0  0 1 1 1
Two complement of subtrahend = 1 1 1 0  0 1 1 0
                           ───────────────────
                         1  0 0 0 0  1 1 0 1 = 13₁₀
```

Carry means that the answer is positive and ignore the carry.

Number Systems and Boolean Logic   27

No carry means that the answer is negative and the final answer is the twos complement of the result of adding the minuend and the twos complement of the subtrahend.

Logic Operations

Boolean operations between two numbers of same length (each consisting of more than 1 bit) can be carried out by performing the operation starting from the least significant bit.

For example:

```
                    0 1 0 1   0 0 1 1
                  V 0 0 1 1   1 0 1 1
   OR operation    0 1 1 1   1 0 1 1
```

Consider another example:

```
                    0 1 1 0   1 0 1 0
                  ∧ 0 1 1 0   0 1 0 1
   AND operation   0 1 1 0   0 0 0 0
```

2.2.7 Number Representations

Microprocessor-based systems are often used to perform elaborate mathematical functions on a wide range of numbers, as in electronic calculators. However, the programs that have been used in this chapter are limited to positive integers between 0 and 255, and the functions are limited to simple logic, addition, and subtraction. This section discusses the techniques used to represent a wider range of numbers and perform complex mathematical operations.

Negative Numbers

Consider the problem of representing both negative and positive integers using an 8-bit word. Since there is no way to represent more than 256 different numbers using 8 bits, the range is limited to about ±127. The first 128 numbers, 0 through 127 (7F hex), are defined as positive numbers. Negative numbers are generated by counting "backward" from 0. Like a hardware up/down counter, if a register is at 0000 0000 and is decremented, the next count is 1111 1111 (FF hex). FF hex is therefore the representation for −1. This representation is called twos complement. Table 2.5 shows the twos complement representation for −8 through +7.

Note that the most significant bit indicates the sign. If the MSB is 0, then the number is positive. If the MSB is 1, then the number is negative.

Table 2.5. Twos Complement Representation of −8 Through +7

Decimal	Two Complement
7	0000 0111
6	0000 0110
5	0000 0101
4	0000 0100
3	0000 0011
2	0000 0010
1	0000 0001
0	0000 0000
−1	1111 1111
−2	1111 1110
−3	1111 1101
−4	1111 1100
−5	1111 1011
−6	1111 1010
−7	1111 1001
−8	1111 1000

The procedure to calculate the twos complement representation is simple. For positive numbers, the twos complement and binary representation are the same (as shown by the first eight entries in Table 2.5). For negative numbers, the procedure for calculating the twos complement representation is as follows:

1. Write the binary representation of the absolute value (e.g., for −5 write 0000 0101).
2. Complement the binary number (this is called the ones complement, e.g., 0000 0101 = 1111 1010).
3. Add one to form the twos complement (e.g., 1111 1010 + 1 = 1111 1011 = −5 twos complement).

The procedure to get the absolute value of a negative twos complement number is the same: complement the number and then add 1.

For example, consider the twos complement number 1111 1011:

$$\overline{1111\ 1011} = 0000\ 0100 \qquad 0000\ 0100 + 1 = 0000\ 0101 = 5$$

Therefore, 1111 1011 is the twos complement representation of negative 5.

Note that the number 1111 1011 could also be interpreted as 251 decimal, if it were considered to be straight binary rather than twos complement. It is therefore necessary to define the data as being twos complement and remember to treat it appropriately.

The twos complement representation is very convenient for arithmetic. Twos complement numbers, when added, subtracted, multiplied, or

Number Systems and Boolean Logic   29

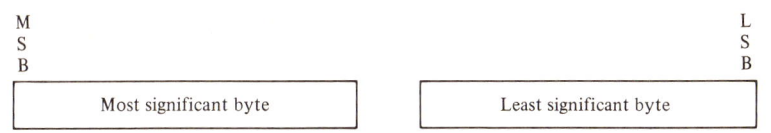

```
M                                        L
S                                        S
B                                        B
```
| Most significant byte | | Least significant byte |

Figure 2.8 Double precision.

divided, yield results in twos complement. It is commonly used in microprocessor systems that must represent both positive and negative numbers.

Large and Small Numbers

While twos complement provides a representation for negative numbers, the range is still limited to integers with absolute values of less than 129. This range can be extended in several different ways, depending upon how wide a range is required and the degree of precision needed.

The simplest technique for extending the range of numbers that can be represented is simply to increase the number of bits used to represent each number. This is often done by using pairs of words to represent a single number (see Figure 2.8). With the 8085, this can be done using the register pair instructions, which operate on 16 bits at a time. Using two words for one number is called double precision. With an 8-bit processor, this extends the range from 0 to 65,535, or ±32,767.

Double precision extends the range of magnitudes, but what about numbers less than 1, or between 3 and 4? Figure 2.9 shows a representation called fixed point. In this example, 2 bytes are used to store the number. The first byte is defined as being to the left of the decimal point (actually a binary point), and the second byte is the fractional part (to the right of the binary point). This allows numbers as small as $2^{-8} = 1/256$ to be represented, as well as fractional numbers such as 3.17. The resolution, however, is limited to 1/256th (about 0.004) and the range is limited to ±127.

Fixed point can be extended by using multiple bytes for each part of the number, but unless a large amount of memory is dedicated to each number, it is still incapable of representing numbers such as 360,000,000,000 or 0.000000297. Note that these numbers contain many zeros, which are used as "place holders." These numbers can be easily represented by using "scientific notation," or mantissa and exponent. The mantissa is the

Implied binary point

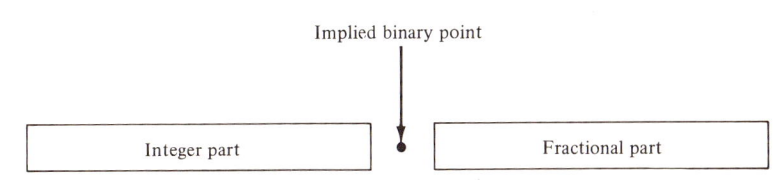

| Integer part | | Fractional part |

Figure 2.9 Fixed point.

| Mantissa | | Exponent |

Figure 2.10 Floating point.

magnitude of the number, adjusted to between 0 and 1. The number 360,000,000,000 for example, can be written as 0.36×10^{12} (0.36 is the mantissa and the exponent is 12), and 0.000000297 can be written as 0.297×10^{-6} (0.297 is the mantissa and -6 is the exponent).

Suppose then, that 2 bytes are used to represent each number as shown in Figure 2.10. One byte is the mantissa, and the other is the exponent. The range of values that can be represented, assuming that both the mantissa and exponent are stored in twos complement form, is about $\pm 10^{\pm 127}$. This is a very large range; 10^{127} is quite a large number, and 10^{-127} is very small.

This technique, called floating point, is commonly used for representing a wide range of numbers. More than 2 bytes are often used to obtain greater resolution (more digits in the mantissa).

Note that, as with all representations, the type of representation must be known in order to decipher the number. The same 2 bytes of data could be very different numbers if interpreted as a pair of twos complement numbers, a single fixed-point number, or a floating point number. The software that operates on the numbers must know which representation is used.

Decimal Number Representation

Most microprocessor systems have decimal I/O devices, such as keyboards and displays. Since decimal is the natural form for most people, most microprocessor systems must accommodate it.

The problem is how to represent the decimal numbers in the binary-oriented processor system. Suppose, for example, that the decimal number 28 is read from a keyboard. The number can be converted to its binary equivalent, 0001 1100 (1C hex). However, if this number is to be displayed on a decimal display, it must be converted back to the two decimal digits, 2 and 8.

An alternative method is to take each of the decimal digits, 2 and 8, and convert them independently to two 4-bit binary numbers. The two 4-bit numbers are then packed into 1 byte. Thus, 28 would be coded as 0010 1000. This is called Binary Coded Decimal (BCD). Note that the binary values 1010 through 1111 are never used in the BCD representation.

BCD is commonly used in systems that utilize decimal I/O, since it avoids the decimal-binary conversion process. One disadvantage is that it is inefficient in terms of storage space. The largest decimal number that can be stored in a byte using BCD is 99, whereas in pure binary it is 255. Arithmetic is also awkward in BCD, since it is not a "natural" number system. However, most microprocessors provide special instructions for accommodating BCD. (See the description of the DAA instruction in Appendix A.)

Representing Alphanumerics

Many microprocessor systems must operate not only on numbers, but also on letters. For example, a computer terminal must read the characters from the keyboard and send them to the computer. Letters must somehow be represented by binary numbers.

The most common code for doing this, called American Standard Code for Information Interchange (ASCII), is shown in Table 2.6. Every character is assigned a binary value. Note that, as with all representations, the context of the information is important. For example, 0101 0100 may be the binary representation of the decimal number 84, or the BCD

Table 2.6. ASCII Codes

00	NUL	20	SPACE	40	@	60	`
01	SOH	21	!	41	A	61	a
02	STX	22	"	42	B	62	b
03	ETX	23	#	43	C	63	c
04	EOT	24	$	44	D	64	d
05	ENQ	25	%	45	E	65	e
06	ACK	26	&	46	F	66	f
07	BEL	27	'	47	G	67	g
08	BS	28	(	48	H	68	h
09	HT	29	)	49	I	69	i
0A	LF	2A	*	4A	J	6A	j
0B	VT	2B	+	4B	K	6B	k
0C	FF	2C	,	4C	L	6C	l
0D	CR	2D	-	4D	M	6D	m
0E	SO	2E	.	4E	N	6E	n
0F	SI	2F	/	4F	O	6F	o
10	DLE	30	0	50	P	70	p
11	DC1	31	1	51	Q	71	q
12	DC2	32	2	52	R	72	r
13	DC3	33	3	53	S	73	s
14	DC4	34	4	54	T	74	t
15	NAK	35	5	55	U	75	u
16	SYN	36	6	56	V	76	v
17	ETB	37	7	57	W	77	w
18	CAN	38	8	58	X	78	x
19	EM	39	9	59	Y	79	y
1A	SUB	3A	:	5A	Z	7A	z
1B	ESC	3B	;	5B	[	7B	{
1C	FS	3C	<	5C	\	7C	|
1D	GS	3D	=	5D	]	7D	}
1E	RS	3E	>	5E	^	7E	~
1F	US	3F	?	5F	_	7F	DELETE

representation of 54 (the ASCII character T). Some codes in Table 2.6 are control codes, which provide special functions. The code 0A, for example, is used to cause a line feed on a printer or display.

The assignment of codes to characters is arbitrary, and there are many other possibilities. ASCII is currently the most widely used code, but another code called BAUDOT was very popular in the past. IBM machines use EBCDIC (Extended Binary Coded Decimal Interchange Code).

Table Look-up

A common programming problem is the conversion of one number representation or code to another. For example, consider the problem of displaying a hexadecimal digit on a seven-segment display. It must somehow be determined which segments to turn on to display the appropriate character. A conversion from binary to seven-segment code is required.

This is done using a technique called table look-up. The segment patterns for each character are stored as a list in memory called a table. The first entry contains the segment pattern for the character 0, the next for the character 1, and so on. To translate a binary code to the corresponding seven-segment code, the code is simply "looked-up" in the table.

Figure 2.11 shows the flowchart for a program that converts binary data to seven-segment code. This program uses a table of seven-segment codes. The first entry in the table contains the seven-segment code for 0, the next entry the seven-segment code for 1, and so forth. First, the binary number to be converted is added to the address of the first entry in the table. The

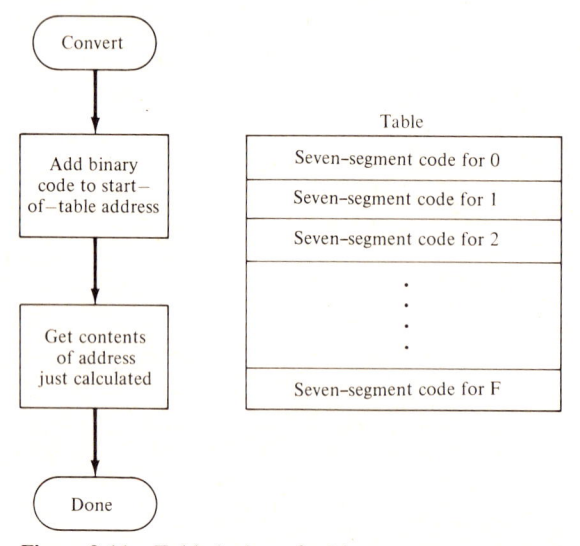

Figure 2.11 Table look-up for binary to seven-segment conversion.

result is the address of the table entry containing the desired seven-segment code. The contents of the addressed location are then read, and the conversion is completed.

2.3 Software Fundamentals

As described in the preceding sections, the microcomputer system consists of both hardware and software. The software (or programming) aspects of the system are discussed in this section.

Programs are first written in a way that is convenient for the person writing the program (the programmer). The program must then be rewritten and stored in the code that the microprocessor understands. The microprocessor then reads the codes from memory, one at a time, and performs the indicated operations.

The important point is that while computers are precise and fast, they are not creative. They can deal with contingencies, but only in ways for which they have been programmed. The apparent intelligence of computers is a function of the large number of programs that they contain. The use of a microprocessor allows some of this simulated intelligence to be incorporated into a product. On the other hand, this type of sophistication is very difficult to obtain using random logic.

2.3.1 The Microcomputer as a Logic Device

Microprocessor systems are often used to replace circuits composed of standard logic devices. In order to illustrate the differences between a

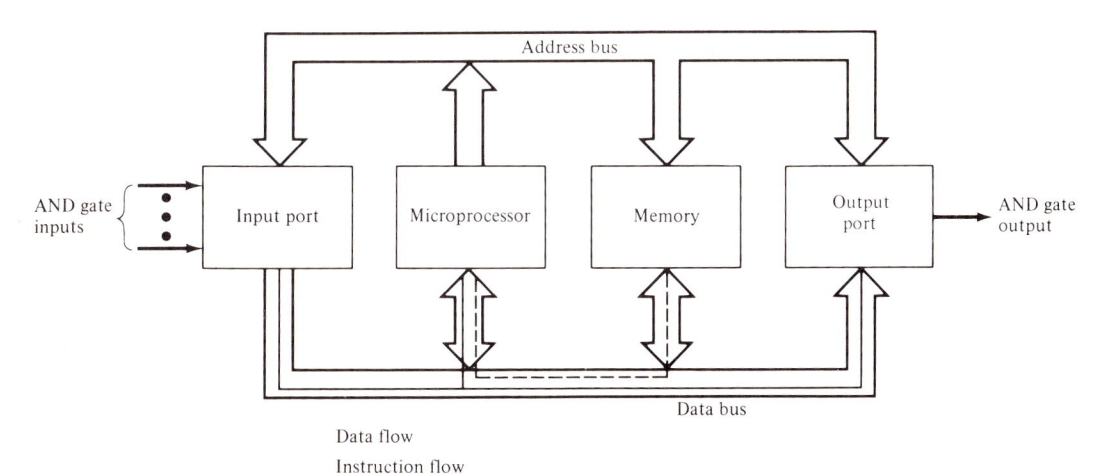

Figure 2.12 Microprocessor-based AND gate.

"programmed" logic device and a traditional logic device, consider using a microprocessor as a simple AND gate.

A microprocessor-based AND gate requires an input port for the gate's inputs and an output port for its output (see Figure 2.12). The microprocessor, using instructions stored in the memory, performs the AND function. Since an AND gate has only one output, only 1 bit of the output port is needed.

An appropriate program is required for the processor-based AND gate. The following is a list of instructions that perform the AND gate function:

1. Read the input port.
2. Go to step 5 if all inputs are high; otherwise continue.
3. Set output low.
4. Go to step 1.
5. Set output high.
6. Go to step 1.

First, the input port is read. Then the inputs are examined to see if they are all high, since that is the function of an AND gate. If the inputs are all high, the output is set high; otherwise, it is set low. Once the procedure has been completed, the program jumps back to step 1 and repeats indefinitely, so the output continuously follows changes in the inputs.

2.3.2 Flowcharts

Flowcharts are a graphic way of describing the operation of a program. They are composed of different types of blocks interconnected with lines. There are three principal types of blocks used for flowcharts, as shown in Figure 2.13. A rectangular block describes each action the program takes. A diamond-shaped block is used for each decision, such as testing the value of a variable. An oval marks the beginning of the flowchart, with the name of the program placed inside it. An oval can also be used to mark the end of the flowchart. There are many other specialized flowcharting symbols, but they will not be used in this section.

Figure 2.14 shows a flowchart for the AND gate. For each line of the program there is a block, except for the two "Go to" instructions. These are

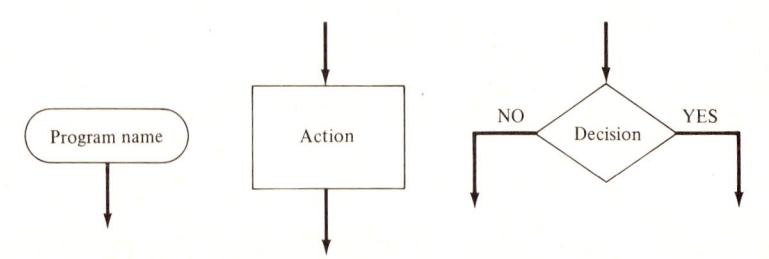

Figure 2.13 Flowcharting symbols.

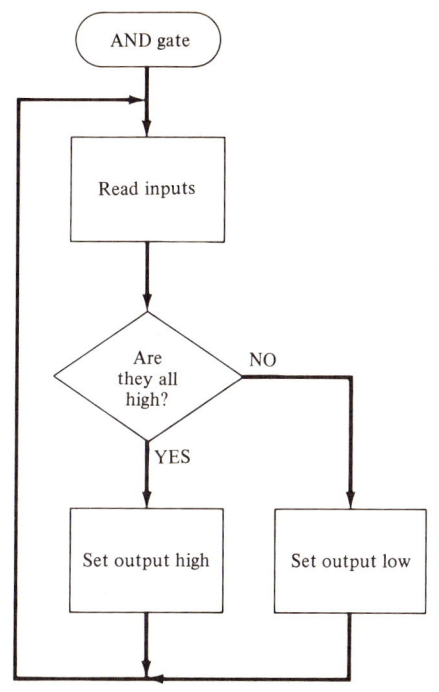

Figure 2.14 AND gate flowchart.

represented simply by a line. The lines show the flow of the program from one block to another.

While the flowchart contains the same information as the program list, it is in a more graphic form. When you first set out to write a program, a flowchart is a good way to organize your thoughts and document what the program must do. By going through the flowchart "by hand," you can check the logic. Then you can write the actual program from the flowchart. Flowcharts are also useful for going back to a program that has been written in the past and figuring out what the program does.

2.3.3 Programming Languages

Writing programs in English is convenient since it is the language most people understand, but unfortunately, it is meaningless to a microprocessor. The language understood by the microprocessor is called machine language (often referred to as machine code). Since microprocessors deal directly only with digital signals, machine language instructions are binary codes (e.g., 00111100). The microprocessor is designed to recognize a specific group of codes called the instruction set.

Machine language is not easy for people to use, since 00111100 has no obvious meaning. It can be made easier to work with by using the hexadecimal representation: 0011 1100 is replaced by 3C. However, this still does not provide any clue to the meaning of the instruction.

The next step is to replace each instruction code with a short name called a mnemonic. The code 3C, for example, which for the 8085 microprocessor means "increment the A register," is represented by INR A. The mnemonics are much easier to remember than the machine codes. By assigning a mnemonic to each instruction code, you can write programs using mnemonics instead of codes. The mnemonics can easily be converted to machine codes after the program is written. Therefore, you do not need to remember the machine codes, and the meaning of each instruction is easier to remember. Programs written using mnemonics are called assembly language programs.

The machine language is generally determined by the design of the microprocessor chip and cannot be modified. The assembly language mnemonics, however, are made up by the microprocessor's manufacturer as a convenience for programmers, and are not set by the processor design. For example, you could write INC A instead of INR A, as long as both were translated to the machine code 3C. In this book, Intel's 8085 assembly language conventions are usually followed.

While assembly language is a vast improvement over machine language, it is still difficult to use for writing complex programs. To make programming easier, high-level languages have been developed. These are similar to English and are generally independent of any particular microprocessor. A typical instruction might be LET COUNT = 10 or PRINT COUNT.

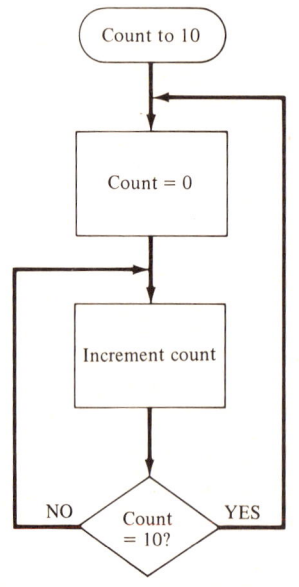

Figure 2.15 Count to ten flowchart.

Software Fundamentals 37

These instructions give a much more complicated command than those that the microprocessor can understand. Therefore, microcomputers on which high-level languages are used also contain long, complex programs (permanently stored in their memory) that translate the high-level language program into a machine language program. A single high-level instruction may translate into dozens of machine language instructions. Such translator programs are called compilers.

A simple programming example will serve to illustrate these concepts. Figure 2.15 shows the flowchart for a program that counts to ten. There is no input or output in this program: the contents of a designated memory location simply count from 0 to 10 and repeat.

The programs that follow are intended to give you an idea of what the various types of languages look like. Do not worry about remembering the details. Programming is discussed in greater detail in the following sections.

High-Level Language

The translation from the flowchart to a high-level language is fairly simple. The following example uses a variant of the high-level language called BASIC, which has the advantage of being simple and similar to English.

Table 2.7 shows the program listing. The first two lines of the program correspond exactly to the first two action blocks of the flowchart. In the first line the memory location called COUNT is set to zero. The second line, LET COUNT = COUNT + 1, is simply a way of saying "increment count." Lines three and four perform the function of the decision block. Line three specifies that if COUNT = 10, then the next instruction executed should be line one. If COUNT ≠ 10, this instruction has no effect, and the program continues with line four. That instruction says "go to line two." Thus, these two instructions perform the actions required by the decision block in the flowchart. Try following the program step by step to see the flow as the count reaches ten.

Assembly Language

Assembly language is not one specific language, but a class of languages. Each microprocessor has its own machine language and therefore its own

Table 2.7. Program in BASIC for Counting to Ten

Line Number	Instruction	Description
1	LET COUNT = 0	Set Count to 0
2	LET COUNT = COUNT + 1	Increment Count
3	IF COUNT = 10 THEN 1	Go to 1 if Count = 10
4	GO TO 2	Otherwise go to 2

assembly language (as defined by the manufacturer). This example uses the assembly language for Intel's 8085 microprocessor which is described later.

Table 2.8 shows the assembly language listing for the count to ten program. This program is certainly more cryptic than the BASIC language program, but it performs the same function. Remember that the characteristics of the assembly language are directly related to the characteristics of the microprocessor. This program is therefore different from the BASIC program, which is designed to be related to English rather than to the microprocessor's machine language.

The three columns are for labels, instructions, and comments. The label provides the same function as the line number. Instead of numbering every line, you simply make up a name (called a label) for each line to which you need to refer. A colon (:) is used to identify the label. A line needs a label only if there is another instruction in the program that refers to that line. The label allows you to easily identify a line that you want to jump to during the execution of a program.

The comments are an aid to understanding the program. A semicolon (;) identifies the beginning of a comment. High-level language programs do not need many comments because the instructions themselves are more descriptive. For assembly language programs, however, comments are an invaluable aid. They are useful for people other than the programmer who need to understand the program, as well as for the programmer, who may need to go back to the program after some time.

The first instruction is MVI A, 0 (move immediate to accumulator the data zero). The accumulator (also called the A register) is a storage location inside the microprocessor. This instruction is the equivalent of LET COUNT = 0, except that, instead of making up a name for the variable (COUNT), we used a preassigned name (A) for a register inside the microprocessor. Later you will see why this register is called the accumulator. For now, think of it simply as a general-purpose storage location in the microprocessor, which this instruction has loaded with the data zero.

The next instruction, INR A, means "increment the value in the

Table 2.8. Program in 8085 Assembly Language for Counting to Ten

LABEL	INSTRUCTION		COMMENTS
START:	MVI	A,0	;Set A register to 0
LOOP:	INR	A	;Increment A register
	CPI	10	;Compare A register to 10
	JZ	START	;Go to beginning if A = 10
	JMP	LOOP	;Repeat

Software Fundamentals

accumulator." The accumulator contains the count, so this is the equivalent of LET COUNT = COUNT + 1.

The next three instructions together implement the decision function. The instruction CPI 10 (compare immediate) means "compare the value in the accumulator with the value ten." It does not directly cause any jumps, regardless of the outcome of the comparison. Instead it sets a special flip-flop (called a flag) in the microprocessor if the value in the A register is equal to ten. Then the next instruction, JZ START, tests this flag. If the values are equal, this instruction detects that the flag is set and causes a jump to the line with the label START. These two instructions together (CPI 10 and JZ START) perform the function of the BASIC statement IF COUNT = 0 THEN 1. The last instruction, JMP LOOP, simply causes a jump to the line with the label LOOP. It is the equivalent of the BASIC statement GO TO 2.

Machine Language

As the last step of this example, Table 2.9 shows a listing of the machine language that corresponds to the assembly language program just discussed. The function of this program has become thoroughly obscured, and the problems of dealing with machine language should now be apparent. However, the compelling reason to use it is that it is the only language that the microprocessor understands directly. Note that we began with an English program description and ended with a sequence of 1's and 0's suitable for storing in the microcomputer's memory.

To understand the machine code, refer to Table 2.10 which compares the three programs. Each memory location holds 8 bits of data. (Eight bits can be represented by two hex characters.) Each instruction begins with an op code (short for operation code). The op code specifies the operation to be performed. All 8085 op codes are 8 bits (1 byte) each, and therefore occupy

Table 2.9. 8085 Machine Language Program for Counting to Ten

MEMORY ADRESS (HEX)	MEMORY CONTENTS (HEX)	(BINARY)
07F0	3E	00111110
07F1	00	00000000
07F2	3C	00111100
07F3	FE	11111110
07F4	0A	00001010
07F5	CA	11001010
07F6	F0	11110000
07F7	07	00000111
07F8	C3	11000011
07F9	F2	11110010
07FA	07	00000111

TABLE 2.10. Counting to Ten in Three Languages

BASIC LANGUAGE		8085 ASSEMBLY LANGUAGE			8085 MACHINE LANGUAGE		
LINE NUMBERS	INSTRUCTION	LABEL	INSTRUCTION		ADDRESS	CONTENTS	
1	LET COUNT = 0	START:	MVI	A,0	07F0	3E	Op code
					07F1	00	Data
2	LET COUNT = COUNT + 1	LOOP:	INR	A	07F2	3C	Op code
3	IF COUNT = 10 THEN 1		CPI	10_{10}	07F3	FE	Op code
					07F4	0A	Data
			JZ	START	07F5	CA	Op code
					07F6	F0	Address
					07F7	07	
4	GO TO 2		JMP	LOOP	07F8	C3	Op code
					07F9	F2	Address
					07FA	07	

one memory location. An op code may be followed by zero, one, or two bytes of data, depending upon the instruction.

The first byte (3E) at address 07F0 is the op code for the instruction MVI A. It is, however, only part of the complete instruction. It specifies that you want to move some data into the accumulator. Now you need another memory location to specify this data. Therefore, the next memory location (address 07F1) contains 00, the data to be moved to the accumulator.

The third location contains the op code for the second instruction, INR A. This op code (3C) tells the microprocessor to increment the accumulator. Since there is no additional data associated with this instruction, it occupies only one memory location.

The code FE is the op code for the compare instruction, CPI. Just as with the MVI A, 0 instruction, the memory location that follows the op code contains the data required by the instruction. Because the machine language is shown in hexadecimal notation, the data (10 decimal) appears as 0A (hex). This instruction compares the accumulator with the value 10 and sets a flag (as described earlier) if they are equal.

The JZ instruction has the op code CA, which appears at address 07F5. This opcode tells the microprocessor to jump if the flag is set. The next two memory locations tell it what address to jump to. Since addresses in an 8085 system are 16 bits long, it takes two memory locations (8 bits each) to store an address. The two parts of the address are stored in the reverse of the order you might expect. The least significant half is stored first and then the most significant half. Thus, the address 07F0 is stored as F0 07. The assembly language instruction JZ START means that the processor should jump to the instruction labeled START. The machine code must then use the actual address that corresponds to the label START (07F0 in this case).

The last instruction, JMP LOOP, is coded in the same way. The only difference is that this jump is independent of any conditions. The code for this type of jump is C3. The jump address (07F2) is stored in the same way as for the JZ instruction.

Note that the machine language program consists of a series of bytes, each of which may have one of three meanings. Some are op codes, some are data, and some are jump addresses. You must know the context of the information to know which type it is. Circuits within the microprocessor determine whether a particular op code should be followed by data or an address, so it can keep track of the three types.

High-level languages are the easiest for programmers to use and can be independent of any particular microprocessor. However, lengthy translation programs must be stored in the microcomputer's memory to translate the programs to machine code. High-level languages are also less efficient in terms of speed of operation and memory usage. An equivalent program written in assembly language normally runs faster and occupies less memory.

Assembly language is widely used for programming microcomputers. It is more difficult to write programs in assembly language than in a high-level language. However, it is much easier to translate from assembly to machine language than from high-level to machine language. In applications in which the program must run as rapidly as possible or fit into as small a memory as possible, assembly language is usually the best choice. From an educational viewpoint, programming in assembly language gives you a much better idea of how the microprocessor system works.

Machine language is the only language directly understood by the microprocessor, but people have a hard time using it. It is difficult to program directly in machine language. Programs are usually written in assembly language and then translated to machine code. The translation may be performed by a special program (called an assembler).

PROBLEMS AND QUESTIONS

2.1   Name one advantage that makes microprocessor-based systems flexible over random logic designs.
2.2   Identify the three groups of signals that interconnect the components of a microprocessor system.
2.3   What is the difference between a byte and a word for an 8-bit microprocessor?
2.4   What is the difference between a microprocessor and a microcomputer?

2.5 Why are both ROMs and RAMs used with microprocessors?

2.6 What is the difference between the accumulator and program counter?

2.7 Identify the main differences among the machine language, assembly language, and high-level language.

2.8 Name one advantage of the microprocessor-based AND gate over a standard AND gate.

2.9 What is the purpose of the labels in an assembly language program?

2.10 Perform the following operations. Include answers in hexadecimal.

$$3F_{16} \quad A9 \quad 35_{10} \quad 6E_{16}$$
$$-2A_{16} \quad +A1 \quad -49_{10} \quad \cdot 7A_{16}$$

2.11 1111 0001 is the twos complement representation of:
(a) F1.
(b) −F1.
(c) 0E.
(d) 0F

2.12 For a processor that uses 4-bit words, what is the largest number that can be represented using double precision?

2.13 What is the advantage of using BCD?

CHAPTER 3

MICROCOMPUTER SYSTEM HARDWARE AND I/O TECHNIQUES

This chapter contains basic types of microcomputer hardware and typical I/O techniques. These include the bus concept, address decoding techniques, memories and peripherals, and the basic input/output methods.

3.1 Basic Hardware Concepts

This section describes basic microprocessor system hardware. Bus structures and address decoding are discussed. The emphasis is on understanding the fundamental parts of a typical system, rather than considering a variety of design possibilities.

3.1.1 The Bus Concept

Microprocessor systems are designed around buses, which are not usually found in traditional random logic designs. In a microprocessor system, many devices must exchange data with the processor. Figure 3.1 shows how this can be done using traditional design techniques. The processor must have a set of data outputs for each device and a multiplexer to select a particular device for data input. This method very quickly gets unwieldy as more and more devices are added. The data paths commonly carry 8 bits of data, so each path requires eight lines. Therefore, for the simple three-device system shown, 48 lines are required: 24 for data input and 24 for data output. A more complicated system might have dozens of memory devices and I/O ports and require hundreds of interconnecting lines.

A solution to this interconnection problem is the use of a bus, as shown in

This chapter contains material reprinted from *Practical Microprocessors—Hardware, Software and Troubleshooting,* copyright © 1979. Reprinted by permission of Hewlett-Packard.

43

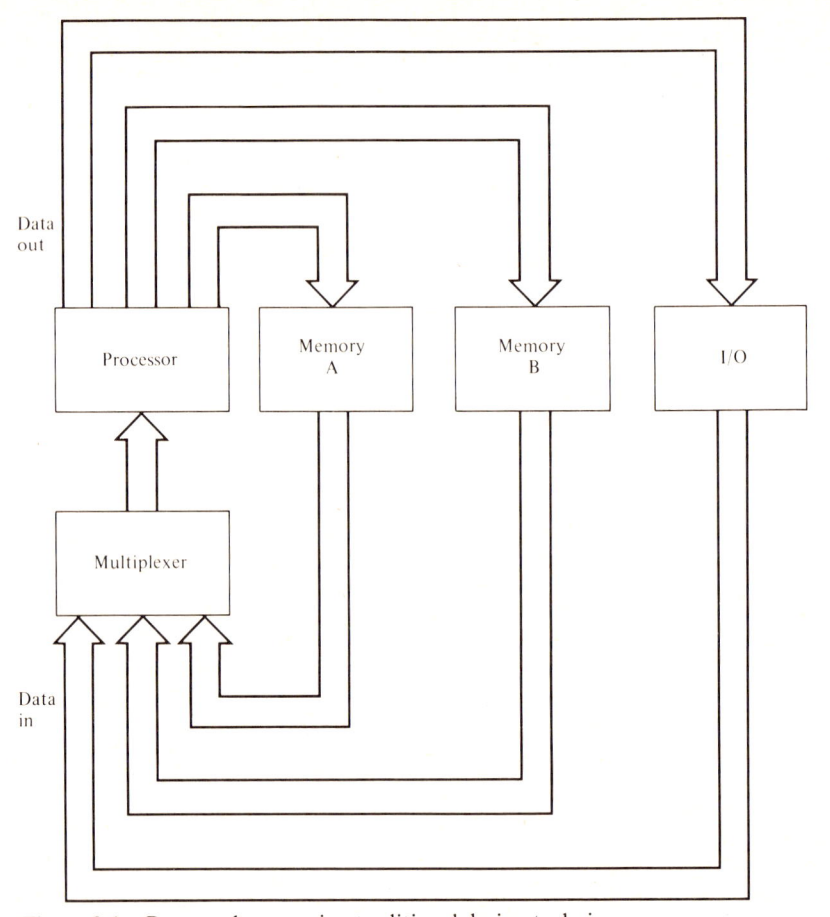

Figure 3.1 Data exchange using traditional design techniques.

Figure 3.2. Note how much simpler the interconnections are. A single set of eight lines is used to interconnect all the devices, and the same set of lines is used for data traveling into or out of the processor. This structure can be expanded indefinitely with little increase in interconnection complexity. A consequence of this technique is that, since all devices share the same data lines, only one may supply data at any given time. The address and control lines (driven by the microprocessor) provide the necessary control to select a particular device.

3.1.2 The Three-State Bus

The three-state driver makes the shared data bus possible. For the sake of simplicity, a single-line bus is discussed first. However, the concept is

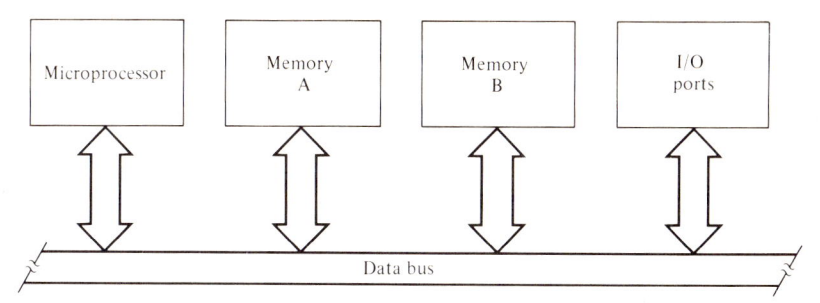

Figure 3.2 Data exchange using a bus to reduce the number of interconnecting lines.

exactly the same regardless of the number of lines in the bus. (A typical data bus has eight lines.)

The three-state bus is like a telephone party line. The bus can have many talkers and many listeners connected to it. Figure 3.3 shows a digital circuit bus with four talkers (three-state drivers) and two listeners (ordinary gates). The control logic chooses only one driver (talker) to be active at any given time. If more than one talker were enabled, the data on the bus would

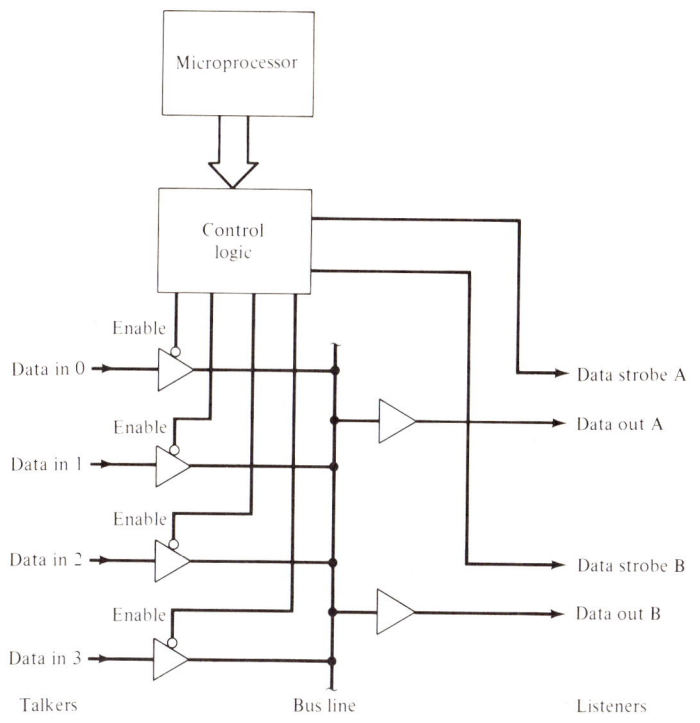

Figure 3.3 Three-state single-line bus with four talkers and two listeners.

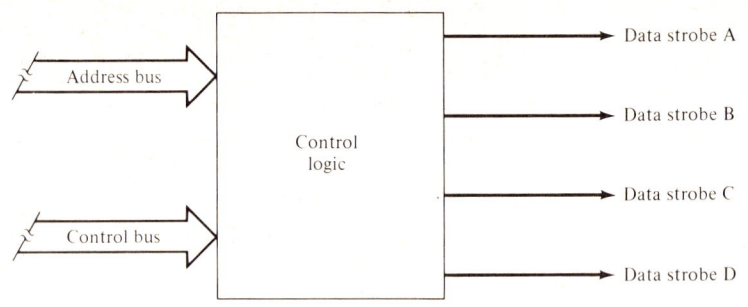

Figure 3.4 Control logic selects device to be involved in data transfer.

be meaningless. When a driver is enabled, the data at its input are placed on the bus. All of the other drivers are disabled. Their outputs are in a high-impedance (floating) state, so they have no effect on the logic state of the bus.

There can be many listeners on the bus. Since all they do is listen, more than one of them can be enabled at the same time. In general, however, the data on the bus is intended for one of them in particular. The control logic generates signals (data strobes) to tell selected listeners that the data on the bus is intended for them. A data strobe can be used, for example, to clock the data from the bus into a flip-flop. The inputs to the control logic are the address and control buses coming from the microprocessor (see Figure 3.4).

The devices just described are unidirectional. They are either talkers or

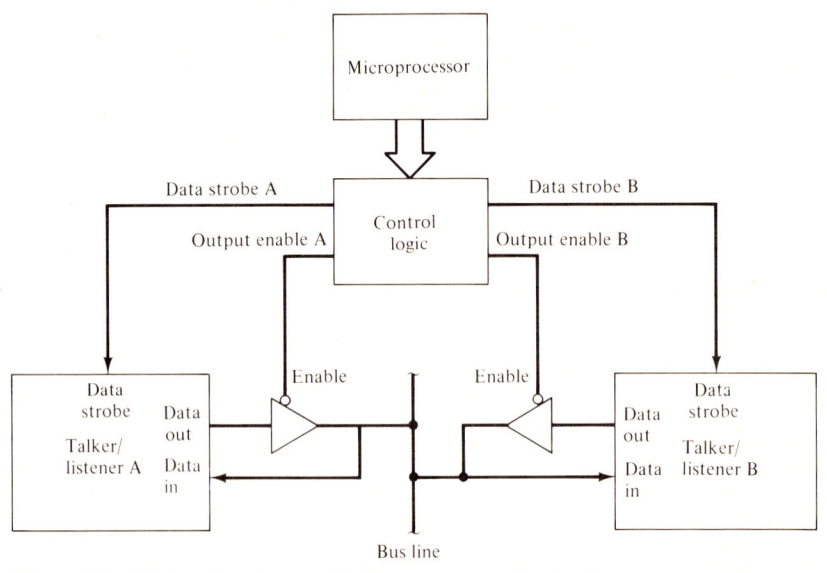

Figure 3.5 Bidirectional talker/listeners connected to bus lines.

Basic Hardware Concepts   47

listeners, but not both. Bidirectional devices also exist, which are both talkers and listeners. Figure 3.5 shows a bus with two talker/listeners. For the sake of simplicity, only two have been shown, but there could be many more. Each talker/listener is provided with two control signals; the output enable signal for the three-state driver and the data strobe for the input. An example of a bidirectional device is a RAM, which can read and write data.

As an example of how this procedure works, suppose device A in Figure 3.5 must send a piece of data to device B. The control logic sets output enable A true (enabled) and output enable B false (not enabled). Then, after enough settling time has elapsed for the data to reach device B's data input, the controller sends a pulse on the data strobe B line. This causes device B to read the data from the bus, which were supplied by device A. Note that many other devices can be connected to the bus. As long as their enables are false, they have no effect.

3.1.3 The System Bus

The microprocessor system's data bus is a bidirectional, three-state bus. It is the same as a single-line bus except that there are eight lines instead of just one. To utilize all the data bus lines, each talker must have eight drivers (one for each line) and each listener must have eight inputs. The microprocessor and RAM are talker/listeners. Input ports are talkers that take inputs from outside the system and put them on the bus. Output ports are listeners that take data off the bus and send it outside the system. The ROM is only a talker.

Figure 3.6 shows how these devices communicate with the data bus. The microprocessor, ROM, RAM, and input ports contain three-state drivers

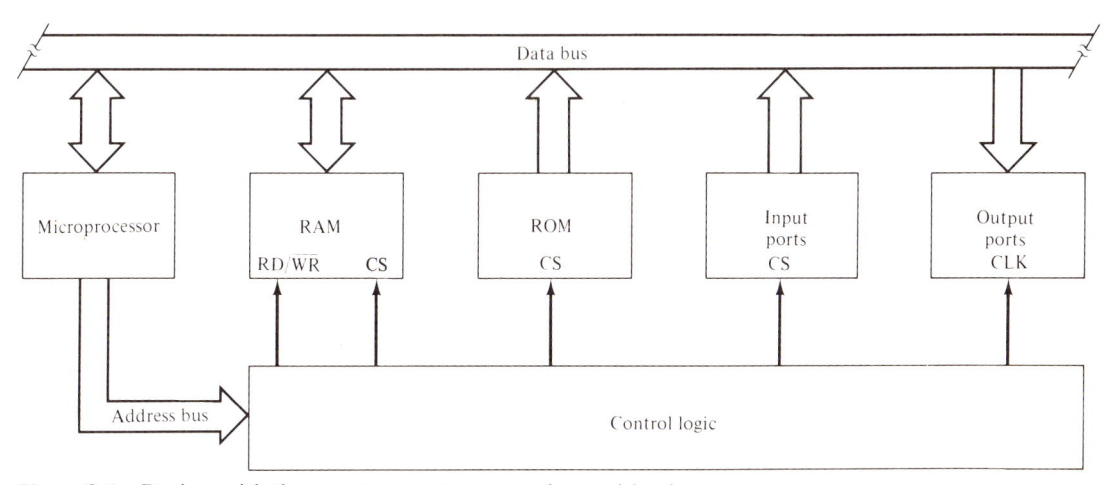

Figure 3.6 Devices with three-state outputs communicate with microprocessor through data bus.

on their outputs. The Chip Select (CS) inputs enable the drivers and cause the data from the selected device to appear on the data bus.

The microprocessor acts as the controller for the system. It ensures that no more than one device is trying to use the bus at any given time. If the microprocessor wants to read data from the ROM, it first disables its own data outputs and then generates the control signals required to enable the ROM. The ROM's outputs then appear on the data bus, and the microprocessor reads the data. Reading the RAM or the input port is done in a similar manner.

To write data to a device (such as the RAM or output port), the microprocessor first places the data to be written onto the data bus. It then generates control signals that send a write pulse to the appropriate device. The write pulse causes that device to internally latch the data.

In general, data flows through the microprocessor. For example, to transfer data from the input port to the RAM, the microprocessor first reads the data from the input port and then writes it to the RAM. Because data cannot be transferred directly from the input port to the RAM, it must be temporarily stored within the microprocessor.

To summarize, the data bus is used for all transfers of data within the microprocessor system. All devices share the same bus. The control logic, operating from signals generated by the microprocessor, directs each device as to when it should place data on the bus or read data from the bus.

The 8085 is capable of handling 8 bits of data at a time and is therefore called an 8-bit processor. Other microprocessors exist which handle more or less data. Many of the early microprocessors used a 4-bit data bus and some of the newer devices use a 16-bit data bus.

You have seen how the data bus is used by many devices to exchange data. Now a method is needed by which the microprocessor can select the particular device that communicates with the data bus. The address bus (in conjunction with the control bus) provides this function.

Since the address bus is unidirectional, its operation is simpler than the data bus. Every memory location (and I/O port) has a unique address. Before any data transfer can take place (via the data bus), the microprocessor must output an address. The address specifies the exact memory location (or I/O port) which the processor wishes to access. In this way, the microprocessor can select any part of the system with which it must communicate.

The 8085's address bus has 16 lines, allowing direct addressing of 2^{16} = 65,536 memory locations and I/O ports. These lines are referred to as A_0, $A_1, A_2, \ldots, A_{15}$, with A_0 being the least significant bit.

The address decoder is a part of the control logic. It generates device select signals when a certain address (or range of addresses) is present on the address bus. For example, Figure 3.7 shows an address decoder for

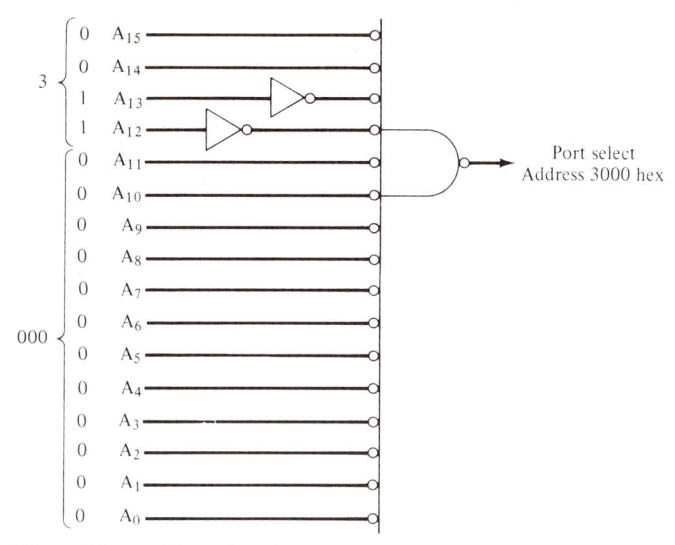

Figure 3.7 Address decoder configured to control port assigned to address 3000.

address 3000 hex (0011 0000 0000 0000 binary). The output of this decoder is true (logic 0) only when this exact address is present on the address bus. This output is then used to enable the port that is assigned address 3000.

You have seen how the address bus is used to select a particular memory location or I/O port and how the data bus carries the data. The entire process is coordinated by the control bus, consisting of a number of control signals, most of which are generated by the microprocessor (a few are inputs to the processor). In this section only the signals that control the reading and writing of I/O ports and memory are discussed.

The two main control signals generated by the 8085 are $\overline{\text{READ}}$ and $\overline{\text{WRITE}}$. If $\overline{\text{READ}}$ is low, it indicates that a read operation is in progress, and the microprocessor signals the addressed device to place data on the data bus. If $\overline{\text{WRITE}}$ is low, then a write operation is in progress, and the microprocessor puts data on the data bus and signals the addressed device to store this data.

The major difference between the control bus and the address and data buses is that each wire in the control bus has a unique function. For the address and data buses, each line carries the same type of information (1 bit of the address or data).

Keep in mind that we are describing the 8085's control signals and that other microprocessors may differ. The data transfers are the same, but they can be achieved in different ways.

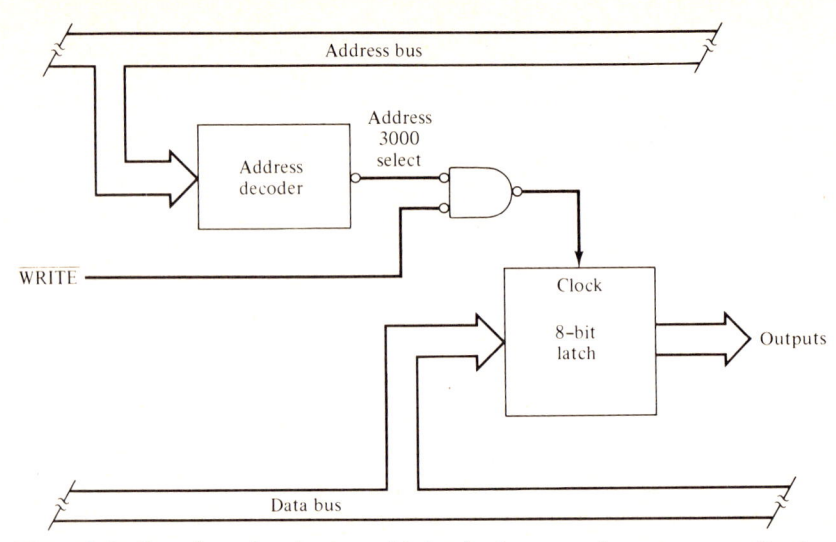

Figure 3.8 Data from data bus stored in latch whenever microprocessor writes to address 3000.

3.1.4 Input and Output Ports

Figure 3.8 shows an output port latch with an assigned address of 3000. The latch is clocked whenever address 3000 is present on the address bus (as indicated by the address decoder) and a low-to-high transition occurs on the $\overline{\text{WRITE}}$ control signal. When the latch is clocked, the data from that

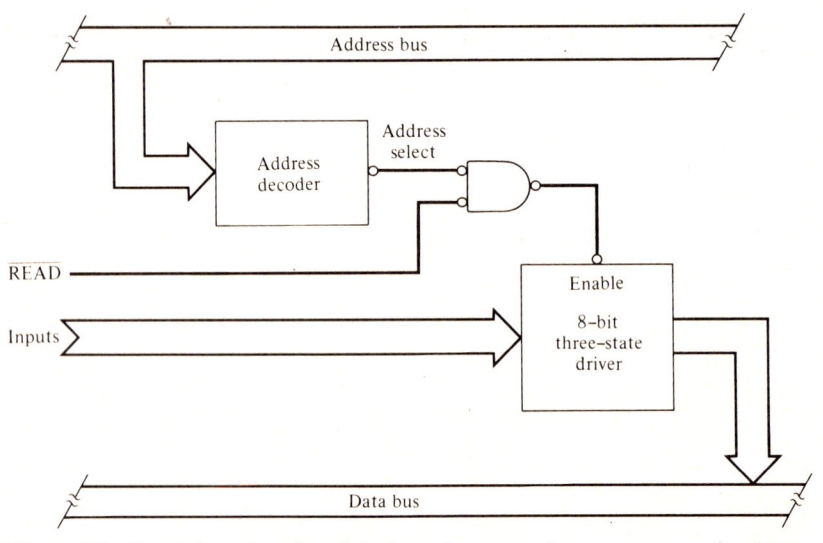

Figure 3.9 Input data placed on data bus whenever microprocessor reads address assigned to three-state driver.

data bus is stored on it. The microprocessor can therefore cause data specified by a program to appear at the output of the latch by writing the data to address 3000.

Input ports are connected in a similar manner, as shown in Figure 3.9. The output of the address decoder is ANDed with $\overline{READ}$ instead of $\overline{WRITE}$ to generate the port enable. The input port is an eight-line three-state driver which places the input signals on the data bus when enabled. The microprocessor can read the input signals on the data bus when enabled. The microprocessor can read the input signals by performing the read operation from the appropriate address. The processor then stores this data in one of its internal registers.

3.1.5 Address Decoding for Multiple Devices and Memories

Suppose that an address decoder is required to control eight I/O ports instead of just one. Eight address decoders similar to the one in Figure 3.7 could be used, but there is a simpler method. Figure 3.10 shows an address decoder that generates select signals for addresses 3000, 3001, 3002, ..., 3007. For these eight addresses, only the three low-order address bits (A_0, A_1, and A_2) of the 16-bit address are changed. The upper 13 bits can therefore be decoded by a common circuit similar to the one in Figure 3.7. The output of this circuit is used to enable a decoder such as a 74LS138. This decoder then generates eight separate outputs, one for each possible

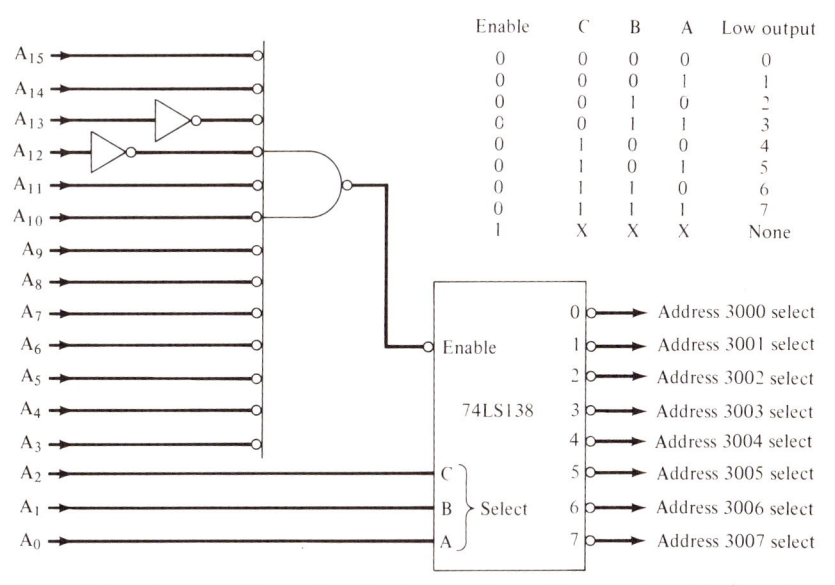

Figure 3.10 Decoder IC provides simple way of extending number of devices that can be selected.

combination of A_0, A_1, and A_2. The decoder is disabled (all outputs are false) if the upper 13 address bits are not of the specified value. In most cases, you do not need to decode the entire 16 bits of the address to select a specific device. All 16 bits are shown in the examples to emphasize that the system does have this amount of addressing capability if required.

Address decoding for memories is similar to that used for a group of I/O ports. For example, think of a ROM as a device with hundreds of 8-bit input ports on a single chip, with one port for each memory location. When the ROM is programmed, the ROM memory locations are permanently set to a desired pattern of 1's and 0's. For a RAM, each memory location can be thought of as having both an input and an output port tied together.

Suppose an address decoder is required for a small ROM containing 256 bytes. Figure 3.11 shows a circuit that accomplishes this. The low-order bits of the address bus connect directly to the ROM. The ROM has an internal address decoder that selects one of the $2^8 = 256$ locations. The high-order 8 bits of the address bus are decoded by an external address decoder to enable the ROM when its particular range of addresses is present on the upper half of the address bus. Notice that all 16 address bits are decoded: half by the address decoder in the ROM and half by the external address decoder. The $\overline{\text{READ}}$ signal is ANDed with the address decoder output to generate the ROM enable. This is identical to the technique used for input ports.

Because most microprocessor systems use more than one memory chip, they need a more complex address decoder. Suppose that four of these 256-byte ROMs were connected with the addresses assigned to each chip as shown in Figure 3.12(a).

The address lines must now indicate which memory chip should be

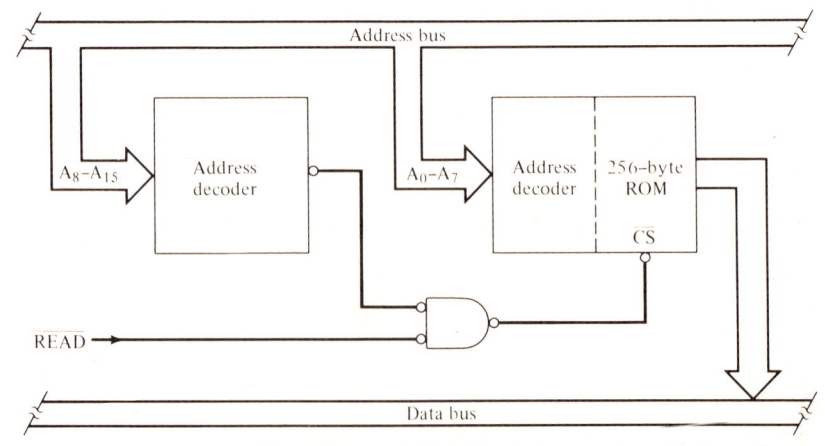

Figure 3.11 Internal address decoder in ROM reduces number of address lines needed by external address decoder.

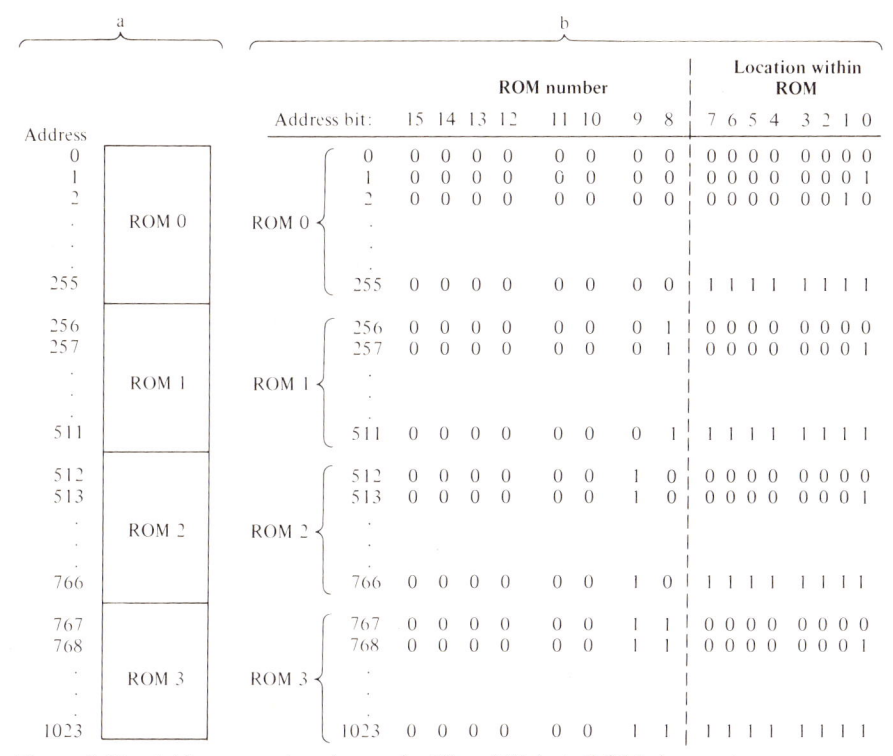

Figure 3.12 Addresses assigned to each of four 256-byte ROMs in a system.

		Address bit:	15	14	13	12	11	10	9	8	7	6	5	4	3	2	1	0
Address 0			0	0	0	0	0	0	0	0	0	0	0	0	0	0	0	0
1			0	0	0	0	0	0	0	0	0	0	0	0	0	0	0	1
2	ROM 0	ROM 0 — 2	0	0	0	0	0	0	0	0	0	0	0	0	0	0	1	0
255		255	0	0	0	0	0	0	0	0	1	1	1	1	1	1	1	1
256		256	0	0	0	0	0	0	0	1	0	0	0	0	0	0	0	0
257	ROM 1	257	0	0	0	0	0	0	0	1	0	0	0	0	0	0	0	1
511		ROM 1 — 511	0	0	0	0	0	0	0	1	1	1	1	1	1	1	1	1
512		512	0	0	0	0	0	0	1	0	0	0	0	0	0	0	0	0
513	ROM 2	513	0	0	0	0	0	0	1	0	0	0	0	0	0	0	0	1
766		ROM 2 — 766	0	0	0	0	0	0	1	0	1	1	1	1	1	1	1	1
767		767	0	0	0	0	0	0	1	1	0	0	0	0	0	0	0	0
768	ROM 3	768	0	0	0	0	0	0	1	1	0	0	0	0	0	0	0	1
1023		ROM 3 — 1023	0	0	0	0	0	0	1	1	1	1	1	1	1	1	1	1

(a) left block; (b) right block — ROM number (bits 15–8), Location within ROM (bits 7–0).

selected and which word within that chip should be addressed. Figure 3-12(b) shows the addresses in binary, so that you can see how to deal with each individual bit. The lower 8 bits of address specify the location within each chip, and the upper 8 bits specify which chip is being addressed.

Observe that only bits A_8 and A_9 vary in decoding one chip from another. The reason that only these two address bits vary is that it takes exactly 10 bits to decode 1024 addresses ($2^{10} = 1024$). A_9 is the tenth bit. The four possible combinations of A_8 and A_9 therefore specify one of four blocks of 256 addresses each (the size of each ROM). The full 16-bit address bus is shown because the microprocessor has the capability of addressing up to 64K locations.

Figure 3.13 shows how this addressing is implemented. The lower 8 bits of address go directly to the address lines of all four ROMs, since these bits specify the location within the chip. The address decoder then looks at the upper 8 bits of address and generates the chip selects. The two least significant bits (of the upper half), A_8 and A_9, are used for the binary inputs to the decoder. The rest of the high-order address bits are used to enable the decoder only when they are all low. Study this diagram and the address-mapping table in Figure 3.12(b); you should be able to see how they

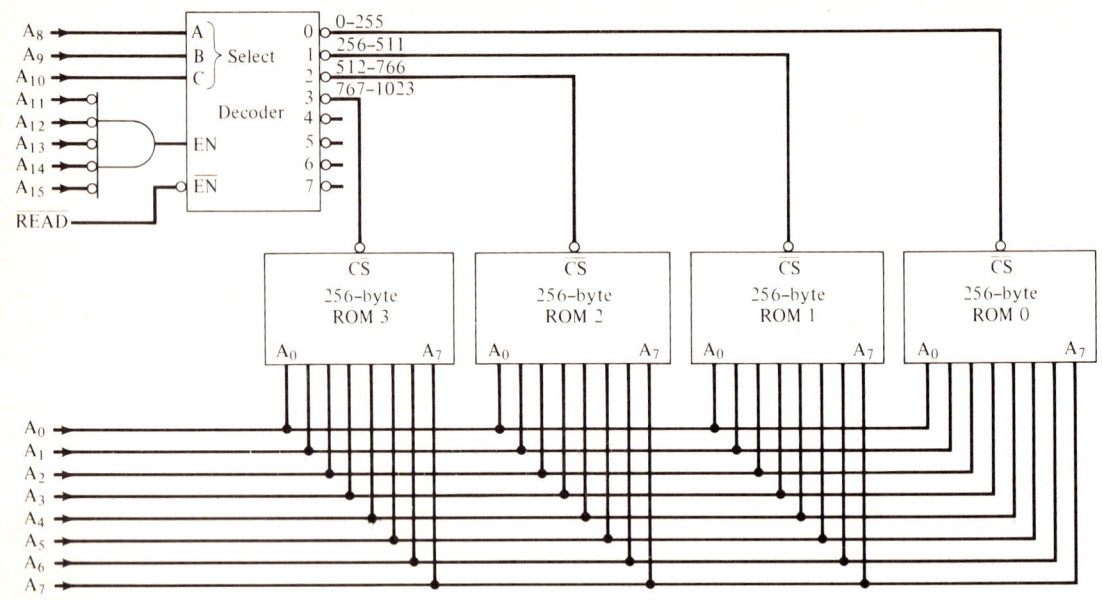

54 Chapter 3 MICROCOMPUTER SYSTEM HARDWARE AND I/O TECHNIQUES

Figure 3.13 Address decoding for four 256-byte ROM example in Figure 3.12.

correspond. Notice that the $\overline{\text{READ}}$ control signal is used as a decoder enable. This is equivalent to ANDing this signal with each of the decoder's outputs.

Although there are numerous variations to this approach, this is a complete and straightforward address decoding technique. It serves to illustrate the basic principle: the low-order address bits are sent directly to the memory's address lines, and the high-order bits are decoded to generate the chip selects. No more than one chip can be selected at any given time. Other designs vary in the number of bits fed directly to the memory devices (a function of the number of words in each memory chip) and in the way the high-order bits are decoded to generate the chip selects.

RAMs are decoded in a manner similar to ROMs, but with some extra control circuits to write (input to the RAM) as well as read (output from the RAM). RAMs have a $\overline{\text{WRITE}}$ input in addition to the $\overline{\text{CS}}$ input.

$\overline{\text{CS}}$	WR	Function
0	0	Write
0	1	Read
1	X	No operation

0 = Low
1 = High
x = Don't care

Figure 3.14 Truth table for controlling RAM.

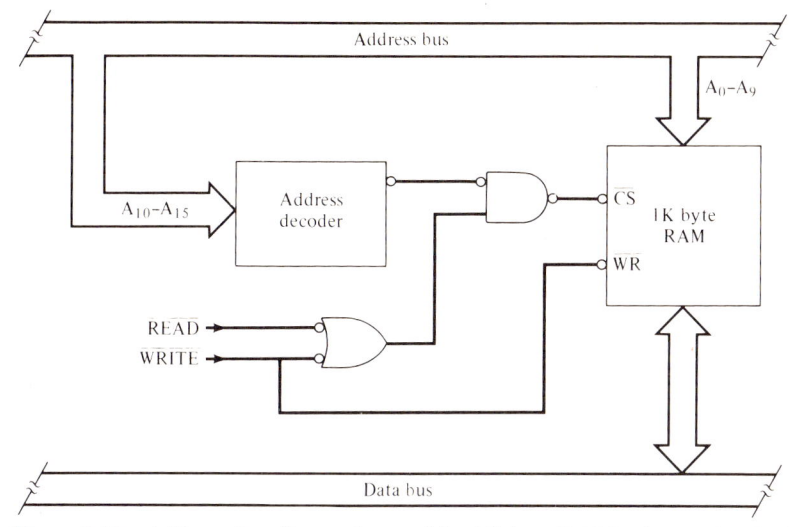

Figure 3.15 Address decoding and control for 1K-byte RAM using truth table in Figure 3.14.

Figure 3.14 shows the truth table for the $\overline{\text{RAM}}$ control. $\overline{\text{CS}}$ must be low for either a read or write to take place. If $\overline{\text{WRITE}}$ is high (not true) when $\overline{\text{CS}}$ is low, the RAM outputs data to the data bus so that the processor can read it. To do this, $\overline{\text{CS}}$ enables the RAM's three-state output drivers. If $\overline{\text{WRITE}}$ is low, $\overline{\text{CS}}$ does not turn on the RAM's output drivers. Instead, the data on the data bus is stored in (written into) the memory at the location specified by the address bus.

A circuit to perform the desired gating is shown in Figure 3.15. $\overline{\text{CS}}$ is low if the RAM address select and either $\overline{\text{READ}}$ or $\overline{\text{WRITE}}$ are low. The $\overline{\text{WRITE}}$ line is connected directly to the RAM's $\overline{\text{WRITE}}$ input. The $\overline{\text{WRITE}}$ input is internally gated with the $\overline{\text{CS}}$ input, so that it is ignored unless $\overline{\text{CS}}$ is low.

3.2 Address Decoding

All devices that communicate with the microprocessor have specific addresses assigned to them. The address decoding circuits ensure that the correct device is on the bus when it is addressed by the microprocessor.

3.2.1 The Address Decoder

An examination of the hardware used to implement the address decoding will show why this approach has simplified the circuits. Figure 3.16 shows the address decoding and control circuits of a typical microprocessor.

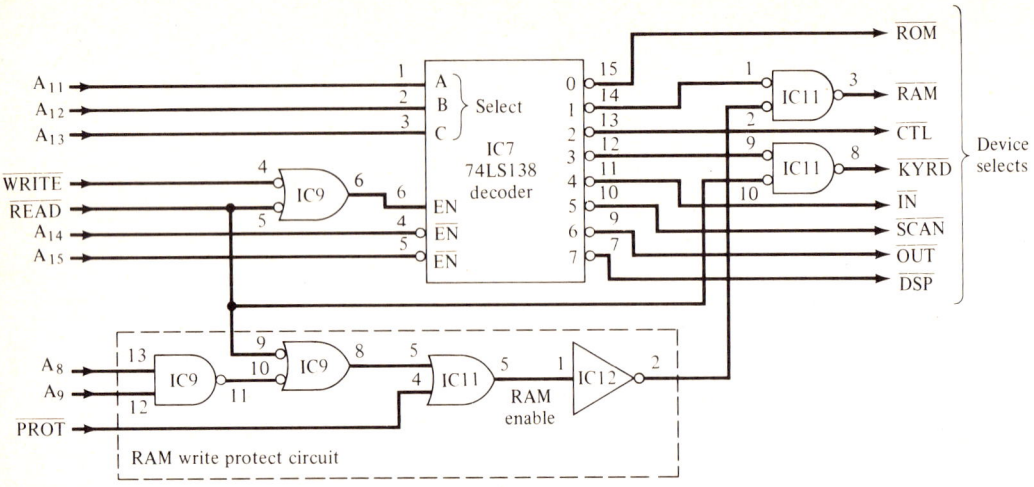

Figure 3.16 Address decoding circuit of a typical microprocessor.

Notice that the A_{11}, A_{12}, and A_{13} lines specify which of eight sections is addressed. These three lines are used to provide the binary select inputs to the 74LS138 binary to one-of-eight decoder. This device provides eight separate outputs, one for each of the 2K blocks the system uses. This method results in a relatively simple address decoding circuit. The simplicity is a direct consequence of the fact that each device is assigned a block of addresses of equal length.

The 74LS138 has three enable inputs: two active low and one active high. All three must be true to allow any of the outputs to be true. The A_{14} and A_{15} lines (connected to the two active low enables) prevent any of the outputs from being true unless both A_{14} and A_{15} are low. This restricts the devices to the lower 16K of the 64K address field.

Connecting the $\overline{READ}$ and $\overline{WRITE}$ lines to decoder enable inputs ensures that the bus devices can be enabled only during a read or write operation. This eliminates the need to gate the $\overline{READ}$ or $\overline{WRITE}$ lines directly into many of the device select signals. For this reason the decoder's third enable input is connected to a gate that generates the OR of $\overline{READ}$ and $\overline{WRITE}$. This allows the device select outputs to be true only when either a read or a write is in progress. The address bus contains meaningful information only during these periods. Enabling the device select outputs only at these times prevents the devices from reading or writing data at the wrong time. Some microprocessor-based systems may not require this type of enabling to be done.

Additionally, the ROM and the input ports must be selected only if a read is being performed. If they responded to either a read or a write, a bus conflict could occur. For example, if a write to the ROM is performed, the microprocessor places data on the data bus. A write to a ROM is impossible. So if the ROM is enabled during the write operation, it will also try to put data on the data bus. This is an unacceptable situation which could even result in electrical circuit damage.

To solve this problem, the $\overline{\text{READ}}$ signal must be ANDed with the ROM device select. This is implemented by connecting $\overline{\text{READ}}$ to one of the ROM's enables. Figure 3.16 shows how this is done for the keyboard input port (KYRD).

For the output ports, the situation is slightly different. Consider the $\overline{\text{OUT}}$ line in Figure 3.16. Since the output port controlled by this line can be enabled by either a $\overline{\text{READ}}$ or a $\overline{\text{WRITE}}$ signal, a write enable to the port would occur for either command. If an attempt is made to read the output port (which is not a meaningful operation), a write is performed instead of a read, loading the port with undefined data. This operation is acceptable because it does not cause a hardware conflict (i.e., it does not make any difference from an electrical standpoint). Therefore, it is not necessary to AND the $\overline{\text{WRITE}}$ signal with the device selects for the output ports.

The RAM's device select is somewhat different. It must be true when either a read or a write to the RAM's address space is in progress. The gate (IC11A) on the RAM's device select line is for the write protect circuit, which is described in the following section.

The write protect circuit helps prevent the RAM's contents from being accidentally destroyed. Occasionally, a relatively simple programming error causes the microprocessor to run amuck (usually by interpreting data as instructions). This error often results in the storing of garbage data into the entire RAM, which could erase the program just entered.

To prevent this problem, a latch can be used for protecting the memory. The output of this latch provides the $\overline{\text{PROT}}$ input to the circuit in Figure 3.16. When the latch is set, the RAM is protected. In this mode, the RAM can be read but not written to. The monitor automatically sets the protect latch whenever you run a program. Otherwise, it is reset to allow you to enter data or modify programs.

Because you may want to use the RAM to store data during program execution, only the first three-fourths of the RAM is protected. Address lines A_8 and A_9 determine which fourth of the RAM is addressed. When they are both high, the last quarter of RAM is addressed and therefore not protected. The A_8 and A_9 lines are ANDed together, and the result is then ORed with $\overline{\text{READ}}$ and ORed with $\overline{\text{PROT}}$. This output produces the RAM enable signal.

There are a number of other techniques for performing address decoding. The technique used for a particular application depends on many factors, including the amount of memory, the number of peripherals, the need for expandability, the types of memory and I/O devices used, and the speed requirements. In some cases these devices have enable pins on them which can be used as part of the address decoding.

3.2.2 Linear Select Decoding

Linear select, the simplest of all decoding techniques, uses no address decoding logic. The high-order address bits act directly as chip selects. Figure 3.17 shows an example of linear select decoding. The RAM is selected whenever A_{15} is high. This corresponds to all addresses from 8000 to FFFF. The ROM is selected whenever A_{14} is high. This is true for addresses 4000 to 7FFF.

Notice that the ROM is also selected if A_{14} and A_{15} are high, corresponding to addresses C000 through FFFF. This overlaps the RAM's space. Both devices are enabled if an attempt is made to read from any of these addresses and will cause a bus conflict. This is one disadvantage of linear select decoding. Because of this potential problem, the software must never read any address in which more than one of the two most significant bits are true. Another disadvantage of this method is that it wastes a large amount of address space. The technique is therefore limited to small systems.

3.2.3 Logic Comparator Decoding

One of the most straightforward and flexible techniques, logic comparator decoding, selects a single portion of 2^N possible address fields from N address inputs. Figure 3.18 shows a circuit that generates a single device select from the six high-order address bits of a system. Each comparator A input is compared to its respective B input. When they all match (all six input pairs are coincident) the comparator output goes low. The switches are used to set the logic level at the B inputs to the comparator. This technique is particularly useful on memory and peripheral boards where

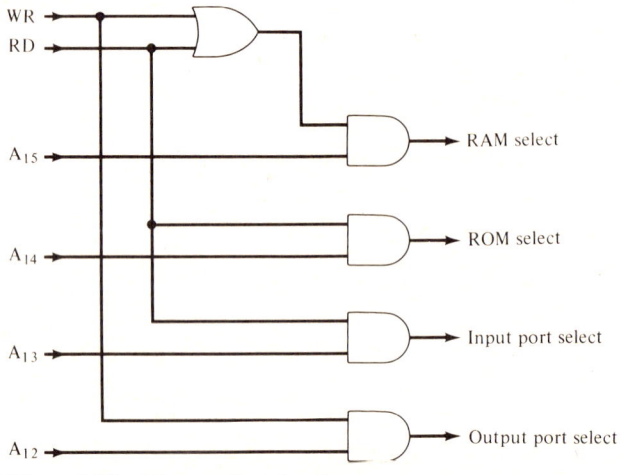

Figure 3.17 Linear select decoder.

Address Decoding 59

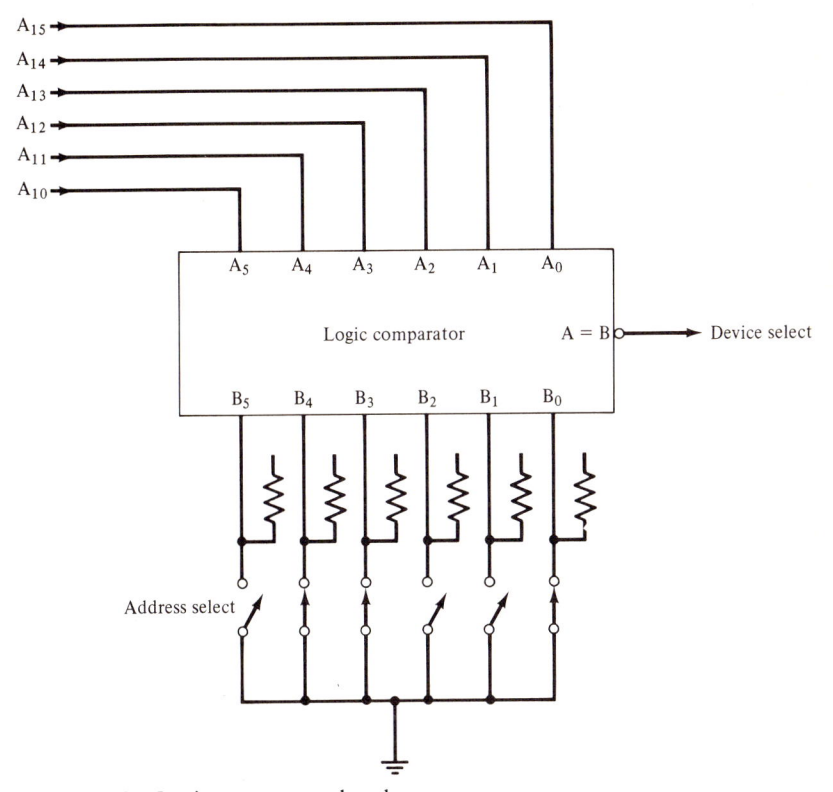

Figure 3.18 Logic comparator decoder.

there are switches or jumpers that set the address of each board in a system. Exclusive OR gates can also be used to accomplish the comparator function.

3.2.4 Combinational Logic Decoding

In systems with very limited decoding requirements, standard logic gates are often used. Figure 3.19 shows a four-input NAND gate preceded by inverters which decodes addresses 9000 through 9FFF. The output goes low whenever the A_{15} to A_{12} address lines are in the state 1, 0, 0, 1. By

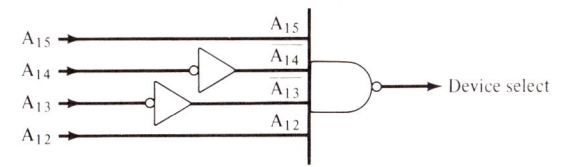

Figure 3.19 Logic gate decoder.

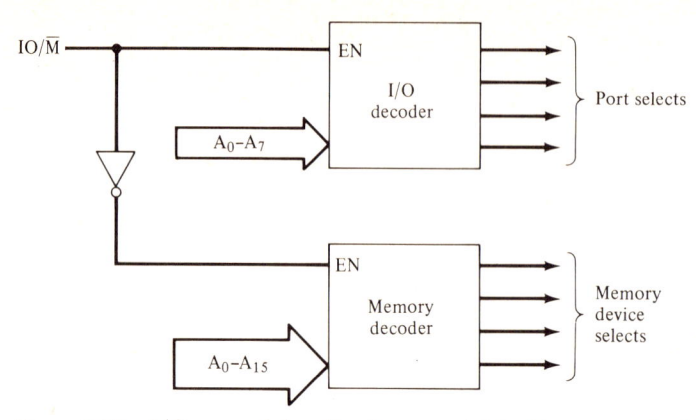

Figure 3.20 I/O mapped decoding increases total address space by 256 bytes.

complementing or not complementing the address inputs to the gate, any one of 16 (2^4) devices can be enabled.

3.2.5 I/O Mapped Decoding

A few microprocessors (including the 8080 and 8085) use an extra control line to specify that the address is for either I/O or memory. In the 8085, this line is called IO/$\overline{\text{M}}$ (see Figure 3.20). The instruction being executed controls this line. During all memory transfers, IO/$\overline{\text{M}}$ is low. When one of the two I/O instructions (IN or OUT) is executed, IO/$\overline{\text{M}}$ goes high, enabling the I/O ports. When IO/$\overline{\text{M}}$ is low, the memory is enabled. When IO/$\overline{\text{M}}$ is high, the I/O is enabled, and eight of the address lines contain the I/O port address. By using this method, memory and I/O have separate address spaces, thereby increasing the total addressable space in a system (by $2^8 = 256$ bytes) and permitting a greater degree of decoder design flexibility. Also, IN and OUT are 2-byte instructions (specifying 1 of 256 I/O ports). This saves 1 byte of program memory for each I/O transfer, as compared to using 3-byte memory instructions such as LDA and STA used in memory-mapped I/O. Finally note that in memory-mapped I/O, the most significant bit of the address A_{15} is used for distinguishing between memory or I/O. When $A_{15} = 0$, it is memory operation; otherwise I/O operations are performed.

3.3 Memories and Peripherals

3.3.1 Types of Memories

If you think of the microprocessor as the heart of the system, then the data bus is the bloodstream and the memories and peripherals are the organs.

Semiconductor memories are available in two fundamentally different types: RAMs and ROMs. Within each of these categories, there are many varieties. Some of the more commonly used memory devices are discussed in this section.

3.3.2 ROMs and RAMs

RAMs are used for the user "programmable" memory and the data storage in nearly all microcomputer systems. There are two different types of RAMs: static and dynamic. Static RAMs use a flip-flop for each memory element. A 1K RAM IC therefore has 1024 flip-flops in it. Each flip-flop can be set to store a 1 or reset to store a 0. Address decoding circuits inside the RAM chip select the particular flip-flop specified by the address lines. The state of the flip-flop does not change unless new data are stored in it or power to the RAM is interrupted.

Dynamic RAMs use an on-chip capacitor for each storage element. In general, a charge is stored on the capacitor to indicate a 1; no charge indicates a 0. This technique simplifies the storage cell, permitting denser memory chips. There is a problem, however: the charge leaks off the capacitor and, after a few milliseconds, a 1 can become a 0. They must therefore be refreshed. Refreshing consists of reading a sequence of RAM address locations within a specified time. In the process of reading the data, the RAM chip automatically rewrites the same data back into the location read. As a result, all the 1 bits are restored to full charge and the 0 bits to no charge. Dynamic memories are typically refreshed at least every 2 ms.

Because dynamic memories must be continually refreshed, special circuits are added to do this, resulting in a more complex system. Small systems tend to use the simpler static memories because of this factor. However, dynamic memories have a number of advantages. They are less expensive than static RAMs of the same size and usually consume less power. The largest RAMs (greatest number of bits) are often available only in the dynamic type. Systems with large amounts of memory often use the cheaper, lower-power dynamic memories. Dynamic memories are almost always 1 bit wide. Some microprocessors contain on-chip refresh circuits to simplify the use of dynamic RAMs.

Many common memory chips are only 1 bit wide. The 2102 was the first inexpensive static memory and is organized 1K × 1. Since each chip reads or writes only 1 bit at a time, eight chips are required to read and write 1K bytes of data. Figure 3.21 shows a 1K × 8 memory using 2102s. As with the 2114 circuit, all the address and control lines are bused together. Each chip takes care of 1 bit of the data bus. The 2102 has separate data in and data out pins which are useful in special systems that do not use a bidirectional data bus. For most microprocessor applications, these pins are simply tied together.

Other common memory chips are the 2141 (4K × 1 static), the 2104

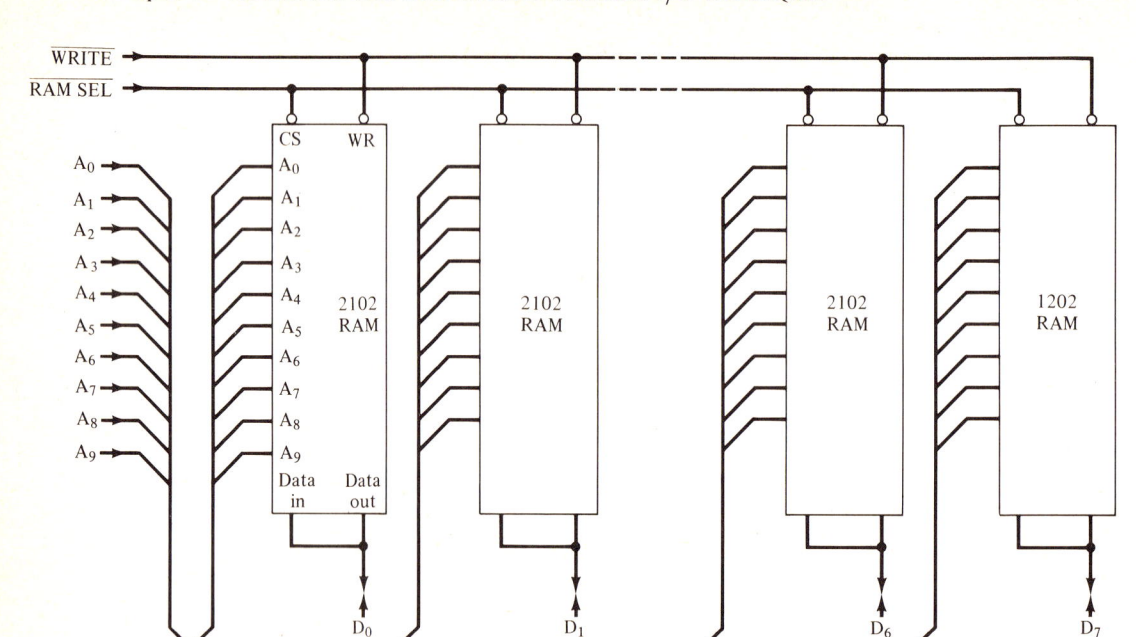

Figure 3.21 1K × 8 memory using 2102 (1K × 1) RAMs.

(4K × 1 dynamic), and the 2116 (16K × 1 dynamic). Eight 2116s will provide 16K bytes of memory, which would require 128 2102s!

ROMs provide a means of permanently storing programs and data. Since RAMs lose their contents when power is removed, they are not very useful for storing permanent programs. Most ROMs intended for use with microprocessors are 8 bits wide.

There are four different types of ROMs. Mask-programmed ROMs are programmed by the IC manufacturer by customizing the actual chip. There is usually a one-time charge to generate the mask for a particular program, but thereafter, the ROMs are relatively inexpensive. Mask-programmed ROMs are often used in reasonably high-volume products because they are the least expensive and the highest in bit density.

The second type is the Programmable Read-Only Memory (PROM). The user programs the ROMs electrically utilizing a special device called a PROM programmer. Once they are programmed, however, they cannot be changed.

The Erasable Programmable Read-Only Memory (EPROM) is similar to a PROM, except that it can be erased and reprogrammed. Programmed bits are stored as charge on a near-zero-leakage capacitor. Erasing is performed by shining ultraviolet light through a clear window in the IC package. These devices are most useful for prototypes or small-volume production runs.

The newest ROM type is the Electrically Alterable Read-Only Memory

(EAROM). The EAROM can be erased electrically while in the circuit. One advantage of this type over the EPROM is that small sections of the EAROM can be erased, whereas EPROMs must be completely erased. But EAROMs are not yet as easy to use as EPROMs and are more expensive. Many systems which require data to be stored for a long period of time, but which must change this data occasionally, use EAROMs. Typical applications include digital TV tuners, calibrated transducers, and automatic telephone dialers.

3.4 Typical Microprocessor I/O Techniques

There are basically three types of I/O techniques by which a microprocessor can communicate with the external world. These are programmed I/O, interrupt I/O, and Direct Memory Access (DMA).

Programmed I/O is a microprocessor-initiated I/O transfer. In this technique, data transfer between the microprocessor and an external device is controlled by the microprocessor. A program is executed by the microprocessor to accomplish this.

The interrupt I/O is a device-initiated technique. Typically, an external device is connected to the interrupt pin of the microprocessor. In order to transfer data, the device raises or lowers (depending on the microprocessor) the signal of the interrupt pin. In response to this, the microprocessor completes execution of the current instruction, saves at least the program counter onto the stack, and executes a program called the interrupt service routine to complete the transfer.

Direct memory access is also a device-initiated technique. Data transfer between the microprocessor memory and the I/O device occurs without any microprocessor involvement. Typically, DMA controller chips are required to complete the transfer.

PROBLEMS AND QUESTIONS

3.1 What is the difference between the data bus and control bus?
3.2 In a system with a 16-bit address bus, what is the maximum number of 1K byte memory devices it could contain?
3.3 What is the address of the device selected in Figure 3.22?
3.4 Modify the circuit of Figure 3.22 in order that it works with an output port.
3.5 Define the term memory-mapped I/O.
3.6 Name the decoding technique that is most wasteful of available address space.

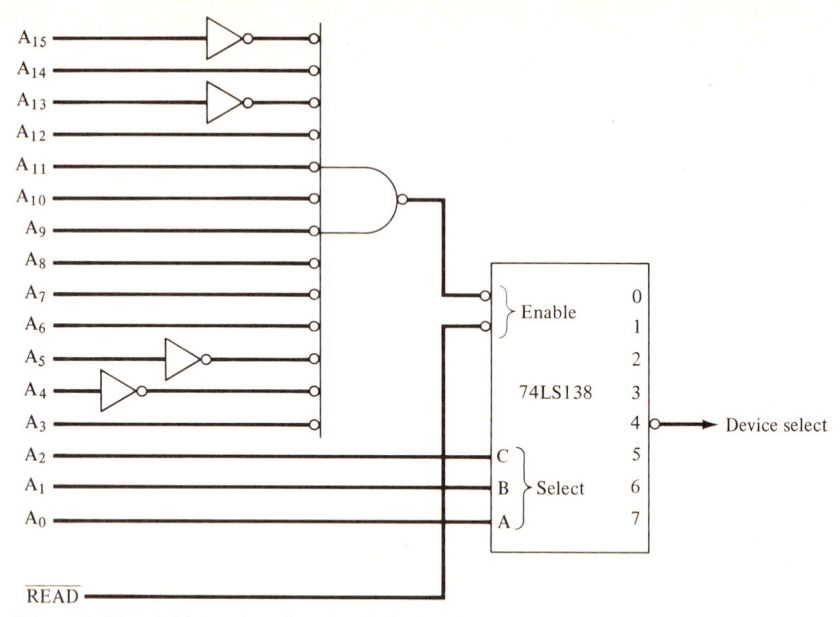

64 Chapter 3 MICROCOMPUTER SYSTEM HARDWARE AND I/O TECHNIQUE

Figure 3.22 Address decoder circuit for Problems 3.3 and 3.4.

3.7 What decoding technique can be used to address the greatest number of memory and I/O locations?

3.8 Identify the main differences between the static RAM and dynamic RAM.

3.9 Identify functionally the advantages and disadvantages of each one of the address decoding techniques discussed in Section 3.2.

3.10 Discuss the various types of I/O techniques.

CHAPTER 4

TYPICAL 8-BIT MICROPROCESSORS AND MICROCOMPUTERS

So far, the microprocessor is treated as a black box; a device with known characteristics whose internal structure is of no concern. However, some knowledge of the internal operation of the microprocessor is helpful in obtaining a clear understanding of the system's operation.

> This chapter takes a brief look inside some of the popular 8-bit microprocessors and microcomputers. Intel, Motorola, and Zilog processors are used for this purpose.

The Intel 8085 is covered in more detail, since in later chapters, hardware and software design using typical microcomputer development systems are demonstrated using this processor. This chapter includes 8085 architecture and programming concepts. Details of the 8085 I/O are covered in Chapter 5.

Note that all 8-bit microprocessors require separate DMA chips to perform DMA data transfer. Single chip 8-bit microcomputers are not intended for DMA-type data transfer.

> Finally, the concepts described in this chapter can be used to understand any 8-bit microprocessor and microcomputer.

66 Chapter 4 Typical 8-Bit Microprocessors and Microcomputers

4.1 Intel 8085

4.1.1 Introduction*

Figure 4.1 shows a simplified block diagram of the 8085 microprocessor. The accumulator connects to the data bus and the Arithmetic and Logic Unit (ALU). The ALU performs all data manipulation, such as incrementing a number or adding two numbers.

The temporary register feeds the ALU's other input. This register is invisible to the programmer and is controlled automatically by the microprocessor's control circuitry.

The flags are a collection of flip-flops that indicate certain characteristics of the result of the most recent operation performed by the ALU. For

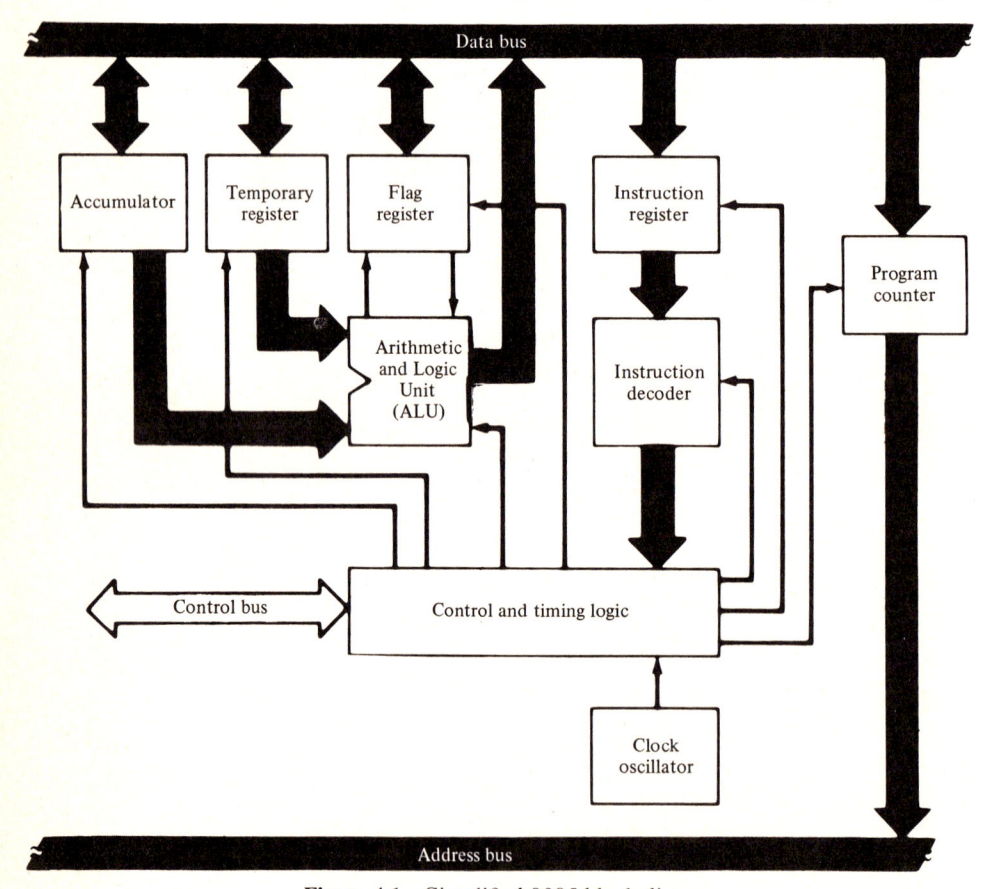

Figure 4.1 Simplified 8085 block diagram.

* This section contains material modified from *Practical Microprocessors—Hardware, Software and Troubleshooting,* copyright © 1979. Reprinted by permission of Hewlett-Packard.

example, the zero flag is set if the result of an operation is zero. The zero flag is tested by the JZ instruction.

The instruction register, instruction decoder, program counter, and control and timing logic are used for fetching instructions from memory and directing their execution. For example, suppose that an instruction is about to be read from location 0200. First the op code must be read from memory; this is the instruction fetch, as shown in Figure 4.2. The PC, which contains the address 0200, is output to the address bus and causes memory location 0200 to be selected. The ROM will then place the contents of location 0200 (presumably an op code) on the data bus, and the microprocessor will store the op code in the instruction register.

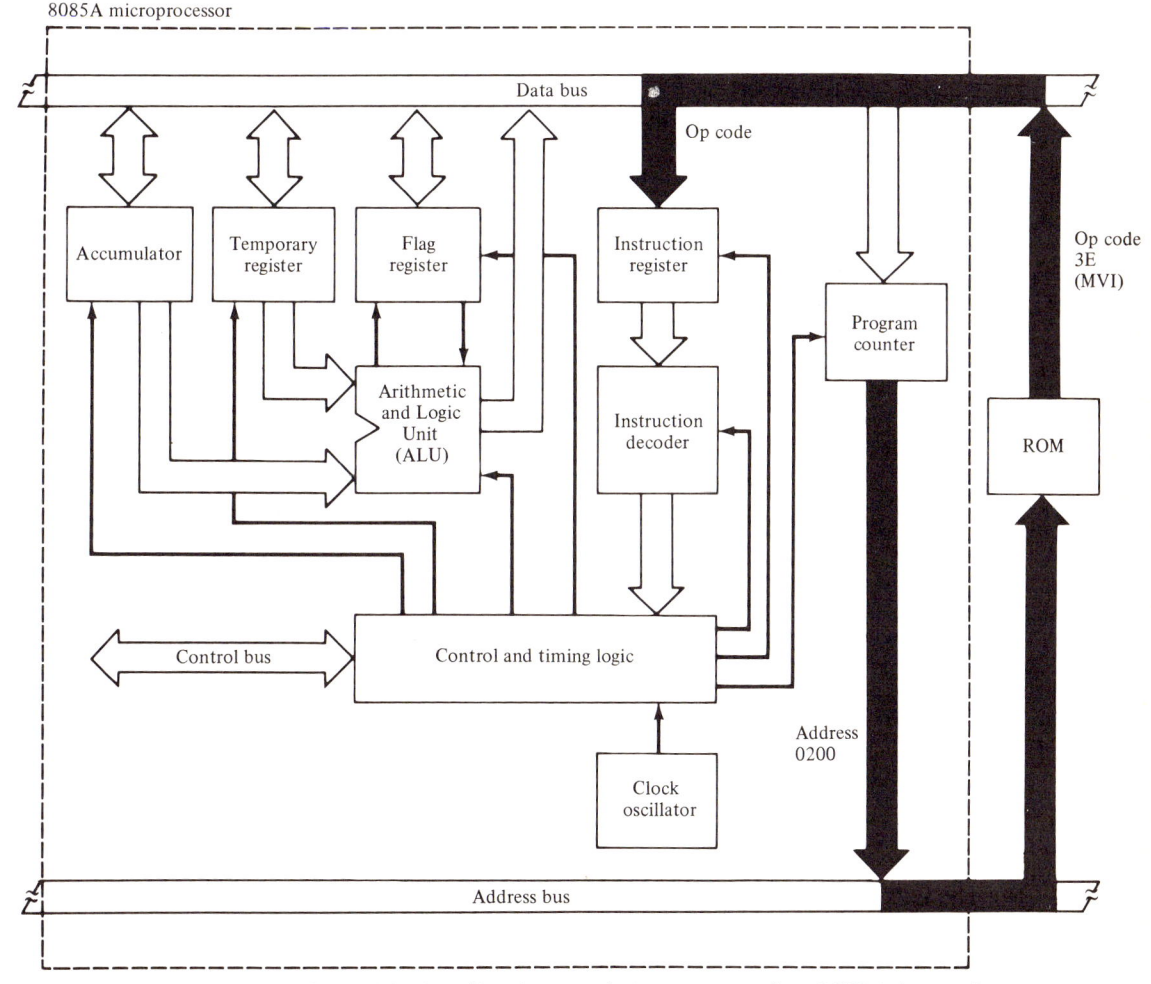

Figure 4.2 Reading the op code from memory for a MVI A instruction.

68 Chapter 4 Typical 8-Bit Microprocessors and Microcomputers

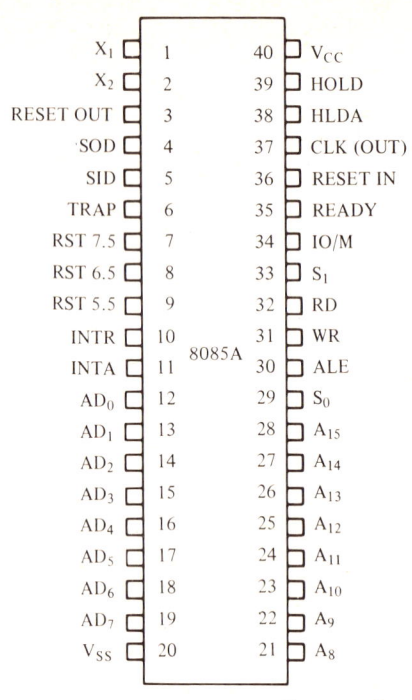

```
              X₁  ▭  1      40 ▭  V_CC
              X₂  ▭  2      39 ▭  HOLD
       RESET OUT ▭  3       38 ▭  HLDA
             SOD ▭  4       37 ▭  CLK (OUT)
             SID ▭  5       36 ▭  RESET IN
            TRAP ▭  6       35 ▭  READY
          RST 7.5 ▭ 7       34 ▭  IO/M
          RST 6.5 ▭ 8       33 ▭  S₁
          RST 5.5 ▭ 9       32 ▭  RD
            INTR ▭ 10       31 ▭  WR
            INTA ▭ 11 8085A 30 ▭  ALE
            AD₀  ▭ 12       29 ▭  S₀
            AD₁  ▭ 13       28 ▭  A₁₅
            AD₂  ▭ 14       27 ▭  A₁₄
            AD₃  ▭ 15       26 ▭  A₁₃
            AD₄  ▭ 16       25 ▭  A₁₂
            AD₅  ▭ 17       24 ▭  A₁₁
            AD₆  ▭ 18       23 ▭  A₁₀
            AD₇  ▭ 19       22 ▭  A₉
            V_SS ▭ 20       21 ▭  A₈
```

Figure 4.3 8085A pinout diagram. Source: Reprinted by permission of Intel Corporation, copyright © 1976.

4.1.2 8085 Pins and Signals*

Figure 4.3 shows 8085 pins and signals. The following table describes the function of each pin:

Symbol	Function
A_8–A_{15} (Output, three-state)	Address bus: The most significant 8 bits of the memory address or the 8 bits of the I/O address.
AD_{0-7} (Input/output, three-state)	Multiplexed address/data bus: Lower 8-bits of the memory address (or I/O address) appear on the bus during the first clock cycle (T state) of a machine cycle. It then becomes the data bus during the second and third clock cycles.
ALE (Output)	Address Latch Enable: It occurs during the first clock state of a machine cycle and enables the address to get latched into the on-chip latch.
S_0, S_1 and IO/$\overline{M}$ (Output)	Machine cycle status:

IO/$\overline{M}$	S_1	S_0	Status
0	0	1	Memory write
0	1	0	Memory read
1	0	1	I/O write

* This section contains material reprinted courtesy of Intel Corporation.

Symbol	Function			
	IO/$\overline{M}$	S_1	S_0	Status
	1	1	0	I/O read
	0	1	1	Op code fetch
	1	1	1	Interrupt acknowledge
	*	0	0	Halt
	*	X	X	Hold
	*	X	X	Reset

* = 3-state (high impedance)
X = unspecified

S_1 can be used as an advanced R/$\overline{W}$ status. IO/$\overline{M}$, S_0, and S_1 become valid at the beginning of a machine cycle and remain stable throughout the cycle. The falling edge of ALE may be used to latch the state of these lines.

$\overline{RD}$ (Output, three-state): READ control: A low level on $\overline{RD}$ indicates the selected memory or I/O device is to be read.

$\overline{WR}$ (Output, three-state): WRITE control: A low level on $\overline{WR}$ indicates the data on the data bus is to be written into the selected memory or I/O location.

READY (Input): If READY is high during a read or write cycle, it indicates that the memory or peripheral is ready to send or receive data. If READY is low, the CPU will wait an integral number of clock cycles for READY to go high before completing the read or write cycle.

HOLD (Input): HOLD indicates that another master is requesting the use of the address and data buses. The CPU, upon receiving the hold request, will relinquish the use of the bus as soon as the completion of the current bus transfer. Internal processing can continue. The processor can regain the bus only after the HOLD is removed. When the HOLD is acknowledged, the address, data, $\overline{RD}$, $\overline{WR}$, and IO/$\overline{M}$ lines are three-stated.

HLDA (Output): HOLD ACKNOWLEDGE: Indicates that the CPU has received the HOLD request and that it will relinquish the bus in the next clock cycle. HLDA goes low after the HOLD request is removed. The CPU takes the bus one-half clock cycle after HLDA goes low.

INTR (Input): INTERRUPT REQUEST: Is used as a general-purpose interrupt. It is sampled only during the next to the last clock cycle of an instruction and during HOLD and HALT states. If it is active, the PC will be inhibited from incrementing and an $\overline{INTA}$ will be issued. During this cycle a RESTART or CALL instruction can be inserted to jump to the interrupt service routine. The INTR is enabled and disabled by software. It is disabled by RESET and immediately after an interrupt is accepted.

$\overline{INTA}$ (Output): INTERRUPT ACKNOWLEDGE: Is used instead of (and has the same timing as) $\overline{RD}$ during the instruction cycle after an INTR is accepted. It can be used to activate the 8259 interrupt chip or some other interrupt port.

RST5.5
RST6.5
RST7.5 (Inputs): RESTART INTERRUPTS: These three inputs have the same timing as INTR except they cause an internal RESTART to be automatically inserted.

TRAP (Input): Trap interrupt is a nonmaskable RESTART interrupt. It is recognized at the same time as INTR or RST5.5–7.5. It is unaffected by any mask or interrupt enable. It has the highest priority of any interrupt.

$\overline{RESET\ IN}$ (Input): Sets the program counter to zero and resets the interrupt enable and HLDA flip-flops.

RESET OUT (Output): Indicates CPU is being reset. Can be used as a system reset.

Symbol	Function
X_1, X_2 (Input)	X_1 and X_2 are connected to a crystal, LC, or RC network to drive the internal clock generator. X_1 can also be an external clock input from a logic gate. The input frequency is divided by 2 to give the processor's internal operating frequency.
CLK (Output)	Clock output for use as a system clock. The period of CLK is twice the X_1, X_2 input period.
SID (Input)	Serial Input Data line. The data on this line is loaded into accumulator bit 7 whenever a RIM instruction is executed.
SOD (Output)	Serial Output Data line. The output SOD is set or reset as specified by the SIM instruction.
V_{CC}	+5 V supply.
V_{SS}	Ground reference.

4.1.3 The Instruction Cycle and Execution*

The instruction register feeds the instruction decoder, which recognizes the op code and provides control signals to the timing and control circuitry. The timing and control circuits are like a processor within the processor. A ROM within the microprocessor IC contains the microcode (or microprogram), which tells the processor exactly what to do to execute each machine language instruction. The microcode, which is part of the design of the microprocessor and generally cannot be changed, defines the microprocessor's machine language. Writing microcode (which is usually done by the microprocessor manufacturer) is called microprogramming and should not be confused with writing programs to be executed by the microprocessor.

For example, for a MVI A instruction, the control and timing logic first reads the op code 3E, and then increments the address in the PC. The instruction decoder determines that this op code is followed by a byte of data, so the contents of the memory location pointed to by the PC are read into the accumulator (see Figure 4.4).

The microprogram now indicates to the control logic that the instruction is completed. The PC is incremented, and the next byte of the program (the next op code) is read into the instruction register. The execution of this instruction then begins. This repetitive sequence performed by the microprocessor is called the fetch-execute cycle.

In the execute phase of the instruction the real work is done. There are four basic types of operations that can be performed by the 8085:

1. Read data from memory or an input port.
2. Write data to memory or an output port.

* This section contains material modified from *Practical Microprocessors—Hardware, Software and Troubleshooting,* copyright © 1979. Reprinted by permission of Hewlett-Packard.

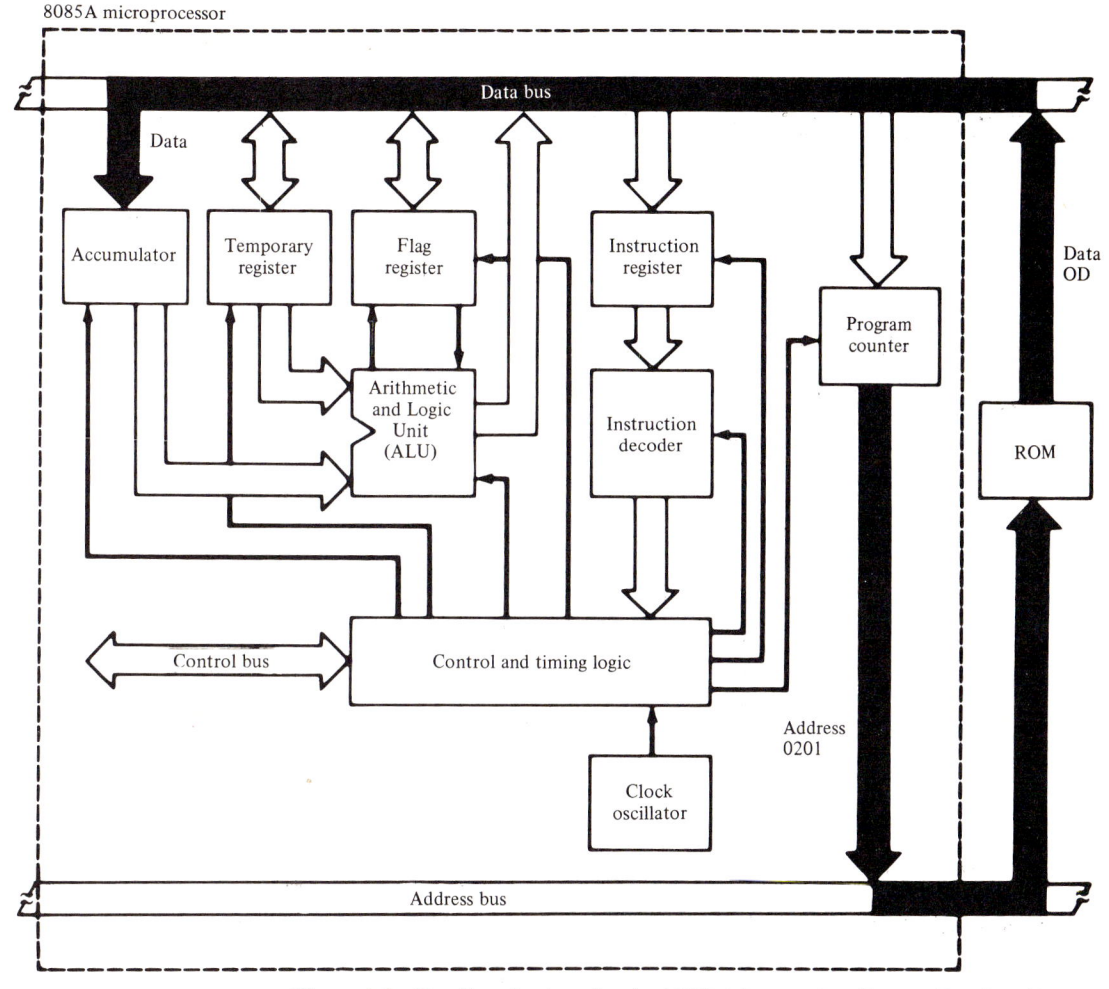

Figure 4.4 Reading the data for the MVI A instruction. Source: Reprinted by permission of Intel Corporation, copyright © 1976.

3. Do an operation internal to the microprocessor.
4. Transfer control to another memory location.

The first two types are self-explanatory. The third, internal operations, involves manipulating the registers (such as the accumulator) without accessing the memory or I/O ports. For example, the contents of one register may be moved to another register, or the contents of a register may be incremented or decremented. The fourth group includes instructions such as JMP, CALL, and RET.

4.1.4 Machine Cycles*

The fetching and execution of instructions is divided into machine cycles. The first machine cycle of every instruction is the op code fetch. An additional machine cycle is then required for each memory or I/O reference to provide time for the data transfer. A machine cycle consists of setting the address on the address bus and then transferring information over the data bus. Most operations internal to the microprocessor (such as incrementing the accumulator) are completed in the same machine cycle as the op code fetch. A simple instruction such as INR A thus requires only one machine cycle, while STA requires four cycles: three to read the instruction and one to write the accumulator to memory.

4.1.5 Program Execution*

In general, the microprocessor keeps reading sequentially through the memory, one location after another, performing the indicated operations. Exceptions to this occur when a jump, call, or return instruction is executed. Another exception is the occurrence of an interrupt. Any of these events will cause the microprocessor to interrupt the sequential flow and begin executing instructions from another address.

Note that op codes and data are intermixed in memory. One address might contain an op code, the next two a jump address, the next one an op code, and the next one a piece of data. This, of course, is done by the assembler. It is the programmer's responsibility to be sure that the memory contains a valid sequence of op codes and data. The microprocessor can distinguish between them only by their context. The op codes, jump addresses, and data are all simply bit patterns stored in the memory. All such information is read in exactly the same way, and it all travels over the same data bus. The microprocessor must always keep track of whether it is reading an op code or data and treat each appropriately. The processor assumes that the first location it reads contains an op code and goes from there. If the op code requires a byte of data, the microprocessor "knows" (from the instruction decoder) that the next byte is data and treats it accordingly. It then assumes that the byte following the data is the next op code. If a piece of data is misinterpreted as an op code, the system usually goes completely out of control (crashes).

4.1.6 Review of 8085 Instruction Set*

Table 4.1 provides a summary of the 8085 instruction set. Several of the 8085's instructions have already been discussed. In this section, these instructions are reviewed to provide a foundation from which to describe

---

* This section contains material modified from *Practical Microprocessors—Hardware, Software and Troubleshooting,* copyright © 1979. Reprinted by permission of Hewlett-Packard.

some new instructions. For a complete description of the 8085 instruction set, refer to Appendix A.

Some shorthand notation is useful in describing instructions. In the following text, the term data is used to indicate any 8-bit quantity, and adrs to indicate any 16-bit address.

1. Some Commonly Used 8085 Instructions

Data Manipulation: MVI, INR, CMA. One of the most fundamental microprocessor operations is to load the accumulator with data. This is done by the MVI A, data instruction (move immediate to the accumulator). The data to be moved to the accumulator are stored in the byte following the op code.

Once the data are in the accumulator, instructions are needed to manipulate them. The two instructions that have been used so far are INR A (increment accumulator) and CMA (complement accumulator).

Testing and Jumping: CPI, JMP, JZ. To test the value in the accumulator, the CPI data (compare immediate) instruction can be used. This compares the data specified in the second byte of the instruction with the contents of the accumulator and sets the processor flags accordingly. The only flag that you have used so far is the zero flag, which is set if the result of an operation is zero. The JZ adrs (jump if zero) instruction tests the zero flag (presumably set by a previous instruction, such as CPI) and causes a jump if the flag is set. There is also an unconditional jump instruction JMP adrs that causes a jump regardless of the state of the flags. The address for both jump instructions is stored in the two memory bytes following the op code.

Memory and I/O: LDA, STA. The LDA adrs and STA adrs (load accumulator and store accumulator) instructions transfer data between the accumulator and memory or I/O ports. The address of the memory location or I/O port is specified in the two bytes following the op code.

Subroutines: CALL, RET. To use subroutines, two more instructions are needed. CALL adrs is used to jump to a subroutine, and RET (return) is used to end a subroutine. The CALL instruction specifies an address exactly like a jump instruction. The RET instruction does not specify an address, but causes a jump to the instruction that follows the previously executed CALL.

Interrupt Control: SIM, EI, DI. Control of the interrupts requires three instructions. Set Interrupt Mask (SIM) is used to specify which interrupts should be enabled and which should not. It copies the contents of the accumulator into the processor's interrupt mask register. Enable Interrupts (EI) causes the selected interrupts to be enabled. Disable Interrupts (DI) disables all interrupts.

Table 4.1. 8085 Instruction Set

INSTRUCTION		CODE	BYTES	T STATES 8085	MACHINE CYCLES
ACI	DATA	CE data	2	7	F R
ADC	REG	1000 1SSS	1	4	F
ADC	M	8E	1	7	F R
ADD	REG	1000 0SSS	1	4	F
ADD	M	86	1	7	F R
ADI	DATA	C6 data	2	7	F R
ANA	REG	1010 0SSS	1	4	F
ANA	M	A6	1	7	F R
ANI	DATA	E6 data	2	7	F R
CALL	LABEL	CD addr	3	18	S R R W W*
CC	LABEL	DC addr	3	9/18	S R•/S R R W W*
CM	LABEL	FC addr	3	9/18	S R•/S R R W W*
CMA		2F	1	4	F
CMC		3F	1	4	F
CMP	REG	1011 1SSS	1	4	F
CMP	M	BE	1	7	F R
CNC	LABEL	D4 addr	3	9/18	S R•/S R R W W*
CNZ	LABEL	C4 addr	3	9/18	S R•/S R R W W*
CP	LABEL	F4 addr	3	9/18	S R•/S R R W W*
CPE	LABEL	EC addr	3	9/18	S R•/S R R W W*
CPI	DATA	FE data	2	7	F R
CPO	LABEL	E4 addr	3	9/18	S R•/S R R W W*
CZ	LABEL	CC addr	3	9/18	S R•/S R R W W*
DAA		27	1	4	F
DAD	RP	00RP 1001	1	10	F B B
DCR	REG	00SS S101	1	4	F*
DCR	M	35	1	10	F R W
DCX	RP	00RP 1011	1	6	S*
DI		F3	1	4	F
EI		FB	1	4	F
HLT		76	1	5	F B
IN	PORT	DB data	2	10	F R I
INR	REG	00SS S100	1	4	F*
INR	M	34	1	10	F R W
INX	RP	00RP 0011	1	6	S*
JC	LABEL	DA addr	3	7/10	F R/F R R†
JM	LABEL	FA addr	3	7/10	F R/F R R†
JMP	LABEL	C3 addr	3	10	F R R
JNC	LABEL	D2 addr	3	7/10	F R/F R R†
JNZ	LABEL	C2 addr	3	7/10	F R/F R R†
JP	LABEL	F2 addr	3	7/10	F R/F R R†
JPE	LABEL	EA addr	3	7/10	F R/F R R†
JPO	LABEL	E2 addr	3	7/10	F R/F R R†
JZ	LABEL	CA addr	3	7/10	F R/F R R†
LDA	ADDR	3A addr	3	13	F R R R
LDAX	RP	000X 1010	1	7	F R
LHLD	ADDR	2A addr	3	16	F R R R R

Machine cycle types:
- F   Four clock period instr fetch
- S   Six clock period instr fetch
- R   Memory read
- I   I/O read
- W   Memory write
- O   I/O write
- B   Bus idle
- X   Variable or optional binary digit

Instruction		Code	Bytes	T States 8085	Machine Cycles
LXI	RP, DATA16	00RP 0001 data16	3	10	F R R
MOV	REG, REG	01DD DSSS	1	4	F*
MOV	M, REG	0111 0SSS	1	7	F W
MOV	REG, M	01DO D110	1	7	F R
MVI	REG, DATA	000D D110 data	2	7	F R
MVI	M, DATA	36 data	2	10	F R W
NOP		00	1	4	F
ORA	REG	1011 0SSS	1	4	F
ORA	M	BG	1	7	F R
ORI	DATA	F6 data	2	7	F R
OUT	PORT	D3 data	2	10	F R 0
PCHL		E9	1	6	S*
POP	RP	11RP 0001	1	10	F R R
PUSH	RP	11RP 0101	1	12	S W W*
RAL		17	1	4	F
RAR		1F	1	4	F
RC		D8	1	6/12	S/S R R*
RET		C9	1	10	F R R
RIM (8085A only)		20	1	4	F
RLC		07	1	4	F
RM		F8	1	6/12	S/S R R*
RNC		D0	1	6/12	S/S R R*
RNZ		C0	1	6/12	S/S R R*
RP		F0	1	6/12	S/S R R*
RPE		E8	1	6/12	S/S R R*
RPO		E0	1	6/12	S/S R R*
RRC		0F	1	4	F
RST	N	11XX X111	1	12	S W W*
RZ		C8	1	6/12	S/S R R*
SBB	REG	1001 1SSS	1	4	F
SBB	M	9E	1	7	F R
SBI	DATA	DE data	2	7	F R
SHLD	ADDR	22 addr	3	16	F R R W W
SIM (8085A only)		30	1	4	F
SPHL		F9	1	6	S*
STA	ADDR	32 addr	3	13	F R R W
STAX	RP	000X 0010	1	7	F W
STC		37	1	4	F
SUB	REG	1001 0SSS	1	4	F
SUB	M	96	1	7	F R
SUI	DATA	D6 data	2	7	F R
XCHG		EB	1	4	F
XRA	REG	1010 1SSS	1	4	F
XRA	M	AE	1	7	F R
XRI	DATA	EE data	2	7	F R
XTHL		E3	1	16	F R R W W

DDD   Binary digits identifying a destination register
       B = 000, C = 001, D = 010 Memory = 110
SSS   Binary digits identifying a source register
       E = 011, H = 100, L = 101 A = 111
RP   Register Pair BC = OO, HL = 10, DE = 01, SP = 11
*Five clock period instruction fetch with 8080A.
†The longer machine cycle sequence applies regardless of condition evaluation with 8080A.
•An extra READ cycle (R) will occur for this condition with 8080A.
Source: All mnemonics copyright © 1976 by the Intel Corporation.

76 Chapter 4 Typical 8-Bit Microprocessors and Microcomputers

2. The Variety of Instructions

This relatively small set of instructions demonstrates most of the 8085's basic capabilities. As you become familiar with more instructions, it will become apparent that there are more instructions than are necessary. The variety of instructions available makes it easier to write programs, since you can choose from several alternatives. There is a direct parallel in hardware design; it is possible to build any logic circuit using only NAND gates. In fact, entire computers have been built this way. However, the system is greatly simplified by using other devices such as NOR gates, flip-flops, multiplexers, counters, and adders.

3. The General-Purpose Registers

Up to this point, one major feature of the 8085 microprocessor has been ignored: its general-purpose registers. There are six 8-bit registers within the 8085, which can be used for temporary data storage. Figure 4.5 shows

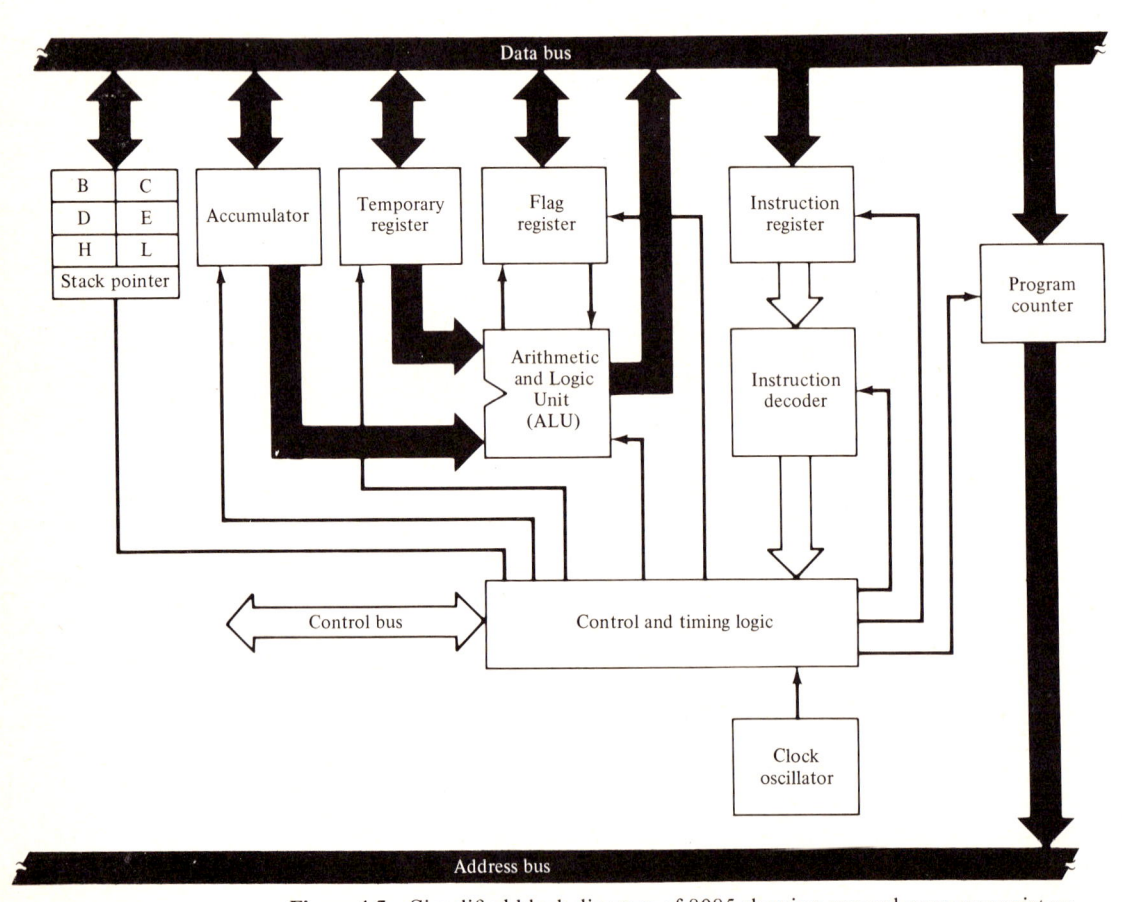

Figure 4.5 Simplified block diagram of 8085 showing general-purpose registers.

the 8085 block diagram including these registers. They are called the B, C, D, E, H, and L registers. The stack pointer is also shown.

To use these registers, some new instructions are needed. The MVI instruction, which loads data into the accumulator, can in fact be used with any register. For example, MVI D, data causes the data to be moved to the D register. The general form of this instruction is MVI r, data where r indicates any of the registers (A, B, C, D, E, H, or L). Although the accumulator is special in that it is used for the results of computations, it may also be used as a general-purpose register. The INR instruction can also be used on any register. The general form is INR r. For example, INR H increments the H register.

Now that all these registers are available, it is useful to have a way to move data from one register to another. The general form of the instruction that does this is MOV r1,r2. Register r1 is the destination, and register r2 is the source. For example, MOV A,H moves the contents of the H register into the accumulator, but the contents of H are not changed. Note that the source and destination are listed in the opposite order from what you might expect. You can think of the instruction MOV A,H as "move into the accumulator the contents of the H register."

The assembly language reference card provided by Intel lists all of the 8085's instructions in mnemonic and hexadecimal forms and shows all the various MOV instructions. This is your guide for translating assembly language mnemonics into hexadecimal machine code, and vice versa. It also provides a convenient list of all available instructions.

The general-purpose registers are useful when a program uses several different variables. Each register can be used for a different purpose. RAM locations are not needed for data storage as long as the six registers are sufficient. For example, a program that counts six different events can use one register for counting each event.

Notice that in Table 4.1 there is an M "register" listed in the MOV instructions. This is not really a register, but refers to a memory location whose address is stored in the H and L registers. The H and L registers hold an address that points to a location in memory. This is called indirect addressing, which means that the instruction specifies where the address is stored (the H and L registers in this case) rather than the actual address.

For example, if H contains 12 and L contains 37 (see Figure 4.6), the instruction MOV A,M will load the accumulator with the contents of memory location 1237. The effect is exactly the same as the instruction LDA 1237.

This is an example of how the same operation can be performed in two different ways. MOV A,M is a single-byte instruction, but requires that the H and L registers be previously set to the desired address. LDA 1237, on the other hand, is a 3-byte instruction. However, it is often preferable because it does not require that the address be stored in the H and L

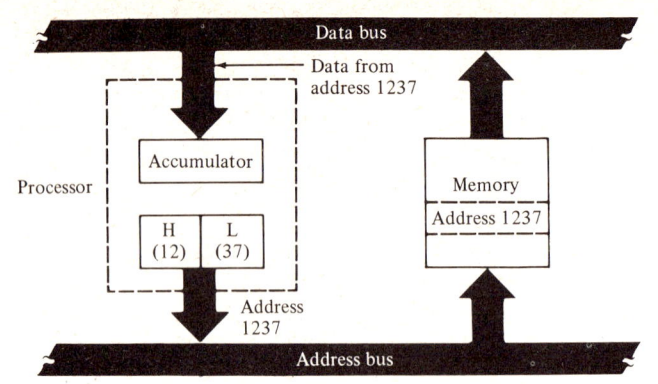

Figure 4.6 Indirect addressing using H and L registers.

registers. Indirect addressing is particularly useful for table-oriented operations.

One of the most common building blocks for digital hardware is the logic gate. Four basic gate functions are NOT, AND, OR, and exclusive OR. Each of these functions can also be performed by software.

The NOT function is performed by the CMA (complement accumulator) instruction. Each bit of the accumulator is inverted. The AND function is performed by the ANA r (and accumulator) instruction. For example, ANA D causes the contents of the D register to be ANDed with the contents of the accumulator. The result is left in the accumulator. Note that the other register (D in this example) is not changed. Each variation (to operate on each register) has its own op code.

As mentioned before, the AND function is performed individually on each bit of the accumulator. For example, if A = 1011 0110 and D = 0011 1100, then the result of the instruction ANA D is:

```
        0011 1100 (D register)
AND     1011 0110 (Accumulator)
        0011 0100 (Accumulator)
```

The OR function is performed by the OR accumulator (ORA r) instructions. Exclusive OR is performed by XRA r. The operation of these instructions is similar to the ANA instruction, except that the logic function is different. Since no address or data is specified, all of these instructions require only a single byte of code. Refer to the instruction set for the list of op codes.

A common use for logical instructions is to select certain bits of a word. This is called masking. For example, suppose that eight switches are connected to an input port. To test only a single bit (a single switch), the processor must disregard the other bits. Figure 4.7 shows the flowchart for a program that tests the switch connected to bit 3 of the input port. If the

Intel 8085

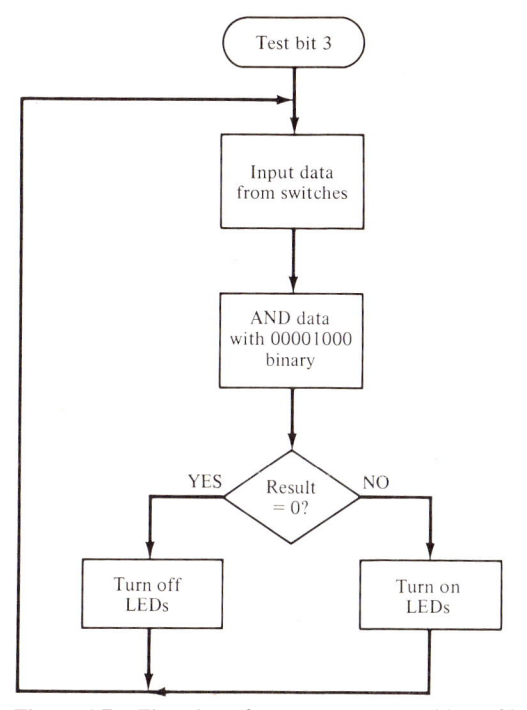

Figure 4.7 Flowchart for program to test bit 3 of input port.

switch is off, the output LEDs are turned on; otherwise, they are turned off.

Figure 4.8 shows the program listing. The program first reads the data from the input port into the accumulator. It then sets the B register to the mask value and ANDs the B register with the accumulator. The result is that all bits except bit 3 are forced to zero. (Since 0 AND 1 = 0 and 1 AND 1 = 1, any bit ANDed with a 1 is unchanged.) Finally, the program uses the JZ instruction to jump if the zero flag is set. The zero flag indicates that the entire byte (and therefore bit 3) is zero. Figure 4.8 gives a program for testing bit 3.

The XRA A instruction exclusive ORs the accumulator with itself. Since the exclusive OR of anything with itself is zero, this instruction clears the accumulator using only 1 byte of memory. The alternative, MVI A,0 requires 2 bytes of memory.

Another commonly required function is the shifting of data to the right or the left. This is performed in hardware using a shift register. The 8085 has instructions that shift the data in the accumulator. Rotate Right Circular (RRC) performs the right shift and Rotate Left Circular (RLC) performs the left shift. These instructions operate only on the accumulator.

80 Chapter 4 Typical 8-Bit Microprocessors and Microcomputers

Address	Contents	Label	Instruction		Comments
0800	_____	START:	LDA	2000	;Read input port to accumulator
0801	_____				
0802	_____				
0803	_____		MVI	B,08	;Set B to mask value (0000
0804	_____				1000 binary)
0805	_____		ANA	B	;Set all bits except no. 3 to zero
0806	_____		JZ	OFF	;Test for accumulator = 0
0807	_____				
0808	_____				
0809	_____	ON:	____	____	;Turn on LEDs
080A	_____				
080B	_____		____	____	
080C	_____				
080D	_____				
080E	_____		JMP	START	
080F	_____				
0810	_____				
0811	_____	OFF:	____	____	;Turn off LEDs
0812	_____				
0813	_____		____	____	
0814	_____				
0815	_____				
0816	_____		JMP	START	
0817	_____				
0818	_____				

Figure 4.8 Program to test bit 3.

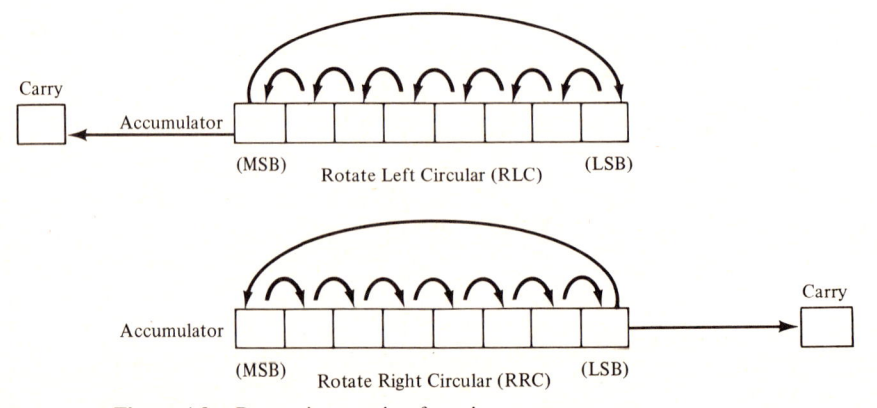

Figure 4.9 Rotate instruction function.

"Circular" refers to the fact that the LSB shifted to the MSB (or vice versa) as shown in Figure 4.9.

For example, suppose that the accumulator contains the value 0010 0001. After an RRC is executed, it will contain 1001 0000. Note that the LSB is moved to the MSB. This happens because the data are rotated as if the bits were arranged in a circle, with the MSB and LSB adjacent to each other. Also, the least significant bit (1) goes to carry.

Write a program following the flowchart in Figure 4.10 to demonstrate the operation of the rotate instructions. The most basic arithmetic function is the addition of two numbers. The ADD r instruction adds the contents of the specified register to the contents of the accumulator and stores the result in the accumulator.

For example, ADD D adds the contents of the D register to the contents of the accumulator. Suppose that the D register contains 1001 0011 and the accumulator contains 1010 1010. The result is:

Decimal	Binary
147	1001 0011 (D register)
+170	+ 1010 1010 (Accumulator)
317	1 0011 1101 (Accumulator)

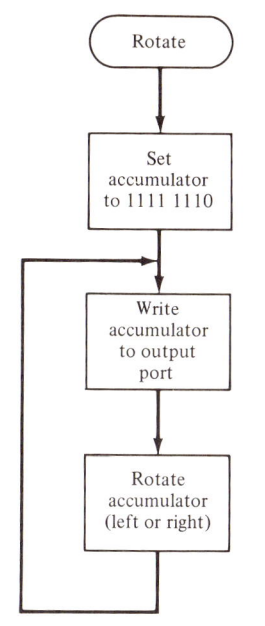

Figure 4.10 Flowchart for programming exercise.

Note that the result is greater than 255 decimal, so it is more than 8 bits long. To accommodate this overflow, the processor contains a carry flag. This flag acts as the ninth bit of the accumulator and can be tested by the Jump if Carry (JC) and Jump if No Carry (JNC) instructions. This test is similar to the test of the zero flag.

For example, the following instructions will add the D register to the accumulator and jump to location 0820 if a carry is generated:

```
ADD D
JC  0820
```

If no carry is generated (result <256 decimal), then the program will continue with the next instruction.

The carry flag is also used when adding numbers longer than 8 bits. Two (or more) registers are used to represent each number. The least significant bytes are added first. Then the most significant bytes are added. The carry from the least significant byte (if any) is added to the most significant byte. The carry bit thus functions as a link between the two bytes.

The flags are all combined into 1 byte, as shown in Figure 4.11. Only the carry and zero flags are used in this section. The sign flag is just a copy of the MSB and is used for twos complement arithmetic. Not all instructions affect all flags. MOV instructions, for example, do not affect any flags. The instruction descriptions in Appendix A indicate which flags are affected by each instruction.

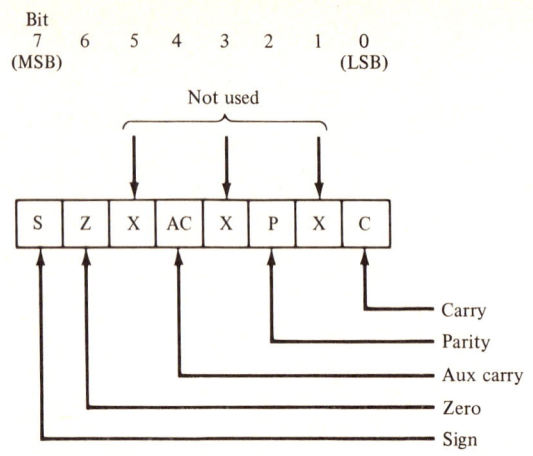

82 Chapter 4 Typical 8-Bit Microprocessors and Microcomputers

```
Bit
 7   6   5   4   3   2   1   0
(MSB)                      (LSB)

         Not used

| S | Z | X | AC | X | P | X | C |
                              └── Carry
                          └────── Parity
                  └────────────── Aux carry
          └────────────────────── Zero
      └────────────────────────── Sign
```

Figure 4.11 Microprocessor flags.

The SUB r instruction subtracts the contents of the specified register from the accumulator. For example, SUB B subtracts the contents of the B register from the accumulator.

The subtract instruction uses the carry flag as a borrow flag. If the carry flag is set after a SUB B instruction, it indicates that the value in the B register is greater than the value in the accumulator.

It is important to note that the DCX and INX instructions do not affect any status flags. They are typically used as a counter in a loop with a value of 256 or more. Since none of the flags are modified by the DCX or INX, other instructions are used to check for a zero counter value. This is illustrated in the following:

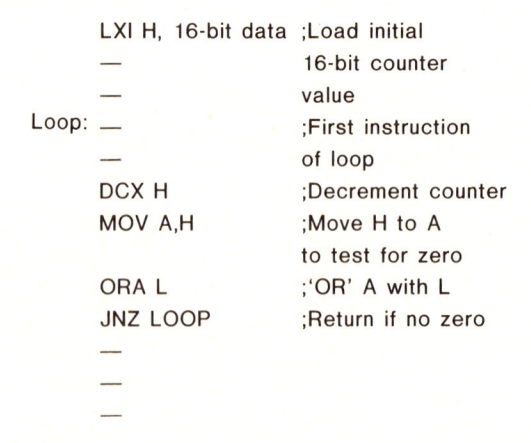

```
        LXI H, 16-bit data   ;Load initial
        —                    16-bit counter
        —                    value
Loop:   —                    ;First instruction
        —                    of loop
        DCX H                ;Decrement counter
        MOV A,H              ;Move H to A
                             to test for zero
        ORA L                ;'OR' A with L
        JNZ LOOP             ;Return if no zero
        —
        —
        —
```

Note that in the above INX can be used instead of DCX by loading the 16-bit counter H–L with twos complement of the counter value.

4.1.7 Subroutines and the Stack*

Large programs can be simplified by using subroutines to perform repetitive tasks. For example, suppose a program must do a series of calculations involving several multiplications. One general-purpose multiplication subroutine can be written, which is then used any time a multiplication must be performed. Subroutines are also useful for dividing a program into small modules.

The CALL instruction is used in 8085 to access a subroutine. When a CALL instruction is executed, the microprocessor saves the contents of the program counter (the return address) in the stack, a specially accessed part of memory. The microprocessor goes back to this return address when a RET instruction is executed at the end of the subroutine. The program then resumes execution at the instruction immediately following the CALL.

Suppose that a 16-bit register were used for storing the return address. Can you see the problem this causes? If the subroutine calls another subroutine (referred to as nested subroutines), then the first return address is lost. The solution to this problem is to use a group of memory locations (called the stack). As one routine calls another, the return addresses are stored in sequential memory locations. Figure 4.12 shows the sequence of operations as routine A calls routine B which calls routine C. The contents of the stack and the PC at each step are shown in Figure 4.13. The sequence of events is as follows:

a. The main program is being executed.
b. The main program calls subroutine A. The return address is stored in the stack, and the PC is loaded with the starting address of routine A.

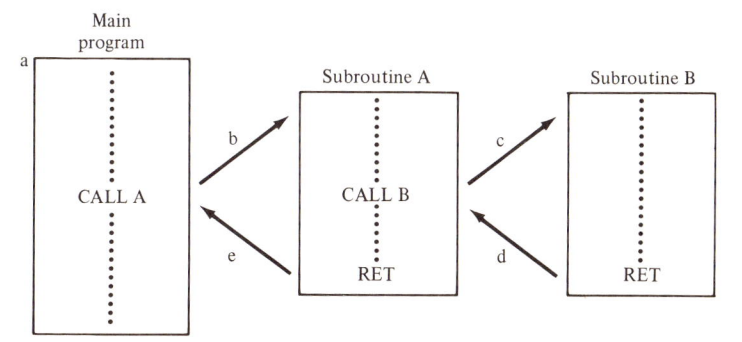

Figure 4.12 Sequence of events as main program calls routine A which calls routine B.

* Source: Kenneth L. Short, *Microprocessors and Programmed Logic,* copyright © 1981. Reprinted by permission of Prentice-Hall, Inc., Englewood Cliffs, N.J.

84 Chapter 4 TYPICAL 8-BIT MICROPROCESSORS AND MICROCOMPUTERS

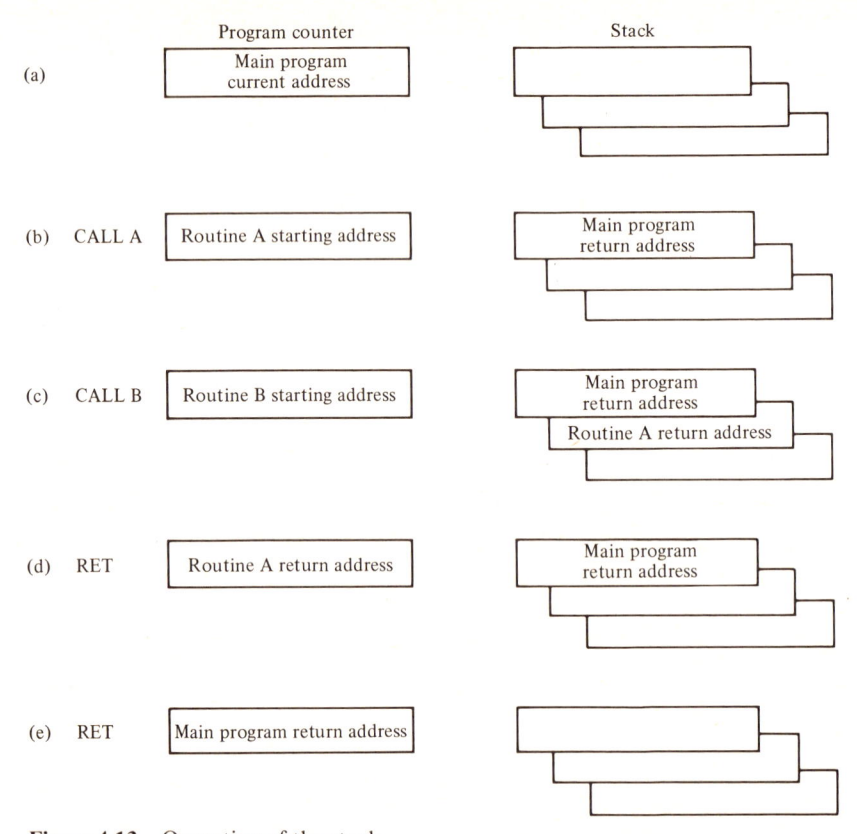

		Program counter	Stack
(a)		Main program current address	
(b)	CALL A	Routine A starting address	Main program return address
(c)	CALL B	Routine B starting address	Main program return address / Routine A return address
(d)	RET	Routine A return address	Main program return address
(e)	RET	Main program return address	

Figure 4.13 Operation of the stack.

    c. Routine A calls routine B. The return address for routine A is placed on the stack, and the PC is loaded with the starting address of routine B.
    d. Routine B returns. The last entry in the stack is loaded into the PC, and control has returned to routine A.
    e. Routine A returns control to the main program.

You can think of the stack as a pile of plates; any number of plates can be piled on, and they are removed in the reverse order. This is called a push-down, or Last In First Out (LIFO), stack. Since the 8085 uses the RAM for the stack, it can be arbitrarily large. A special register in the processor (the stack pointer) contains the address of the top of the stack. The location of the stack is established by setting the stack pointer to the desired address.

    The CALL and RET instructions manipulate the stack pointer automatically. It is also possible to use the stack manually. The PUSH instruction stores a pair of registers in the stack, and the POP instruction reads the data back into the registers. Since the stack is designed for storing addresses, which are 16 bits long, registers are stored two at a time. PUSH B, for example, pushes the B and then the C register onto the stack. POP B restores both of these registers from the top of the stack.

These registers are commonly used for temporarily saving the contents of registers. For example, suppose that a program uses the B and C registers to store some data. It then calls a subroutine which also must use these registers. The subroutine can save the original contents of these registers (as set by the calling program) by using PUSH B. The B and C registers can now be used by the subroutine. Then, near the end of the subroutine, a POP B instruction is used to restore the registers to their initial values. Alternatively, the saving and restoring can be done by the main program just before and after the CALL instruction.

4.1.8 Mathematical Algorithms

As has been seen, the instruction set of the 8085 (as well as most other 8-bit microprocessors) is limited to a very basic set of simple instructions. The direct arithmetic capability of the 8085 is limited to addition and subtraction only. The power of the microprocessor would be severely limited if the only functions it could perform were just addition and subtraction. The microprocessor is given greater power by using the simple addition and subtraction instructions in organized sequences to simulate the complex mathematical functions. The routine that allows a complex mathematical function to be expressed in simple calculations is called an algorithm.

To create an algorithm, the function to be performed must be defined in a set of simple steps of the type that the microprocessor can execute. As an example of breaking up a complex operation, consider multiplication.

When multiplication is performed by hand, the multiplicand is multiplied by just one digit of the multiplier (Figure 4.14). As each successive digit of the multiplier is used, the partial result is shifted to the left. When all of the digits of the multiplier have been used, the partial products are added together. In the case of binary multiplication, multiplication may be performed using only shift and add instructions. A full example is shown in the section on multiplication of unsigned binary numbers.

Most functions, no matter how complicated, may be expressed as a series

```
        1 0 1 1    ←—— Multiplicand
     ×  1 0 0 1    ←—— Multiplier
        1 0 1 1
      0 0 0 0
     0 0 0 0
   1 0 1 1
   1 1 0 0 0 1 1   ←—— Product
```
Figure 4.14 Binary multiplication.

of simpler functions. For example, the sine function may be expressed as

$$\sin x = x - \frac{x^3}{3!} + \frac{x^5}{5!} - \frac{x^7}{7!} + \frac{x^9}{9!} - \ldots$$

The series expressing the sine function is an infinite series, and to obtain an exact result for the sine of an angle, the calculations must be carried out infinitely. No matter what the speed of a microprocessor, infinite calculations cannot be performed, but the series may be truncated at some point that will be an approximation as close as the programmer desires. Therefore, the microprocessor may approximate the sine function by performing a large number of multiplication and division operations, which in turn are algorithms consisting of shifts, adds, and subtracts. The large number of calculations that must be performed are not difficult for the current microprocessors which are capable of performing hundreds of thousands of instructions per second.

While the 8-bit microprocessors usually only provide addition and subtraction instructions, the current trend is toward 16- and 32-bit microprocessors that do provide the multiplication and division routines in single instructions.

As an example of the power of an 8085 in performing complex functions, some common algorithms are presented.

1. Multiplication for Unsigned Binary Numbers

When integers are represented as unsigned binary, only positive numbers are possible because all bits in the word are representing magnitude, and none represent the sign of the number.

A simple algorithm may be used if the multiplier is known to be a power of two (2^n). If the multiplier is a power of two, the multiplicand may simply be shifted to the left n times, provided a 1 is not shifted out of the most significant bit. This routine proves very powerful under conditions where simple multiplications (such as ×2 or ×4) need to be performed.

Another simple algorithm for multiplication uses addition only. Since multiplication is really repeated addition, an algorithm may be made to perform repeated addition. If the calculation 23 × 5 has to be made, the following addition could be made:

```
      23
      23
      23
      23
    +23
     115
```

To perform the repeated addition algorithm on a microprocessor, the multiplicand would be stored in one register and the multiplier stored in another register. The result register would be cleared and the multiplier register used as a counter. The multiplicand would be added to the result and then the multiplier register decremented by 1. If the result of the decrement is 0, then the multiplication is finished; otherwise the process is repeated.

EXAMPLE 4.1*

Write an 8085 assembly language program to multiply two 8-bit unsigned numbers.

SOLUTION

The multiplication routine is set up as a subroutine that may be called by another program. When calling the subroutine, the multiplicand is held in the D register and the multiplier is held in the E register. The result, which may be a 16-bit quantity, is returned in the HL register pair.

Since the result may be a 16-bit quantity, it is easier to perform 16-bit arithmetic on the multiplicand using the 8085 double add (DAD) instruction.

The complete program is shown in Figure 4.15. Note that if the multiplier holds large values, the subroutine will take a long time to complete the multiplication.

2. Division for Unsigned Binary Numbers

Similar to multiplication by a power of two, an unsigned binary number may be easily divided by a power of two (2^n) by shifting to the right n times. Care must be taken to see that a 1 is not shifted out of the least significant bit position.

```
MULT:    LXI   H,0       ; INITIALIZE RESULT TO ZERO
         MOV   C,D       ; PUT THE MULTIPLICAND LOW BYTE OF 'BC'
         MVI   B,0       ; NOW BC PAIR HOLDS MULTIPLICAND
MULT05:  MOV   A,E
         ANA   A         ; REST THE MULTIPLIER FOR ZERO
         RZ              ; ROUTINE IS DONE IF ZERO
         DAD   B         ; NOT DONE SO ADD MULTIPLICAND
         DCR   E         ; SUBTRACT 1 FROM MULTIPLIER
         JMP   MULT05    ; AND REPEAT LOOP
```

Figure 4.15 8085 Routine for 8-bit unsigned multiplication.

* Source: Kenneth L. Short, *Microprocessors and Programmed Logic,* copyright © 1981. Reprinted by permission of Prentice-Hall, Inc., Englewood Cliffs, N.J.

In the same manner that multiplication is repeated addition, division may be performed by repeated subtraction. The divisor may be subtracted from the dividend until the result of a subtraction is less than the divisor. When the result is less than the divisor, the result is stored as the remainder and the number of times the subtraction was performed is stored as the quotient. For example, when 9 is divided by 2, it is found that after 2 has been subtracted from 9 four times, the result of the subtraction is 1. This result is less than the divisor (2) and is therefore the remainder. The answer is therefore 4 with a remainder of 1.

EXAMPLE 4.2*

Write an 8085 routine to divide a 16-bit unsigned number by an 8-bit unsigned number.

SOLUTION

An 8085 subroutine is written that is called with the 16-bit dividend held in the HL register pair and the 8-bit divisor held in the D register. When the subroutine returns, the B register holds the quotient of the division and the C register holds the remainder. If the quotient is greater than an 8-bit number, the subroutine returns an erroneous result. To denote the erroneous data, the subroutine returns with the carry flag set if an error has been

```
DIVIDE: MVI   B,0      ; INITIALIZE QUOTIENT TO ZERO
DIV05:  MOV   A,L      ; GET LS BYTE OF DIVIDEND
        ANA   A        ; AND CLEAR CARRY FLAG FOR SUBTRACT
        SBB   E        ; SUBTRACT LS BYTE OF DIVISOR
        MOV   L,A      ; AND SAVE NEW LS BYTE OF DIVIDEND
        MOV   A,H      ; GET MS BYTE OF DIVIDEND AND
        SBB   D        ; SUBTRACT MS BYTE OF DIVISOR
        MOV   H,A      ; AND SAVE NEW MS BYTE OF DIVIDEND
        JP    DIV10    ; BRANCH IF DIVIDEND STILL > 0
        MOV   A,L      ; GET LS BYTE OF DIVIDEND
        ADD   E        ; AND RESTORE IT TO PROPER VALUE
        MOV   C,A      ; OF REMAINDER
        RET            ; RETURN WITH CARRY FLAG RESET
DIV10:  INR   B        ; ADD 1 TO QUOTIENT TO REFLECT SUB.
        JNZ   DIV05    ; LOOP IF QUOTIENT > 0
        STC            ; SET CARRY IF 256 SUBTRACTIONS HAVE
        RET            ; TAKEN PLACE (ERROR CONDITION)
```

Figure 4.16 8085 unsigned binary division subroutine.

* Source: Kenneth L. Short, *Microprocessors and Programmed Logic,* copyright © 1981. Reprinted by permission of Prentice-Hall, Inc., Englewood Cliffs, N.J.

detected. In this manner the user may check the carry flag after the subroutine has executed to know if the results are valid. The complete subroutine is shown in Figure 4.16.

3. Multiplication and Division for Signed Binary Numbers*

The previous routines for multiplication and division for unsigned numbers cannot be used for signed numbers because the sign bit (the MSB) will be interpreted as a magnitude bit and the results will be in error. One method of multiplying signed numbers is the *sign and magnitude* method. Before any multiplication takes place, the sign of both numbers is checked. Negative numbers are made positive and the multiplication routine for unsigned numbers may be used. If the multiplicand and the multiplier have opposite signs, the result of the unsigned multiplication will be made negative to reflect the correct sign. If both multiplicand and multiplier have the same sign, the result of the unsigned multiplication is positive.

Booth's algorithm for multiplying signed numbers is a more straightforward method because the numbers may be multiplied directly as signed numbers without conversion. In the previous example of a shift and add algorithm for multiplication, there was a shift and a bit test for 1 or 0 regardless of the bit pattern of the multiplier. Booth's algorithm takes advantage of the properties of bit patterns to perform multiple shifts without any additions.

Booth's algorithm is based on the fact that a string of 0's in the multiplier requires shifting, but no addition, while a string of 1's in the multiplier running from bit 2^p to 2^q may be treated as the quantity $(2^{q+1} - 2^p)$. For example, consider the multiplier $X = 00011110$. In this case, $p = 1$ and $q = 4$. By the rule, $2^{q+1} - 2^p = 2^5 - 2^1 = 32 - 2 = 30$, which is the value of X. With Booth's algorithm, multiplication requires only two operations in addition to the shifts: one subtraction and one addition. Compare this to the add and shift algorithm which required four additions plus the shifts. Because Booth's algorithm requires fewer operations to perform, the execution time of the algorithm is faster.

Booth's algorithm may be stated as follows. Let X_i be the *i*th bit of an *n*-bit multiplier. Bit X_{n-1} is the most significant bit, and X_0 is the least significant bit. Bit X_{-1} is assumed to be equal to zero. The multiplicand is referred to as Y. Depending on the result of the comparison of the multiplier bit, one of the following actions occurs:

X_i	X_{i-1}	
0	0	; shift Y (left with respect to partial product)
0	1	; add Y to partial product, and shift Y
1	0	; subtract Y from partial product, and shift Y
1	1	; shift Y

* Source: Kenneth L. Short, *Microprocessors and Programmed Logic,* copyright © 1981. Reprinted by permission of Prentice-Hall, Inc., Englewood Cliffs, N.J.

The process is repeated until *n* comparisons have been made, which completes the multiplication. The procedure is valid for the twos complement numbers *X* and *Y* because of the following reasons. It is valid for *Y* because the logic for addition and subtraction of unsigned numbers and twos complement numbers is identical. It is valid for *X* because if *X* ends in a string of 1's, the last operation is a subtraction of 2^{n-1} which will compensate for twos complement arithmetic.

EXAMPLE 4.3*

Write an 8085 assembly language program to multiply two 8-bit signed numbers using Booth's algorithm.

```
SMULT:  MVI   B,0   ; CLEAR MSB OR RESULT
        MVI   E,8   ; SET BIT COUNTER
        XRA   A     ; CLEAR CARRY, X₋₁ = 0
        MOV   A,C   ; PLACE MULTIPLIER IN 'A' REGISTER
LLA:    JC    LLB   ; CHECK Xᵢ₋₁ BIT
        RRC         ; Xᵢ₋₁ BIT = 0, PLACE Xᵢ BIT IN CARRY
        MOV   A,B   ; MOVE PARTIAL PRODUCT TO 'A' REGISTER
        JNC   LLC   ; CHECK X BIT
        SUB   D     ; Xᵢ = 1 AND Xᵢ₋₁ = 0, SUBTRACT MULTIPLICAND
        JMP   LLC   ; CONTINUE
LLB:    RRC         ; Xᵢ₋₁ = 1, PLACE Xᵢ IN CARRY
        MOV   A,B   ; MOVE PARTIAL PRODUCT TO 'A' REGISTER
        JC    LLC   ; CHECK Xᵢ
        ADD   D     ; Xᵢ = 0 AND Xᵢ₋₁ = 1, SO ADD MULTIPLICAND
LLC:    MOV   B,A   ; SAVE MSB OF PARTIAL PRODUCT IN 'B' REGISTER
        RAL         ; SET CARRY FLAG TO MSB
        MOV   A,B   ; LOAD MSB OF PARTIAL PRODUCT
        RAR         ; ARITHMETIC SHIFT RIGHT
        MOV   B,A   ; SAVE SHIFTED MSB
        MOV   A,C   ; LOAD LSB OF PARTIAL PRODUCT
        RAR         ; RIGHT SHIFT LSB, NEW Xᵢ₋₁ IN CARRY FLAG
        MOV   C,A   ; SAVE RESULT
        DCR   E     ; TEST FOR END (ALL 8 BITS TESTED)
        JNZ   LLA   ; LOOP IF NOT DONE
        RET         ; FINISHED SO RETURN TO CALLER
```

Figure 4.17 Subroutine to implement signed multiplication using Booth's algorithm.

* Source: Kenneth L. Short, *Microprocessors and Programmed Logic,* copyright © 1981. Reprinted by permission of Prentice-Hall, Inc., Englewood Cliffs, N.J.

SOLUTION

The program to solve Example 4.3 is shown in Figure 4.17. Upon calling the subroutine, the multiplicand is stored in the D register and the multiplier is stored in the C register. The 16-bit result is returned in the BC register pair.

Several different algorithms are used for division of twos complement numbers. The simplest routine uses the sign and magnitude approach, similar to the procedure described for multiplication. Algorithms are available that directly divide twos complement numbers, but they are primarily designed for implementation with hardware, and therefore there is little benefit in implementing them with software.

4. Floating-Point Arithmetic Routines*

A typical floating-point software package contains the subroutines to perform addition, subtraction, multiplication, division, and negation. The subroutines will also handle overflow and underflow error conditions.

For the floating-point package described in this section, the following conventions will be used:

1. Operands will be expressed as a number (called the mantissa) raised to a power (called the exponent).
2. When operands are passed in registers, the first register will hold the exponent, the second byte will hold the MSB of the mantissa, and the third byte will hold the LSB of the mantissa.
3. At the start of a routine, the first operand is held in registers B, D, and E. The second operand, if any, is held in registers A, H, and L.
4. At the conclusion of a routine, the result is returned in the B, D, and E registers.
5. The C register holds the count of the negations performed, as well as a copy of the carry bit from the exponent calculations. The carry bit may be used to determine overflow or underflow.

Overflow and underflow conditions are handled by the OUFLW subroutine (shown in Figure 4.18). OUFLW checks the MSB of register C, which holds the copy of the carry produced during exponent calculations. If the carry result is 0, an overflow condition exists, and a call is made to a user subroutine, EOFLW. EOFLW will take any appropriate actions programmed by the user for the overflow error condition. Upon return from EOFLW, the result registers hold either the largest possible positive number or the largest possible negative number.

* Source: Kenneth L. Short, *Microprocessors and Programmed Logic,* copyright © 1981. Reprinted by permission of Prentice-Hall, Inc., Englewood Cliffs, N.J.

```
OUFLW:  XRA   A         ; TEST CARRY STORED IN MSB OF C
        ADD   C
        JM    UFLW
OFLW:   CALL  EOFLW     ; CALL ERROR ROUTINE FOR OVERFLOW
        LXI   H,7FFFH   ; SET TO LARGEST POSITIVE VALUE
        MVI   B,7FH
STSGN:  MOV   A,C       ; CHECK IF VALUE SHOULD BE NEGATIVE
        RAR
        XCHG            ; PLACE MANTISSA IN DE
        CC    NGDE1     ; NEGATE
        RET
UFLW:   CALL  EUFLW     ; CALL ERROR ROUTINE FOR UNDERFLOW
        LXI   D,0H      ; SET MANTISSA TO ZERO
UFLWE:  MVI   B,0H      ; SET EXPONENT TO ZERO (2^-64)
        RET
```

Figure 4.18 Subroutine for handling overflow and underflow conditions for floating-point operations.

If the copy of the carry is a 1 when OUFLW is called, a call is made to the user subroutine EUFLW, which takes the appropriate actions for an underflow error. Upon return from EUFLW, the result registers are all set to 0, which gives a result value of 0×2^{-64}, which makes 0 less significant than the smallest possible nonzero number.

The UFLWE entry point is used to set the result exponent to 0 if the result of a calculation is 0, in which case no call to EUFLW will be made.

The subroutine OUFLW, as well as the subroutine NORM (which normalizes a floating-point number), require an additional subroutine that will negate a floating-point number. The negation subroutine, NGDE, has two entry points, one that increments the negation count (held in C) and another that does nothing to the negation count. The NGDE subroutine is shown in Figure 4.19.

The process of normalizing a floating-point number consists of making the number positive, and then shifting it left until its magnitude MSB is 1. In order to maintain the original value of the number, the exponent is

```
NGDE:   INR   C         ; INCREMENT NEGATION COUNT
NGDE1:  XRA   A         ; SUBTRACT DE FROM 0
        SUB   E
        MOV   E,A       ; LEAVE RESULT IN DE
        MVI   A,0
        SBB   D
        MOV   D,A
        RET
```

Figure 4.19 Subroutine to negate a floating-point number.

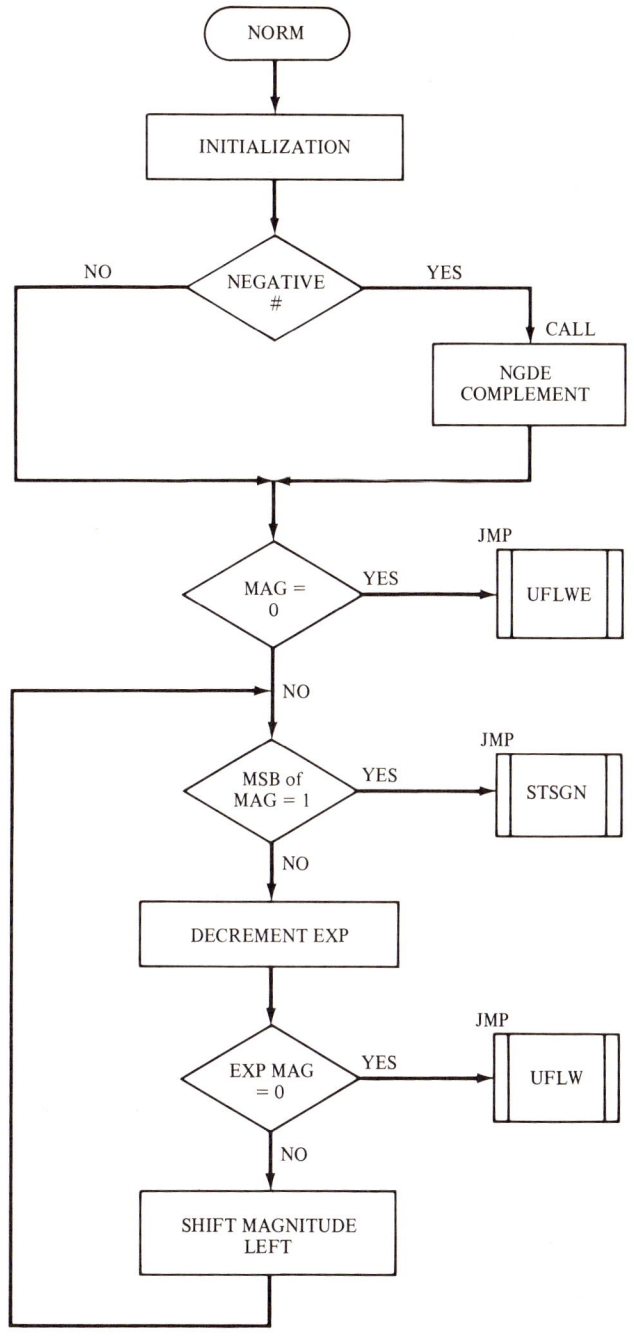

Figure 4.20 Flowchart for normalization subroutine.

```
NORM:   XRA     A       ; CLEAR C FOR NORMALIZATION
        MOV     C,A     ; CHECK FOR NEGATIVE NUMBER
        ORA     D       ; MAKE IT POSITIVE
        CM      NGDE    ; CHECK FOR ZERO MAGNITUDE
        ORA     E       ; IF MAGNITUDE IS ZERO, SET EXP. TO 0
        JZ      UFLWE   ; NORMALIZE IN HL
        XCHG            ; ENTRY FOR POSITIVE NONZERO NUMBERS
NORM1:  MOV     A,H
        ADD     H       ; NORMALIZATION COMPLETE, SET SIGN
        JM      STSGN   ; DECREMENT EXPONENT
        DCR     B       ; UNDERFLOW
        JM      UFLW    ; SHIFT LEFT
        DAD     H
        JMP     NORM1
```

Figure 4.21 Subroutine to normalize a floating-point number; (a) assume number is in B and DE; (b) C must be initialized to 0.

decremented each time a shift is performed. If the original number is negative, the normalized floating-point number must be negated. A flowchart for the normalization routine is shown in Figure 4.20 and the subroutine is shown in Figure 4.21.

Before two floating-point numbers may be added, they must be aligned. Alignment refers to the exponents, and is accomplished by shifting the smaller number to the right and incrementing its exponent until the values of the two exponents are equal. Due to the limits in precision of the floating-point routines, if more than 16 shifts are required, the actual addition is unnecessary because the smaller number will not change the value of the larger number when they are added together. In this case, the sum is simply the larger of the two numbers. A flowchart for the addition routine, FADD, is shown in Figure 4.22.

When aligned numbers are added, the sign of the result and the carry bit as well as the signs of the original operands, are checked for magnitude overflow. If the modulo$_2$ sum of the carry bit and the three sign bits is 1, then there is an overflow. The overflowed bit is the same as the sign bit of the operands and must be shifted into the result, as well as incrementing the exponent of the result. The exponent is also checked for overflow after being incremented. In all calculations, the result may need normalizing, in which case the NORM subroutine is called. The FADD subroutine is shown in Figure 4.23.

Floating-point subtraction is easily accomplished by negating the subtrahend and then performing floating-point addition. Floating-point multiplication and division routines may be developed by applying the rules for scientific notation.

Since floating-point numbers are all stored and manipulated in mantissa

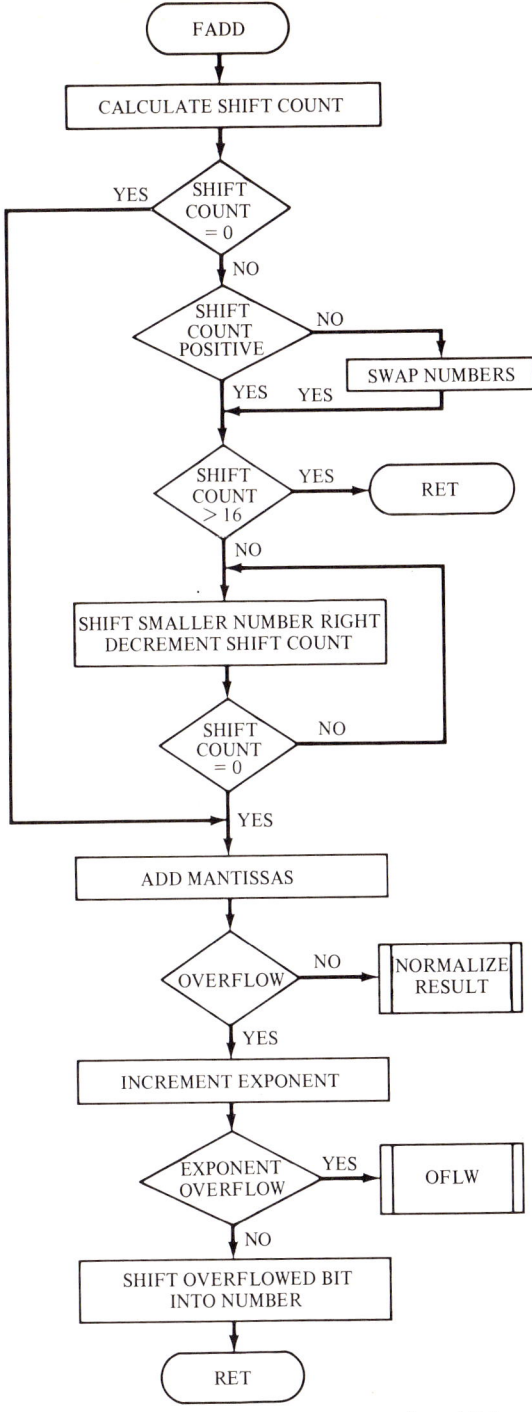

Figure 4.22 Flowchart for a floating-point addition subroutine.

```
FADD:   MOV   C,A      ; SAVE EXPONENT
        MOV   A,B
        SUB   C
        JZ    FADD3    ; NO SHIFT REQUIRED
        JP    FADD1    ; OPERANDS IN RIGHT ORDER
        CMA            ; MAKE SHIFT COUNT POSITIVE
        ADI   O1H
        XCHG           ; SWAP OPERANDS
        MOV   B,C
FADD1:  CPI   16
        RP             ; SHIFT > 16 ADDITION UNNECESSARY
        MOV   C,A      ; SAVE SHIFT COUNT
FADD2:  MOV   A,H      ; LOOP TO SHIFT SMALLER NUMBER RIGHT
        RAL              GET SIGN
        MOV   A,H
        RAR
        MOV   H,A
        MOV   A,L
        RAR            ; LEAVES LSB IN CARRY
        MOV   L,A
        DCR   C
        JNZ   FADD2
FADD3:  MOV   C,H      ; SAVE SIGN OF H,L
        DAD   D        ; ADD MANTISSAS
        XCH   G        ;
        SBB   A        ; SAVE CARRY/OVERFLOW A = 0 OR FF
        XRA   A
        XRA   D
        XRA   H
        JP    NORM
FADD4:  MOV   A,H      ; SUPER NORMAL OR NEGATIVE MAX
        RLC
        MOV   C,A
        INR   B        ; ADJUST EXPONENT FOR CARRY
        JM    OFLW     ; REAL OVERFLOW
        MOV   A,D      ; SHIFT OVERFLOW BIT INTO RESULT
        RAR
        MOV   D,A
        MOV   A,E
        RAR
        MOV   E,A
        RET
```

Figure 4.23 Subroutine for floating-point addition.

Intel 8085   97

and exponent form, additional routines are needed to convert the values to and from the decimal form that is required by the user.

When greater precision is required, the operands can no longer be passed between subroutines in registers, and are therefore stored in memory locations that are accessed by each subroutine.

5. Square Root Algorithm

One of the simplest ways of finding the square root of a number is by using the successive approximation algorithm. Successive approximation works as follows.

Let B be the value for which the square root is desired and A be the guess value of B. The value of A is squared and compared to the value of B. If A^2

```
137                     *SQUARE ROOT ROUTINE
138                     *
139                     *
140  0347  26    80     SQRT    MVI    H,80H       ;SET MSB OF SHIFT COUNTER
141  0349  2E    00             MVI    L,0         ;CLEAR THE BINARY VALUE
142  0348  70           SQRT1   MOV    A,L         ;GET BINARY VALUE
143  034C  B4                   ORA    H           ;SET A BIT IN L
144  034D  6F                   MOV    L,A
145  034E  47                   MOV    B,A         ;SQUARE BINARY VALUE
146  034F  CD    037A           CALL   SQRB
147  0352  7A                   MOV    A,D         ;IS B > D? YES, RESET BIT
148  0353  B8                   CMP    B           ;NO, LEAVE BIT
149  0354  DA    035F           JC     RSTBIT
150  0357  C2    0362           JNZ    SHFTCTR     ;IS B = D? NO, LEAVE BIT SET
151  035A  7B                   MOV    A,E         ;YES, COMPARE LO BYTE
152  035B  B9                   CMP    C           ;IS C > E? YES, RESET BIT
153  035C  D2    0362           JNC    SHFTCTR     ;NO, LEAVE BIT SET
154  035F  7D           RSTBIT  MOV    A,L         ;GET THE BIT SET LAST
155  0360  AC                   XRA    H           ;RESET THAT BIT IN BINARY VALUE
156  0361  6F                   MOV    L,A
157  0362  7C           SHFTCTR MOV    A,H         ;GET THE COUNTER
158  0363  1F                   RAR                ;SHIFT RIGHT
159  0364  67                   MOV    H,A         ;HAS IT BEEN SHIFTED 8 TIMES?
160  0365  D2    034B           JNC    SQRT1       ;YES, FALL THRU
161  0368  45                   MOV    B,L         ;SQUARE L
162  0369  CD    037A           CALL   SQRB
163  036C  7B                   MOV    A,E         ;GET LO BYTE OF HL
164  036D  91                   SUB    C           ;SUBTRACT LO BYTE L**2
165  036E  BD                   CMP    L           ;IS DIFFERENCE < L OR = L
```

Figure 4.24 8085 program for square root algorithm (continued on next page).

98 Chapter 4 Typical 8-Bit Microprocessors and Microcomputers

```
166 036F DA    0376            JC      DONE        ;YES, L**2 IS CLOSER
167 0372 CA    0376            JZ      DONE
168 0375 2C                    INR     L           ;NO, (L + 1)**2 IS CLOSER
169 0376 4D            DONE    MOV     C,L         ;SQUARE ROOT TO REG C
170 0377 C3    0397            HLT     CDA         ;HALT
171                    *
172                    *
173                    *
174                    *SUBROUTINE FOR SQUARING REGISTER B
175                    *RESULT IN RP B_C
176                    *
177 037A D5            SQRB    PUSH    D
178 037B 1E    08              MVI     E,08H       ;MULTIPLY COUNT
179 037D 0E    00              MVI     C,00H
180 037F 50                    MOV     D,B
181 0380 B7            SHIFT1  ORA     A           ;CLEAR CARRY
182 0381 79                    MOV     A,C         ;SHIFT 16 BITS LEFT
183 0382 17                    RAL
184 0383 4F                    MOV     C,A
185 0384 78                    MOV     A,B
186 0385 17                    RAL
187 0386 47                    MOV     B,A
188 0387 D2    0391            JNC     SQRB1
189 038A 7A                    MOV     A,D         ;GET DATA
190 038B 81                    ADD     C
191 038C 4F                    MOV     C,A
192 038D 78                    MOV     A,B
193 038E CE    00              ACI     00H
194 0390 47                    MOV     B,A
195 0391 1D            SQRB1   DCR     E           ;CHECK IF DONE
196 0392 C2    0380            JNZ     SHIFT1
197 0395 D1                    POP     D
198 0396 C9                    RET                 ;DONE
199                    *
```

Figure 4.24 Continued

is greater than B, A is decreased, but if A^2 is less than B, then A is increased by an arbitrary number (user choice). This procedure is repeated until A^2 is approximately equal to B. The user decides how close A^2 needs to be compared to B before the loop is terminated. When the loop is terminated, A is the value of the square root of B. Figure 4.24 shows the 8085 assembly language routine (along with the machine code) to implement the square root algorithm. In the following program, assume that the 'DE' pair contains the number whose square root is desired.

4.2 INTEL 8048 Microcomputer*

4.2.1 Introduction

The Intel MCS-48 microcomputers incorporate all the functions of a microcomputer on a single chip. The 8048 contains an 8-bit CPU, 1K × 8 ROM program memory, 64 × 8 data memory, 27 I/O lines, and an 8-bit timer/counter. The 8748, fully compatible with the 8048 but with EPROM program memory, is used for software development and nonproduction applications such as test and burn-in fixtures. The 8049 is equivalent to the 8048 but with twice the program and data memory capacity. The 8035 and 8029 are equivalent to the 8048 and 8049, respectively, yet have no internal program memory. All the devices are code compatible. Advantages of these processors include extensive bit manipulating instructions, program memory efficiency (no instruction over 2 bytes in length), and low cost. Disadvantages are restricted program memory addressing due to the 8-bit address argument and limited arithmetic functions (i.e., no subtract function) compared to other processors.

Figure 4.25 shows the 8048 block diagram and the pinout. The arithmetic section of the processor contains the basic data manipulation functions of the 8048 and can be divided into the following blocks: Arithmetic and Logic Unit (ALU), accumulator, carry flag, and instruction decoder.

Resident program memory consists of 1024 or 2048 words 8 bits wide which are addressed by the program counter. In the 8748, this memory is EPROM, and in the 8048, this memory is ROM.

Resident data memory is organized as 64 or 128 words 8 bits wide. All locations are indirectly addressable through eight of two RAM pointer registers which reside at address 0 or 1 of the register array. In addition, the first eight locations (0–7) of the array are designated as working registers and are directly addressable by several instructions.

By executing a register bank switch instruction (SEL RB), RAM locations 24–31 are designated as the working registers in place of locations 0–7 and are then directly addressable.

There are four user accessible flags in the 8048. These are carry, auxiliary carry, F0, and F1. Carry and auxiliary carry have the same meaning as in the 8085. F0 and F1 are undedicated general-purpose flags to be used as the program desires. Both of these flags can be cleared, complemented, and tested by conditional jump instructions.

We now describe some of the 8048 pins and signals.

V_{CC}, V_{DD}, and V_{SS} are power and ground signals. V_{SS} is ground, V_{CC}

---

* This section contains material modified from Intel manuals, courtesy of Intel Corporation.

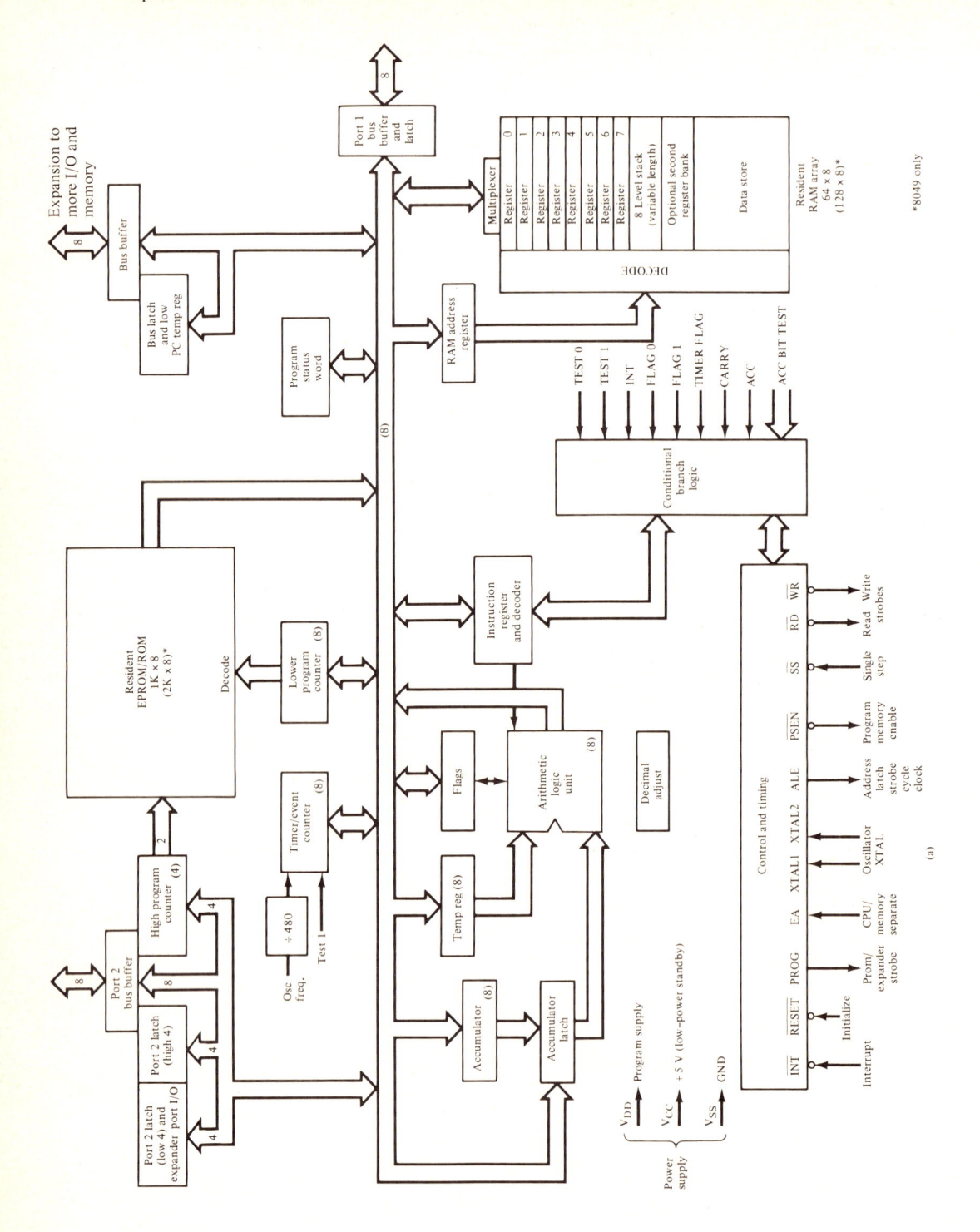

100 Chapter 4 Typical 8-Bit Microprocessors and Microcomputers

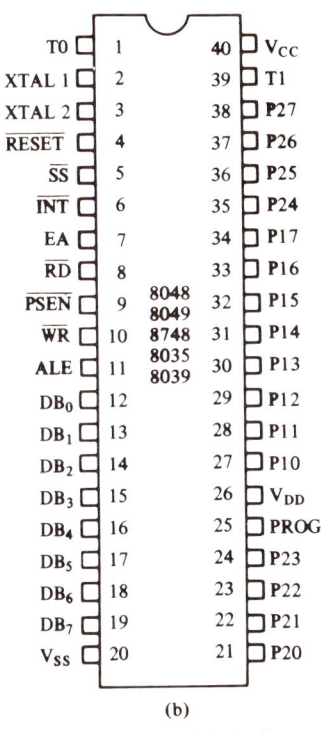

```
         ┌───∪───┐
   T0 ──┤1     40├── V_CC
XTAL 1 ─┤2     39├── T1
XTAL 2 ─┤3     38├── P27
 RESET ─┤4     37├── P26
    SS ─┤5     36├── P25
   INT ─┤6     35├── P24
    EA ─┤7     34├── P17
    RD ─┤8     33├── P16
  PSEN ─┤9  8048 32├── P15
        │   8049   │
    WR ─┤10 8748 31├── P14
        │   8035   │
   ALE ─┤11 8039 30├── P13
   DB0 ─┤12     29├── P12
   DB1 ─┤13     28├── P11
   DB2 ─┤14     27├── P10
   DB3 ─┤15     26├── V_DD
   DB4 ─┤16     25├── PROG
   DB5 ─┤17     24├── P23
   DB6 ─┤18     23├── P22
   DB7 ─┤19     22├── P21
   V_SS ┤20     21├── P20
        └─────────┘
             (b)
```

Figure 4.25 8048 block diagram and pinout. (a) Microcomputer internal block diagram. (b) Device pinout. Source: Reprinted by permission of Intel Corporation, copyright © 1982.

is +5 V, and V_{DD} is +25 V during program, and +5 V during operation.

PROG is the pin on which +23 V input pulse is applied during programming.

P10–P17 and P20–P27 are two 8-bit quasi-bidirectional ports.

D0–D7 is the data BUS.

T0 and T1 are two input pins that can be listed using the conditional transfer instructions JT0, JNT0 and JT1, JNT1 instructions.

PSEN (program store enable) is an output. This occurs only during a fetch to external program memory.

SS is a single-step input and can be used in conjunction with ALE to single step the processor through each instruction.

EA is the external access input which forms all program memory fetches to reference external memory

4.2.2 Instruction Set

A summary of the 8048 instruction set is given in Table 4.2. Highlights of the 8048 instruction set, some of which are unique to this processor include:

> DA A: Decimal Adjust Accumulator—provides single instructions binary to BCD conversion within the accumulator. Carry is generated for contents larger than decimal 99.
> SWAP A: Low-order 4 bits are exchanged with high-order 4 bits within the accumulator.

Table 4.2. 8048 Instruction Set

Mnemonic	Description	Bytes	Cycles
Accumulator			
ADD A, R	Add register to A	1	1
ADD A, @R	Add data memory to A	1	1
ADD A, #data	Add immediate to A	2	2
ADDC A, R	Add register with carry	1	1
ADDC A, @R	Add data memory with carry	1	1
ADDC A, #data	Add immediate with carry	2	2
ANL A, R	And register to A	1	1
ANL A, @R	And data memory to A	1	1
ANL A, #data	And immediate to A	2	2
ORL A, R	Or register to A	1	1
ORL A, @R	Or data memory to A	1	1
ORL A, #data	Or immediate to A	2	2
XRL A, R	Exclusive Or register to A	1	1
XRL A, @R	Exclusive Or data memory to A	1	1
XRL A, #data	Exclusive Or immediate to A	2	2
INC A	Increment A	1	1
DEC A	Decrement A	1	1
CLR A	Clear A	1	1
CPL A	Complement A	1	1
DA A	Decimal adjust A	1	1
SWAP A	Swap nibbles of A	1	1
RL A	Rotate A left	1	1
RLC A	Rotate A left through carry	1	1
RR A	Rotate A right	1	1
RRC A	Rotate A right through carry	1	1
Input/Output			
IN A, P	Input port to A	1	2
OUTL P, A	Output A to port	1	2
ANL P, #data	And immediate to port	2	2
ORL P, #data	Or immediate to port	2	2
INS A, BUS	Input BUS to A	1	2
OUTL BUS, A	Output A to BUS	1	2
ANL BUS, #data	And immediate to BUS	2	2
ORL BUS, #data	Or immediate to BUS	2	2

Table 4.2. Continued

Mnemonic	Description	Bytes	Cycles
MOVD A, P	Input expander port to A	1	2
MOVD P, A	Output A to expander port	1	2
ANLD P, A	And A to expander port	1	2
ORLD P, A	Or A to expander port	1	2
Registers			
INC R	Increment register	1	1
INC @R	Increment data memory	1	1
DEC R	Decrement register	1	1
Branch			
JMP addr	Jump unconditional	2	2
JMPP @A	Jump indirect	1	2
DJNZ R, addr	Decrement register and skip	2	2
JC addr	Jump on carry = 1	2	2
JNC addr	Jump on carry = 0	2	2
J Z addr	Jump on A zero	2	2
JNZ addr	Jump on A not zero	2	2
JT0 addr	Jump on T0 = 1	2	2
JNT0 addr	Jump on T0 = 0	2	2
JT1 addr	Jump on T1 = 1	2	2
JNT1 addr	Jump on T1 = 0	2	2
JF0 addr	Jump on F0 = 1	2	2
JF1 addr	Jump on F1 = 1	2	2
JTF addr	Jump on timer flag	2	2
JNI addr	Jump on $\overline{INT}$ = 0	2	2
JBb addr	Jump on accumulator bit	2	2
Subroutine			
CALL	Jump to subroutine	2	2
RET	Return	1	2
RETR	Return and restore status	1	2
Flags			
CLR C	Clear carry	1	1
CPL C	Complement carry	1	1
CLR F0	Clear flag 0	1	1
CPL F0	Complement flag 0	1	1
CLR F1	Clear flag 1	1	1
CPL F1	Complement flag 1	1	1
Data Moves			
MOV A, R	Move register to A	1	1
MOV A, @R	Move data memory to A	1	1
MOV A, #data	Move immediate to A	2	2
MOV R, A	Move A to register	1	1
MOV @R, A	Move A to data memory	1	1
MOV R, #data	Move immediate to register	2	2
MOV @R, #data	Move immediate to data memory	2	2
MOV A, PSW	Move PSW to A	1	1
MOV PSW, A	Move A to PSW	1	1
XCH A, R	Exchange A and register	1	1
XCHA, @R	Exchange A and data memory	1	1

Table 4.2. Continued

MNEMONIC	DESCRIPTION	BYTES	CYCLES
XCHD A, @R	Exchange nibble of A and register	1	1
MOVX A, @R	Move external data memory to A	1	2
MOVX @R, A	Move A to external data memory	1	2
MOVP A, @A	Move to A from current page	1	2
MOVP3 A, @A	Move to A from page 3	1	2
TIMER/COUNTER			
MOV A, T	Read timer/counter	1	1
MOV T, A	Load timer/counter	1	1
STRT T	Start timer	1	1
STRT CNT	Start counter	1	1
STOP TCNT	Stop timer/counter	1	1
EN TCNTI	Enable timer/counter Interrupt	1	1
DIS TCNTI	Disable timer/counter Interrupt	1	1
CONTROL			
EN I	Enable external interrupt	1	1
DIS I	Disable external interrupt	1	1
SEL RB0	Select register bank 0	1	1
SEL RB1	Select register bank 1	1	1
SEL MB0	Select memory bank 0	1	1
SEL MB1	Select memory bank 1	1	1
ENT0 CLK	Enable clock output on T0	1	1
NOP	No Operation	1	1

Source: All mnemonics copyright Intel Corporation © 1982.

ANL P and ORL P: Logical AND, Logical OR with port—allows single bits of a port to be modified without changing other bits.

MOVD: Special instructions used to access the 8243 I/O expander.

DJNZ R and DJZ R: Single-instruction decrements register and checks for zero (or nonzero) executing a jump to in-page address. Very useful in interactive loops.

JT0, JT1, JNT0, and JNT1: Executes a jump to page address based on the value of a test input. This provides a simple means to change execution based on an external logic level.

JBb: Invokes a jump to address when a particular bit of the accumulator is value 1. This allows any port bit to be easily used as a test input.

MOVP3 A, @A: Causes a move from page 3 of the currently selected memory bank into A as addressed by A. Look-up tables, for example, can be stored in page 3 with this instruction providing a means to get around the 8048 page boundaries.

ENT0 CLK: Designates T0 as an output for the system clock. Can be used to provide a time base for external devices.

SEL RB0 and SEL RB1: Allows selection of one of two register banks. RB0 can be used for normal execution with RB1 reserved for interrupt processing.

4.2.3 Addressing Modes

Twelve address bits are required to access the 4K bytes of program memory. Since all instructions are 1 to 2 bytes in length, some instructions are limited in jump capability. Conditional jumps are restricted within a 256-byte page boundary since only the lower 8 bits of the program counter are modified. Jump within a 2K block is provided in the JMP instruction by using 3 bits of instruction byte as part of the jump address. Selection of upper or lower 2K block is done with the SEL MB0 and SEL MB1 instructions, which modify only the high-order program counter bit.

The advantage of this type of addressing is efficient use of program memory due to the maximum 2-byte instruction size. The disadvantage is that the programmer must take care to provide a JMP instruction at each page boundary and SEL MB instruction at the block boundary. These restrictions hold true for both internal and external memory access. Subroutine CALL instructions address within a 2K block.

External program memory can be extended beyond 4K bytes if memory bank switching is provided via an I/O port. Care should be taken to avoid having subroutines cross the boundaries since the programmer must keep track of which bank the routine was called from.

4.2.4 I/O Capability

Programmed I/O

Several I/O modes are available—static I/O ports P1 and P2, memory-mapped I/O, and 8243 I/O expander.

1. Ports P1 and P2 are two 8-bit input/output ports. An 8-bit word can be outputted using the OUT1 instruction or individual bits can be set with masks using the ANL or ORL instructions. Since outputs are of relatively high impedance (about 50K ohms), they can be externally driven to serve as inputs. BUS can also be used as a static port if external memory or memory-mapped I/O are not used.
2. Memory-mapped I/O is accomplished using the MOVX instruction. An address latch is required for device selection:
   a. Content of RD is strobed into an external address latch from BUS as ALE falls low. Address value is used to select an external device.
   b. Accumulator data are outputted to BUS.
   c. WR is strobed to latch data in the external device.
3. The 8243 I/O expander is accessed using the MOVD, ANLD, ORLD instructions as ports P3–P7. Four-bit port select and data appear on P23–P20 and data are latched through the PROG pin. Figures 4.26 and 4.27 demonstrate the 8048 I/O capabilities.

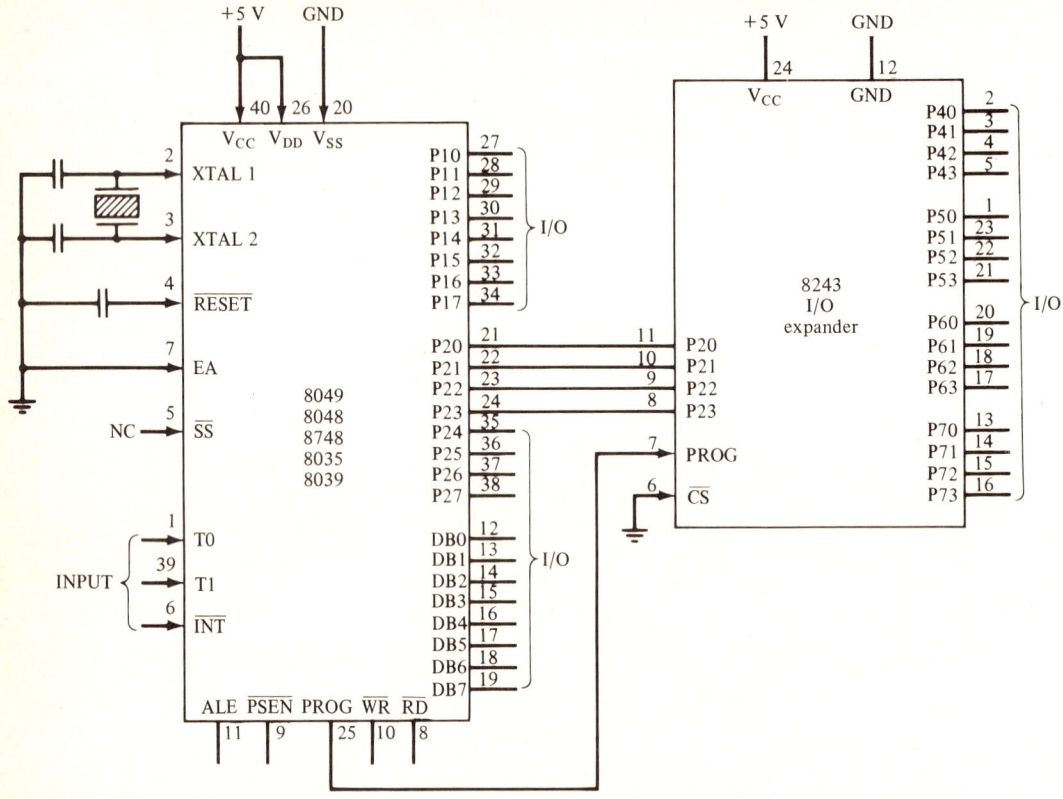

Figure 4.26 I/O expansion using the low-cost 8243 I/O expander. Source: Reprinted by permission of Intel Corporation, copyright © 1982.

Interrupt I/O

The 8048 is provided with two independent interrupt functions—hardware interrupt and timer/counter interrupt.

A low level on the INT pin forces a jump to location 3 of program memory (if interrupts have been enabled by an ENI instruction). The jump occurs at the completion of the instruction being executed when the interrupt occurs. Location 3 should contain an unconditional jump to an interrupt service routine. The basic sequence of events is as follows:

1. External device initiates interrupt by driving INT low.
2. Processor executes a subroutine call to location 3, then ignores the interrupt signal.
3. Interrupt service routine is executed.
4. RETR instruction returns to main program at the point where execution was interrupted. Interrupt is reenabled and program status word is restored.

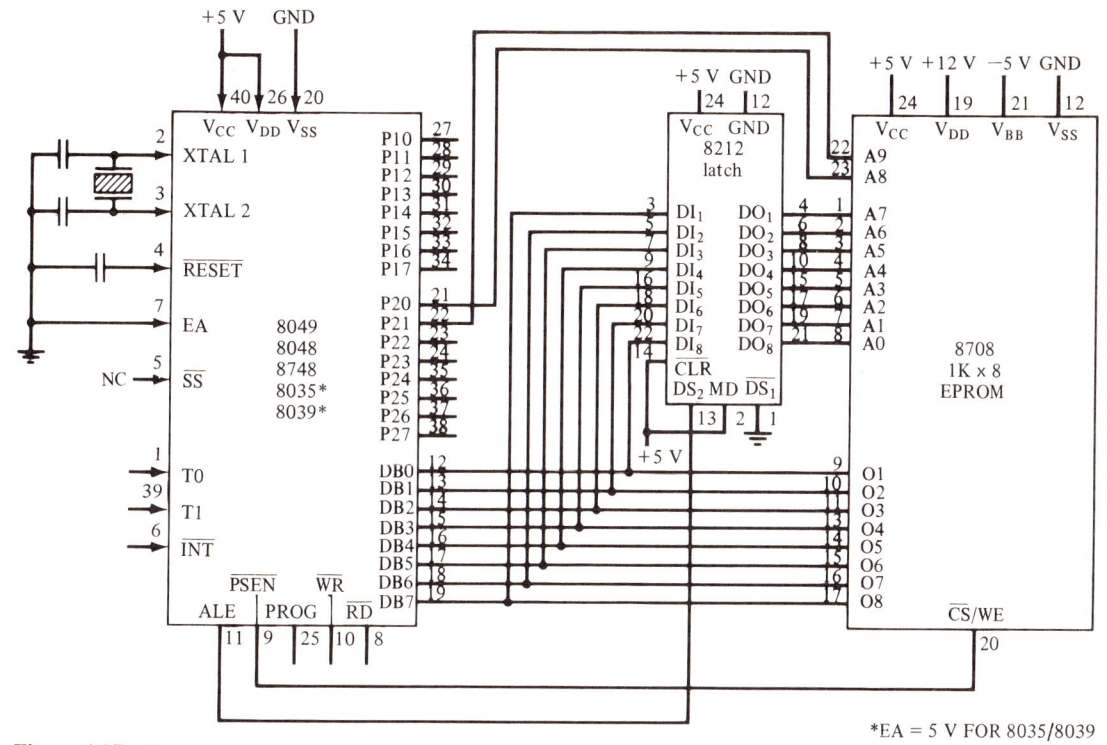

Figure 4.27 Program memory expansion showing the use of an external address latch. Source: Reprinted by permission of Intel Corporation, copyright © 1982.

There are several important points to remember when using interrupt on the 8048:

Interrupt always vectors to location 3 on the first page, regardless of current page or block selection.
The external interrupt pin must be high when returning from interrupt service or else the interrupt will be immediately reexecuted.
It is useful to use register bank 1 for interrupt service exclusively thus avoiding loss of main program data stored in register bank 0.

Operation of the timer/counter interrupt is similar to that of the hardware interrupt except that it vectors to memory location 7 and is initiated by overflow of the 8-bit timer/counter. Priority of this interrupt is below that of the hardware interrupt; hardware interrupt is serviced first and the timer/counter interrupt remains pending.

In the timer mode the time interval per count depends on the crystal frequency (92.6 μs with 5.185-MHz crystal). To yield a given time interval in the range of 92.6 μs to 23.7 ms (256 counts), the timer is loaded with the ones complement of the number of single intervals as calculated by:

$$N = \text{total}/92.6 \ \mu s$$

Longer intervals can be obtained by performing any number of interrupts sequentially.

Applications of the timer include time-of-day clock, stepper motor timing, and process timing. This approach frees the processor to perform other functions, such as numerical calculations, instead of waiting in a timing loop. The timer register also functions as a counter clocked by an external pulse at T1. The counter is incremented for each high to low transition at T1. Applications would include a frequency counter reference.

EXAMPLE 4.4

Write an 8048 assembly language program for BCD to binary conversion. Assume R5 contains BCD data. Use the algorithm as follows: Let AB be the BCD number. "AB" in BCD is equivalent to $A \times 10' + B \times 10°$ in binary. In the following program, the binary equivalent of "AB" is calculated by multiplying A by 8 and adding A twice (which gives $A \times 10$) and then adding B.

SOLUTION

The program is given in the following:

```
BCDBIN: MOV A, R5      ; R5 contains two digit BCD data.
        SWAP A         ; Move tens digit to low nibble.
        ANL A, #0FH    ; Mask off high nibble.
        MOV R1, A      ; Tens digit in low nibble of A and R1.
        RL A
        RL A
        RL A           ; Multiply by 8.
        ADD A, R1
        ADD A, R1      ; No, make it 10.
        MOV R1, A      ; Move converted tens to R1.
        MOV A, R5
        ANL A, #0FH    ; Mask off tens digit.
        ADD A, R1      ; Add ones to converted tens.
        MOV R5, A      ; Move result to R5.
        RET            ; R5 now contains binary data.
```

EXAMPLE 4.5

Write an 8048 assembly language program to perform a division with remainder. Assume R5 contains dividend and R6 contains divisor.

SOLUTION

The program is given in the following:

```
DIVD:   MOV A, R5      ; Save R5 contents.
        MOV R5, #00H   ; Clear R5.
DIVD1:  INC R5         ; Count passes for result.
        CPL A
        ADD A, R6
        CPL A          ; Subtract R6 from A.
        JNC DIVD1      ; Finished if carry generated.
        ADD A, R6
        DEC R5         ; R5 was 1 too large.
        RET            ; R5 contains result.
                       ; A contains remainder.
```

4.3 Zilog Z80*

4.3.1 Introduction

The architecture of the Zilog Z80 is based on that of the 8080 and can perform all the 78 instructions of that processor plus an additional 80 instructions. In all, the Z80 has 696 op codes compared to 244 op codes for 8080. The construction is ion-implanted NMOS. Features include single +5-V supply operation, a single-phase external clock, 17 internal registers, paged-memory and built-in RAM refresh circuitry. Three modes of interrupt response are provided. There is a second set of eight 8-bit registers that mirrors the eight registers of the 8080. All timing generation is on the processor chip with the exception of a single external oscillator. The address BUS is structured so that dynamic RAM refresh addresses appear on the lower half of the BUS. The minimal system would consist of the processor, a clock source, and some external memory. The Z80 block diagram and pinout are shown in Figures 4.28 and 4.29.

All the 8080 registers are duplicated within the Z80, and in addition to the 8-bit registers (A, B, C, D, E, H, and L) of the 8080, there is an alternate set (A', F', B', C', D', E', H', and L') and several other special-purpose registers. The additional registers include two 16-bit index registers (IX and IY), an 8-bit interrupt-vector register (I), and an 8-bit memory refresh register (R). Also, there are one 16-bit PC and one 16-bit SP. A special feature of the Z80 is its ability to refresh dynamic memory automatically using the R register.

There are two identical 8-bit flag registers in the Z80. There are four

---

* This section contains material reprinted courtesy of Zilog, Inc.

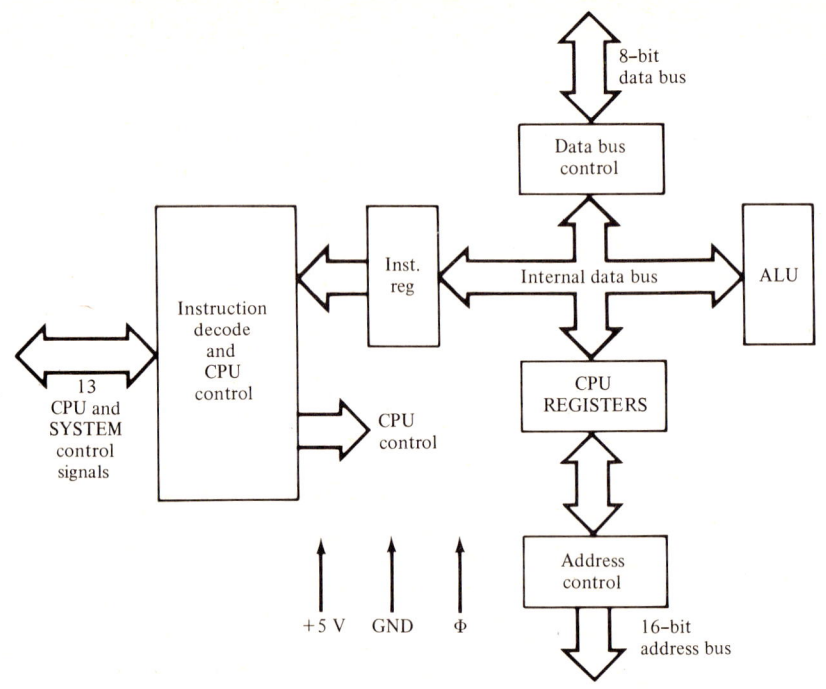

Figure 4.28 Z80 CPU block diagram. Source: Reprinted by permission of Zilog Inc., copyright © 1982.

testable and two nontestable flag bits. The four testable flags are carry, zero, negative sign, and parity/overflow flag. The two nontestable bits are half-carry (same as auxiliary carry in the 8085) and subtract flag. The subtract flag corrects for BCD operations by helping to identify the previous instruction. The correction differs for addition and subtraction.

We now describe some of the Z80 pins and signals.

$\overline{\text{BUSRQ}}$ is an input that requests not only the Z80's address and data buses but also memory request, I/O request, and so on, to go to the high impedance state so that other devices can use the bus.

$\overline{\text{BUSAK}}$ is an output signal which goes high to indicate when the lines go into a high impedance state.

$\overline{M_1}$ (machine cycle 1) goes low to indicate when the microprocessor is in the op code fetch part of an instruction.

$\overline{\text{MREQ}}$ (memory request line) goes low when the address bus holds a valid address for a memory read or write operation.

The $\overline{\text{RFSH}}$ (refresh signal) line goes low to indicate that the lower 7 bits of the address bus contain a refresh address for dynamic memories; the current $\overline{\text{MREQ}}$ signal should be used to do a refresh read to all dynamic memory.

$\overline{\text{HALT}}$ is output low to indicate execution of the HALT instruction.

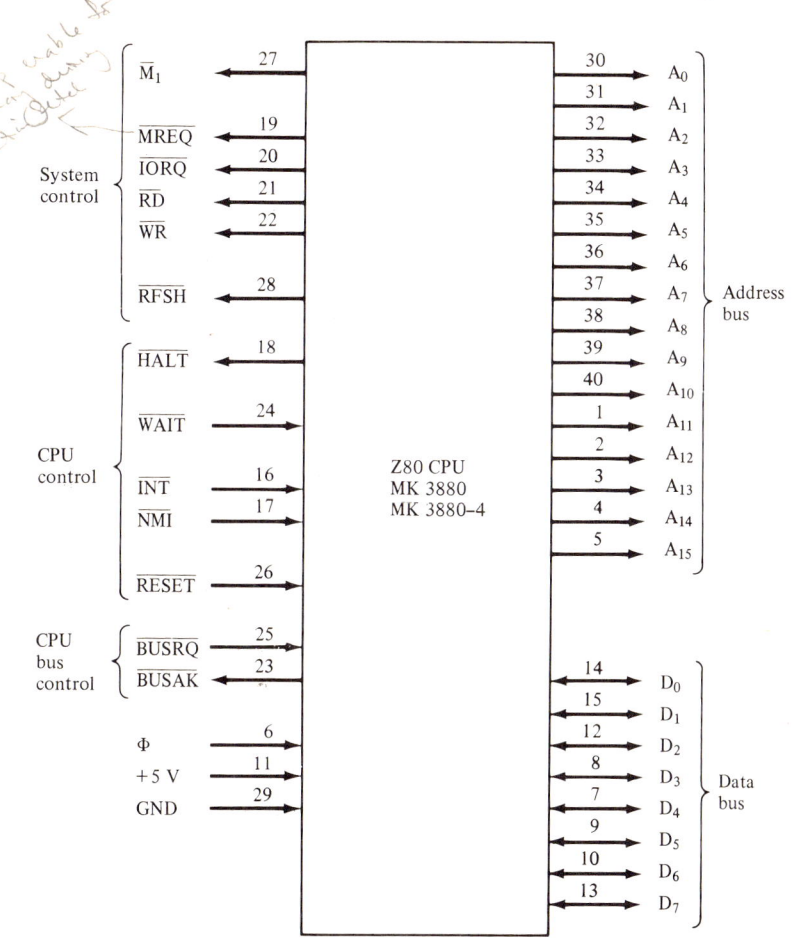

Figure 4.29 Z80 CPU pinout. Source: Reprinted by permission of Zilog Inc., copyright © 1982.

4.3.2 Addressing Modes

The Z80 CPU contains a 16-line address BUS capable of accessing 64K of program memory. The various modes of addressing are as follows:

1. Instruction fetch: The program counter value (PC) is outputted to the address bus. MREQ goes low and is used as chip enable for program memory. RD goes low to enable data from memory onto the data bus. As the instruction is being decoded, a 7-bit refresh address is outputted to the address bus and RFSH goes low, indicating dynamic RAM refresh should be performed.
2. Immediate mode: The location following the op code contains the data operand.

3. Extended immediate mode: The locations following the op code contain the 16-bit data operand.
4. Modified page zero addressing: This instruction, called a restart, is used to initiate a subroutine jump to any of eight locations in page zero. Commonly called subroutines can be placed at these locations and be accessed by a single-byte instruction.
5. Relative addressing: This uses a 1-byte displacement address in range of +127 to −128 from current address plus 2, thereby allowing a 2-byte call to nearby subroutines and allowing for relocatable code.
6. Extended addressing: The full 16-bit destination address is specified in two operand bytes. A call or jump to any location in memory can be executed.
7. Indexed addressing: A displacement is added to one of the two index registers forming a memory pointer. This is useful for look-up table operations.
8. Register addressing: The op code contains data specifying a particular register.
9. Implied addressing: The addressed register, such as the accumulator, is implied within the instruction.
10. Register indirect addressing: A 16-bit register pair, such as HL, contains the operand address.
11. Bit addressing: Three bits of the op code specify a particular bit of a memory location to be manipulated.

4.3.3 Instruction Set

Table 4.3 shows a summary of the Z80 instruction set. Highlights of the Z80 instruction set are as follows:

1. Data can be moved directly from register to register, memory to register, register to memory, or memory to memory. Contents can also be exchanged without the use of temporary storage.
2. The primary and auxiliary registers (R and R′) can be exchanged using the EX and EXX instructions, allowing the separation of register data between different procedures.
3. A full repertoire of stack operations are included. The Stack Pointer (SP) is used both to store and retrieve data and for subroutine address linkage. The stack operates on a last in first out basis and can be as large as required up to the system memory capacity. Thus subroutine nesting and data storage in the stack are essentially unlimited.
4. Sixteen-bit operations, such as DAD (register pair add), INX and DCX (increment and decrement register pair), LHLD (load register pair direct), and others are provided to aid in 16-bit arithmetic operations and in control of addressing.

Table 4.3. Z80 Instruction Set

EXCHANGE GROUP AND BLOCK TRANSFER AND SEARCH GROUP

Mnemonic	Symbolic Operation	C	Z	P/V	S	N	H	Op-Code 76 543 210	No. of Bytes	No. of M Cycles	No. of T States	Comments
EX DE, HL	DE ↔ HL	•	•	•	•	•	•	11 101 011	1	1	4	
EX AF, AF'	AF ↔ AF'	•	•	•	•	•	•	00 001 000	1	1	4	
EXX	(BC)↔(BC') (DE)↔(DE') (HL)↔(HL')	•	•	•	•	•	•	11 011 001	1	1	4	Register bank and auxiliary register bank exchange
EX (SP), HL	H ↔ (SP+1) L ↔ (SP)	•	•	•	•	•	•	11 100 011	1	5	19	
EX (SP), IX	IX_H ↔ (SP+1) IX_L ↔ (SP)	•	•	•	•	•	•	11 011 101 11 100 011	2	6	23	
EX (SP), IY	IY_H ↔ (SP+1) IY_L ↔ (SP)	•	•	•	•	•	•	11 111 101 11 100 011	2	6	23	
LDI	(DE) ← (HL) DE ← DE+1 HL ← HL+1 BC ← BC-1	•	•	↕ ①	•	0	0	11 101 101 10 100 000	2	4	16	Load (HL) into (DE), increment the pointers and decrement the byte counter (BC)
LDIR	(DE) ← (HL) DE ← DE+1 HL ← HL+1 BC ← BC-1 Repeat until BC = 0	•	•	0	•	0	0	11 101 101 10 110 000	2 2	5 4	21 16	If BC ≠ 0 If BC = 0
LDD	(DE) ← (HL) DE ← DE-1 HL ← HL-1 BC ← BC-1	•	•	↕ ①	•	0	0	11 101 101 10 101 000	2	4	16	
LDDR	(DE) ← (HL) DE ← DE-1 HL ← HL-1 BC ← BC-1 Repeat until BC = 0	•	•	0	•	0	0	11 101 101 10 111 000	2 2	5 4	21 16	If BC ≠ 0 If BC = 0
CPI	A - (HL) HL ← HL+1 BC ← BC-1	•	↕	↕ ② ①	↕	1	↕	11 101 101 10 100 001	2	4	16	
CPIR	A - (HL) HL ← HL+1 BC ← BC-1 Repeat until A = (HL) or BC = 0	•	↕	↕ ② ①	↕	1	↕	11 101 101 10 110 001	2 2	5 4	21 16	If BC ≠ 0 and A ≠ (HL) If BC = 0 or A = (HL)

Zilog Z80   113

Table 4.3. Continued

Mnemonic	Symbolic Operation	Flags C	Z	P/V	S	N	H	Op-Code 76 543 210	No. of Bytes	No. of M Cycles	No. of T States	Comments
CPD	A − (HL) HL ← HL−1 BC ← BC−1	•	↕	↕ ②	↕ ①	1	↕	11 101 101 10 101 001	2	4	16	
CPDR	A − (HL) HL ← HL−1 BC ← BC−1 Repeat until A = (HL) or BC = 0	•	↕	↕	↕	1	↕	11 101 101 10 111 001	2 2	5 4	21 16	If BC ≠ 0 and A ≠ (HL) If BC = 0 or A = (HL)

Notes: ① P/V flag is 0 if the result of BC−1 = 0, otherwise P/V = 1
② Z flag is 1 if A = (HL), otherwise Z = 0.

Flag Notation: • = flag not affected, 0 = flag reset, 1 = flag set, X = flag is unknown,
↕ = flag is affected according to the result of the operation.

8-BIT ARITHMETIC AND LOGICAL GROUP

Mnemonic	Symbolic Operation	Flags C	Z	P/V	S	N	H	Op-Code 76 543 210	No. of Bytes	No. of M Cycles	No. of T States	Comments
ADD A, r	A ← A + r	↕	↕	V	↕	0	↕	10 [000] r	1	1	4	r Reg.
ADD A, n	A ← A + n	↕	↕	V	↕	0	↕	11 [000] 110 ← n →	2	2	7	000 B 001 C 010 D
ADD A, (HL)	A ← A + (HL)	↕	↕	V	↕	0	↕	10 [000] 110	1	2	7	011 E 100 H
ADD A, (IX+d)	A ← A + (IX+d)	↕	↕	V	↕	0	↕	11 011 101 10 [000] 110 ← d →	3	5	19	101 L 111 A
ADD A, (IY+d)	A ← A+(IY+d)	↕	↕	V	↕	0	↕	11 111 101 10 [000] 110 ← d →	3	5	19	
ADC A, s	A ← A + s + CY	↕	↕	V	↕	0	↕	[001]				s is any of r, n, (HL), (IX+d), (IY+d) as shown for ADD instruction
SUB s	A ← A − s	↕	↕	V	↕	1	↕	[010]				
SBC A, s	A ← A − s − CY	↕	↕	V	↕	1	↕	[011]				
AND s	A ← A ∧ s	0	↕	P	↕	0	1	[100]				The indicated bits replace the 000 in the ADD set above.
OR s	A ← A ∨ s	0	↕	P	↕	0	0	[110]				
XOR s	A ← A ⊕ s	0	↕	P	↕	0	0	[101]				
CP s	A − s	↕	↕	V	↕	1	↕	[111]				
INC r	r ← r + 1	•	↕	V	↕	0	↕	00 r [100]	1	1	4	
INC (HL)	(HL) ← (HL)+1	•	↕	V	↕	0	↕	00 110 [100]	1	3	11	
INC (IX+d)	(IX+d) ← (IX+d)+1	•	↕	V	↕	0	↕	11 011 101 00 110 [100] ← d →	3	6	23	

Table 4.3. Continued

Mnemonic	Symbolic Operation	Flags C	Z	P/V	S	N	H	Op-Code 76 543 210	No. of Bytes	No. of M Cycles	No. of T States	Comments
INC (IY+d)	(IY+d) ← (IY+d) + 1	•	↕	V	↕	0	↕	11 111 101 00 110 [100] ← d →	3	6	23	
DEC m	m ← m−1	•	↕	V	↕	1	↕	[101]				m is any of r, (HL), (IX+d), (IY+d) as shown for INC. Same format and states as INC. Replace 100 with 101 in OP code.

Notes: The V symbol in the P/V flag column indicates that the P/V flag contains the overflow of the result of the operation. Similarly the P symbol indicates parity. V = 1 means overflow, V = 0 means not overflow. P = 1 means parity of the result is even, P = 0 means parity of the result is odd.

Flag Notation: • = flag not affected, 0 = flag reset, 1 = flag set, X = flag is unknown,
↕ = flag is affected according to the result of the operation.

8-BIT LOAD GROUP

Mnemonic	Symbolic Operation	C	Z	P/V	S	N	H	OP-Code 76 543 210	No. of Bytes	No. of M Cycles	No. of T Cycles	Comments
LD r, r'	r ← r'	•	•	•	•	•	•	01 r r'	1	1	4	r, r' Reg.
LD r, n	r ← n	•	•	•	•	•	•	00 r 110 ← n →	2	2	7	000 B 001 C
LD r, (HL)	r ← (HL)	•	•	•	•	•	•	01 r 110	1	2	7	010 D
LD r, (IX+d)	r ← (IX+d)	•	•	•	•	•	•	11 011 101 01 r 110 ← d →	3	5	19	011 E 100 H 101 L
LD r, (IY+d)	r ← (IY+d)	•	•	•	•	•	•	11 111 101 01 r 110 ← d →	3	5	19	111 A
LD (HL), r	(HL) ← r	•	•	•	•	•	•	01 110 r	1	2	7	
LD (IX+d), r	(IX+d) ← r	•	•	•	•	•	•	11 011 101 01 110 r ← d →	3	5	19	
LD (IY+d), r	(IY+d) ← r	•	•	•	•	•	•	11 111 101 01 110 r ← d →	3	5	19	
LD (HL), n	(HL) ← n	•	•	•	•	•	•	00 110 110 ← n →	2	3	10	
LD (IX+d), n	(IX+d) ← n	•	•	•	•	•	•	11 011 101 00 110 110 ← d → ← n →	4	5	19	
LD (IY+d), n	(IY+d) ← n	•	•	•	•	•	•	11 111 101 00 110 110 ← d → ← n →	4	5	19	

Chapter 4 TYPICAL 8-BIT MICROPROCESSORS AND MICROCOMPUTERS

Table 4.3. Continued

Mnemonic	Symbolic Operation	Flags C	Z	P/V	S	N	H	OP-Code 76 543 210	No. of Bytes	No. of M Cycles	No. of T Cycles	Comments
LD A, (BC)	A ← (BC)	•	•	•	•	•	•	00 001 010	1	2	7	
LD A, (DE)	A ← (DE)	•	•	•	•	•	•	00 011 010	1	2	7	
LD A, (nn)	A ← (nn)	•	•	•	•	•	•	00 111 010 ← n → ← n →	3	4	13	
LD (BC), A	(BC) ← A	•	•	•	•	•	•	00 000 010	1	2	7	
LD (DE), A	(DE) ← A	•	•	•	•	•	•	00 010 010	1	2	7	
LD (nn), A	(nn) ← A	•	•	•	•	•	•	00 110 010 ← n → ← n →	3	4	13	
LD A, I	A ← I	•	↕	IFF	↕	0	0	11 101 101 01 010 111	2	2	9	
LD A, R	A ← R	•	↕	IFF	↕	0	0	11 101 101 01 011 111	2	2	9	
LD I, A	I ← A	•	•	•	•	•	•	11 101 101 01 000 111	2	2	9	
LD R, A	R ← A	•	•	•	•	•	•	11 101 101 01 001 111	2	2	9	

Notes: r, r' means any of the registers A, B, C, D, E, H, L

IFF the content of the interrupt enable flip-flop (IFF) is copied into the P/V flag

Flag Notation: • = flag not affected, 0 = flag reset, 1 = flag set, X = flag is unknown,

↕ = flag is affected according to the result of the operation.

16-BIT LOAD GROUP

Mnemonic	Symbolic Operation	Flags C	Z	P/V	S	N	H	Op-Code 76 543 210	No. of Bytes	No. of M Cycles	No. of T States	Comments
LD dd, nn	dd ← nn	•	•	•	•	•	•	00 dd0 001 ← n → ← n →	3	3	10	dd Pair 00 BC 01 DE 10 HL 11 SP
LD IX, nn	IX ← nn	•	•	•	•	•	•	11 011 101 00 100 001 ← n → ← n →	4	4	14	
LD IY, nn	IY ← nn	•	•	•	•	•	•	11 111 101 00 100 001 ← n → ← n →	4	4	14	
LD HL, (nn)	H ← (nn+1) L ← (nn)	•	•	•	•	•	•	00 101 010 ← n → ← n →	3	5	16	
LD dd, (nn)	dd$_H$ ← (nn+1) dd$_L$ ← (nn)	•	•	•	•	•	•	11 101 101 01 dd1 011 ← n → ← n →	4	6	20	
LD IX, (nn)	IX$_H$ ← (nn+1) IX$_L$ ← (nn)	•	•	•	•	•	•	11 011 101 00 101 010 ← n → ← n →	4	6	20	

Table 4.3. Continued

Mnemonic	Symbolic Operation	C	Z	P/V	S	N	H	Op-Code 76 543 210	No. of Bytes	No. of M Cycles	No. of T States	Comments
LD IY, (nn)	IY$_H$ ← (nn+1) IY$_L$ ← (nn)	•	•	•	•	•	•	11 111 101 00 101 010 ← n → ← n →	4	6	20	
LD (nn), HL	(nn+1) ← H (nn) ← L	•	•	•	•	•	•	00 100 010 ← n → ← n →	3	5	16	
LD (nn), dd	(nn+1) ← dd$_H$ (nn) ← dd$_L$	•	•	•	•	•	•	11 101 101 01 dd0 011 ← n → ← n →	4	6	20	
LD (nn), IX	(nn+1) ← IX$_H$ (nn) ← IX$_L$	•	•	•	•	•	•	11 011 101 00 100 010 ← n → ← n →	4	6	20	
LD (nn), IY	(nn+1) ← IY$_H$ (nn) ← IY$_L$	•	•	•	•	•	•	11 111 101 00 100 010 ← n → ← n →	4	6	20	
LD SP, HL	SP ← HL	•	•	•	•	•	•	11 111 001	1	1	6	
LD SP, IX	SP ← IX	•	•	•	•	•	•	11 011 101 11 111 001	2	2	10	
LD SP, IY	SP ← IY	•	•	•	•	•	•	11 111 101 11 111 001	2	2	10	
PUSH qq	(SP-2) ← qq$_L$ (SP-1) ← qq$_H$	•	•	•	•	•	•	11 qq0 101	1	3	11	qq Pair 00 BC 01 DE
PUSH IX	(SP-2) ← IX$_L$ (SP-1) ← IX$_H$	•	•	•	•	•	•	11 011 101 11 100 101	2	4	15	10 HL 11 AF
PUSH IY	(SP-2) ← IY$_L$ (SP-1) ← IY$_H$	•	•	•	•	•	•	11 111 101 11 100 101	2	4	15	
POP qq	qq$_H$ ← (SP+1) qq$_L$ ← (SP)	•	•	•	•	•	•	11 qq0 001	1	3	10	
POP IX	IX$_H$ ← (SP+1) IX$_L$ ← (SP)	•	•	•	•	•	•	11 011 101 11 100 001	2	4	14	
POP IY	IY$_H$ ← (SP+1) IY$_L$ ← (SP)	•	•	•	•	•	•	11 111 101 11 100 001	2	4	14	

Notes: dd is any of the register pairs BC, DE, HL, SP
qq is any of the register pairs AF, BC, DE, HL
(PAIR)$_H$, (PAIR)$_L$ refer to high order and low order eight bits of the register pair respectively.
E.g. BC$_L$ = C, AF$_H$ = A

Flag Notation: • = flag not affected, 0 = flag reset, 1 = flag set, X = flag is unknown,
‡ flag is affected according to the result of the operation.

GENERAL PURPOSE ARITHMETIC AND CPU CONTROL GROUPS

Mnemonic	Symbolic Operation	C	Z	P/V	S	N	H	Op-Code 76 543 210	No. of Bytes	No. of M Cycles	No. of T States	Comments
DAA	Converts acc. content into packed BCD following add or subtract with packed BCD operands	‡	‡	P	‡	•	‡	00 100 111	1	1	4	Decimal adjust accumulator

Table 4.3. Continued

Mnemonic	Symbolic Operation	C	Z	P/V	S	N	H	Op-Code 76 543 210	No. of Bytes	No. of M Cycles	No. of T States	Comments
CPL	A ← Ā	•	•	•	•	1	1	00 101 111	1	1	4	Complement accumulator (one's complement)
NEG	A ← 0 − A	↕	↕	V	↕	1	↕	11 101 101 01 000 100	2	2	8	Negate acc. (two's complement)
CCF	CY ← $\overline{CY}$	↕	•	•	•	0	X	00 111 111	1	1	4	Complement carry flag
SCF	CY ← 1	1	•	•	•	0	0	00 110 111	1	1	4	Set carry flag
NOP	No operation	•	•	•	•	•	•	00 000 000	1	1	4	
HALT	CPU halted	•	•	•	•	•	•	01 110 110	1	1	4	
DI	IFF ← 0	•	•	•	•	•	•	11 110 011	1	1	4	
EI	IFF ← 1	•	•	•	•	•	•	11 111 011	1	1	4	
IM 0	Set interrupt mode 0	•	•	•	•	•	•	11 101 101 01 000 110	2	2	8	
IM 1	Set interrupt mode 1	•	•	•	•	•	•	11 101 101 01 010 110	2	2	8	
IM 2	Set interrupt mode 2	•	•	•	•	•	•	11 101 101 01 011 110	2	2	8	

Notes: IFF indicates the interrupt enable flip-flop
CY indicates the carry flip-flop.

Flag Notation: • = flag not affected, 0 = flag reset, 1 = flag set, X = flag is unknown,
↕ = flag is affected according to the result of the operation.

16-BIT ARITHMETIC GROUP

Mnemonic	Symbolic Operation	C	Z	P/V	S	N	H	Op-Code 76 543 210	No. of Bytes	No. of M Cycles	No. of T States	Comments	
ADD HL, ss	HL ← HL+ss	↕	•	•	•	0	X	00 ss1 001	1	3	11	ss 00 01 10 11	Reg. BC DE HL SP
ADC HL, ss	HL←HL+ss+CY	↕	↕	V	↕	0	X	11 101 101 01 ss1 010	2	4	15		
SBC HL, ss	HL←HL-ss-CY	↕	↕	V	↕	1	X	11 101 101 01 ss0 010	2	4	15		
ADD IX, pp	IX ← IX + pp	↕	•	•	•	0	X	11 011 101 00 pp1 001	2	4	15	pp 00 01 10 11	Reg. BC DE IX SP
ADD IY, rr	IY←IY+rr	↕	•	•	•	0	X	11 111 101 00 rr1 001	2	4	15	rr 00 01 10 11	Reg. BC DE IY SP

Table 4.3. Continued

Mnemonic	Symbolic Operation	Flags C	Z	P/V	S	N	H	Op-Code 76 543 210	No. of Bytes	No. of M Cycles	No. of T States	Comments
INC ss	ss ← ss + 1	•	•	•	•	•	•	00 ss0 011	1	1	6	
INC IX	IX ← IX + 1	•	•	•	•	•	•	11 011 101 00 100 011	2	2	10	
INC IY	IY ← IY + 1	•	•	•	•	•	•	11 111 101 00 100 011	2	2	10	
DEC ss	ss ← ss - 1	•	•	•	•	•	•	00 ss1 011	1	1	6	
DEC IX	IX ← IX - 1	•	•	•	•	•	•	11 011 101 00 101 011	2	2	10	
DEC IY	IY ← IY - 1	•	•	•	•	•	•	11 111 101 00 101 011	2	2	10	

Notes: ss is any of the register pairs BC, DE, HL, SP
pp is any of the register pairs BC, DE, IX, SP
rr is any of the register pairs BC, DE, IY, SP.

Flag Notation: • = flag not affected, 0 = flag reset, 1 = flag set, X = flag is unknown,
‡ = flag is affected according to the result of the operation.

ROTATE AND SHIFT GROUP

Mnemonic	Symbolic Operation	Flags C	Z	P/V	S	N	H	Op-Code 76 543 210	No. of Bytes	No. of M Cycles	No. of T States	Comments
RLCA		‡	•	•	•	0	0	00 000 111	1	1	4	Rotate left circular accumulator
RLA		‡	•	•	•	0	0	00 010 111	1	1	4	Rotate left accumulator
RRCA		‡	•	•	•	0	0	00 001 111	1	1	4	Rotate right circular accumulator
RRA		‡	•	•	•	0	0	00 011 111	1	1	4	Rotate right accumulator
RLC r		‡	‡	P	‡	0	0	11 001 011 00 000 r	2	2	8	Rotate left circular register r
RLC (HL)		‡	‡	P	‡	0	0	11 001 011 00 000 110	2	4	15	r Reg. 000 B 001 C
RLC (IX+d)		‡	‡	P	‡	0	0	11 011 101 11 001 011 ← d → 00 000 110	4	6	23	010 D 011 E 100 H 101 L 111 A
RLC (IY+d)		‡	‡	P	‡	0	0	11 111 101 11 001 011 ← d → 00 000 110	4	6	23	

120 Chapter 4 Typical 8-Bit Microprocessors and Microcomputers

Table 4.3. Continued

Mnemonic	Symbolic Operation	C	Z	P/V	S	N	H	76 543 210	No. of Bytes	No. of M Cycles	No. of T States	Comments
RL m	m ≡ r, (HL), (IX+d), (IY+d)	↕	↕	P	↕	0	0	010				Instruction format and states are as shown for RLC,m. To form new OP-code replace 000 of RLC,m with shown code
RRC m	m ≡ r, (HL), (IX+d), (IY+d)	↕	↕	P	↕	0	0	001				
RR m	m ≡ r, (HL), (IX+d), (IY+d)	↕	↕	P	↕	0	0	011				
SLA m	m ≡ r, (HL), (IX+d), (IY+d)	↕	↕	P	↕	0	0	100				
SRA m	m ≡ r, (HL), (IX+d), (IY+d)	↕	↕	P	↕	0	0	101				
SRL m	m ≡ r, (HL), (IX+d), (IY+d)	↕	↕	P	↕	0	0	111				
RLD		•	↕	P	↕	0	0	11 101 101 01 101 111	2	5	18	Rotate digit left and right between the accumulator and location (HL). The content of the upper half of the accumulator is unaffected
RRD		•	↕	P	↕	0	0	11 101 101 01 100 111	2	5	18	

Flag Notation: • = flag not affected, 0 = flag reset, 1 = flag set, X = flag is unknown, ↕ = flag is affected according to the result of the operation.

BIT SET, RESET AND TEST GROUP

Mnemonic	Symbolic Operation	C	Z	P/V	S	N	H	76 543 210	No. of Bytes	No. of M Cycles	No. of T States	Comments
BIT b, r	Z ← $\overline{r}_b$	•	↕	X	X	0	1	11 001 011 01 b r	2	2	8	
BIT b, (HL)	Z ← $\overline{(HL)}_b$	•	↕	X	X	0	1	11 001 011 01 b 110	2	3	12	
BIT b, (IX+d)	Z ← $\overline{(IX+d)}_b$	•	↕	X	X	0	1	11 011 101 11 001 011 ← d → 01 b 110	4	5	20	
BIT b, (IY+d)	Z ← $\overline{(IY+d)}_b$	•	↕	X	X	0	1	11 111 101 11 001 011 ← d → 01 b 110	4	5	20	

r	Reg.
000	B
001	C
010	D
011	E
100	H
101	L
111	A

b	Bit Tested
000	0
001	1
010	2
011	3
100	4
101	5
110	6
111	7

Table 4.3. Continued

Mnemonic	Symbolic Operation	C	Z	P/V	S	N	H	Op-Code 76 543 210	No. of Bytes	No. of M Cycles	No. of T States	Comments
SET b, r	$r_b \leftarrow 1$	•	•	•	•	•	•	11 001 011 [11] b r	2	2	8	
SET b, (HL)	$(HL)_b \leftarrow 1$	•	•	•	•	•	•	11 001 011 [11] b 110	2	4	15	
SET b, (IX+d)	$(IX+d)_b \leftarrow 1$	•	•	•	•	•	•	11 011 101 11 001 011 ← d → [11] b 110	4	6	23	
SET b, (IY+d)	$(IY+d)_b \leftarrow 1$	•	•	•	•	•	•	11 111 101 11 001 011 ← d → [11] b 110	4	6	23	
RES b, m	$s_b \leftarrow 0$ m≡r, (HL), (IX+d), (IY+d)							[10]				To form new OP-code replace [11] of SET b,m with [10]. Flags and time states for SET instruction

Notes: The notation s_b indicates bit b (0 to 7) or location s.

Flag Notation: • = flag not affected, 0 = flag reset, 1 = flag set, X = flag is unknown,
‡ = flag is affected according to the result of the operation.

CALL AND RETURN GROUP

Mnemonic	Symbolic Operation	C	Z	P/V	S	N	H	Op-Code 76 543 210	No. of Bytes	No. of M Cycles	No. of T States	Comments
CALL nn	$(SP-1) \leftarrow PC_H$ $(SP-2) \leftarrow PC_L$ $PC \leftarrow nn$	•	•	•	•	•	•	11 001 101 ← n → ← n →	3	5	17	
CALL cc, nn	If condition cc is false continue, otherwise same as CALL nn	•	•	•	•	•	•	11 cc 100 ← n → ← n →	3 3	3 5	10 17	If cc is false If cc is true
RET	$PC_L \leftarrow (SP)$ $PC_H \leftarrow (SP+1)$	•	•	•	•	•	•	11 001 001	1	3	10	

Table 4.3. Continued

Mnemonic	Symbolic Operation	Flags C	Z	P/V	S	N	H	Op-Code 76 543 210	No. of Bytes	No. of M Cycles	No. of T States	Comments
RET cc	If condition cc is false continue, otherwise same as RET	•	•	•	•	•	•	11 cc 000	1 1	1 3	5 11	If cc is false If cc is true
RETI	Return from interrupt	•	•	•	•	•	•	11 101 101 01 001 101	2	4	14	
RETN	Return from non maskable interrupt	•	•	•	•	•	•	11 101 101 01 000 101	2	4	14	
RST p	(SP-1)←PC$_H$ (SP-2)←PC$_L$ PC$_H$←0 PC$_L$←P	•	•	•	•	•	•	11 t 111	1	3	11	

cc	Condition
000	NZ non zero
001	Z zero
010	NC non carry
011	C carry
100	PO parity odd
101	PE parity even
110	P sign positive
111	M sign negative

t	P
000	00H
001	08H
010	10H
011	18H
100	20H
101	28H
110	30H
111	38H

Flag Notation: • = flag not affected, 0 = flag reset, 1 = flag set, X = flag is unknown
‡ = flag is affected according to the result of the operation.

JUMP GROUP

Mnemonic	Symbolic Operation	Flags C	Z	P/V	S	N	H	Op-Code 76 543 210	No. of Bytes	No. of M Cycles	No. of T States	Comments
JP nn	PC ← nn	•	•	•	•	•	•	11 000 011 ← n → ← n →	3	3	10	
JP cc, nn	If condition cc is true PC ←nn, otherwise continue	•	•	•	•	•	•	11 cc 010 ← n → ← n →	3	3	10	
JR e	PC ← PC + e	•	•	•	•	•	•	00 011 000 ← e-2 →	2	3	12	
JR C, e	If C = 0, continue	•	•	•	•	•	•	00 111 000 ← e-2 →	2	2	7	If condition not met
	If C = 1, PC ← PC+e								2	3	12	If condition is met

cc	Condition
000	NZ non zero
001	Z zero
010	NC non carry
011	C carry
100	PO parity odd
101	PE parity even
110	P sign positive
111	M sign negative

Zilog Z80 123

Table 4.3. Continued

Mnemonic	Symbolic Operation	Flags C Z P/V S N H	Op-Code 76 543 210	No. of Bytes	No. of M Cycles	No. of T States	Comments
JR NC, e	If C = 1, continue	• • • • • •	00 110 000 ← e-2 →	2	2	7	If condition not met
	If C = 0, PC ← PC + e			2	3	12	If condition is met
JR Z, e	If Z = 0 continue	• • • • • •	00 101 000 ← e-2 →	2	2	7	If condition not met
	If Z = 1, PC ← PC + e			2	3	12	If condition is met
JR NZ, e	If Z = 1, continue	• • • • • •	00 100 000 ← e-2 →	2	2	7	If condition not met
	If Z = 0, PC ← PC + e			2	3	12	If condition met
JP (HL)	PC ← HL	• • • • • •	11 101 001	1	1	4	
JP (IX)	PC ← IX	• • • • • •	11 011 101 11 101 001	2	2	8	
JP (IY)	PC ← IY	• • • • • •	11 111 101 11 101 001	2	2	8	
DJNZ,e	B ← B-1 If B = 0, continue	• • • • • •	00 010 000 ← e-2 →	2	2	8	If B = 0
	If B ≠ 0, PC ← PC + e			2	3	13	IF B ≠ 0

Notes: e represents the extension in the relative addressing mode.

e is a signed two's complement number in the range $<-126, 129>$

e-2 in the op-code provides an effective address of pc +e as PC is incremented by 2 prior to the addition of e.

Flag Notation: • = flag not affected, 0 = flag reset, 1 = flag set, X = flag is unknown,

‡ = flag is affected according to the result of the operation.

INPUT AND OUTPUT GROUP

Mnemonic	Symbolic Operation	Flags C Z P/V S N H	Op-Code 76 543 210	No. of Bytes	No. of M Cycles	No. of T States	Comments
IN A, (n)	A ← (n)	• • • • • •	11 011 011 ← n →	2	3	11	n to $A_0 \sim A_7$ Acc to $A_8 \sim A_{15}$
IN r, (C)	r ← (C) if r = 110 only the flags will be affected	• ‡ P ‡ 0 ‡ ①	11 101 101 01 r 000	2	3	12	C to $A_0 \sim A_7$ B to $A_8 \sim A_{15}$

124 Chapter 4 TYPICAL 8-BIT MICROPROCESSORS AND MICROCOMPUTERS

Table 4.3. Continued

Mnemonic	Symbolic Operation	C	Z	P/V	S	N	H	76 543 210	No. of Bytes	No. of M Cycles	No. of T States	Comments
INI	(HL) ← (C) B ← B - 1 HL ← HL + 1	X	↕	X	X	1	X	11 101 101 10 100 010	2	4	16	C to $A_0 \sim A_7$ B to $A_8 \sim A_{15}$
INIR	(HL) ← (C) B ← B - 1 HL ← HL + 1 Repeat until B = 0	X	1	X	X	1	X	11 101 101 10 110 010	2 2	5 (If B ≠ 0) 4 (If B = 0)	21 16	C to $A_0 \sim A_7$ B to $A_8 \sim A_{15}$
IND	(HL) ← (C) B ← B - 1 HL ← HL - 1	X	↕	X	X	1	X	11 101 101 10 101 010	2	4	16	C to $A_0 \sim A_7$ B to $A_8 \sim A_{15}$
INDR	(HL) ← (C) B ← B - 1 HL ← HL - 1 Repeat until B = 0	X	1	X	X	1	X	11 101 101 10 111 010	2 2	5 (If B ≠ 0) 4 (If B = 0)	21 16	C to $A_0 \sim A_7$ B to $A_8 \sim A_{15}$
OUT (n), A	(n) ← A	•	•	•	•	•	•	11 010 011 ← n →	2	3	11	n to $A_0 \sim A_7$ Acc to $A_8 \sim A_{15}$
OUT (C), r	(C) ← r	•	•	•	•	•	•	11 101 101 01 r 001	2	3	12	C to $A_0 \sim A_7$ B to $A_8 \sim A_{15}$
OUTI	(C) ← (HL) B ← B - 1 HL ← HL + 1	X	↕	X	X	1	X	11 101 101 10 100 011	2	4	16	C to $A_0 \sim A_7$ B to $A_8 \sim A_{15}$
OTIR	(C) ← (HL) B ← B - 1 HL ← HL + 1 Repeat until B = 0	X	1	X	X	1	X	11 101 101 10 110 011	2 2	5 (If B ≠ 0) 4 (If B = 0)	21 16	C to $A_0 \sim A_7$ B to $A_8 \sim A_{15}$
OUTD	(C) ← (HL) B ← B - 1 HL ← HL - 1	X	↕	X	X	1	X	11 101 101 10 101 011	2	4	16	C to $A_0 \sim A_7$ B to $A_8 \sim A_{15}$
OTDR	(C) ← (HL) B ← B - 1 HL ← HL - 1 Repeat until B = 0	X	1	X	X	1	X	11 101 101 10 111 011	2 2	5 (If B ≠ 0) 4 (If B = 0)	21 16	C to $A_0 \sim A_7$ B to $A_8 \sim A_{15}$

Notes: ① If the result of B - 1 is zero the Z flag is set, otherwise it is reset.

Flag Notation: • = flag not affected, 0 = flag reset, 1 = flag set, X = flag is unknown,
↕ = flag is affected according to the result of the operation.

Source: Copyright © 1982 Advanced Micro Devices, Inc. Reproduced by permission.

4.3.4 Input/Output

Programmed I/O

The Z80 uses a port-mapped I/O configuration. The lower 8-bits of the address bus are used to select a given I/O device (up to 256 separate devices). The sequence for an input operation is as follows:

1. Port address is placed on the lower 8-bits of the address bus.
2. IORQ goes low and RD goes low for an input operation to activate the external device.
3. A wait state is provided to give the I/O device time to respond (i.e., put data on the bus).
4. The CPU inputs the 8-bit data from the data bus.

If a longer wait period is required, the I/O device can be configured to generate a wait signal, causing the CPU to extend this period.

Interrupt I/O

Several interrupt modes are provided by the Z80 processor as follows:

1. Nonmaskable interrupt: The CPU executes a restart to location 0066H. The nonmaskable interrupt will be accepted at all times by the CPU.
2. Maskable interrupts: Any one of three possible modes can be selected by the programmer:
    a. Mode 0: This mode is automatically entered after RESET and is identical to the 8080A interrupt response. The interrupting device can place any instruction (usually a restart or 3-byte jump) on the data bus and the CPU will execute it.
    b. Mode 1: This mode initiates a restart to location 0038H. This response, although to a different address, is identical to that of the nonmaskable interrupt.
    c. Mode 2: In this mode the interrupting device sends an 8-bit word to the CPU which points to an address of an interrupt service routine stored in program memory. The upper 8 bits of this address are stored in the I register by the programmer. This is the most powerful mode since one 8-bit argument can specify a routine anywhere in program memory.

EXAMPLE 4.6

Write a program in Z80 assembly language to convert a BCD number into binary. Assume that the register B contains BCD data.

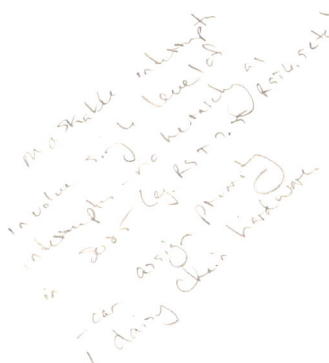

SOLUTION

The assembly language program is given in the following:

```
BCDBIN:  LD A, B    ; B contains two digit BCD data.
         RRC
         RRC
         RRC
         RRC        ; Move tens digit to low nibble.
         ANI 0FH    ; Mask high nibble.
         LD C, A    ; Tens digit in low nibble of A and C.
         RLC
         RLC
         RLC        ; Multiply by 8.
         ADD C
         ADD C      ; No, make it 10.
         LD C, A    ; Load converted tens to C.
         LD A, B
         ANI 0FH    ; Mask off tens.
         ADD C      ; Add ones to converted tens.
         LD B, A    ; Move result to B.
         RET        ; B contains binary data.
```

EXAMPLE 4.7

Write a program in Z80 assembly language to divide the dividend contained in register B by the divisor in register C.

SOLUTION

The program is given in the following:

```
DIVD:    LD A, B     ; Save B contents.
         LD B, 00H   ; Clear B.
DIVD1:   INC B       ; B is pass counter.
         SUB C       ; Subtract C from A.
         CMC
         JC DIVD1    ; Jump if no carry.
         ADD C
         DCR B       ; B was 1 too large.
         RET         ; B contains result.
                     ; A contains remainder.
```

4.4 Motorola 6800*

4.4.1 Introduction

The Motorola 6800 (Figure 4.30) is an 8-bit general-purpose microprocessor with an instruction set of 72 commands. The processor incorporates an 8-bit bidirectional data bus, a full 16-bit address bus, and features single +5-V supply operation. The minimum system would consist of the processor, a clock circuit, some ROM and RAM, and some I/O circuits. All lines except the clock lines are Transistor Transistor Logic (TTL) compatible and the data bus, R/W line, and address bus have tristate capability. All stack space must be in user-supplied RAM. A two-phase clock is required.

The 6800 has two accumulators (accumulators A and B), three 16-bit registers (PC, SP, and index register) and an 8-bit condition code or status register. The 6800 status flags are carry, overflow, zero, negative, interrupt mask, and half-carry (auxiliary carry) flags. We now describe some of the 6800 pins and signals.

A low output on the Valid Memory Address (VMA) indicates that the address on the bus is valid. The Three State Control (TSC) is usually held LOW. When it is high, the address bus is floated. A low on the Data Bus Enable (DBE) and a high on the TSC are used to flat the buses for DMA operations. The other pins are self-explanatory.

4.4.2 Addressing Modes

Several means of addressing data are provided in the instruction set as follows:

1. Inherent addressing—The address of a register is specified as part of the op code (i.e., ADDA, ADDB).
2. Immediate mode—The byte following the op code contains immediate data to be operated on (i.e., ORA #76, SUB #22).
3. Direct mode—The byte following the op code contains the address in memory of where the operand can be found (i.e., ADD 30, where 30 is the operand address).
4. Extended mode—This is identical to direct mode except the operand address is 2 bytes long, allowing access over the full 64K memory size (i.e., JMP 6400).
5. Relative mode—Addressing is done relative to the program counter in the range of -125 to $+129$ from the position of the JMP instruction. Use of this mode allows relocatable code.

* This section contains material reprinted courtesy of Motorola.

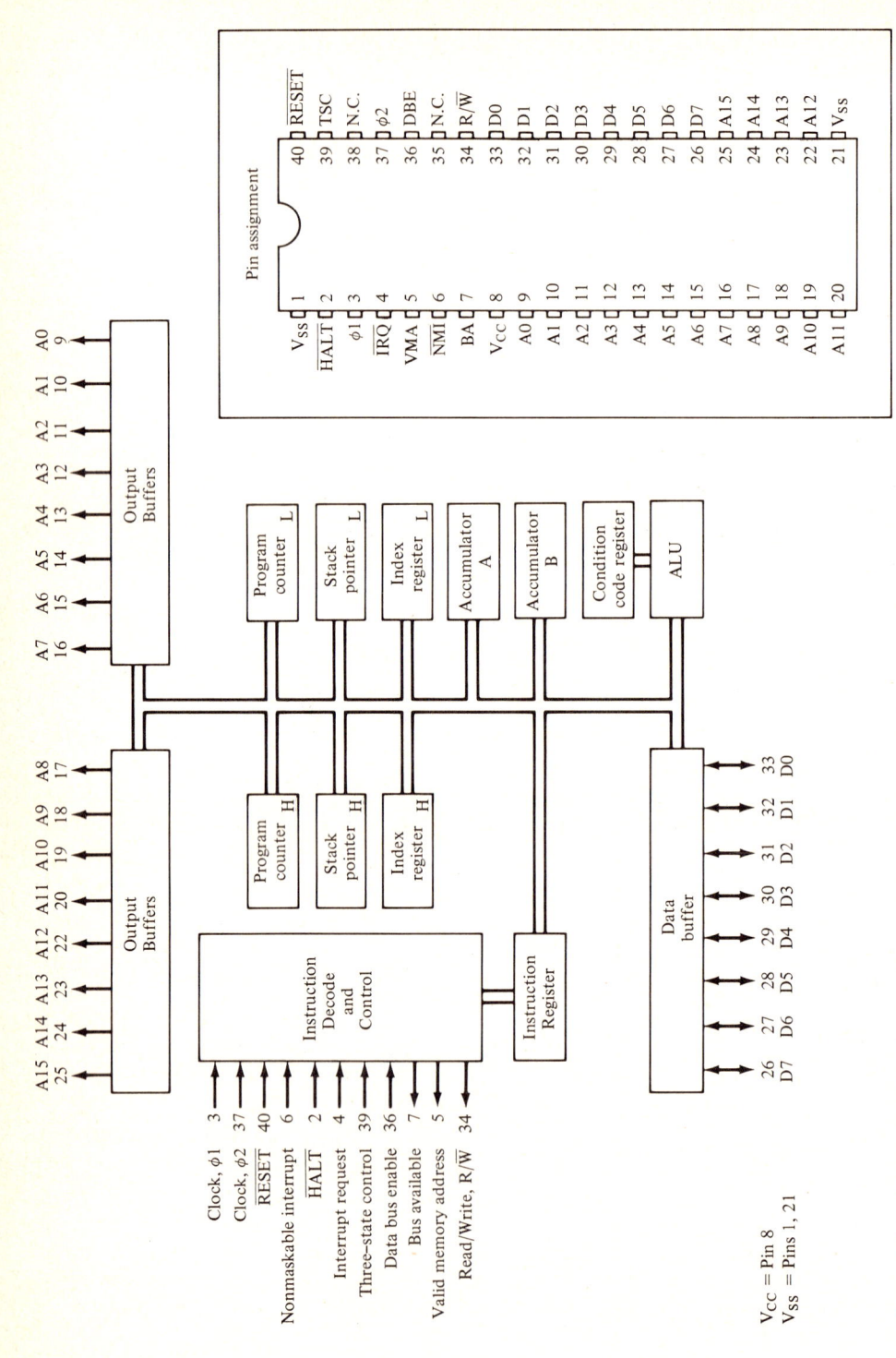

128 Chapter 4 TYPICAL 8-BIT MICROPROCESSORS AND MICROCOMPUTERS

Figure 4.30 Motorola 6800. Source: Reprinted by permission of Motorola Semiconductor Products, Inc., copyright © 1975.

6. Indexed mode—The address is calculated from the predefined value of the index register and an offset operand. This mode generates relocatable code.

4.4.3 Instruction Set

The 6800 (Table 4.4) contains 72 instructions of 1 to 3 bytes each. All I/O is memory mapped, thus no I/O (IN's or OUT's) are included. Highlights of the instruction set are as follows:

1. Stack operations—The stack is organized as part of external memory and can be as large as required up to the memory size. The 16-bit Stack Pointer (SP) can be loaded with the LDS instruction, thus allowing the use of multiple stacks. PUSH and PULL instructions are provided for both the A and B accumulators. The stack is also used to store the Program Counter (PC) during a subroutine call; thus essentially unlimited subroutine nesting is possible.
2. Software interrupt—The SWI instruction provides a single-byte call to subroutine to the address contained in locations FFFA and FFFB hex. This can be used with a frequently called subroutine to conserve program memory.
3. Wait for interrupt—This instruction (WAI) yields fast interrupt response by saving PC, A, and B prior to a hardware interrupt request.
4. Conditional branch—Testable flags include sign bit (N), zero flag (Z), overflow flag (V), and carry flag (C). Combinations of flags can be tested using branch on higher (BHI) where C and Z = 0, branch on less than zero (BLT) where $N \oplus V = 1$, and others are provided. These instructions provide straightforward testing of the flags.

4.4.4 I/O Capability

Programmed I/O

All I/O on the 6800 is memory mapped; thus a portion of memory space is used to access I/O ports. In order to utilize this type of I/O, peripheral devices, such as the 6821 Peripheral Interface Adapter, are required. The 6821 contains two 8-bit I/O ports which can be programmed by the processor to function as either input or output. Inputs can be configured to interrupt the processor or disabled under program control. Output strobe capability is also provided. Other I/O chips are also available, such as the 6835 CRT Controller and the 6852 Synchronous Serial Data Adapter which provide various specialized I/O functions. Although the 6800 has no true I/O capability within itself, these devices can be used to make it a versatile I/O processor.

Table 4.4. 6800 Instruction Set

ACCUMULATOR AND MEMORY OPERATIONS	MNEMONIC	IMMED OP	~	#	DIRECT OP	~	#	INDEX OP	~	#	EXTND OP	~	#	INHER OP	~	#	BOOLEAN/ARITHMETIC OPERATION (All register labels refer to contents)	H 5	I 4	N 3	Z 2	V 1	C 0
Add	ADDA	8B	2	2	9B	3	2	AB	5	2	BB	4	3				A + M → A	↕	•	↕	↕	↕	↕
	ADDB	CB	2	2	DB	3	2	EB	5	2	FB	4	3				B + M → B	↕	•	↕	↕	↕	↕
Add Acmltrs	ABA													1B	2	1	A + B → A	↕	•	↕	↕	↕	↕
Add with Carry	ADCA	89	2	2	99	3	2	A9	5	2	B9	4	3				A + M + C → A	↕	•	↕	↕	↕	↕
	ADCB	C9	2	2	D9	3	2	E9	5	2	F9	4	3				B + M + C → B	↕	•	↕	↕	↕	↕
And	ANDA	84	2	2	94	3	2	A4	5	2	B4	4	3				A • M → A	•	•	↕	↕	R	•
	ANDB	C4	2	2	D4	3	2	E4	5	2	F4	4	3				B • M → B	•	•	↕	↕	R	•
Bit Test	BITA	85	2	2	95	3	2	A5	5	2	B5	4	3				A • M	•	•	↕	↕	R	•
	BITB	C5	2	2	D5	3	2	E5	5	2	F5	4	3				B • M	•	•	↕	↕	R	•
Clear	CLR							6F	7	2	7F	6	3				00 → M	•	•	R	S	R	R
	CLRA													4F	2	1	00 → A	•	•	R	S	R	R
	CLRB													5F	2	1	00 → B	•	•	R	S	R	R
Compare	CMPA	81	2	2	91	3	2	A1	5	2	B1	4	3				A − M	•	•	↕	↕	↕	↕
	CMPB	C1	2	2	D1	3	2	E1	5	2	F1	4	3				B − M	•	•	↕	↕	↕	↕
Compare Acmltrs	CBA													11	2	1	A − B	•	•	↕	↕	↕	↕
Complement, 1's	COM							63	7	2	73	6	3				$\overline{M}$ → M	•	•	↕	↕	R	S
	COMA													43	2	1	$\overline{A}$ → A	•	•	↕	↕	R	S
	COMB													53	2	1	$\overline{B}$ → B	•	•	↕	↕	R	S
Complement, 2's (Negate)	NEG							60	7	2	70	6	3				00 − M → M	•	•	↕	↕	①	②
	NEGA													40	2	1	00 − A → A	•	•	↕	↕	①	②
	NEGB													50	2	1	00 − B → B	•	•	↕	↕	①	②
Decimal Adjust, A	DAA													19	2	1	Converts Binary Add. of BCD Characters into BCD Format	•	•	↕	↕	↕	③
Decrement	DEC							6A	7	2	7A	6	3				M − 1 → M	•	•	↕	↕	④	•
	DECA													4A	2	1	A − 1 → A	•	•	↕	↕	④	•
	DECB													5A	2	1	B − 1 → B	•	•	↕	↕	④	•
Exclusive OR	EORA	88	2	2	98	3	2	A8	5	2	B8	4	3				A ⊕ M → A	•	•	↕	↕	R	•
	EORB	C8	2	2	D8	3	2	E8	5	2	F8	4	3				B ⊕ M → B	•	•	↕	↕	R	•
Increment	INC							6C	7	2	7C	6	3				M + 1 → M	•	•	↕	↕	⑤	•
	INCA													4C	2	1	A + 1 → A	•	•	↕	↕	⑤	•
	INCB													5C	2	1	B + 1 → B	•	•	↕	↕	⑤	•
Load Acmltr	LDAA	86	2	2	96	3	2	A6	5	2	B6	4	3				M → A	•	•	↕	↕	R	•
	LDAB	C6	2	2	D6	3	2	E6	5	2	F6	4	3				M → B	•	•	↕	↕	R	•
Or, Inclusive	ORAA	8A	2	2	9A	3	2	AA	5	2	BA	4	3				A + M → A	•	•	↕	↕	R	•
	ORAB	CA	2	2	DA	3	2	EA	5	2	FA	4	3				B + M → B	•	•	↕	↕	R	•
Push Data	PSHA													36	4	1	A → M$_{SP}$, SP − 1 → SP	•	•	•	•	•	•
	PSHB													37	4	1	B → M$_{SP}$, SP − 1 → SP	•	•	•	•	•	•
Pull Data	PULA													32	4	1	SP + 1 → SP, M$_{SP}$ → A	•	•	•	•	•	•
	PULB													33	4	1	SP + 1 → SP, M$_{SP}$ → B	•	•	•	•	•	•
Rotate Left	ROL							69	7	2	79	6	3				M	•	•	↕	↕	⑥	↕
	ROLA													49	2	1	A	•	•	↕	↕	⑥	↕
	ROLB													59	2	1	B	•	•	↕	↕	⑥	↕
Rotate Right	ROR							66	7	2	76	6	3				M	•	•	↕	↕	⑥	↕
	RORA													46	2	1	A	•	•	↕	↕	⑥	↕
	RORB													56	2	1	B	•	•	↕	↕	⑥	↕
Shift Left, Arithmetic	ASL							68	7	2	78	6	3				M	•	•	↕	↕	⑥	↕
	ASLA													48	2	1	A	•	•	↕	↕	⑥	↕
	ASLB													58	2	1	B	•	•	↕	↕	⑥	↕
Shift Right, Arithmetic	ASR							67	7	2	77	6	3				M	•	•	↕	↕	⑥	↕
	ASRA													47	2	1	A	•	•	↕	↕	⑥	↕
	ASRB													57	2	1	B	•	•	↕	↕	⑥	↕
Shift Right, Logic.	LSR							64	7	2	74	6	3				M	•	•	R	↕	⑥	↕
	LSRA													44	2	1	A	•	•	R	↕	⑥	↕
	LSRB													54	2	1	B	•	•	R	↕	⑥	↕
Store Acmltr.	STAA				97	4	2	A7	6	2	B7	5	3				A → M	•	•	↕	↕	R	•
	STAB				D7	4	2	E7	6	2	F7	5	3				B → M	•	•	↕	↕	R	•
Subtract	SUBA	80	2	2	90	3	2	A0	5	2	B0	4	3				A − M → A	•	•	↕	↕	↕	↕
	SUBB	C0	2	2	D0	3	2	E0	5	2	F0	4	3				B − M → B	•	•	↕	↕	↕	↕
Subract Acmltrs.	SBA													10	2	1	A − B → A	•	•	↕	↕	↕	↕
Subtr. with Carry	SBCA	82	2	2	92	3	2	A2	5	2	B2	4	3				A − M − C → A	•	•	↕	↕	↕	↕
	SBCB	C2	2	2	D2	3	2	E2	5	2	F2	4	3				B − M − C → B	•	•	↕	↕	↕	↕
Transfer Acmltrs	TAB													16	2	1	A → B	•	•	↕	↕	R	•
	TBA													17	2	1	B → A	•	•	↕	↕	R	•
Test, Zero or Minus	TST							6D	7	2	7D	6	3				M − 00	•	•	↕	↕	R	R
	TSTA													4D	2	1	A − 00	•	•	↕	↕	R	R
	TSTB													5D	2	1	B − 00	•	•	↕	↕	R	R

Table 4.4. Continued

INDEX REGISTER AND STACK POINTER OPERATIONS	MNEMONIC	IMMED OP ~ #	DIRECT OP ~ #	INDEX OP ~ #	EXTND OP ~ #	INHER OP ~ #	BOOLEAN/ARITHMETIC OPERATION	5 H	4 I	3 N	2 Z	1 V	0 C
Compare Index Reg	CPX	8C 3 3	9C 4 2	AC 6 2	BC 5 3		$(X_H/X_L) - (M/M+1)$	•	⑦	‡	⑧	•	•
Decrement Index Reg	DEX					09 4 1	$X - 1 \to X$	•	•	•	‡	•	•
Decrement Stack Pntr	DES					34 4 1	$SP - 1 \to SP$	•	•	•	•	•	•
Increment Index Reg	INX					08 4 1	$X + 1 \to X$	•	•	•	‡	•	•
Increment Stack Pntr	INS					31 4 1	$SP + 1 \to SP$	•	•	•	•	•	•
Load Index Reg	LDX	CE 3 3	DE 4 2	EE 6 2	FE 5 3		$M \to X_H, (M+1) \to X_L$	•	•	⑨	‡	R	•
Load Stack Pntr	LDS	8E 3 3	9E 4 2	AE 6 2	BE 5 3		$M \to SP_H, (M+1) \to SP_L$	•	•	⑨	‡	R	•
Store Index Reg	STX		DF 5 2	EF 7 2	FF 6 3		$X_H \to M, X_L \to (M+1)$	•	•	⑨	‡	R	•
Store Stack Pntr	STS		9F 5 2	AF 7 2	BF 6 3		$SP_H \to M, SP_L \to (M+1)$	•	•	⑨	‡	R	•
Indx Reg → Stack Pntr	TXS					35 4 1	$X - 1 \to SP$	•	•	•	•	•	•
Stack Pntr → Indx Reg	TSX					30 4 1	$SP + 1 \to X$	•	•	•	•	•	•

JUMP AND BRANCH OPERATIONS	MNEMONIC	RELATIVE OP ~ #	INDEX OP ~ #	EXTND OP ~ #	INHER OP ~ #	BRANCH TEST	5 H	4 I	3 N	2 Z	1 V	0 C
Branch Always	BRA	20 4 2				None	•	•	•	•	•	•
Branch If Carry Clear	BCC	24 4 2				$C = 0$	•	•	•	•	•	•
Branch If Carry Set	BCS	25 4 2				$C = 1$	•	•	•	•	•	•
Branch If = Zero	BEQ	27 4 2				$Z = 1$	•	•	•	•	•	•
Branch If ≥ Zero	BGE	2C 4 2				$N \oplus V = 0$	•	•	•	•	•	•
Branch If > Zero	BGT	2E 4 2				$Z + (N \oplus V) = 0$	•	•	•	•	•	•
Branch If Higher	BHI	22 4 2				$C + Z = 0$	•	•	•	•	•	•
Branch If ≤ Zero	BLE	2F 4 2				$Z + (N \oplus V) = 1$	•	•	•	•	•	•
Branch If Lower Or Same	BLS	23 4 2				$C + Z = 1$	•	•	•	•	•	•
Branch If < Zero	BLT	2D 4 2				$N \oplus V = 1$	•	•	•	•	•	•
Branch If Minus	BMI	2B 4 2				$N = 1$	•	•	•	•	•	•
Branch If Not Equal Zero	BNE	26 4 2				$Z = 0$	•	•	•	•	•	•
Branch If Overflow Clear	BVC	28 4 2				$V = 0$	•	•	•	•	•	•
Branch If Overflow Set	BVS	29 4 2				$V = 1$	•	•	•	•	•	•
Branch If Plus	BPL	2A 4 2				$N = 0$	•	•	•	•	•	•
Branch To Subroutine	BSR	8D 8 2					•	•	•	•	•	•
Jump	JMP		6E 4 2	7E 3 3		} See Special Operations	•	•	•	•	•	•
Jump To Subroutine	JSR		AD 8 2	BD 9 3			•	•	•	•	•	•
No Operation	NOP				01 2 1	Advances Prog. Cntr. Only	•	•	•	•	•	•
Return From Interrupt	RTI				3B 10 1		⑩
Return From Subroutine	RTS				39 5 1	} See special Operations	•	•	•	•	•	•
Software Interrupt	SWI				3F 12 1		•	S	•	•	•	•
Wait for Interrupt	WAI				3E 9 1		•	⑪	•	•	•	•

CONDITIONS CODE REGISTER OPERATIONS	MNEMONIC	INHER OP ~ =	BOOLEAN OPERATION	5 H	4 I	3 N	2 Z	1 V	0 C
Clear Carry	CLC	0C 2 1	$0 \to C$	•	•	•	•	•	R
Clear Interrupt Mask	CLI	0E 2 1	$0 \to I$	•	R	•	•	•	•
Clear Overflow	CLV	0A 2 1	$0 \to V$	•	•	•	•	R	•
Set Carry	SEC	0D 2 1	$1 \to C$	•	•	•	•	•	S
Set Interrupt Mask	SEI	0F 2 1	$1 \to I$	•	S	•	•	•	•
Set Overflow	SEV	0B 2 1	$1 \to V$	•	•	•	•	S	•
Acmltr A → CCR	TAP	06 2 1	$A \to CCR$	⑫
CCR → Acmltr A	TPA	07 2 1	$CCR \to A$	•	•	•	•	•	•

CONDITION CODE REGISTER NOTES:
(Bit set if test is true and cleared otherwise)

① (Bit V) Test: Result = 10000000?
② (Bit C) Test: Result = 00000000?
③ (Bit C) Test: Decimal value of most significant BCD Character greater than nine? (Not cleared if previously set.)
④ (Bit V) Test: Operand = 10000000 prior to execution?
⑤ (Bit V) Test: Operand = 01111111 prior to execution?
⑥ (Bit V) Test: Set equal to result of N ⊕ C after shift has occurred.
⑦ (Bit N) Test: Sign bit of most significant (MS) byte of result = 1?
⑧ (Bit V) Test: 2's complement overflow from subtraction of LS bytes?
⑨ (Bit N) Test: Result less than zero? (Bit 15 = 1)
⑩ (All) Load Condition Code Register from Stack. (See Special Operations)
⑪ (Bit I) Set when interrupt occurs. If previously set, a Non-Maskable Interrupt is required to exit the wait state.
⑫ (ALL) Set according to the contents of Accumulator A.

LEGEND:

OP	Operation Code (Hexadecimal);	00	Byte = Zero;
~	Number of MPU Cycles;	H	Half-carry from bit 3;
#	Number of Program Bytes;	I	Interrupt mask
+	Arithmetic Plus;	N	Negative (sign bit)
−	Arithmetic Minus;	Z	Zero (byte)
•	Boolean AND;	V	Overflow, 2's complement
M$_{SP}$	Contents of memory location pointed to be Stack Pointer;	C	Carry from bit 7
		R	Reset Always
+	Boolean Inclusive OR;	S	Set Always
⊕	Boolean Exclusive OR;	‡	Test and set if true, cleared otherwise
$\overline{M}$	Complement of M;	•	Not Affected
→	Transfer Into;	CCR	Condition Code Register
0	Bit = Zero;	LS	Least Significant
		MS	Most Significant

Source: Reprinted by permission of Motorola Semiconductor Products, Inc., copyright © 1975.

Interrupt I/O

Four separate interrupts are provided as follows. All interrupts vector to address values contained in the highest (FFF8 to FFFF) 8 bytes of memory.

1. Interrupt request—A low level on the IRQ pin initiates an interrupt request, providing the software-controllable interrupt mask bit is not set. Address of the service routine is contained in addresses FFF8 and FFF9 of external memory. The index register, program counter, accumulators, and condition code register are saved on the stack.
2. Software interrupt—This is initiated by the SWI instruction and causes a jump to subroutine vectored by the address contained at FFFA and FFFB hex.
3. Nonmaskable interrupt—This is identical to the interrupt request except that the nonmaskable interrupt cannot be software disabled and vectors to addresses at FFFC and FFFD. Wait for interrupt (WAI) allows faster service by saving registers prior to the hardware interrupt.
4. RESET—The RESET line is usually used for power-up initialization and vectors to addresses at FFFE and FFFF hex. As with all interrupts the initialization routine can be located anywhere in memory. The memory at FFFE and FFFF must be nonvolatile (e.g., ROM, EPROM) if RESET is to be used for power-up initialization.
5. DMA/BREQ functions as an interrupt of sorts. When this line is activated by an external device the processor relinquishes the address and data buses (goes to tristate). This allows the external device to access memory or use the data bus. Applications include a DMA floppy disk controller, memory refresh operations, and multiprocessing systems.

EXAMPLE 4.8

Write a program in 6800 assembly language to convert a BCD number into binary. Assume that location 000FH contains the BCD number.

SOLUTION

The program is given in the following:

```
BCDBIN: LDDA 000FH; A contains the two digit BCD data.
        RORA
        RORA
        RORA
        RORA         ; Move tens digit to the low nibble.
```

```
        ANDA #0FH ; Mask high nibble.
        TAB        ; Tens digit in low nibble of A and B.
        ROLA
        ROLA
        ROLA       ; Multiply by 8.
        ABA
        ABA        ; No, make it 10.
        TAB        ; Load converted tens to B.
        LDDA 000FH ; Move result back to memory.
        RTS        ; Location 000FH now contains binary data.
```

EXAMPLE 4.9

Write a program in 6800 assembly language to divide a number contained in the accumulator by another number in register B.

SOLUTION

The program is given below:

```
DIVD:   CLR 000FH   ; Clear counter
DIVD1:  INC 000FH   ; Increment pass counter
        CBA         ; Subtract B from A
        BLD DIVD1   ; Branch on underflow
        ABA
        DECB        ; B was 1 too large
        RTS         ; B contains the result
                    ; A contains the remainder
```

4.5 Motorola 6809*

4.5.1 Introduction

The Motorola 6809 (Figure 4.31) is an 8-bit microprocessor which can perform a full range of 16-bit arithmetic operations. The 6800 is upward compatible to the 6809 and thus software for the 6800 can be executed on the 6809. Enhancements beyond the 6800 instruction set include extra addressing modes, 16-bit arithmetic, and an 8 × 8 multiply instruction. The processor is also hardware compatible with the 6800 and thus can use all existing peripheral devices. An on-chip clock oscillator is also included.

According to Motorola, the 6809 has the largest variety of addressing modes of any microprocessor available today. Most of the added modes provide greater code efficiency and generate relocatable code.

* This section contains material reprinted courtesy of Motorola.

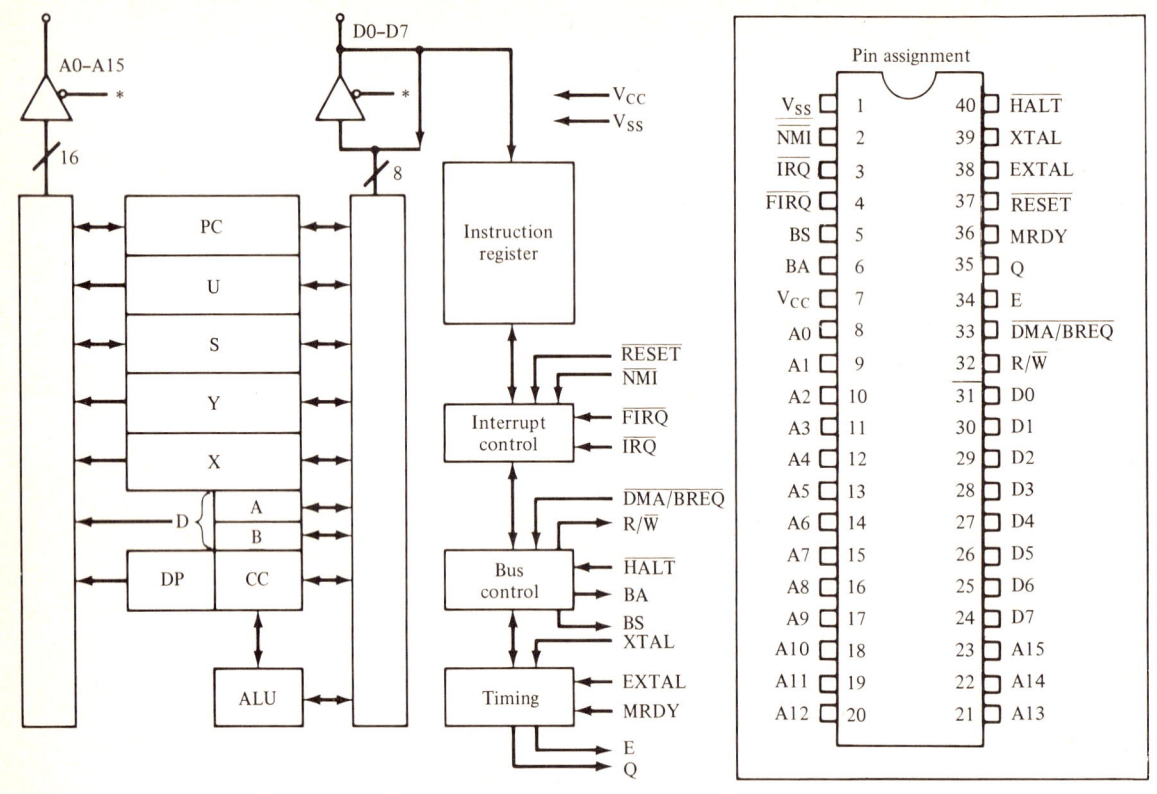

Figure 4.31 Motorola 6809. Source: Reprinted by permission of Motorola Semiconductor Products, Inc., copyright © 1980.

The 6809 has two 8-bit accumulators (A and B), one 8-bit direct page register, one 8-bit condition code register, and five 16-bit registers. The 16-bit registers are two index registers (X and Y), two stack pointers (U and S), and one program counter. U and S are the user and hardware stack pointers, respectively. Both of the SPs make use of push and pull instructions to stack CPU registers under program control. However, it is the hardware stack pointer, S, which corresponds to the 6800's stack pointer for handling return addresses and CPU registers automatically during subroutine calls and interrupts.

The two accumulators can be combined to provide one 16-bit accumulator called the D register. The 8-bit Direct Page (DP) register contains the most significant byte of the address to be used in the direct addressing mode.

The 6809's 8-bit condition code register provides eight flags, namely, carry, overflow, zero, negative, IRQ mask, half-carry, FIRQ mask, and entire flag. The entire flag is used to indicate how many registers were stacked. When this flag is set, all the registers were stacked during the last interrupt stacking operation. When this flag is clear, only the program counter and condition code registers were stacked during the last interrupt. The F (FIRQ mask) and I (IRQ mask) are used to disable the $\overline{\text{FIRQ}}$ and $\overline{\text{IRQ}}$ interrupts, respectively. The other flags are self-explanatory. We now describe some of the 6809 pins and signals.

There are three interrupt pins, namely, $\overline{\text{FIRQ}}$ (fast interrupt request), $\overline{\text{IRQ}}$ (interrupt request), and $\overline{\text{NMI}}$ (nonmaskable interrupt). During servicing of $\overline{\text{NMI}}$ and $\overline{\text{IRQ}}$, all registers are saved on the hardware stack, whereas during servicing of the $\overline{\text{FIRQ}}$ only the contents of the condition code register and the PC are saved on the hardware stack.

A low on $\overline{\text{RESET}}$ fetches the high and low bytes of the starting address from the locations $FFFF_{16}$ and $FFFE_{16}$, respectively.

The $\overline{\text{DMA/BREQ}}$ input is used to suspend program execution and make the buses available for other usage such as DMA or a dynamic memory refresh.

E and Q are, respectively, the enable and quadrature clock inputs. The E clock is similar to the phase 2 clock of the 6800. The Q clock leads the E clock by approximately one-half of the E clock time. A low in the MRDY input allows extension of the E and Q clocks used for interfacing slow devices.

The Bus Available (BA) and Bus Status (BS) outputs are encoded to indicate the present state of the processor such as interrupt acknowledge, and so on.

4.5.2 Addressing Modes

Several means of addressing data are provided in the instruction set as follows:

1. Inherent addressing—The address of a register is specified as part of the op code (i.e., ADDA, ADDB).
2. Immediate mode—The byte following the op code contains immediate data to be operated on (i.e., ORA #76, SUB #22).
3. Direct mode—The byte following the op code contains the address in memory of where the operand can be found (i.e., ADD 30, where 30 is the operand address). Direct Page register specifies high address byte.
4. Extended mode—This is identical to direct mode except the operand address is 2 bytes long, allowing access over the full 64K memory size (i.e., JMP 6400).
5. Relative mode—Addressing is done relative to the program counter in the range of -125 to $+129$ from the position of the JMP instruction. Use of this mode allows relocatable code.
6. Indexed mode—The address is calculated from the predefined value

of the index register and an offset operand. This mode generates relocatable code.
7. Register addressing—Some op codes are following by a byte which defines a register or set of registers to be manipulated by the instruction (i.e., EXG A, B exchanges A with B).
8. Zero offset indexed mode—A selected pointer register contains the address of the data. This is the fastest of the indexing modes.
9. Constant offset indexed mode—This is the same as zero offset indexing except that a constant offset is added to the address value. Three sizes of offset specifications are available to provide efficient memory usage—5-bit contained in the second byte of the instruction, 8-bit contained after the instruction, and 16-bit contained in 2 bytes after the instruction. The assembler selects the optimum size automatically. This type of addressing is ideal for use where memory efficiency and relocatable code are desired.
10. Accumulator offset indexing—This is the same as constant offset indexing except the value of an accumulator (A, B, or D) is used as the offset. Using this mode the offset can be dynamically modified, finding uses in fast look-up tables, for example.
11. Auto increment/decrement indexing—The pointer register contains the address. Each time the register is used its value is incremented or decremented by 1 or 2. Several applications immediately become apparent—implementation of auxiliary stacks, block data moves, and look-up tables. It has the ability to use 1 or 2 as the step size allows the use of either 8- or 16-bit data.
12. Program counter relative addressing—The address is obtained by adding an 8- or 16-bit signed offset to the program counter. The code utilizing this addressing is fully relocatable.

4.5.3 Instruction Set

The 6809 (Table 4.5) contains 59 instructions of 1 to 4 bytes each. All I/O is memory-mapped, thus no I/O (INs or OUTs) are included. Highlights of the instruction set are as follows:

1. Stack operations—The stack is organized as part of external memory and can be as large as required up to the memory size. The 16-bit Stack Pointer (SP) can be loaded with the LDS instruction thus allowing the use of multiple stacks. PUSH and PULL instructions are provided for both the A and B accumulators. The stack is also used to store the Program Counter (PC) during a subroutine call, thus essentially unlimited subroutine nesting is possible.
2. Software interrupt—The SWI instruction provides a single-byte call to subroutine to the address contained in locations FFFA and FFFB

Table 4.5. Motorola 6809 Instruction Set

8-BIT ACCUMULATOR AND MEMORY INSTRUCTIONS

Mnemonic(s)	Operation
ADCA, ADCB	Add memory to accumulator with carry
ADDA, ADDB	Add memory to accumulator
ANDA, ANDB	And memory with accumulator
ASL, ASLA, ASLB	Arithmetic shift of accumulator or memory left
ASR, ASRA, ASRB	Arithmetic shift of accumulator or memory right
BITA, BITB	Bit test memory with accumulator
CLR, CLRA, CLRB	Clear accumulator or memory location
CMPA, CMPB	Compare memory from accumulator
COM, COMA, COMB	Complement accumulator or memory location
DAA	Decimal adjust A accumulator
DEC, DECA, DECB	Decrement accumulator or memory location
EORA, EORB	Exclusive or memory with accumulator
EXG R1, R2	Exchange R1 with R2 (R1, R2 = A, B, CC, DP)
INC, INCA, INCB	Increment accumulator or memory location
LDA, LDB	Load accumulator from memory
LSL, LSLA, LSLB	Logical shift left accumulator or memory location
LSR, LSRA, LSRB	Logical shift right accumulator or memory location
MUL	Unsigned multiply (A × B → D)
NEG, NEGA, NEGB	Negate accumulator or memory
ORA, ORB	Or memory with accumulator
ROL, ROLA, ROLB	Rotate accumulator or memory left
ROR, RORA, RORB	Rotate accumulator or memory right
SBCA, SBCB	Subtract memory from accumulator with borrow
STA, STB	Store accumulator to memory
SUBA, SUBB	Subtract memory from accumulator
TST, TSTA, TSTB	Test accumulator or memory location
TFR R1, R2	Transfer R1 to R2 (R1, R2 = A, B, CC, DP)

NOTE: A, B, CC or DP may be pushed to (pulled from) either stack with PSHS, PSHU (PULS, PULU) instructions.

16-BIT ACCUMULATOR AND MEMORY INSTRUCTIONS

Mnemonic(s)	Operation
ADDD	Add memory to D accumulator
CMPD	Compare memory from D accumulator
EXG D, R	Exchange D with X, Y, S, U or PC
LDDA	Load D accumulator from memory
SEX	Sign Extend B accumulator into A accumulator
STD	Store D accumulator to memory
SUBD	Subtract memory from D accumulator
TFR D, R	Transfer D to X, Y, S, U or PC
TFR R, D	Transfer X, Y, S, U or PC to D

NOTE: D may be pushed (pulled) to either stack with PSHS, PSHU (PULS, PULU) insructions.

Table 4.5. Continued

INDEX REGISTER/STACK POINTER INSTRUCTIONS

Mnemonic(s)	Operation
CMPS, CMPU	Compare memory from stack pointer
CMPX, CMPY	Compare memory from index register
EXG R1, R2	Exchange D, X, Y, S, U or PC with D, X, Y, S, U or PC
LEAS, LEAU	Load effective address into stack pointer
LEAX, LEAY	Load effective address into index register
LDS, LDU	Load stack pointer from memory
LDX, LDY	Load index register from memory
PSHS	Push A, B, CC, DP, D, X, Y, U, or PC onto hardware stack
PSHU	Push A, B, CC, DP, D, X, Y, S, or PC onto user stack
PULS	Pull A, B, CC, DP, D, X, Y, U or PC from hardware stack
PULU	Pull A, B, CC, DP, D, X, Y, S or PC from hardware stack
STS, STU	Store stack pointer to memory
STX, STY	Store index register to memory
TFR R1, R2	Transfer D, X, Y, S, U or PC to D, X, Y, S, U or PC
ABX	Add B accumulator to X (unsigned)

BRANCH INSTRUCTIONS

Mnemonic(s)	Operation
	SIMPLE BRANCHES
BEQ, LBEQ	Branch if equal
BNE, LBNE	Branch if not equal
BMI, LBMI	Branch if minus
BPL, LBPL	Branch if plus
BCS, LBCS	Branch if carry set
BCC, LBCC	Branch if carry clear
BVS, LBVS	Branch if overflow set
BVC, LBVC	Branch if overflow clear
	SIGNED BRANCHES
BGT, LBGT	Branch if greater (signed)
BGE, LBGE	Branch if greater than or equal (signed)
BEQ, LBEQ	Branch if equal
BLE, LBLE	Branch if less than or equal (signed)
BLT, LBLT	Branch if less than (signed)
	UNSIGNED BRANCHES
BHI, LBHI	Branch if higher (unsigned)
BHS, LBHS	Branch if higher or same (unsigned)
BEQ, LBEQ	Branch if equal
BLS, LBLS	Branch if lower or same (unsigned)
BLO, LBLO	Branch if lower (unsigned)
	OTHER BRANCHES
BSR, LBSR	Branch to subroutine
BRA, LBRA	Branch always
BRN, LBRN	Branch never

Table 4.5. Continued

MISCELLANEOUS INSTRUCTIONS

Mnemonic(s)	Operation
ANDCC	AND condition code register
CWAI	AND condition code register, then wait for interrupt
NOP	No operation
ORCC	OR condition code register
JMP	Jump
JSR	Jump to subroutine
RTI	Return from interrupt
RTS	Return from subroutine
SWI, SWI2, SWI3	Software interrupt (absolute indirect)
SYNC	Synchronize with interrupt line

Source: Reprinted by permission of Motorola Semiconductor Products, Inc., copyright © 1980.

hex. This can be used with a frequently called subroutine to conserve program memory.

3. Wait for interrupt—This instruction (WAI) yields fast interrupt response by saving PC, A, and B prior to a hardware interrupt request.
4. Conditional branch—Testable flags include sign bit (N), zero flag (Z), overflow flag (V), and carry flag (C). Combinations of flags can be tested using branch on higher (BHI) where C and Z = 0, branch on less than zero (BLT) where N XOR V = 1, and others are provided. These instructions provide straightforward testing of the flags.
5. TFR and EXG instructions allow any register to be transferred or exchanged with any other of equal size. This allows complete versatility in the selection of register functions.
6. LEA (Load Effective Address) instruction allows software look-up tables to be totally relocatable.
7. MUL (Multiply) executes an 8 × 8 unsigned multiple of A and B storing the result in the 16-bit accumulator D. This instruction allows for a great increase in speed and program simplicity when many arithmetic calculations are required.
8. Full 16-bit arithmetic capability is included with load, compare, add, subtract, store, transfer, exchange, push, and pull instructions. This eliminates the need to write routines for double add, double store, and so on which is the case with most 8-bit processors.

4.5.4 I/O Capability

Programmed I/O

All I/O on the 6809 is memory mapped, thus a portion of memory space is used to access I/O ports. In order to utilize this type of I/O peripheral devices, such as the 6821 Peripheral Interface Adapter, are required. The

6821 contains two 8-bit I/O ports which can be programmed by the processor to function as either input or output. Inputs can be configured to interrupt the processor or disabled under program control. Output strobe capability is also provided. Other I/O chips are also available, such as the 6835 CRT Controller and the 6852 Synchronous Serial Data Adapter which provide various specialized I/O functions. Although the 6809 has no true I/O capability within itself these devices can be used to make it a versatile I/O processor.

Interrupt Capability

Four separate interrupts are provided as follows. All interrupts vector to address values contained in the highest (FFF8 to FFFF) 8 bytes of memory:

1. Interrupt request—A low level on the IRQ pin initiates an interrupt request, providing the software-controllable interrupt mask bit is not set. Address of the service routine is contained in addresses FFF8 and FFF9 of external memory. The index register, program counter, accumulators, and condition code register are saved on the stack.
2. Software interrupt—This is initiated by the SWI instruction and causes a jump to subroutine vectored by the address contained at FFFA and FFFB hex.
3. Nonmaskable interrupt—This is identical to the interrupt request except that the nonmaskable interrupt cannot be software disabled, and vectors to addresses at FFFC and FFFD. Wait for interrupt (WAI) allows faster service by saving registers prior to the hardware interrupt.
4. RESET—The RESET line is usually used for power-up initialization and vectors to addresses at FFFE and FFFF hex. As with all interrupts the initialization routine can be located anywhere in memory. The memory at FFFE and FFFF must be nonvolatile (e.g., ROM, EPROM) if RESET is to be used for power-up initialization.
5. DMA/BREQ functions as an interrupt of sorts. When this line is activated by an external device the processor relinquishes the address and data buses (goes to tristate). This allows the external device to access memory or use the data bus. Applications include a DMA floppy disk controller, memory refresh operations, and multiprocessing systems.

EXAMPLE 4.10

Write a program in 6809 assembly language to convert a BCD number into binary. Assume that memory location 000FH contains the BCD number.

SOLUTION

The program is given in the following:

```
BCDBIN: LDDA 000FH  ; A contains the two digit BCD data.
        RORA
        RORA
        RORA
        RORA        ; Move tens digit to the low nibble.
        ANDA #0FH   ; Mask high nibble.
        TAB         ; Tens digit in low nibble of A and B.
        ROLA
        ROLA
        ROLA        ; Multiply by 8.
        ABA
        ABA         ; No, make it 10.
        TAB         ; Load converted tens to B.
        LDDA 000FH  ; Move result back to memory.
        RTS         ; Location 000FH now contains binary data.
```

EXAMPLE 4.11

Write a program in 6809 assembly language to divide the dividend contained in the accumulator by the divisor in register B.

SOLUTION

The program is given below:

```
DIVD:   CLR 000FH   ; Clear counter
DIVD1:  INC 000FH   ; Increment pass counter
        SUBA        ; Subtract B from A
        BLE DIVD1   ; Branch on underflow
        ABA
        DECB        ; B was 1 too large
        RTS         ; B contains the result
                    ; A contains the remainder
```

PROBLEMS AND QUESTIONS

4.1 Compare the register structure of:
    (a) 8085 versus Z80.
    (b) 6800 versus 6809.

4.2 What is the difference between the 8085 and the 8048?

4.3 Consider the 8085 microprocessor. If the B register contains 37 hex

and the accumulator contains 14 hex, what will be the contents of the accumulator after executing:
(a) ANA B.
(b) ORA B.

4.4 Find the value in hex of an 8-bit number which should be ANDed with another number contained in the accumulator of an 8-bit microprocessor to keep its most significant bit unchanged and set all other bits to 0.

4.5 If the accumulator initially contains E5 and Z = 0, which location will a program jump to after execution of the following instructions? Assume a 8048 microcomputer.

$$\vdots$$

```
JZ    0200
JMP   0205
```

$$\vdots$$

4.6 Write programs in 8085, Z80, 8048, 6800, and 6809 assembly languages to perform the following:
(a) Add two 32-bit numbers and store the result in four consecutive memory locations.
(b) Subtract two 16-bit numbers and store the result in two consecutive memory locations.
(c) 16 bit × 16 bit signed multiplication using any algorithm of your choice.
(d) 16-bit dividend divided by 8-bit divisor for signed numbers using any algorithm of your choice.

4.7 Using the following algorithm, write an 8085 assembly language program to find the square root of a number from a Taylor series approximation as follows:

$$\text{Let } X = \text{any number}$$
$$f(X) = \text{a function of } X$$
$$= \sqrt{x} \text{ (in this case)}$$
$$a = \text{known number close to } X$$
$$f(a) = \text{known function of } a$$

Then using Taylor series,

$$f(X) = f(a) + (X - a)f'(a) + \frac{(x-a)^2}{2!}f''(a) + \cdots + \frac{(X-a)^n}{n!}f^n(a)$$

Let $X = N =$ the number whose square root is desired. Then
$$f(X) = \sqrt{N}$$
$$a = \text{known number close to } N$$

$f(a) = \sqrt{a}$ = known number close to $\sqrt{N}$

$f(X) = \sqrt{a} + \dfrac{(N-a)}{2\sqrt{a}} + \cdots$

$= \dfrac{2a + N - a}{2\sqrt{a}} = \dfrac{a + N}{2\sqrt{a}}$, neglecting all other terms in the series

In the above equation, $f(X)$ or the square root of the number can be found by guessing $\sqrt{a}$ and then computing $f(X)$. The square of this $f(X)$ can be compared to the original number N. If two consecutive guesses are approximately equal, then that guess gives the square root of the number.

4.8 Compare the I/O techniques of:
(a) 8085 versus Z80.
(b) 6800 versus 6809.

CHAPTER 5

8085 INPUT/OUTPUT

The 8085 I/O transfer techniques are discussed. The 8355/8755 and 8155 I/O ports and the 8085 SID and SOD lines are also included.

> The 8085 I/O techniques are discussed in detail since the 8085 is used in the subsequent chapters to develop hardware and software for typical microcomputer-based applications. Once the reader understands the 8085 I/O, it will be easier to design applications with other microprocessors.

5.1 8085 Programmed I/O

The 8085 has two input/output instructions namely, IN and OUT. Each of these instructions requires 2 bytes. The first byte contains the op code followed by the second byte defining the I/O port number. The IN PORT instruction loads a byte into the accumulator from an I/O port defined in the instruction. The OUT PORT outputs a byte from the accumulator into an I/O port defined in the instruction.

The 8085's programmed I/O capabilities are obtained via its support chips, namely 8355/8755 and 8155. The specifications for these chips are given in Chapter 8. We now describe the I/O ports in the 8355/8755 and 8155.

This chapter contains material modified from *Microcomputer Theory and Applications with the Intel SDK-85*, by M. Rafiquzzaman, Wiley, 1982.

5.1.1 8355/8755 I/O Ports

Two 8-bit I/O ports are provided with the 8355/8755. These are ports A and B. The direction of data flow into or out of each of these data registers is controlled by another register called the data direction register. For example, a 0 written into a bit position of the data direction register sets up the corresponding bit in the data register as the input. A 1 written in a specific bit position in the data direction register configures the corresponding bit in the data register as output. In order to understand the 8355/8755 I/O ports, consider the following instruction sequence.

```
MVI A, 1AH
OUT DDRA
```

The above instruction sequence assumes DDRA as the data direction register for PORT A. The bits of port 00 are configured as follows:

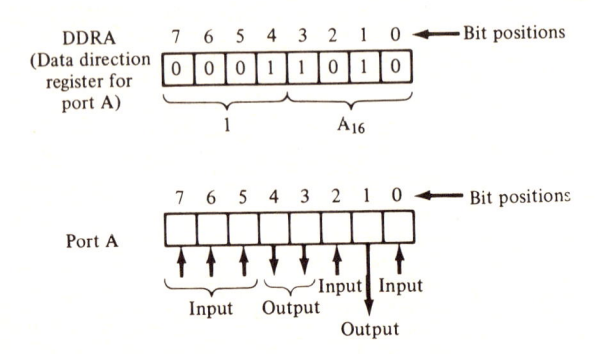

```
DDRA            7 6 5 4 3 2 1 0  ← Bit positions
(Data direction [0|0|0|1|1|0|1|0]
 register for
   port A)         1     A₁₆
```

```
              7 6 5 4 3 2 1 0  ← Bit positions
Port A       [ | | | | | | | ]
              ↑ ↑ ↑ ↓ ↓ ↓ ↑ ↑
              └─┬─┘ └─┬─┘ Input Input
              Input Output  ↓
                         Output
```

5.1.2 8155 I/O Ports

Three I/O ports are provided with the 8155. These are port A, port B, and port C. Ports A and B are 8 bits long and port C is 6 bits long.

The 8155 I/O ports are controlled by another register known as the command status register. A thorough description of this register is given in the 8155 specification in Chapter 8. At this point, we will only be interested in bits 0 through 3 of the command/status register.

Bits 0 and 1 of the Command/Status Register (CSR) control the direction of data flow in ports A and B, respectively. For example, a 0 written at bit position 0 of CSR configures all 8 bits of port A as inputs. Similarly, a 1 at bit 0 of CSR sets up all 8 bits of port A as outputs. Bit 1 of CSR controls port B in the same way.

Table 5.1 provides a list of the 8155 and 8355 I/O ports to be used in subsequent examples.

Table 5.1. Addresses of the 8355 and 8155 I/O Ports To Be Used in Subsequent Examples

Port	
00	8355 port A
01	8355 port B
02	8355 port A data direction register
03	8355 port B data direction register
20	8155 command/status register
21	8155 port A
22	8155 port B
23	8155 port C

EXAMPLE 5.1

An 8085-8355-based microcomputer is required to drive an LED connected to bit 0 of port 0 based on the input conditions set by a switch on bit 1 of port 0 as shown in Figure 5.1. The input/output conditions are as follows: If the input to bit 1 of port 0 is HIGH then the LED will be turned ON; otherwise the LED will be turned OFF.

1. Design the hardware interface.
2. Flowchart the problem.
3. Convert the flowchart to an 8085 assembly language program.

SOLUTION

1. The hardware interface can be designed as follows: From 8355 specifications, the 8355 can source up to 400 μA of current at a minimum output high of 2.4 V. In practice, the true sourcing capability into a transistor base as shown above is almost never specified and has to be estimated (guessed). A conservative estimate is 1.5 mA at 5 V. Assume that the LED requires a current of 10 mA at 1.7 V.

   The basic design problem now is to determine the β for the transistors (Q_1) and the values of R_1 and R_2. A hex driver or an inverter/chip such as the 7406 or 7407 could have been used in place of the transistor. Now, assume

$$V_{CE}(\text{sat}) \simeq 0, \quad R_1 = \frac{(2.4 - 0.7)\text{ V}}{400\text{ }\mu\text{A}} = 4.25\text{ kohms}$$

$$R_2 = \frac{5\text{ V} - 1.7\text{ V} - V_{CE}(\text{sat})}{10\text{ mA}}$$

$$= \frac{5 - 1.7}{10\text{ mA}}$$

$$= 330\text{ ohms}$$

Chapter 5 8085 Input/Output

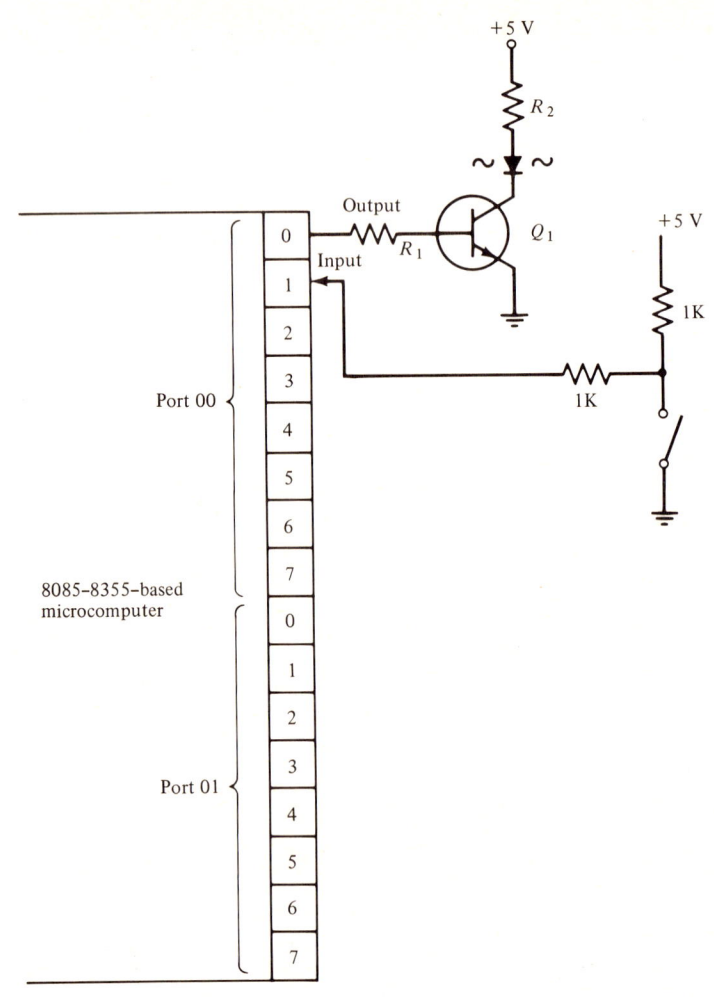

Figure 5.1 The circuit for Example 5.1.

We know

$$I_C = \beta I_B$$

$$I_B = I_{\text{source}} = 400 \ \mu A$$

$$= 400 \times 10^{-6}$$

$$I_C = I_{\text{LED}} = 10 \text{ mA}$$

$$= 10 \times 10^{-3}$$

$$\beta = \frac{I_C}{I_B} = \frac{10 \times 10^{-3}}{400 \times 10^{-6}}$$

$$= 25$$

Therefore use $R_1 = 4.25$ kohms, $R_2 = 330$ ohms, and select a transistor with a minimum saturation β of 25.

As far as the input switch is concerned, a HIGH is input when the switch is open and a LOW is input when the switch is closed (active low). The hardware interface design is now complete.

2. The flowchart can be drawn as follows:

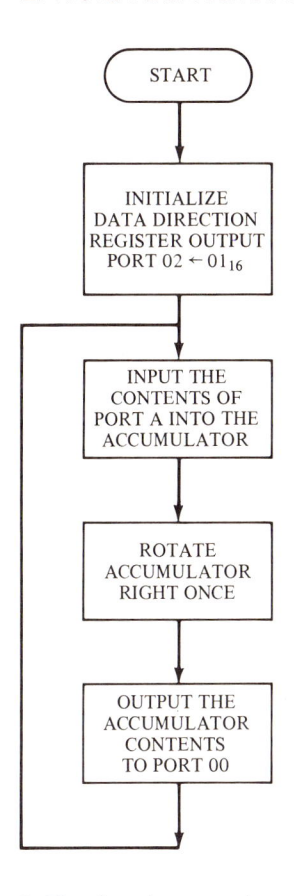

```
              START
                │
                ▼
        ┌───────────────┐
        │  INITIALIZE   │
        │ DATA DIRECTION│
        │REGISTER OUTPUT│
        │  PORT 02 ← 01₁₆│
        └───────────────┘
                │
      ┌─────────▼─────────┐
      │                   │
      │  ┌─────────────┐  │
      │  │  INPUT THE  │  │
      │  │ CONTENTS OF │  │
      │  │PORT A INTO THE│ │
      │  │ ACCUMULATOR │  │
      │  └─────────────┘  │
      │         │         │
      │         ▼         │
      │  ┌─────────────┐  │
      │  │   ROTATE    │  │
      │  │ ACCUMULATOR │  │
      │  │ RIGHT ONCE  │  │
      │  └─────────────┘  │
      │         │         │
      │         ▼         │
      │  ┌─────────────┐  │
      │  │ OUTPUT THE  │  │
      │  │ ACCUMULATOR │  │
      │  │  CONTENTS   │  │
      │  │ TO PORT 00  │  │
      │  └─────────────┘  │
      │         │         │
      └─────────┘         
```

3. The flowchart can be translated into an assembly language program as follows:

```
       PORT A  EQU  00H
       PORT C  EQU  02H
               MVI  A, 01H
               OUT  PORT C
       START:  IN   PORT A
               RAR
               OUT  PORT A
               JMP  START
```

EXAMPLE 5.2

Write an 8085 assembly language program that turns on an LED connected to bit 4 of the 8155 I/O port B.

SOLUTION

```
PORT B  EQU  22H
PORT D  EQU  20H
        MVI  A, 02H
        OUT  PORT D
        MVI  A, 10H
        OUT  PORT B
        HLT
```

5.2 8085 Interrupt System

The 8085 chip has five interrupt pins namely, TRAP, RST7.5, RST6.5, RST5.5, and INTR. If the signals on these interrupt pins go to HIGH simultaneously, then TRAP will be serviced first (i.e., highest priority) followed by RST7.5, RST6.5, RST5.5, and INTR. Note that once an interrupt is serviced, all the interrupts except TRAP are disabled. They can be enabled by executing the Enable Interrupts (EI) instruction. We will now describe the 8085 interrupts in detail.

5.2.1 TRAP

TRAP is a nonmaskable interrupt. That is, it cannot be disabled by an instruction. In order for the 8085 to service this interrupt, the signal on the TRAP pin must have a sustained HIGH level with a leading edge. If this condition occurs, then the 8085 completes execution of the current instruction, pushes the program counter onto the stack, and branches to location 0024_{16} (interrupt address vector for the TRAP). Note that the TRAP interrupt is disabled by the falling edge of the signal on the pin.

5.2.2 RST7.5

RST7.5 is a maskable interrupt. This means that it can be enabled or disabled using the SIM instruction. The 8085 responds to the RST7.5 interrupt when the signal on the RST7.5 pin has a leading edge. In order to service RST7.5, the 8085 completes execution of the current instruction, pushes the program counter onto the stack, and branches to $003C_{16}$. The 8085 remembers the RST7.5 interrupt by setting an internal D flip-flop by the leading edge.

5.2.3 RST6.5

RST6.5 is a maskable interrupt. It can be enabled or disabled using the SIM instruction. RST6.5 is HIGH level sensitive. In order to service this interrupt, the 8085 completes execution of the current instruction, saves the program counter onto the stack, and branches to location 0034_{16}.

5.2.4 RST5.5

RST5.5 is a maskable interrupt. It can be enabled or disabled by the SIM instruction. RST5.5 is HIGH level sensitive. In order to service this interrupt, the 8085 completes execution of the current instruction, saves the program counter onto the stack, and branches to 0020_{16}.

5.2.5 INTR

INTR is a maskable interrupt. This is also called handshake interrupt. INTR is HIGH level sensitive. When no other interrupts are active and the signal on the INTR pin is HIGH, the 8085 completes execution of the current instruction, and generates an interrupt acknowledge, $\overline{\text{INTA}}$, LOW pulse on the control bus. The 8085 then expects either a 1-byte CALL (RST0 through RST7) or a 3-byte CALL. This instruction must be provided by external hardware. In other words, the $\overline{\text{INTA}}$ can be used to enable a tristate buffer. The output of this buffer can be connected to the 8085 data lines. The buffer can be designed to provide the appropriate op code on the data lines. Note that the occurrence of $\overline{\text{INTA}}$ turns off the 8085 interrupt system in order to avoid multiple interrupts from a single device. Also note that there are eight RST instructions (RST0 through RST7). Each of these RST instructions has a vector address. These are shown in Table 5.2.

Table 5.2. Restart Instructions and Interrupt Inputs

Instruction or Input	Code (Hex)	Vector Address (Hex)
RST0	C7	0000
RST1	CF	0008
RST2	D7	0010
RST3	DF	0018
RST4	E7	0020
TRAP	Hardware interrupt	0024
RST5	EF	0028
RST5.5	Hardware interrupt	0020
RST6	F7	0030
RST6.5	Hardware interrupt	0034
RST7	FF	0038
RST7.5	Hardware interrupt	0030

152 Chapter 5   8085 INPUT/OUTPUT

Let us now identify the characteristics of an interrupt acknowledge ($\overline{\text{INTA}}$) machine cycle. The $\overline{\text{INTA}}$ machine cycle is same as the instruction fetch cycle with the following differences:

1. The 8085 generates an $\overline{\text{INTA}}$ pulse rather than $\overline{\text{MEMR}}$ pulse. An RST instruction is then fetched and executed.
2. The 8085 does not increment the program counter contents in order to return to the proper location after servicing the interrupt.
3. The generation of $\overline{\text{INTA}}$ disables the 8085 interrupt capability in order to avoid multiple interrupts.

The interrupt acknowledge timing diagram is shown in Figures 5.2 and 5.3. In response to a HIGH on the INTR, the 8085 proceeds with the

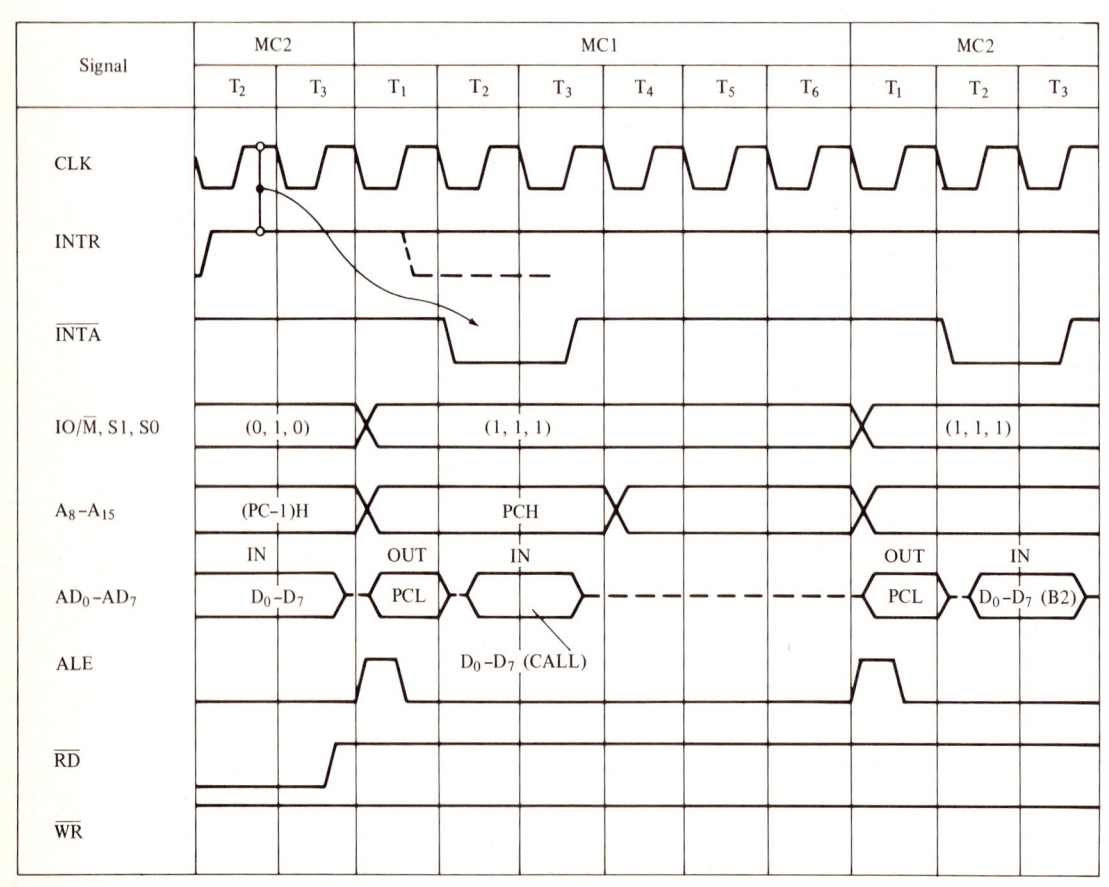

Figure 5.2 Interrupt acknowledge machine cycles (with CALL instruction in response to INTR). Source: Reprinted by permission of Intel Corporation, copyright © 1976.

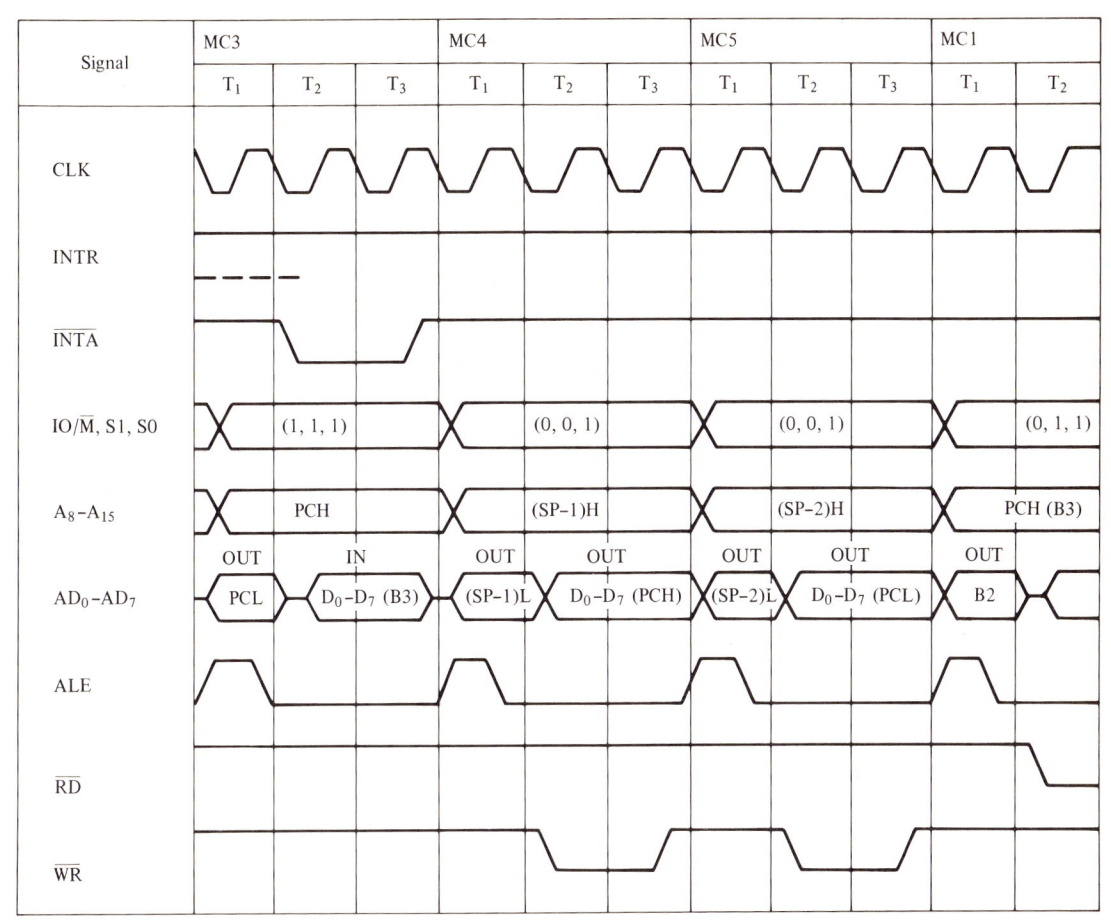

Figure 5.3 Interrupt acknowledge machine cycles (with CALL instruction in response to INTR). Source: Reprinted by permission of Intel Corporation, copyright © 1976.

sequence of events shown in Figures 5.2 and 5.3 (a continuation of 5.2), if the 8085 system interrupt is enabled by the EI instruction. Before the MC1.T1 cycle, the 8085 checks all the interrupts. If INTR is the only interrupt and if the 8085 system interrupt is enabled, the 8085 will turn off the system interrupt and then make the $\overline{\text{INTA}}$ LOW for about two T-states (T2 and T3 cycles of MC1 in Figure 5.2). This $\overline{\text{INTA}}$ signal can be used to enable an external hardware to provide an op code on the data bus. The 8085 can then read this op code. Typically, the 1-byte RST or 3-byte CALL instruction can be used as the op code. If the 3-byte CALL is used then the 8085 will generate two additional $\overline{\text{INTA}}$ cycles in order to fetch all 3 bytes of the instruction. However, on the other hand, if RST is used, then no additional $\overline{\text{INTA}}$ is required. Figures 5.2 and 5.3 show that in response to $\overline{\text{INTA}}$, a CALL op code is generated on the data bus during MC1. The call op code could have been placed there by a device like the 8259 programmable interrupt controller. At this point, only the op code for the CALL (CD_{16}) is fetched by the 8085. The 8085 executes this instruction and determines that it needs two more bytes (the address portion of the 3-byte instruction). The 8085 then generates a second $\overline{\text{INTA}}$ cycle in MC2 followed by a third $\overline{\text{INTA}}$ cycle in MC3 in order to fetch the address portion of the CALL instruction from the 8259. The 8085 executes the CALL instruction and branches to the interrupt service routine located at an address specified in the CALL instruction. Note that the 8085 does not increment the program counter contents during the three $\overline{\text{INTA}}$ cycles so that the appropriate program counter value is pushed in the stack during MC4 and MC5. Also note that the recognition of any maskable interrupt (RST7.5, RST6.5, RST5.5, and TRAP) disables all interrupts.

Therefore, in order that the 8085 can accept another interrupt, the last two instructions of the interrupt service routine will be EI followed by RET.

One can produce a single RST instruction, say RST7 (op code FF in hex), using an 8212 I/O port as an instruction I/O port. The inputs I_0 through I_7 of the 8212 are connected to HIGH and its select line, DS1, is tied to a LOW. In response to $\overline{\text{INTA}}$ LOW, the 8212 port places FF in hex (RST7) on the data bus. Figure 5.4 shows a typical circuit.

An 8 to 3 encoder such as the 74LS148 can be used along with the 8212 in order to generate all eight RST instructions. This is shown in Figure 5.5. The encoder generates active LOW outputs. This means that if the input $\overline{R_4}$ is connected to the 74LS148, the encoder converts the 3-bit binary code 100_2 (4) into 011_2 (3_{10}).

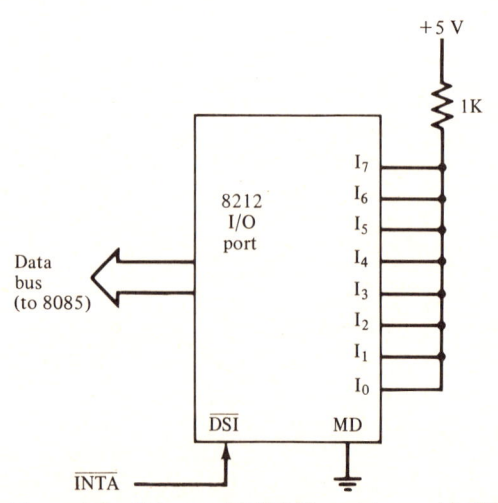

Figure 5.4 Using an 8212 I/O port to provide RST7 instruction. Source: *8080A/8085 Assembly Language Programming* by Lance Leventhal. Copyright © 1978, McGraw-Hill, Inc.

8085 Interrupt System

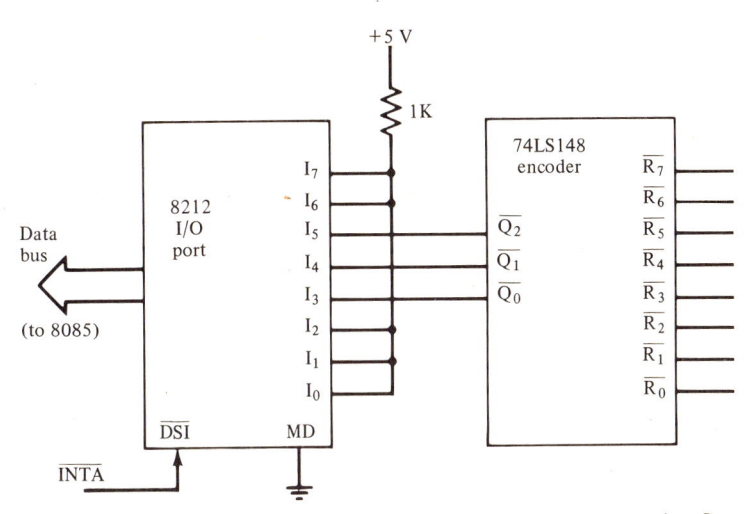

Figure 5.5 Forming eight RST instructions with a priority encoder. Source: *8080A/8085 Assembly Language Programming* by Lance Leventhal. Copyright © 1978, McGraw-Hill, Inc.

As mentioned before the op code for RST instruction is:

11 CCC 111
where CCC is 000 for RST0
001 for RST1
010 for RST2
011 for RST3
100 for RST4
101 for RST5
110 for RST6
111 for RST7

In the above circuit, the output of the encoder $\overline{Q_2}, \overline{Q_1}, \overline{Q_0}$ provides CCC for the RST instruction.

Table 5.2 provides a summary of the 8085 interrupts and the regular RST instructions. Figure 5.6 shows the 8085 interrupt structure. Now in Figure 5.5, the encoder provides three active-low output bits to an 8212 port. The result is to place one of the eight RST instructions on the data bus of the 8085 in response to the $\overline{INTA}$ signal. Note that in Figure 5.5, the inputs to the encoder should be synchronized to INTA in order to avoid any erratic results. Now, we know that the inputs and outputs of a 74LS148 encoder are active LOW. As a result, a LOW level on input $\overline{R_0}$ produces the RST7 instruction (op code FF_{16}) and input $\overline{R_7}$ produces the RST0 instruction (op code $C7_{16}$) which has the same address as RESET. The encoder only differentiates between simultaneous active inputs and produces an output which corresponds to the highest priority input.

Let us elaborate on Figure 5.6. Execution of the EI instruction sets the RS flip-flop of Figure 5.6 and makes one of the inputs to the AND gates #1

156 Chapter 5 8085 INPUT/OUTPUT

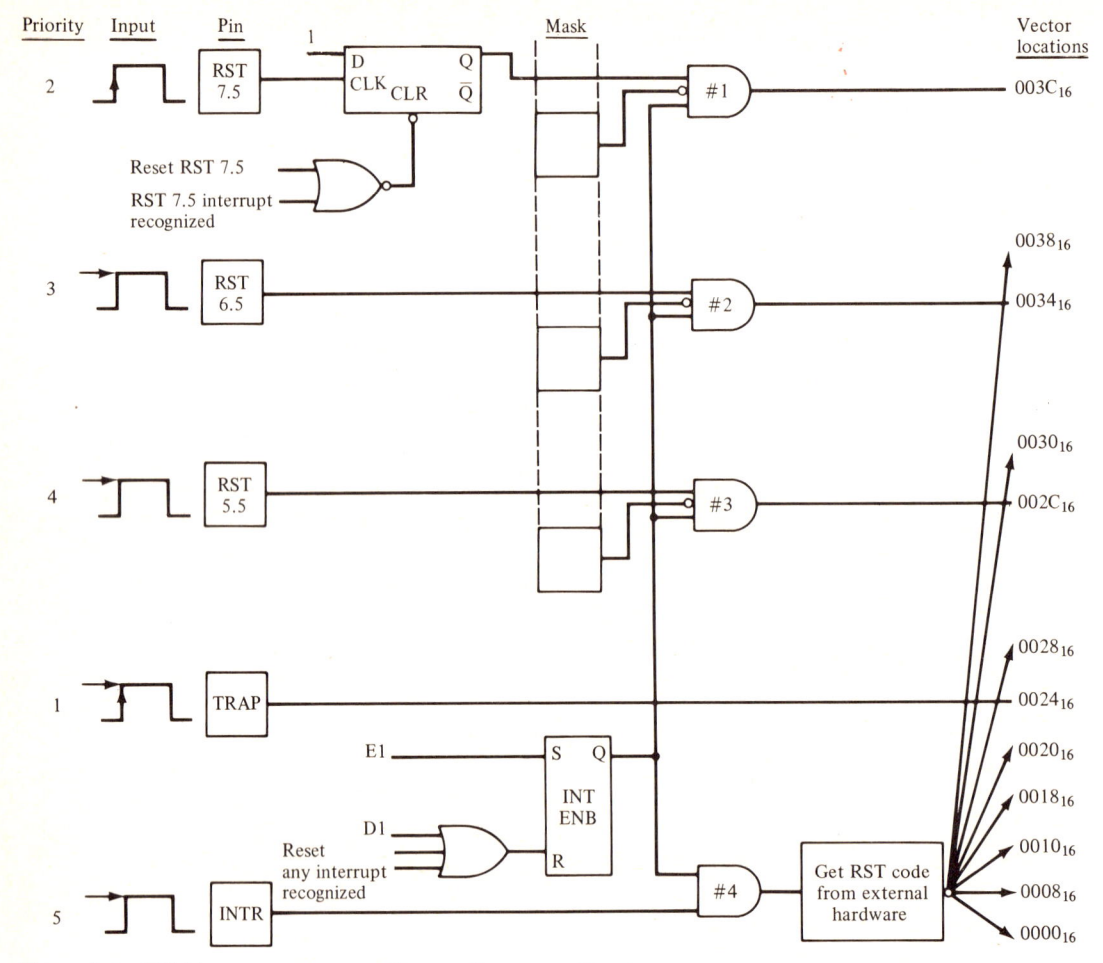

Figure 5.6 8085 interrupt structure. Source: Courtesy of Intel.

through #4 HIGH. Hence, in order for all the interrupts (except TRAP) to work, the interrupt system must be enabled. Execution of Disable Interrupts (DI) clears the RS flip-flop and disables all interrupts except TRAP. As mentioned in Chapter 4, the SIM instruction outputs the contents of the accumulator which can be interpreted as shown in Figure 5.7. The interrupt mask function is only executed if the mask set enable bit is 1. Suppose if 06_{16} is stored in the accumulator and the SIM instruction is executed, 1 will be sent to the interrupt mask for RST7.5 and RST6.5 and 0 will be sent to RST5.5. That is, in Figure 5.6, 1 will be sent to the inputs of the AND gates #1 and #2, and 0 will be sent to the AND gate #3, then inverted at the AND gate inputs (shown by circles), giving two LOW outputs disabling RST7.5, RST6.5, and a HIGH input to AND gate #3. Therefore, in order to enable RST7.5, RST6.5, or RST5.5, the interrupt

8085 Interrupt System

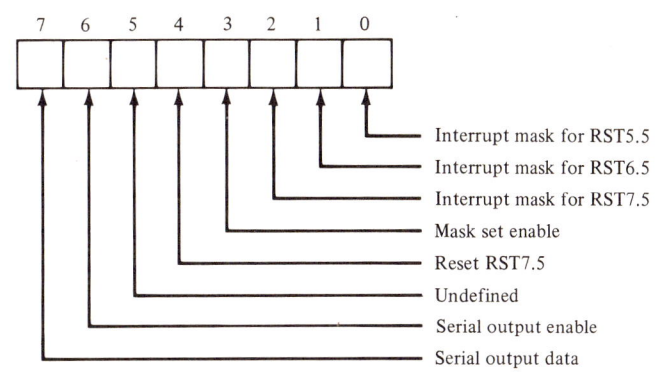

```
 7   6   5   4   3   2   1   0
┌───┬───┬───┬───┬───┬───┬───┬───┐
│   │   │   │   │   │   │   │   │
└─┬─┴─┬─┴─┬─┴─┬─┴─┬─┴─┬─┴─┬─┴─┬─┘
```

- Interrupt mask for RST5.5
- Interrupt mask for RST6.5
- Interrupt mask for RST7.5
- Mask set enable
- Reset RST7.5
- Undefined
- Serial output enable
- Serial output data

Figure 5.7 Interpretation of data output by the SIM instruction.

system must be enabled, the appropriate interrupt mask bit must be LOW, and the appropriate interrupt signal (leading edge or high level) at the respective pins must be available. For example, consider the RST7.5 interrupt. When the EI and SIM instructions are executed, the interrupt system can be enabled and also the interrupt mask bit for RST7.5 can be set to a LOW, making the two inputs to AND gate #1 HIGH. The third input to this AND gate can be set to a HIGH by a leading edge at the RST7.5 pin. This sets the D flip-flop, thus making the output of the AND gate #1 HIGH, enabling the RST7.5. The 8085 branches to location $003C_{16}$ where a 3-byte JMP instruction takes the program to the service routine. The RST5.5 and RST6.5 can similarly be explained from Figure 5.6.

From Figure 5.6, it can also be seen that a leading edge and a HIGH level at the TRAP interrupt pin takes the 8085 to location 0024_{16} where a 3-byte CALL can be executed to go to the service routine. Note that TRAP cannot be disabled by any instruction and is nonmaskable.

Finally, if the INTR is HIGH and the interrupt system is enabled, the output of the AND gate #4 is HIGH, interrupting the 8085. After executing the current instruction, the 8085 puts the $\overline{\text{INTA}}$ signal to a LOW. As mentioned before, this LOW at the $\overline{\text{INTA}}$ can be used to enable an external device such as the 8212 to provide an RST code on the 8085 data lines.

EXAMPLE 5.3

The 8085 is required to read the output of a tristate Analog-Digital (A/D) converter, such as the Teledyne 8703, through port A of the 8155. It uses bit 0 of port A of the 8355 to send an output to start the conversion. The 8085 is then interrupted by the DATA VALID signal. The microcomputer reads the output of A/D through I/O port A of the 8155 by enabling the tristate output through bit 1 of 8355 port A.

158 Chapter 5 8085 INPUT/OUTPUT

Design the interface hardware using a simplified block diagram between the 8085-based microcomputer and the A/D converter. Use RST6.5 interrupt first and then repeat the example using INTR (say RST6) interrupt.

SOLUTION

The A/D converter used is the Teledyne 8703 8-bit with tristate outputs. The timing diagrams of the Teledyne 8703 A/D Converter can be drawn from the manufacturer's specification as shown in Figure 5.8. The 8085 can be programmed to send an INITIATE CONVERSION pulse to the 8703 for at least 500 ns. This can be accomplished by sending a HIGH and then a LOW to the INITIATE CONVERSION pin of the 8703. Either the DATA VALID or the BUSY signal can be connected to the interrupt pin (RST6.5 or INTR in this example) of the 8085 to interrupt the processor after the conversion is complete.

Figure 5.9 shows the interfacing of the 8703 A/D to the 8085-based microcomputer using RST6.5 and data valid signals. In the above interface circuit, the 8085 can be programmed to send a HIGH output through bit 0 of port 00 and a LOW output through bit 0 of port 00 to provide the INITIATE CONVERSION pulse for at least 500 ns. The 8085 then waits for the DATA VALID signal to go to a LOW, indicating the conversion is complete. This waiting can be accomplished using the HLT instruction in the program. When the DATA VALID signal goes to a LOW, and the RST6.5 is unmasked and enabled, the 8085 will be interrupted. The 8085 will complete the current instruction and branch to location 0034_{16} where a 3-byte JMP instruction can be placed to branch to the interrupt service routine. The first few instructions of the service routine will be to send a LOW output through bit 1 of port 00 to enable the output of the A/D converter. Then the 8085 can be programmed to input the A/D converter output through port 21.

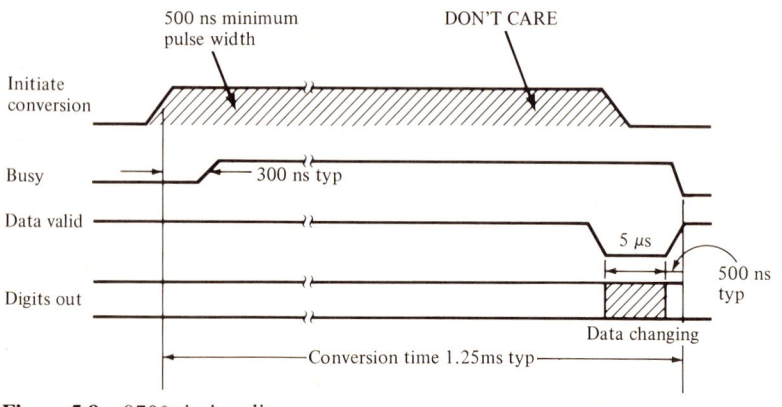

Figure 5.8 8703 timing diagram.

8085 Interrupt System

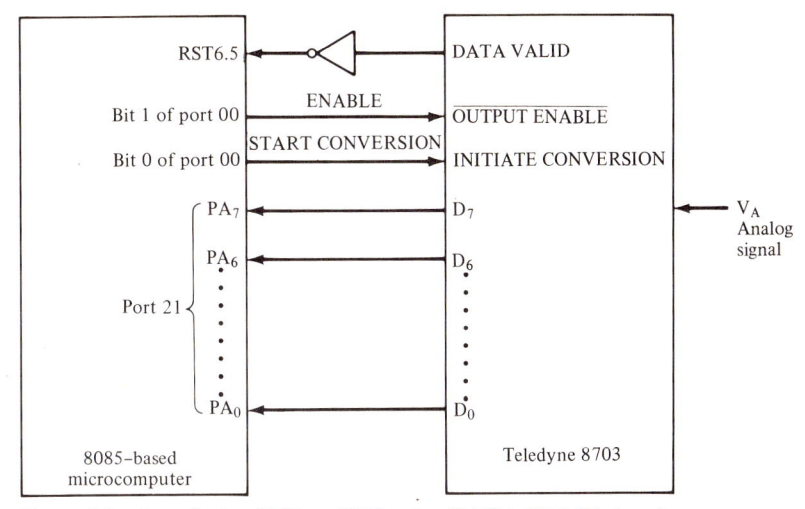

Figure 5.9 Interfacing 8703 to 8085 using DATA VALID signal.

Note that the 8703 latches the data when the DATA VALID signal goes to a HIGH after 5 μs. Therefore, the data must be input into the 8085 5 μs after the occurrence of the interrupt. In the above, the duration between the occurrence of the interrupt and the outputting of the A/D output into the 8085 is much more than 5 μs.

Next we consider using the INTR and the DATA VALID signals.

Using the 8085 INTR (RST 6) Interrupt and the DATA VALID Signal

The hardware interface can be designed as shown in Figure 5.10. In Figure 5.10 as before, the 8085 can be programmed to send a HIGH output through bit 0 of port 00 and a LOW output through bit 0 of port 00 to provide the INITIATE CONVERSION pulse. The HLT instruction can then be used in the program for the 8085 to wait until the conversion is complete. As soon as the DATA VALID signal goes to a LOW, indicating the conversion is complete, the INTR is set to a HIGH. Now, if the interrupt is enabled, the 8085 will be interrupted. The processor will complete the current instruction and will output the interrupt acknowledge ($\overline{\text{INTA}}$) LOW, which will enable the 74LS244 tristate buffer where the op code for RST6 ($F7_{16}$) can be placed by means of DIP switches. Thus, upon enabling the 74LS244 by the $\overline{\text{INTA}}$ signal, the RST6 instruction will be strobed on to the data lines. This will cause the processor to jump to location 8085 where a 3-byte CALL instruction can be executed to branch to the interrupt service routine. The interrupt service routine can be written to send a LOW output through bit 1 of port 00 to enable the $\overline{\text{OUTPUT ENABLE}}$ and then input the 8-bit A/D output through the I/O port 21.

Note that as in the RST6.5, the duration between the occurrence of the INTR and inputting of the A/D output into the 8085 is much more than 5 μs.

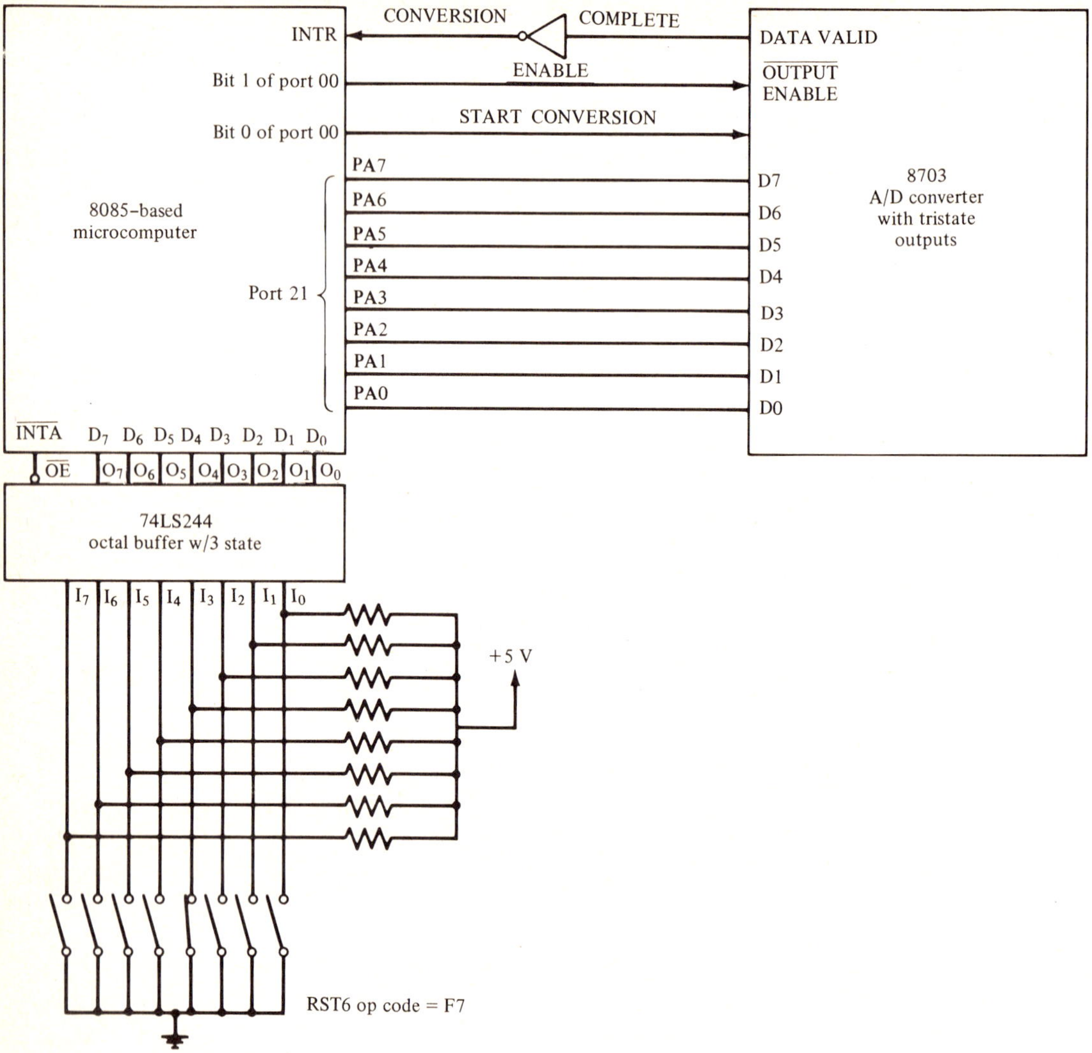

Figure 5.10 8085-8703 schematic.

This means that the A/D output is input into the 8085 after the 8703 latches the data.

5.3 8085 DMA

Direct Memory Access (DMA) is commonly used for three types of data transfer: burst, cycle stealing, and transparent. Burst DMA transfers a block of data at the highest rate possible.

In cycle-stealing DMA, data are transferred concurrently with other processing being carried out by the microprocessor. Typically, 1 byte is transferred at a time.

Transparent DMA contains logic that detects the occurrence of microprocessor states, such as during ALU operation, which involve only internal processing. During this interval, data transfer takes place via the system bus.

For any type of DMA transfer, the microprocessor must use an external chip known as the DMA controller. This chip contains its own address register, word count register, and logic for reading or writing data to or from memory. For the three types of DMA transfer, the only software required is that necessary for initializing the DMA controller's address and word count registers.

In the 8085, a DMA controller requests a DMA operation by bringing the HOLD input of the microprocessor HIGH. The microprocessor then synchronizes the asynchronous HOLD request and, at the proper time in the machine cycle, provides a HOLD ACKNOWLEDGE (HLDA) signal to the DMA controller and floats its address and data buses and the $\overline{RD}$, $\overline{WR}$, and IO/$\overline{M}$ control lines. The 8085 continues internal processing and enters a HOLD state. By floating its address, data, and control buses, the 8085 disconnects itself from the memory. From this point on, it is up to the DMA controller to provide address, data, and control signals to the memory to implement the data transfer. The DMA controller then enables its tristate buffers, which connect it to the address, data, and control buses. When the DMA processor is through using memory, it floats its address, data, and control buses, and then brings the HOLD input of the 8085 LOW. The 8085 exits the HOLD state and continues its previous operation from the point at which it was suspended by the HOLD request. The DMA controller subsequently interrupts the 8085, indicating that the DMA transfer is complete.

DMA controllers range from random logic structures to special Large-Scale Integration (LSI) devices and even to dedicated microprocessors. An LSI DMA controller such as the Intel 8257 is programmable and controls the DMA operations of several I/O devices. Details of the 8257 are included in Chapter 8.

5.4 8085 SID and SOD Lines

Serial I/O is extensively used for data transfer between a peripheral device and the microprocessor. Since microprocessors perform internal operations in parallel, conversions of data from parallel to serial and vice versa is required to provide communication between the microprocessor and the serial I/O. The 8085 provides serial input/output capabilities via Serial Input Data (SID) and Serial Output Data (SOD) lines.

One can transfer data to or from the SID or SOD lines using the instructions RIM (20_{16}) and SIM (30_{16}). We discussed these two instructions in Chapter 4. After executing the RIM instruction, the bits in the accumulator are interpreted as follows:

Serial input bit is bit 7 of the accumulator.
Bits 0 through 6 are interrupt masks, the interrupt enable bit, and pending interrupts.

The SIM instruction sends the contents of the accumulator to the interrupt mask register and serial input line. Therefore, before executing the SIM, the accumulator must be loaded with proper data. The contents of the accumulator are interpreted as follows:

Bit 7 of the accumulator is the serial output bit.
The SOD enable bit is bit 6 of the accumulator.
This bit must be 1 in order to output bit 7 of the accumulator to the SOD line.
Bits 0 through 5 are interrupt masks, enables, and resets.

The SID line (pin 5) can be interfaced to a debounced switch as shown in Figure 5.11. An LED can be interfaced to a SOD line (pin 4) as shown in Figure 5.12. Assuming that the LED takes 10 mA at 1.7 V, the value of R is calculated as 330 ohms.

PROBLEMS AND QUESTIONS

5.1 What are the differences between the 8355 I/O ports and 8155 I/O ports?

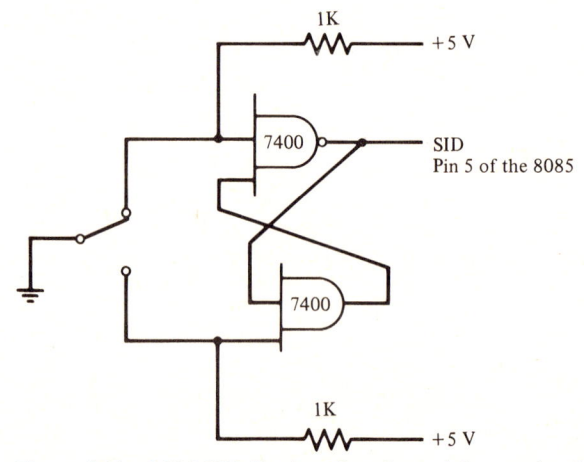

Figure 5.11 8085 SID line interfaced to a debounced switch.

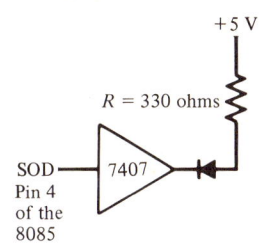

Figure 5.12 8085-driven LED via SOD line.

5.2 Identify all the maskable and nonmaskable interrupts on the 8085 and also the signals by which they are activated.

5.3 Is the TRAP interrupt affected by the execution of EI or DI instruction? Comment.

5.4 The 8085 and 8355 are required to perform the following function:

Port 00 has two switch inputs (connected to bits 1 and 2) and one LED output (connected to bit 0).

Port 01 has an LED connected to bit 0.

The LED at port 00 is to be turned ON and the LED at port 01 is to be turned OFF if port 00 has an even number of HIGH inputs.

Port 00 LED is to be OFF and port 01 LED ON if port 00 has an odd number of HIGH inputs.

(a) Flowchart the problem.

(b) Convert the flowchart to an 8085 assembly language program.

5.5

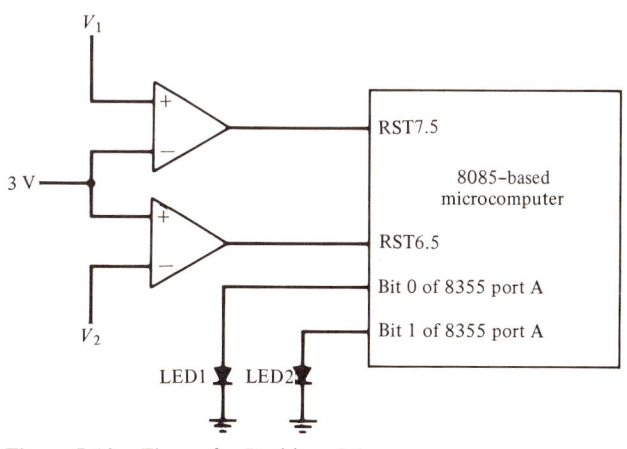

Figure 5.13 Figure for Problem 5.5.

In the above circuit, the 8085 is required to perform the following functions:

1. Turn LED1 ON and LED2 OFF if $V_1 > 3$ V and $V_2 > 3$ V.
2. Turn LED1 OFF and LED2 ON if $V_1 < 3$ V and $V_2 < 3$ V.

3. Turn both LEDs OFF if $V_1 < 3$ V and $V_2 > 3$ V.
(a) Flowchart the problem.
(b) Convert the flowchart to 8085 assembly language program.

5.6 Write an 8085 assembly language program which will input a switch via the SID line and output it through bit 3 of 8355 port B to turn on an LED if the switch input is HIGH. Otherwise the LED will be turned OFF.

CHAPTER 6

INTEL 8086 AND ZILOG Z8000

Chapters 6 and 7 describe the various 16-bit and 32-bit microprocessors. Three major manufacturers, namely, Intel, Motorola, and Zilog are included for this purpose. The 16- and 32-bit microprocessors are designed using the HMOS (high-density, short-channel MOS) technology. The HMOS is achieved by reducing the channel length of the NMOS transistor. HMOS has the following advantages over NMOS:

1. Speed-power products of HMOS are four times better than those of standard NMOS.

$$NMOS \approx 4 \text{ pJ (pico Joules)}$$

$$HMOS \approx 1 \text{ pJ (pico Joules)}$$

2. Circuit densities of HMOS are approximately twice compared to those of standard NMOS:

$$NMOS = 4128 \ \mu m^2/\text{gate}$$

$$HMOS = 1852.5 \ \mu m^2/\text{gate}$$

where $1 \ \mu m$ (micrometer) $= 10^{-6}$ meter

The Intel 8086, Zilog Z8000, and the Motorola 68000 are typical examples of popular 16-bit microprocessors.

Since the 16-bit microprocessors can directly address large amounts of memory, the manufacturers of these microprocessors provide high-level

165

language compilers and interpreters on separate ROM chips. Typical compilers and interpreters include FORTRAN, BASIC, PL/M, and PASCAL. These ROM chips can be interfaced to the appropriate microprocessors to provide them with the capabilities of programming in high-level languages.

This chapter focuses on the architectures, instruction sets, CPU pins, and signals and interfacing characteristics of the 8086 and Z8000 microprocessors. Furthermore, enough material is included on each of the above 16-bit microprocessors along with some programming examples. This will help the reader to design simple systems using these processors. For more detailed information, the reader should consult the manufacturers' manuals.

6.1 Intel 8086*

The 8086 is the first 16-bit microprocessor. Its design is based on the 8080, but is not directly compatible with the 8080. The 8086 can directly address up to 1 megabyte of memory. The 8086 uses a paged memory. An interesting feature of the 8086 is that it prefetches up to six instruction bytes from memory and queues them in order to speed up instruction execution.

The 8086 family consists of two types of 16-bit microprocessors—the 8086 and 8088. They are closely related third-generation microprocessors. The fundamental difference is how the processors communicate to the outside world. The 8088 has an 8-bit external data path to memory and I/O, while the 8086 has a 16-bit external data path. In most other respects the processors are identical. No alterations are needed to run software written for one CPU on the other processor. Because of the similarities only the 8086 will be considered here.

An 8086 can be configured in a small uniprocessor minimal memory system (Figure 6.1) or in a multiprocessor system (Figure 6.2) capable of addressing up to a megabyte of memory. This wide range of applications is made possibly by the processor's dual operating mode (minimum and maximum mode) and built-in multiprocessing features. Some of the CPU pins have dual functions depending on the selection on the strapping pin. In minimum mode these pins transfer control signals directly to memory and input/output devices. In maximum mode, these same pins have different functions which facilitate medium to large systems, especially multiprocessor systems. In maximum mode, the control functions normally present in minimum mode are assumed by a support chip, the 8288 bus controller.

* This section contains material reprinted courtesy of Intel Corporation.

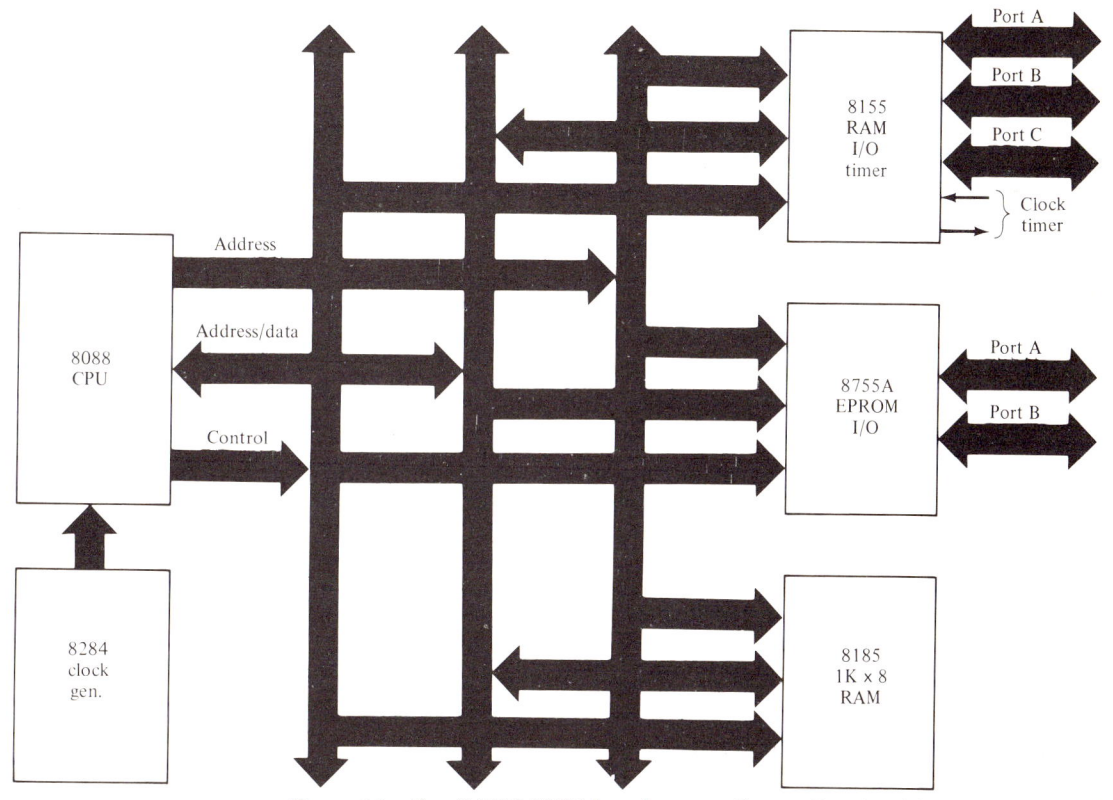

Figure 6.1 Small 8088/8086-based system. Source: Reprinted by permission of Intel Corporation, copyright © 1979.

Actual performance of the 8086 varies from application to application, but comparison to the industry standard 2-MHz 8080A shows the 8086 seven to ten times more powerful than the 8080A. Because of its 8-bit external data bus, the 8088 rates at about four to six times the 8080A's performance. In applications that manipulate 8-bit quantities extensively the 8088 comes close to the 8086's processing throughput.

The 8086 uses a 16-bit internal data path with a pipe-lined architecture that allows it to prefetch instructions during spare bus cycles. This, and a more compact instruction format enabling more instructions to be fetched in a given amount of time, contribute to the 8086's higher performance.

The 8086 is designed to provide direct hardware support for programs written in high-level languages such as PL/M and PASCAL. Routines with critical performance requirements that cannot be met with the high-level language may be written in assembly code and linked with the high-level language program.

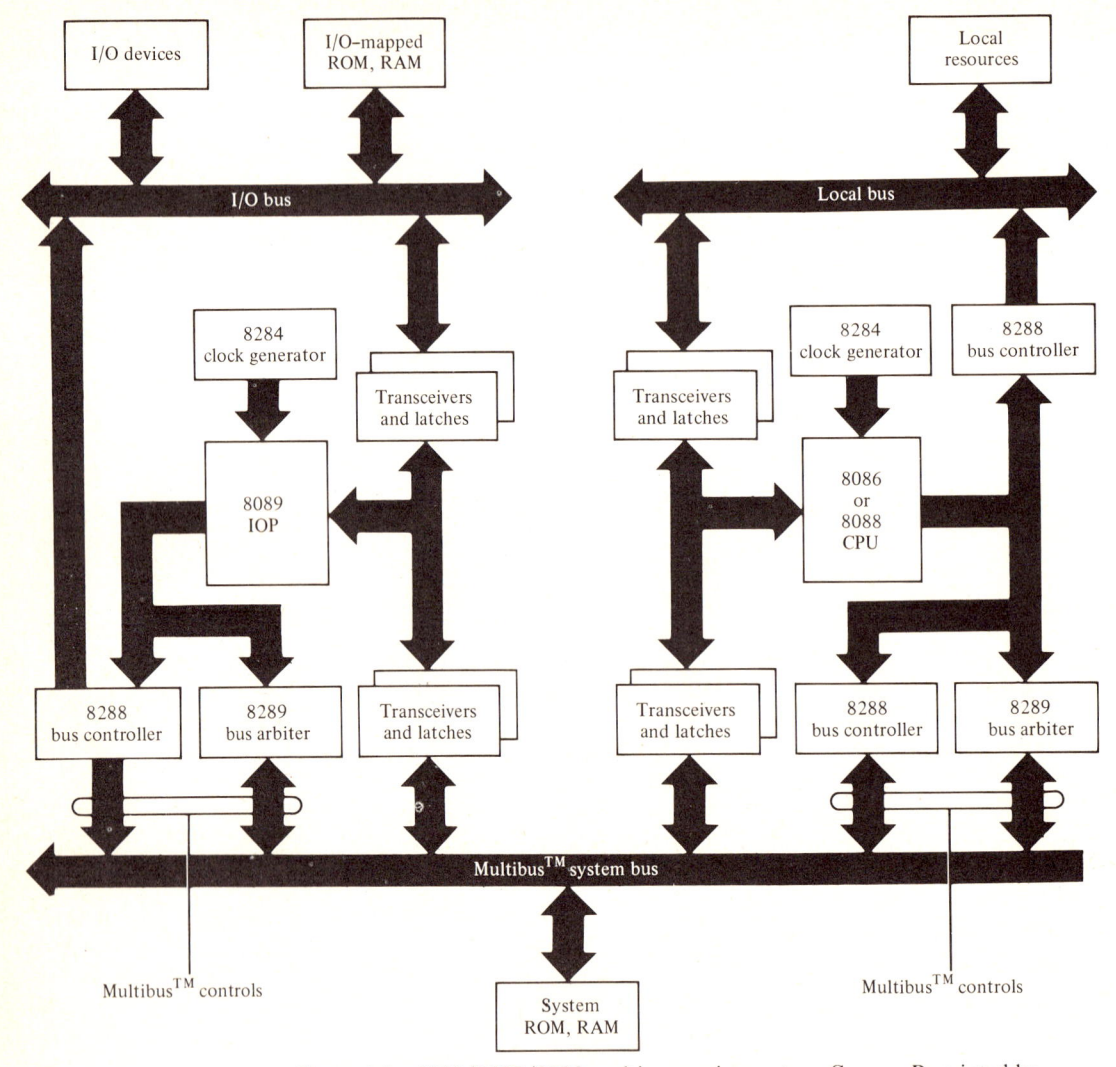

Figure 6.2 8086/8088/8089 multiprocessing system. Source: Reprinted by permission of Intel Corporation, copyright © 1979.

6.1.1 8086 Architecture

A simplified sequence of events for a microprocessor executing a program would go as follows:

1. Fetch the next instruction from memory.
2. Read an operand (if needed by instruction).
3. Execute the instruction.
4. Write the result (if required by instruction).

In most previous CPU architectures, these steps have been performed serially, or with only a single bus cycle fetch overlap. The 8086 architecture performs the same steps but allocates them to separate internal processing units. The Execution Unit (EU) executes instructions; the Bus Interface Unit (BIU) fetches instructions, reads operands, and writes results (Figure 6.3). These two units operate independently and in most cases extensively overlap instruction fetch with execution. The EU executes instructions that have already been fetched by the BIU so the instruction fetch time is essentially eliminated.

A 16-bit Arithmetic and Logic Unit (ALU) in the EU maintains the CPU status and control flags, and manipulates the general registers and instruction operands. The register and data paths in the EU are 16 bits wide for fast internal transfers.

The EU has no connection to the system bus, but obtains its instructions

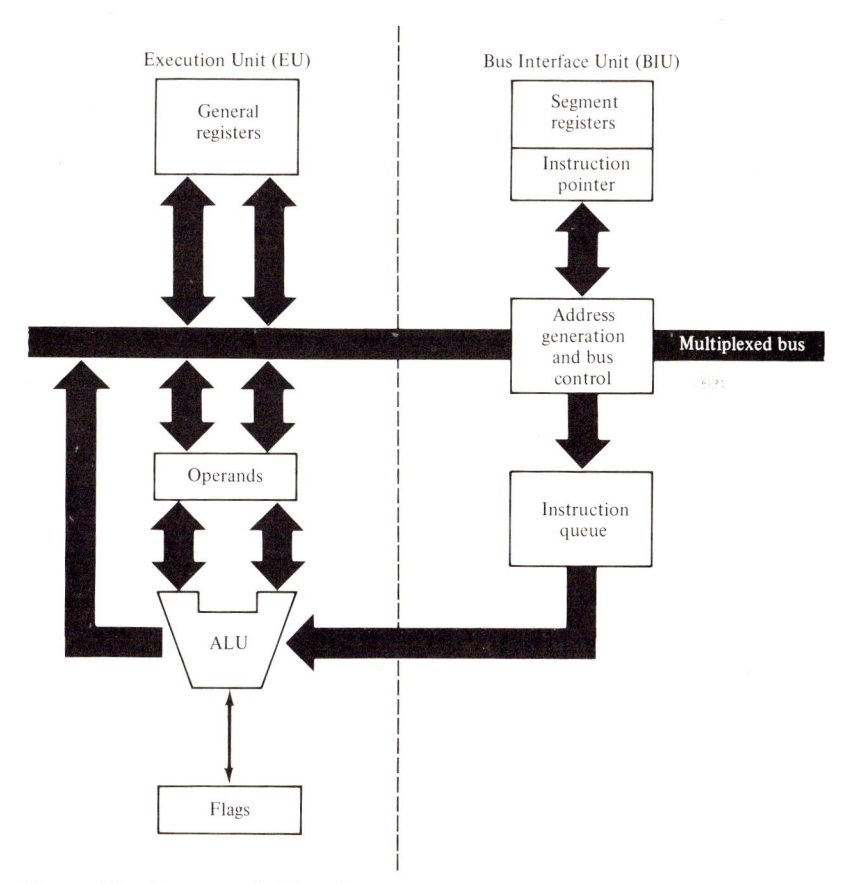

Figure 6.3 Processor division. Source: Reprinted by permission of Intel Corporation, copyright © 1979.

from a queue maintained by the BIU. When an instruction requires access to memory or some type of input/output, the EU requests the BIU to obtain or store the data. The EU only manipulates 16-bit addresses but the BIU can perform address relocation giving the EU access to a full megabyte of memory space. The BIU performs all bus operations for the EU. Data are transferred between the CPU and memory or peripheral devices when so demanded by the EU.

When the EU is executing instructions, the BIU is fetching more instructions from memory. The instructions are stored in an internal RAM array called the instruction stream queue. The 8086 queue can store up to six instruction bytes. The queue allows the BIU to keep the EU supplied with prefetched instructions under most conditions, without tying up the system bus.

Under most circumstances, the queue contains at least 1 byte of the sequence of instructions so the EU does not have to wait for instructions to be fetched. The instructions stored in the queue are those stored in memory locations immediately adjacent to and higher than the currently executing instruction. They are the next logical instructions if execution proceeds serially. If an instruction transfers control to another location, the BIU will reset the queue and begin refilling after passing the new instruction to the EU.

There are eight 16-bit registers in the EU. These registers are divided into two groups of four each: (1) the data registers (H and L group), and (2) the pointer and index registers (P and I group). Each data register can be used as two 8-bit registers or a one 16-bit register. The other CPU registers are always accessed as 16-bit units. There are two pointer registers: the Stack Pointer (SP) which contains the current stack address, and the Base Pointer (BP) which is usually used when the 8086 addresses memory. The two index registers, the Source Index (SI) and Destination Index (DI) are used in indexed addressing. All eight registers can be used as a so-called "accumulator."

The BIU contains four 16-bit segment registers and one 16-bit Instruction Pointer (IP). The IP is analogous to the 8080/8085 program counter. The 8086's megabyte of memory space is divided into segments of up to 64K bytes each. The CPU has direct access to four segments at a time. The base addresses for these four segments are contained in the segment registers. The Code Segment (CS) register points to current code segment from which instructions are fetched. The effective address of an instruction in the memory is obtained by adding the contents of CS to the contents of IP. The Stack Segment (SS) register points to the current stack segment. Stack operations will occur in this segment of memory. The effective address of the stack is obtained by adding the contents of SS to the contents of SP register in EU. The DS register points to the current data segment, where program variables are usually kept. The Extra Segment (ES)

```
AX  | AH | AL |  Accumulator
BX  | BH | BL |  Base
CX  | CH | CL |  Count
DX  | DH | DL |  Data
```

```
| SP |  Stack pointer
| BP |  Base pointer
| SI |  Source index
| DI |  Destination index
```

```
| IP    |  Instruction pointer
| FLAGS |  Status flags
```

```
| CS |  Code segment
| DS |  Data segment
| SS |  Stack segment
| ES |  Extra segment
```

Figure 6.4 Register structure. Source: Reprinted by permission of Intel Corporation, copyright © 1979.

register points to the current extra segment (fourth 64K block of memory) where data are typically stored. The segment registers are accessible to programs and can be manipulated in software. Figure 6.4 shows the 8086 register structure.

The 8086 has six 1-bit status flags (Figure 6.5). The EU sets/resets these flags to reflect certain properties of the results of arithmetic and logic operations. The flags can be used to alter a program's execution depending on their status. In general, the flags reflect the following conditions:

1. If AF (Auxiliary carry Flag) is set, there has been a carry out of the low nibble into the high nibble, or a borrow from the high nibble into the low nibble of an 8-bit quantity (low-order byte of a 16-bit quantity). This flag is used by decimal arithmetic instructions. (Bit 4 of the Flag register)
2. If CF (Carry Flag) is set, there has been a carry out of, or a borrow into, the high-order bit of the result (8- or 16-bit). The flag is used by instructions that add and subtract multibyte numbers. Rotate in-

```
Control flags         Status flags
| TF | DF | IF | OF | SF | ZF | AF | PF | CF |
                                           |— Carry
                                      |——— Parity
                                 |———————— Auxiliary carry
                            |————————————— Zero
                       |—————————————————— Sign
                  |——————————————————————— Overflow
        |———————————————————————————————— Interrupt enable
   |————————————————————————————————————— Direction
|——————————————————————————————————————— Trap
```

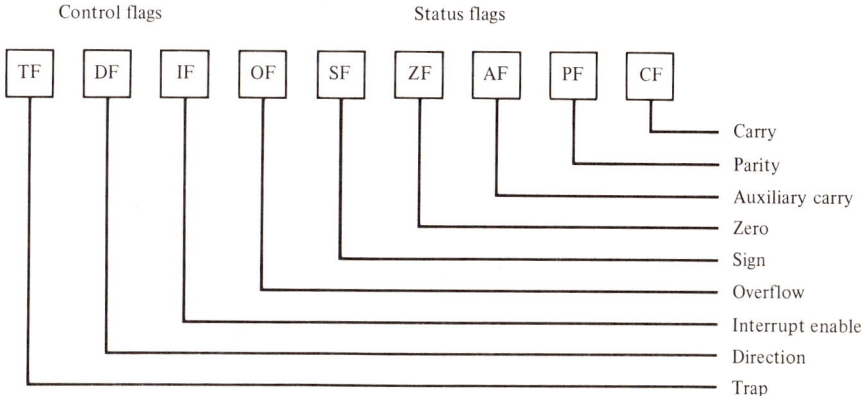

Figure 6.5 Flags. Source: Reprinted by permission of Intel Corporation, copyright © 1979.

structions can also isolate a bit in memory or a register by placing it in the carry flag. (Bit 0)

3. If OF (Overflow Flag) is set, an arithmetic overflow has occurred; that is, a significant digit has been lost because the size of the result exceeded the capacity of its destination location. An interrupt on overflow instruction is available that will generate an interrupt in this situation. (Bit 11)
4. If SF (Sign Flag) is set, the high-order bit of the result is a 1. Since negative binary numbers are represented in the 8086 in standard twos complement, SF indicates the sign of the result (0 = positive, 1 = negative). (Bit 7)
5. If PF (Parity Flag) is set, the result has even parity, an even number of 1 bits. This flag can be used to check for data transmission errors. (Bit 2)
6. If ZF (Zero Flag) is set, the result of the operation is 0. (Bit 6)

Three additional control flags can be set and cleared by programs to alter processor operations:

1. Setting DF (Direction Flag) causes string instructions to autodecrement, that is, to process strings from high addresses to low addresses, or from "right to left." Clearing DF causes string instructions to autoincrement, or to process strings from "left to right." (Bit 10)
2. Setting IF (Interrupt enable Flag) allows the CPU to recognize external (maskable) interrupt requests. Clearing IF disables these interrupts. IF has no effect on either nonmaskable external or internally generated interrupts. (Bit 9)
3. Setting TF (Trap Flag) puts the processor into the single-step mode for debugging. In this mode, the CPU automatically generates an internal interrupt after each instruction, allowing a program to be inspected as it executes instruction by instruction. (Bit 8)

The status flag is 16-bit long. But, only 9 bits are currently used. The 8086 stack is implemented in memory and is located by the stack segment register SS and the stack pointer register SP. A system can have an unlimited number of stacks that can be a maximum length of 64K bytes each. Going beyond the 64K causes an overwrite at the beginning of the stack. Only one stack is directly addressable at a time. SS contains the base address of the current stack and SP points to the Top Of the Stack (TOS).

The stack is 16 bits wide. The stack operations add and remove stack items one word at a time. Pushing an item on the stack decrements SP by 2 and then writes the item at the new TOS. An item is popped off the stack by copying it from TOS and then incrementing the SP by 2. Stack memory is never altered by popping the stack. The top of the stack changes only as a result of updating the stack pointer.

Two areas in extreme low and high memory are dedicated to specific processor functions or are reserved for use by hardware and software products, namely those produced by Intel. These locations are 00H–7FH (128 bytes) and FFFF0 through FFFFFH (16 bytes). These areas are used for interrupt and system reset processing. Using these areas may make a system incompatible with future Intel products.

6.1.2 Addressing Modes

The 8086 provides various ways to access instruction operands. Operands may be contained in registers, within the instruction op code, in memory, or in I/O ports. The addresses of memory and I/O port operands can be calculated in several different ways.

1. Register and Immediate Operands

Registers can be used for source operands, destination operands, or both. Immediate operands are constant data contained as part of the instruction. Data words may be 8- or 16-bit quantities.

2. Memory Addressing Modes

The EU has direct access to register and immediate operands but it cannot directly access memory. Memory operands must be transferred to or from the CPU over the bus. When the EU needs to read or write a memory operand, it must pass an offset value to the BIU. This offset is added to the content of a segment register (after shifting it four times to left) producing a 20-bit physical address and then executes the bus cycles needed to access the operand.

The EU calculates an offset for a memory operand which is called the operand's effective address or EA. It is a 16-bit number which represents the operand's distance in bytes from the beginning of the segment in which it resides. The EU can calculate the effective address in several different ways. Information encoded in the second byte of the instruction tells the EU how to calculate the effective address of each memory operand.

We now describe the memory addressing modes.

Direct Addressing

In direct addressing, the effective address is taken directly from the displacement field (8 or 16-bit) of the instruction. No registers are involved.

Register Indirect Addressing

The effective address of a memory operand may be taken directly from one of the base or index registers. One instruction can operate on many different memory locations if the value in the base or index register is updated appropriately. The Load Effective Address (LEA) and arithmetic instructions might be used to change the register value. Any 16-bit general register may be used for register indirect addressing with the JMP or CALL instructions.

Based Addressing

In based addressing, the effective address is the sum of a displacement value and the content of register BX or register BP. Specifying BP as a base register directs the BIU to obtain the operand from the current stack segment (unless a segment override prefix is present).

Indexed Addressing

In indexed addressing, the effective address is calculated from the sum of a displacement plus the content of an index register (SI or DI). Indexed addressing often is used to access elements in an array.

Based Indexed Addressing

An effective address is generated from the sum of a base register, an index register, and a displacement in based indexed addressing. Two address components can be varied at execution time.

String Addressing

String instructions use the index register implicitly instead of using normal addressing modes to access their operands. SI is assumed to point to the first byte or word of the source string, and DI is assumed to point to the first byte or word of the destination string when a string instruction is executed. The SI and DI are automatically adjusted to obtain subsequent bytes or words in repeated string operations.

3. I/O Port Addressing

In memory-mapped I/O, any memory addressing modes may be used to access the port. String instructions can also be used to transfer data to memory-mapped ports with an appropriate hardware interface. Two different addressing modes can be used to access ports located in the I/O space. In direct port addressing, the port number is an 8-bit immediate operand allowing fixed access to ports numbered 0–255. Indirect port addressing is similar to register indirect addressing of memory operands. The port number is taken from register DX allowing a range of 0 to 65,535. One instruction can access any port in the I/O space by previously adjusting the content of DX.

6.1.3 Instruction Set

The 8086 instruction set includes equivalents to the instructions typically found in previous microprocessors, such as the 8080/8085. Significant new operations include:

1. Multiplication and division of signed and unsigned binary numbers as well as unpacked decimal numbers.
2. Move, scan, and compare operations for strings up to 64K bytes in length.
3. Nondestructive bit testing.
4. Byte translation from one code to another.
5. Software-generated interrupts.
6. A group of instructions to help with coordinating the activities of multiprocessor systems.

Almost all instructions can operate on either byte (8-bit) or word (16-bit) data. Register, memory, and immediate operands may be specified interchangeably in most instructions. Memory variables can be added to, subtracted from, shifted, compared, and so on, in place, without moving them in and out of registers.

The 8086 has about 100 different instructions with about 300 different op codes.

1. Data Transfer Instructions (Figure 6.6)

The 14 data transfer instructions move single bytes and words between memory and registers as well as between register AL or AX and I/O ports. Stack manipulation instructions as well as instructions for transferring flag contents and for loading segment registers are included in this group.

	GENERAL PURPOSE
MOV	Move byte or word
PUSH	Push word onto stack
POP	Pop word off stack
XCHG	Exchange byte or word
XLAT	Translate byte
	INPUT/OUTPUT
IN	Input byte or word
OUT	Output byte or word
	ADDRESS OBJECT
LEA	Load Effective Address
LDS	Load pointer using DS
LES	Load pointer using ES
	FLAG TRANSFER
LAHF	Load AH register from flags
SAHF	Store AH register in flags
PUSHF	Push flags onto stack
POPF	Pop flags off stack

Figure 6.6 Data transfer instructions. Source: Reprinted by permission of Intel Corporation, copyright © 1979.

2. Arithmetic Instructions (Figure 6.7)

8086 arithmetic operations may be performed on four types of numbers: unsigned binary, signed binary (integers), unsigned packed decimal, and unsigned unpacked decimal. Binary numbers may be 8 or 16 bits long. Decimal numbers are stored in bytes, two digits per byte for packed decimal and one digit per byte for unpacked decimal. The processor assumes correct data format for the particular instruction execution desired.

In unsigned binary numbers, which may be 8 or 16 bits long, all bits are considered in determining a number's magnitude. Sixteen bits can represent values from 0 through 65,536. Addition, subtraction, multiplication, and division operations are available for unsigned binary numbers.

Signed binary numbers (integers) can also be 8 or 16 bits long. The high-order (left-most) bit is interpreted as the number's sign: 0 = positive, 1 = negative. Negative numbers are represented in standard twos complement notation. Since 1 bit is lost in sign representation, the range of an 8-bit integer is −128 to +127 and 16-bit integers may range from −32,768 to 32,767. Zero is considered a positive number. Multiplication and division operations are available for signed binary numbers. Addition and subtrac-

	ADDITION
ADD	Add byte or word
ADC	Add byte or word with carry
INC	Increment byte or word by 1
AAA	ASCII adjust for addition
DAA	Decimal adjust for addition
	SUBTRACTION
SUB	Subtract byte or word
SBB	Subtract byte or word with borrow
DEC	Decrement byte or word by 1
NEG	Negate byte or word
CMP	Compare byte or word
AAS	ASCII adjust for subtraction
DAS	Decimal adjust for subtraction
	MULTIPLICATION
MUL	Multiply byte or word unsigned
IMUL	Integer multiply byte or word
AAM	ASCII adjust for multiply
	DIVISION
DIV	Divide byte or word unsigned
IDIV	Integer divide byte or word
AAD	ASCII adjust for division
CBW	Convert byte to word
CWD	Convert word to doubleword

Figure 6.7 Arithmetic instructions. Source: Reprinted by permission of Intel Corporation, copyright © 1979.

tion operations are performed with the unsigned binary instructions. Therefore the overflow flag must be checked to determine the sign status of the result.

Packed decimal numbers are stored as unsigned byte quantities. The upper 4 bits are the high-order decimal digit while the lower 4 bits are the low-order decimal digit. The digits 0 to 9 are valid in each half-byte. The range of a packed decimal number is 0 to 99. Multiplication and division are not available for packed decimal numbers.

Unpacked decimal numbers are stored as unsigned byte quantities. The magnitude of the number is determined from the low-order half-byte while the upper 4 bits must remain 0 for multiplication and division instructions. The results of an arithmetic instruction set and reset the six status flags accordingly.

3. Bit Manipulation Instructions (Figure 6.8)

The 8086 provides three groups of instructions for manipulating bits within bytes or words. These are logicals, shifts, and rotates.

- Logicals. The logical instructions include the Boolean operators "not," "and," "exlusive or," and "inclusive or," plus a TEST instruction that sets the flags, but does not alter any of their operands.
- Shifts. Bits in bytes and words may be shifted arithmetically or logically. Up to 255 shifts can be performed depending on the values specified in the operand.
- Rotates. Bits in bytes and words may also be rotated. Bits rotated out of the operand are cycled around into the other end of the operand.

	Logicals
NOT	"Not" byte or word
AND	"And" byte or word
OR	"Inclusive or" byte or word
XOR	"Exclusive or" byte or word
TEST	"Test" byte or word
	Shifts
SHL / SAL	Shift logical / arithmetic left byte or word
SHR	Shift logical right byte or word
SAR	Shift arithmetic right byte or word
	Rotates
ROL	Rotate left byte or word
ROR	Rotate right byte or word
RCL	Rotate through carry left byte or word
RCR	Rotate through carry right byte or word

Figure 6.8 Bit manipulation instructions. Source: Reprinted by permission of Intel Corporation, copyright © 1979.

4. String Instructions (Figure 6.9)

Strings of up to 64K bytes may be manipulated with five basic string instructions, called primitives, allowing strings of bytes or words to be operated on one element at a time. Instructions are available to move, compare, and scan for a value as well as move string elements to and from the accumulator. These instructions contain prefixes which cause the instruction to be repeated in hardware, allowing long strings to be processed much faster than if done in a software loop.

5. Unconditional Transfers (Figure 6.10)

Unconditional transfer instructions can transfer control to a target instruction either in the current executing segment of memory or to a different code segment (called intrasegment and intersegment transfers, respectively).

6. Conditional Transfers (Figure 6.10)

These 18 instructions each test a different combination of flags for a condition and may or may not transfer control depending on the status of the CPU flags at the time the instruction is executed. The instruction transfers control if the condition is "true," otherwise it will pass to the instruction that follows the conditional jump.

All conditional jumps are relative and must be within -128 to $+127$ bytes of the first byte of the next instruction. They also must remain within the current executing code segment. Routines using conditional jumps can be used for position-independent coding since they are self-relative.

7. Interrupt Instructions (Figure 6.10)

Interrupt instructions allow interrupt service routines to be accessed by program control as well as by external hardware devices. The effect of a software-generated interrupt is similar to a hardware interrupt but no interrupt acknowledge but cycle is executed by the processor.

REP	Repeat
REPE/REPZ	Repeat while equal/zero
REPNE/REPNZ	Repeat while not equal/not zero
MOVS	Move byte or word string
MOVSB/MOVSW	Move byte or word string
CMPS	Compare byte or word string
SCAS	Scan byte or word string
LODS	Load byte or word string
STOS	Store byte or word string

Figure 6.9 String instructions. Source: Reprinted by permission of Intel Corporation, copyright © 1979.

UNCONDITIONAL TRANSFERS	
CALL	Call procedure
RET	Return from procedure
JMP	Jump
CONDITIONAL TRANSFERS	
JA/JNBE	Jump if above/not below nor equal
JAE/JNB	Jump if above or equal/not below
JB/JNAE	Jump if below/not above nor equal
JBE/JNA	Jump if below or equal/not above
JC	Jump if carry
JE/JZ	Jump if equal/zero
JG/JNLE	Jump if greater/not less nor equal
JGE/JNL	Jump if greater or equal/not less
JL/JNGE	Jump if less/not greater nor equal
JLE/JNG	Jump if less or equal/not greater
JNC	Jump if not carry
JNE/JNZ	Jump if not equal/nor zero
JNO	Jump if not overflow
JNP/JPO	Jump if not parity/parity odd
JNS	Jump if not sign
JO	Jump if overflow
JP/JPE	Jump if parity/parity even
JS	Jump if sign
ITERATION CONTROLS	
LOOP	Loop
LOOPE/LOOPZ	Loop if equal/zero
LOOPNE/LOOPNZ	Loop if not equal/not zero
JCXZ	Jump if register CX = 0
INTERRUPTS	
INT	Interrupt
INTO	Interrupt if overflow
IRET	Interrupt return

Figure 6.10 Transfer instructions. Source: Reprinted by permission of Intel Corporation copyright © 1979.

8. Processor Control Instructions (Figure 6.11)

These instructions allow control of various CPU functions. One group updates flags and another group is used primarily for synchronizing the 8086 with external events. The NOP causes the CPU to do nothing.

6.1.4 Input/Output

1. Programmed I/O

The 8086 I/O space can accommodate up to 64K byte I/O locations which can be configured as 64K 8-bit ports or up to 32K 16-bit ports. The IN and OUT instructions transfer data between the accumulator (AL for byte transfers, AX for word transfers) and ports located in the I/O space. To access a port, the BIU places the port address (0–64K) on the lower 16 lines of the address bus. Different forms of the I/O instructions allow the address to be specified directly or taken from register DX.

The 8086 can transfer either 8 or 16 bits at a time to a device located in the I/O space. A 16-bit device should be located at an even address so that the word will be transferred in a single bus cycle. An 8-bit device may be located at either an even or odd address. The internal registers in a given device must be assigned all even or all odd addresses. I/O devices may be placed in 8086 memory space. As long as they respond as memory the processor does not know the difference. This allows more programming flexibility as all memory reference instructions are now essentially I/O instructions.

2. Direct Memory Access (DMA)

When the 8086 is configured in minimum mode, the HOLD (hold) and HLDA (hold acknowledge) signals can be used to control the system bus

	FLAG OPERATIONS
STC	Set carry flag
CLC	Clear carry flag
CMC	Complement carry flag
STD	Set direction flag
CLD	Clear direction flag
STI	Set interrupt enable flag
CLI	Clear interrupt enable flag
	EXTERNAL SYNCHRONIZATION
HLT	Halt until interrupt or reset
WAIT	Wait for $\overline{\text{TEST}}$ pin active
ESC	Escape to external processor
LOCK	Lock bus during next instruction
	NO OPERATION
NOP	No operation

Figure 6.11 Processor control instructions. Source: Reprinted by permission of Intel Corporation, copyright © 1979.

for DMA applications. The 8086 addresses memory that is physically organized in two separate banks, one containing even-addressed bytes and one containing odd-addressed bytes. An 8-bit DMA controller must alternatively select these banks to access logically adjacent bytes in memory.

3. 8089 Input/Output Processor (IOP)

The 8089 is designed to be used in conjunction with the 8086. It conceptually resembles a microprocessor with two DMA channels and an instruction set specifically tailored for I/O operations. The 8089 can service I/O devices directly, removing this task from the CPU. It can transfer data on its own bus or on the system bus. It can match 8- or 16-bit peripherals to 8- or 16-bit buses and can transfer data from memory to memory and from I/O device to I/O device.

4. Interrupts

The 8086 assigns every interrupt a type code so the CPU can identify it. It can handle up to 256 different interrupt types. Interrupts can be initiated by devices external to the CPU or triggered by software interrupt instructions.

a. External Interrupts. The 8086 has two lines that devices may use to signal interrupts. These are interrupt request (INTR), and Non-Maskable Interrupt (NMI). When INTR is active, the CPU will respond according to the state of the Interrupt enable Flag (IF). No action will occur until the current executing instruction is completed. INTR is not latched so it must be held high until recognized. The CPU acknowledges the interrupt request by executing two consecutive interrupt acknowledge (INTA) bus cycles. The first cycle signals that the interrupt request has been honored. In the second cycle the processor reads the data-bus-expected type code between 0 and 255 to show which device is requesting service. The CPU uses this type code to call the corresponding interrupt procedure.

NMI is edge triggered and is generally used to trigger a "catastrophic" event since it cannot be masked. The catastrophic events usually include power failure, memory error detection, or bus parity error. The NMI interrupt takes priority over INTR.

b. Internal Interrupts. An interrupt (INT) instruction causes an interrupt to be generated at the end of executing the instruction. The type code is specified as part of the instruction. The INT can be used to test an interrupt service routine written for an external interrupt.

If the OF is set, the interrupt on overflow (INTO) instruction generates a type 4 interrupt immediately upon completion of its execution. The CPU itself generates a type 0 interrupt immediately following execution of a

DIV or IDIV (divide or integer divide) instruction if the calculated quotient is larger than the specified destination.

If the Trap Flag (TF) is set, the CPU automatically generates a type 1 interrupt following every instruction. This single-step execution is a powerful debugging tool.

All internal interrupts (INTO, INT, divide error, and single-step) have the following characteristics:

- The interrupt type code is contained in the instruction or is predefined.
- No INTA bus cycles are run.
- Internal interrupts cannot be disabled except for single-step.
- Any internal interrupt (except single-step) has higher priority than any external interrupt. If an interrupt occurs on NMI or INTR while an instruction is executed which causes an internal interrupt, the internal interrupt will be serviced first.

c. Interrupt Pointer Table. The interrupt pointer (interrupt vector) table is the link between an interrupt type code and processing of the interrupt that is associated with that code. The interrupt pointer table can use up to the first 1K bytes of low memory. There may be up to 256 entries in the table, one for each type that can occur in the system. Each entry in the table is a 32-bit address of the service routine where control will be transferred. The higher word is the base address of the segment, while the low word is the address within the 64K segment.

d. Interrupt Procedures. When an interrupt service procedure is entered, the flags, CS, and IP are pushed onto the stack and TF and IF are cleared. The STI (set interrupt enable flag) instruction will reenable external interrupts allowing itself to be interrupted by a request on INTR. An interrupt procedure is always interrupted by a request on NMI. Software interrupts occurring during the procedure will also interrupt the procedure. Enough stack space must be available to accommodate the maximum depth of interrupt nesting that can occur in the system.

Interrupt procedures should be terminated with an IRET (interrupt return) instruction. It pops the top three stack words into the IP, CS, and the flags, thus returning to the next instruction to be executed when interrupted.

e Single-Step (Trap) Interrupt. When the trap flag is set the 8086 is said to be in the single-step mode. In this mode the processor generates a type 1 interrupt after every instruction. Since the CPU automatically pushes the flags onto the stack then clears TF and IF, the processor will not be in the single-step mode when going to the interrupt procedure. Returning from the single-step interrupt procedure will restore the TF flag, putting it back in the single-step mode.

To set or clear TF, the flag image on the stack, must be modified since no 8086 instructions exist for this purpose.

f. Breakpoint Interrupt. Breakpoints are typically inserted into programs during debugging as a way of displaying or modifying registers, memory locations, and so on. It can be inserted anywhere in the program. A type 3 interrupt is dedicated to the breakpoint. The INT3 (breakpoint) instruction is 1 byte long. This makes it easier to insert a breakpoint into the program when debugging.

6.1.5 8086 Pins and Signals (Figure 6.12)

AD0–AD15 lines are a 16-bit multiplexed address/data bus. During the first clock cycle AD0–AD15 are the low order 16-bits of address. The 8086 has a total of 20 address lines. The upper four are multiplexed with the status signals for the CPU. These are the A16/S3, A17/S4, A18/S5, and A19/S6. During the first clock signal the entire 20-bit address is available on the combination of these lines. During the other clock cycles of the system AD0–AD15 contain the 16-bit data bus and S3, S4, S5, S6 are status lines decoded as follows:

A17/S4	A16/S3	FUNCTION
0	0	Extra segment
0	1	Stack segment
1	0	Code or no segment
1	1	Data segment

- A18/S5 provides the status of the 8086 interrupt enable flag and A19/S6 may be used for controlling the system bus.
- BHE/S7 is used as bus high enable during the first clock period of an instruction. This signal can be used, along with AD0 for selecting memory banks. S7 is undefined.
- RD is low whenever the processor is reading data from memory or an I/O location.
- READY is used by slow external devices to inform the processor to insert wait states into the execution cycle.
- TEST is used by the WAIT instruction. The processor enters a wait state after execution of the WAIT instruction until a low is seen on TEST.
- INTR is the maskable interrupt input. This line is not latched so INTR must be held at a high level until recognized to generate an interrupt.
- NMI is the nonmaskable interrupt input activated by a leading edge. The interrupt address vector is 00008H.

Chapter 6 INTEL 8086 AND ZILOG Z8000

COMMON SIGNALS		
NAME	FUNCTION	TYPE
AD15–AD0	Address/data bus	Bidirectional, tristate
A19/S6–A16/S3	Address/status	Output, tristate
$\overline{BHE}$/S7	Bus high enable/status	Output, tristate
MN/$\overline{MX}$	Minimum/maximum mode control	Input
$\overline{RD}$	Read control	Output, tristate
TEST	Wait on test control	Input
READY	Wait state control	Input
RESET	System reset	Input
NMI	Nonmaskable interrupt request	Input
INTR	Interrupt request	Input
CLK	System clock	Input
V_{CC}	+5 V	Input
GND	Ground	

MINIMUM MODE SIGNALS (MN/$\overline{MX}$ = V_{CC})

Name	Function	Type
HOLD	Hold request	Input
HLDA	Hold acknowledge	Output
$\overline{WR}$	Write control	Output, tristate
M/$\overline{IO}$	Memory/IO control	Output, tristate
DT/$\overline{R}$	Data transmit/receive	Output, tristate
$\overline{DEN}$	Data enable	Output, tristate
ALE	Address latch enable	Output
$\overline{INTA}$	Interrupt acknowledge	Output

MAXIMUM MODE SIGNALS (MN/$\overline{MX}$ = GND)

NAME	FUNCTION	TYPE
$\overline{RQ}/\overline{GT}$1,0	Request/grant bus access control	Bidirectional
$\overline{LOCK}$	Bus priority lock control	Output, tristate
$\overline{S2}$–$\overline{S0}$	Bus cycle status	Output, tristate
QS1, QS0	Instruction queue status	Output

```
GND   1      40  Vcc
AD14  2      39  AD15
AD13  3      38  A16/S3
AD12  4      37  A17/S4
AD11  5      36  A18/S5
AD10  6      35  A19/S6
AD9   7      34  BHE/S7
AD8   8      33  MN/MX
AD7   9      32  RD
AD6  10 8086 31  HOLD   (RQ/GT0)
AD5  11 CPU  30  HLDA   (RQ/GT1)
AD4  12      29  WR     (LOCK)
AD3  13      28  M/IO   (S2)
AD2  14      27  DT/R   (S1)
AD1  15      26  DEN    (S0)
AD0  16      25  ALE    (QS0)
NMI  17      24  INTA   (QS1)
INTR 18      23  TEST
CLK  19      22  READY
GND  20      21  RESET
```

MAXIMUM MODE PIN FUNCTIONS (e.g., $\overline{LOCK}$) ARE SHOWN IN PARENTHESES

Figure 6.12 8086 pins and signals. Source: Reprinted by permission of Intel Corporation, copyright © 1979.

RESET is the system reset signal. This signal must be active for four clock cycles to be recognized. It causes the 8086 to fetch and execute the instruction at location FFFF0H.

MN/$\overline{\text{MX}}$ is an input used to select the CPU structure. When MN/$\overline{\text{MX}}$ is high it is in the minimum mode. In this mode the 8086 is configured to support small, single-processor systems using a few devices that use the system bus.

When MN/$\overline{\text{MX}}$ is low the 8086 is configured in the maximum mode. In this case the Intel 8288 bus controller is added to provide sophisticated bus controls and compatibility with the multibus architecture.

In minimum mode, the 8086 itself generates all bus control signals. These signals are:

DT/R   (Data transmit/receive)
DEN   (Data enable)
ALE   (Address Latch Enable)
M/IO   (Memory/I/O control)
WR   (Write)
INTA   (Interrupt acknowledge)
HOLD   (Hold)
HLDA   (Hold acknowlege)

In maximum mode, the 8288 Bus controller uses S0, S1, and S2 status bit outputs from the 8086 to generate all bus control and command output signals required for a bus cycle.

RQ/GT0 and RQ/GT11 provide 8086's bus access control in maximum mode.
LOCK output used in conjunction with the 8289 bus arbiter guarantees exclusive access of a shared system bus.
QS1 and QS0 (Queue Status) allow external monitoring of the internal instruction queue RAM.
CLK is an input requiring an externally generated clock source.

EXAMPLE 6.1

Write a program in 8086 assembly language to add two BCD numbers and store the result in a location addressed by the DI register.

SOLUTION

```
CLC          ; Clear carry
MOV AL,(SI)  ; Load first data
```

```
              ADC AL,(DI)  ; Add second data
              DAA          ; Decimal adjust
              MOV(DI),AL   ; Store result
       START: JMP START    ; Halt
```

EXAMPLE 6.2*

Write a program in 8086 assembly language to perform 32 bit by 32 bit unsigned multiplication. Assume that the BX register points to this block. Also assume that the data has the following form (see Figure 6.13)

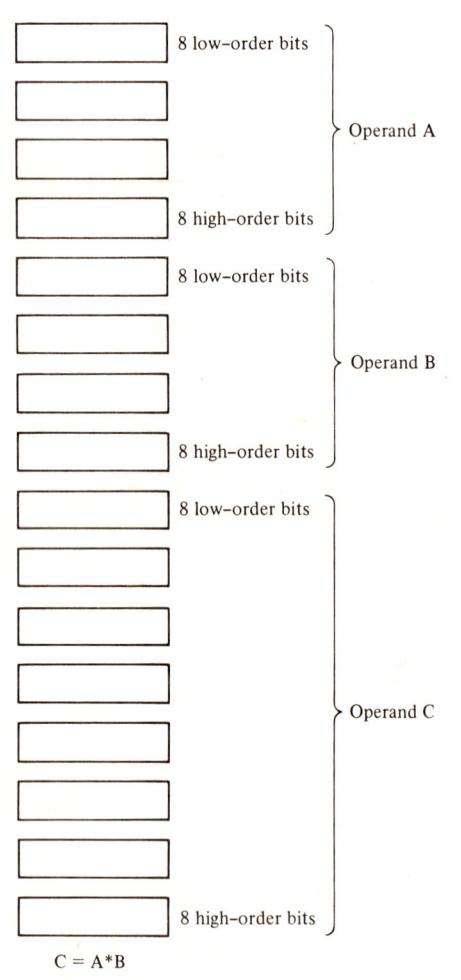

C = A*B

Figure 6.13 32-bit × 32-bit unsigned multiplication.

* Source: *The 8086 Book* by R. Rector and G. Alexy, 1980. Reprinted by permission of Osborne/McGraw-Hill.

SOLUTION

The assembly language program is given below:

	MOV	AX, (BX)	; MULTIPLY LOW-ORDER 16 BITS
	MUL	(BX + 4)	; BY LOW-ORDER 16 BITS
	MOV	(BX + 8), AX	; SAVE RESULT, WHICH IS IN AX
	MOV	(BX + 10), DX	; AND DX
	MOV	AX, (BX)	; MULTIPLY LOW-ORDER 16 BITS OF OPERAND A BY HIGH-ORDER 16 BITS
	MUL	(BX + 6)	; OF OPERAND B
	ADD	(BX + 10), AX	; ADD TO PREVIOUS RESULT
	ADC	(BX + 12), DX	; ASSUME RESULT BYTES
	JNC	NEXT$SMUL	; ARE INITIALLY ZERO
	INC	(BX + 14)	
NEXT$SMUL:	MOV	AX, (BX + 2)	; MULTIPLY HIGH ORDER 16 BITS OF OPERAND A BY LOW-ORDER 16 BITS
	MUL	(BX + 4)	; OF OPERAND B
	ADD	(BX + 10), AX	; ADD TO PREVIOUS RESULT
	ADC	(BX + 12), DX	
	INC	HIGH$ORDER$SMUL	
	INC	(BX + 14)	; SAVE CARRY
HIGH$ORDER $SMUL	MOV	AX, (BX + 2)	; MULTIPLY HIGH-ORDER 16 BITS OF OPERAND A BY HIGH-ORDER 16 BITS OF OPERAND B
	MUL	(BX + 6)	; BITS OF OPERAND B
	ADD	(BX + 12), AX	; ADD TO PREVIOUS RESULT
	ADC	(BX + 14), DX	; ADD TO PREVIOUS RESULT
	RET		

6.2 Zilog Z8000*

The Z8000 is a 16-bit microprocessor manufactured by Zilog and second sourced by Advanced Micro Devices. There are two versions of the Z8000: the Z8001 48-pin segmented CPU and the Z8002 40-pin nonsegmented CPU. They differ only in the manner and range of memory addressing.

The Z8001 and Z8002 are two different chips but are both referred to as "Z8000." The main difference is the addressable memory space of each processor. The Z8000's are both register oriented. The Z8002 contains 21 16-bit registers, 14 of which can be considered to be general purpose, because they store either data or addresses. There is a system and a normal stack pointer, flag word, program counter, refresh counter, instruction register, and a status pointer. The Z8002 is the nonsegmented version of the Z8000 family. It does not have segment registers and cannot use segmented addresses to address memory. Thus it can only address 64K bytes of memory (the program counter is 16 bits).

The Z8001 is the segmented CPU chip, and as with the 8086, a memory address is determined by both a segment value and an effective or offset address. The Z8001, using a 7-bit segment value and a 16-bit offset, can address 8 megabytes of memory. The segment value and effective address are not added internally, thus external logic is required.

The Z8000 family, like the 8086, has both standard I/O and memory-mapped I/O. The Z8001 and Z8002 (to be called Z8001/2 from this point) have many general-purpose registers and a powerful instruction set. They can operate on bit, byte, word, long-word (32 bits), and quad-word (64 bits) value. Most of the instructions use 8- and 16-bit values.

The Z8001/2 have the standard data transfer, math and logic instructions, bit, processor control, and control transfer instructions. The Z8001/2 also have multiplication and division instructions, including 32-bit multiply and divide. The processors have block transfer and string manipulation instructions, some of which can autoincrement and decrement pointers. The processors also incorporate a number of I/O and processor control instructions.

The Z8001/2 operate in one of two modes: system (privileged) or normal (nonprivileged). The CPU is in the normal mode when executing the user's program. In the normal mode, only a subset of the processors' instructions can be executed. I/O and some of the processors' control instructions cannot be executed. The CPU is in the system mode when executing the operating system software. In the system mode, all instructions can be executed.

6.2.1 Z8000 CPU Organization

The Z8000 CPU is organized around a general-purpose register file (Figure 6.14). The register file is a group of registers, any one of which can

---

* This section contains material reprinted courtesy of Zilog, Inc., and Advanced Micro Devices, Inc.

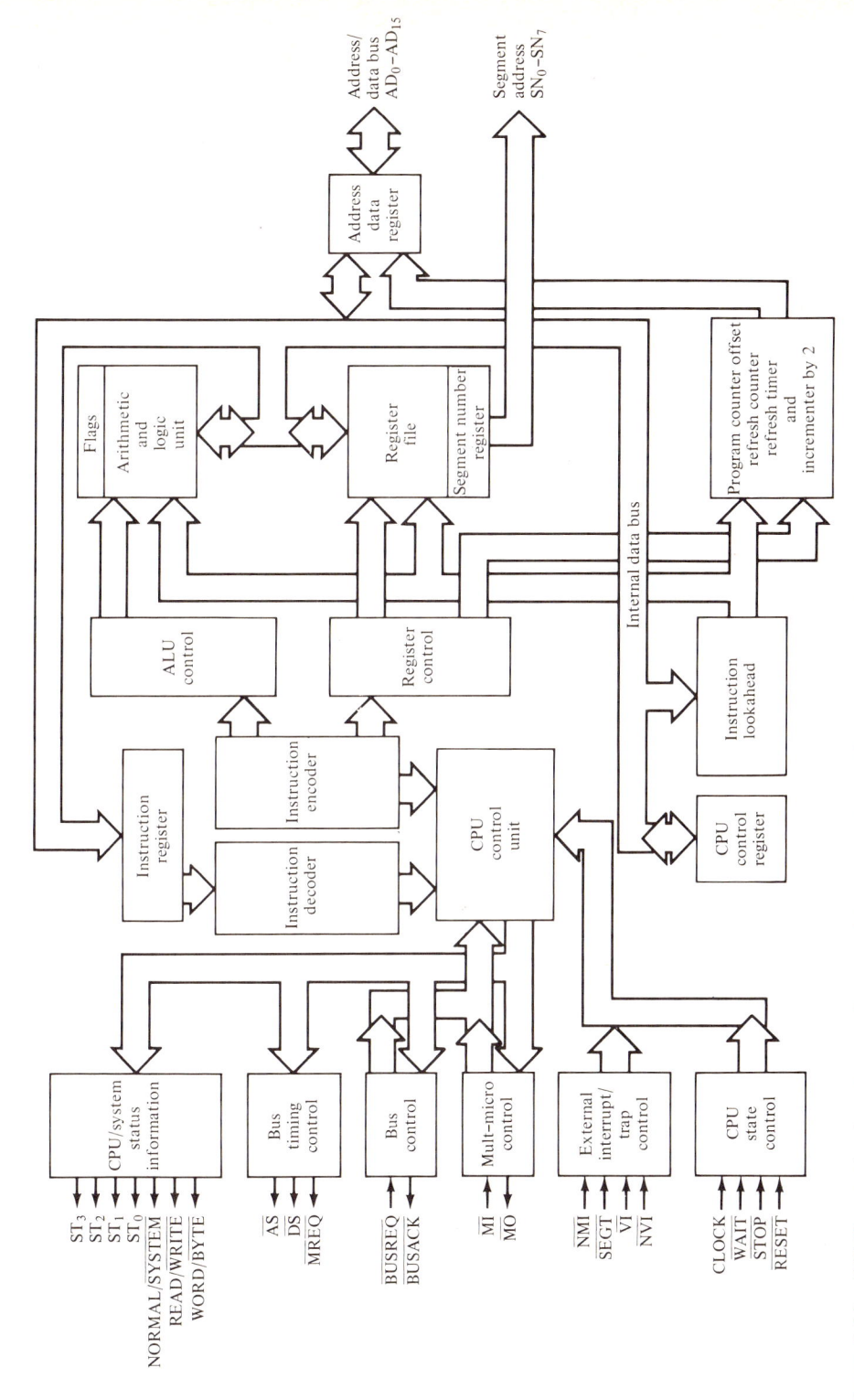

Figure 6.14 Z8000 organization. Source: Reprinted by permission of Zilog, Inc., copyright © 1981.

be used as an accumulator, index register, memory pointer, stack pointer, and so on. The only exception is register 0, as will be explained later. In addition, the registers of the Z8000 are organized to process 8-bit bytes, 16-bit words, 32-bit long words, and 64-bit quadruple words.

Although all registers can—in general—be used for any purpose, certain instructions such as subroutine call and string translation make use of specific registers in the general register file, and this must be taken into account when these instructions are used.

The Z8000 CPU also contains a number of special-purpose registers in addition to the general-purpose ones. These include the program counter, program status registers, and the refresh counter. These registers are accessible through software and provide some of the interesting features of Z8000 CPU architecture.

6.2.2 Register Architecture

The Z8001/2 have a number of 16-bit registers (Figure 6.14). When these registers are used with 16-bit quantities, they are labeled R0–R15. R15 is the normal stack pointer and R15' is used for the system mode stack pointer. In the Z8001, two additional registers, R14 and R14', are also used to store segment values for two stack pointers. For byte operations, each of the first eight registers is divided into two 8-bit registers. Thus, R0 is divided into RH0 and RL0. For long-word operations (32-bit), two 16-bit registers are grouped together such that R0 and R1 become RR0. In this case, the most significant bits are stored in the even-numbered register while the least significant bits are stored in the odd-numbered word. For 64-bit operations, four registers are grouped together. The most significant bits are stored in the lowest even-numbered register and the least significant bits reside in the highest odd-numbered register. The registers are not assigned a specific function. Any register can be used to store a count, displacement, offset, or base register. But stack operations always use R15 and R15' (and R14 and R14' in the Z8001).

Since the Z8001 has to specify a segment value, the registers are used in a slightly different manner. In many instructions, two registers in the Z8001 have to be used to store a memory address, rather than one register as in the Z8002. One register contains the 7-bit segment value, while the other register has the 16-bit displacement, offset, or effective address.

The Z8000 processors have a flag and control word, program status area pointer, and a refresh counter (register), along with a program counter and instruction register. The program status registers refer to the grouping of the Flag and Control Word (FCW) and the Program Counter (PC). The Program Status Area Pointer (PSAP) is primarily used when the microprocessor is interrupted. The refresh counter is used by the Z8001/2 processors to automatically refresh dynamic memory. The time between refresh cycles can be adjusted for different memories by loading the refresh counter. Automatic refresh can be disabled if desired.

The FCW contains six condition code flags. Most of these flags can be tested by transfer of control instructions. The six flags (which are in the least significant byte of the FCW) are the Carry (C), Zero (Z), Sign (S), parity/overflow (P/V), Decimal Adjust (DA), and Half-carry (H) flags.

The most significant byte of the FCW contains control bits. The segmentation bit (SEG, Z8001 only) allows the Z8001 to operate in the unsegmented mode so it can execute Z8002 programs. The Normal/System (N/S) flag indicates the present mode of the processor.

The Vectored Interrupt Enable (VIE) and Non-Vectored Interrupt Enable (NVIE) flags control whether or not the microprocessor will be interrupted by signals coming in on these pins. Figure 6.15 shows the Z8000 register structure.

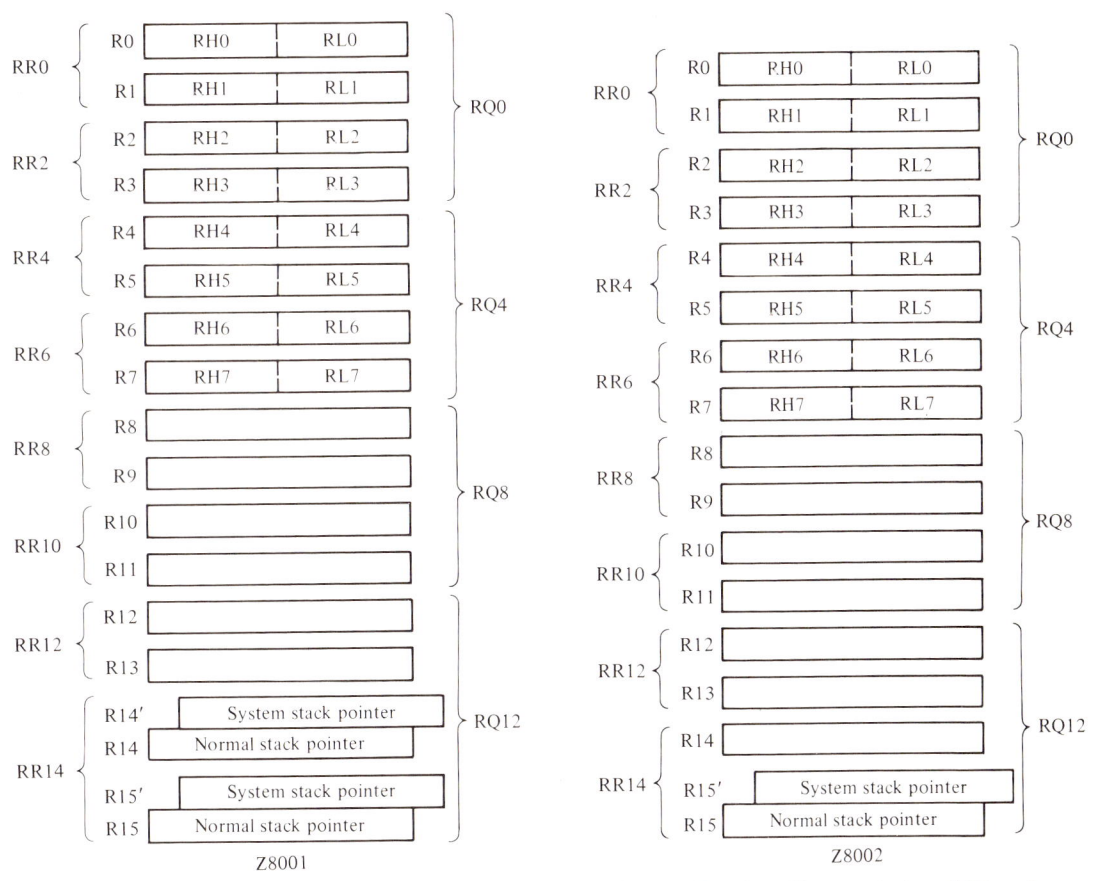

Figure 6.15 Register structure. Source: Reprinted by permission of Zilog, Inc., copyright © 1981.

6.2.3 Addressing Modes

Memory addressing for the Z8002 is straightforward since it only addresses 64K memory spaces. It just has to generate a 16-bit address which can be fully contained in a single register or memory location, or in the instruction itself (Figure 6.16).

The Z8001 can address 8 megabytes of memory so it must generate a

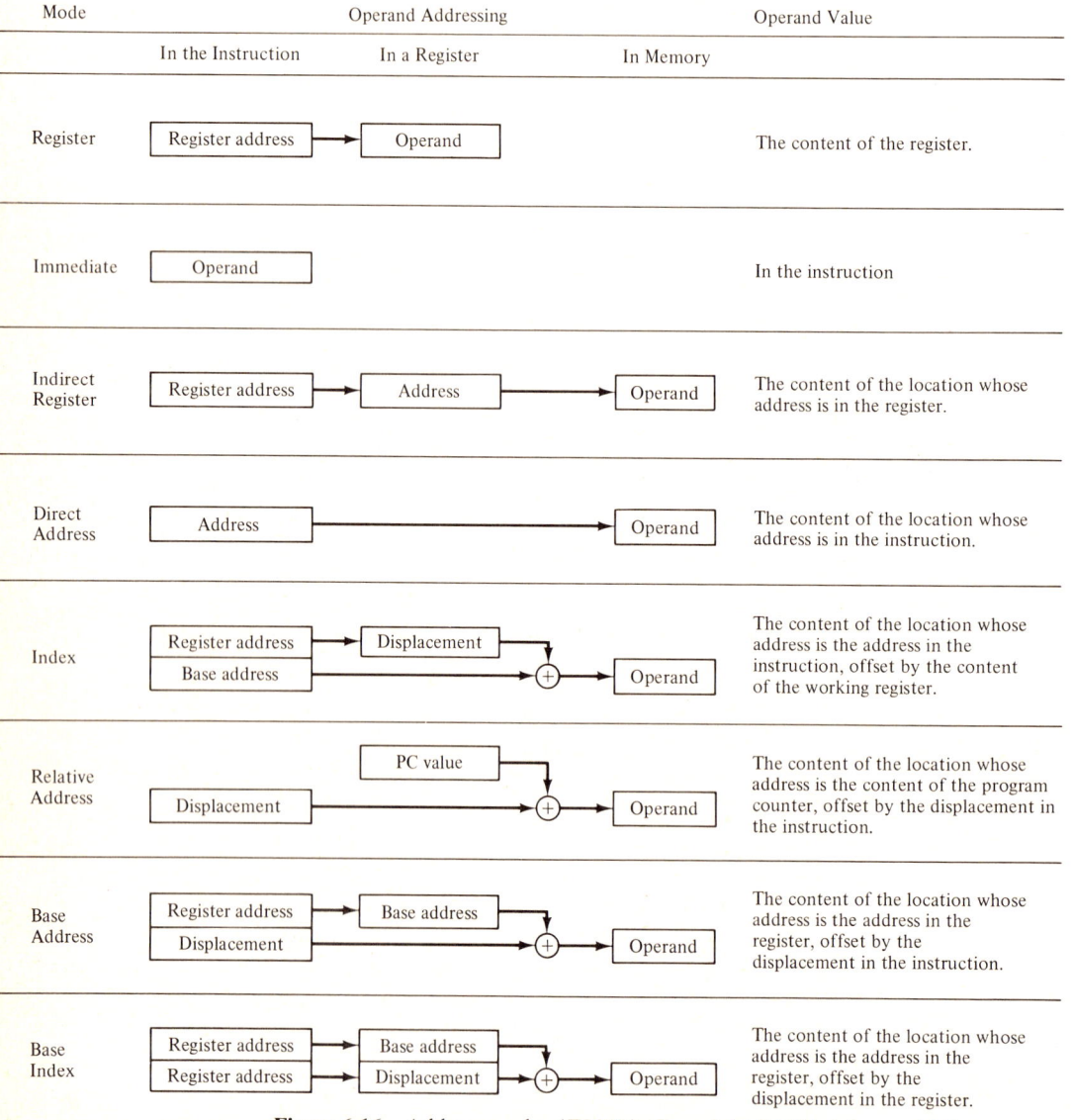

Mode	Operand Addressing			Operand Value
	In the Instruction	In a Register	In Memory	
Register	Register address → Operand			The content of the register.
Immediate	Operand			In the instruction
Indirect Register	Register address → Address → Operand			The content of the location whose address is in the register.
Direct Address	Address → Operand			The content of the location whose address is in the instruction.
Index	Register address / Base address → Displacement ⊕ → Operand			The content of the location whose address is the address in the instruction, offset by the content of the working register.
Relative Address	Displacement → PC value ⊕ → Operand			The content of the location whose address is the content of the program counter, offset by the displacement in the instruction.
Base Address	Register address / Displacement → Base address ⊕ → Operand			The content of the location whose address is the address in the register, offset by the displacement in the instruction.
Base Index	Register address / Register address → Base address / Displacement ⊕ → Operand			The content of the location whose address is the address in the register, offset by the displacement in the register.

Figure 6.16 Address modes (Z8002). Copyright © 1981 Advanced Micro Devices, Inc. Reproduced with permission of copyright owner. All rights reserved.

7-bit segment number along with the 16-bit offset. The 7-bit segment number must be used by external memory management hardware. This hardware combines the 16-bit offset and generates the 23-bit memory address. The memory management hardware could consist of the special function 8010 memory management unit chip, or it could be built with standard TTL logic.

To address an I/O device a 16-bit port address is either contained within an instruction or in a general-purpose register. This allows 64K addressable I/O ports without interfering with the memory space of the processor. All I/O instructions are privileged so they can only be expected when the processor is in the system mode.

The Z8001/2 do not have special base and index registers. These values are taken from the processors' general-purpose registers. A 4-bit field in the op code is used to indicate which register contains the base address, index, displacement, absolute address, I/O address, or count. A brief description of the various addressing modes is given below:

1. *Register addressing*. In this mode, the instruction contains a register address of a register containing the operand.
2. *Immediate addressing*. In immediate addressing the instruction contains an 8-, 16-, or 32-bit operand.
3. *Indirect addressing*. In this mode, a general-purpose register defined in the instruction contains a memory address. For the Z8002, this address is stored in a 16-bit register. On the other hand, for the Z8001, two registers are required for this address; one register is used for the offset and the other for the segment value.
4. *Direct addressing*. In direct addressing, the address is part of the instruction.
5. *Indexed addressing*. For the Z8002, the effective memory address is determined by adding the contents of a general-purpose register to a 16-bit address specified in the instruction.
   For the Z8001, a 16-bit number is first obtained by adding the contents of a general-purpose register and a 16-bit offset contained in the instruction. This 16-bit number along with a 7-bit segment number specified in the instruction is used to determine effective address.
6. *Based addressing*. In based addressing, the effective address is the sum of an address (called the base address) contained in a specified register and a displacement defined in the instruction. In based indexed addressing, the effective address is the sum of a displacement and an address (called base address)—both contained in registers as specified in the instruction.
7. *Relative addressing*. In relative addressing, an 8- or 16-bit signed displacement is added to the updated program counter. This mode is available for jump and call relative instructions.

6.2.4 Instruction Set

The main difference between Z8001 and Z8002 is the addressing capability of different memory sizes. The processors execute similar instructions.

An interesting feature of the Z8000 is the extended instruction facility where the basic instructions such as the floating-point arithmetic, data base search, and so on, are stored. When the CPU encounters an extended instruction op code, it tells the external device, called the Extended Processing Unit (EPU), to execute it. The EPU helps the CPU perform complex and time-consuming tasks in order to unburden the CPU. Table 6.1 lists all the abbreviations used in the subsequent figures for instructions. Some typical Z8000 instructions are discussed below.

Table 6.1. Abbreviations Used

ADDRESSING MODE	
ABBREVIATION	MEANING
R	Register
IM	Immediate
IR	Indirect register
DA	Direct addressing
X	Indexed
RA	Relative addressing
BA	Base addressing
BX	Base indexed addressing

SEGMENTATION INFORMATION	
ABBREVIATION	MEANING
S	Segmented (Z8001)
NS	Nonsegmented (Z8002)
SS or SSO	Segmented, short offset (Z8001)
SL or SLO	Segmented, long offset (Z8001)

GENERAL INFORMATION
Numbers to the right of instructions are the number of clock cycles required to execute it.
Letters and symbols just above or to the right of each instruction op code are the format of the instruction (mnemonic) to be used when writing programs.

OPERAND INFORMATION	
ABBREVIATION	MEANING
dst	Destination
src	Source
R	Register
cc	Condition code (for decision-making instructions
n	An integer
IM	Immediate data value

Source: Reprinted by permission of Zilog, Inc., copyright © 1981.

N registers can be saved in one instruction by using the load multiple (LDM) instruction. Using the INC or DEC, we can increment or decrement the contents of a register by N, where N is a 4-bit number. This instruction is used for address and pointer manipulation. The MULT instruction supports the signed multiplication of a two-word operand to obtain a long-word result, or two long-word operands to obtain a quadruple-word result. The DIV instruction provides a signed division of a long word by a word, or a quadruple word by a long word. The call relative (CALR) and Jump Relative (JR) are shorter and faster versions of a call and a jump instruction, respectively, but the range is limited.

Any bit in a register or memory can be set, reset, or tested by using the instructions SET, RES, and BIT, respectively. The Z8000 also has instructions to synchronize the access by a multiple microprocessor system to a shared resource, such as a common memory, bus, or I/O device. These instructions are MBIT (test multi-micro bit), MREQ (multi-micro request), MSET (multi-micro set), and MRES (multi-micro reset).

The Z8000 has several instructions that are very handy in block transfer or string manipulations. For example, the instructions TRDB and TRIB (translate and decrement/increment) are used for code conversion, such as from ASCII to EBCDIC. These instructions decrement or increment a length register after each conversation. TRTDB and TRTIB (translate and test decrement/increment) are used to test a character match with a translation table.

We now describe the various Z8001/2 instructions in more detail in the following.

1. Load and Exchange Instructions (Figure 6.17)

With the Z8001/2, data can be moved to a register from a register, to a register from memory, or to memory from a register. An immediate data byte (word or long word) can be moved to a register or memory location. The content of a register, immediate data word, or memory word can be saved on the stack (push), or data from the stack may be retrieved (pop) off the stack into a register or memory.

2. Arithmetic Instructions (Figure 6.18)

The Z8001/2 can perform arithmetic operations for both signed and unsigned numbers. Typical operations include add, subtract, multiply, and divide.

3. Logical Instructions (Figure 6.19)

The logical instructions include AND, OR, exclusive OR, or complement. A word or byte can also be tested, which "ores" the operand with zero and sets appropriate status flags. The data value is not altered and the

Mnemonics	Operands	Address Modes	Operation
CLR CLRB	dst	R IR DA X	Clear dst ← 0
EX EXB	R, src	R IR DA X	Exchange R ← src
LD LDB LDL	R, src	R IM IM IR DA X BA BX	Load into register R ← src
LD LDB LDL	dst, R	IR DA X BA BX	Load into memory (store) dst ← R
LD LDB	dst, IM	IR DA X	Load immediate into memory dst ← IM
LDA	R, src	DA X BA BX	Load address R ← source address
LDAR	R, src	RA	Load address relative R ← source address
LDK	R, src	IM	Load constant R ← n (n = 0 · · · 15)
LDM	R, src, n	IR DA X	Load multiple R ← src (n consecutive words) (n = 1 · · · 16)
LDM	dst, R, n	IR DA X	Load multiple (store multiple) dst ← R (n consecutive words) (n = 1 · · · 16)
LDR LDRB LDRL	R, src	RA	Load relative R ← src (range −32768 · · · −32767)
LDR LDRB LDRL	dst, R	RA	Load relative (store relative) dst ← R (range −32768 · · · +32767)
POP POPL	dst, R	R IR DA X	Pop dst ← IR Autoincrement contents of R
PUSH PUSHL	IR, src	R IM IR DA X	Push Autodecrement contents of R IR ← src

Figure 6.17 Z8001/Z8002 load and exchange instructions. Source: Reprinted by permission of Zilog, Inc., copyright © 1981.

Mnemonics	Operand	Address Modes	Operation
ADC ADCB ADD ADDB ADDL	R, src	R R IM IR DA X	Add with carry R ← R + src + carry Add R ← R + src
CP CPB CPL	R, src	R IM IR DA X	Compare with register R − src
CP CPB	dst, IM	IR DA X	Compare with immediate dst − IM
DAB	dst	R	Decimal adjust
DEC DECB	dst, n	R IR DA X	Decrement by n dst ← dst − n (n = 1 · · · 16)
DIV DIVL	R, src	R IM IR DA X	Divide (signed) Word $R_{n+1} ← R_{n,n+1} ÷ src$ R_n ← remainder Long word: $R_{n+2,n+3}$ $← R_{n...n+3} ÷ src$ $R_{n,n+1}$ ← remainder
EXTS EXTSB EXTSL	dst	R	Extend sign Extend sign of low-order half of st through high-order half of dst
INC INCB	dst, n	R IR DA X	Increment by n dst ← dst + n (n = 1 · · · 16)
MULT MULTI	R, src	R IM IR DA X	Multiply (signed) Word: $R_{n,n+1} ← R_{n+1} • src$ Long word: $R_{n...n+3}$ $← R_{n+2,n+3} • src$ *Plus seven cycles for each 1 in the multiplicand
NEG NEGB	dst	R IR DA X	Negate dst ← 0 − dst
SBC SBCB SUB SUBB SUBL	R, src	R R IM IR DA X	Subtract with carry R ← R − src − carry Subtract R ← R − src

Figure 6.18 Z8001/Z8002 arithmetic instructions. Source: Reprinted by permission of Zilog, Inc., copyright © 1981.

198 Chapter 6 INTEL 8086 AND ZILOG Z8000

MNEMONICS	OPERANDS	ADDRESS MODES	OPERATION
AND ANDB	R, src	R IM IR DA X	AND R ← R AND src
COM COMB	dst	R IM IR DA X	Complement dst ← NOT dst
OR ORB	R, src	R IM IR DA X	OR R ← R OR src
TEST TESTB TESTL	dst	R IR DA X	TEST dst OR 0
TCC TCCB	cc, dst	R	Test condition code Set LSB if cc is true
XOR XORB	R, src	R IM IR DA X	Exclusive OR R ← R XOR src

Figure 6.19 Z8001/Z8002 logical instructions. Source: Reprinted by permission of Zilog, Inc., copyright © 1981.

zero value is not stored in memory or a register. These test instructions are not the same as compare instructions.

4. Shift and Rotate Instructions (Figure 6.20)

The processor can shift or rotate a memory location or register by the number of bits specified in the instruction. The instruction also specifies the direction of the shift or rotate.

5. I/O Instructions (Figure 6.21)

The Z8000 processors can only execute I/O instructions when they are in the system mode.

The I/O instructions can be used to input or output byte or word data to and from memory and registers. The Z8001/2 can address 64K separate I/O ports, which is more than enough for most applications.

6. Bit Manipulation Instructions (Figure 6.22)

These Z8001/Z8002 instructions can be used to check a bit for 0 or 1, set or clear the bit, in either a register or memory location.

Mnemonics	Operand	Address Modes	Operation
RLDB	R, src	R	Rotate digit left
RRDB	R, src	R	Rotate digit right
RL	dst, n	R	Rotate left
RLB		R	by n bits (n = 1, 2)
RLC	dst, n	R	Rotate left through carry
RLCB		R	by n bits (n = 1, 2)
RR	dst, n	R	Rotate Right
RRB		R	by n bits (n = 1, 2)
RRC	dst, n	R	Rotate right through carry
RRCB		R	by n bits (n = 1, 2)
SDA	dst, R	R	Shift dynamic arithmetic
SDAB			Shift dst left or right by
SDAL			contents of R
SDL	dst, R	R	Shift dynamic logical
SDLB			Shift dst left or right by
SDLL			contents of R
SLA	dst, n	R	Shift left arithmetic
SLAB			by n bits
SLAL			
SLL	dst, n	R	Shift left logical
SLLB			by n bits
SLLL			
SRA	dst, n	R	Shift right arithmetic
SRAB			by n bits
SRAL			
SRL	dst, n	R	Shift right logical
SRLB			by n bits
SRLL			

Figure 6.20 Z8001/Z8002 shift and rotate instructions. Source: Reprinted by permission of Zilog, Inc., copyright © 1981.

7. Program Control (Figure 6.23)

The program control instructions include jump conditional, CALL, RETURN, and other similar instructions.

The Z8000 processors have an unconditional jump along with 16 conditional jump instructions (Figure 6.24). The conditional jumps are limited to displacements of $+127$ to -128.

8. Block Transfer Instructions (Figure 6.25)

The block transfer instructions use three registers. The first register is used as the source of data, second register as the destination, and the third register contains the number of data to be moved. With these instructions, 1 byte or word can be transferred and then the count decremented or the transfer can continue until the count is decremented to zero. For the Z8002, three registers are used (two for address, one for the count). On the other hand, for the Z8001, five registers are used, since each address needs two registers (one for the offset and one for the segment).

Mnemonics	Operands	Address Modes	Operation
IN* INB*	R, src	IR DA	Input R ← src
IND* INDB*	dst, src, R	IR	Input and decrement dst ← src Autodecrement dst address R ← R − 1
INDR* INDRB*	dst, src, R	IR	Input, decrement, and repeat dst ← src Autodecrement dst address R ← R − 1 Repeat until R = 0
INI* INIB*	dst, src, R	IR	Input and increment dst ← src Autoincrement dst address R ← R − 1
INIR* INIRB*	dst, src, R	IR	Input, increment, and repeat dst ← src Autoincrement dst address R ← R − 1 Repeat until R = 0
OUT* OUTB*	dst, R	IR DA	Output dst ← R
OUTD* OUTDB*	dst, src, R	IR	Output and decrement dst ← src Autodecrement src address R ← R − 1
OTDR* OTDRB*	dst, src, R	IR	Output, decrement, and repeat dst ← src Autodecrement src address R ← R − 1 Repeat until R = 0
OUTI* OUTIB*	dst, src, R	IR	Output and increment dst ← src Autoincrement src address R ← R − 1
OTIR* OTIRB*	dst, src, R	IR	Output, increment, and repeat dst ← src Autoincrement src address R ← R − 1 Repeat until R = 0
SIN* SINB*	R, src	DA	Special input R ← src
SIND* SINDB*	dst, src, R	IR	Special input and decrement dst ← src Autodecrement dst address R ← R − 1
SINDR* SINDRB*	dst, src, R	IR	Special input, decrement, and repeat dst ← src Autodecrement dst address R ← R − 1 Repeat until R = 0

Figure 6.21 (Continued on next page.)

Mnemonics	Operand	Address Modes	Operation
SINI* SINIB*	dst, src, R	IR	Special input and increment dst ← src Autoincrement dst address R ← R − 1
SINIR* SINIRB*	dst, src, R	IR	Special input, Increment, and repeat dst ← src Autoincrement dst address R ← R − 1 Repeat until R = 0
SOUT* SOUTB*	dst, src	DA	Special output dst ← src
SOUTD* SOUTDB*	dst, src, R	IR	Special output and decrement dst ← src Autodecrement src address R ← R − 1
SOTDR* SOTDRB*	dst, src, R	IR	Special output, Decrement, and repeat dst ← src Autodecrement src address R ← R − 1 Repeat until R = 0
SOUTI* SOUTIB*	dst, src, R	IR	Special output and increment dst ← src Autoincrement src address R ← R − 1
SOTIR* SOTIRB*	dst, src, R	R	Special output, Increment, and repeat dst ← src Autoincrement src address R ← R − 1 Repeat until R = 0

Figure 6.21 Z8001/Z8002 I/O instructions. Source: Reprinted by permission of Zilog, Inc., copyright © 1981.

Mnemonics	Operand	Address Modes	Operation
BIT BITB	dst, b	R IR DA X	Test bit static Z flag ← NOT dst bit specified by b
BIT BITB	dst, R	R	Test bit dynamic Z flag ← NOT dst bit specified by contents of R
RES RESB	dst, b	R IR DA X	Rest bit static Reset dst bit specified by b
RES RESB	dst, R	R	Reset bit dynamic Reset dst bit specified by contents of R
SET	dst, b	R	Set bit static

Figure 6.22 (Continued on next page.)

202   Chapter 6   INTEL 8086 AND ZILOG Z8000

Mnemonics	Operands	Address Modes	Operation
SETB		IR DA X	Set dst bit specified by b
SET	dst, R	R	Set bit dynamic
SETB			Set dst bit specified by contents of R
TSET	dst	R	Test and set
TSETB		IR DA X	S flag ← MSB of dst dst ← all 1s

Figure 6.22 Z8001/Z8002 bit manipulation instructions. Reprinted by permission of Zilog, Inc., copyright © 1981.

Mnemonics	Operands	Address Modes	Operation
CALL	dst	IR DA X	Call subroutine Autodecrement SP @ SP ← PC PC ← dst
CALR	dst	RA	Call relative Autodecrement SP @ SP ← PC PC ← PC + dst (range −4094 to +4096)
DJNZ DBJNZ	R, dst	RA	Decrement and jump if nonzero R ← R − 1 IF R = 0: PC ← PC + dst (range −254 to 0)
IRET*	—	—	Interrupt return PS ← @ SP Autoincrement SP
JP	cc, dst	IR IR DA X	Jump conditional if cc is true: PC ← dst
JR	cc, dst	RA	Jump conditional relative If cc is true: PC ← PC + dst (range −256 to +254)
RET	cc	—	Return conditional If cc if true: PC ← @ SP Autodecrement SP
SC	src	IM	System call Autodecrement SP @ SP ← old PS Push instruction PS ← System Call PS

Figure 6.23 Z8001/Z8002 program control instructions. Source: Reprinted by permission of Zilog, Inc., copyright © 1981.

Code	Meaning	Flag Settings	CC Field
	Always false	—	0000
	Always true	—	1000
Z	Zero	Z = 1	0110
NZ	Not zero	Z = 0	1110
C	Carry	C = 1	0111
NC	No carry	C = 0	1111
PL	Plus	S = 0	1101
MI	Minus	S = 1	0101
NE	Not equal	Z = 0	1110
EQ	Equal	Z = 1	0110
OV	Overflow	P/V = 1	0100
NOV	No overflow	P/V = 0	1100
PE	Parity is even	P/V = 1	0100
PO	Parity is odd	P/V = 0	1100
GE	Greater than or equal (signed)	(S XOR P/V) = 0	1001
LT	Less than (signed)	(S XOR P/V) = 1	0001
GT	Greater than (signed)	[Z OR (S XOR P/V)] = 0	1010
LE	Less than or equal (signed)	[Z OR (S XOR P/V)] = 1	0010
UGE	Unsigned greater than or equal	C = 0	1111
ULT	Unsigned less than	C = 1	0111
UGT	Unsigned greater than	[(C = 0) AND (Z = 0)] = 1	1011
ULE	Unisgned less than or equal	(C OR Z) = 1	0011

Note that some condition codes have identical flag settings and binary fields in the instruction:
Z = EQ, NZ = NE, C = ULT, NC = UGE, OV = PE, NOV = PO

Figure 6.24 Conditional Tests. Source: Reprinted by permission of Zilog, Inc., copyright © 1981.

Mnemonics	Operands	Address Modes	Operation
LDI LDIB	dst, src, R	IR	Load and increment dst ← src Autoincrement dst and src addresses R ← R − 1
LDIR LDIRB	dst, src, R	IR	Load, increment, and repeat dst ← src Autoincrement dst and src addresses R ← R − 1 Repeat until R = 0
LDD LDDB	dst, src, R	IR	Load and decrement dst ← src Autodecrement dst and src addresses R ← R − 1
LDDR LDDRB	dst, src, R	IR	Load, decrement, and repeat dst ← src Autodecrement dst and src addresses R ← R − 1 Repeat until R = 0

Figure 6.25 Z8001/Z8002 Block transfer instructions. Reprinted by permission of Zilog, Inc., copyright © 1981.

9. String Instructions (Figure 6.26)

Some of the string instructions compare a value in a register to a value or values stored in memory.

Also some string comparison instructions compare two strings that are stored in memory.

Mnemonics	Operands	Address Modes	Operation
CPD CPDB	R_x, src, R_y, cc	IR	Compare and decrement $R_x - $ src Autodecrement src address Ry ← Ry − 1
CPDR CPDRB	R_x, src, Ry, cc	IR	Compare, decrement, and repeat $R_x - $ src Autodecrement src address Ry ← Ry − 1 Repeat until cc is true or Ry = 0
CPI CPIB	R_x, src, Ry, cc	IR	Compare and increment $R_x - $ src Autoincrement src address R_y ← Ry − 1
CPIR CPIRB	R_x, src, Ry, cc	IR	Compare, increment, and repeat Rx − src Autoincrement src address Ry ← Ry − 1 Repeat until cc is true or Ry = 0
CPSD CPSDB	dst, src, R, cc	IR	Compare string and decrement dst − src Autodecrement dst and src addresses R ← R − 1
CPSDR CPSDRB	dst, src, R, cc	IR	Compare string, decrement, and repeat dst − src Autodecrement dst and src addresses R ← R − 1 Repeat until cc is true or R = 0
CPSI CPSIB	dst, src, r, cc	IR	Compare string and increment dst − src Autoincrement dst and src addresses R ← R − 1
CPSIR CPSIRB	dst, src, R, cc	IR	Compare string, increment, and repeat dst − src Autoincrement dst and src addresses R ← R − 1 Repeat until cc is true or R = 0

Figure 6.26 String instructions. Reprinted by permission of Zilog, Inc., copyright © 1981.

10. Translate Instructions (Figure 6.27)

The translate instructions are essentially look-up table instructions. The translate instructions can be used to translate a single byte or a whole string of instructions from one data type such as ASCII to another data type such as EBCDIC before transferring this data to another microcomputer or peripheral. These instructions use look-up tables to accomplish this translation.

Mnemonics	Operands	Address Modes	Operation
TRDB	dst, src, R	IR	Translate and decrement dst ← src (dst) Autodecrement dst address R ← R − 1
TRDRB	dst, src, R	IR	Translate, decrement, and repeat dst ← src (dst) Autodecrement dst address R ← R − 1 Repeat until R = 0
TRIB	dst, src, R	IR	Translate and increment dst ← src (dst) Autoincrement dst address R ← R − 1
TRIRB	dst, src, R	IR	Translate, increment, and repeat dst ← src (dst) Autoincrement dst address R ← R − 1 Repeat until R = 0
TRTDB	src 1, src 2, R	IR	Translate and test, decrement RH1 ← src 2 (src 1) Autodecrement src 1 address R ← R − 1
TRTDRB	src 1, src 2, R	IR	Translate and test, decrement, and repeat RH1 ← src 2 (src 1) Autodecrement src 1 address R ← R − 1 Repeat until R = 0 or RH1 = 0
TRTIB	src 1, src 2, R	IR	Translate and test, increment RH1 ← src 2 (src 1) Autoincrement src 1 address R ← R − 1
TRTIRB	src 1, src 2, R	IR	Translate and test, increment, and repeat RH1 ← src 2 (src 1) Autoincrement src 1 address R ← R − 1 Repeat until R = 0 or RH1 = 0

Figure 6.27 Translate instructions. Source: Reprinted by permission of Zilog, Inc., copyright © 1981.

11. Interrupt Instructions

Interrupt enable (EI) and disable (DI) are the only two interrupt instructions on the Z8001/2. The Z8001/2 have three interrupt inputs: nonmaskable (NMI), vectored (VI), and nonvectored (NVI). The NMI interrupt can never be disabled by the DI instruction. Both the NVI and VI interrupts can be enabled and disabled in any combination.

When an interrupt occurs the processor saves the program counter, the FCW, and a 16-bit interrupt identifier word. When the IRET instruction is performed, all this information is popped off the stack.

12. Processor Control Instructions (Figure 6.28)

These instructions are used to set, clear, and complement individual flags in the FCW. They are also used to control the processor in a multiprocessor environment.

The load instructions are used to read and write information to and from the FCW, and refresh counter, PSAP, and both stack pointers (system and normal).

6.2.5 Interrupts

The Z8001/2 can be interrupted by both internal and external events. The following events cause a trap (internal interrupt): (1) a System Call (SC) instruction is executed; (2) an unimplemented op code is executed in a program; (3) the processor attempts to execute a privileged instruction in the normal mode; and (4) a segmentation error occurs (as determined by the 8010 MMU). When any trap occurs, the program counter, FCW, and a 16-bit identifier (identifying the trap that occurred) are pushed onto the stack. The processor then fetches from memory new program status information. The PSAP is used to address this section of memory. From this section of memory, the CPU fetches a new program counter value and FCW value. For an interrupting peripheral device, its interface must provide the eight least significant bits that are used with the program status area pointer to address memory.

The user has NMI, NVI, and VI available for external interrupts. When NMI and NVI are used the processor always goes to a specific memory location within the program status area for the new value of the program counter and FCW. If the VI is used, the interrupting hardware provides the low 8 bits that are used with the rest of the bits in the PSAP to address memory. The processor then begins to execute the interrupt service subroutine for that peripheral.

6.2.6 Z8000 Pins and Signals

To address memory the Z8001/2 generate a 7-bit segment number and a 16-bit offset, or a 16-bit address. To address peripherals, both processors

Mnemonics	Operands	Address Modes	Operation
COMFLG	flags	—	Complement flag (Any combination of C, Z, S, P/V)
DI*	int	—	Disable interrupt (Any combination of NVI, VI)
EI*	int	—	Enable interrupt (Any combination of NVI, VI)
HALT*	—	—	HALT
LDCTL*	CTLR, src	R	Load into control register CTLR ← src
LDCTL*	dst, CTLR	R	Load from control register dst ← CTLR
LDCTLB	FLGR, src	R	Load into flag byte register FLGR ← src
LDCTLB	dst, FLGR	R	Load from flag byte register dst ← FLGR
LDPS*	src	IR DA X	Load program status PS ← src
MBIT*	—	—	Test multi-micro bit Set S if μl is High; reset S if $\overline{\mu l}$ is low.
MREQ*	dst	R	Multi-micro request
MRES*	—	—	Multi-micro reset
MSET*	—	—	Multi-micro set
NOP	—	—	No operation
RESFLG	flag	—	Reset flag (Any combination of C, Z, S, P/V)
SETFLG	flag	—	Set flag (Any combination of C, Z, S, P/V)

*Privileged instructions. Executed in system mode only.

Figure 6.28 Z8001/Z8002 processor control instructions. Reprinted by permission of Zilog, Inc., copyright © 1981.

generate a 16-bit peripheral address. The processors also communicate with memory and peripherals with a 16-bit data bus. The 16 data lines are multiplexed with the lower 16 address lines. AD_0–AD_{15} are the lower 16 address lines multiplexed with the data lines. Figure 6.29 shows the Z8000 pins and signals.

- The AS (Address Strobe) signal is low when an address is present on the multiplexed addr/data lines.
- ST_0–ST_3 are four outputs which must be externally decoded with some TTL logic, to indicate when a memory operation or peripheral operation is taking place, among other possibilities (Figure 6.30).

Chapter 6 INTEL 8086 AND ZILOG Z8000

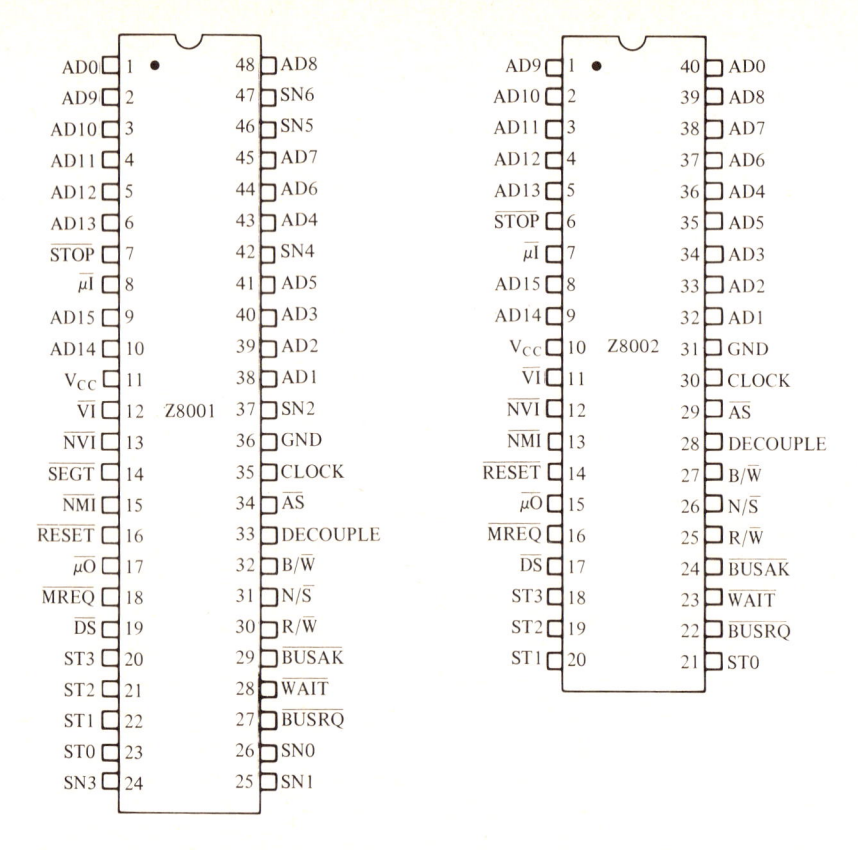

```
        Z8001                                    Z8002
  AD0  ⌐1  •    48⌐ AD8           AD9  ⌐1  •    40⌐ AD0
  AD9  ⌐2       47⌐ SN6           AD10 ⌐2       39⌐ AD8
  AD10 ⌐3       46⌐ SN5           AD11 ⌐3       38⌐ AD7
  AD11 ⌐4       45⌐ AD7           AD12 ⌐4       37⌐ AD6
  AD12 ⌐5       44⌐ AD6           AD13 ⌐5       36⌐ AD4
  AD13 ⌐6       43⌐ AD4           STOP ⌐6       35⌐ AD5
  STOP ⌐7       42⌐ SN4           μI   ⌐7       34⌐ AD3
  μI   ⌐8       41⌐ AD5           AD15 ⌐8       33⌐ AD2
  AD15 ⌐9       40⌐ AD3           AD14 ⌐9       32⌐ AD1
  AD14 ⌐10      39⌐ AD2           Vcc  ⌐10      31⌐ GND
  Vcc  ⌐11      38⌐ AD1           VI   ⌐11      30⌐ CLOCK
  VI   ⌐12      37⌐ SN2           NVI  ⌐12      29⌐ AS
  NVI  ⌐13      36⌐ GND           NMI  ⌐13      28⌐ DECOUPLE
  SEGT ⌐14      35⌐ CLOCK         RESET⌐14      27⌐ B/W
  NMI  ⌐15      34⌐ AS            μO   ⌐15      26⌐ N/S
  RESET⌐16      33⌐ DECOUPLE      MREQ ⌐16      25⌐ R/W
  μO   ⌐17      32⌐ B/W           DS   ⌐17      24⌐ BUSAK
  MREQ ⌐18      31⌐ N/S           ST3  ⌐18      23⌐ WAIT
  DS   ⌐19      30⌐ R/W           ST2  ⌐19      22⌐ BUSRQ
  ST3  ⌐20      29⌐ BUSAK         ST1  ⌐20      21⌐ ST0
  ST2  ⌐21      28⌐ WAIT
  ST1  ⌐22      27⌐ BUSRQ
  ST0  ⌐23      26⌐ SN0
  SN3  ⌐24      25⌐ SN1
```

Figure 6.29 Z8000 pins and signals. Source: Reprinted by permission of Zilog, Inc., copyright © 1981.

The $\overline{STOP}$ input pin provides single-step operation of the chip. External hardware must be used for achieving this facility.

The decouple pin is an output signal from the internal bias generator circuitry of the chip. The user should not use this signal.

R/$\overline{W}$ (Read/Write) signal controls read and write operation.

B/$\overline{W}$ (byte/word not) is used to indicate whether a byte or word is being transferred.

DS (Data Strobe) indicates when data are on the addr/data bus.

MREQ (memory request) is an output signifying that the processor is communicating with memory.

N/$\overline{S}$ (normal/system not) signal indicates which mode of operation the processor is in (normal or system).

NMI, NVI, VI are the three interrupt inputs. These were discussed previously.

BUSAK, WAIT, BUSRQ control the system bus. These lines are similar to the Z80 signals.

ST3	ST2	ST1	ST0	
L	L	L	L	Internal operation
L	L	L	H	Memory refresh
L	L	H	L	Normal I/O transaction
L	L	H	H	Special I/O transaction
L	H	L	L	Reserved
L	H	L	H	Nonmaskable interrupt acknowledge
L	H	H	L	Nonvectored interrupt acknowledge
L	H	H	H	Vectored interrupt acknowledge
H	L	L	L	Memory Transaction for Operand
H	L	L	H	Memory Transaction for Stack
H	L	H	L	Reserved
H	L	H	H	Reserved
H	H	L	L	Memory Transaction for Instruction Fetch (Subsequent Word)
H	H	L	H	Memory Transaction for Instruction Fetch (First Word)
H	H	H	L	Reserved
H	H	H	H	Reserved

Figure 6.30 Status outputs. Reprinted by permission of Zilog, Inc., copyright © 1981.

CLOCK input requires an external clock. This clock input is not TTL compatible, and requires therefore additional circuitry.

6.2.7 A Typical Z8000 System*

This section describes the hardware design implementation of a small computer using the Zilog Z8002 16-bit microprocessor, ROMs/EPROMs, and dynamic RAMs plus parallel and serial I/O devices. The interface requirements of the Z8002 to memory and to Z80A peripherals are described and design alternatives are given whenever possible. Figure 6.31 shows a block diagram of the design. The Z8002 16-bit microprocessor is the heart of the system.

Fixed program and data information is stored in an array of 2K × 8 ROMs or EPROMs; sixteen 16K × 1 dynamic RAMs provide 32K bytes of read/write storage. Input/output is handled by five I/O devices. Two Z80A PIOs provide 4-byte-wide bidirectional ports (32 lines) with handshake control. A Z80A SIO provides two fully independent full-duplex asynchronous or synchronous serial data communications channels. Four counter/timers in the Z80A Conditional Transfer of Control (CTC) relieve the processor from simple counting and timing tasks and generate the programmable baud-rates for the serial I/O channels. Eight switches can be interrogated and interpreted by the program.

The block diagram also indicates the various support functions. A crystal-controlled clock circuit generates a Z8002 and Z80A compatible

---

* Source: B. Pettner, *Sample Programs in the MACRO 8000 Assembly Language for the Z8002,* Advanced Micro Devices, 1981. Reprinted by permission.

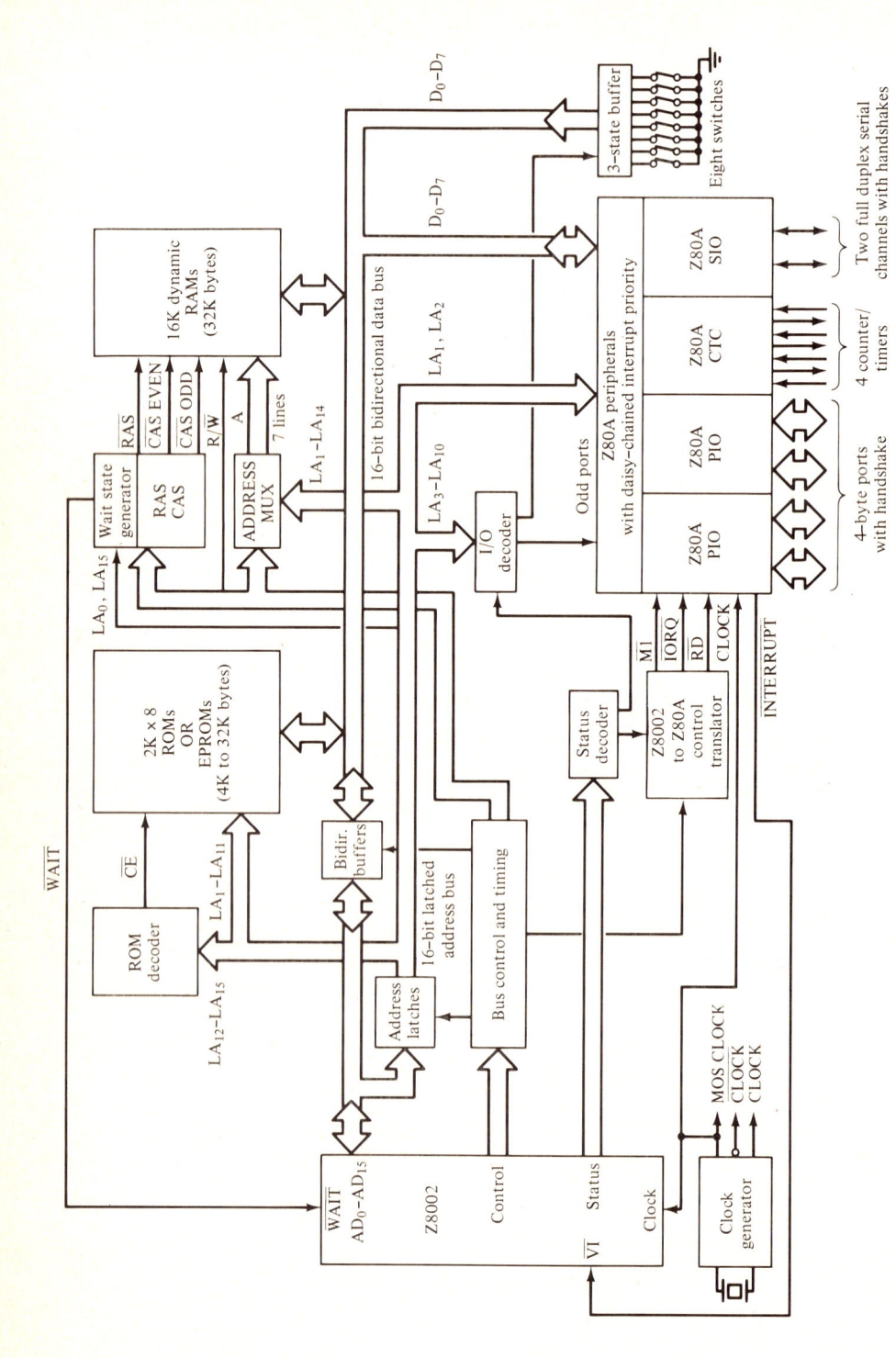

Figure 6.31 Z8002-based microcomputer. Source: Reprinted by permission of Zilog, Inc., copyright © 1981.

clock signal plus two complementary TTL clocks. Address buffers drive the memory and I/O devices; address latches demultiplex the time-shared address/data bus.

The ROM array uses a one-of-eight address decoder and the RAMs are driven by an address multiplexer and a $\overline{RAS/CAS}$ generator. The timing for all these functions originates in the bus control and timing circuit. The I/O devices are selected by an I/O decoder and receive Z80A equivalent control signals generated by the Z8002 to Z80A control translater. The following sections contain detailed descriptions of these circuits.

1. Clock Generation

The Z8002 requires a continuously running clock with a frequency between 500 KHz and 4 MHz. For best performance, the clock rate is usually set close to the maximum limit of 4 MHz.

2. CPU Output Buffering

The Z8002 outputs can sink 2 mA and can drive five Large Scale (LS) TTL inputs. Very small systems can be built without TTL buffering, but most systems require TTL buffering of the address/data lines and major control outputs like $\overline{AS}$, $\overline{DS}$, $\overline{MREQ}$, and $R/\overline{W}$.

3. Address Latching

The Z8002 uses a 16-bit time-shared address/data bus that must be demultiplexed, that is, latched for use with standard memories. $\overline{AS}$ and $\overline{BUSACK}$ signals along with two LS 373 octal transparent latches are used to achieve the address latching.

4. ROM Addressing

The program status information for the Z8002 is read after reset from locations 0002_{16} and 0004_{16}. Therefore, the lower half of the addressing space is used for ROM or EPROM. The circuit in Figure 6.24 uses 2716-type 2K × 8 EPROMs addressed by the Latched Addresses LA_1–LA_{11}. LA_{15} is used as a chip select input to separate the ROM and RAM areas.

5. RAM Addressing

Sixteen 16K × 1 dynamic RAMs are used for the upper half of the addressable memory space (LA_{15} = HIGH). These RAMs use address multiplexing to reduce the package pin count, thus requiring seven address inputs plus strobe inputs $\overline{RAS}$ and $\overline{CAS}$. The $\overline{MREQ}$ and $\overline{DS}$ lines of the Z8002 are used as $\overline{RAS}$ and $\overline{CAS}$, respectively.

6. Status Decoding

The Z8002 provides encoded status information on four outputs (ST_0–ST_3) as per Figure 6.29. Two LS 138 one-of-eight decoders can generate all the individual status signals.

7. Interfacing Peripheral Devices

Z-bus compatible peripheral devices that require no external logic to interface with a Z8002 can be used. In Figure 6.31, TTL chips and a few lines of code are used to make the Z8002 emulate the typical Z80A control signals such as the $\overline{\text{IORQ}}$, $\overline{\text{M1}}$, $\overline{\text{RD}}$, and RETI.

EXAMPLE 6.3*

Write a program in Z8002 assembly language to add a 64-bit number starting at location 3000H to another 64-bit number starting at location 3008H.

SOLUTION

The program can be written as follows:

```
LD     R8, 3008H      ;SET POINTER TO FIRST VALUE
POPL   RR4, R8        ;MOST SIGNIFICANT HALF
POPL   RR6, R8        ;LEAST SIGNIFICANT HALF
ADDL   RR6, 3004H     ;ADD LOWER HALF
PUSHL  R8, RR6        ;SAVE RESULT ON STACK
LDL    RR0, 3000H     ;GET REST OF SECOND VALUE
ADC    R5, R1         ;ADD LSW UPPER HALF WITH CARRY
PUSH   R8, R5         ;SAVE IT ON THE STACK
ADC    R4, R0         ;ADD MSW UPPER HALF WITH CARRY
PUSH   R8, R4         ;SAVE IT ON THE STACK
HALT                  ;HALT
```

EXAMPLE 6.4

Write a program in Z8002 assembly language to add the contents of the top of the stack and the second value on the stack. Place the result onto the stack.

SOLUTION

The assembly language program can be written as follows:

```
POP   R0, R15   ;LOAD THE VALUE INTO A REGISTER
POP   R1, R15   ;AND DECREMENT R15
ADD   R0, R1    ;ADD THE VALUES
```

* Source: B. Pettner, *Sample Programs in the MACRO 8000 Assembly Language for the Z8002,* Advanced Micro Devices, 1981. Reprinted by permission.

```
        PUSH  R15, R0  ;INCREMENT R15 AND LOAD THE RESULT ON
        HALT            THE STACK
                        ;HALT
```

PROBLEMS AND QUESTIONS

6.1 Using 8086 and Z8002 assembly language instruction sets, write programs to perform the following:

*(a) Using indirect register mode, perform a 32-bit addition.

(b) Divide the low-order byte of the value on top of the stack into two 4-bit nibbles and store them on the stack. The low-order 4 bits of the byte will be in the low-order 4 bits of the first word pushed onto the stack. The high-order 4 bits of the byte will be in the low-order 4 bits of the second stack word.

(c) Find ones complement of the contents of the top of the stack and store the result onto the stack.

*(d) Find the sum of a string of ten 16-bit numbers. The first number is stored in location 3000H. Store the sum onto the stack.

*(e) Find the number of negative elements in a series of five numbers given as: $F100_{16}$, 0155_{16}, $A011_{16}$, 0005_{16}, and $71FF_{16}$. Note that a negative number is identified by a "1" in the most significant bit of the number. The numbers are stored in consecutive memory locations starting at 3000H. Store the result onto the stack.

(f) Find the minimum value of a string of ten numbers using indexed addressing.

*(g) Find the length of a string of ASCII characters (7 bits plus most significant bit 0). The numbers are stored in consecutive memory locations starting at 3000H. The length of the numbers is stored in memory location 2000H. The end of the string is marked by a carriage return character ('cr', $0D_{16}$).

(h) Compare two strings of ASCII characters to check if they are identical. The length of the first string is stored in 3000H followed by the string. The length of the second string is in 4000H followed by the string. If the two strings are the same, store $EEEE_{16}$ onto the top of the stack; otherwise, store 0000H.

*(i) Provide a delay of 1 ms.

(j) Output the contents of memory locations 3000H through 300A on ten multiplexed 7-segment displays.

(k) Multiply a 64-bit unsigned number by another 32-bit unsigned number.

* Source: B. Pettner, *Sample Programs in the MACRO 8000 Assembly Language for the Z8002,* Advanced Micro Devices, Inc., 1981. Reprinted by permission.

†(1) Divide a 32-bit dividend by a 16-bit divisor taking overflow into consideration. Assume all numbers are unsigned. You may use the following as the guidelines:

$$X\overline{|YZ} = X\overline{|Y \times 16^4 + Z}$$

$$\Rightarrow X\overline{\begin{array}{c} Q_1 \times 16^4 + Q_0 \\ |Y \times 16^4 + Z \\ \cdots \\ \overline{R_1 \times 16^4 + Z} \\ \cdots \\ \overline{R_0} \end{array}}$$

6.2 What is meant by the $\overline{\text{TEST}}$, $\text{MN}/\overline{\text{MX}}$, and $\overline{\text{DEN}}$ pins on the 8086?
6.3 What is the purpose of ST_0–ST_3, $\overline{\text{STOP}}$, $\overline{\text{BUSRQ}}$, and $\overline{\text{BUSAK}}$ pins on the Z8002?
6.4 Identify functionally the main differences between the 8086 and Z8000.
6.5 Compare the interrupt structures of the 8086 and Z8000.

† Reprinted courtesy of Motorola.

CHAPTER 7

MOTOROLA 68000 AND INTEL 432

This chapter describes the basic features of the Motorola 68000 and Intel 432. The architectures, instruction sets, CPU pins and signals, and interfacing characteristics of these microprocessors are included. As mentioned before, the Motorola 68000 is a 16-bit microprocessor and the Intel 432 is a 32-bit microprocessor. Both are designed using the HMOS technology.

Intel recently announced a 32-bit microprocessor—the Intel 432. Sufficient data on the processor is not yet available to provide a complete description for various characteristics as we have done with the 16-bit processors. We, therefore, provide a functional description of the 432.

7.1 Motorola 68000*

The 68000 is a 16-bit microprocessor with a 32-bit internal architecture. It has direct memory addressing of 16 megabytes of nonsegmented memory. It has 17 general-purpose 32-bit registers, a 16-bit status register, and a 32-bit program counter. Eight of the general-purpose registers are data registers, seven are address registers, and two are stack pointers.

The eight data registers can be configured to perform 8-bit byte, 16-bit word, and 32-bit long-word operations. Address registers can function as base address registers and software stack pointers which can address bytes, words, and long words. All of the 17 general-purpose registers can be used as index registers.

The address bus is 24 bits wide, giving the 68000 the ability to directly address 16 megabytes of memory. The program counter is 32 bits long, but

---
* This section contains material modified from Motorola manuals.

only the low 24 bits are used. The lowest 8 bytes of memory hold the reset vector. Additional locations in the low 1K bytes are allocated to interrupt vectors, error vectors, and vectors for other types of exceptions. The remainder of the 16 megabyte memory locations can be used for whatever is desired by the user.

The 68000 has a 16-bit data bus, asynchronous control lines for 68000 peripheral devices, and synchronous control lines for slower devices such as the MC-6800 8-bit peripheral devices. The 68000 provides both hardware and software interrupts and a trace mode for software debugging.

The 68000 was designed with operating systems support in mind. It has two operating states: a user state for normal functions and a supervisor state for executing certain privileged instructions.

The 68000 can operate on five different types of data: bits, 4-bit Binary Coded Decimal (BCD) digits, 8-bit bytes, 16-bit words, and 32-bit long words. The instruction set contains 56 basic instruction types. With the 14 addressing modes and five data types, there are more than 1000 instructions the processor can execute. The fastest instruction is one that copies the contents of one register into the contents of another register. It executes in four clock cycles or 50 ns at a 8-MHz clock rate. The slowest instruction is a 32 by 16-bit divide which can take up to 170 clock cycles or 21.25 μs at 8 MHz.

The 68000 has no I/O instructions making all I/O memory mapped. All memory reference instructions can be used to access I/O as long as the I/O responds as memory.

7.1.1 Processor Architecture

1. Internal Registers

The 68000 provides many features of both a 32-bit and a 16-bit microprocessor. It has seventeen 32-bit registers (eight data registers, seven address registers, and two stack pointers). The program counter is also 32 bits wide, though only the low-order 24 bits are used. The status register is a 16-bit register (Figure 7.1).

2. Data and Address Registers (D0 through D7 and A0 through A6)

The contents of the eight data registers (D0 through D7) may be accessed as 8-bit bytes, 16-bit words, or 32-bit long words. The seven address registers can be accessed as 16-bit words or 32-bit long words.

All registers are general purpose but the instruction set is geared toward using the data registers to hold data and using the address registers as storage for memory addresses.

3. Stack Pointers

Address register A7 operates as the stack pointer. The stack pointers have the same address designation because only one stack is used in each of

Motorola 68000

```
 31         16 15        8 7         0
┌──────────┬──────────┬──────────┐ D0
├──────────┼──────────┼──────────┤ D1
├──────────┼──────────┼──────────┤ D2
├──────────┼──────────┼──────────┤ D3   Eight
├──────────┼──────────┼──────────┤ D4   data
├──────────┼──────────┼──────────┤ D5   registers
├──────────┼──────────┼──────────┤ D6
└──────────┴──────────┴──────────┘ D7

 31         16 15                 0
┌──────────┬─────────────────────┐ A0
├──────────┼─────────────────────┤ A1
├──────────┼─────────────────────┤ A2
├──────────┼─────────────────────┤ A3   Seven address
├──────────┼─────────────────────┤ A4   registers
├──────────┼─────────────────────┤ A5
└──────────┴─────────────────────┘ A6

          User stack pointer
     Supervisory stack pointer       A7   Two stack pointers

 31                                 0
┌─────────────────────────────────┐  Program counter

      15          8 7           0
      ┌───────────┬────────────┐     Status register
      │System byte│ User byte  │
      └───────────┴────────────┘
```

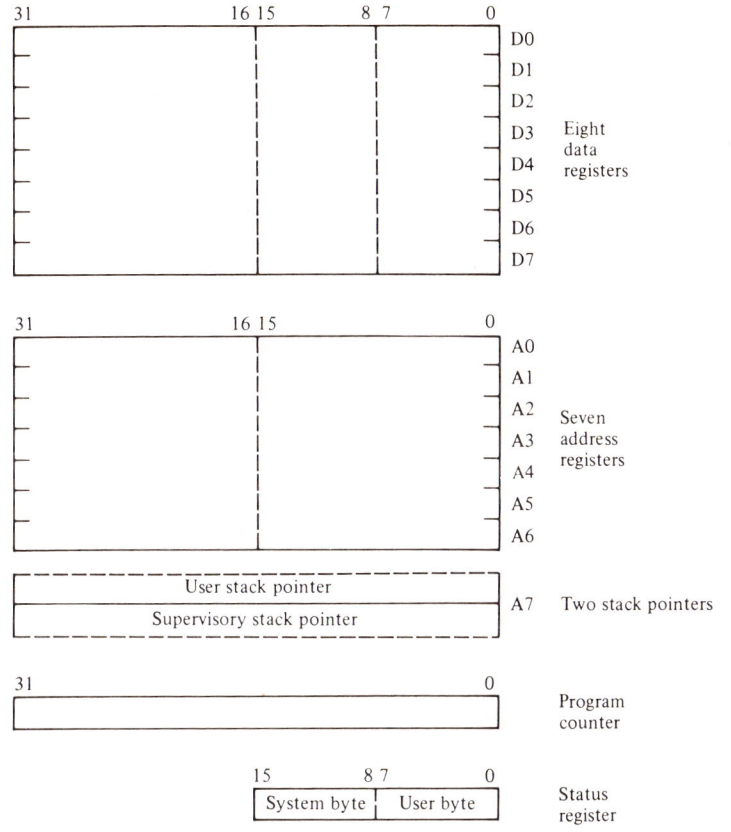

Figure 7.1 Internal registers. Source: Reprinted by permission of Motorola Semiconductor Products, Inc., copyright © 1982.

the two states of the processor. When the 68000 is in the user state then A7 is the user stack pointer. When the processor is in the supervisor state then the address register A7 is the supervisory stack pointer.

4. Program Counter

Since the program counter is 24 bits long in the current 68000 implementation, memory addresses of 000000H to FFFFFFH can be used with the 68000 utilizing external memory. Bytes can be accessed using either even- or odd-memory addresses. Only even addresses are used to access word and long-word operands. Bits 1 through 23 are provided by A1 through A23 on the 68000 chip. A0 is internally encoded to generate two data strobe signals, called Upper Data Strobe (UDS) and Lower Data Strobe (LDS). For word transfers, both data strobes are asserted. For byte transfers, only one of the data strobes is asserted; UDS if an even-numbered byte is being transferred, and LDS if an odd-numbered byte is being transferred.

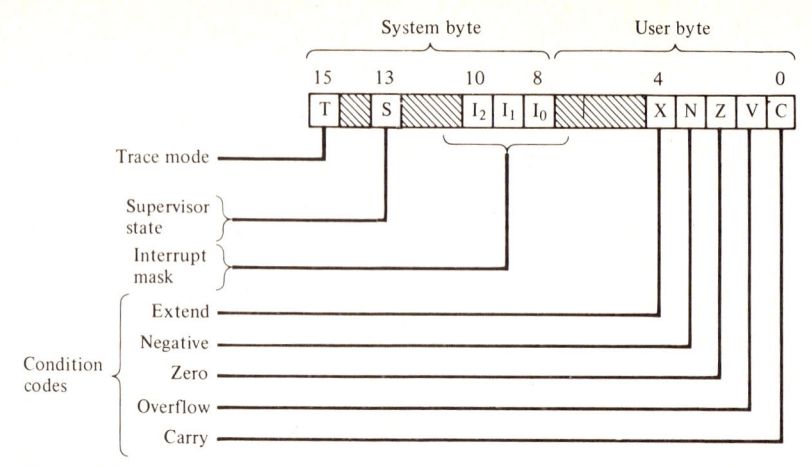

Figure 7.2 Status register. Source: Reprinted by permission of Motorola Semiconductor Products, Inc., copyright © 1982.

5. The Status Register

The 68000 status register consists of a system byte and a user byte (Figure 7.2). The user byte contains five condition code flags:

- The carry flag (C) indicates any carry generated by an addition instruction, any borrow produced by a subtract operation, or the value of a bit after a shift operation, and so on.
- The overflow flag (V) is used for operations involving signed numbers. It is set if an add or subtract operation has produced a result that exceeds twos complement range of numbers; otherwise the overflow flag is 0.
- The zero flag (Z) is set to 1 if execution of an instruction generates a zero result.
- The negative flag (N) is set to 1 if the most significant bit of an operand is 1 (negative numbers); this flag is 0 if the most significant bit of an operand is 0 (positive numbers). The operand can be 8, 16 or 32 bits long.
- The extend flag (X) is used in multiprecision operation to reflect the carry.

These flags are used in conditional branch instructions which may or may not transfer control, depending on the state of the flags.

The system byte of the status register is divided into three fields.

- The interrupt masks (I0, I1, I2) provides a numeric value for the interrupt request priority. Any interrupts having a numeric value above that specified by I0, I1, and I2 will be serviced by the microprocessor.

The supervisory flag (S) is a set when the 68000 is in the supervisory mode. When S is clear, the 68000 is in the user mode.

The trace mode flag (T) when set to 1 enables the internal debug circuitry on the 68000. When T is set to 1, the processor will single step through the instructions. After each instruction is executed, the 68000 will enter the supervisory mode and jump to a user-written trace routine. The routine could be used to look at the contents of specific registers or memory or any other desired debug operations. All unused flags in the status register will always be read as zeros.

7.1.2 Addressing Modes

The 68000 provides 14 addressing modes. These 14 modes can be divided into six basic addressing groups: register direct, address register indirect, absolute, program counter relative, immediate, and implied (Figure 7.3).

Some of the 68000 addressing modes facilitate the programming to implement stacks and queues. For example, one way to implement the user stack is by using the address register indirect with predecrement or postincrement addressing mode. The high to low stack can be implemented using An@− to push data on the stack and An@+ to pop data from the stack. On the other hand, low to high stack is implemented with An@+ to push and An@− to pop.

Queue can be implemented by using two address register indirect with postincrement and predecrement modes. One register is used as the "put" pointer and the other as the "get" pointer. The queue can be from low to high memory or from high to low memory.

We now describe the various 68000 addressing modes in more detail.

1. Register Direct Addressing

In this mode, the data operand is contained in one of the eight data registers (D0–D7) or address registers (A0–A7).

2. Address Register Indirect Addressing

In this mode, the operand is contained in an address register. There are five different types of address register indirect addressing mode. For example, the basic address register indirect mode (known as the address register indirect) contains the effective address.

Postincrement address register indirect increments an address register by 1, 2, or 4 after the register has been used. The increment value varies based on whether a byte, word, or long word is specified in the instruction.

The predecrement address register indirect mode decrements 1, 2, or 4 from an address register before the register is used. The decrement value is defined by the operand length (8-, 16-, or 32-bit) specified in the instruction.

Mode	Generation	Assembler Syntax
Register Direct Addressing		
Data register direct	EA = Dn	Dn
Address register direct	EA = An	An
Address Register Indirect Addressing		
Register indirect	EA = (An)	(An)
Postincrement register indirect	EA = (An), An ← An + N	(An)+
Predecrement register indirect	An ← An − N, EA = (An)	−(An)
Register indirect with offset	EA = (An) + d_{16}	d(An)
Indexed register indirect with offset	EA = (An) + (Ri) + d_8	d(An,Ri)
Absolute Data Addressing		
Absolute short	EA = (Next word)	xxxx
Absolute long	EA = (Next two words)	xxxxxxxx
Program Counter Relative Addressing		
Relative with offset	EA = (PC) + d_{16}	d
Relative with index and offset	EA = (PC) + (Ri) + d_8	d(Ri)
Immediate Data Addressing		
Immediate	DATA = Next word(s)	#xxxx
Quick immediate	Inherent data	#xx
Implied Addressing		
Implied register	EA = SR, USP, SP, PC	

Notes:
EA = effective address
An = address register
Dn = data register
Ri = address or data register used as index register
SR = status register
PC = program counter
SP = active system stack pointer
USP = user stack pointer
d_8 = 8-bit offset (displacement)
d_{16} = 16-bit offset (displacement)
N = 1 for byte, 2 for words, and 4 for long words
( ) = contents of
← = replaces

Figure 7.3 Addressing modes. Source: Reprinted by permission of Motorola Semiconductor Products, Inc., copyright © 1982.

The two other address register indirect modes provide accessing of data tables by allowing offsets and indexes to be included to an indirect address pointer. The address register indirect with offset mode determines the effective address by adding a 16-bit signed integer to the contents of an address register.

The indexed address register indirect with offset determines the effective address by adding an 8-bit signed integer and the contents of a register (a data or address register) to the contents of an address register.

3. Absolute Addressing

In this mode, the effective address is part of the instruction. The 68000 has two absolute addressing modes; absolute short addressing, in which a 16-bit address is used, and absolute long addressing, in which a 32-bit address is used.

4. Program Counter Relative Addressing

The 68000 has two program counter relative address modes: relative with offset and relative with index and offset. In relative with offset, the effective address is obtained by adding the contents of the integer number.

In relative with index and offset the effective address is obtained by adding the contents of the program counter, a signed 8-bit displacement integer number, and the contents of an index register.

5. Immediate Data Addressing

In this mode, the operand is constant data which are part of the instruction. If the constant is an 8-bit byte it is called "quick immediate"; otherwise it is referred to as immediate.

6. Implicit Addressing

The 68000 has some instructions that implicitly use the Program Counter (PC), the system Stack Pointer (SP), the Supervisor Stack Pointer (SSP), the User Stack Pointer (USP), or the Status Register (SR). For example, the JMP instruction allows loading a value into the program counter although the program counter is not explicitly identified in the instruction (Figure 7.4). Note that the stack pointer is defined as the system Stack Pointer (SP) in Figure 7.4 when stack pointer is automatically used during execution of an instruction such as PEA, RTE, and so on.

Instruction	Implied Register(s)
Branch conditional (B_{cc}), Branch always (BRA)	PC
Branch to subroutine (BSR)	PC, SP
Check register against bounds (CHK)	SSP, SR
Test condition, decrement and branch (DB_{cc})	PC
Signed divide (DIVS)	SSP, SR
Unsigned divide (DIVU)	SSP, SR
Jump (JMP)	PC
Jump to subroutine (JSR)	PC, SP
Link and allocate (LINK)	SP
Move condition codes (MOVE CCR)	SR
Move States Register (MOVE SR)	SR
Move User Stack Pointer (MOVE USP)	USP
Push effective address (PEA)	SP
Return from exception (RTE)	PC, SP, SR
Return and restore condition codes (RTR)	PC, SP, SR
Return from subroutine (RTS)	PC, SP
Trap (TRAP)	SSP, SR
Trap on overflow (TRAPV)	SSP, SR
Unlink (UNLK)	SP

Figure 7.4 Implicit instructions. Source: Reprinted by permission of Motorola Semiconductor Products, Inc.

Table 7.1. 68000 Instruction Set

MNEMONIC	DESCRIPTION
ABCD	Add decimal with extend
ADD	Add
AND	Logical and
ASL	Arithmetic Shift Left
ASR	Arithmetic Shift Right
B_{cc}	Branch conditionally
BCHG	Bit test and change
BCLR	Bit test and clear
BRA	Branch always
BSET	Bit test and set
BSR	Branch to subroutine
BTST	Bit test
CHK	Check register against bounds
CLR	Clear operand
CMP	Compare
DB_{cc}	Test cond., decrement and branch
DIVS	Signed divide
DIVU	Unsigned divide
EOR	Exclusive or
EXG	Exchange registers
EXT	Sign extend
JMP	Jump
JSR	Jump to subroutine
LEA	Load Effective Address
LINK	Link stack
LSL	Logical Shift Left
LSR	Logical Shift Right
MOVE	Move
MOVEM	Move multiple registers
MOVEP	Move peripheral data
MULS	Signed multiply
MULU	Unsigned multiply
NBCD	Negate decimal with extend
NEG	Negate
NOP	No operation
NOT	Ones complement
OR	Logical or
PEA	Push Effective Address
RESET	Reset external devices
ROL	Rotate left without extend
ROR	Rotate right without extend
ROXL	Rotate left with extend
ROXR	Rotate right with extend
RTE	Return from exception
RTR	Return and restore
RTS	Return from subroutine
SBCD	Subtract decimal with extend
S_{cc}	Set conditional
STOP	Stop
SUB	Subtract

Table 7.1. Continued

Mnemonic	Description
SWAP	Swap data register halves
TAS	Test and set operand
TRAP	Trap
TRAPV	Trap on overflow
TST	Test
UNLK	Unlink

Source: Reprinted by permission of Motorola Semiconductor Products, Inc., copyright © 1982.

7.1.3 Instruction Set

Table 7.1 shows the 68000 instruction set. The length of an instruction varies from one to five words in memory (Figure 7.5). The 68000 has 56 basic instruction types.

The following are some of the 68000 instructions. Although there are no increment or decrement instructions, MC68000 provides one-word instructions ADDQ and SUBQ which can be used to increment or decrement a number by as much as 8. Besides the ADDQ and SUBQ, it also has MOVEQ which is used to load a register with a sign-extended constant smaller than 8-bits. For efficient programs, the 68000 allows some dual operand instructions to have both source and destination in memory; these instructions are ADDX, CMP M, MOVE, ABCD, SBCD, and SUBX. The MOVE is a one-word instruction that allows the transfer data from register to register to register, memory to register, register to memory, and memory to memory. The MOVE M instruction is a one-word instruction used to save data or address registers in memory, and vice versa. The instruction DB_{CC} (test condition decrement, and branch) is a very useful instruction to implement looping. It first tests the condition to see if the termination condition is met. If the counter is not equal to -1, it will execute the

15 14 13 12 10 9 8 7 6 5 4 3 2 1 0
Operation word (first word specifies operation and modes)
Immediate operand (if any, one or two words)
Source effective address extension (if any, one or two words)
Destination effective address extension (if any, one or two words)

Figure 7.5 Instruction format. Source: Reprinted by permission of Motorola Semiconductor Products, Inc., copyright © 1982.

instruction indicated by the PC plus the sign-extended 16-bit displacement.

Data movements are achieved through instructions MOVE, EXG (to exchange the contents of two registers), and SWAP (to swap the lower half of a data register with the upper half).

There are three types of return instructions provided: (1) RTS (return from subroutine) will restore PC, (2) RTR (return and restore) will restore PC and condition code register, and (3) RTE (return from exception) will restore the PC and status register.

Software interrupt is accomplished through TRAP and TRAPV. TRAP has 16 unique vector addresses that allow 16 kinds of exception processing. TRAPV is executed when the overflow bit is set as a result of an operation.

Using the shift and rotate instructions, one can shift and rotate a byte, word, or long word by a count in the range of 1 to 8.

The CHK instruction implemented in the 68000 is very useful for array processing. This instruction performs the bound check which compares an array index against zero and the limit value addressed by the instruction. If the index is out of bounds, a trap will occur. We now describe the 68000 instructions in more detail.

Note that in order to identify the operand site of an instruction, the following is placed after a 68000 mnemonic: .B for byte, .W for word (default), .L for long word. For example;

CLR .B
CLR .W or CLR
CLR .L

We now describe the 68000 instructions in more details.

1. Data Movement Instructions

These instructions are used to move information between memory and the general-purpose registers (Figure 7.6)

2. Arithmetic Instructions

Figure 7.7 shows the 68000 arithmetic instructions. The 68000 can add and subtract 8-, 16-, or 32-bit quantities. It can do a 16 by 16 bit multiply yielding a 32-bit result. It can also perform a 32 by 16 bit divide. The compare instruction subtracts two operands but does not save the result. Instead, the condition code flags in the status register are set or closed, based on the result of the subtraction.

3. Logical Instructions

The basic instructions in this group are logical AND, logical OR, logical exclusive OR, and logical complement (NOT). These instructions can operate on byte, word, and long-word operands (Figure 7.8).

Motorola 68000

Instruction	Operand Size	Operation
EXG	32	Rx → Ry
LEA	32	EA → An
LINK	—	An → SP@−
		SP → An
		SP + d → SP
MOVE	8, 16, 32	(EA)s → EAd
MOVEM	16, 32	(EA) → An, Dn
		An, Dn → EA
MOVEP	16, 32	(EA) → Dn
		Dn → EA
MOVEQ	8	#Imm → Dn
PEA	32	EA → SP@−
SWAP	32	Dn [31:16] ↔ Dn [15:0]
UNLK	—	An → SP
		SP @+ → An

Notes: S = source, d = destination, [ ] = bit numbers.

Figure 7.6 Data movement instructions. Source: Reprinted by permission of Motorola Semiconductor Products, Inc., copyright © 1982.

Instruction	Operand Size	Operation
ADD	8, 16, 32	Dn + (EA) → Dn
		(EA) + Dn → EA
		(EA) + #xxx → EA
	16, 32	An + (EA) → An
ADDX	8, 16, 32	Dx + D6 + X → Dx
	16, 32	Ax@− Ay@− + X → Ax@
CLR	8, 16, 32	0 → EA
CMP	8, 16, 32	Dn − (EA)
		(EA) − #xxx
		Ax@+ − Ay@+
	16, 32	An − (EA)
DIVS	32 ÷ 16	Dn / (EA) → Dn
DIVU	32 ÷ 16	Dn / (EA) → Dn
EXT	8 → 16	$(Dn)_8 → Dn_{16}$
	16 → 32	$(Dn)_{16} → Dn_{32}$
MULS	16 * 16 → 32	Dn * (EA) → Dn
MULU	16 * 16 → 32	Dn * (EA) → Dn
NEG	8, 16, 32	0 − (EA) → EA
NEGX	8, 16, 32	0 − (EA) - X → EA
SUB	8, 16, 32	Dn − (EA) → Dn
		(EA) − Dn → EA
		(EA) − #xxx → EA
	16, 32	An − (EA) → An
SUBX	8, 16, 32	Dx − Dy − X → Dx
		Ax@− − Ay@− − X → Ax@
TAS	8	(EA) − 0, 1 → EA[7]
TST	8, 16, 32	(EA) − 0

Note: [ ] = bit number.

Figure 7.7 Arithmetic instructions. Source: Reprinted by permission of Motorola Semiconductor Products, Inc., copyright © 1982.

Instruction	Operand Size	Operation
AND	8, 16, 32	Dn ∧ (EA) → Dn (EA) 3p Dn → EA (EA) ∧ #xxx → EA
OR	8, 16, 32	Dn ∨ (EA) → Dn (EA) ∨ Dn → EA (EA) ∨ #xxx → EA
EOR	8, 16, 32	(EA) ⊕ Dy → EA (EA) ⊕ #xxx → EA
NOT	8, 16, 32	~(EA) → EA

Note: ~ = invert.

Figure 7.8 Logical instructions. Source: Reprinted by permission of Motorola Semiconductor Products, Inc., copyright © 1982.

4. Shift and Rotate Instructions

The 68000 has a group of shift and rotate instructions that can shift or rotate an operand in a register or memory to the right or to the left (Figure 7.9).

5. Bit Manipulation Instructions

The 68000 has four instructions that test the state of a specified bit in a memory location or register. The state of a specified bit is stored in a memory location or register or in the zero (Z) flag, and performs some operation based on the result (Figure 7.10).

Instruction	Operand Size	Operation
ASL	8, 16, 32	X/C ← ← ← 0
ASR	8, 16, 32	→ → X/C
LSL	8, 16, 32	X/C ← ← ← 0
LSR	8, 16, 32	0 → → → X/C
ROL	8, 16, 32	C ← ←
ROR	8, 16, 32	→ → C
ROXL	8, 16, 32	C ← ← ← X
ROXR	8, 16, 32	X → → C

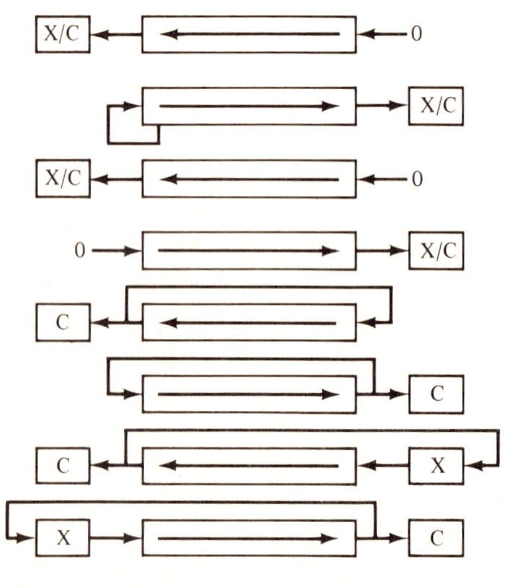

Figure 7.9 Shift and rotate instructions. Source: Reprinted by permission of Motorola Semiconductor Products, Inc., copyright © 1982.

Instruction	Operand Size	Operation
BTST	8, 32	$\sim$ bit of (EA) $\to$ Z
BSET	8, 32	$\sim$ bit of (EA) $\to$ Z
		1 $\to$ bit of EA
BCLR	8, 32	$\sim$ bit of (EA) $\to$ Z
		0 $\to$ bit of EA
BCHG	8, 32	$\sim$ bit of (EA) $\to$ Z
		$\sim$ bit of (EA) $\to$ bit of EA

Figure 7.10 Bit manipulation instructions. Source: Reprinted by permission of Motorola Semiconductor Products, Inc., copyright © 1982.

6. Binary Coded Decimal Instructions

The 68000 provides three BCD arithmetic operations. These are add, subtract, and negate (Figure 7.11). Because these instructions always include the extend (X) flag in the operation, the X bit must be cleared before operating on the least significant BCD bytes.

7. Program Control Instructions

The program control instructions contain branches, jumps, and subroutine calls (Figure 7.12).

Figure 7.13 shows the various conditional test instructions.

8. System Control Instructions

The 68000 operation can be controlled by system control instructions which include privileged instructions, trap generating instructions, and instructions that use or modify the status register (Figure 7.14). Note that the 68000 can execute the privileged instructions only in the supervisory mode.

7.1.4 68000 Pins and Signals

The 68000 is packaged in a 64-pin Dual In-line Package (DIP) (Figure 7.15).

The 68000 is provided with two V_{CC} (+ 5 V) and two ground pins. Power

Instruction	Operand Size	Operation
ABCD	8	$Dx_{10} + Dy_{10} + X \to Dx$
		$Ax@-_{10} + Ay@-_{10} + X \to Ax@$
SBCD	8	$Dx_{10} - Dy_{10} - X \to Dx$
		$Ax@-_{10} - Ay@-_{10} - X \to Ax@$
NBCD	8	$0 - (EA)_{10} - X \to EA$

Figure 7.11 BCD instructions. Source: Reprinted by permission of Motorola Semiconductor Products, Inc., copyright © 1982.

Instruction	Operation
CONDITIONAL	
B$_{CC}$	Branch conditionally (14 conditions) 8- and 16-bit displacement
DB$_{CC}$	Test condition, decrement counter, and branch. 16-bit displacement
S$_{CC}$	Set byte conditionally (16 conditions)
UNCONDITIONAL	
BRA	Branch always 8- and 16-bit displacement
BSR	Branch to subroutine 8- and 16-bit displacement
JMP	Jump
JSR	Jump to subroutine
RETURNS	
RTR	Return and restore condition codes
RTS	Return from subroutine

Figure 7.12 Program control instructions. Source: Reprinted by permission of Motorola Semiconductor Products, Inc., copyright © 1982.

is thus distributed in order to reduce noise problems at high frequencies.

D0–D15 is the 16-bit data bus. All transfers to and from memory and I/O devices are conducted over the 16-bit bus. To transfer more than 16 bits requires additional transfer instructions.

Mnemonic	Condition	Encoding	Test
T	True	0000	1
F	False	0001	0
HI	High	0010	$\overline{C} \cdot \overline{Z}$
LS	Low or Same	0011	$C + Z$
CC	Carry Clear	0100	$\overline{C}$
CS	Carry Set	0101	C
NE	Not Equal	0110	$\overline{Z}$
EQ	Equal	0111	Z
VC	Overflow clear	1000	$\overline{V}$
VS	Overflow set	1001	V
PL	Plus	1010	$\overline{N}$
MI	Minus	1011	N
GE	Greater or Equal	1100	$N \cdot V + \overline{N} \cdot \overline{V}$
LT	Less Than	1101	$N \cdot \overline{V} + \overline{N} \cdot V$
GT	Greater Than	1110	$N \cdot V \cdot \overline{Z} + \overline{N} \cdot \overline{V} \cdot \overline{Z}$
LE	Less or Equal	1111	$Z + N \cdot \overline{V} + \overline{N} \cdot V$

Figure 7.13 Conditional test instructions. Source: Reprinted by permission of Motorola Semiconductor Products, Inc., copyright © 1982.

Instruction	Operation
PRIVILEGED	
RESET	Reset external devices
RTE	Return from exception
STOP	Stop program execution
ORI to SR	Logical OR to status register
MOVE USP	Move user stack pointer
ANDI to SR	Logical AND to status register
EORI to SR	Logical EOR to status register
MOVE EA to SR	Load new status register
TRAP GENERATING	
TRAP	Trap
TRAPV	Trap on overflow
CHK	Check register against bounds
STATUS REGISTER	
ANDI to CCR	Logical AND to condition codes
EORI to CCR	Logical EOR to condition codes
MOVE EA to CCR	Load new condition codes
ORI to CCR	Logical OR to condition codes
MOVE SR to EA	Store status register

Figure 7.14 System control instructions. Source: Reprinted by permission of Motorola Semiconductor Products, Inc., copyright © 1982.

A1–A23 are the 23 address lines. Being 23 bits wide, the address range is 8 megawords and 16 megabytes. Note that A0 is obtained by encoding $\overline{UDS}$ and $\overline{LDS}$.

AS (Address Strobe) is used to notify system devices that a valid address is on the address bus.

The 68000 can be interfaced to either synchronous or asynchronous devices, and it has a set of control lines for each.

The 68000 accepts a single-phase TTL level clock that can range from dc to 8 MHz. Motorola also has the MC6800212 version of the MC68000, which goes up to 12.5 MHz.

1. Asynchronous Control Lines

Upper Data Strobe (UDS) and Lower Data Strobe (LDS) are used to segment the memory into bytes instead of words. When UDS is asserted, information is transferred on the high-order eight lines of the data bus, D8–D15. When LDS is asserted, information is transferred on the low-order eight lines of the data bus, D0–D7. During word length transfer operations, both strobe lines, UDS and LDS, are asserted, and information is transferred on all 16 data lines, D0–D15.

R/W (read not write) is high during a read cycle and low during a write cycle. DTACK (data transfer acknowledge) is used to tell the 68000 that a

230 Chapter 7 MOTOROLA 68000 AND INTEL 432

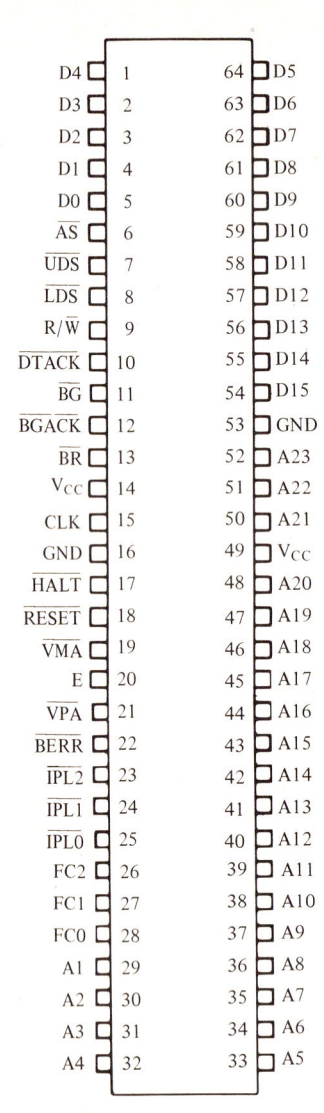

```
D4   — 1          64 — D5
D3   — 2          63 — D6
D2   — 3          62 — D7
D1   — 4          61 — D8
D0   — 5          60 — D9
AS   — 6          59 — D10
UDS  — 7          58 — D11
LDS  — 8          57 — D12
R/W  — 9          56 — D13
DTACK — 10        55 — D14
BG   — 11         54 — D15
BGACK — 12        53 — GND
BR   — 13         52 — A23
Vcc  — 14         51 — A22
CLK  — 15         50 — A21
GND  — 16         49 — Vcc
HALT — 17         48 — A20
RESET — 18        47 — A19
VMA  — 19         46 — A18
E    — 20         45 — A17
VPA  — 21         44 — A16
BERR — 22         43 — A15
IPL2 — 23         42 — A14
IPL1 — 24         41 — A13
IPL0 — 25         40 — A12
FC2  — 26         39 — A11
FC1  — 27         38 — A10
FC0  — 28         37 — A9
A1   — 29         36 — A8
A2   — 30         35 — A7
A3   — 31         34 — A6
A4   — 32         33 — A5
```

Figure 7.15 68000 pins and signals. Source: Reprinted by permission of Motorola Semiconductor Products, Inc., copyright © 1982.

transfer is finished. When an external device has placed data on the bus for a read operation, or has gated data off the data bus during a write operation, the device notifies the 68000 by asserting DTACK. After receiving the DTACK the 68000 will terminate the bus cycle. This makes the 68000 speed dependent on the speed of external devices.

2. Synchronous Control Lines

The 68000 contains three control lines that facilitate interfacing to synchronous peripheral devices such as Motorola's MC6800 family.

- The Enable (E) line is used to synchronize data transfer for 6800 peripherals. This clock corresponds to phase 2 clock in existing 6800 systems. The E clock is output at a frequency that is one-tenth of the 68000 input clock.
- Valid Peripheral Address (VPA) is an input which tells the 68000 that a 6800 device is being addressed, and therefore data transfers should be synchronized with the E clock.
- Valid Memory Address (VMA) is the processor's response to VPA. When the memory address is valid then VMA will be asserted.

For both synchronous and asynchronous transfer operations, the 68000 accompanies the address bus information with qualitative information on three function code lines (FC0, FC1, and FC2). These lines tell external devices whether user data, a user program, supervisor data, or a supervisor program is being addressed. These lines can be decoded and used to extend the address space of the 68000 to four 16-megabyte segments, for a total of 64 megabytes (Figure 7.16).

BR, BG, and BGACK are bus arbitration lines used for DMA purposes, gaining control of the microprocessor's buses.

RESET, BERR, and HALT are used to control the 68000 or indicate its state. RESET and HALT are bidirectional and so can be used to reset or halt the processor or indicate that the 68000 is in this state.

IPL0, IPL1, and IPL2 are interrupt control lines. These lines input the encoded priority level of an active interrupt request to the processor. If the level reflected in these bits is higher than the interrupt mask value in the

FUNCTION CODE OUTPUT			
FC2	FC1	FC0	REFERENCE CLASS
0	0	0	(Unassigned)
0	0	1	User data
0	1	0	User program
0	1	1	(Unassigned)
1	0	0	(Unassigned)
1	0	1	Supervisor data
1	1	0	Supervisor program
1	1	1	Interrupt acknowledge

Figure 7.16 Function code lines. Source: Reprinted by permission of Motorola Semiconductor Products, Inc., copyright © 1982.

status register, the 68000 will call an associated interrupt service routine through a vector memory.

7.1.5 68000 System Diagram

Figure 7.17 shows a simplified version of the 68000 basic system diagram.

7.1.6 68000 Byte Addressing

Figure 7.18 shows the 68000 byte addressing scheme. The address strobe line is used in conjunction with three other pins on the 68000, namely, the read/write line, the upper-data strobe and lower-data strobe. The $R/\overline{W}$ line defines the data bus operation and controls external bus buffers, while the $\overline{UDS}$ and $\overline{LDS}$ lines identify the byte or bytes to be operated on.

7.1.7 System Features

The 68000 includes features beyond instruction execution. It also has system features for program and memory management, and for handling of exceptional conditions

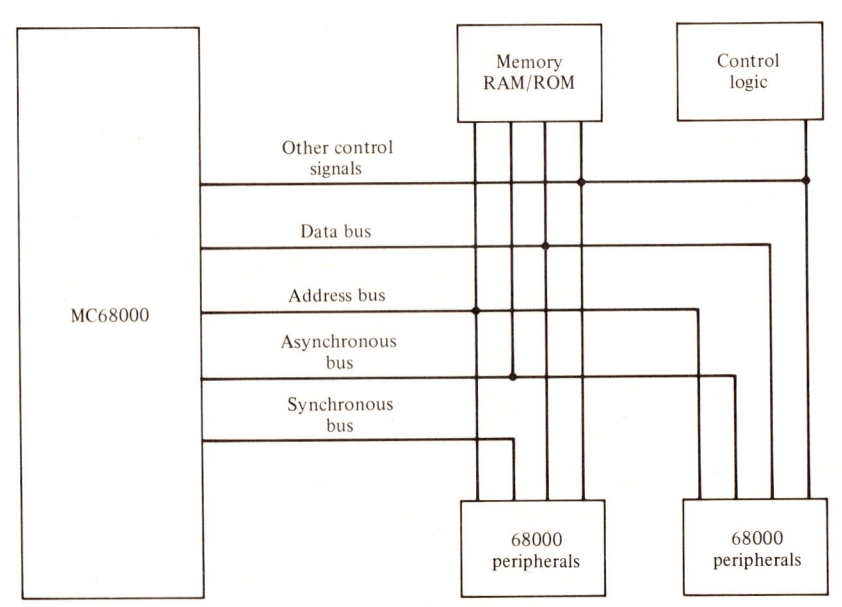

Figure 7.17 68000 basic system design. Source: Reprinted by permission of Motorola Semiconductor Products, Inc., copyright © 1982.

Motorola 68000   233

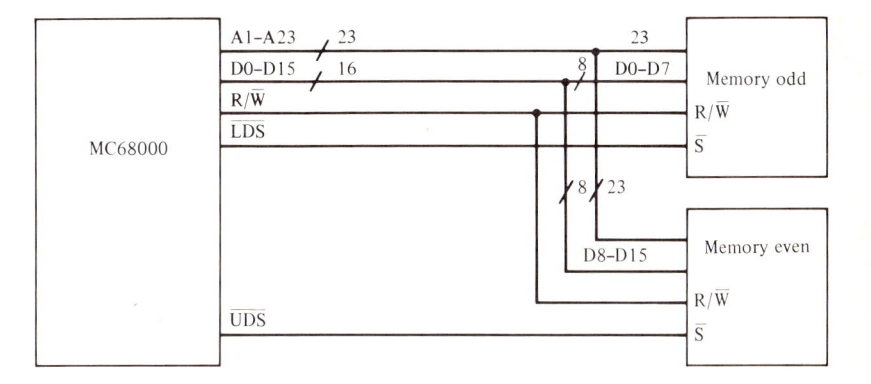

UDS	LDS	R/W		
0	0	0	VALID WRITE DATA	VALID WRITE DATA
0	0	1	VALID READ DATA	VALID READ DATA
0	1	0	VALID WRITE DATA	*SAME AS D8-D15
0	1	1	VALID READ DATA	INVALID DATA
1	0	0	*SAME AS D0-D7	VALID WRITE DATA
1	0	1	INVALID DATA	VALID READ DATA
1	1	0	INVALID DATA	INVALID DATA
1	1	1	INVALID DATA	INVALID DATA

Figure 7.18 MC68000 byte addressing. (*This feature is not part of the 68000 specification, and is not assured in future versions.)

1. Privilege States

The 68000 processor operates in one of two states of privilege: the "user" state or the "supervisor" state. The privilege state determines which operations are legal. It is used to choose between the supervisor stack pointer and the user stack pointer in instruction references.

When the processor starts a bus cycle, it classifies the reference via an encoding on the three function code pins. This allows external translation of addresses, control of access, and differentiation of special processor states, such as interrupt acknowledge (Figure 7.16).

a. Supervisor/User State. For instruction execution, the supervisor state is determined by the S bit of the status register; if the S bit is on, the processor is in supervisor state, otherwise, it is in the user state. The supervisor state is the higher state of privilege. All instructions can be executed in supervisor state. The bus cycles generated by instructions executed in supervisor state are classified as supervisor references. While the processor is in the supervisor privilege state, those instructions that use either the system stack pointer implicitly or address register seven (A7) explicitly access the supervisor stack pointer.

Table 7.2. Privileges of the 68000's User and Supervisor Levels

	USER LEVEL	SUPERVISOR LEVEL
Enter level by	Clearing status bit S	Recognition of a trap, reset, or interrupt
Function code output (FC2 =)	0	1
System stack pointer	User stack pointer	Supervisor stack pointer
Other stack pointers	Registers A0–A6	User stack pointer and registers A0–A6
Status bits available		
(Read)	C, V, Z, N, X, I_0-I_2, S,	C, V, Z, N, X, I_0-I_2, S, T
(Write)	T, C, V, Z, N, X	C, V, Z, N, X, I_0-I_2, S, T
Instructions available	All, except those listed at right	All, including: STOP, RESET, MOVE to SR, ANDI to SR, ORI to SR, EORI to SR, MOVE USP to (ea), MOVE to USP, RTE

The user state is the lower state of privilege. Most instructions execute the same in user state as in supervisor state. However, some instructions that have important system effects are made "illegal" (Table 7.2). For example, to ensure that a user program cannot enter the privileged state except in a controlled manner, the instructions that modify the entire status register are privileged. The bus cycles generated by an instruction executed in user state are classified as user-state references. While the processor is in the user privilege state, those instructions that use either the system stack pointer implicitly, or address register seven (A7) explicitly access the user stack pointer.

b. Change of Privilege State. Once the processor is in the user state executing instructions, only exception processing (described below) can change the privilege state. During exception processing the current setting of the S bit of the status register is saved, and the S bit is forced on, putting the processor in supervisor state. Thus when instruction excution resumes at the address specified to process the exception, the processor is in the supervisor privilege state.

The transition from supervisor to user state can be accomplished by any of four instructions: RTE, MOVE to status register, ANDI to status register, and EORI to status register. The RTE instruction fetches the new status register and program counter from the supervisor stack, loads each into its respective register, and then begins the instruction fetch at the new program counter address in the privilege state determined by the S bit of the new status register. The MOVE, ANDI, and EORI to status register instructions each fetch all operands in the supervisor state, perform the appropriate update to the status register, and then fetch the next instruction at the next sequential program counter address in the privilege state determined by the new S bit.

The function code pins are employed to classify processor bus cycles. Two bits in the microcontrol store classify an access as data space, program space, interrupt acknowledge, or unknown. The unknown state is combined with a value from a special decoder to determine whether the associated access is to data or program space. Unknown states occur in microroutines which may be shared by data space access macroinstructions and instruction space access macroinstructions. For example, the base plus displacement addressing mode (data space access) and the program counter plus displacement addressing mode (program space access) share the same microroutine.

The user/supervisor function code information is obtained from the status register. User/supervisor information is not provided by the microcontrol store due to microcontrol store word width constraints. Its exclusion from the microcontrol store implies that there must exist some means in the nanocontrol store for direct manipulation of the user/supervisor bit in the status register during exception processing. In addition, there are several privileged instructions which can change the user/supervisor bit. Any prefetches done prior to manipulation of the status register must be discarded. Since the microroutines manipulate the entire status register, the delay associated with ignoring the prefetches is suffered by both instruction types.

2. Exception Processing

a. Processing States. The processor is always in one of three processing states: normal, exception, or halted. The normal processing state is that associated with instruction execution; the bus cycles are to fetch instructions and operands, and to store results. The STOP instruction is a special case of the normal state in which no further bus cycles are started.

The exception processing state is associated with interrupts, trap instructions, tracing, and other exceptional conditions. The exception may be internally generated by an instruction or by an unusual condition arising during the execution of an instruction. Externally, exception processing can be forced by an interrupt, by a bus error, or by a reset. Exception processing is designed to provide an efficient context switch so that the processor may handle unusual conditions.

Exceptions can be grouped according to their generation. Table 7.3 shows a listing of the various exception groups. The group 0 exceptions are

Table 7.3. Exception Groups

Group 0	Reset Bus error Addr error	Exception processing begins at the next minor cycle
Group 1	Trace Interrupt Illegal Privilege	Exception processing begins before the next instruction
Group 2	TRAP, TRAPV, CHK, Zero divide	Exception processing is started by normal instruction execution

reset, bus error, and address error. These exceptions cause the instruction currently being executed to be aborted, and the exception processing to commence at the next minor cycle of the processor. The group 1 exceptions are trace and interrupt, as well as the privilege violations and illegal instructions. These exceptions allow the current instruction to execute to completion, but preempt the execution of the next instruction by forcing exception processing to occur. The group 2 exceptions occur as part of the normal processing of instructions. The TRAP, TRAPV, CHK, and zero divide exceptions are in this group.

The halted processing state is an indication of catastrophic hardware failure. For example, if during the exception processing of a bus error another bus error occurs, the processor assumes that the system is unusable and halts.

b. Exception Processing Initiation. The processor hardware recognizes three distinct types of exception conditions: internal exceptions (group 2), noncatastrophic exceptions (group 1), and catastrophic exceptions (group 0). Exception processing for group 2 exceptions is initiated through normal instruction execution. Group 2 exceptions are detected and processed via microroutines without the aid of specialized additional hardware.

When a group 1 exception arises, execution of the current macroinstruction continues unaffected (including prefetch and decode of the next macroinstruction). At the end of the current macroinstruction, the microroutine specifies that the next microcontrol store address is to come from the macroinstruction register decoder. However, the existence of a group 1 exception condition will force substitution of a microcontrol store address for the appropriate exception processing microroutine.

Occurrence of any group 0 exception implies that the currently executing microroutine cannot continue; the exception microroutine address preempts the current microroutine at the next minor cycle.

i. Exception Vectors

Exception vectors are memory locations from which the processor fetches the address of a routine which will handle that exception. All exception vectors are two words in length, except for the reset vector, which is four words in length. A vector number is an 8-bit number, which when multiplied by 4 gives the address of an exception vector. Vector numbers are generated internally or externally, depending on the cause of the exception. The exception vectors are assigned to low addresses in the supervisor data space.

ii. Exception Processing Sequence

All exception processing is done in supervisor state, regardless of the setting of the S bit in the status register. The bus cycles generated during exception processing are classified as supervisor references. All stacking operations during exception processing use the supervisor stack pointer.

Exception processing occurs in four identifiable steps. During the first step, an internal copy is made of the status register. After the copy is made, the special processor state bits in the status register are changed. The S bit is forced on (1), putting the processor into supervisor privilege state. Also, the T bit is forced to 0 (off), which will allow the exception handler to execute unhindered by tracing. For the reset and interrupt exceptions, the interrupt priority mask is also updated.

In the second step, the vector number of the exception is determined. For interrupts, the vector number is obtained by a processor fetch, classified as an interrupt acknowledge. For all other exceptions, internal logic provides the vector number. This vector number is then used to generate the address of the exception vector.

The third step is to save the current processor status. Only for the reset exception is this not done. The current program counter value and the saved copy of the status register are stacked using the supervisor stack pointer. The program counter value stacked usually points to the next unexecuted instruction. Additional information defining the current context is stacked for the bus error and address error exceptions.

The last step is the same for all exceptions. The new program counter value is fetched from the exception vector. The processor then resumes instruction execution. The instruction at the address given in the exception vector is fetched, and normal instruction decoding and execution is started.

iii. Reset

Description. The reset pin provides the highest level exception. The processing of the reset signal is designed for system initiation and recovery from catastrophic failure. Whatever processing was in progress at the time of the reset is aborted. The processor interrupt priority mask is set at level seven. The vector number is internally generated to reference the reset exception vector at location 0 in the supervisor program space. Because no assumptions can be made about the validity of register contents, in particular the supervisor stack pointer, neither the program counter nor the status register is saved. The address contained in the first two words of the reset exception vector is used to initialize the supervisor stack pointer, and the address in the next two words is used to initialize the program counter. Finally instruction execution is started at the address in the program counter.

Hardware support. Hardware support for reset permeates the machine because reset must provide machine initialization from any internal state. Activation of the reset pin preempts all other pending conditions and current activities. Normal operation of the control unit is suspended and the control unit is forced to a state from which it begins executing the reset microroutine. Bits in the nanocontrol store are provided to allow the microroutine to obtain the reset vector address, force the machine into supervisor mode, and set the priority mask (to the level specified by a decoder—in this case, level seven). Additionally, since the register designators for the preempted instruction are unknown, the nanocontrol store must provide bits that can directly specify selection of the implicit stack pointer for its initialization.

iv. Interrupts

Description. The 68000 provides seven levels of interrupt priorities. Devices may be chained externally within interrupt priorities, allowing an unlimited number of peripheral devices to interrupt the processor. Interrupt priority levels are numbered from one to seven, level seven being the highest priority. The status register contains a 3-bit mask which indicates the current processor priority, and interrupts are inhibited for all priority levels less than or equal to the current processor priority.

An interrupt request is made to the processor by encoding the interrupt pins IPL0, IPL1, and IPL2; a zero indicates no interrupt request. Interrupt requests arriving at the processor do not force immediate exception processing, but are made pending. Pending interrupts are detected between instruction executions. If the priority of the pending interrupt is lower than or equal to the current processor priority, execution continues with the next instruction and the interrupt exception processing is postponed. (The recognition of level seven is slightly different, as explained below.)

If the priority of the pending interrupt is greater than the current processor priority, the exception processing sequence is started. First a copy of the status register is saved, and the privilege state is set to supervisor, tracing is suppressed, and the processor priority level is set to the level of the interrupt being acknowledged. The processor fetches the vector number from the interrupting device, classifying the access as an interrupt acknowledge and displaying the level number of the interrupt being acknowledged on the address bus. External logic can respond to the interrupt acknowledge read in one of three ways: put a vector number on the data bus, request automatic vectoring, or indicate that no device is responding (bus error). If external logic requests an automatic vectoring, the processor internally generates a vector number which is determined by the interrupt level number. If external logic indicates a bus error, the interrupt is taken to be spurious, and the generated vector number references the spurious interrupt vector. The processor then proceeds with the usual exception processing. Normal instruction execution commences in the interrupt handling routine.

Priority level seven is a special case. Level seven interrupts cannot be inhibited by the interrupt priority mask, thus providing a "nonmaskable interrupt" capability. An interrupt is generated each time the interrupt request level changes from some lower level to level seven.

Hardware support. On-chip logic provides detection and comparison of interrupt requests. Arrival of interrupt requests does not affect execution of the current instruction. If an interrupt of sufficient priority arrives, a pointer to the interrupt microroutine will be substituted for the microroutine pointer from IR decode at the next macroinstruction boundary. An interrupt acknowledge is accomplished by the interrupt microroutine via an internal path involving no less than six separate registers. Support for translation and extension of interrupt vector addresses and creation of interrupt autovector addresses is the responsibility of the field translate hardware in the 68000. The microroutine uses the address from this special function unit as a pointer to the location of the program counter for the particular interrupt. Vectored, autovectored, and spurious interrupts are all handled by the same microroutine; the differences occur in vector generation by the field translate unit.

v. Internally Generated Exceptions

Description. Traps are exceptions caused by instructions. They arise either from processor recognition of abnormal conditions during instruction execution, or from use of instructions whose normal behavior is trapping. There are 16 user-definable trap instructions that, when executed, always direct program counter to a designated trap routine at the supervisory level. These software interrupts are useful for calling the operating system, simulating interrupts during debugging operations, signaling the completion of a task, or indicating that an error condition has appeared in a routine.

Some instructions are used specifically to generate traps. The TRAP instruction always forces an exception, and is useful for implementing system calls for user programs. The TRAPV and CHK instructions force an exception if the user program detects a runtime error, which may be an arithmetic overflow or a subscript out of bounds. The divide instructions will force an exception if a division operation (DIVS—signed and DIVU—unsigned) is attempted with a divisor of zero.

The attempt to execute certain instructions not implemented in current versions of the 68000 can cause one of two traps to occur. These instructions have op codes whose first 4 bits are 1010 (A_{16}) or 1111 (F_{16}) and are reserved for future enhancements to the instruction set. In anticipation of the expanded instruction set, the "line 1010 emulator" and the "line 1111 emulator" traps are provided to allow the user to imitate the operation of future instructions with macroinstructions. When specific op codes become available for the additional instructions, those can be included in programs. Currently, when an instruction op code is fetched whose first 4 bits are 1010 or 1111, a trap is made to the emulator routine—the line 1010 emulator and line 1111 emulator. When the operation becomes available as a machine primitive, the macroinstruction routine can be eliminated.

There are other op codes that would otherwise cause problems but instead initiate exception processing. Those, for example, that neither decode into valid instructions nor fall into the line 1010/1111 category are considered illegal, and the attempted execution of one will result in a trap. This is a particularly valuable exception because it helps to catch incorrect machine code. Most microprocessors perform some unknown of variable operation when an undefined op code is fetched, inviting the destruction of program or data. Software integrity is improved by forcing an operating system call to be made upon receipt of an invalid op code.

Unlike most instructions, which may execute at either the user or the supervisor level, privileged instructions, listed in Table 7.4, may execute only at the supervisor level. Privileged instructions are designed for system control; hence any instruction that modifies the entire status register is privileged. This privilege prevents a user-level program from turning on or off the trace feature, from changing the privilege level, or from changing the interrupt mask level.

Table 7.4. Privileged Instructions

PRIVILEGED INSTRUCTION	OPERATION
RESET	Reset external devices
RTE	Return from exception
STOP	Stop program execution
ORI to SR	Logical OR to status register
MOVE USP	Move user stack pointer
ANDI to SR	Logical AND to status register
EORI to SR	Logical EOR to status register
MOVE EA to SR	Load new status register

Trace, privilege violation, illegal instruction, and all instructions that cause a trap are handled in much the same fashion as an autovectored interrupt by the hardware. They all share (except for some small initial differences) a single microroutine. Again, as with interrupts, the field translate unit provides the vector address for the program counter. The decode of an illegal instruction, or a privileged instruction in user mode causes the macroinstruction decode logic to generate a pointer to a special microroutine which returns the machine to supervisor mode and effects a trap. Considerable additional hardware is required to detect these errors and to create the address of the exception vector; and increased control store space is necessary for the special microroutine.

vi. Bus Error/Address Error

Bus error exceptions occur when external logic requests that a bus error be processed by an exception. The current bus cycle that the processor is making is aborted. Whatever processing the processor was doing, instruction or exception, is terminated, and the processor immediately begins exception processing.

c. Multiple Exceptions. This section describes the processing that occurs when multiple exceptions arise simultaneously. Group 0 exceptions have highest priority; group 2 exceptions have lowest priority. Within group 0, reset has highest priority, followed by bus error and address error. Within group 1, trace has priority over external interrupts, which in turn takes priority over illegal instruction and privilege violation. Since only one instruction can be executed at once, there is no priority relation within group 2.

3. High-Level Language Support

On various occasions, the exact state of the stack prior to return from a subroutine might not be known to the programmer. Also, the execution of a subroutine will not save temporary data on the stack in an orderly manner. The LINK and UNLK instructions on the 68000 are used to take care of the above problems. The LINK instructions dynamically allocates up to 32,768 bytes of storage on the stack and also assigns a pointer to the top of the reserved area. Furthermore, the LINK instruction saves the current value of the pointer. The UNLK instruction reverses the effects of the LINK instruction and therefore, it restores the stack and address registers. Note that while using LINK and UNLK instruction, the displacement for data storage and offsets to the pointer register must be negative. This is because the stack grows toward low address memory and the address register addresses the top of the temporary data area.

Therefore, LINK and UNLK allow for the allocation and deallocation, respectively, of local variable storage for procedure calls. LINK uses an address register as a frame pointer to mark the beginning of local variable storage on the stack. The stack space for local variables is automatically reserved through incrementing the stack pointer by the number of bytes used for local storage. Access to the local variables is accomplished by using the frame pointer as a base register. Upon completion of the procedure, UNLK decrements the stack pointer to remove the local storage and then restores the previous frame pointer, to allow nesting of procedures.

Boundary checking can be accomplished using the CHK instruction (check register against bounds). Execution of CHK compares the contents of the data register with zero and an upper limit. If the register contents is less than zero or greater than the limit, a trap to the CHK routine is invoked.

Bounds testing is useful for maintaining arrays. The upper limit used in the CHK instruction could be set equal to the dimension of the array. The data register contains the element number of the array and the address register contains the starting address of the array. Prior to array access, the CHK instruction is executed to ensure that the array bounds have not been violated. If valid, then access to the array would be accomplished by using indirect addressing with index, where the starting address added with the index would point to the memory location of the array element. If not valid, the CHK routine would generate an error message.

Often it is desirable to pass parameters from one procedure to another. This may be accomplished by simply pushing the parameter on the stack. Another technique involves pushing the address of the parameter on the stack. The 68000 allows effective address calculation with a Push Effective Address (PEA) and Load Effective Address (LEA) instruction. These instructions perform the address calculation automatically and place it either on the stack (PEA) or in an address register (LEA).

Another operation frequently encountered by compilers involves performing Boolean operations on integer values. For instance, let X, Y, and Z be integers:

$$\text{If } (X > Y) \text{ and } (Y \leq Z) \text{ then}$$

This PASCAL statement requires that each expression contained in parentheses be evaluated and converted to a Boolean variable. Then the Boolean AND function is applied to these variables. The compiled assembly code might look like this:

CMP X, Y	Compare X and Y
SGT TEMP1	Set memory location TEMP1 to all ones if greater than; otherwise set to zero
CMP Y,Z	Compare Y and Z
SLE TEMP2	Set memory location Temp2 to all ones if less than or equal; otherwise set to zero
AND TEMP1, TEMP2	AND Temp1 and Temp2; Temp1 holds result

At this point the compiler knows the result of the IF statement and can proceed accordingly.

Multiprocessing often requires that two or more processors share a common memory. The Test And Set (TAS) instruction allows a processor to interrogate a trap to supervisor state (by stacking the current program and status word and loading a new context from a preassigned trap vector). Illegal instructions, unimplemented instructions, interrupts, and traps (operating as system calls) all cause the processor to trap and switch to supervisor state.

a. The 68000 design supports high-level languages, at both compilation time and execution time, with a clean, consistent instruction set; with hardware implementation of commonly used functions (multiply, divide, and address calculation); and with a set of special-purpose instructions designed to manipulate the runtime environment of a high-level language program. The language constructs aided by these special-purpose instructions include array accessing, limited-precision arithmetic, looping, Boolean expression evaluation, and procedure calls.

Array Accessing. The BOUNDS CHECK instruction compares a previously calculated array index (in a data register) against zero and a limit value addressed by the instruction. A trap occurs if the index is out of bounds for that array. This replaces a common sequence of instructions (at least four) with a single instruction.

Limited-precision Arithmetic. The TRAP ON OVERFLOW instruction causes a trap if the preceding operation resulted in overflow. This allows efficient overflow testing to encourage proper checking of arithmetic results.

Looping. A restricted form of the FOR-loop construct is implemented in a single instruction that decrements a count and branches backward if the result is nonzero.

Boolean-expression Evaluation. The CONDITIONAL SET instructions assign a true or false value to a Boolean variable on the same conditions that are used by the CONDITIONAL BRANCH instructions. These instructions help implement Boolean-expression evaluation by avoiding extra conditional branches, especially in the case (as with Pascal) where "short-circuited" evaluation may be undesirable because of possible side effects.

Procedure Calls. The 68000 uses a stack—pointed to by one of the address registers, called the stack pointer—to build the nested environments of called procedures. Three instructions (plus an additional one for each parameter) implement a high-level-language procedure call. The entire call mechanism uses only the stack and is completely reentrant. These instructions are described in more detail below.

Push Parameter Values or Addresses onto the Stack. The MOVE instruction pushes a value onto the stack, and the PUSH EFFECTIVE ADDRESS (see LOAD EFFECTIVE ADDRESS explained earlier) pushes the result of an arbitrary address calculation onto the stack for call by reference.

Call Procedure. The JUMP to SUBROUTINE instruction pushes the return address on the stack and jumps to the procedure entry point.

Establish New Local Environment. The LINK instruction does all of the following: saves the old contents of the frame pointer (an arbitrary address register) on the stack, points the frame pointer to the new top of stack, and subtracts the number of bytes of local storage required by the procedure from the stack pointer. This establishes local storage for the called procedure and a frame pointer (address register) for index addressing of local variables and parameters.

b. *Save an Arbitrary Subset of the Registers on the Stack.* The MOVE MULTIPLE REGISTERS instruction saves an arbitrary subset of the registers on the stack (or anywhere in memory) in a single instruction. The registers to be saved are indicated by setting the corresponding bits in a 16-bit field of the instruction.

A set of at most four instructions reverses the process for procedure return:

Reload saved registers. The MOVE MULTIPLE REGISTERS instruction is used here also.
Reestablish previous environment. The UNLINK instruction undoes the work of the LINK instruction.
Return from procedure. The RETURN instruction pops the return address from the stack and returns to the calling procedure.
Pop parameters from the stack. The ADD IMMEDIATE instruction used on the stack pointer pops any number of values off the stack.

7.1.8 Looping

Repetitive looping is one of the most common techniques used in computer programming. The test condition, decrement, and branch instruction (DB_{CC}) allows the efficient looping with a variety of features. The instruction is two words long and consists of three parameters: a condition based on status flags, a data register, and a displacement.

The process begins by initializing a data register with the number of loop iterations. The body of the loop follows, with the DB_{CC} instruction appearing at the end of the loop. Specified in the instruction is one of 16 conditions and the data register that holds the count. When DB_{CC} is encountered, the processor tests to see if the condition is true, decrements the data register, and also checks to see if the specified data register equals -1. If neither of these criteria is met, the processor branches backward or forward up to 32K bytes. If one or both are true, however, looping is terminated and normal processing continues.

Consider the following code segment:

```
      MOVE  #50, D1     INITIALIZE LOOP COUNT
LOOP  FIRST STATEMENT   BEGINNING OF LOOP (BODY OF LOOP)
      DBLE  D1, LOOP    END OF LOOP
```

The loop count is equal to 50 and resides in data register, D1. Upon completion of the loop, the condition-code register is checked for the less-than-or-equal-to condition. If true, the loop is terminated; if false D1 is decremented. If D1 equals zero, the loop is terminated. If not, the processor branches back to the label LOOP and executes the loop's body again. Note that DBLE is DB_{CC} instruction. CC is replaced by the appropriate condition. In this case, CC is LE, that is, less or equal.

Since the 68000 has so many data and address registers, saving them all during exceptions or subroutine calls could prove to be time consuming so register saving is left up to the programmer. This is easily facilitated with the MOVEM instruction. Any or all of the registers may be moved to a contiguous memory block with MOVEM, and contiguous memory may similarly be moved to selected registers. For instance,

```
MOVEM.L D1, D5, D6, A3, A4, SAVE
```

moves the contents of registers D1, D5, D6, A3, and A4 to the memory beginning at location SAVE. Likewise,

```
MOVEM.L SAVE, D1, D5, D6, A3, A4
```

restores the same registers with the data starting at location SAVE. Thus, only the critical registers need be saved, thereby maximizing context switching.

7.1.9 68000 Peripheral Circuits

The 68000 also has its own family of peripheral devices. Some of the currently available devices are shown in Figure 7.19.

Part No.	Description
68120	Intelligent peripheral controller (IPC)
68122	Cluster terminal controller (CTC)
68540	Error detection and correction circuit (EDCC)
68451	Memory-management unit (MMU)
68450	Direct memory access controller (DMAC)
68230	Parallel interface/timer (PI/T)
68561	Multiprotocol communications controller (MPCC)
68341	Floating-point read-only memory
68340	Dual-port RAM (DPR)
68453	Bubble memory controller
68560	Serial direct memory access processor (SDMA)

Figure 7.19 68000 peripheral circuits. Source: Reprinted by permission of Motorola Semiconductor Products, Inc., copyright © 1982.

7.1.10 Interfacing the 68000 to the 6846 ROM I/O Timer (RIOT)

The MC6846 ROM I/O Timer (RIOT) provides several versatile functions which the MC68000 may use with minimal effort. The RIOT features a 2K by 8 mask-programmable ROM, an 8-bit I/O port, and a 16-bit programmable timer/counter, in one 40-pin package. The MC68000 has the option of addressing the RIOT singly or in pairs, depending on the desired bus width. The 8-bit bus can be used if the upper and lower data strobes are used. Note that if a single RIOT is used, the MC68000 will not be able to obtain executable code from the ROM within the RIOT. This is due to the limitation introduced by the width of the data bus on the RIOT. Therefore, to effectively interface the ROM in the RIOT to the MC68000, a 16-bit data bus is used in this application. This configuration makes three 16-bit capabilities available to the MC68000. They are:

2K by 16 bits of mask-programmable ROM.
Two parallel, 8-bit I/O ports, or one parallel, 16-bit I/O port.
Two 16-bit timers that can be used together or independently.

1. Hardware

The basic connections needed for the RIOT to function with the MC68000 are: the lower ten address lines (A1–A10), the 16 data lines (D0–D15), and the R/$\overline{\text{W}}$, $\overline{\text{RESET}}$, E, and chip select signals. All of these may be obtained directly from the MC68000 with the exception of the chip select signals. As shown in Figure 7.20, the eight high-order data lines go to one RIOT and the eight low-order data lines go to the other RIOT. All other connections between the RIOTs are made in parallel. To obtain the chip select signals, some decoding circuitry must be provided. The RIOT may be run synchronously with the MC68000.

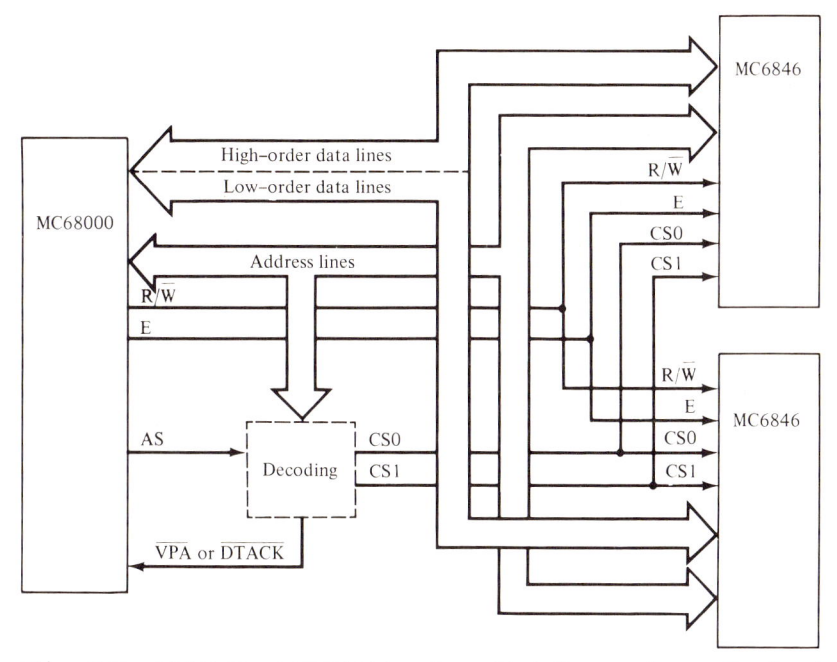

Figure 7.20 MC6846 to MC68000 interface—block diagram. Source: Reprinted by permission of Motorola Semiconductor Products, Inc., copyright © 1982.

a. Synchronous Operation. To run the RIOT synchronously, some decoding circuitry must be used to provide a low input to the $\overline{\text{VPA}}$ pin of the 68000 when the RIOT is selected. This synchronizes the 68000 with E and generates the $\overline{\text{VMA}}$ signal.

To use the synchronous output of the MC68000, the decoding circuitry must also generate a $\overline{\text{VPA}}$ signal, in addition to the chip selects. This signal informs the MC68000 that it is addressing a M6800 peripheral and synchronizes the processor with the E clock. The $\overline{\text{VPA}}$ signal also causes $\overline{\text{VMA}}$ to be generated which can be used for other M6800 peripherals.

b. Asynchronous Operation. Operating the RIOTs asynchronously with the MC68000 allows the processor to begin executing the next instruction without waiting to synchronize with the E clock. To operate asynchronously, the decoding circuitry must generate a $\overline{\text{DTACK}}$ signal in addition to the chip selects.

2. Software

The software needed for the MC68000 to use the RIOT is straightforward. One point to keep in mind is that the MC68000 addresses every 8 bits, even though it executes 16-bit instructions. This means that the least significant byte of an instruction is always located at an odd address, and

248 Chapter 7 MOTOROLA 68000 AND INTEL 432

likewise the most significant byte is always located at an even address. Since the hardware writes to all 16 bits at once, the addresses for the control registers are located two addresses apart (i.e., PCR: 11882, DDR: 11884, etc.). In using the ROM, no preliminary software is necessary. However, to use the I/O lines, the peripheral control register must be initialized and the data direction register must be configured before data may be transmitted to or received from the peripheral data register.

The software for the sample circuit is given in Figure 7.21. The I/O lines are connected to four, seven-segment displays through MC14511 BCD-to-decimal decoders. The software initializes the I/O lines (as outputs) and then outputs the first 10 bytes of each ROM. Since the decoder cannot decode hexadecimal numbers greater than 9, the software subtracts 8 if the

```
REVII     MC68000 ASM REV= 1.1—COPYRIGHT BY MOTOROLA 1978

 1        00001000              ORG    $1000
 2        00010000    ROMSTR    EQU    $1000         *STARTING ADDR.
 3                    *                              OF '46 ROM
 4        00011882    PCR       EQU    $11882        *'46 PERIPH.
 5                    *                              CNTR. REG.
 6        00011884    DDR       EQU    $11884        *'46 DATA DIR.
 7                    *                              REGISTER
 8        00011886    PDR       EQU    $11886        *'46 PERIPH.
 9                    *                              DATA REG.
10 001000 33FC0000
           00011882             MOVE.W #$0,PCR       CONFIG. '46 PCR'S
11 001008 33FCFFFF
           00011884             MOVE.W #$FFFF,DDR    CONFIG. '46 DOR'S
12 0010101 303C0009             MOVE.W #$0A-1,D0     SET NUMB. OF
13                    *                              WORDS FROM ROM
14                    *                              TO DISPLAY
15                    * * * * * * * * * *
16                    *
17                    *         DISPLAY ROUTINE—USES REGS. A1, D0, D1, D2, D3
18                    *
19                    * * * * * * * * * *
20                    *
21                    *         HEX TO DECIMAL MODIFICATION—IF HEX DIGIT GT 9,
22                    *                                     SUBTRACT 8
23 001014 227C00010000 CVRCHK   MOVE.L #ROMSTR,A1    LOAD IN STR. ADDR.
24 00101A 3211         BYTE1    MOVE.W (A1),D1       FETCH WD. FM ROM
25 00101C 3401                  MOVE.W D1,D2         MOVE TO SCTCH AREA
26 00101E 0242000F             AND.W  #$000F,D2      ISOLATE L.S. DIG.
27 001022 0C420009             CMP.W  #$0009,D2      CHCK IF NEEDS MOD
```

```
28 001026   6F000004              BLE      BYTE2          IF NOT, BRANCH
29 00102A   5142                  SUB.W    #$0008,D2      IF SO, SUBT. 8
30 00102C   3601         BYTE2    MOVE.W   D1,D3          GET SECOND BYTE
31 00102E   024300F0              AND.W    #$00F0,D3        TO SCRATCH AREA
32 001032   0C430090              CMP.W    #$0090,D3        AND REPEAT PROC
33 001036   6F000006              BLE      BYTE3
34 00103A   04430080              SUB.W    #$0080,D3
35 00103E   8443         BYTE3    OR.W     D3,D2
36 001040   3601                  MOVE.W   D1,D3
37 001042   02430F00              AND.W    #$0F00,D3
38 001046   0C430900              CMP.W    #$0900,D3
39 00104A   6F000006              BLE      BYTE4
40 00104E   04430080              SUB.W    #$0800,D3
41 001052   8443         BYTE4    OR.W     D3,D2
42 001054   2601                  MOVE.L   D1,D3          USE LONG WD. FOR MSB.
43 001056   02830000F000          AND.L    #$F000,D3
44 00105C   0C8300009000          CMP.L    #$9000,D3
45 001062   6F000006              BLE      DONE
46 001066   04438000              SUB.W    #$8000,D3
47 00106A   8443         DONE     OR.W     D3,D2          DISPYD DATA IN D2
48 00106C   33C200011886          MOVE.W   D2,PDR         WRITE DATA TO PIA
49 001072   2E3C0003D090          MOVE.L   #250000,D7     DLY FOR 5 SEC
50 001078   5387         DLY      SUB.L    #1,D7
51 00107A   6AFC                  BPL      DLY
52 00107C   51C8FF9C              DBRA     D0,BYTE1       GO AGN IF <> 10
53                       *
54                       *                 BACK TO MACSBUG
55                       *
56 001080   4E4F                  TRAP     15
57 001082   0000                  DC.W     0
58                       *
59                       * THE PIA ADRESSES ARE $11882 PCR
60                       *                    $11884 DDR
61                       *                    $11886 TO WRITE TO THE DISPL
62                                END

******TOTAL ERRORS 0— 0

SYMBOL TABLE

BYTE1    00101A  BYTE2  00102C  BYTE3    00103E  BYTE4  001052
CVRCHK   001014  DDR    011884  DLY      001078  DONE   00106A
PCR      011882  PDR    011886  ROMSTR   010000
```

Figure 7.21 Program listing. Source: Reprinted by permission of Motorola Semiconductor Products, Inc., copyright © 1982.

number is greater than 9. Then the code is output to the display for operator inspection. This software in included to give an idea of the simplicity involved in interfacing to these M6800 peripherals.

EXAMPLE 7.1

Write a program in 68000 assembly language to move a block of data from source to destination. D0 contains the number of long words to be moved. A0 contains the source address and A1 contains the destination address.

Solution

The program can be written as follows:

```
AGAIN:  MOVE.L  (A0)+, (A1)+
        SUBQ    #1, D0
        BNE     AGAIN
END:    JMP     END
```

EXAMPLE 7.2

Write a program in 68000 assembly language to add a string of words pointed to by A0 (+2) to A1 (+2). The sum is to be stored at A1. A2 contains the address of the end of the string.

Solution

The program can be written as follows:

```
        AND.W   #EFH, CCR    ; X, CCR BECOMES ZERO
REPEAT: ADDX.W  -(A0), -(A1) ; ADD TWO WORDS + X
        CMPA.L  A2, A1       ; IF NOT THE END OF STRING
        BHI     REPEAT       ; THEN LOOP AGAIN
END:    JMP     END          ; HALT
```

Note that in the above # represents immediate addressing mode.

7.2 Intel 432*

The Intel 432 is a true 32-bit microprocessor manufactured using Intel's HMOS-1 process. The processor unit consists of three chips, each packaged in 64-pin Quad In-Line Packages (a QUIP has four staggered rows of pins on 0.1-in. centers which gives greater density than standard DIP

---
* This section contains material modified from Intel manuals.

packages). The two data processor chips (iAPX43201 and iAPX43202) and single interface processor (iAPX43203) are all VLSI chips. The chip set contains over 200,000 devices, which is nearly six times the size of the 8086 microprocessor.

The two data processor chips (iAPX43201 and iAPX43202) are together referred to as a General Data Processor (GDP). Multiple GDPs may be added to the system to give increased processing power. A single GDP will yield 200,000 instructions per second while the performance of six GDPs is almost 2 million instructions per second, giving them the performance of a midrange main frame computer such as the IBM 370/148; hence the iAPX432's designation as a micro main frame computer.

The GDP uses a pipelined architecture which overlaps the instruction fetch and instruction execute cycles for increased performance. In this manner an instruction may be executed while the next instruction is being fetched. The instruction decode chip (iAPX43201) and the instruction execution chip (iAPX43202) communicate over a bidirectional 16-bit microinstruction bus which serves to pass the data and control signals between the two chips.

The 32-bit architecture of the GDP gives it a logical address capability of more than 4 billion bytes (2^{32}). The GDP can select one of the 2^{24} entries in its object table (the iAPX432 is an object-based machine) and each entry can specify a single segment of up to 2^{16} bytes, giving the iAPX432 a virtual address space of over a terabyte (2^{40}). This addressing scheme allows the use of high-speed main memory and slow-speed mass storage.

The 432 handles 32-bit data words similar to those handled by the larger minicomputers and some main frames (a main frame has a larger word size and higher execution speed than a minicomputer). The processor can operate on 32-bit integers or on 32-, 64-, or 80-bit floating-point data. Using multiplication as a benchmark, the 432 can multiply two 32-bit integers in 6.25 μs or two 80-bit floating-point words in 26.125 μs. This high speed exceeds the performance of many contemporary main frame computers.

The instruction set of the 432 has been specially tailored for high-level languages and will manipulate Boolean and string data as well as floating-point and integer data.

The 432 utilizes a "capability-based" memory protection system that ensures that all data structures are protected as far as what programs may access the data and to what extent the data may be modified.

Input/output communications are controlled by the interface processor (iAPX43203), the third of the three chip set. The interface processor controls satellite processors called "attached processors." Each attached processor handles a particular I/O operation independently of other attached processors. By use of as many attached processors as desired, a system of any size may easily be designed. Midrange Intel processors such as the 8086 are ideally suited for attached processor use.

Two 432's may be wired in parallel to check for hardware failures. The processors run at full speed with one processor checking the computations of the other. If the processors do not agree on a result, the processors may be halted to pinpoint system failure.

Hardware features of the 432 perform functions such as storage allocation and interprogram communications which are usually performed by operating system software. Single instructions such as "send" or "receive" transfer data between programs, which yields much faster program execution. Hardware is also used to synchronize the GDPs, allowing the processors to be "self-dispatching." The GDPs automatically find their own work and share the workload between GDPs. The workload per GDP is automatically redistributed as more GDPs are added to the system.

ADA, an object-oriented language, was developed by the United States Department of Defense, private industries, and universities as the 432s programming language. ADA is oriented toward systems programming, numerical problem solving, and real-time applications involving concurrent execution requirements. The elegance and simplicity of PASCAL is combined with the structure and expressive capabilities of multifunction software to provide a powerful language that is expected to decrease software development time.

7.2.1 General Data Processors (GDP)—iAPX43201 and iAPX43202

The instruction decoder (Figure 7.22) and instruction execution unit (Figure 7.23) are both fabricated with 5-V, N-channel, silicon gate HMOS (high-performance MOS) technology and packaged in 64-pin QUIPs.

1. Functional Description

The GDP is internally organized as a three-stage microprogrammed pipeline:

Stage 1—Instruction Decoder (ID)
Stage 2—Microinstruction Sequencer (MS)
Stage 3—Execution Unit (EU)

Each stage of the pipeline is an independent subprocessor with stages 1 and 2 located on the iAPX43201 (Figure 7.24) and stage 3 located on the iAPX43202. Each stage will operate until the pipeline is full and then halt until more work is available.

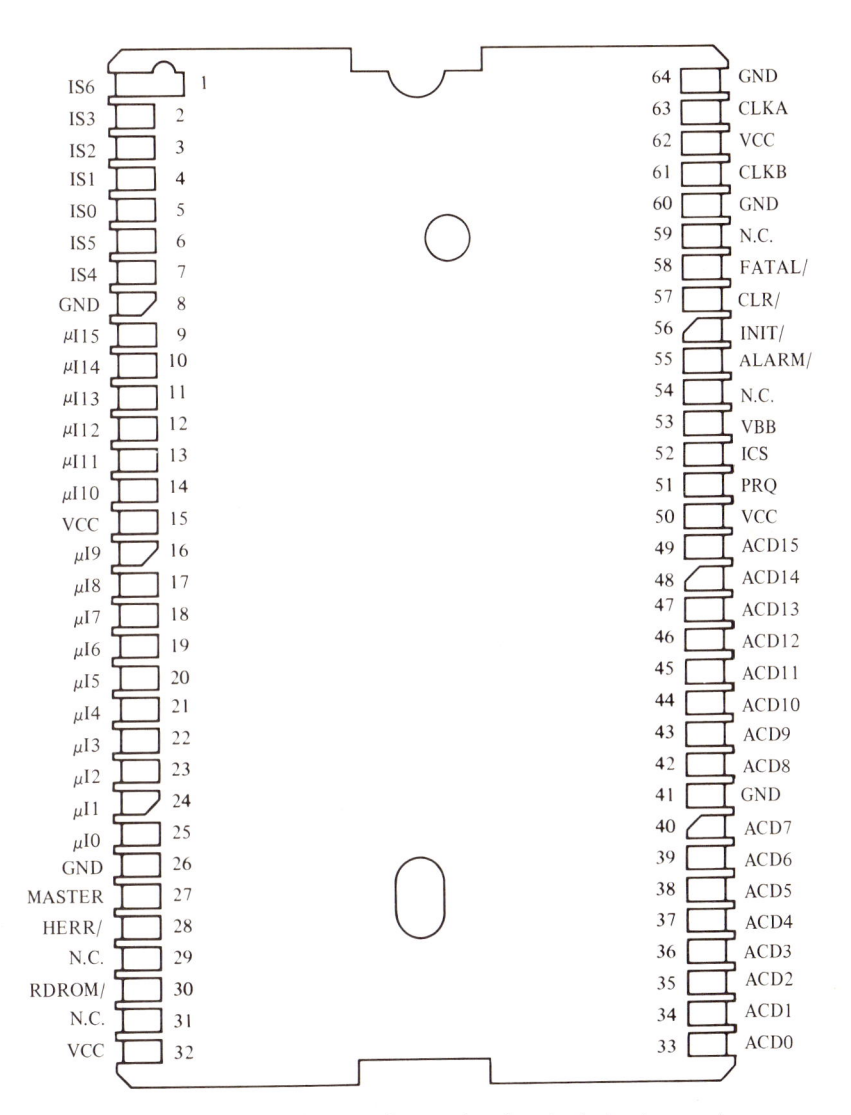

```
IS6  ─┤ 1          64 ├─ GND
IS3  ─┤ 2          63 ├─ CLKA
IS2  ─┤ 3          62 ├─ VCC
IS1  ─┤ 4          61 ├─ CLKB
IS0  ─┤ 5          60 ├─ GND
IS5  ─┤ 6          59 ├─ N.C.
IS4  ─┤ 7          58 ├─ FATAL/
GND  ─┤ 8          57 ├─ CLR/
µI15 ─┤ 9          56 ├─ INIT/
µI14 ─┤ 10         55 ├─ ALARM/
µI13 ─┤ 11         54 ├─ N.C.
µI12 ─┤ 12         53 ├─ VBB
µI11 ─┤ 13         52 ├─ ICS
µI10 ─┤ 14         51 ├─ PRQ
VCC  ─┤ 15         50 ├─ VCC
µI9  ─┤ 16         49 ├─ ACD15
µI8  ─┤ 17         48 ├─ ACD14
µI7  ─┤ 18         47 ├─ ACD13
µI6  ─┤ 19         46 ├─ ACD12
µI5  ─┤ 20         45 ├─ ACD11
µI4  ─┤ 21         44 ├─ ACD10
µI3  ─┤ 22         43 ├─ ACD9
µI2  ─┤ 23         42 ├─ ACD8
µI1  ─┤ 24         41 ├─ GND
µI0  ─┤ 25         40 ├─ ACD7
GND  ─┤ 26         39 ├─ ACD6
MASTER ─┤ 27       38 ├─ ACD5
HERR/ ─┤ 28        37 ├─ ACD4
N.C. ─┤ 29         36 ├─ ACD3
RDROM/ ─┤ 30       35 ├─ ACD2
N.C. ─┤ 31         34 ├─ ACD1
VCC  ─┤ 32         33 ├─ ACD0
```

Figure 7.22 43201 pin assignment instruction decoder/microinstruction sequencer. Source: Reprinted by permission of Intel Corporation, copyright © 1982.

a. Instruction Decoder (ID). The instruction decoder is the first subprocessor in the pipeline. The ID receives the macroinstructions and processes them to generate the microinstructions needed to execute the macroinstruction.

Instructions for the 432 vary in length depending on their complexity. Instructions range from only a few bits to several hundred bits and extend

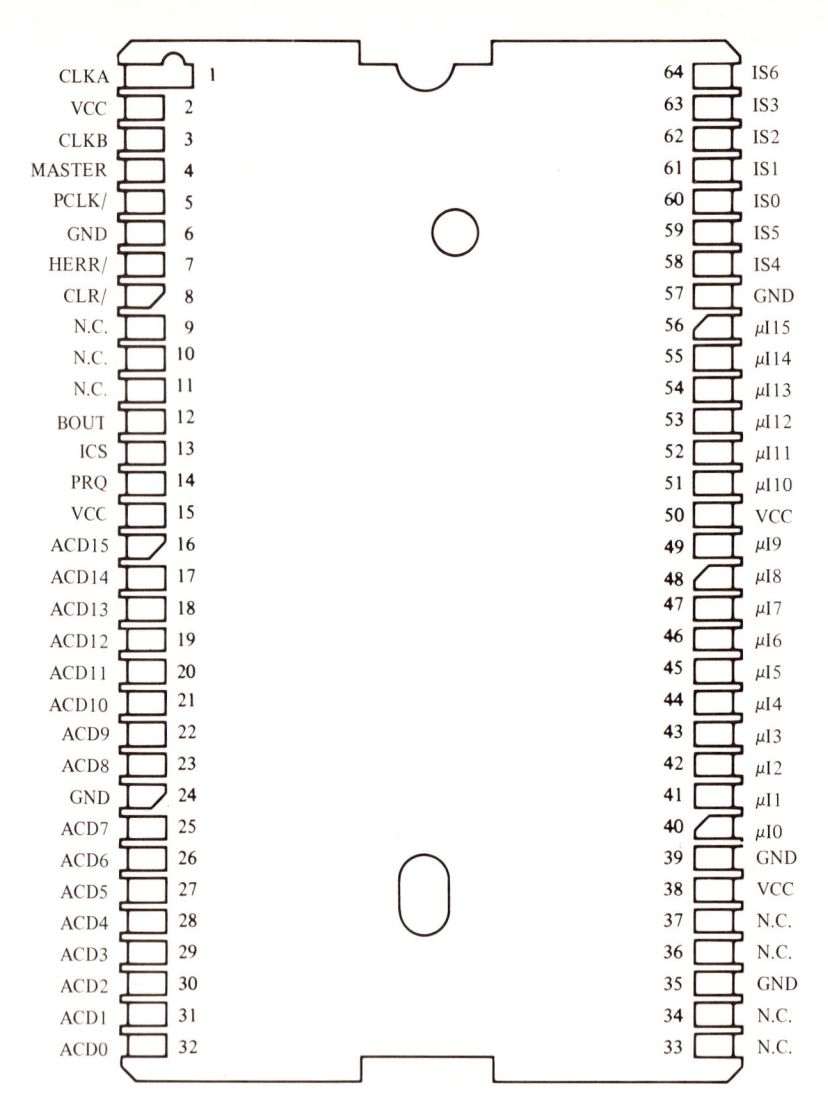

```
                    ┌──────────────────┐
         CLKA  │  1                64  │  IS6
          VCC  │  2                63  │  IS3
         CLKB  │  3                62  │  IS2
       MASTER  │  4                61  │  IS1
        PCLK/  │  5                60  │  IS0
          GND  │  6                59  │  IS5
        HERR/  │  7                58  │  IS4
         CLR/  │  8                57  │  GND
         N.C.  │  9                56  │  µI15
         N.C.  │ 10                55  │  µI14
         N.C.  │ 11                54  │  µI13
         BOUT  │ 12                53  │  µI12
          ICS  │ 13                52  │  µI11
          PRQ  │ 14                51  │  µI10
          VCC  │ 15                50  │  VCC
        ACD15  │ 16                49  │  µI9
        ACD14  │ 17                48  │  µI8
        ACD13  │ 18                47  │  µI7
        ACD12  │ 19                46  │  µI6
        ACD11  │ 20                45  │  µI5
        ACD10  │ 21                44  │  µI4
         ACD9  │ 22                43  │  µI3
         ACD8  │ 23                42  │  µI2
          GND  │ 24                41  │  µI1
         ACD7  │ 25                40  │  µI0
         ACD6  │ 26                39  │  GND
         ACD5  │ 27                38  │  VCC
         ACD4  │ 28                37  │  N.C.
         ACD3  │ 29                36  │  N.C.
         ACD2  │ 30                35  │  GND
         ACD1  │ 31                34  │  N.C.
         ACD0  │ 32                33  │  N.C.
                    └──────────────────┘
```

Figure 7.23 43202 pin assignment execution unit. Source: Reprinted by permission of Intel Corporation, copyright © 1982.

over as many words in memory as needed. The ID requests words from memory as needed to process each instruction. Instructions to the GDP contain a variable number of fields, each of which are in turn variable in length. In most cases the ID can decode a field to determine its length. When the ID detects an instruction boundary, it begins to execute the next instruction.

The 432 instruction set contains several branch instructions, each of

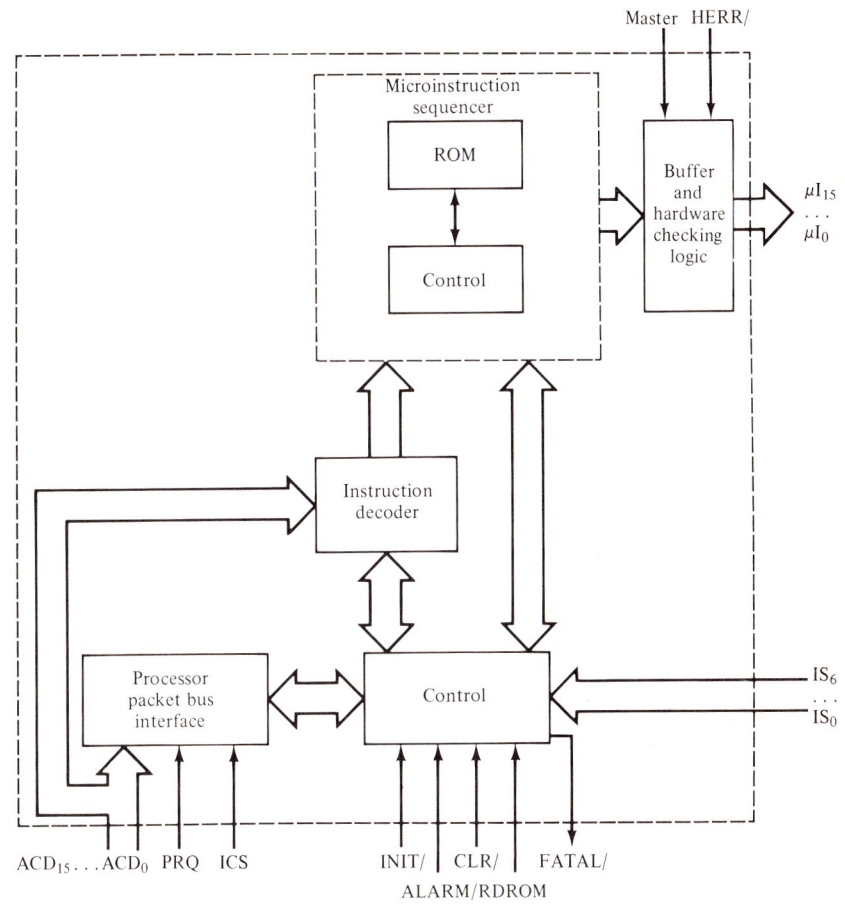

Figure 7.24 43201 block diagram. Source: Reprinted by permission of Intel Corporation, copyright © 1982.

which may start at any bit in the segment. Since branches occur often in a typical instruction stream, the start-up time after a branch is minimized.

Instruction fault recovery is also provided in the ID. The fault recovery information is retained in the ID until the instruction is successfully completed.

b. Microinstruction Sequencer (MS). The microinstruction sequencer issues the series of microinstructions to the execution unit (iAPX43202). The MS decides which microinstruction should be sent for each cycle and must consider the following to generate and process the correct microinstruction:

256 CHAPTER 7 MOTOROLA 68000 AND INTEL 432

- Whether the source for microinstructions is from the instruction decoder or from a ROM contained in the MS.
- The address of the next microinstruction, if it comes from the ROM.
- Length of time needed for the execution unit to complete the microinstruction.

c. Execution Unit (EU). The third stage of the GDP pipeline is contained in the execution unit (Figure 7.25). The EU receives the microinstructions from the iAPX43201 and routes them to one of its two independent subprocessors, the Data Manipulation Unit (DMU) and the Reference Generator Unit (RGU).

The EU executes most microinstructions in a single clock cycle while the internal sequencers of its subprocessors may run for many clock cycles (depending on the microinstruction). Complicated arithmetic operations invoke the sequencer in the DMU and processor packet bus transactions invoke the sequencer in the RGU. The processor packet concept is designed to reduce bus use. The processors request and receive information over the bus in discrete packages. In this manner a task may be requested from one subprocessor and the bus will be released after the request is made. When

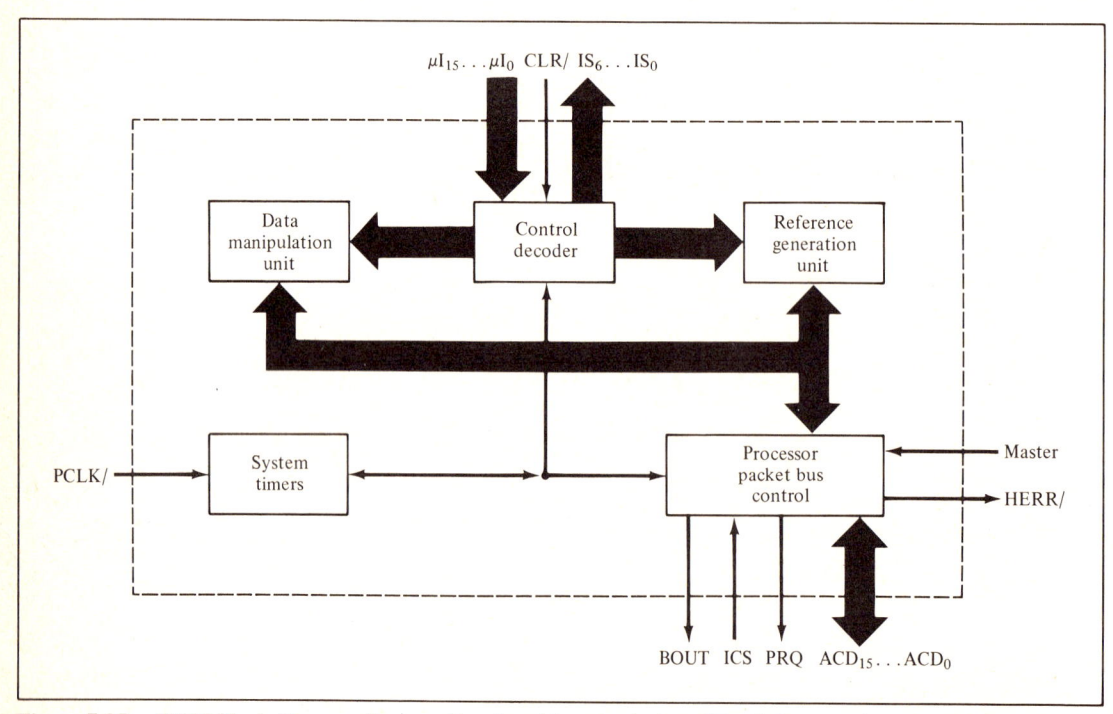

Figure 7.25 43202 block diagram. Source: Reprinted by permission of Intel Corporation, copyright © 1982.

the result is ready, the subprocessor can return its reply with a separate "packet."

The data manipulation unit contains the registers and arithmetic capabilities to execute the following functions:

1. Recognition of nine data types.
2. State machine execution of 16- and 32-bit multiply, divide, and remainder.
3. Control functions for 32-, 64-, and 80-bit floating-point arithmetic.

The reference generation unit provides the translations of 40-bit virtual addresses to 24-bit physical addresses as well as providing sequencing for the 8-, 16-, 32-, 64-, and 80-bit memory accesses. The physical address is the maximum amount of memory that the processor can access without referring to the mass storage device (disk, etc.).

Figure 7.26 shows how both the iAPX43201 and iAPX43202 interface to the packet bus as a single processing unit.

2. 432 Instructions

The 432 views instructions as groups of fields, each field consisting of a variable number of bits. A unified form is used for all instructions.

GDP instructions generally consist of four main fields: the class field, the format field, the reference field, and the op code field. Depending on the complexity of the operand references, the reference field may contain several additional fields.

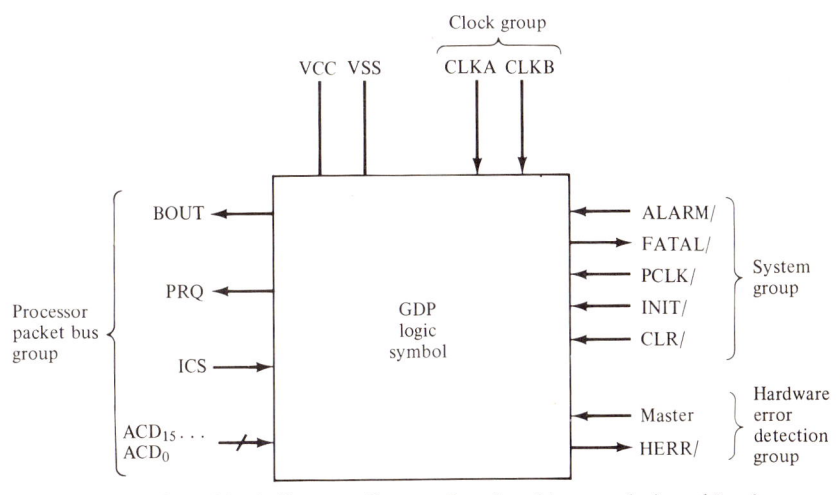

Figure 7.26 GDP block diagram. Source: Reprinted by permission of Intel Corporation, copyright © 1982.

The class field is either 4 or 6 bits long, depending on its encoding. The class field specifies the number of operands required, the primitive types of the operands, and the number of references (0–3).

If the class field indicates one or more references, a format field is required to specify whether the references are implicit or explicit as well as their uses. Explicit references are used when the operand is supplied by the instruction and implicit references are used when one or more of the operands are implied by the instruction.

If an explicit reference is used, the format field can indicate whether the reference is direct or indirect. The format field may also indicate that a single operand plays more than one role in the execution of the instruction. For example, an instruction to increment the value of an integer in memory contains the following:

1. A class field which specifies that the operator is of order two and that the operands both occupy a word of memory.
2. A format field which indicates that a single reference specifies a logical address to be used for fetching the source operand and storing the result.
3. An explicit data reference to the integer to be incremented.
4. An op code field to specify the two-order operator "increment integer."

It is possible for a format field to indicate that an instruction contains fewer explicit data references than are indicated by the instruction's class field, in which case the other data references required are implicit references and the corresponding source or result operands are obtained from, or returned to, the top of the operand stack.

The following high-level statement can be used to illustrate the use of implicit references:

A = A + B*C

The instruction stream segment for the above statement consists of two instructions and each instruction has the following form:

OP CODE	REFERENCE	FORMAT	CLASS

Assuming that A, B, and C are integer operands, the first class field (right-most field) specifies that the operator requires three references, each of which are to word operands (A, B, and C).

The first format field contains the code specifying the two explicit data references (the source operands A and B). The destination is referenced implicitly so that the result of the multiplication (designated in the op code field) is to be pushed onto the operand stack. The second class field, identical to the first, again specifies the three references required by the operator. The second format field specifies one explicit data reference (A) to be used for the first source operand and the destination (A). The second source operand is referenced implicitly and is to be popped from the operand stack (which holds the result of the previous instruction: B*C) when the instruction is executed.

The reference fields can be of various lengths and can appear in various numbers, consistent with their specification in the class and format fields. If implicit references are specified, reference fields for them will not appear. Direct references will require more bits than indirect references.

The op code field follows the class, format, and reference fields and specifies the operator to be applied to the operands specified in the other fields.

Modes of Generation. System modes of generation, selector generation and displacement generation, are illustrated in Figures 7.27 and 7.28, respectively.

The four modes of selector generation are concerned with the object structure and how they are accessed by the operands:

1. Short direct.
2. Long direct.
3. Stack indirect.
4. General indirect.

The four modes of displacement generation specify the physical location and displacement of objects within a given segment(s):

1. Scalar data reference mode.
2. Record item reference mode.
3. Static vector element reference mode.
4. Dynamic vector element reference mode.

3. Hardware Error Detector for iAPX432 Processors

iAPX432 processors include the hardware necessary to detect errors by Functional Redundancy Checking (FRC). As the name implies, FRC uses a redundant system (in this case another iAPX432) to check the functions of the primary system. At initialization, each iAPX432 processor is configured as either a master or as a checker processor. A master operates in the normal manner while the checker operates with all output pins to be checked in the high-impedance state. The pins to be checked on the master are parallel connected to the checker so that the checker can compare its

260 Chapter 7 MOTOROLA 68000 AND INTEL 432

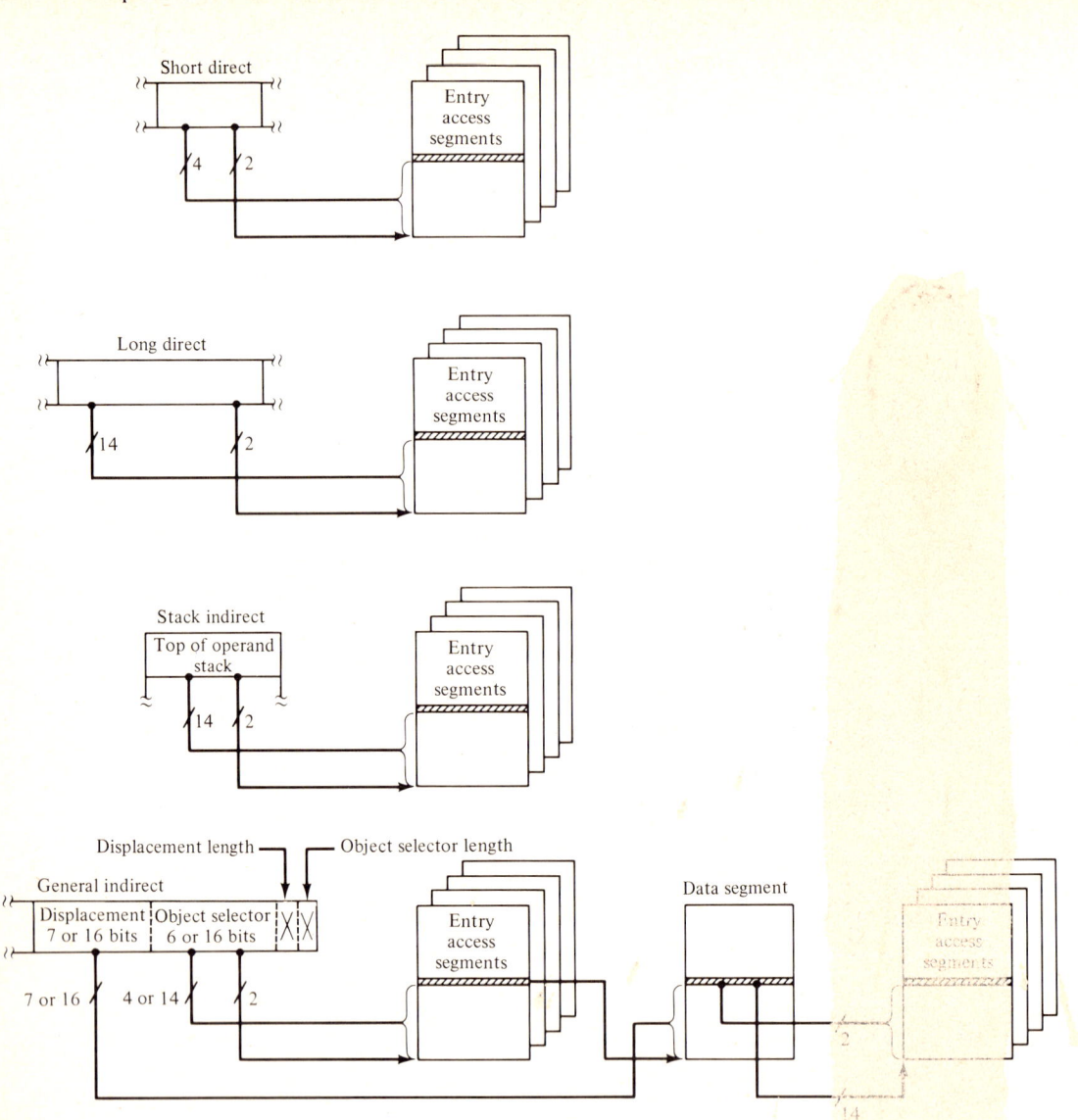

Figure 7.27 Modes of selector generation. Source: Reprinted by permission of Intel Corporation, copyright © 1982.

output values with the master's output values. Any comparison error causes the checker to assert its hardware error (HERR/) output (refer to Figure 7.29).

4. iAPX432 Information Structure

This section discusses the information structure for an iAPX432 system including memory system requirements, physical addressing, data formats,

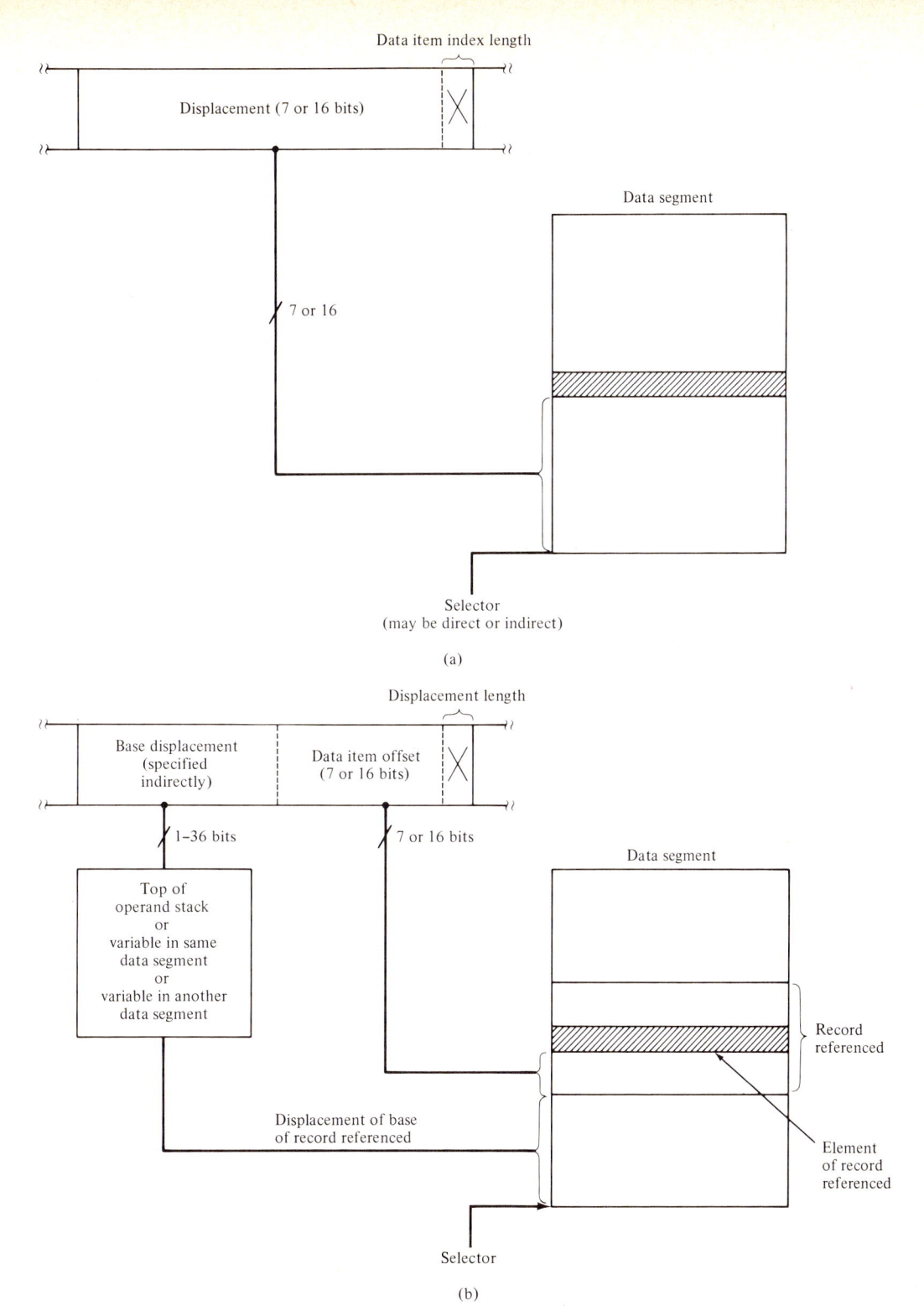

Figure 7.28 Modes of displacement generation. (a) Scalar data reference mode. (b) Record item reference mode. (c) Static vector element reference mode. (d) Dynamic vector element reference mode. Source: Reprinted by permission of Intel Corporation, copyright © 1982.

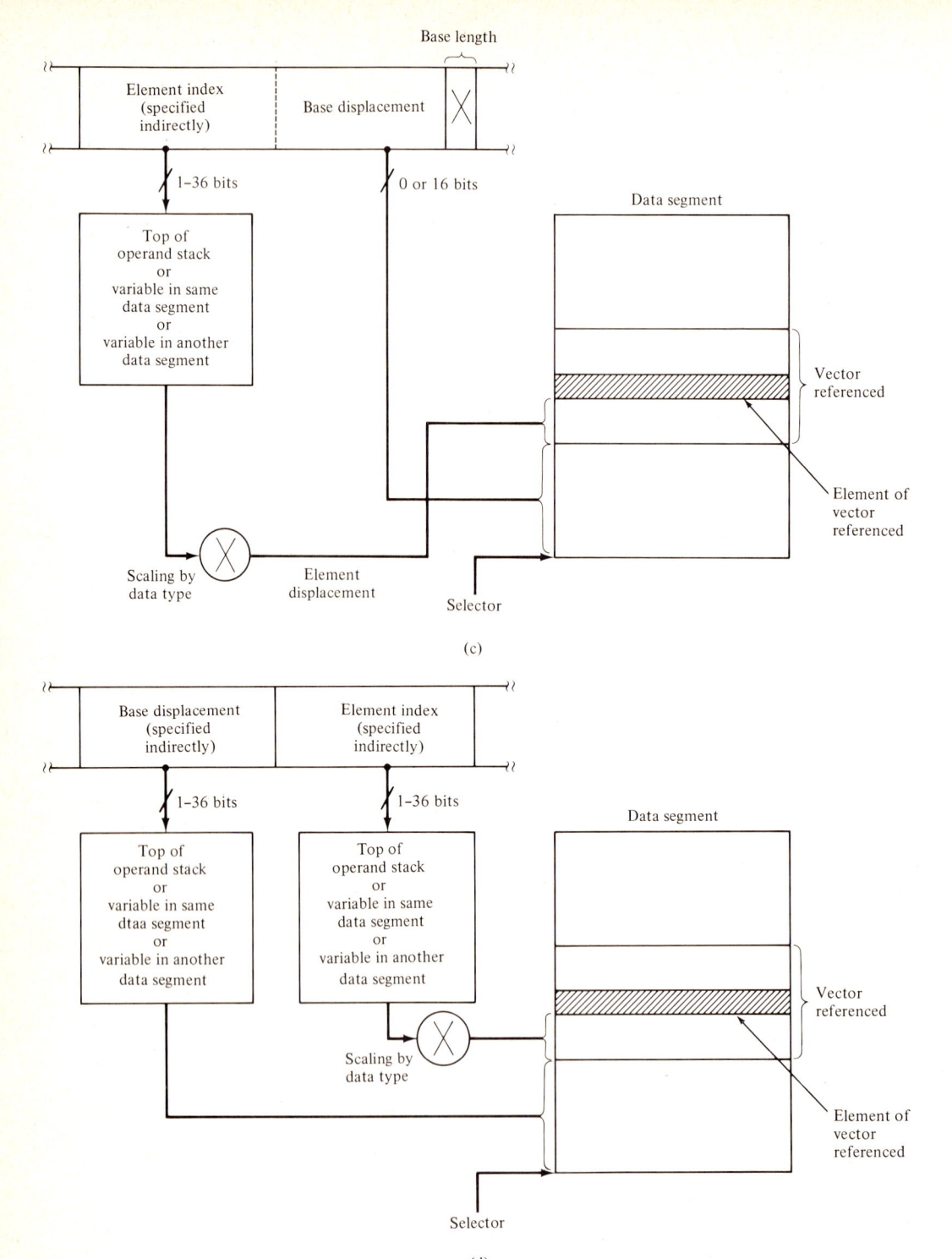

Figure 7.28 Continued

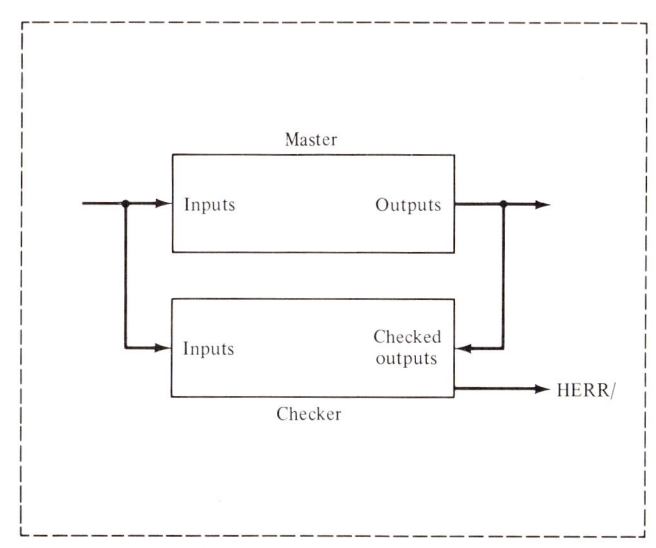

Figure 7.29 Hardware error detection. Source: Reprinted by permission of Intel Corporation, copyright © 1982.

and data representation. Any iAPX432 processor in the system can access all the contents of physical memory.

a. Memory. The iAPX432 implements a two-level memory structure where the software exists in a segmented environment in which a logical address specifies the location of a data item. The processor automatically translates this logical address into a physical address for accessing the value from physical memory. Since the iAPX432 can specify an address in its logical space of 2^{40} but only has an actual memory size of 2^{24}, the iAPX432 hardware will check to see if the address needed is already in its actual memory. If the address is not present, the memory segment needed will be loaded from auxiliary storage into the physical memory segment. This implementation is referred to as virtual memory.

b. Physical Addressing. Logical addresses are translated into physical addresses by the processor by transmitting a 24-bit physical address to the memory to select the beginning byte of a memory value to be referenced. The maximum physical memory is 16 megabytes (2^{24}).

c. Data Formats. When a processor executes the instructions of an operation within a context, operands found in the logical address space of the context may be manipulated. An individual operand may occupy 1 (byte), 2 (doubt-byte), 4 (word), 8 (double-word), or 10 (extended-word) bytes of memory. All operands are referenced by a logical address which is translated into a physical address. The displacement of such an address is the displacement in bytes from the base address of the data segment to the first byte of the operand. For operands consisting of multiple bytes, the address locates the low-order byte while the higher-order bytes are found at the next higher consecutive addresses.

d. Data Representation. A convention for representing data in the iAPX432 has been adopted where the bits in a field are numbered by increasing numeric significance, with the least significant bit shown on the right. Increasing byte addresses are shown from right to left (see Figure 7.30 for examples).

e. Requirements of an iAPX432 Memory System. The multiprocessor architecture of the iAPX432 places certain requirements on the operation of the memory system to ensure the integrity of the operation of data items that may be accessed simultaneously. Indivisible Read-Memory-Write (RMW) operations to both double-byte and word operands in memory are necessary for manipulating system objects. When an RMW-read is

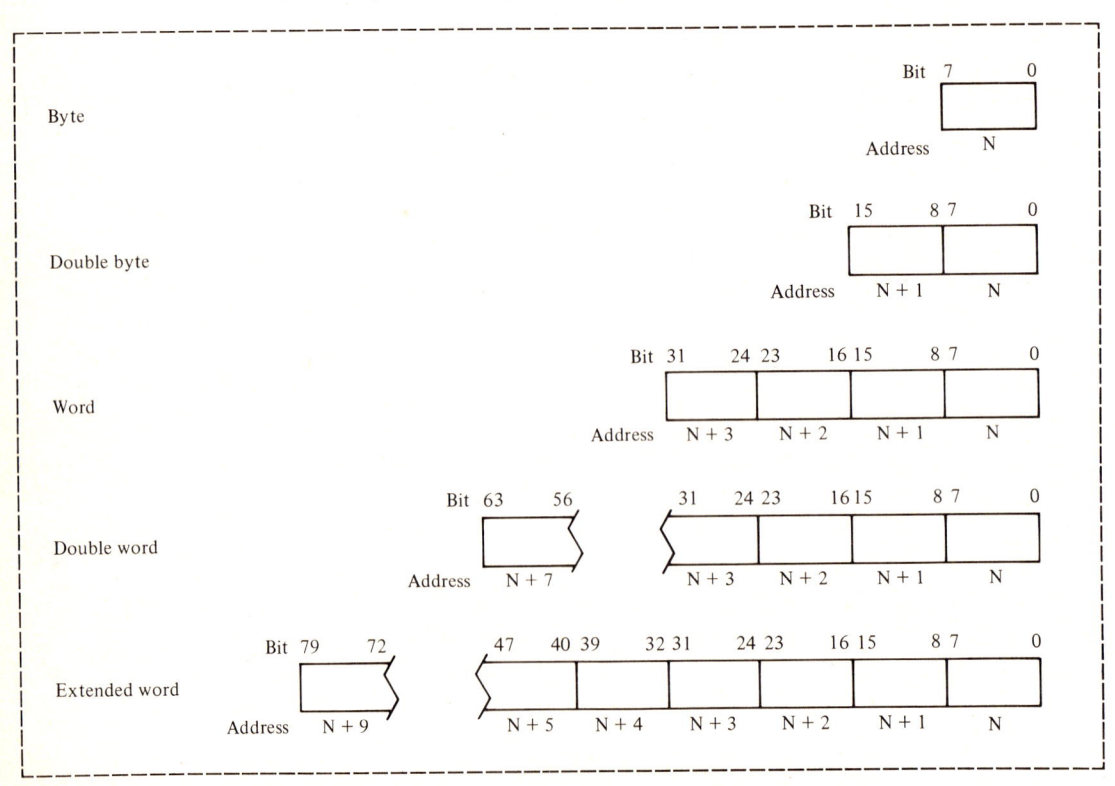

Figure 7.30 Basic iAPX432 data lengths. Source: Reprinted by permission of Intel Corporation, copyright © 1982.

processed for a location in memory, any other RMW-reads from that location must be held off by the memory system until an RMW-write to that location is received (or until an RMW time-out occurs). While the memory system is awaiting the RMW-write, other types of reads and writes are still allowed. For ordinary reads and writes of double-byte or longer operands, the memory system must ensure the entire operand has either been read or written before beginning to process another access to the same location. For example, if two simultaneous writes to the same location occur, the memory system must ensure that the set of locations used to store the operand does not get changed to some interleaved combination of the two written values.

5. Instruction Set Summary

Table 7.5 gives a summary of the iAPX432 General Data Processor operator set.

Table 7.5. General Data Processor Operator Set Summary

CHARACTER OPERATORS	SHORT-INTEGER OPERATORS	INTEGER OPERATORS
Move character	Move short integer	Move integer
Zero character	Zero short integer	Zero integer
One character	One short integer	One integer
Save character	Save short integer	Save integer
AND character	Add short integer	Add integer
OR character	Subtract short integer	Subtract integer
XOR character	Increment short integer	Increment integer
XNOR character	Decrement short integer	Decrement integer
Complement character	Negate short integer	Negate integer
	Multiply short integer	Multiply integer
Add character	Divide short integer	Divide integer
Subtract character	Remainder short integer	Remainder integer
Increment character		
Decrement character	Equal short integer	Equal integer
	Not equal short integer	Not equal integer
Equal character	Equal zero short integer	Equal zero integer
Not equal character	Not equal zero short integer	Not equal zero integer
Equal zero character		Greater than integer
Not equal zero character	Greater than short integer	Greater than or equal integer
Greater than character	Greater than or equal short integer	Positive integer
Greater than or equal character	Positive short integer	Negative integer
Convert character to short ordinal	Negative short integer	
	Convert short integer to integer	Convert integer to short integer
	Convert short integer to temporary real	Convert integer to ordinal
		Convert integer to temporary real

Table 7.5. Continued

SHORT-ORDINAL OPERATORS	ORDINAL OPERATORS	SHORT-REAL OPERATORS
Move short ordinal	Move ordinal	Move short real
Zero short ordinal	Zero ordinal	Zero short real
One short ordinal	One ordinal	Save short real
Save short ordinal	Save ordinal	
		Add short real—short real
AND short ordinal	AND ordinal	Add short real—temporary real
OR short ordinal	OR ordinal	Add temporary real—short real
XOR short ordinal	XOR ordinal	Subtract short real—short real
XNOR short ordinal	XNOR ordinal	Subtract short real—temporary real
Complement short ordinal	Complement ordinal	Subtract temporary real—short real
		Multiply short real—short real
Extract short ordinal	Extract ordinal	Multiply short real—temporary real
Insert short ordinal	Insert ordinal	Multiply temporary real—short real
Significant bit short ordinal	Significant bit ordinal	Divide short real—short real
		Divide short real—temporary real
Add short ordinal	Add ordinal	Divide temporary real—short real
Subtract short ordinal	Subtract ordinal	Negate short real
Increment short ordinal	Increment ordinal	Absolute value short real
Decrement short ordinal	Decrement ordinal	
Multiply short ordinal	Multiply ordinal	
Divide short ordinal	Divide ordinal	
Remainder short ordinal	Remainder ordinal	
Equal short ordinal	Equal ordinal	
Not equal short ordinal	Not equal ordinal	
Equal zero short ordinal	Equal zero ordinal	
Not equal zero short ordinal	Not equal zero ordinal	
Greater than short ordinal	Greater than ordinal	
Greater than or equal short ordinal	Greater than or equal ordinal	
Convert short ordinal to character	Convert ordinal to short ordinal	
Convert short ordinal to ordinal	Convert ordinal to integer	
Convert short ordinal to temporary real	Convert ordinal to temporary real	

SHORT-REAL OPERATORS	REAL OPERATORS	TEMPORARY-REAL OPERATORS
Equal short real	Move real	Move temporary real
Equal zero short real	Zero real	Zero temporary real
Greater than short real	Save real	Save temporary real
Greater than or equal short real		
Positive short real	Add real—real	Add temporary real
Negative short real	Add real—temporary real	Subtract temporary real
	Add temporary real—real	Multiply temporary real

Table 7.5. Continued

SHORT-REAL OPERATORS	REAL OPERATORS	TEMPORARY-REAL OPERATORS
Convert short real to temporary real	Subtract real—real	Divide temporary real
	Subtract real—temporary real	Remainder temporary real
	Subtract temporary real—real	Negate temporary real
	Multiply real—real	Square root temporary real
	Multiply real—temporary real	Absolute value temporary real
	Multiply temporary real—real	
	Divide real—real	Equal temporary real
	Divide real—temporary real	Equal zero temporary real
	Divide temporary real—real	Greater than temporary real
	Negate real	Greater than or equal temporary real
	Absolute value real	Positive temporary real
		Negative temporary real
	Equal real	
	Equal zero real	Convert temporary real to ordinal
	Greater than real	Convert temporary real to integer
	Greater than or equal real	Convert temporary real to short
	Positive real	Convert temporary real to real
	Negative real	
	Convert real to temporary real	

ACCESS DESCRIPTOR MOVEMENT OPERATORS	RIGHTS MANIPULATION OPERATORS	TYPE DEFINITION MANIPULATION OPERATORS
Copy access descriptor	Amplify rights	Create public type
Null access descriptor	Restrict rights	Create private type
		Retrieve public type representation
		Retrieve type representation
		Retrieve type definition

REFINEMENT OPERATORS	SEGMENT CREATION OPERATORS	ACCESS PATH INSPECTION OPERATORS
Create generic refinement	Create data segment	Inspect access descriptor
Create typed refinement	Create access segment	Inspect access
Retrieve refined object	Create typed segment	
	Create access descriptor	

OBJECT INTERLOCK OPERATORS	BRANCH OPERATORS	INTERCONNECT OPERATORS
Lock object	Branch	Move to interconnect
Unlock object	Branch true	Move from interconnect
Indivisibly add short ordinal	Branch false	
Indivisibly add ordinal	Branch indirect	
Indivisibly insert short ordinal	Branch intersegment	
Indivisibly insert ordinal	Branch intersegment without trace	
	Branch intersegment and link	

Table 7.5. Continued

Process Communication Operators	Processor Communication Operators	Context Communication Operators
Send	Send to processor	Enter access segment
Receive	Broadcast to processors	Enter global access segment
Conditional send	Read processor status and clock	Set context mode
Conditional receive		Call context
Surrogate send		Call context with message
Surrogate receive		Return from context
Delay		
Read process clock		

Source: Reprinted by permission of Intel Corporation, copyright © 1982.

7.2.2 Interface Processor (IP)—iAPX43203

The iAPX43203 Interface Processor (IP) provides I/O capabilities for iAPX432 peripheral subsystems. The interface processor operates with its own address space and interfaces to an iAPX432 system by mapping a portion of the subsystem memory into the main system memory. As with the other iAPX432 processors, the IP operates in an object-oriented, capability-based, multiprocessing environment.

The iAPX43203, like the iAPX43201 and iAPX43202, is a VLSI device manufactured using the Intel HMOS-1 technology and is packaged in a 64-pin QUIP (see Figure 7.31).

1. Functional Description

The internal architecture of the iAPX43203 is shown in the block diagram (Figure 7.32). The IP interfaces to the processor packet bus and peripheral subsystem as shown in Figure 7.33. An attached processor (e.g., an 8086) is used with the IP to form an I/O processor unit for the iAPX432 system.

The interface processor acts as a slave processor to the attached processor and functions to map part of the peripheral subsystem memory into the iAPX432 main memory. The same memory protection properties of other iAPX432 processors apply to the IP. Up to five subsystem memory packets (referred to as windows 0–4) may be mapped into iAPX432 main memory. The attached processor usually references memory with a logical address but under special circumstances may use a direct 24-bit physical address.

2. A Basic I/O Model

The typical application for the iAPX432 micro main frame consists of the main system (general data processors) and one or more peripheral subsystems (Interface Processors). Figure 7.34 shows the architecture of a

Intel 432   269

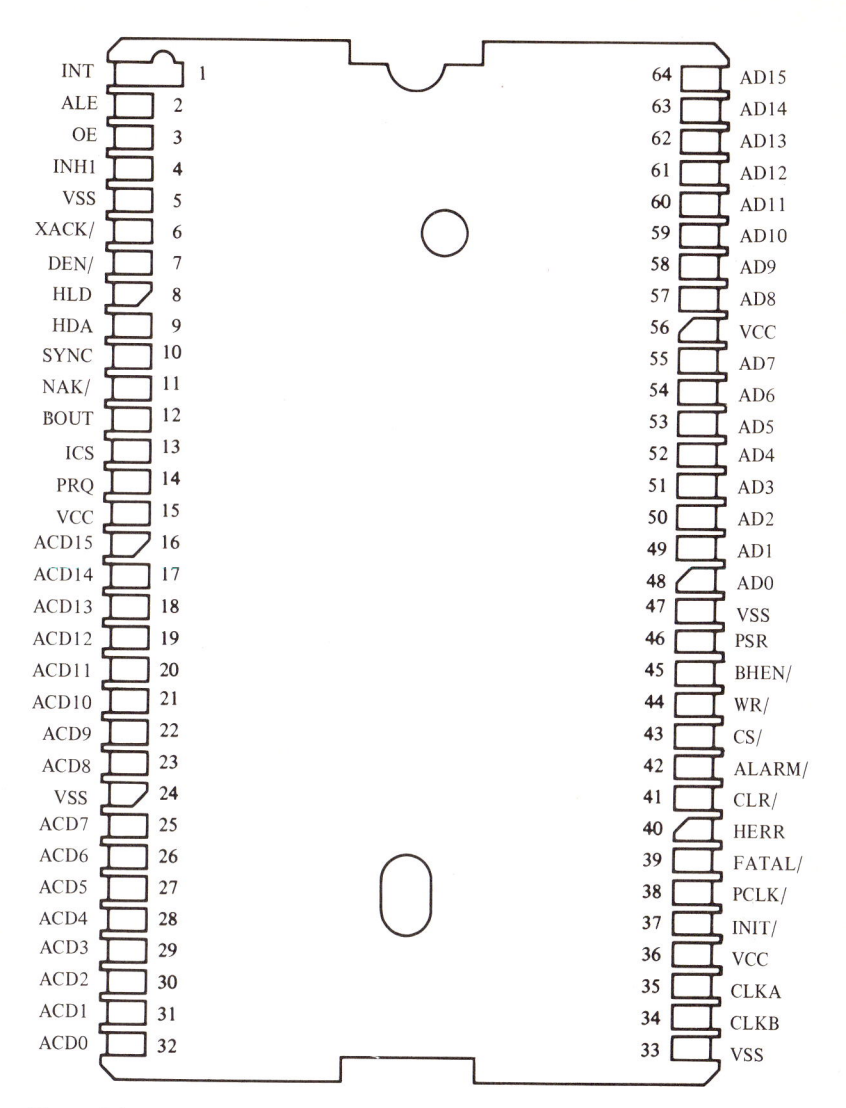

```
         INT  ⌐⌐  1            64  ⌐⌐  AD15
         ALE  ⌐⌐  2            63  ⌐⌐  AD14
          OE  ⌐⌐  3            62  ⌐⌐  AD13
        INH1  ⌐⌐  4            61  ⌐⌐  AD12
         VSS  ⌐⌐  5            60  ⌐⌐  AD11
       XACK/  ⌐⌐  6            59  ⌐⌐  AD10
        DEN/  ⌐⌐  7            58  ⌐⌐  AD9
         HLD  ⌐⌐  8            57  ⌐⌐  AD8
         HDA  ⌐⌐  9            56  ⌐⌐  VCC
        SYNC  ⌐⌐ 10            55  ⌐⌐  AD7
        NAK/  ⌐⌐ 11            54  ⌐⌐  AD6
        BOUT  ⌐⌐ 12            53  ⌐⌐  AD5
         ICS  ⌐⌐ 13            52  ⌐⌐  AD4
         PRQ  ⌐⌐ 14            51  ⌐⌐  AD3
         VCC  ⌐⌐ 15            50  ⌐⌐  AD2
       ACD15  ⌐⌐ 16            49  ⌐⌐  AD1
       ACD14  ⌐⌐ 17            48  ⌐⌐  AD0
       ACD13  ⌐⌐ 18            47  ⌐⌐  VSS
       ACD12  ⌐⌐ 19            46  ⌐⌐  PSR
       ACD11  ⌐⌐ 20            45  ⌐⌐  BHEN/
       ACD10  ⌐⌐ 21            44  ⌐⌐  WR/
        ACD9  ⌐⌐ 22            43  ⌐⌐  CS/
        ACD8  ⌐⌐ 23            42  ⌐⌐  ALARM/
         VSS  ⌐⌐ 24            41  ⌐⌐  CLR/
        ACD7  ⌐⌐ 25            40  ⌐⌐  HERR
        ACD6  ⌐⌐ 26            39  ⌐⌐  FATAL/
        ACD5  ⌐⌐ 27            38  ⌐⌐  PCLK/
        ACD4  ⌐⌐ 28            37  ⌐⌐  INIT/
        ACD3  ⌐⌐ 29            36  ⌐⌐  VCC
        ACD2  ⌐⌐ 30            35  ⌐⌐  CLKA
        ACD1  ⌐⌐ 31            34  ⌐⌐  CLKB
        ACD0  ⌐⌐ 32            33  ⌐⌐  VSS
```

Figure 7.31 iAPX43203 interface processor pin configuration. Source: Reprinted by permission of Intel Corporation, copyright © 1982.

system utilizing two IPs. The main memory shown is shared by all processors and contains the main system software that executes on the GDPs.

As shown in Figure 7.34, the main system may be conceived as self-contained and isolated from the actual I/O or "real world." The function of the "wall" around the main system is to protect objects in memory from damage by accidental I/O operations.

270 Chapter 7 MOTOROLA 68000 AND INTEL 432

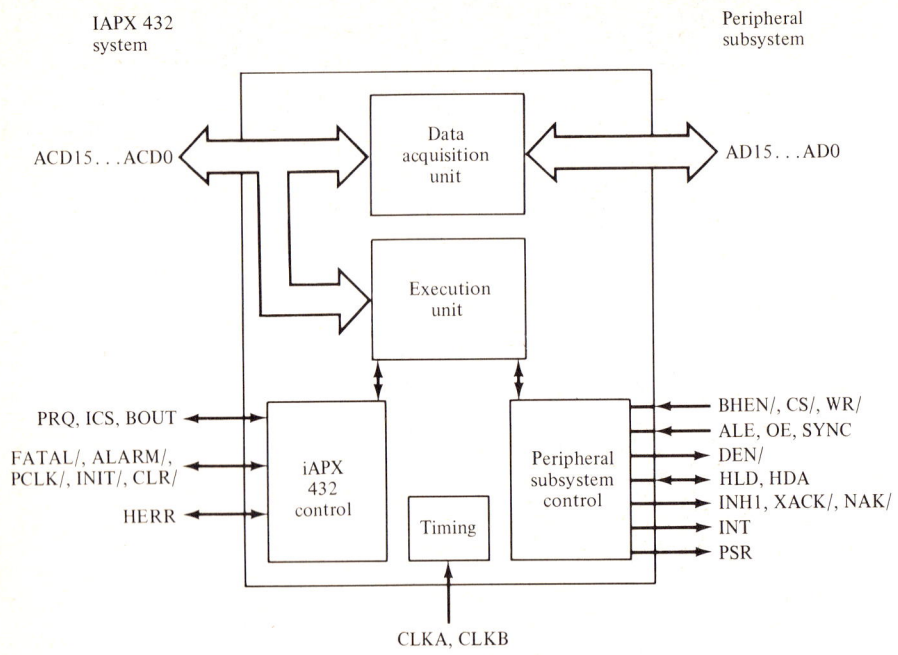

Figure 7.32 iAPX43203 IP functional block diagram. Source: Reprinted by permission of Intel Corporation, copyright © 1982.

All I/O controls (timing, interrupts, buffering, etc.) are the responsibility of the peripheral subsystems and do not require the attention of the GDPs. The peripheral subsystem is a complete processor in its own right with its own memory, processor, I/O, and so on. The subsystems are independent of the GPDs and the number of subsystems may be increased or decreased as needed to meet system criteria.

A peripheral subsystem is analogous to a main frame channel in that it executes in parallel with the main processor and handles all low-level I/O support, but it differs from a standard channel in that the subsystem can be configured to meet any system requirements by changing the subsystem hardware or software.

At the hardware level, the interface processor attaches the subsystem to the main system by two separate busses, the iAPX432 processor Packet Bus and a general-system interface. In general, any system using an 8- or 16-bit bus (e.g., Intel's Mutlibus) may serve as a peripheral subsystem.

The IP provides software that controls the "windows" through which the subsystem may communicate with main system memory. The "window" will allow a single object in main memory to be examined or modified by the subsystem.

The IP also provides a varied set of software functions that may be used for such purposes as manipulating objects in main memory and enabling

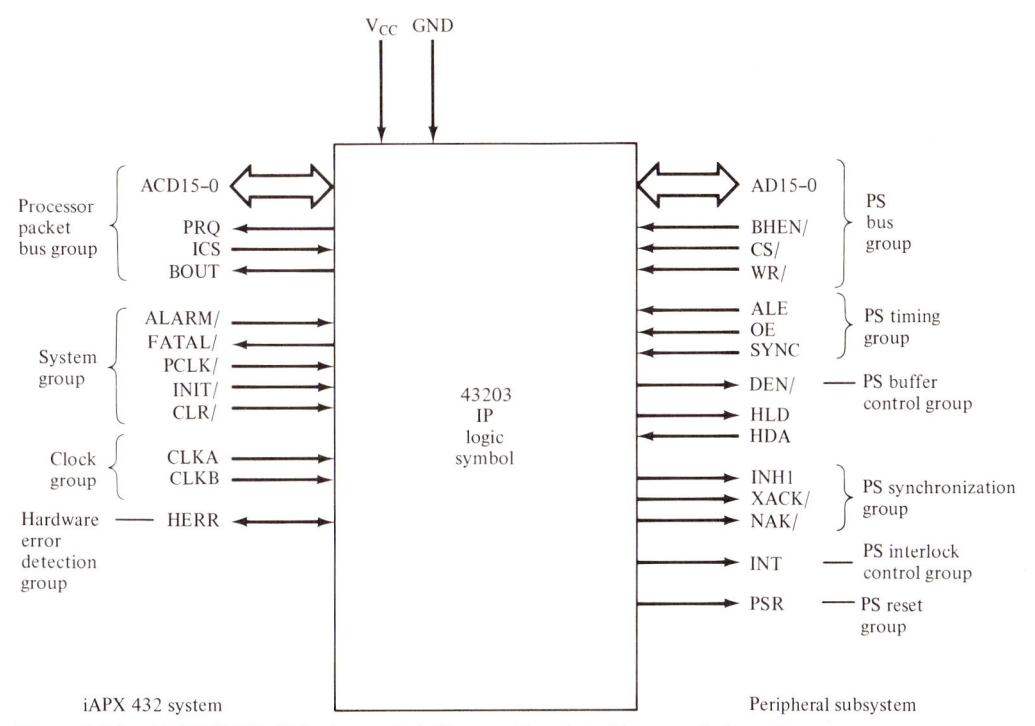

Figure 7.33 iAPX43203 IP logic symbol. Source: Reprinted by permission of Intel Corporation, copyright © 1982.

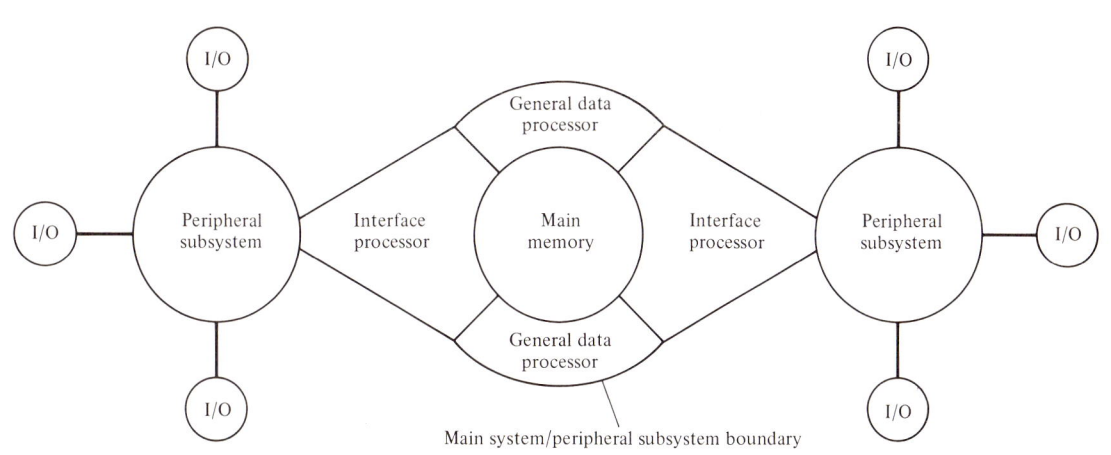

Figure 7.34 Main system and peripheral subsystem. Source: Reprinted by permission of Intel Corporation, copyright © 1982.

communications between processes executing in the main system and processes executing in the subsystem.

A main feature of the iAPX432 system is data integrity and therefore the "window" and "special function" capabilities of the IP both operate using the standard memory addressing and protection features of the iAPX432 system.

As shown in Figure 7.35, I/O communication is accomplished by passing messages between the main system and device interfaces located in the subsystems. The device interface is the hardware and software that controls an I/O device such as a user peripheral (e.g. a terminal), a file, or a psuedo device such as a spooler.

The message sent from the main system to the subsystem contains the information necessary to describe the I/O operation (read or write to console, for example). The device interface interprets the command and sends the message to the I/O in the case of a write operation or returns a message from the I/O device to the main system in the case of a read operation. Handshaking acknowledgments may also be used between the device interface and the main system.

3. iAPX432 System Interface

The interface processor actually exists in two environments, the protected environment of the iAPX432 system and the normal processor environment of the peripheral subsystem. It is this dual environment that

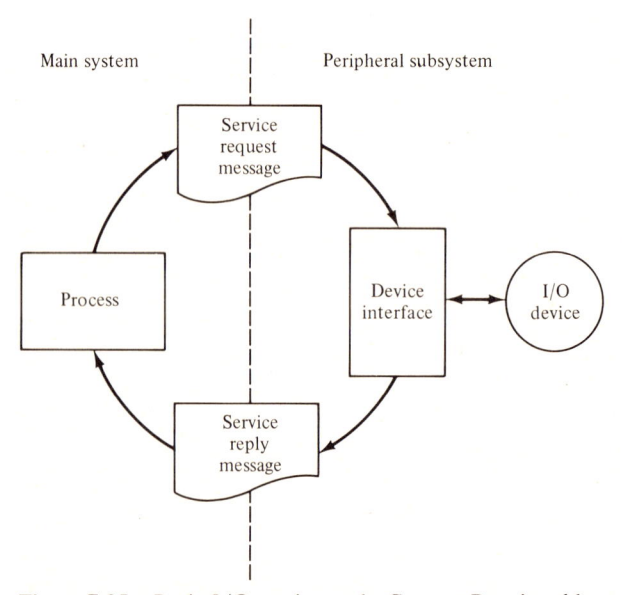

Figure 7.35 Basic I/O service cycle. Source: Reprinted by permission of Intel Corporation, copyright © 1982.

allows the IP to pass data between the two systems. As is shown in Figure 7.34, the IP operates on the boundary between the main system and the subsystem. From the main system side, the IP acts and interfaces like any of the other processors in the system. The main difference between the GDPs and the IPs is that the GDP operates on instructions from the main system while the IP operates on instructions from its attached processor.

4. Peripheral Subsystem Interface

The Peripheral Subsystem Interface (PSI shown in Figure 7.36) is a system of hardware and software that enables the message communication between the main system and an I/O device in the subsystem.

a. Hardware. The PSI hardware consists of an interface processor, an attached processor, and local memory.

i. Attached Processor (AP)

Most general-purpose 8- or 16-bit processors (8085 or 8086, for example) may be used as an attached processor. The AP is not dedicated to use with the IP only but may also be used to execute device interface software. In this manner the peripheral subsystem interface may consist of only one processor or may use multiple processors.

The AP is attached to the IP in a logical sense only (see Figure 7.37) with physical communications between IP and AP being carried out over a

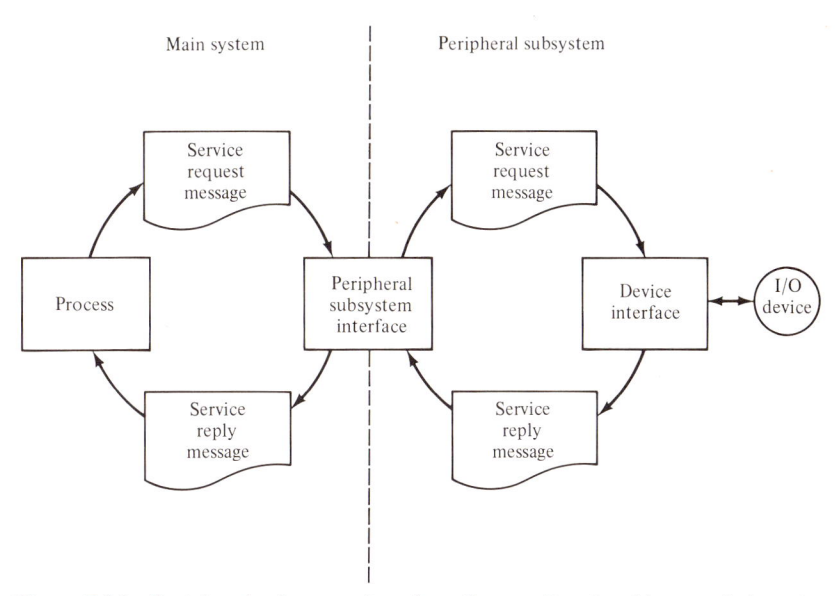

Figure 7.36 Peripheral subsystem interface. Source: Reprinted by permission of Intel Corporation, copyright © 1982.

274 Chapter 7 MOTOROLA 68000 AND INTEL 432

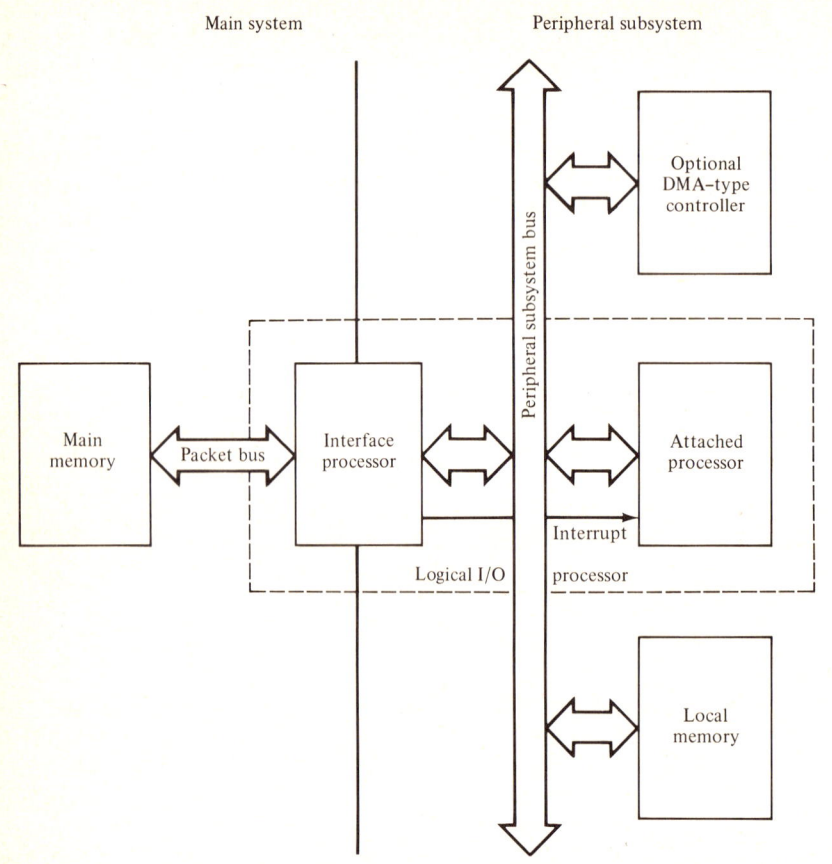

Figure 7.37 Peripheral subsystem interface hardware. Source: Reprinted by permission of Intel Corporation, copyright © 1982.

standard bus system (such as is available on the Intel Multibus). The interrupt from the IP allows the AP to work independently as an I/O processor, processing its own software until the IP requests a main system interface process.

ii. Interface Processor (IP)

The IP completes the subsystem package by providing the communications between the main system and the peripheral subsystem. The IP also extends the AP's instruction set to allow the software running on the I/O processor to operate in the main system.

As shown in Figure 7.37, the IP bridges the packet bus and the subsystem bus to provide a hardware link that permits software-controlled data flow between the main system and the subsystem.

Since the IP interfaces to the main system in the same manner as the

GDPs, the IP supports iAPX432 hardware facilities such as processor communication, alarm signal, and functional redundancy checking.

The IP appears as a memory block to the attached processor and acts passively except when the IP detects a communication request from the main system, in which case an interrupt is generated to the AP. Since the IP appears as memory, other subsystem processors may access the IP (e.g., DMA) and in turn access the main system memory.

b. Software

i. IP Controller

The subsystem peripheral software, referred to as the IP controller, executes on the attached processor and uses the facilities of the IP and the AP to control data flow between the main system and the subsystem.

If the IP controller is organized as a collection of tasks running under RMX-80 or some other multitasking operating system, software development and maintenance is simplified. Multitasking of the IP controller supports asynchronous message-based communications within the IP controller which allows the subsystem to be structured similarly to the main iAPX432 system. Communications between the IP controller and actual device interfaces are completely arbitrary and defined by application of the subsystem. Synchronous procedure calls may also be used with the "messages" being passed between software blocks as parameters.

No matter how the IP controller is structured, it interacts with main system memory through the IP by the following IP facilities: execution environments, windows, and functions.

ii. Execution Environments

The IP provides an environment in the main system that supports the operation of the IP controller within the main system. The environment consists of a set of system objects that are used and manipulated by the IP. The IP controller is represented in main memory by a process object and a context object and like a GDP, the IP itself is represented by a processor object. Representing the IP and the IP controller as objects creates an execution environment that is analogous to the environment of a process running on a GDP and provides a standard framework for addressing, protection, and communication within the main system.

As with the GDP, the IP supports multiple-process environments and the IP controller selects the environment in which a function is to run. This allows the establishment of separate environments for individual device interfaces within the peripheral subsystem. The use of separate environments allows an error to occur in one device interface without affecting the processes controlling other device interfaces.

iii. Windows

Transfer of data between the main system and a subsystem may only occur with the use of an IP window. The window defines the correspondence (or mapping) between a subrange of subsystem memory (within the range of addresses occupied by the IP) and an object in the main system memory (see Figure 7.38). When a process in the subsystem (the IP controller for example) reads a logical windowed address, data are obtained from the associated object in the main system memory. Similarly, writing to a windowed address writes data from the subsystem to the main

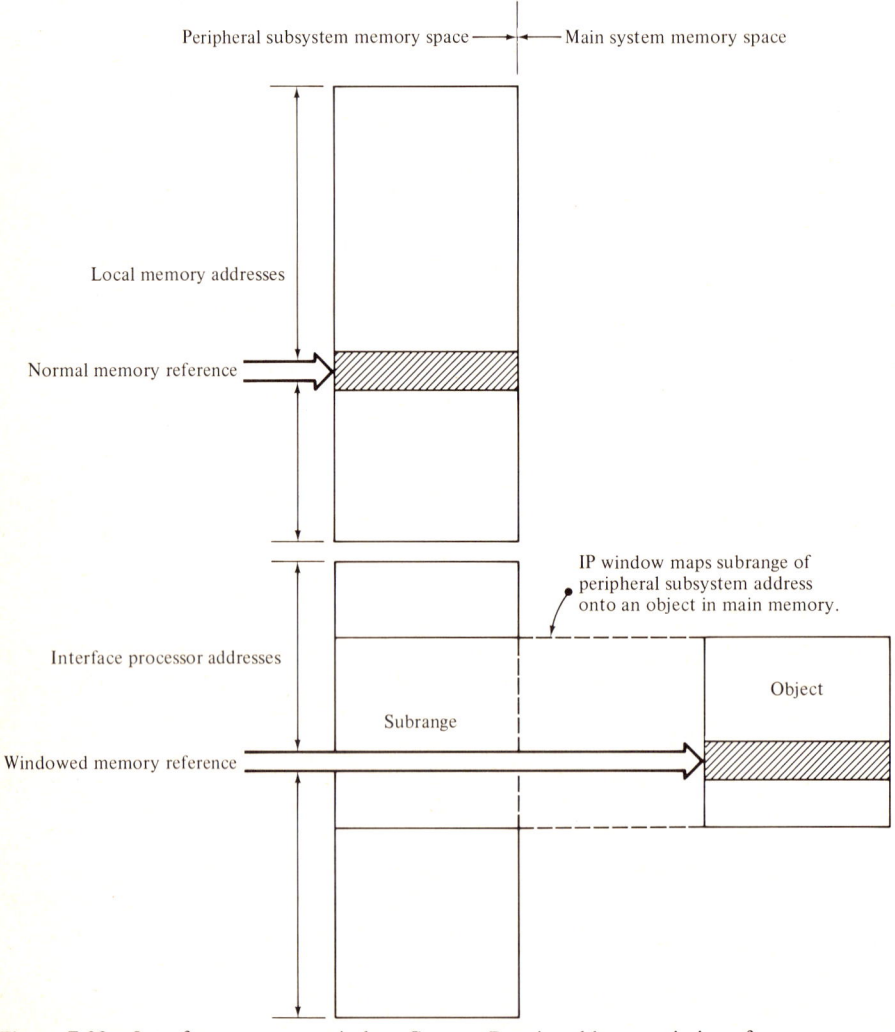

Figure 7.38 Interface processor window. Source: Reprinted by permission of Intel Corporation, copyright © 1982.

system object. There are four IP windows that may be mapped onto four different jobs.

iv. Functions

A fifth window (previously mentioned as the extensions to the AP software facilities) provides the IP controller with access to the IP's function facility. By writing operands and op codes into set locations in the fifth window, the IP controller causes the IP to execute one of its built-in functions. This procedure is analogous to the operation of a standard memory-mapped peripheral (such as a floppy disk controller). The IP provides status information back to the IP controller upon the completion of a function. The IP may still perform transfers through the other four windows while it is executing a function through the fifth window.

The IP's functions allow the IP controller to alter windows, manipulate objects, and exchange messages with GDP processes in the main system.

c. Supplementary Interface Processor Facilities

Along with the previously listed facilities, the IP provides two additional capabilities that are used only in exceptional circumstances: the physical reference mode and the interconnect access.

i. Physical Reference Mode

The IP normally operates in the logical reference mode which is characterized by its object-oriented addressing and protection system. There are times when the objects used by the hardware to perform logical-to-physical address conversion are absent or sometimes damaged. In these cases, logical address reference cannot be used and the IP must be put in the physical reference mode.

In the physical reference mode the IP provides a reduced set of functions whereby its windows still operate in the logical reference mode except that they are mapped onto memory segments that are specified directly by a 24-bit address as in traditional computer addressing techniques.

Physical reference mode is most often used during initialization to load binary images of objects from a subsytem into main system memory. Logical reference operations may be used after the needed object images have been loaded.

ii. Interconnect Address

In addition to main memory, the iAPX432 architecture allows the use of a second address space called the processor-memory interconnect address space. One of the four IP windows is software selectable to access either space. When the interconnect space is addressed in the logical reference mode, normal object-oriented techniques are used. In the physical reference mode the interconnect address space is addressed as an array of 16-bit registers with each register selected by a 24-bit physical address.

7.2.3 432 Operating System—iMAX

The object orientation of the iAPX432 architecture is embodied in the structure and implementation of iMAX, the 432 operating system provided by Intel to complement the new architecture embodied in the iAPX432. The benefits of an object-based system over a conventional system are improved system configuration, extensibility, and robustness.

Being an object-based computer, the 432 views its memory as a collection of data structures called objects. The capability-based protection scheme used by the 432 limits access to objects based on a routine's authorization. In this manner, unauthorized processes cannot modify the wrong objects. Certain object types are predefined in the architecture and are used by the hardware to control the system's operation. The iMAX operation system is designed to complement these 432 features.

iMAX is designed to be an OEM operating system rather than an end-user system and in its minimal form supplies the operations necessary to complete the support for the objects defined by the hardware. iMAX is used for creation, alteration, and destruction of all system objects including process objects, ports, and storage resource objects. iMAX also supplies basic device independent I/O for a selected set of devices. Above the minimal level, iMAX will support virtual memory if it is available to the system as well as providing for long-term storage of objects in an object filing system. iMAX will also provide utility functions such as process scheduling, I/O spooling, and human interfacing.

The iMAX operating system is made up of "packages" of software tools that the user needs to build a particular application. If a particular package is not sufficient for a purpose, it may be replaced with a package of a different design.

7.2.4 432 Applications

The 432 is available in a multibus compatible single-board computer (Intellec 432/100) for an evaluation tool to be used with an Intel development system. The 432/100 contains an RS-232 port and an object builder for execution of 432 symbolic machine instructions that will allow the user to become familiar with 432 architecture and programming.

The micro main frame is aimed at usage for multifunction, software intensive designs such as modern banking transaction systems. Such systems have grown from simple, single-transaction systems to large systems expected to handle data security, on-line funds transfer, accounting, credit authorizations, and many other simultaneous operations.

Other future applications will include telecommunications switching systems (PABX), on-line office information systems, Computer-Aided Design (CAD), multiuser business systems, and factory automation and control systems.

7.2.5 Conclusion

The 432 is a new device and many of its applications have not even been discovered yet. Detailed information on the 432 instruction set, I/O techniques, and other features is still to be released by Intel.

PROBLEMS AND QUESTIONS

7.1 Repeat Problem 6.1 using the 68000 instruction set.
7.2 Define the $\overline{\text{BERR}}$, $\overline{\text{UDS}}$, $\overline{\text{LDS}}$, $\overline{\text{BGAC}}$, and $\overline{\text{VMA}}$ pins on the 68000
7.3 Identify functionally the main differences between the 68000 and the 8086.
7.4 Define the LINK, UNLINK, and CHK instructions on the 68000.
7.5 Compare the interrupt structures of the 68000 with the Z8000.
7.6 Design hardware and software for the 68000 to provide dual 16-bit ports using two Motorola 6821 chips.
7.7 How many (minimum) chips are required to design a 432-based microcomputer? Describe them functionally.
7.8 Discuss functionally the basic features of the 432.

CHAPTER 8

TYPICAL MICROPROCESSOR INTERFACE CHIPS

This chapter describes the functional capabilities and interfacing characteristics of typical microprocessor support chips. These include Intel 2716, 8355/8755, 8155/8156, 8257, 8279, and Motorola 6850. Appendix B provides manufacturers' specification for the Intel 8279.

8.1 Typical EPROM, RAM, and I/O Chips*

This section includes functional characteristics of typical ROM/EPROM, RAM, and I/O chips. These include Intel 2716, 8355/8755, and 8155/8156 chips. The main characteristic of EPROMs is that they can be repeatedly programmed by applying a special sequence of varying voltage levels to the appropriate pins of the chips using an EPROM programmer. Another important feature of EPROMs is that they are nonvolatile. This means that they retain the information in case of power failure. EPROMs are designed using the FAMOS (floating gate avalanche injection MOS) technology. This technology utilizes a field effect transistor with a floating gate (a gate with no connections to it) for each bit. The presence or absence of electrons on the floating gate is used to represent a 1 or 0, respecitvely. By applying special voltage levels to the appropriate pins of an EPROM chip, electrons with high energy are injected into the floating gate storing a 0. Since the gate is floating, these electrons cannot be removed electrically. These electrons are removed by exposing the EPROM chip to ultraviolet (UV) light. The UV light causes a photocurrent to flow from the floating gate to the silicon substrate of the transistor, thus discharging the floating

---
* This section contains material reprinted courtesy of Intel Corporation.

gate and storing a 1. Note that since there is no way of exposing a single floating gate to UV light, the entire chip must be erased. One cannot erase and reprogram a specific word or bit. Also, note that the EPROM must be erased before each reprogramming.

There are basically two types of RAMs—static and dynamic. Static RAMs store information in flip-flops whereas dynamic RAMs store information in capacitors. Therefore, dynamic RAMs need to be refreshed using typically on-chip refresh circuitry. RAMs are usually volatile. That is, these chips cannot retain information in case of power failure.

Typically, ROM/EPROM and I/O (8355/8755) or RAM and I/O (8155/8156) are contained in a single chip. We now describe these chips in more detail.

8.1.1 Intel 2716 EPROM

The Intel 2716 is a 2K × 8 bit ultraviolet erasable and electrically programmable read-only memory (EPROM). It requires a single 5-V power supply. The 2716 can be programmed in any sequence. Single address location or blocks of locations can be programmed. There is no need to program all locations within the 2716 during a programming session. Therefore, errors in programming a particular location can easily be rectified. The 2716 has an access time of up to 350 ns and is compatible with most of the Intel microprocessors.

Figure 8.1 shows the pin diagram, block diagram, and mode selection features of the 2716. Figure 8.2 shows a typical 16K 2716-based memory interfaced to the 8085. Note that eight 2716's are required for 16K memory. Since the AD0–AD7 lines of the 8085 are multiplexed, an external 8212 address latch is necessary which is enabled by the falling edge of ALE to latch AD0–AD7 for addressing the 2716. A8–A10 lines of the 8085 are directly connected to the 2716 A8–A10 lines. This will provide the 11 address lines required by the 2716's.

A 3604A PROM decoder is used to decode the 8085 A8–A15 lines for providing the chip enable signals (CE_0–CE_7) of the 2716's. The 8085 $\overline{RD}$ line is used to enable the output line ($\overline{OE}$) of the 2716's. The 3604A has two chip select signals—CS_1 (edge-triggered) and CS_2 (low). The 8085 ALE is connected to CS_1 and IO/$\overline{M}$ is connected to CS_2 for enabling the PROM decoder.

1. Programming

Initially, and after each erasure, all bits of the 2716 are in the "1" state. Data is introduced by selectively programming 0's into the desired bit locations. Although only 0's will be programmed, both 1's and 0's can be presented in the data word.

The 2716 is in the programming mode when the V_{pp} power supply is at 25 V and $\overline{OE}$ is at V_{IH}. The data to be progammed is applied 8 bits in parallel

Typical EPROM, RAM, and I/O Chips 283

Pin configuration
2716

A7	1	24	Vcc
A6	2	23	A8
A5	3	22	A9
A4	4	21	Vpp
A3	5	20	$\overline{OE}$
A2	6 16K	19	A10
A1	7	18	$\overline{CE}$
A0	8	17	O7
O0	9	16	O6
O1	10	15	O5
O2	11	14	O4
GND	12	13	O3

Mode selection

Pins / Mode	CE/PGM (18)	$\overline{OE}$ (20)	Vpp (21)	Vcc (24)	Outputs (9–11, 13–17)
Read	V_{IL}	V_{IL}	+5	+5	D_{OUT}
Standby	V_{IH}	Don't care	+5	+5	High Z
Program	Pulsed V_{IL} to V_{IH}	V_{IH}	+25	+5	D_{IN}
Program verify	V_{IL}	V_{IL}	+25	+5	D_{OUT}
Program inhibit	V_{IL}	V_{IH}	+25	+5	High Z

Block diagram

Vcc ○→
GND ○→
Vpp ○→

$\overline{OE}$ ○→
$\overline{CE}$/PGM ○→

A0–A10 address inputs →

Output Enable Chip Enable and prog logic
Y decoder
X decoder
Output buffers
Y gating
16,384 bit cell matrix

Data outputs O0–O7

Pin names

A0–A10	Addresses
CE/PGM	Chip Enable/program
$\overline{OE}$	Output Enable
O0–O7	Outputs

Figure 8.1 The 2716. (*Pin 18 and pin 20 have been renamed to conform with the entire family of 16K, 32K, and 64K EPROMs and ROMs. The die, fabrication process, and specifications remain the same and are totally unaffected by this change. Source: Reprinted by permission of Intel Corporation, copyright © 1982.

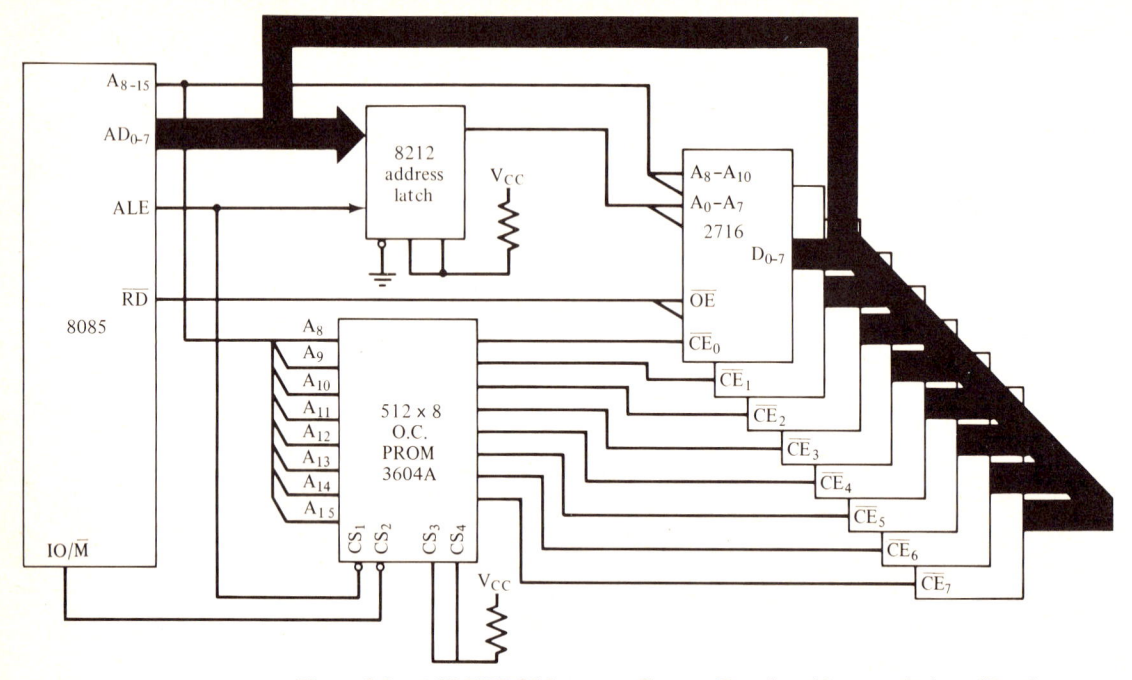

Figure 8.2 16K EPROM system. Source: Reprinted by permission of Intel Corporation, copyright © 1982.

to the data output pins. The levels required for the address and data inputs are TTL.

2. Program Verify

A verify should be performed on the programmed bits to determine that they were correctly programmed. The verify may be performed with V_{PP} at 25 V. Except during programming and program verify, V_{PP} must be at 5 V.

8.1.2 Intel 8355/8755 ROM/EPROM with I/O

The 8355 contains 2K × 8 bit (16,384 bits) ROM and two 8-bit I/O ports with each I/O port line individually programmable as input or output.

The 8755 is similar to the 8355 with the following differences:

8355	8755
2K × 8 ROM	2K × 8 EPROM
Pin 1 is used for $\overline{CE}_1$	Pin 1 is used for PROG/$\overline{CE}_1$
Pin 5 is not used	Pin 5 is used for V_{DD}

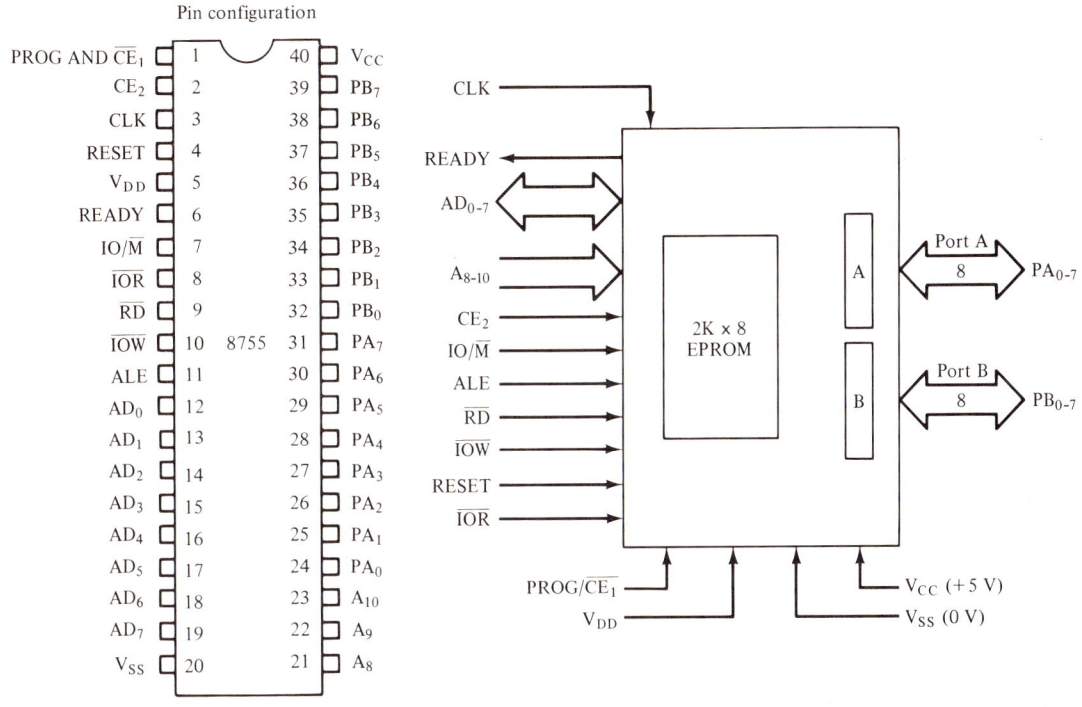

Figure 8.3 8755 pin and block diagrams. Source: Reprinted by permission of Intel Corporation, copyright © 1982.

Since a user would normally use the 8755 chip, we describe the 8755 in detail in the following.

1. **8755 Pin Diagram**

   Figure 8.3 shows the pin diagram and block diagram of the 8755. The functions of the pins are self-explanatory.

2. **Functional Description**

a. PROM Section. The 2K × 8 memory is addressed by the 11-bit address, and chip enables. The addresses, CE_1 and CE_2, are latched into the address latches on the falling edge of ALE.

b. I/O Section. There are two 8-bit I/O ports in the 8755, namely, port A and port B. Each bit in an I/O port can be configured as an input or output by a Data Direction Register (DDR). A 0 in a particular bit position of a DDR signifies that the corresponding I/O port bit is in the input mode. A 1 in a particular bit position signifies that the corresponding I/O port bit is in the output mode. In this manner, the I/O ports of the 8755 are bit-by-bit programmable as inputs or outputs. Note that DDRs cannot be read. AD_0 and AD_1 lines are decoded to address the I/O ports and DDRs as follows:

AD_1	AD_0	SELECTION
0	0	Port A
0	1	Port B
1	0	Port A Data Direction Register (DDR A)
1	1	Port B Data Direction Register (DDR B)

3. **Programming**

Initially, and after each erasure, all bits of the EPROM portions of the 8755 are in the 1 state. The 8755 can be programmed by either a PROM programmer or a PROM programming module on a microcomputer development system. It is very easy to program the 8755 by a development system. One would typically enter the starting and ending addresses of the program via the development system keyboard. Then, pressing a control key such as the PROG key would burn the 8755 with the desired object program. Note that the 8755 must be erased after each programming by exposing it to the ultraviolet light for about 15 minutes.

4. **Typical Applications**

Figures 8.4 and 8.5 show how the 8755 can be used with the 8085 by memory-mapped I/O and standard I/O, respectively. If a standard I/O technique is used, the system can use the features of both CE_2 and $\overline{CE_1}$. By

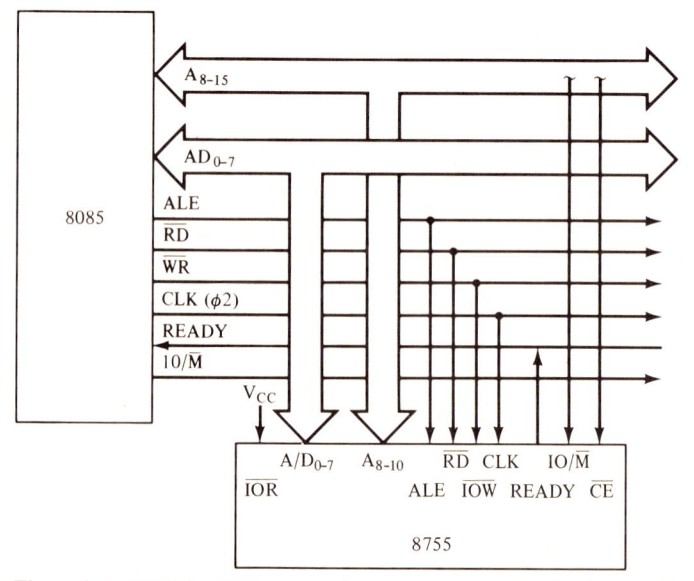

Figure 8.4 8755 in 8085 system (memory-mapped I/O). Source: Reprinted by permission of Intel Corporation, copyright © 1982.

Typical EPROM, RAM, and I/O Chips   287

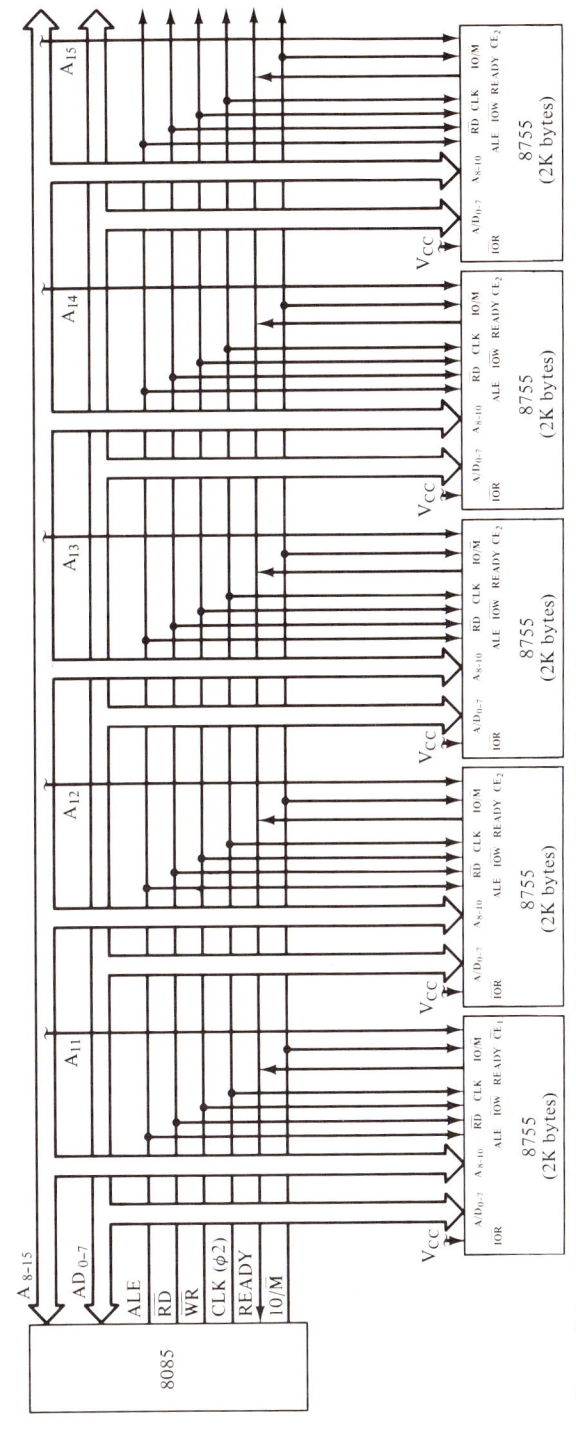

Figure 8.5 8755 in 8085 system (standard I/O). Note: Use CE_1 for the first 8755 in the system, and CE_2 for the other 8755's. Permits up to five 8755's in a system without CE decoder. Source: Reprinted by permission of Intel Corporation, copyright © 1982.

using a combination of unused address lines A_{11-15} and the chip enable inputs, the 8085 system can use up to five 8755's each without requring a CE decoder (Figure 8.5).

If a memory-mapped I/O approach is used the 8755 will be selected by the combination of both the chip enables and $\overline{IO/M}$ using the AD_{8-15} address lines (Figure 8.4).

8.1.3 Intel 8155/8156 RAM with I/O and Timer

The Intel 8155 contains 256×8 (2048 bits) static RAM, two 8-bit and one 6-bit parallel I/O ports (the 6-pit port may be used to control the two 8-bit ports to operate in handshake mode), and a 14-bit programmable counter/timer.

The 8156 is exactly the same as the 8155 except that the chip enable on the 8156 is active HIGH whereas the chip enable on the 8155 is active LOW.

1. 8155/8156 Pin and Block Diagrams

Figure 8.6 shows the 8155/8156 pin diagram and block diagram. The functions of all the pins on the chip are self-explanatory.

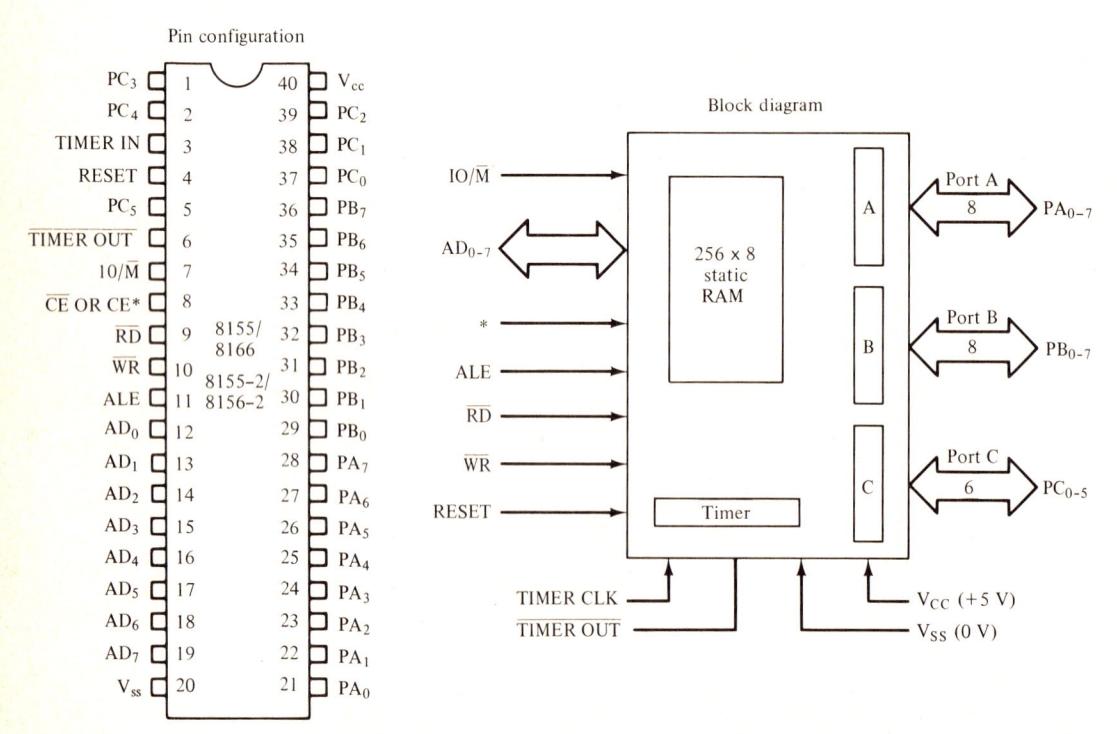

Figure 8.6 8155/8156 pin diagram and block diagram. (*: 8155/8155-2 = $\overline{CE}$, 8156/8156-2 = CE.) Source: Reprinted by permission of Intel Corporation, copyright © 1982.

2. Command/Status Register

The command register is 8 bits long. Four bits (0–3) configure the ports as inputs or outputs, two bits (4–5) enable or disable the interrupt from port C when it acts as handshake port, and the last two bits (6–7) are for the timer.

The command register contents can be altered at any time by using the I/O address XXXXX000 during a WRITE operation with the chip enable active and $IO/\overline{M} = 1$. The meaning of each bit of the command byte is defined in Figure 8.7. The contents of the command register may never be read.

The status register consists of seven latches, one for each bit, six (0–5) for the status of the ports and one (6) for the status of the timer.

The status of the timer and the I/O section can be polled by reading the status register (address XXXXX000). Status word format is shown in Figure 8.8. Note that you may never write to the status register since the command register shares the same I/O address and the command register is selected when a write to that address is issued.

7	6	5	4	3	2	1	0
TM$_2$	TM$_1$	IEB	IEA	PC$_2$	PC$_1$	PB	PA

- Defines PA$_{0-7}$: 0 = Input
- Defines PB$_{0-7}$: 1 = Output

- Defines PC$_{0-5}$:
  - 00 = ALT 1
  - 11 = ALT 2
  - 01 = ALT 3
  - 10 = ALT 4

- Enable port A interrupt
- Enable port B interrupt
  - 1 = Enable
  - 0 = Disable

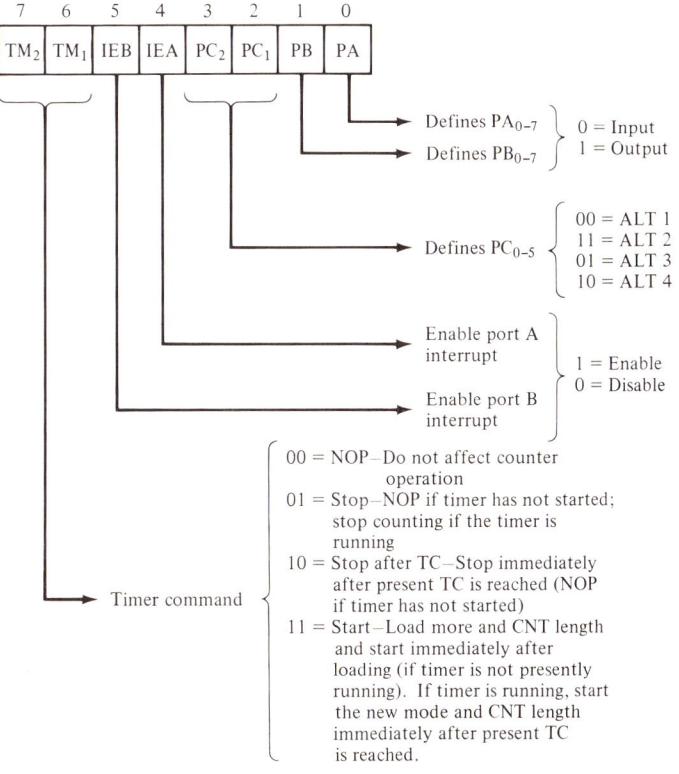

- Timer command:
  - 00 = NOP–Do not affect counter operation
  - 01 = Stop–NOP if timer has not started; stop counting if the timer is running
  - 10 = Stop after TC–Stop immediately after present TC is reached (NOP if timer has not started)
  - 11 = Start–Load more and CNT length and start immediately after loading (if timer is not presently running). If timer is running, start the new mode and CNT length immediately after present TC is reached.

Figure 8.7 Command register bit assignment. Source: Reprinted by permission of Intel Corporation, copyright © 1982.

290 Chapter 8 TYPICAL MICROPROCESSOR INTERFACE CHIPS

```
AD₇ AD₆ AD₅ AD₄ AD₃ AD₂ AD₁ AD₀
┌────┬────┬────┬────┬────┬────┬────┬────┐
│ ╳  │TIMER│INTE│ B  │INTR│INTE│ A  │INTR│
│    │    │ B  │ BF │ B  │ A  │ BF │ A  │
└────┴────┴────┴────┴────┴────┴────┴────┘
```

— Port A interrupt request
— Port A buffer full/empty (input/output)
— Port A interrupt enable
— Port B interrupt request
— Port B buffer full/empty (input/output)
— Port B interrupt enabled
— Timer interrupt (this bit is latched high when terminal count is reached, and is reset to low upon reading of the C/S register and by hardware reset).

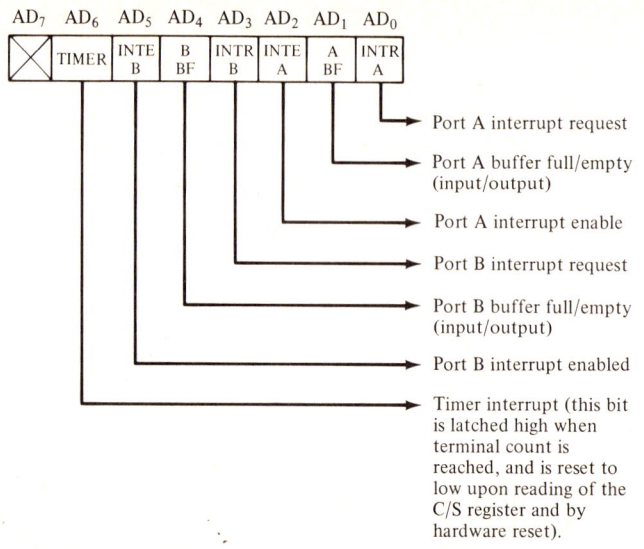

Figure 8.8 Status register bit assignment. Source: Reprinted by permission of Intel Corporation, copyright © 1982.

3. I/O

All ports in the 8155/8156 are parallel ports. It is not possible to configure each bit in an 8155/8156 I/O port as input or output. Each port must be configured in parallel. Figure 8.9 shows the register structure of the 8155/8156. Note that the lines AD_0–AD_2 are decoded to define the 8155/8156 I/O ports.

a. Command/Status (C/S) Register. Both registers are assigned the address XXXXX000. The C/S address serves the dual purpose. When the C/S registers are selected during WRITE operation, a command is written

\multicolumn{7}{c}{I/O Address}	SELECTION
A7	A6	A5	A4	A3	A2	A1	A0	
X	X	X	X	X	0	0	0	Internal command/status register
X	X	X	X	X	0	0	1	General purpose I/O port A
X	X	X	X	X	0	1	0	General purpose I/O port B
X	X	X	X	X	0	1	1	Port C—general purpose I/O or control
X	X	X	X	X	1	0	0	Low-order & bits of timer count
X	X	X	X	X	1	0	1	High 6 bits of timer count and 2 bits of timer mode

X: Don't Care
†: I/O Address must be qualified by CE = 1 (8156) or $\overline{CE}$ = 0(8155) and IO/$\overline{M}$ = 1 in order to select the appropriate register.

Figure 8.9 I/O port and timer addressing scheme. Source: Reprinted by permission of Intel Corporation, copyright © 1982.

Table 8.1. Table of Port Control Assignment

Pin	ALT 1	ALT 2	ALT 3	ALT 4
PC_0	Input port	Output port	A INTR (port A interrupt)	A INTR (port A interrupt)
PC_1	Input port	Output port	A BF (port A buffer full)	A BF (port A buffer full)
PC_2	Input port	Output port	A STB (port A strobe)	A STB (port A strobe)
PC_3	Input port	Output port	Output port	B INTR (port B interrupt)
PC_4	Input port	Output port	Output port	B BF (port B buffer full)
PC_5	Input port	Output port	Output port	B STB (port B strobe)

Source: Reprinted by permission of Intel Corporation.

into the command register. The contents of this register are *not* accessible through the pins. When the C/S (XXXXX000) is selected during a READ operation, the status information of the I/O ports and the timer becomes available on the AD_{0-7} lines.

b. Port A. This register can be programmed to be either input or output ports depending on the status of the contents of the C/S register. Also depending on the command, this port can operate in either the basic I/O mode or the handshake mode. The I/O pins assigned in relation to this register are PA_{0-7}. The address of this register is XXXXX001.

c. Port B. This register functions the same as port A. The I/O pins assigned are PB_{0-7}. The address of this register is XXXXX010.

d. Port C. This register has the address XXXXX011 and contains only 6 bits. The 6 bits can be programmed to be either input ports or output ports, or as handshake signals for ports A and B by properly programming the AD_2 and AD_3 bits of the C/S register.

When PC_{0-5} is used as a handshake port, 3 bits are assigned for port A and 3 for port B. The first bit is an interrupt that the 8155 sends out. The second is an output signal indicating whether the buffer is full or empty, and the third is an input pin to accept a strobe for the strobed input mode. (Table 8.1).

4. Timer

The timer is a 14-bit down-counter that counts the TIMER IN pulses and provides either a square wave or pulse when Terminal Count (TC) is reached. The timer has the I/O address XXXXX100 for the low-order byte of the register and the I/O address XXXXX101 for the high-order byte of the register.

To program the timer, the COUNT LENGTH REG is loaded first, 1 byte at a time, by selecting the timer addresses. Bits 0–13 of the high-order count register will specify the length of the next count and bits 14–15 of the high-order register will specify the timer output mode (Figure 8.10).

There are four modes to choose from: M_2 and M_1 define the timer modes, as shown in Figure 8.11.

292 Chapter 8 TYPICAL MICROPROCESSOR INTERFACE CHIPS

7	6	5	4	3	2	1	0
M_2	M_1	T_{13}	T_{12}	T_{11}	T_{10}	T_9	T_8

Timer mode   MSB of count length

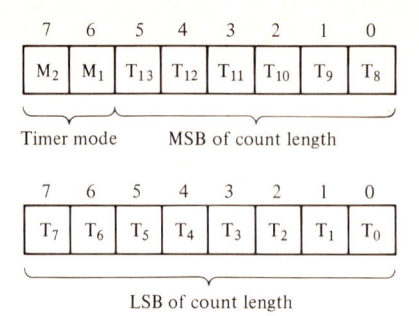

7	6	5	4	3	2	1	0
T_7	T_6	T_5	T_4	T_3	T_2	T_1	T_0

LSB of count length

Figure 8.10 Timer format. Source: Reprinted by permission of Intel Corporation, copyright © 1982.

In mode 0, timer out is HIGH for the first half and LOW for the second half of the time out.

Mode 1 is the same as mode 0 except the timer is automatically reloaded after each time out.

Mode 2 generates a low timer out pulse on terminal count.

Mode 3 is the same as mode 2 except timer is automatically reloaded after each time out.

Bits 6–7 (TM_2 and TM_1) of command register contents are used to start and stop the counter. There are four commands to choose from:

TM_2	TM_1	
0	0	NOP—Do not affect counter operation.
0	1	STOP—NOP is timer has not started; stop counter if the timer is running.
1	0	STOP AFTER TC—Stop immediately after present TC is reached (NOP if timer has not started).
1	1	START—Load mode and CNT length and start immediately after loading (if timer is not presently running). If timer is running, start the new mode and CNT length immediately after present TC is reached.

Note that in the above TC stands for Terminal Count. Also note that while the counter is counting, you may load a new count and mode into the count length registers. Before the new count and mode will be used by the counter, you *must* issue a START command to the counter. This applies even though you may only want to change the count and use the previous mode.

In case of an odd-numbered count, the first half-cycle of the square-wave output, which is high, is one count longer than the second (low) half-cycle, as shown in Figure 8.12.

The counter in the 8155 is not initialized to any particular mode or count when hardware RESET occurs, but RESET does stop the counting.

Typical EPROM, RAM, and I/O Chips   293

TIMER OUT waveforms:

Mode bits			Start count	Terminal count	(Terminal count)
M_2	M_1				
0	0	1. Single square wave			
0	1	2. Continuous square wave			
1	0	3. Single pulse on terminal count			
1	1	4. Continuous pulses			

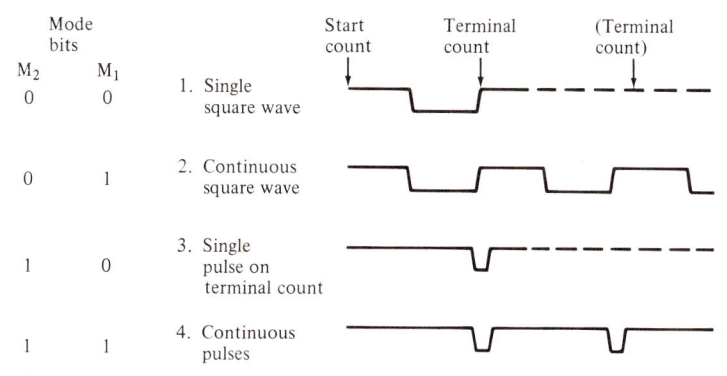

Figure 8.11 Timer modes. Source: Reprinted by permission of Intel Corporation, copyright © 1982.

Therefore, counting cannot begin following RESET until a START command is issued via the C/S register.

Note that the timer circuit on the 8155/8156 chip is designed to be a square-wave timer, not an event counter. To achieve this, it counts down by twos twice in completing one cycle. Thus, its registers do not contain values directly representing the number of TIMER IN pulses received. You cannot load an initial value of 1 into the count register and cause the timer to operate, as its terminal count value is 10 (binary) or 2 (decimal). (For the detection of single pulses, it is suggested that one of the hardware interrupt pins on the 8085 be used.) After the timer has started counting down, the values residing in the count registers can be used to calculate the actual number of TIMER IN pulses required to complete the timer cycle if desired. To obtain the remaining count, perform the following operations in order:

1. Stop the count.
2. Read in the 16-bit value from the count length registers.
3. Reset the upper two mode bits.

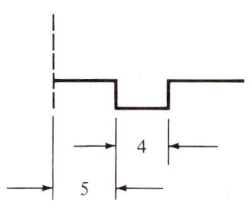

Figure 8.12 Asymmetrical square-wave output resulting from count of 9. Note: 5 and 4 refer to the number of clocks in that time period. Source: Reprinted by permission of Intel Corporation, copyright © 1982.

4. Reset the carry and rotate right one position all 16 bits through carry.
5. If carry is set, add one-half of the full original count (one-half full count—1 if full count is odd).

5. Example Program

Following is an acutal sequence of program steps that adjusts the 8155/8156 count register contents to obtain the count. First store the value of the full original count in register HL of the 8085. Then stop the count to avoid getting an incorrect count value. Then sample the timercounter, storing the lower-order byte of the current count register in register C and the higher-order count byte in register B. Then, call the following 8085 subroutine:

```
ADJUST, 78  MOV A,B      ;Load accumulator with upper half
                         ;of count.
        E63F ANI 3F      ;Reset upper 2 bits and clear carry.
        1F   RAR         ;Rotate right through carry.
        47   MOV B,A     ;Store shifted value back in B.
        79   MOV A,C     ;Load accumulator with lower half.
        1F   RAR         ;Rotate right through carry.
        4F   MOV C,A     ;Store lower byte in C.
        D0   RNC         ;If in 2nd half of count, return.
                         ;If in 1st half, go on.
        3F   CMC         ;Clear carry.
        7C   MOV A,H     ;Divide full count by 2. (If HL
                         ;is odd, disregard remainder.)
        1F   RAR
        67   MOV H,A
        7D   MOV A,L
        1F   RAR
        6F   MOV L,A
        09   DAD B       ;Double-precision add HL and BC.
        44   MOV B,H     ;Store results back in BC.
        4D   MOV C,L
        C9   RET         ;Return.
```

After executing the subroutine, BC will contain the *remaining count* in the current count cycle.

6. 8085-based Microcomputer

Figure 8.13 shows a minimum system using three chips (8085, 8155/8156, and 8355/8755).

7. A Typical 8155/8156 Handshake Application

The Universal Asynchronous Receiver/Transmitter (UART) (Western Digital 1602) will be used as both the input and output device for

Typical EPROM, RAM, and I/O Chips 295

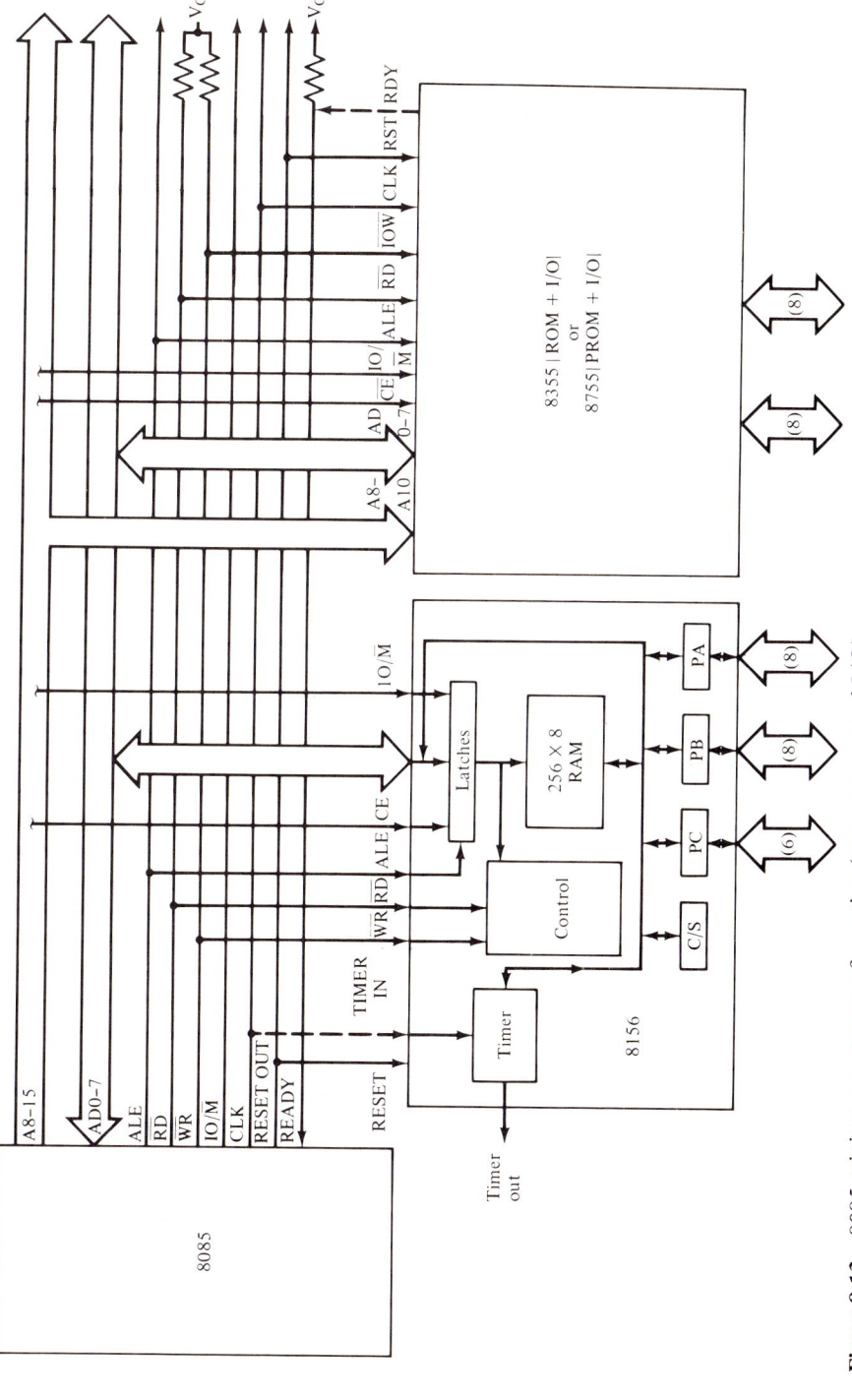

Figure 8.13 8085 minimum system configuration (memory-mapped I/O). (*Note: Optional connections.) Source: Reprinted by permission of Intel Corporation, copyright © 1982.

296 Chapter 8 Typical Microprocessor Interface Chips

handshaking with the 8155. The transmitter section converts parallel data into a serial word. The receiver section converts a serial word into parallel data. Figure 8.14 provides a schematic for the desired handshaking.

Figures 8.15 through 8.18 provide the timing diagrams, flowchart, and program for the send/receive station utilizing the 8155/8156 handshake signals.

TRANSMIT HANDSHAKE OPERATION

1. When the BF signal is low, data are being transmitted because the low level is tied to THRL line (which allows data to be transmitted at a low level).
2. When the TRE (Transmitter Register Empty) goes high, the $\overline{\text{BSTB}}$ goes low.

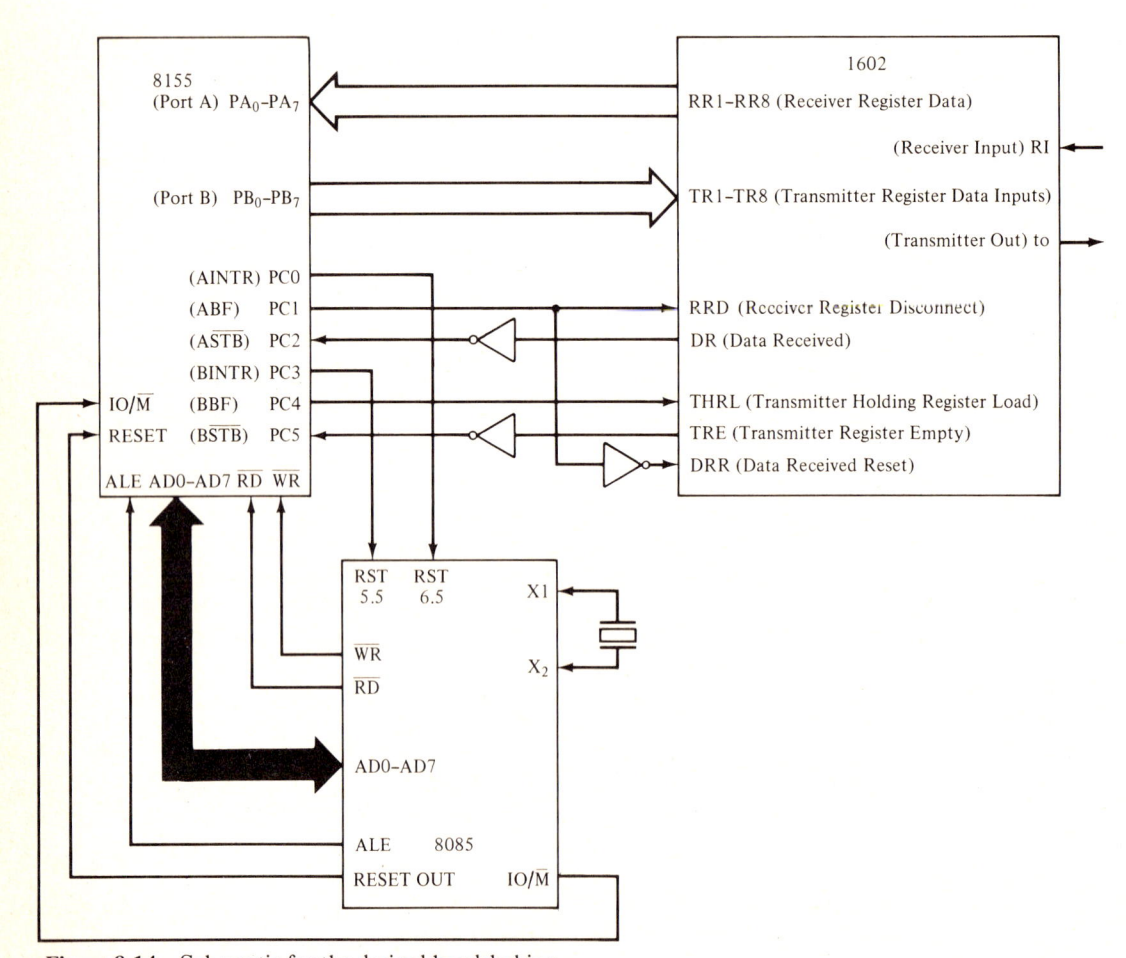

Figure 8.14 Schematic for the desired handshaking.

Typical EPROM, RAM, and I/O Chips **297**

Lines Used for Handshaking of the Western Digital 1602 UART

Pin No.	Name	Symbol	Function
5-12	Receiver holding Register data	RR8-RR1	Contents of receiving data
4	Receiver Register Disconnect	RRD	A high level disables RR8-RR1
18	Data Received Reset	DRR	A low level resets DR
19	Data Received	DR	A high level indicates a word has been received
20	Receiver Input	RI	Serial input data received
23	Transmitter Holding Register Load	THRL	A low level enters a character; a high level stops entering characters
24	Transmitter Register Empty	TRE	A high level on this line indicates that serial transmission of a word has been completed
25	Transmitter Register Output	TRO	The content is read out
26-33	Transmitter Register data inputs	TR1-TR8	The word to be transmitted is loaded into these pins

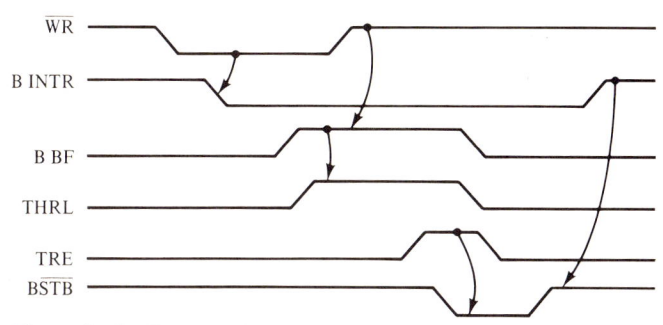

Figure 8.15 Transmit handshake timing diagram.

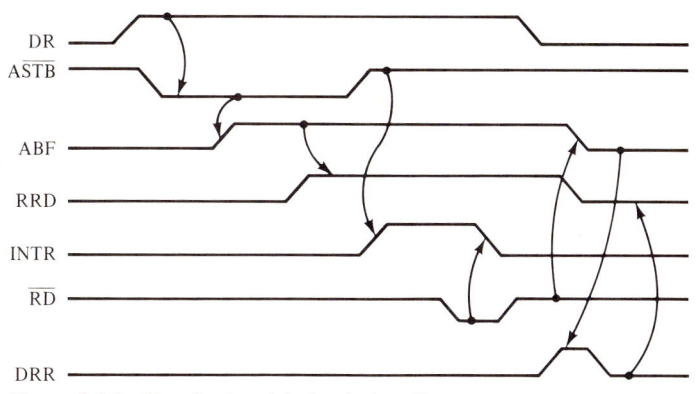

Figure 8.16 Receive handshake timing diagram.

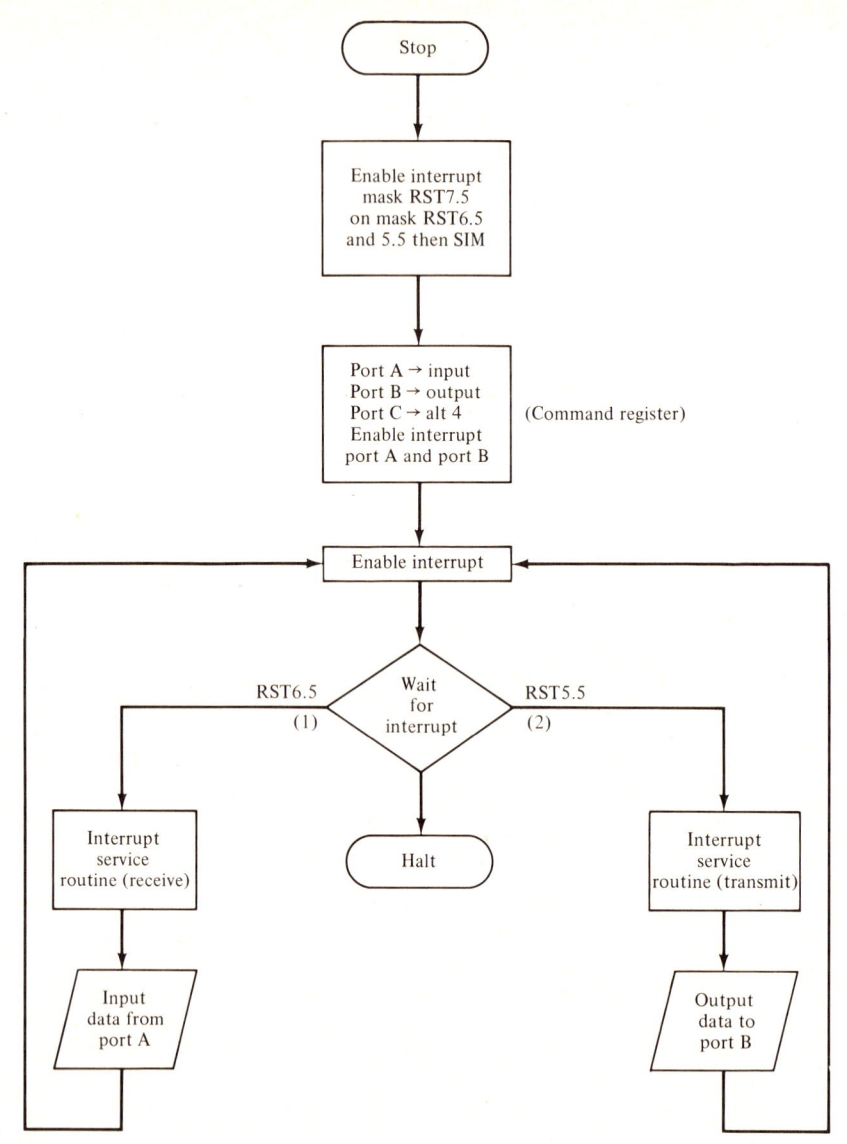

298   Chapter 8   TYPICAL MICROPROCESSOR INTERFACE CHIPS

Figure 8.17 Send/receive station flowchart for handshaking. Note: (1) Data received line goes high as soon as data are received, therefore there is no need for initialization, and $\overline{\text{ASTB}}$ goes low and activated interrupt. (2) As soon as TRE goes low, indicating room for more data, $\overline{\text{BSTB}}$ is activated and interrupt occurs.

3. When the $\overline{\text{BSTB}}$ goes high, the BINTR is triggered, allowing for more data to be transmitted.
4. Also note when the $\overline{\text{WR}}$ goes to a high transition the BF signal goes high which triggers the THRL line (this allows the discontinuation of more data).

Typical Serial I/O Interface Chips

```
0000 FB   EI              ;enable interrupts
0001 3E   MVI A, FB       ;unmask RST6.5 and RST5.5
0002 FB
0003 3D   SIM             ;set interrupt mask
0004 00   NOP
0005 3E   MVI A, 3A       ;set up command register
0006 3A                   ;for port A input, port B
                          ;output, interrupt enable F & B
0007 D3   OUT 40          ;dump to port command
0008 40                   ;register
0009 FB   EI
000A 76   HLT             ;halt
000B DB   IN 41           ;read data in port A
000C 41                              **Interrupt service routine**
000D C3   JMP 0009 ;start process over   002C C3 JMP 0010 (transmit)
000E 09                              002D 10
000F 00                              002E 00
0010 3E   MVIA, XX        ;set up some data
0011 XX
0012 D3   OUT 41          ;send data to port B   0034 C3 JMP 000B (receive)
0013 41                              0035 0B
0014 C3   JMP 0009 ;start process over   0036 00
0015 09
0016 00
```

Figure 8.18 Send/receive station program.

RECEIVE HANDSHAKE OPERATION

1. As soon as DR Goes high (indicating data has been received including stop bit), a low signal is transferred to $\overline{ASTB}$.
2. The $\overline{ASTB}$ then triggers the ABF which in turn triggers the RRD signal of the UART (which disables all receiving data).
3. As soon as the $\overline{ASTB}$ goes high, the RST6.5 is triggered and data are read in the microprocessor ($\overline{RD}$ goes low).
4. As soon as the $\overline{RD}$ line goes high, the BF line goes low which triggers the DRR (Data Received Reset), which allows for the continuation of more data.

8.2 Typical Serial I/O Interface Chips

Serial I/O interface chips are typically used to interface serial I/O devices to microprocessors. The purpose of the serial I/O interface chip is to convert 8-bit parallel data from the microprocessor into a serial data for the serial I/O device. Furthermore, the interface chip also has to convert the serial data from the serial I/O device into 8-bit parallel data that the microprocessor can understand. The interface chip can carry out these transformations synchronously or asynchronously. In synchronous communication, the microprocessor and the serial I/O device must be synchronized during data transmission. On the other hand, in asynchronous communication, the transmitting device (microprocessor or serial I/O device) can transmit data at any time to the receiving device (microprocessor or serial I/O device) without being synchronized to the receiver. Synchronous serial transmit and receive timing is essentially the same as the asynchronous timing. The only differences are in formatting the data. In synchronous communication, a block of synchronous data is preceded by SYNC characters. Note that SYNC characters are included into the data stream whenever valid data are not ready to be transmitted. On the other hand, in asynchronous format, each data word (typically 5 to 8 bits) is framed by adding a LOW start bit, followed by 5 to 8 data bits (representing the actual data), an optional parity bit for detecting any error, and 1, $1\frac{1}{2}$ (which is 1.5 times the bit interval), or 2 stop bits which are always HIGH. Because of the popularity of asynchronous communications, mainly because of their simplicity, the manufacturers have developed a number of interface chips called Universal Asynchronous Receiver Transmitter (UART) or Asynchronous Communications Interface Adapter (ACIA). ACIA is typically a Motorola term. However, the terms UART or ACIA are used interchangeably. They typically perform all the asynchronous functions such as framing each data word, all necessary transformations and timing, and error detection capabilities for asynchronous data communication between a microprocessor and a serial I/O device. A typical example of such an interface chip is the Motorola 6850. Some manufacturers such as Intel provide both synchronous and asynchronous communication capabilities on the same chip. This chip is usually called Universal Synchronous/Asynchronous Receiver Transmitter (USART). The Intel 8251 is a typical example.

In the following, we describe the Motorola 6850 and its interfacing characteristics to the 68000 (16-bit microprocessor). Learning the concepts described will help the reader to understand other serial interface chips.

8.2.1 Motorola MC6850 Asynchronous Communications Interface Adapter (ACIA)*

The MC6850 ACIA interfaces the microcomputer to devices using asynchronous, serial data format. The MC6850 provides the capabilities of interfacing Motorola microprocessors to typical peripherals such as CRT terminals, teletypes, and so on. Figure 8.19 shows the 6850 block diagram.

* This section contains material reprinted courtesy of Motorola Corporation.

Typical Serial I/O Interface Chips   301

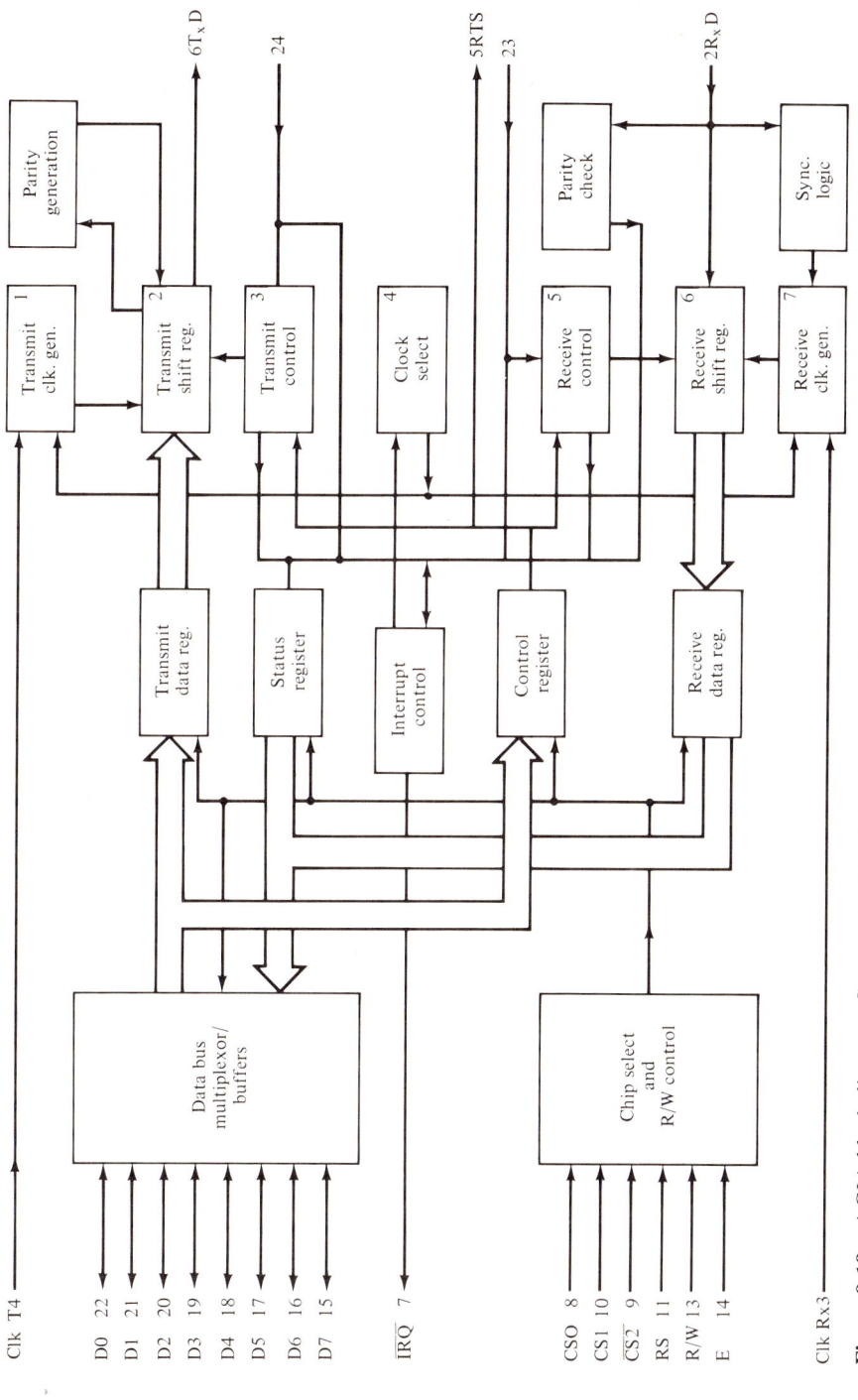

Figure 8.19 ACIA block diagram. Source: Reprinted by permission of Motorola Semiconductor Products, Inc., copyright © 1975.

The main blocks of Figure 8.19 are:

1. Chip select and read/write control.
2. Data bus multiplexor/buffers.
3. Transmitter Section consisting of transmit data register and transmit shift register.
4. Receiver section consisting of receive data register and receive shift register.
5. Status and control registers.

We now describe these functional blocks.

1. Chip Select and Read/Write Control

The microprocessor would typically be interfaced with more than one I/O device. The three chip select signals CS0, CS1, and $\overline{CS2}$ are used for addressing a particular 6850. The microprocessor typically carries out one of the following functions after the MC6850 is selected by CS0 and CS1 HIGH, and $\overline{CS2}$ LOW:

1. Input the receiver data register.
2. Input the status register.
3. Output to the transmit data register.
4. Output to the control register.

The above functions are performed based on the status of the Chip Select lines ($\overline{CS2}$, CS1, and CS0), Enable (E), Register Select (RS), and Read/Write (R/W) as follows:

$\overline{CS2}$	CS1	CS0	R/W	E	RS	Function
0	1	1	1	1	1	Input the receive data register
0	1	1	1	1	0	Input the status register
0	1	1	0	1	1	Output to transmit register
0	1	1	0	1	0	Output to the control register

2. Data Bus Multiplexor/Buffer

The data bus multiplexor/buffer is 8-bit bidirectional. It converts parallel data from the microprocessor to the transmit data register or from receive data register to the microprocessor over the data bus.

3. Transmitter Section

The transmitter in the ACIA is serial. It inputs parallel data from the transmit data register and transforms it to a serial format transmission.

In order to transmit a data word to a serial device, the microprocessor outputs the data word to the 6850's transmit data register. Control logic within the transmitter section formats this data by adding a START bit, a parity bit, and the STOP bits. This formatted word is then transferred into the transmit shift register which is shifted at the transmit clock rate. This generates serial data (T_xD) which is transferred to the serial device.

4. Receiver Section

The receiver section contains a receive data register and a receive shift register. It transforms serial data from the serial device into parallel format and transfers this data into the receive data register for ultimate transmission to the microprocessor.

In order to transmit data to the microprocessor, the serial device sends a serial data word to the 6850's receiver section via the R_xD input. As soon as the control logic in the receiver section detects a HIGH to LOW transition on the R_xD input, it translates this as the START bit. It then transfers the rest of the serial data into the receiver shift register at the receive clock rate. When the complete serial word is moved into the receive shift register, the 8-bit data portion is transferred in parallel into the receive data register. The microprocessor would ultimately input the contents of the receive data register via the data bus multiplexor/buffer and the system bus.

5. Status and Control Registers

Figure 8.20 shows the 6850 status register format. This register is 8 bits long. One can detect any errors in data transmission by checking the various bits in this register. For example, after shifting the serial data word into the receiver shift register, the 6850 automatically verifies the required number of STOP bits. If this does not agree with the number that was programmed via the control register, a framing error flag is set. Also, if the parity of the data portion in the receiver shift register does not agree with the desired parity programmed in the control register, a parity error flag is set. The other bits of the 6850 status register of Figure 8.20 are self-explanatory.

The microprocessor can output an 8-bit code via the system data bus into the control register (Figure 8.21). This 8-bit code will tell the 6850 the characteristics of the serial data, such as number of data bits, parity bit (odd, even, or none), number of STOP bits, and so on.

6. Interfacing the 6850 to a 16-bit Microprocessor Such as the 68000

Interfacing the MC6850 Asynchronous Communications Interface Adapter (ACIA) to the MC68000 is easy because the MC68000 has a special cycle to handle M6800 peripherals. The ACIA data bus can be placed on either the upper or lower 8 bits of the MC68000 data bus with

Data carrier detect

b2 = 0: Indicates carrier is present.
b2 = 1: Indicates the loss of carrier.
1. The low-to-high transition of the $\overline{\text{DCD}}$ input causes b2 = 1 and generates an interrupt (b7 = 1), ($\overline{\text{IRQ}}$ = 0)
2. Reading the status register and Rx data register or master resetting the ACIA causes b2 = 0 and b7 = 0.

Receiver data register full

b0 = 0: Indicates that the receiver data register is empty.
b0 = 1: Indicates that data has been transferred to the receiver data register and status bits states are set (PE, OVRN, FE).
1. The read data command on the high-to-low E transition or a master reset causes b0 = 0.
2. A "high" on the DCD input causes b0 = 0 and the receiver to be reset.

Interrupt request

The interrupt request bit is the complement of the $\overline{\text{IRQ}}$ output. Any interrupt that is set and enabled will be available in the status register in addition to the normal $\overline{\text{IRQ}}$ output.

b7	b6	b5	b4	b3	b2	b1	b0
IRQ	PE	OVRN	FE	$\overline{\text{CTS}}$	$\overline{\text{DCD}}$	TxDRE	RxDRF

Framing error

b4 = 1: Indicates the absence of the first stop bit resulting from character synchronization error, faulty transmission, or a break condition.
1. The internal Rx data transfer signal causes b4 = 1 due to the above conditions and causes b4 = 0 on the next Rx data transfer signal if conditions have been rectified.

Overrun error

b5 = 1: Indicates that a character or a number of characters were received but not read from the Rx data register prior to subsequent characters being received.
1. The read data command on the high-to-low E transition causes b5 = 1 and b0 = 1 if an overrun condition exists. The next read data command on the high-to-low E transition causes b5 = 0 and b0 = 0.

Parity error

b6 = 1: Indicates that a parity error exists. The parity error bit is inhibited if no parity is selected.
1. The parity error status is updated during the internal receiver data transfer signal.

Transmitter data register empty

b1 = 1: Indicates that the transmitter data register is empty.
b1 = 0: Indicates that the transmitter data register is full.
1. The internal Tx transfer signal forces b1 = 1.
2. The write data command on the high-to-low E transition causes b1 = 0.
3. A "high" on the $\overline{\text{CTS}}$ input causes b1 = 0.

Clear to send

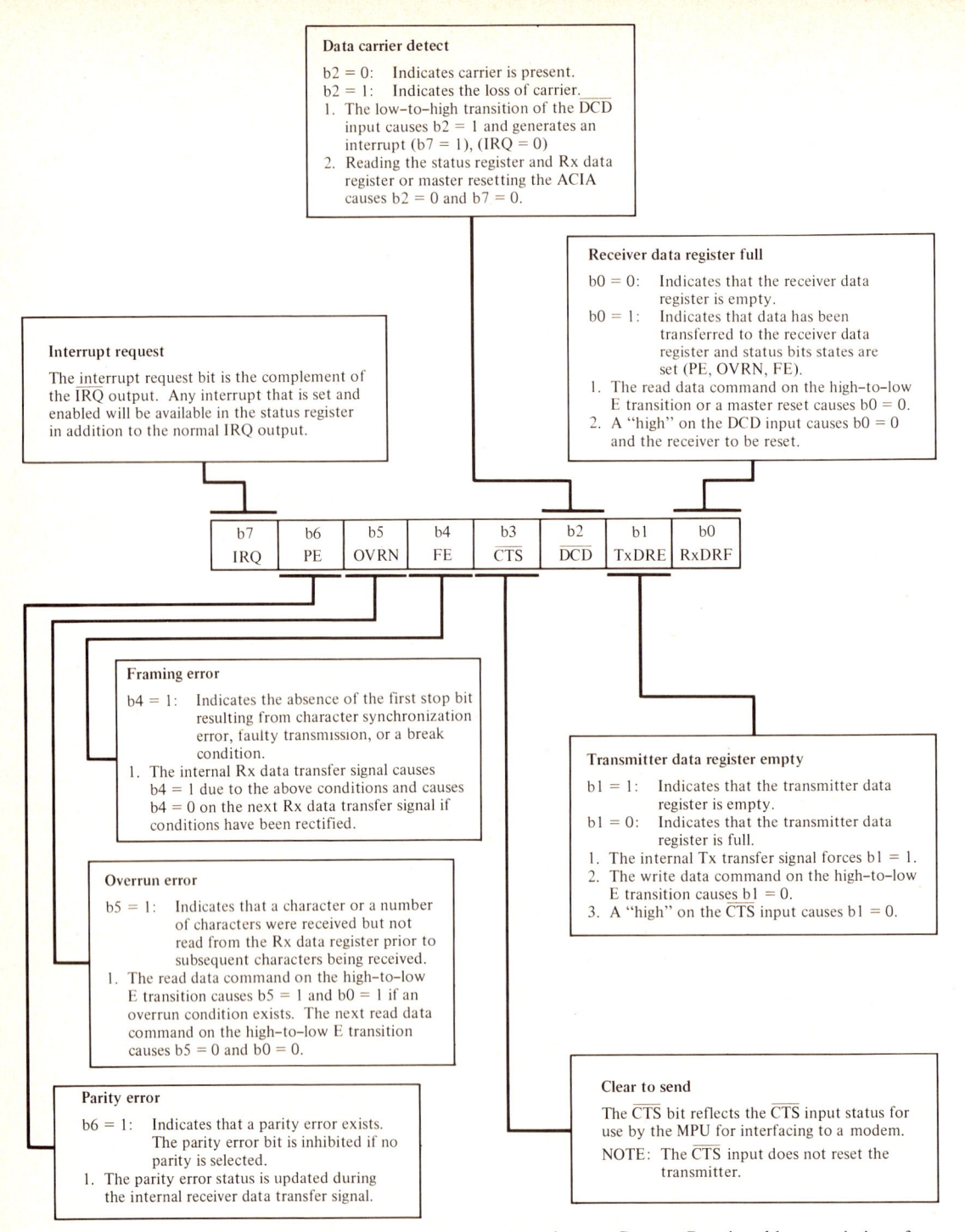

The $\overline{\text{CTS}}$ bit reflects the $\overline{\text{CTS}}$ input status for use by the MPU for interfacing to a modem.
NOTE: The $\overline{\text{CTS}}$ input does not reset the transmitter.

Figure 8.20 ACIA status register format. Source: Reprinted by permission of Motorola Semiconductor Products, Inc., copyright © 1975.

b4 (WS3)	b3 (WS2)	b2 (WS1)	CHARACTER FRAME
0	0	0	7 bit + even parity + 2 stop bits
0	0	1	7 bit + odd parity + 2 stop bits
0	1	0	7 bit + even parity + 1 stop bit
0	1	1	7 bit + odd parity + 1 stop bit
1	0	0	8 bit + no parity + 2 stop bits
1	0	1	8 bit + no parity + 1 stop bit
1	1	0	8 bit + even parity + 1 stop bit
1	1	1	8 bit + odd parity + 1 stop bit

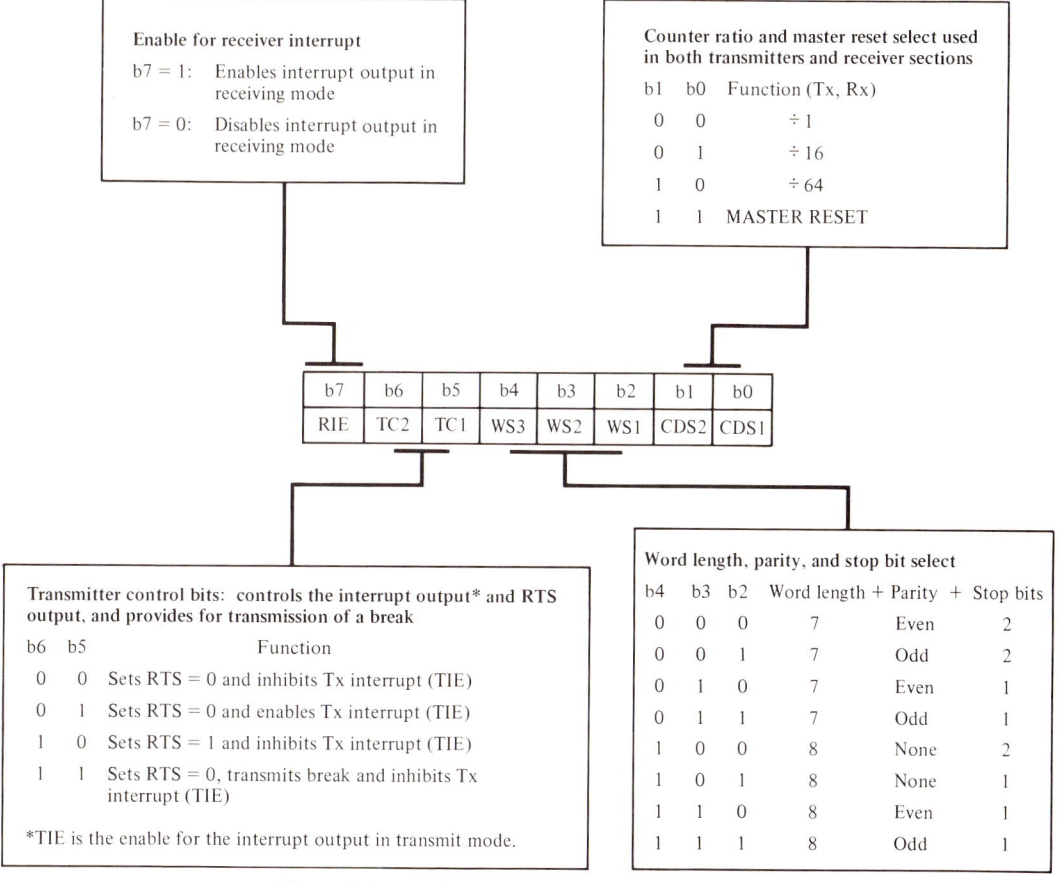

Enable for receiver interrupt

b7 = 1: Enables interrupt output in receiving mode

b7 = 0: Disables interrupt output in receiving mode

Counter ratio and master reset select used in both transmitters and receiver sections

b1	b0	Function (Tx, Rx)
0	0	÷ 1
0	1	÷ 16
1	0	÷ 64
1	1	MASTER RESET

b7	b6	b5	b4	b3	b2	b1	b0
RIE	TC2	TC1	WS3	WS2	WS1	CDS2	CDS1

Transmitter control bits: controls the interrupt output* and RTS output, and provides for transmission of a break

b6	b5	Function
0	0	Sets RTS = 0 and inhibits Tx interrupt (TIE)
0	1	Sets RTS = 0 and enables Tx interrupt (TIE)
1	0	Sets RTS = 1 and inhibits Tx interrupt (TIE)
1	1	Sets RTS = 0, transmits break and inhibits Tx interrupt (TIE)

*TIE is the enable for the interrupt output in transmit mode.

Word length, parity, and stop bit select

b4	b3	b2	Word length	Parity	Stop bits
0	0	0	7	Even	2
0	0	1	7	Odd	2
0	1	0	7	Even	1
0	1	1	7	Odd	1
1	0	0	8	None	2
1	0	1	8	None	1
1	1	0	8	Even	1
1	1	1	8	Odd	1

Figure 8.21 ACIA control register format. Source: Reprinted by permission of Motorola Semiconductor Products, Inc., copyright © 1975.

equivalent results. Using the upper byte implies an even address and use of the Upper Data Strobe ($\overline{\text{UDS}}$), and using the lower byte implies an odd address and the use of the Lower Data Strobe ($\overline{\text{LDS}}$). In this application, the ACIA is placed on the lower byte of the data bus.

Enable (E) and R/$\overline{\text{W}}$ are connected to the corresponding pins of the MC68000. Several signals are generated to form chip selects as shown in Figure 8.22. Valid Memory Address ($\overline{\text{VMA}}$) from the MC68000 is an active low signal (as opposed to active high for the MC6800) as well as $\overline{\text{LDS}}$. The NOR of the two signals is used to develop CS1. The address $F3FFXX is generated by address lines A8 through A23 to enable a SN74LS154 4 to 16 line selector. Address lines A4 through A7 are used to generate a low output at 02 of the SN74LS154 to be used for CS2 of the ACIA. Address line A1 is used for the register select (RS) pin of the ACIA. This puts the ACIA status register at address $F3FF21 and the control register at address $F3FF23. If the ACIA has been placed on the upper byte, the addresses would be $F3FF20 and $F3FF22, respectively. Note that the $ sign represents hexadecimal numbers in the Motorola assembler. To complete the circuit, a signal called Valid Peripheral Address ($\overline{\text{VPA}}$) must be generated and returned to the MC68000 to indicate that a 6800 cycle is being executed. The SN74LS154 has two active low chip enable lines which are driven by the gates that form address $F3FFXX from address lines A8 through A23. Since the SN74LS154 always picks M6800 peripherals, the two chip enable lines can be ORed to develop $\overline{\text{VPA}}$. Since more than 16 peripherals could exist, it is best to make the device actually driving the $\overline{\text{VPA}}$ line an open collector output so that several gates can be wire ORed.

Operating the ACIA is relatively easy as shown in the flowchart given in Figure 8.23. Once the control register is set up, the status register is monitored for Receive Data Register Full (RDRF) and Transmit Data Register Empty (TDRE) indications, as well as error signals and handshake lines. The handshake lines such as Request To Send (RTS), Clear To Send (CTS), and Data Carrier Detect ($\overline{\text{DCD}}$) indicate which conditions are present so that the microprocessor can ascertain when transmission can occur. Once all conditions are ready, transmission or reception or both can begin.

A sample program is given in Figure 8.24 which shows the MC68000 receiving a character from a terminal through the ACIA and then echoing that character back to the terminal. Essentially, the MC68000 checks to see that transmission and reception can occur. The status register is polled until a character is received. The character is read and then written back to the ACIA for transmission to the terminal as soon as the transmit data register is empty. Of course, any number of subroutines or additional code could be executed before looking for the next character from the ACIA.

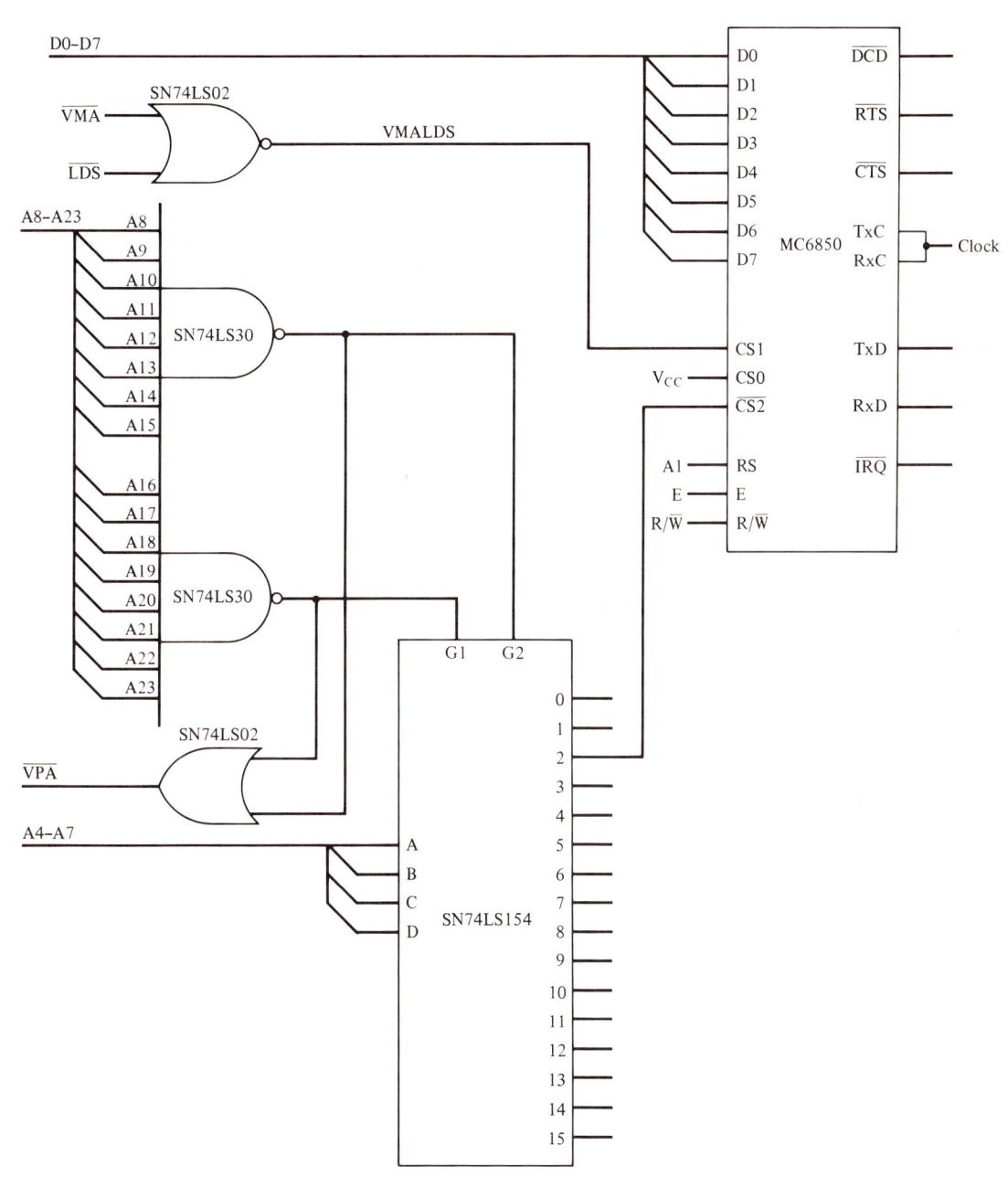

Figure 8.22 MC68000 to MC6850 interconnections. Source: Reprinted by permission of Motorola Semiconductor Products, Inc., copyright © 1982.

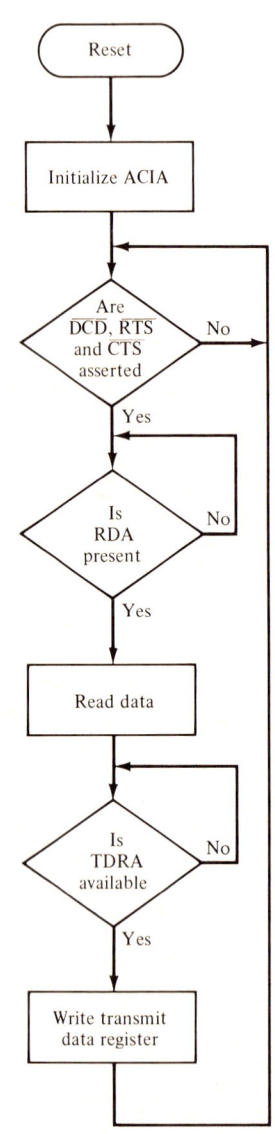

308 Chapter 8 TYPICAL MICROPROCESSOR INTERFACE CHIPS

Figure 8.23 ACIA operation—flowchart. Source: Reprinted by permission of Motorola Semiconductor Products, Inc., copyright © 1982.

```
 1              00000000         ORG $00000000
 2              00F3FF00         ACIASR EQU $00F3FF00
 3              00F3FF00         ACIACR EQU $00F3FF00
 4              00F3FF02         ACIADR EQU $00F3FF02
 5              00F3FF02         ACIATR EQU $00F3FF02
 6              00020000         SYSTACK EQU $00020000
 7              00000008         RESET EQU $00000008
 8  000000      00020000          DC.L SYSTACK
 9  000004      00000008          DC.L RESET
10  000008      13FC0003
                00F3FF00         MOVE.B #$03,ACIACR RESET ACIA
11  000010      13FC0051
                00F3FF00         MOVE.B #$51,ACIACR INITIALIZE ACIA
12  000018      103900F3FF00     ERROR MOVE.B ACIASR,D0 GET STATUS
13  00001E      0200007C         AND.B #$7C,D0 MASK IRQ,TDRA,RDA
14  000022      66F4             BNE ERROR ANY ERRORS?
15  000024      08390001
                00F3FF00         READS1 BTST #01,ACIASR
16  00002C      66F6             BNE READS1
17  00002E      103900F3FF02     MOVE.B ACIADR,D0 READ CHARACTER
18  000034      08390002
                00F3FF00         READS2 BTST #02,ACIASR IS TDRA SET?
19  00003C      66F6             BNE READS2 LOOP IF NO
20  00003E      13C000F3FF02     MOVE.B D0,ACIATR TRANSMIT CHARACTER
21  000044      60D2             BRA ERROR START OVER
22                               END
```

****** TOTAL ERRORS   0—   0

SYMBOL TABLE

ACIACR   F3FF00 ACIADR   F3FF02 ACIASR   F3FF00 ACIATR   F3FF02
ERROR   000018 READS1   000024 READS2   000034 RESET   000008
SYSTACK   020000

Figure 8.24 ACIA operation—sample program.

8.3. Keyboard/Display Controller Chips

A common method of entering programs into a microcomputer is via a keyboard. A popular way of displaying results by the microcomputer is by using seven segment displays. The main functions to be performed for interfacing keyboards to microcomputers are:

1. Sensing a key actuation.
2. Debounce the key.
3. Decode the key.

Let us now elaborate on the keyboard interfacing concepts. A keyboard is arranged in rows and columns. Figure 8.25 shows a 2 × 2 keyboard interfaced to a typical microcomputer. In Figure 8.25, the columns are normally at a HIGH level. A key actuation is sensed by sending a LOW to each row one at a time via PA_0 and PA_1 of port A. The two columns can then be inputted via PB_2 and PB_3 of port B to see whether any of the normally HIGH columns are pulled LOW by a key actuation. If it is, the rows can be checked individually to determine the row in which the key is down. The row and column code in which the key is pressed can thus be found.

The next step is to debounce the key. Key bounce occurs when a key is pressed; it bounces for a short time before making the contact. When this bounce occurs, it may appear to the microcomputer that the same key has been actuated several times instead of just once. This problem can be eliminated by reading the keyboard after 20 ms and then verifying to see if it is still down. If it is, then the key actuation is valid.

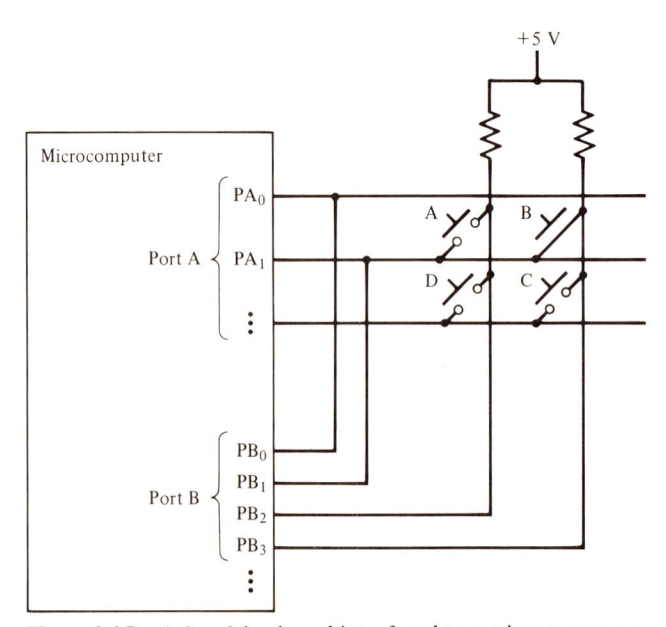

Figure 8.25 A 2 × 2 keyboard interfaced to a microcomputer.

Keyboard/Display Controller Chips   311

The next step is to translate the row and column code into a more popular code such as hexadecimal or ASCII. This can easily be accomplished by a program.

There are certain characteristics associated with keyboard acutations which must be considered while interfacing a keyboard to a microcomputer. Typically, these are two-key lockout and N-key rollover. The two-key lockout takes into account only one key pressed. An additional key pressed and released does not generate any codes. The system is simple to implement and most often used. However, it might slow down the typing since each key must be fully released before the next one is pressed down. On the other hand, the N-key rollover will ignore all keys pressed until only one remains down.

Now let us elaborate on the interfacing characterisics of typical displays. The following functions are to be typically performed for displays:

1. Output the appropriate display code.
2. Output the code via right entry or left entry into the displays if there are more than one display.

The above functions can easily be realized by a microcomputer program. If there are more than one key, they are typically arranged in rows. A row of four displays is shown in Figure 8.26. Note that in Figure 8.26, one has the option of outputting the display code via right entry or left entry. If it is entered via left entry, then the code for the most significant digit of the four-digit display should be outputted first, then the next digit code, and so on. Note that the first digit will be shifted three times, the next digit twice, the next digit once, and the last digit (least significant digit in this case) does not need to be shifted. The shifting operations are so fast that visually all four digits will appear on the display simultaneously. If the displays are entered via left entry then the least significant digit must be outputted first and the rest of the sequence is similar to the right entry.

The keyboard and display concepts described here can be realized by software or hardware. In order to unload the microprocessor of these functions, microprocessor manufacturers developed a number of keyboard/display controller chips. These chips are typically initialized by the microprocessor. The keyboard/display functions are then performed by the chip independent of the microprocessor. The amount of keyboard/display functions performed by the controller chip varies from one manufacturer to

Figure 8.26 A row of four displays.

another. However, these functions are usually shared between the controller chip and the microprocessor.

We describe one such keyboard/display controller chip, namely the Intel 8279, in the following. Appendix B provides Intel's specification for the 8279.

8.3.1 Intel 8279 Keyboard/Display Controller Chip

1. Introduction

This section is intended to aid in the use of the Intel 8279 Programmable Keyboard/Display Controller. All modes of this device will be explained in detail with examples. The 8279 description is split into three main parts: the interface to the 8085 microprocessor, interface to keyboard and display hardware, and software interface.

A block diagram is shown in Figure 8.27. As can be seen, this chip has many features which would normally require extensive external logic to perform these same functions. The chip automatically controls the display refreshing and multiplexing. It contains the debounce circuitry needed for any normal key switch. It also contains an 8×3 bit RAM which can be configured as a First-In-First-Out buffer (FIFO) or it can represent the actual condition of all the switches at any given time.

The chip is fully programmable, and many different modes can be programmed using the same external logic.

2. Interfacing to the 8085

The 8279 was initially designed for the 8080 microprocessor, but it can work with the 8085. As mentioned before, the main difference between the 8085 and the 8080 is the fact that the 8085 multiplexes the lower byte of address and the data on the same eight pins. Since the 8279 requires A_0, the least significant bit of the address bus, we will either have to decode A_0 from the multiplexed lines or use a trick of the 8085.

If the 8279 is to be I/O mapped, that is, to appear as a group of input/output ports, we can use the upper byte of the address bus to provide A_0. The 8085, like the 8080, duplicates the lower byte of the address bus onto the upper byte of the address bus during I/O operations. Thus, A_8 becomes A_0. This is shown in Figure 8.28.

If the 8279 is to be memory mapped, that is, to appear as a group of memory locations, we will have to demultiplex the address/data lines to provide the entire 16-bit address bus. This can be done by using an octal latch such as the Intel 8282 or a TTL 74LS373. The signal from the 8085 specifying the address/data lines that contain address information is ALE, for Address Latch Enable. With ALE, the octal latch can store the lower byte of the address bus, thereby providing the entire 16-bit address bus for decoding. This is shown in Figure 8.29.

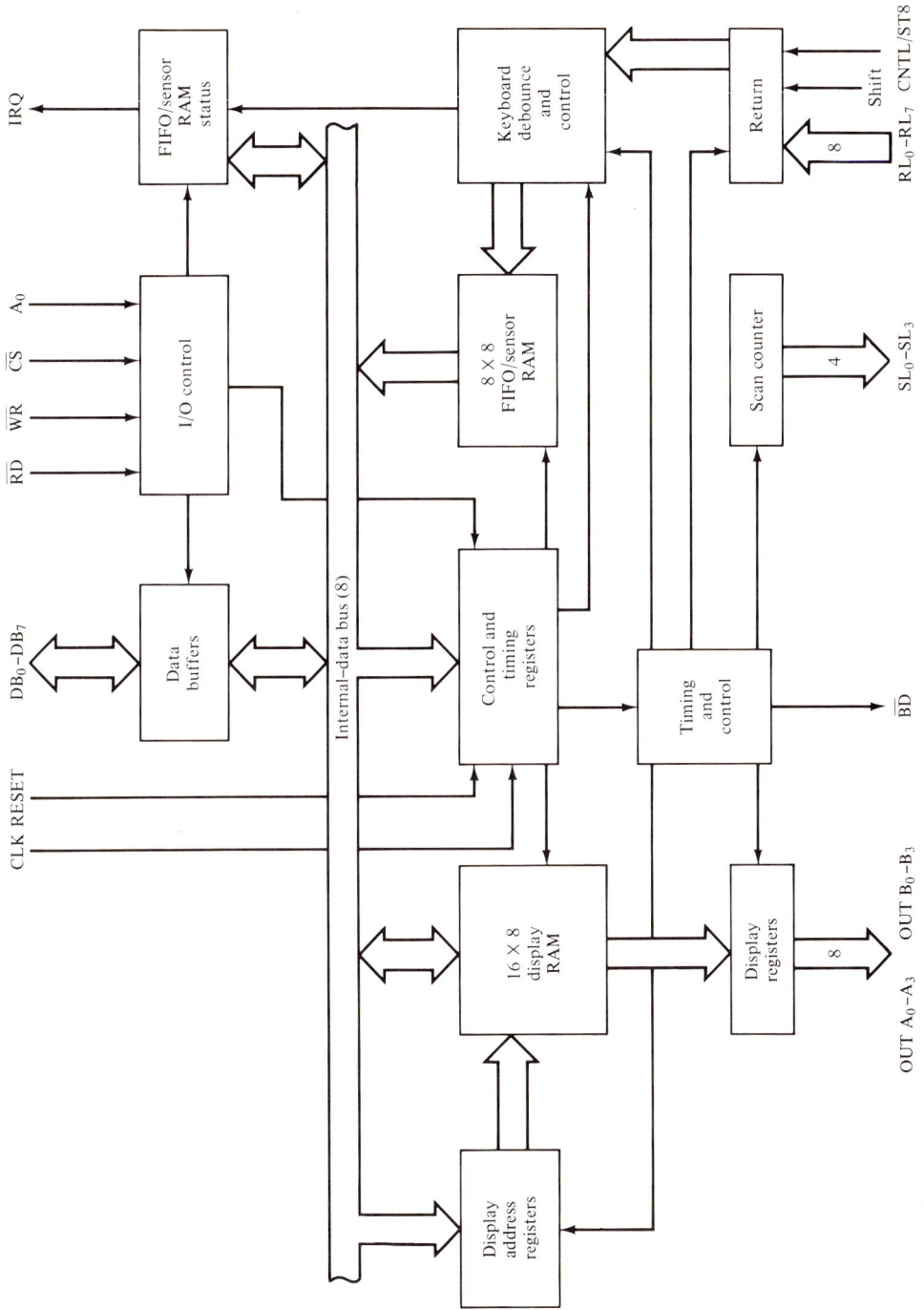

Figure 8.27 8279 block diagram. Source: Reprinted by permission of Intel Corporation, copyright © 1982.

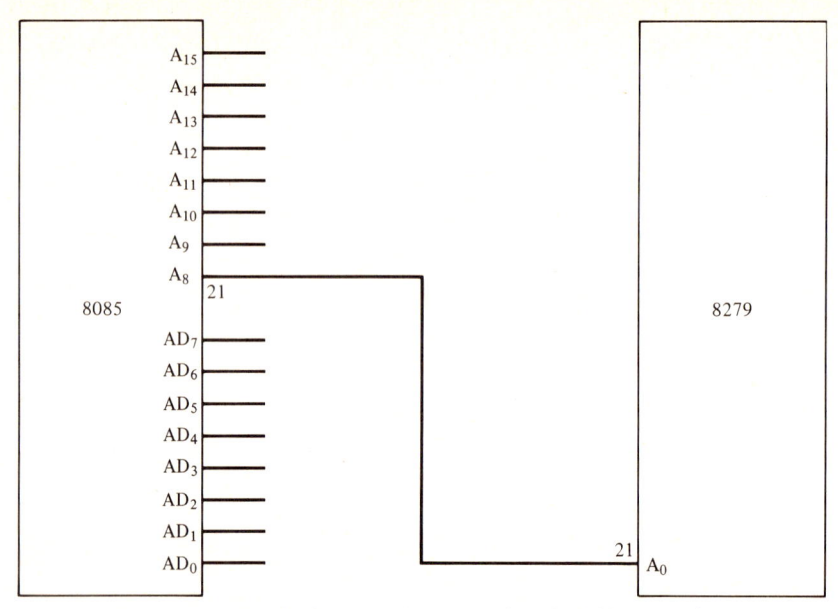

314 Chapter 8 Typical Microprocessor Interface Chips

Figure 8.28 8085/8279 interface when the 8279 is to be I/O mapped.

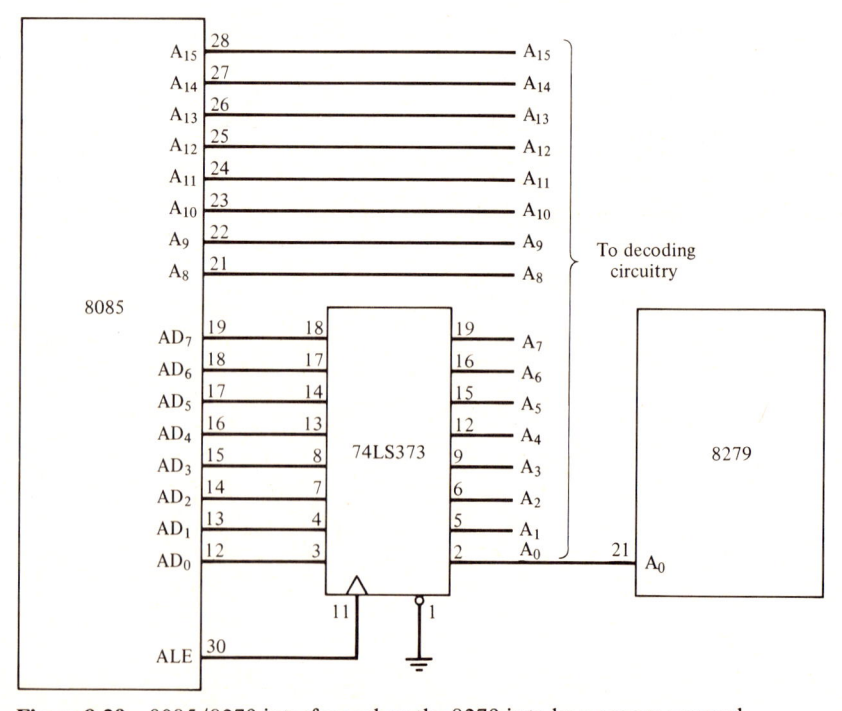

Figure 8.29 8085/8279 interface when the 8279 is to be memory mapped.

The 8279 has an 8-bit data bus which supplies control information and the exchange of data. This must be connected to the 8085's address/data bus.

The 8279 has two signals which control the direction of data flow on the data bus. These signals are $\overline{RD}$ and $\overline{WR}$. When $\overline{RD}$ is true, the CPU is reading data from the 8279. When $\overline{WR}$ is true, the CPU is writing data to the 8279. To simplify the chip select circuitry, these signals should only be active during either an I/O cycle or memory cycle, depending on the mapping selected for the 8279. The 8085 does not generate these two signals directly, but they can be generated easily.

The 8085 provides three signals which define the operation in progress. They are $\overline{WR}$, $\overline{RD}$, and $IO/\overline{M}$. The $\overline{RD}$ and $\overline{WR}$ signals specify the direction of data flow while the $IO/\overline{M}$ signal specifies the operation in progress. The table below shows the decoding of these three signals and the resulting bus operation.

WR	RD	IO/M	OPERATION
0	1	1	I/O write
1	0	1	I/O read
0	1	0	Memory read
1	0	0	Memory write

By using a simple 3 to 8 decoder, such as a 74LS138, we can decode these signals into $\overline{IOWR}$, $\overline{IORD}$, $\overline{MEMR}$, and $\overline{MEMW}$. Figure 8.30 shows this implementation.

The $\overline{CS}$ pin enables the 8279 for a data transfer as specified by its $\overline{RD}$, $\overline{WR}$, and A_0 pins. This line goes true whenever the correct address is present on the address bus. The degree to which the address bus must be

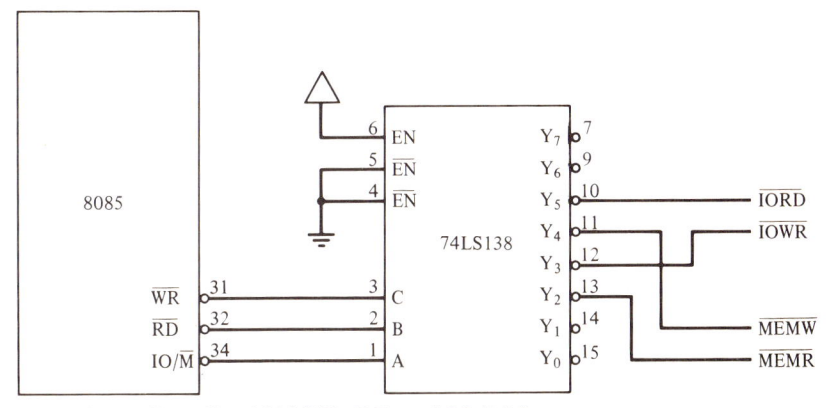

Figure 8.30 Decoding 8085 WR, RD, and IO/M lines.

decoded depends upon how complex the system is. If the system has many I/O devices, a more complete decoding of the address is needed to protect against bus conflicts. But in a simple system with few devices, no real decoding is needed. Each device can occupy many I/O locations.

The reset pin on the 8279 serves to reset the device during power on or reset events. This pin can be connected to the 8085 reset pin.

The CLK pin provides the clock for the internal timing of the 8279. This clock must be greater than 200 kHz for the internal timers to provide the correct delays. This can be connected to the 8085's CLK pin or other frequency source.

The 8279's IRQ pin signals the CPU that the 8279 has data available and needs to be read. In an interrupt driven system, the IRQ signal can be connected to the 8085's RST5.5, RST6.5, or RST7.5 pins to interrupt the 8085 when data are available. This will cause the 8085 to execute an interrupt service routine to read the 8279. In noninterrupt driven systems this line is not used; the CPU can determine if the 8279 needs service by reading the status register of the 8279.

A complete interface of the 8279 to an 8085 can be seen in Figure 8.31. This implementation is I/O mapped, interrupt driven, and uses simple decoding of the address bus.

3. Interfacing to Keyboard/Display Hardware

The 8279 interfaces the CPU to a keyboard and a display device. Since these two sections are separate, we first discuss the display interface.

The display interface is relatively simple. The 8279 provides the buffers, the multiplexing logic, and the refreshing needed to drive the display. This greatly simplifies the necessary hardware. In fact, if you only need a four-character display, you only need to add the display driver necessary for the particular display you are using.

The 8279 has two buffers, the A buffer and the B buffer. These buffers can be used together to form two 4 bit $\times$ 16 word displays, or they can be used together to form an 8 bit $\times$ 16 word display. Writing data into or reading data from the buffer is controlled by the mode selected, and will be discussed in the next section on software interfacing.

The 8279 provides the date from the internal buffer on the out A and out B pins. Each of these ports is 4 bits wide. This data is synchronized with the scan lines, SL_0 through SL_3, to provide multiplexing. These scan lines are either encoded or decoded. In the decoded mode, only one scan line is active at one time. Thus, only four characters are displayed. In the encoded mode, the scan lines form a binary sequence counting from 0 to either 8 or 16, depending on the options selected. In this mode, an external decoder, such as a 4 to 16 line decoder, would have to be used. In the decoded mode, the scan lines are active low, while in the encoded mode they are active high.

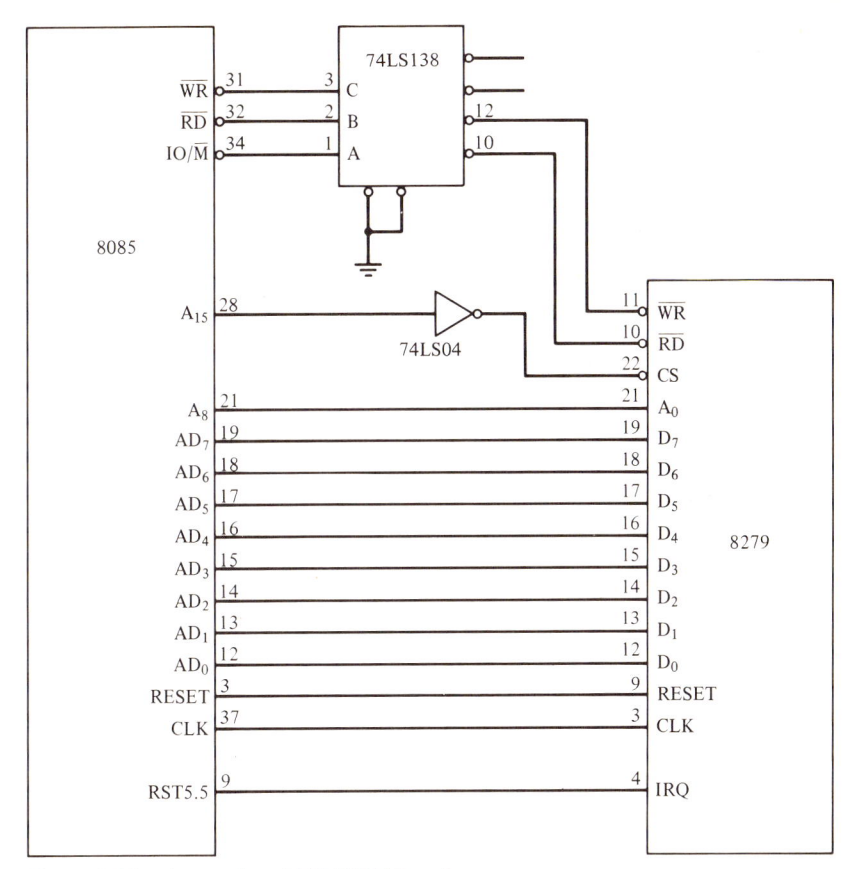

Figure 8.31 A complete 8085/8279 interface.

There is one additional signal provided by the 8279 for the display interface. This is BD or Blank Display. This active low line goes true when the display should be blanked, either by command or between successive words.

If you use the two outputs together to form an 8 bit × 16 word display, you can directly drive a multiplexed LED display. Seven of the bits control the seven segments, and the eighth bit can control the decimal points. With this setup, you can display limited alphanumerics, or even special graphics. (A display much like the simple handheld games could be fashioned in this way.) For this application, you would only need to add anode and cathode drivers to buffer the signals from the 8279 and decoder chip. A sample of this display is shown in Figure 8.32.

The keyboard interface is organized as either an 8 × 8 matrix or a 4 × 8 matrix of SPST switches. The keyboard uses the same four scan lines

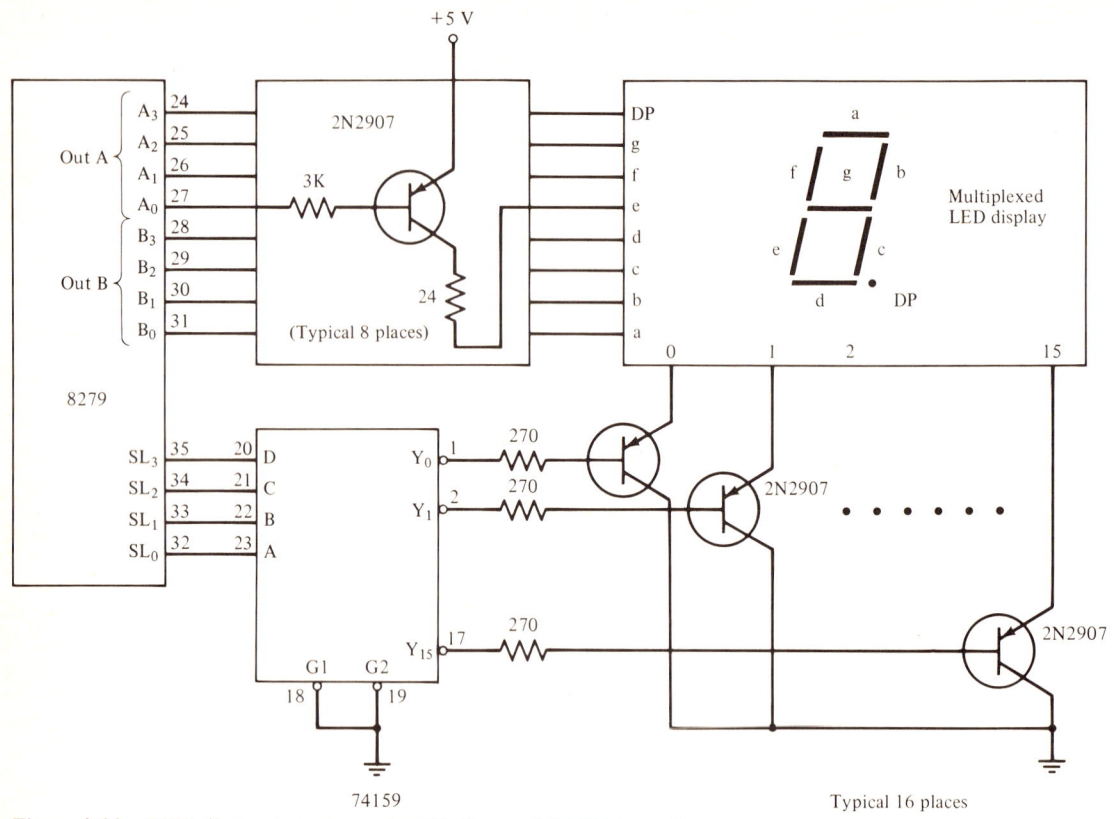

318 Chapter 8 Typical Microprocessor Interface Chips

Figure 8.32 8279 display interface using OUT A and OUT B together.

(SL_{0-3}) that the display uses. The keyboard can operate in two different modes: decoded (4 × 8) or encoded (8 × 8). The scan lines behave exactly as described for the display interface. In the decoded mode, the scan lines directly do the scanning, while in the encoded mode, the scan lines must be externally decoded. Note that in the encoded mode only the first 3 bits or eight lines should be used for the keyboard. Note that the keyboard section and the display section must be in the same scan mode, meaning that if the keyboard scan is encoded, the display scan must be encoded.

Two additional keys are provided for by the 8279. These are for the SHIFT and CONTROL keys. These keys do not trigger the 8279 themselves, but are recorded in the FIFO along with a key in the matrix when that key is pressed. This gives you an effective 256 codes which can be generated by the 8279. A simple circuit for 64 keys, SHIFT, CONTROL, and a 16-character display is shown in Figure 8.33.

In the scanned sensor mode, the FIFO buffer is converted into an 8 × 8 bit map. Each bit in the map represents the state of the switch at the same

Keyboard/Display Controller Chips 319

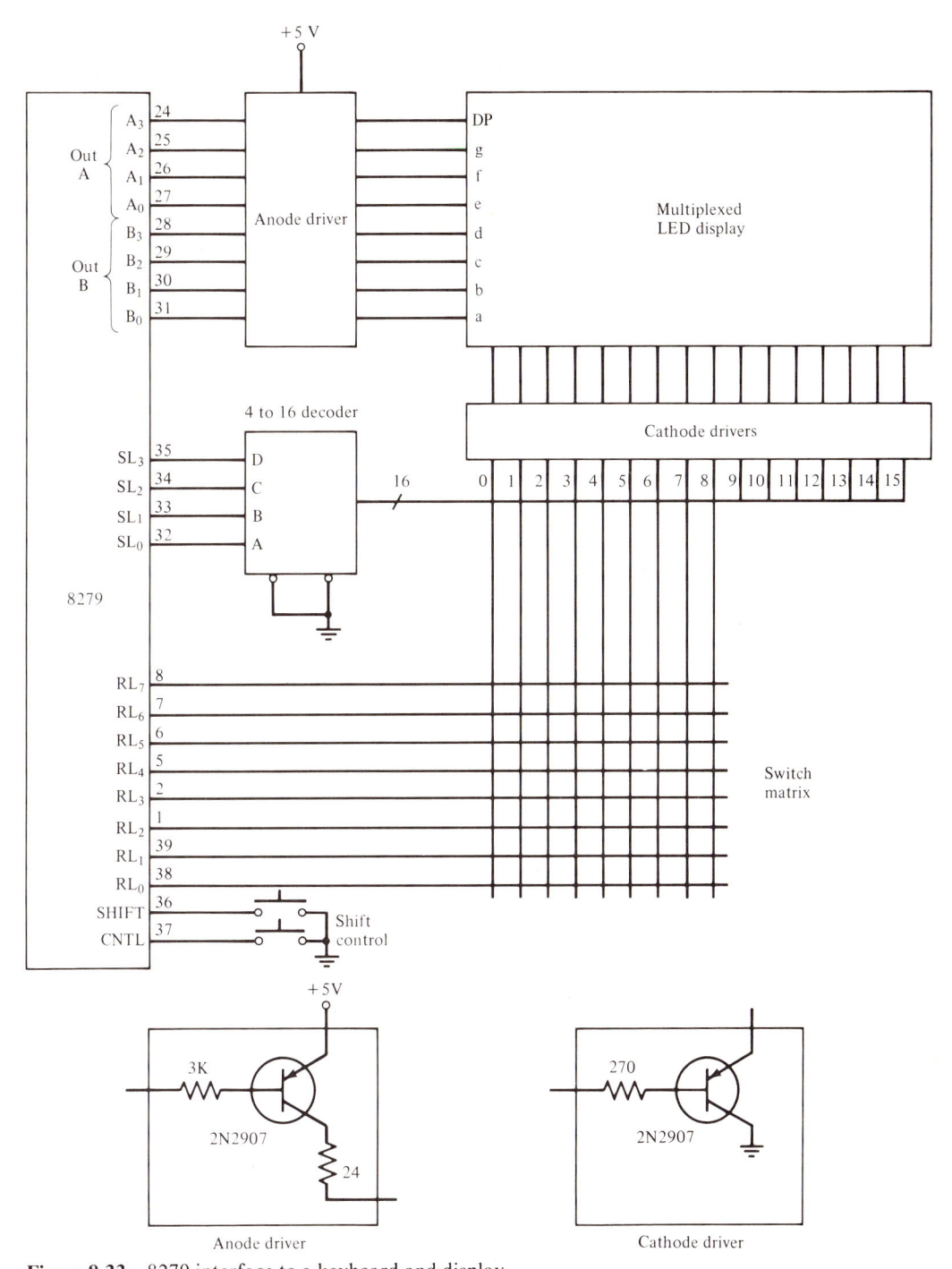

Figure 8.33 8279 interface to a keyboard and display.

320 Chapter 8 Typical Microprocessor Interface Chips

location in the keyboard matrix. If the switch is closed, then the RAM location corresponding to that switch will be a logical zero. No key debouncing is performed by the 8279, and the SHIFT or CONTROL status is not recorded. In this mode, the 8279 signals any change in the matrix by raising IRQ. A bit is also set in the status register.

In the scanned sensor mode, the sensors do not have to be switches, but can be anything that produces a 1 or a 0 in response to the scan lines.

A third mode is available for entering data into the FIFO of the 8279. This is the strobed input mode. In this mode the data present on the Return Lines (RL_{0-7}) are loaded into the FIFO by the rising edge of the CNTL/STB pulse. In this mode the scan lines do not mean anything to the keyboard section; they only control the display hardware.

4. Software Interface

For the 8279 to work properly, it must be sent commands programming it for the specific hardware configuration. These commands are sent to the command port of the 8279 (A_0 = high). The data are read from or sent to the data port of the 8279 (A_0 = low). Status information is read from the command port.

The keyboard/display mode set command defines the mode the 8279 will operate in. This command is diagrammed below:

	MSB							LSB
Keyboard/display mode set	0	0	0	D	D	K	K	K

DD	
0 0	8 8-bit character display—left entry
0 1	16 8-bit character display—left entry
1 0	8 8-bit character display—right entry
1 1	16 8-bit character display—right entry

KKK	
0 0 0	Encoded scan keyboard—two-key lockout
0 0 1	Decoded scan keyboard—two-key lockout
0 1 0	Encoded scan keyboard—N-key rollover
0 1 1	Decoded scan keyboard—N-key rollover
1 0 0	Encoded scan sensor matrix
1 0 1	Decoded scan sensor matrix
1 1 0	Strobed input, encoded display scan
1 1 1	Strobed input, decoded display scan

The DD field sets the display length and the entry mode. The length of the display can be 8 or 16 words long, and we can enter data from the left or the right.

In left-entry mode, characters are entered from the left as on a typewriter. When in the autoincrementing mode, each new character will appear to the right of the old character. If you are using a 16-word display, the seventeenth character will replace the first character entered.

In right-entry mode, the characters are entered at the right side of the display and scrolled to the left with each new character, much like on a calculator. In this mode, the seventeenth character causes the first character entered to scroll off the display.

The KKK field sets the keyboard and scan mode. The scan modes have been discussed in the hardware section, along with the scanned sensor and strobed input modes.

The keyboard mode is either two-key lockout or N-key rollover. These modes determine how the 8279 deals with the problem of rollover; that is, when two or more keys are depressed at once. In two-key lockout the 8279 recognizes the first key pressed, and additional keys pressed are ignored until the first key is released. In N-key rollover, keys pressed simultaneously are entered into the FIFO in the order that the 8279 finds them. In this mode, a special error mode can be set. This error mode will consider a simultaneous key depression as an error. A bit is set in the status register, any further writing into the FIFO is inhibited, and an interrupt is requested. This error mode is set by the end interrupt/error mode set command, described later.

The 8279 has programmable counters to divide the CLK signal to 100 kHz for the internal timing. The value is set by the use of the program clock command. The P field contains the divisor necessary to give a 100-kHz internal clock. This value is in the range 2 to 31. For a 2-MHz CLK signal, the divisor would be 20 or 14K.

	MSB							LSB
Program clock	0	0	1	P	P	P	P	P

When the CPU sends a read FIFO/sensor RAM command, the 8279 responds to each successive read from the FIFO. This command is shown below:

	MSB							LSB	
Read FIFO/sensor RAM	0	1	0	AI	X	A	A	A	X = don't care

In the scanned sensor mode, AAA selects one of the eight rows of the RAM to read. AI is the autoincrement bit. If this is true, the RAM address will automatically increment after the read. If the AI bit is set, reading the RAM will *not* clear the interrupt. The AAA and AI field is ignored during any other mode.

The read display RAM command enables the CPU to read the data from the display buffer. This command is diagrammed below:

```
                  MSB                           LSB
Read display RAM | 0 | 1 | 1 | AI | A | A | A | A |
```

The AAAA field sets the address for this read, and the AI field controls the autoincrement mode. Since the same counter is used for reading and writing to the display RAM, this command also sets the next address and increment mode for both reading and writing.

The write display RAM command sets up the 8279 for a write to the display buffer. The addressing and autoincrement modes are identical to the Read Display RAM command, described before.

```
                   MSB                           LSB
Write display RAM | 1 | 0 | 0 | AI | A | A | A | A |
```

This command does not affect the source of subsequent data reads; the CPU will read from whichever data source (FIFO/sensor RAM or display RAM) was last selected. If the source was the display RAM, the write display RAM command will change the address of the next read location.

The display inhibit/blanking command is used to inhibit writing to the display RAM or in blanking the display. This command makes using two 4-bit ports easier in that the inhibit and blanking functions can be performed on each of the two ports independently.

```
                          MSB                                     LSB
Display inhibit/blanking | 1 | 0 | 1 | X | IW A | IW B | BL A | BL B |    X = don't care
```

The IW bits are used to inhibit writing to the A port or B port. If we are using BCD decoding for the two 4-bit displays, we can inhibit writing to one display while writing to the other. Port B is the lower nibble of the data written to the display, with port A being the upper nibble.

The BL bits blank the display of the selected port. The code that is sent to the display during blanking is specified by the clear command described later. When using the display as a single 8-bit display, both BL bits must be set to blank the display.

The clear command determines the codes sent to the display when it is blanked, and can also clear the display RAM and reset the device. This command, shown below,

```
        MSB                                   LSB
Clear | 1 | 1 | 0 | E_N | C_D | C_D | C_F | C_A |
```

consists of one field and three enable bits. The C_D field determines the blanking code for the displays.

C_D	C_D	BLANKING CODE
0	X	All zeros (X = don't care)
1	0	Hex 20 (ASCII space)
1	1	All ones

The E_N bit enables clearing of the display when true. During display clear, the display RAM may not be written into. This state is recorded in the status register, and remains true until the display is finished clearing.

The C_F bit, if true, clears the FIFO status, the interrupt line is reset, and the sensor RAM pointer is reset to 0.

The C_A bit, when set, has the combined effect to the E_N and C_F bits; in addition, it resynchronizes the internal timing chain.

The end interrupt/error mode set command lowers the interrupt request line and enables further writing into RAM. This command also sets the special error mode for the N-key rollover mode described earlier.

	MSB						LSB	
End interrupt/error mode set	1	1	1	E	X	X	X	X	X = don't care

When the E bit is set, and the keyboard mode is set to N-key rollover, the special error mode is set.

Now that we have discussed all the commands, we will now look at the data formats of the various registers contained within the 8279. The FIFO status word contains information as to the state of the 8279. This word is diagrammed below:

	MSB						LSB
FIFO status word	D_U	S/E	O	U	F	N	N	N

The NNN field indicates the number of characters contained in the FIFO during keyboard or strobed input modes. This field has no meaning during the scanned sensor mode.

The F bit indicates the FIFO is full and needs to be read before another character is entered. This bit has no meaning during the scanned sensor mode.

The U bit indicates an underrun error has occurred. That is, the CPU has read an empty FIFO. This bit has no meaning during the scanned sensor mode.

The 0 bit indicates a FIFO overrun has occurred. That is, a character was entered into a full FIFO. This bit has no meaning during the scanned sensor mode.

The S/E bit has two functions, determined by the mode the 8279 is operating in. During the scanned sensor mode, this bit is set to show that at least one sensor closure indication is contained in the sensor RAM. In the N-key rollover mode, if the special error mode has been set, this bit indicates a simultaneous multiple closure error has occurred.

The D_U bit indicates the display is unavailable because a clear display or clear all command has not completed.

The data format for the FIFO during keyboard mode is shown below:

```
                MSB                            LSB
Keyboard data  | C | S | SC | SC | SC | RL | RL | RL |
```

This byte represents the position of the switch matrix, along with the control and shift lines.

The RL and SC fields represent the position in the matrix of the depressed switch. The SC field is the scan line that was active when the key closure was detected, and the RL field is the return line that sampled the closed keyswitch.

The S and C bits are the noninverted shift and control lines, respectively.

In strobed input mode or scanned sensor mode, the FIFO contains the data present on the return lines when strobed in, with RL_0 being the least significant bit.

For all of the following software examples, we will use the hardware shown in Figures 8.31 and 8.33, which has the 8279's data register at I/O port #80_{16}, and the control register at port #81_{16}.

For the 8279 to operate properly, the internal timing chain must be set and the mode selected. This will be contained in an initialization routine shown in Figure 8.34. Since the 8085's CLK signal is 3 MHz, we must divide this by 30 to get a 100-kHz scan rate. We use the program clock command to set this value.

Next we must set the mode the 8279 will operate in. We will be using a 16-character display, with left entry, and an encoded keyboard scan with

```
MACRO-80 3.36     17-Mar-80      PAGE    1

                  ;
                  ;         INITIALIZATION ROUTINE FOR THE 8279
                  ;
                  ;         THIS ROUTINE SETS THE TIMING CLOCK, THE MODE
                  ;
                  ;         AND ENABLES INTERRUPTS ON THE 8085
                  ;
                  ;
                  ;
0081              C8279  EQU  81H       ;8279 CONTROL REGISTER
0080              D8279  EQU  80H       ;8279 DATA REGISTER
                  ;
0000              MODE   EQU  08H       ;MODE WORD FOR 16 CHAR DISP, ENCODED LEFT ENTRY
                  ;                      2 KEY LOCKOUT MODE
003E              CLOCK  EQU  3EH       ;PROGRAM CLOCK COMMAND, DIVISOR = 30
                  ;
0008              INTM   EQU  08H       ;INTERRUPT MASK, ENABLE RST 5.5,6.5,7.5
                  ;
                  ;
                         ORG  1000H    ;PROGRAM BASE
1000' 3E 3E       START: MVI  A,CLOCK  ;LOAD A REGISTER WITH CLOCK COMMAND
1002' D3 81              OUT  C8279    ;OUTPUT TO 8279 CONTROL REGISTER
1004' 3E 00              MVI  A,MODE   ;LOAD A REGISTER WITH MODE COMMAND
1006' D3 81              OUT  C8279    ;OUTPUT TO 8279
1008' 3E 08              MVI  A,INTM   ;LOAD A WITH INTERRUPT MASK
100A' 30                 SIM           ;ENABLE 5.5,6.5,7.5 INTERRUPTS
100B' FB                 EI            ;ENABLE INTERRUPTS
100C' C9                 RET           ;RETURN TO MAIN PROGRAM
                         END  START

MACRO-80 3.36     17-Mar-80      PAGE    5

Macros:

Symbols:
C8279 0081  CLOCK 003E  D8279 0080  INTM 0008
MODE  0000  START 1000'

No Fatal error(s)
```

Figure 8.34 8279 initialization routine.

326 Chapter 8 Typical Microprocessor Interface Chips

two-key lockout. We use the keyboard/display mode set command for this operation.

Since the 8279 will interrupt the 8085 using the RST5.5 interrupt request, we have to enable interrupts on the 8085 by using the SIM and EI instructions. This routine then returns to the calling program. For the different keyboard/display modes, all we do is change the mode word we sent to the 8279.

The interrupt service routine for the 8279 is shown in Figure 8.35. This routine simply reads the FIFO on the 8279, converts this code to a graphics

```
MACRO-80 3.36      17-Mar-80      PAGE    1

                ;
                ;       INTERRUPT SERVICE ROUTINE FOR THE 8279
                ;
                ;       THIS ROUTINE READS THE CHARACTER FROM THE 8279
                ;
                ;       AND CONVERTS IT TO A HEX DIGIT, THEN OUTPUTS IT
                ;
                ;       TO THE DISPLAY. THIS ROUTINE IS INDEPENDENT OF ANY
                ;
                ;       MODE SELECTED. THIS ROUTINE ONLY USES THE LOWER NIBBLE
                ;
                ;       WHEN FORMING THE HEX CHARACTER.
                ;
                ;
0081            C8279   EQU     81H     ;8279 COMMAND PORT WITH AUTO INCREMENT
0080            D8279   EQU     90H     ;8279 DATA PORT
                ;
0040            RFIFO   EQU     40H     ;READ FIFO COMMAND
                ;
                ;
                        ORG     2CH     ;RST 5.5 VECTOR
002C'  F5       START:  PUSH    PSW     ;SAVE REGISTERS
002D'  E5               PUSH    H       ;
002E'  C5               PUSH    B       ;
002F'  3E 40            MVI     A,RFIFO ;LOAD A WITH READ FIFO COMMAND
0031'  D3 81            OUT     C8279   ;SEND TO 8279
0033'  DB 80            IN      D8279   ;INPUT FROM FIFO
0035'  E6 0F            ANI     0FH     ;CLEAR UPPER NIBBLE
0037'  06 00            MVI     B,00H   ;CLEAR B REGISTER
0039'  4F               MOV     C,A     ;MOVE CHARACTER TO C REGISTER
```

Figure 8.35 Interrupt service routine for 8279.

```
003A'  21 3000'         LXI    H,TABLE    ;LOAD TABLE BASE ADDRESS INTO HL
003D'  09               DAD    B          ;ADD OFFSET TO BASE ADDRESS
003E'  7E               MOV    A,M        ;LOAD TABLE CONTENTS INTO A
003F'  2F               CMA               ;COMPLEMENT TABLE ENTRY
0040'  D3 80            OUT    D8279      ;OUTPUT TO 8279
0042'  C1               POP    B          ;RESTORE REGISTERS
0043'  E1               POP    H          ;
0044'  F1               POP    PSW        ;
0045'  FB               EI                ;ENABLE INTERRUPTS
0046'  C9               RET               ;RETURN TO MAIN PROGRAM
                        ;
                        ORG    3000H      ;TABLE LOCATION
3000'  3F        TABLE: DB     00111111B  ;ZERO
3001'  06               DB     00000110B  ;ONE
3002'  5B               DB     01011011B  ;TWO

    MACRO-80 3.36    17-Mar-80    PAGE    1-1

3003'  4F        DB    01001111B  ;THREE
3004'  66        DB    01100110B  ;FOUR
3005'  6D        DB    01101101B  ;FIVE
3006'  7D        DB    01111101B  ;SIX
3007'  07        DB    00000111B  ;SEVEN
3008'  7F        DB    01111111B  ;EIGHT
3009'  6F        DB    01101111B  ;NINE
300A'  37        DB    00110111B  ;'A'
300B'  7C        DB    01111100B  ;'b'
300C'  58        DB    01011000B  ;'c'
300D'  5E        DB    01011110B  ;'d'
300E'  79        DB    01111001B  ;'E'
300F'  71        DB    01110001B  ;'F'
                 ;
                 END   START

    MACRO-80 3.36    17-Mar-80    PAGE    5

Macros:

Symbols:
C8279  0081   D8279  0080   RFIFO  0040   START  002C'
TABLE  3000'

No Fatal error(s)
```

Figure 8.35 Interrupt service routine for 8279 (continued).

character, and sends this graphics character to the display. Using this routine, almost all the modes can be checked for the keyboard and display.

The scanned matrix mode interrupt service routine is shown in Figure 8.36. This program responds to an interrupt by reading the entire sensor matrix and placing it into a buffer in memory. This matrix can then be used by the main program.

The strobed input mode will not be tested since the hardware is not set up for this mode. However, the service routine of listing 2 will work in this configuration.

For noninterrupt driven systems, the FIFO status word must be read and the NNN field must be decoded to see if any characters are in the FIFO. This routine is shown in Figure 8.37.

8.4 Direct Memory Access (DMA) Controller Chips

A DMA controller chip is typically used to perform the functions required for data transfers between a microprocessor and an external device using DMA. The DMA controller chip may accomplish the data transfer using a number of different techniques. It may suspend a microprocessor, or it may stop it (burst DMA) or it may steal memory cycles from the microprocessor (cycle stealing DMA) or it may stretch clock pulses. Some sophisticated DMAs such as dynamic memory refreshed DMAs can use some portions of the instruction cycle (such as incrementing the program counter) when the microprocessor does not use the address bus and data bus (transparent DMA). The simplest approach, and the one usually implemented for most microprocessors, is to suspend the operation of the microprocessor. This is the reason for the tristate buses used for the data and the address bus. For performing data transfer between memory and a peripheral device, the peripheral device will send an interrupt to the DMA controller rather than to the microprocessor as shown in Figure 8.38.

When the DMA controller receives an interrupt from the peripheral device, it sends a HOLD signal to the microprocessor. The microprocessor completes the current instruction, releases the address and data buses and sends HOLD acknowledge signal to the DMA controller. The DMA controller then places an address on the address bus which specifies the memory address at which the data transfer takes place. The DMA controller then generates a "read" or a "write" signal and allows the peripheral device to generate the data or receive the data on the data bus. For block transfer, the DMA controller chip typically contains an address register and a counter register. The address register is loaded with the initial starting address at which data transfer takes place. The counter register is initialized with the total amount of data to be transferred. These registers are initialized by the programmer. After each word transfer, the

MACRO-80 3.36   17-Mar-80   PAGE   1

```
                ;
                ;           SCANNED SENSOR MODE INTERRUPT SERVICE ROUTINE
                ;
                ;           WHEN CALLED, COPIES SENSOR MATRIX FROM 8279
                ;
                ;           INTO MEMORY BUFFER STARTING AT LOCATION MATRIX
                ;
                ;
0081            C8279   EQU   81H       ;8279 COMMAND PORT
0080            D8279   EQU   80H       ;8279 DATA PORT
                ;
0050            RFIFO   EQU   50H       ;READ FIFO COMMAND, AUTO INCRE., ADD = 0
00E0            INTEND  EQU   0E0H      ;END INTERRUPT COMMAND
                ;
                ;
                        ORG   2CH       ;RST 5.5 RESTART AREA
002C' F5        BEGIN:  PUSH  PSW       ;SAVE REGISTERS
002D' E5                PUSH  H         ;
002E' C5                PUSH  B         ;
002F' 3E 50             MVI   A,RFIFO   ;LOAD REAF FIFO COMMAND INTO A REGISTER
0031' D3 81             OUT   C8279     ;OUTPUT TO 8279 COMMAND PORT
0033' 21 2000'          LXI   H,MATRIX  ;LOAD STARTING ADDRESS OF MATRIX INTO HL
0036' 06 0B             MVI   B,8       ;LOAD COUNT INTO B REGISTER
0038' DB 80     LOOP:   IN    D8279     ;INPUT SENSOR RAM CONTENTS
003A' 77                MOV   M,A       ;SAVE IN MEMORY
003B' 23                INX   H         ;INCREMENT MEMORY POINTER
003C' 05                DCR   B         ;DECREMENT COUNT
003D' C2 0038'          JNZ   LOOP      ;JUMP IF NOT ZERO
0040' C1                POP   B         ;RESTORE REGISTERS
0041' E1                POP   H         ;
0042' F1                POP   PSW       ;
0043' FB                EI              ;ENABLE INTERRUPTS
0044' C9                RET             ;RETURN TO MAIN PROGRAM
                ;
                        ORG   2000H     ;SET FOR MATRIX ADDRESS
2000'           MATRIX: DS    8         ;8 BYTES OF STORAGE
                ;
                        END   BEGIN
```

MACRO-80 3.36   17-Mar-80   PAGE   5

Macros:

Symbols:
BEGIN 002C' C8279 0081 D8279 0080 INTEND 00E0
LOOP 0038' MATRIX 2000' RFIFO 0050

No Fatal error(s)

Figure 8.36 8279 scanned sensor mode interrupt service routine.

330 Chapter 8 Typical Microprocessor Interface Chips

```
MACRO-80 3.36     17-Mar-80     PAGE    1

              ;
              ;         8279 INPUT ROUTINE FOR NON-INTERRUPT DRIVEN SYSTEMS
              ;
              ;         READS THE FIFO STATUS WORD AND DETERMINES IF FIFO
              ;
              ;         HAS A CHARACTER READY. IF NOT, IT WILL WAIT UNTIL
              ;
              ;         ONE IS. WILL RETURN TO CALLING PROGRAM THIS NEXT
              ;
              ;         CHARACTER IN THE A REGISTER
              ;
0081            C8279 EQU 81H      ;8279 COMMAND PORT
0080            D8279 EQU 80H      ;8279 DATA PORT
              ;
0040            RFIFO EQU 40H      ;READ FIFO COMMAND
              ;
0007            MASK  EQU 07H      ;MASK FOR NNN FIELD
              ;
                      DRG  2000H   ;START OF PROGRAM
2000' DB 81    START: IN   C8279   ;INPUT FIFO STATUS
2002' E6 07           ANI  MASK    ;MASK FOR NNN FIELD
2004' CA 2000'        JZ   START   ;IF BITS ARE ZERO, NOTHING IN FIFO
2007' 3E 40           NVI  A,RFIFO ;MOVE READ FIFO COMMAND TO A
2009' D3 81           OUT  C8279   ;SEND IT TO 8279
200B' DB 80           IN   D8279   ;READ FIFO
200D' C9              RET          ;RETURN
                      END  START

MACRO-80 3.36     17-Mar-80     PAGE    5
```

Macros:

Symbols:
C8279 0081 D8279 0080 MASK 0007 RFIFO 0040
START 2000'

No Fatal error(s)

Figure 8.37 8279 input routine for noninterrupt driven systems.

Direct Memory Access (DMA) Controller Chips

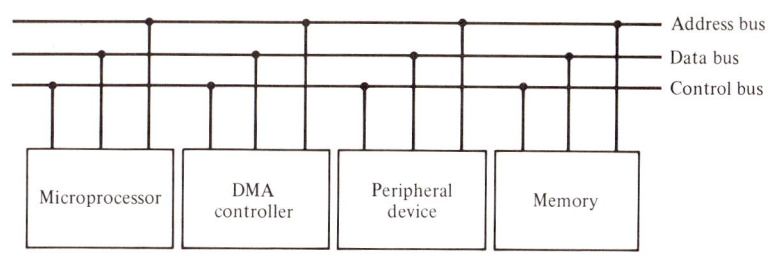

Figure 8.38 DMA controller operation.

address register is incremented and the counter register is decremented. The data transfer stops whenever the counter counts down to 0.

The DMA controller is a very complex and expensive chip. In many cases, it may be cheaper to use a microprocessor and memory to perform block transfer DMA rather than a DMA controller chip.

In the following, we describe the Intel 8257.

8.4.1 Intel 8257 DMA Controller*

The Intel 8257 is a 4-channel DMA controller. Its primary function is to generate, upon a peripheral request, a sequential memory address which will allow the peripheral to read or write data directly to or from memory. Acquisition of the system bus is accomplished via the CPU's hold function. The 8257 has priority logic that resolves the peripheral's requests and issues a composite hold request to the CPU. It maintains the DMA cycle count for each channel and outputs a control signal to notify the peripheral that the programmed number of DMA cycles is complete. It is important to note that the 8257 requires one 8212 I/O port to demultiplex data bus pin outputs. Figure 8.39 shows the 8257 pins, signals, and the functional block diagram.

1. Functional Description

a. General. The 8257 is a programmable, direct memory access device which, when coupled with a single Intel 8212 I/O port device, provides a complete 4-channel DMA controller for use in Intel microcomputer systems. After being initialized by software, the 8257 can transfer a block of data containing up to 16,384 bytes between memory and a peripheral device directly, without further intervention required of the CPU. Upon receiving a DMA transfer request from an enabled peripheral, the 8257:

    i. Acquires control of the system bus.
    ii. Acknowledges that requesting peripheral which is connected to the highest priority channel.

---
* This section contains material reprinted courtesy of Intel Corporation.

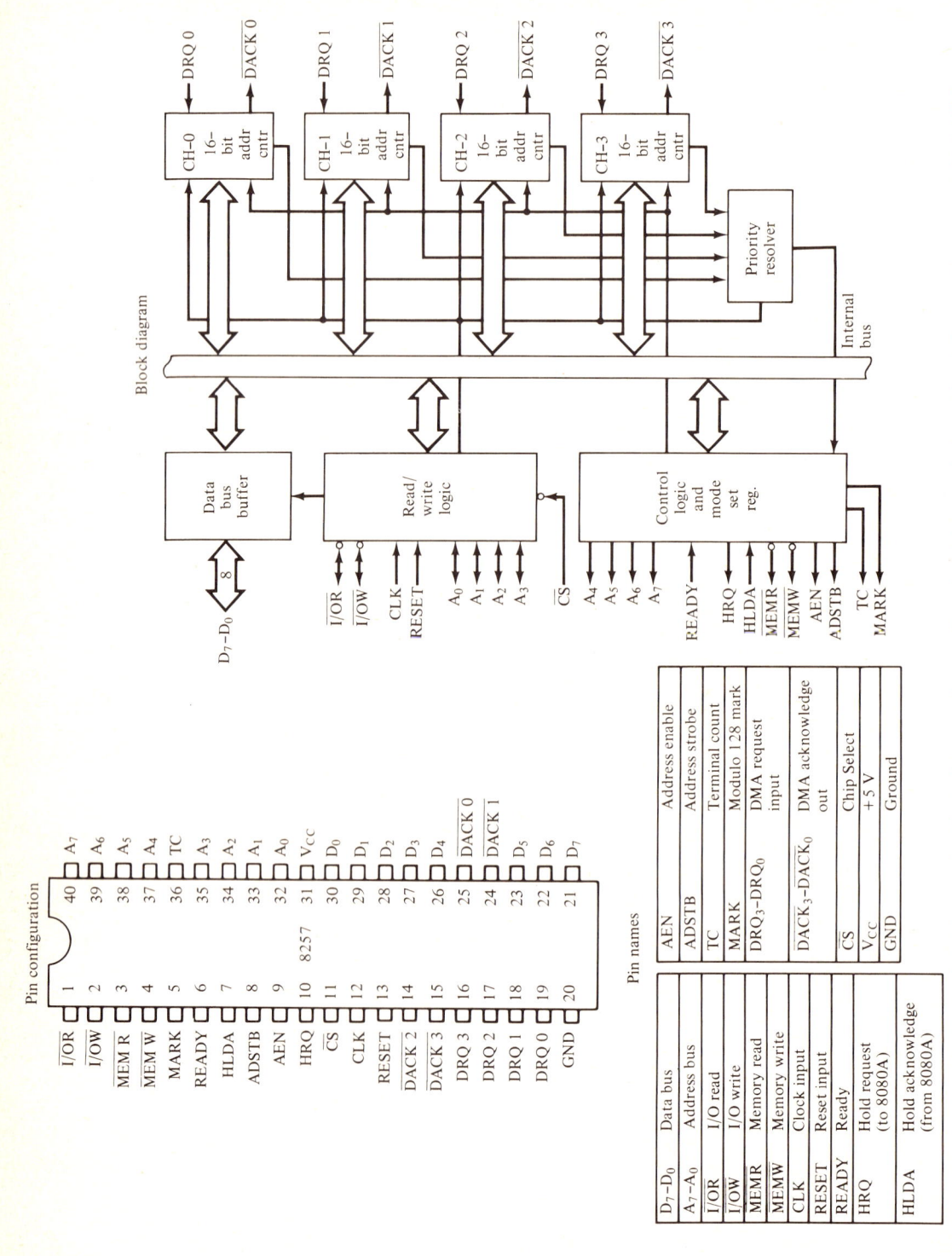

332 Chapter 8 TYPICAL MICROPROCESSOR INTERFACE CHIPS

Figure 8.39 Intel 8257 pin definitions and a block diagram. Source: Reprinted by permission of Intel Corporation, copyright © 1982.

iii. Outputs the least significant 8 bits of the memory address onto system address lines A_0–A-, outputs the most significant 8 bits of the memory address to the 8212 I/O port via the data bus (the 8212 places these address bits on lines A_8–A_{15}).
iv. Generates the appropriate memory and I/O read/write control signals that cause the peripheral to receive or deposit a data byte directly from or to the addressed location in memory.

The 8257 will retain control of the system bus and repeat the transfer sequence, as long as a peripheral maintains its DMA request. Thus, the 8257 can transfer a block of data to/from a high-speed peripheral (e.g., a sector of data on a floppy disk) in a single "burst." When the specified number of data bytes has been transferred, the 8257 activates its Terminal Count (TC) output, informing the CPU that the operation is complete.

The 8257 offers three different modes of operation: (1) DMA read, which causes data to be transferred from memory to a peripheral; (2) DMA write, which causes data to be transferred from a peripheral to memory; and (3) DMA verify, which does not actually involve the transfer of data. When an 8257 channel is in the DMA verify mode, it will respond the same as described for transfer operations, except that no memory or I/O read/write control signals will be generated, thus preventing the transfer of data. The 8257, however, will gain control of the system bus and will acknowledge the peripheral's DMA request for each DMA cycle. The peripheral can use these acknowledge signals to enable an internal access of each byte of a data block in order to execute some verification procedure, such as the accumulation of a Cyclic Redundancy Code (CRC) checkword. For example, a block of DMA verify cycles might follow a block of DMA read cycles (memory to peripheral) to allow the peripheral to verify its newly acquired data.

b. Block Diagram Description

i. DMA Channels

The 8257 provides four separate DMA channels (labeled CH-0 to CH-3). Each channel includes two 16-bit registers: (1) a DMA address register, and (2) a terminal count register. Both registers must be initialized before a channel is enabled. The DMA address register is loaded with the address of the first memory location to be accessed. The value loaded into the low-order 14 bits of the terminal count register specifies the number of DMA cycles minus one before the TC output is activated. For instance, a terminal count of 0 would cause the TC output to be active in the first DMA cycle for that channel. In general, if N = the number of desired DMA cycles, load the value $N - 1$ into the low-order 14 bits of the terminal count register. The most significant 2 bits of the terminal count register specify the type of DMA operation for that channel. These 2 bits are not modified during a DMA cycle, but can be changed between DMA blocks. Each channel accepts a DMA request (DRQn) input and provides a DMA acknowledge (DACKn) output.

ii. Read/Write Logic

When the CPU is programming or reading one of the 8257's registers, the read/write logic accepts the I/O Read ($\overline{I/OR}$) or I/O Write ($\overline{I/OW}$) signal, decodes the least significant 4 address bits, (A_0–A_3), and either writes the contents of the data bus into the addressed register (if $\overline{I/OW}$ is true) or places the contents of the addressed register onto the data bus (if $\overline{I/OR}$ is true).

RESET is an asynchronous input (generally from an 8224 or 8085 device) which disables all DMA channels by clearing the mode register and three-states all control lines.

In the "slave" mode, A_0–A_3 lines are inputs that select one of the registers to be read or programmed. In the "master" mode, they are outputs that constitute the least significant 4 bits of the 16-bit memory address generated by the 8257.

iii. Control Logic

This block controls the sequence of operations during all DMA cycles by generating the appropriate control signals and the 16-bit address that specifies the memory location to be accessed.

- The ADSTB output strobes the most significant byte of the memory address into the 8212 device from the data bus.
- The AEN output is used to disable (float) the system data bus and the system control bus.
- The TC output notifies the currently selected peripheral that the present DMA cycle should be the last cycle for this data block.
- The MARK output notifies the selected peripheral that the current DMA cycle is the one hundred twenty-eighth cycle since the previous MARK output.

iv. Mode Set Register

When set, the various bits in the mode set register enable each of the four DMA channels, and allow four different options for the 8257:

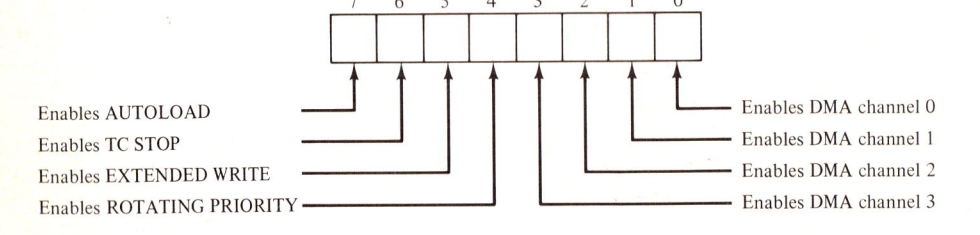

```
        7 6 5 4 3 2 1 0
       ┌─┬─┬─┬─┬─┬─┬─┬─┐
       │ │ │ │ │ │ │ │ │
       └─┴─┴─┴─┴─┴─┴─┴─┘
```

Enables AUTOLOAD — bit 7
Enables TC STOP — bit 6
Enables EXTENDED WRITE — bit 5
Enables ROTATING PRIORITY — bit 4

Enables DMA channel 0 — bit 0
Enables DMA channel 1 — bit 1
Enables DMA channel 2 — bit 2
Enables DMA channel 3 — bit 3

The mode set register is normally programmed by the CPU after the DMA address register(s) and terminal count register(s) are initialized.

v. Status Register

The 8-bit status register indicates which channels have reached a terminal count condition and includes the update flag described previously.

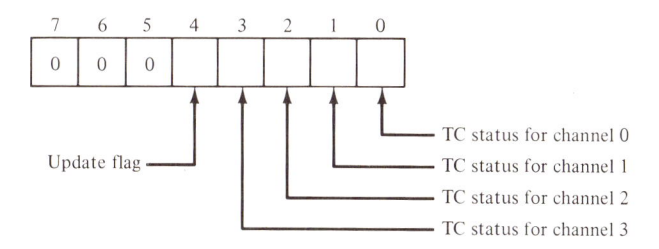

```
 7   6   5   4   3   2   1   0
┌───┬───┬───┬───┬───┬───┬───┬───┐
│ 0 │ 0 │ 0 │   │   │   │   │   │
└───┴───┴───┴───┴───┴───┴───┴───┘
```
- TC status for channel 0
- TC status for channel 1
- TC status for channel 2
- TC status for channel 3
- Update flag

2. Programming and Reading the 8257 Registers

There are four pairs of "channel registers," each pair consisting of a 16-bit DMA address register and a 16-bit terminal count register (one pair for each channel). The 8257 also includes two "general registers," one 8-bit mode set register and one 8-bit status register. The registers are loaded or read when the CPU executes a write or read instruction that addresses the 8257 device and the appropriate register within the 8257. The 8228 generates the appropriate read or write control signal (generally I/OR or I/OW) while the CPU places a 16-bit address on the system address bus, and either outputs the data to be written onto the system data bus or accepts the data being read from the data bus. All or some of the most significant 12 address bits A_4–A_{15} (depending on the systems memory, I/O configuration) are usually decoded to produce the Chip Select ($\overline{CS}$) input to the 8257.

a. DMA Operation

i. Single-Byte Transfers

A single-byte transfer is initiated by the I/O device raising the DRQ line of one channel of the 8257. If the channel is enabled, the 8257 will output a HRQ to the CPU. The 8257 now waits until a HLDA is received, ensuring that the system bus is free for its use. Once HLDA is received the $\overline{DACK}$ line for the requesting channel is activated (LOW). The $\overline{DACK}$ line acts as a chip select for the requesting I/O device. The 8257 then generates the read and write commands and byte transfer occurs between the selected I/O device and memory. After the transfer is complete, the $\overline{DACK}$ line is set HIGH and the HRQ line is set LOW to indicate to the CPU that the bus is now free for use. DRQ must remain HIGH until $\overline{DACK}$ is issued to be recognized and must go LOW before S4 of the transfer sequence to prevent another transfer from occurring (Figure 8.40).

ii. Consecutive Transfers

If more than one channel requests service simultaneously, the transfer will occur in the same way a burst does. No overhead is incurred by switching from one channel to another. In each S4 the DRQ lines are sampled and the highest priority request is recognized during the next transfer. A burst mode transfer in a lower priority channel will be overridden by a higher priority request. Once the high priority transfer has been completed, control will return to the lower priority channel if its DRQ is still active. No extra cycles are needed to execute this sequence and the HRQ line remains active until all DRQ lines go LOW.

iii. Control Override

The continuous DMA transfer mode described above can be interrupted by an external device by lowering the HLDA line. After each DMA transfer the 8257 samples the HLDA line to ensure that it is still active. If it is not active, the 8257 completes the current transfer, releases the HRQ line (LOW), and returns to the idle state. If DRQ lines are still active the 8257 will raise the HRQ line in the third cycle and proceed normally (Figure 8.40).

iv. Not Ready

The 8257 has a ready input similar to the 8080 and the 8085. The ready line is sampled in state 3. If ready is LOW the 8257 enters a wait state. Ready is sampled during every wait state. When ready returns HIGH the 8257 proceeds to state 4 to complete the transfer. Ready is used to interface memory or I/O devices that cannot meet the bus setup times required by the 8257.

v. Speed

The 8257 uses four clock cycles to transfer a byte of data. No cycles are lost in the master-to-master transfer, thus bus efficiency is maximized. A 2-MHz clock input will allow the 8257 to transfer at a rate of 500K bytes/s.

vi. Memory-Mapped I/O Configurations

The 8257 can be connected to the system bus as a memory device instead of as an I/O device for memory-mapped I/O configurations by connecting the system memory control lines to the 8257's I/O control lines and the system I/O control lines to the 8257's memory control lines. Figure 8.41 shows a detailed schematic of the 8085/8257 interface.

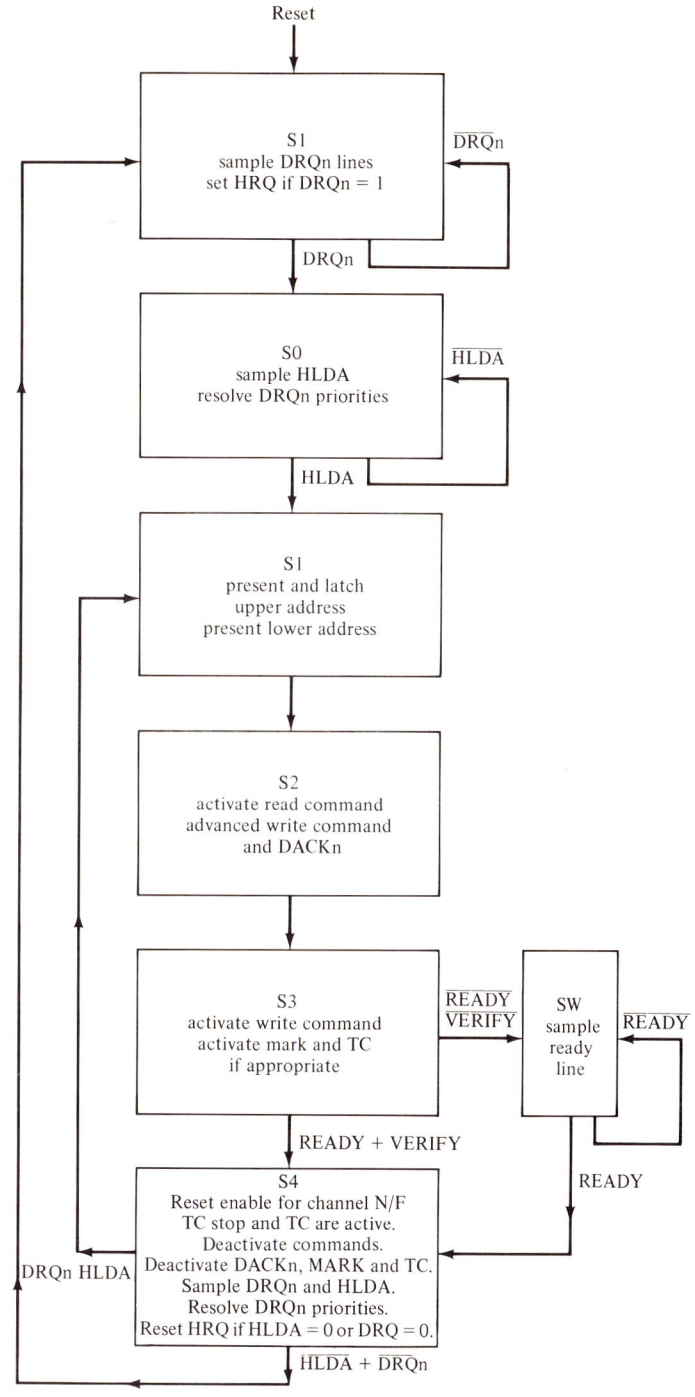

Figure 8.40 DMA operation state diagram. (DRQn refers to any DRQ line on an enabled DMA channel.) Source: Reprinted by permission of Intel Corporation, copyright © 1982.

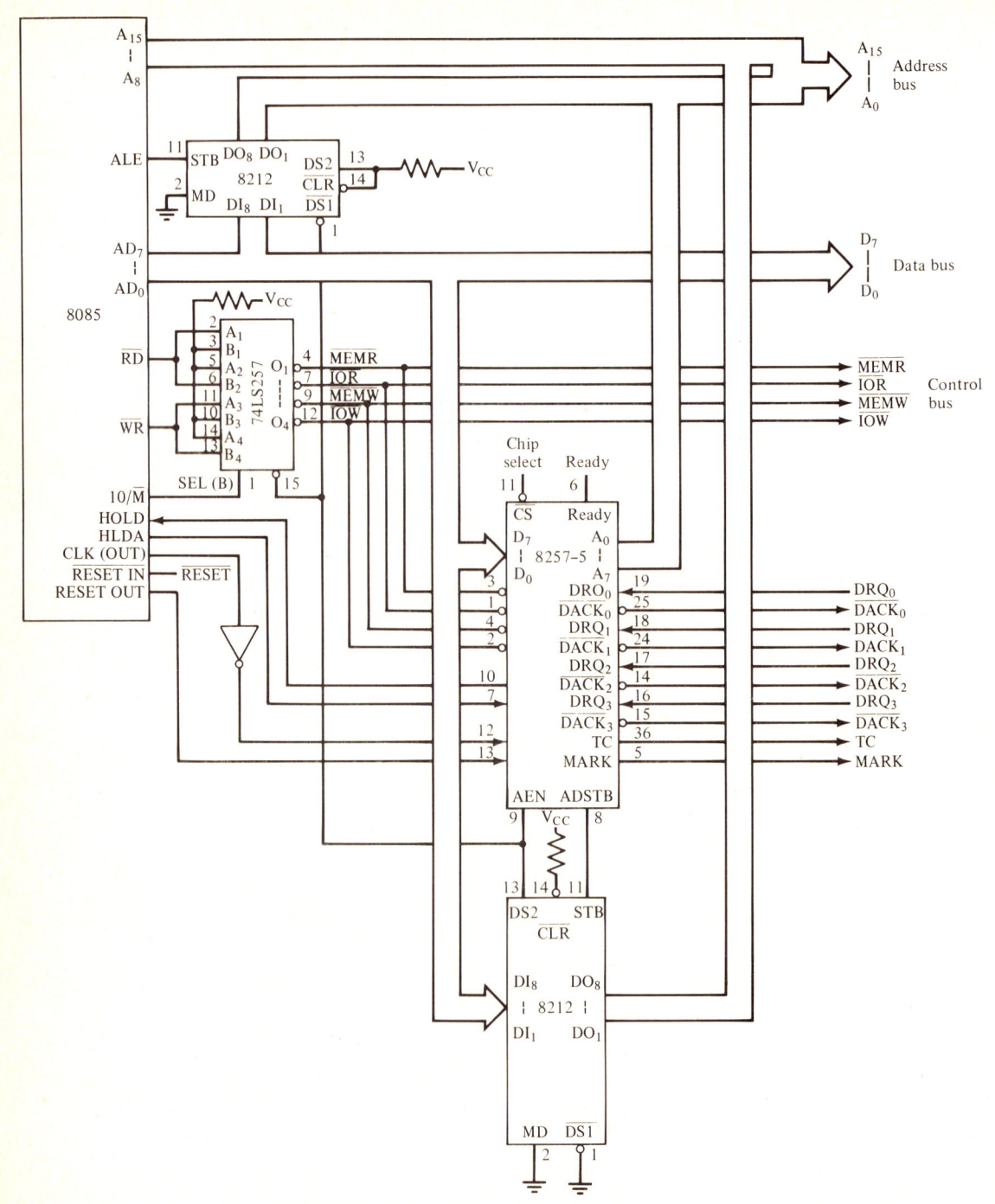

Figure 8.41 Detailed system interface schematic. Source: Reprinted by permission of Intel Corporation, copyright © 1982.

PROBLEMS AND QUESTIONS

8.1 Draw schematics for the following and identify the basic differences:
   (a) Connect one 2716 to the 8085.
   (b) Connect one 8755 to the 8085.

8.2 What are the main differences between the 8155/8156 I/O ports and the 8355/8755 I/O ports?

8.3 Design and develop both hardware and software for interfacing General Instruments Ay-5-1013 UART to an 8085 system using all the signals of the I/O with handshaking mode of the 8155/8156.

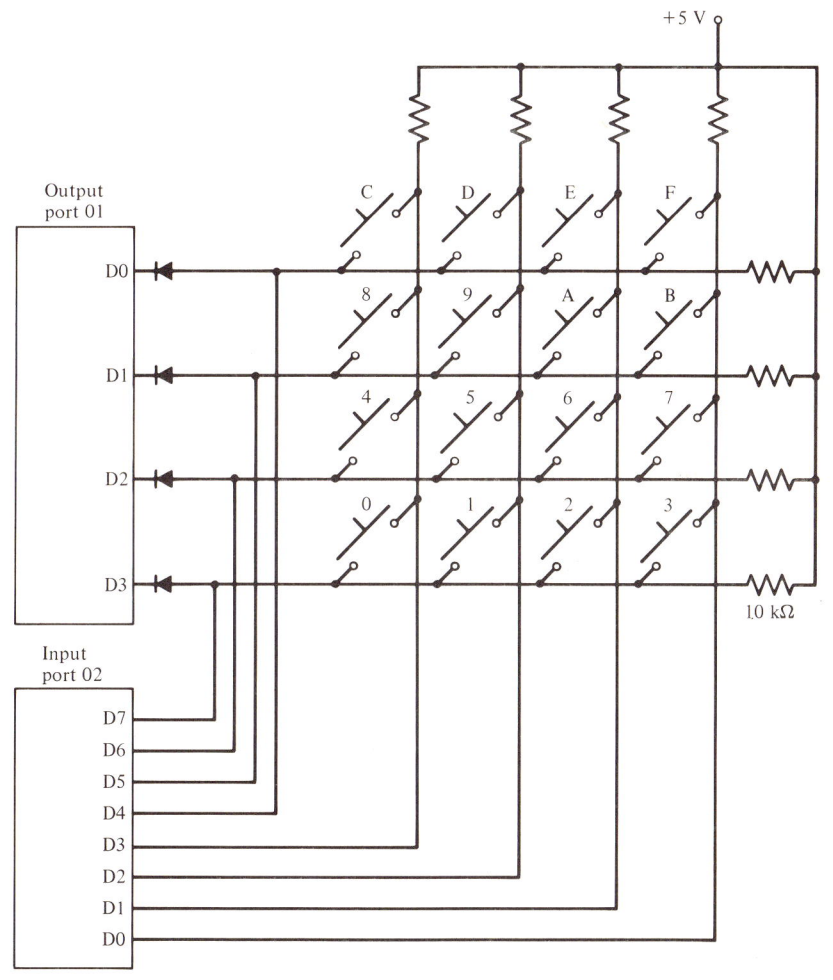

Figure 8.42 Figure for Problem 8.5. Source: D. Hall, *Microprocessors and Digital Systems,* McGraw-Hill, 1982. Reprinted by permission.

8.4 Design and develop both hardware and software for interfacing one 6850 to the 6809.

8.5 An 8085/8155/8755-based microcomputer is to be interfaced to a 4 × 4 keyboard via the I/O ports as shown in Figure 8.42. The microcomputer is required to perform the following by means of software:

Detecting a key actuation.

Debouncing a key (20 ms).

Decoding the key, that is, translating the row and column code into hexadecimal code.

Two-key rollover.

(a) Draw a flowchart.

(b) Convert the flowchart to 8085 assembly language program.

8.6 What is the purpose of A_0, $\overline{BD}$, and IRQ pins on the 8279?

8.7 What is the purpose of SL0–SL3 pins on the 8279? How would you connect an eight-digit display and 8 × 8 keyboard via these lines?

8.8 What are the functional characteristics of the Intel 8257 DMA? Why do you need an 8212 with the 8257?

CHAPTER 9

FUNDAMENTALS OF MICROCOMPUTER DEVELOPMENT SYSTEMS

As microprocessor-based systems became more prominent in the market place, the need for microprocessor development systems increased. The development systems range from inexpensive kits with limited capabilities (usually limited to software development only) to large systems supporting many users simultaneously developing hardware and software.

The purpose of this chapter is to demonstrate the basic features of microcomputer development systems, including such software modules as editors, assemblers, linkers, compilers, and various debugging programs. The hardware features usually include in-circuit emulators and logic analyzers.

9.1 Basic Features

When the microprocessor-based system to be designed is simple, it is usually not productive to design the complete system from the chip level. Microprocessor manufacturers recognize the need for simple microprocessor systems and usually provide a variety of Single-Board Computers (SBC). The single-board computer contains the CPU, memory, and some limited I/O facilities, all complete on a single printed circuit board. Some single-board computers, such as the Intel SDK-85, include a built-in monitor program (contained in ROM) and an input/output combination of a keypad for data entry and LED displays for data output. User programs can be entered into such systems in machine code (hexadecimal) form and debugged using the built-in monitor facilities. The monitor usually contains routines to display register contents of the CPU and allows a program to be executed one instruction at a time (single-stepping). When a program has been developed for the SBC, the machine code can be programmed into a PROM and installed in the SBC.

While SBCs are extremely valuable in some design situations, many specific microprocessor applications demand that the designer develop the system from the chip level. In these cases it is very helpful to have a system to develop the software for the system, and some techniques for debugging the hardware. The microcomputer development system provides all the necessary tools for microprocessor development in a single compact package. Some typical systems available are the Intel 120, 225, 286, and 290, the Tektronix 8540, 8550, 8560, and 8002A, the GenRad 2300 series, and the Hewlett Packard 64000. As noted in Chapter 1, development systems provided by microprocessor manufacturers usually only support chips supplied by the manufacturer (nonuniversal systems) while the systems provided by nonmanufacturers usually support a wide range of microprocessors (universal systems). Some of the more advanced development systems support multiple stations, allowing many users to develop hardware and software simultaneously.

9.1.1 Hardware

A microcomputer development system consists of the hardware necessary to design systems, and the software packages needed to operate the hardware. The main hardware components (shown in block diagram form in Figure 9.1) consist of the following:

1. Microprocessor (one or more depending on system complexity).
2. Main memory.
3. Mass storage (disk or magnetic tape).
4. CRT console(s).
5. In-Circuit Emulator (ICE).
6. Logic analyzers.
7. PROM programmer.
8. Line printer(s).
9. Paper tape reader and punch.
10. MODEM interface.

1. Microprocessor

The number of microprocessors used in the system depends on the system architecture. Multiple processors can be configured in a multiprocessing environment to distribute the workload and thereby increase system throughput. Single-station development systems often contain a single processor which is all that is necessary for small development environments.

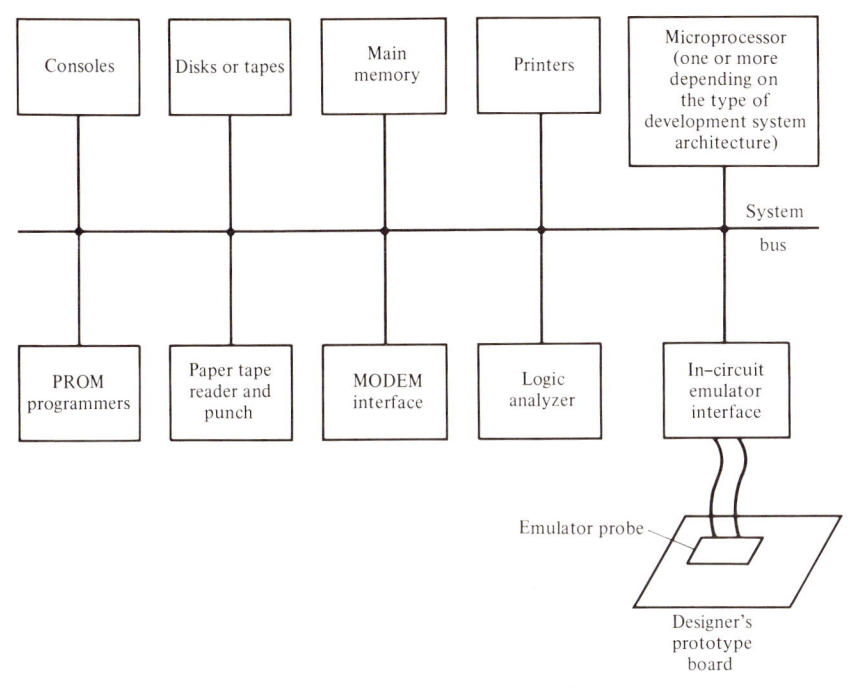

Figure 9.1 Typical microcomputer development system hardware components.

2. Main Memory

The main memory is the directly addressable memory that the system processor uses to store the development software such as editors, assemblers, emulators, and so on. Main memory size ranges from 32K to 64K and may be a combination of ROM and RAM. The ROM will usually contain a basic monitor with routines to interface the system software to the system hardware.

3. Mass Storage

Mass storage for development systems is used to hold system software and user programs when they are not currently in use by the development system. Mass storage is not directly addressable by the system processor and is accessed through an I/O peripheral. Larger development systems use hard disk systems (storage capabilities in megabytes) and smaller systems use flexible disk systems (storage capabilities about 250K–500K bytes).

Each program (whether system software or user program) is stored in an ordered format on the disk. Each separate entry on the disk is called a *file*. The operating system software contains the routines necessary to interface between the user and the mass storage unit. When the user requests a file by a specific *file name,* the operating system finds the program stored on disk by the file name and loads it into main memory. More advanced development systems contain *memory management* software that protects a user's files from unauthorized modification by another user. This is accomplished via a unique user identification code caller USER ID. A user can only access files that have the user's unique code.

4. CRT Console(s)

The CRT console provides all interface between the user and the operating system software. The user inputs data via the CRT keyboard and the CRT screen displays data from the operating system. Program listings, processor status during debugging, and various error messages are all displayed on the CRT screen. CRTs are usually connected to the development system via a serial data path communicating at speeds of 9,600–19,200 bits per second.

5. In-Circuit Emulator

Most development systems support one or more in-circuit emulators. The ICE is one of the most advanced tools for microprocessor hardware development. To use an ICE, the microprocessor chip is removed from the system under development (called the target processor) and the emulator plugged into the socket that the processor was removed from. The ICE will functionally and electrically act identically to the target processor with the exception that the ICE is under the control of development system software. In this manner the development system may exercise the hardware that is being designed and monitor all status information available about the operation of the target processor. Using an ICE, processor register contents may be displayed on the CRT and operation of the hardware observed in a single-stepping mode. In-circuit emulators can find hardware and software bugs quickly that might take many hours using conventional hardware testing methods.

6. Logic Analyzers

Another valuable hardware tool available to the system designer is the logic analyzer. The logic analyzer allows the designer to get a visual representation of the logic levels occurring in real time in the hardware. High-speed logic analyzers are capable of capturing and displaying noise spikes and transient signals that cause the hardware to malfunction. The logic analyzer works by sampling the input lines (usually 16 to 32 lines) at a fixed clock rate and storing the binary logic levels in memory. The logic levels may then be displayed in sequential order as 1's and 0's on the CRT screen.

7. PROM Programmer

After the target system software has been completely developed and debugged, it needs to be permanently stored for execution in the target hardware. The PROM programmer takes the machine code and programs it into a PROM or EPROM. Erasable/Programmable Read Only Memories (EPROMs) are more generally used in system development as they may be erased and reprogrammed if the program changes. PROM programmers usually interface to circuits particularly designed to program a specific PROM. These interface boards are called personality cards and are available for all the popular PROM configurations.

8. Line Printer(s)

Program development and documentation calls for the availability of printed listings of the programs. These listings are referred to as *hard copy* and are printed on the system line printer.

9. Paper Tape Interfaces

On occasion the need arises for data communication between different systems. A paper tape interface allows information to be punched on paper tape on one system and read into another system via a paper tape reader. Paper tape interfaces are generally outdated because of their slow speed and inconvenient storage requirements.

10. MODEM Interfaces

MODEM (MOdulator–DEModulator) interfaces allow serial communication between systems using telephone lines. The modulator on the transmitting end converts the serial data into distinct tones which are demodulated on the receiver end back into serial data. MODEMs are also used to connect a user's CRT to a master development system at a remote installation. Communication rates for MODEMs are usually limited to about 1,200 bits per second and are therefore much slower than directly connected CRTs. Microcomputer development systems can be interfaced to a minicomputer via MODEMs to provide software development capabilities for many different microprocessors.

9.1.2 Operating System and Debugging Techniques

We now describe operating system facilities and debugging techniques available with a typical development system.

1. Operating Systems

The software programs to develop microprocessor systems are all managed by the *operating system*. The operating system software is stored in the system mass storage media and is loaded into main memory upon system power-up. Operating systems are not tailored to individual hardware, but communicate with system hardware through subroutine calls to monitor routines. The operating system will call a subroutine with the necessary parameters passed in registers to provide the needed linkages. By tailoring only the monitor routines to the system hardware, the complicated operating system software may be easily used on systems with different hardware configurations.

The operating system contains the memory management software necessary to keep the files in an orderly structure. The operating system maintains a *directory* that shows all files currently in use, as well as how much storage space is available to the user.

Program development software usually included with the operating system are editors, assemblers, linkers, compilers (for converting high-level languages such as FORTRAN and PASCAL into machine code), and debuggers.

2. Debugging Techniques

Debugging a microprocessor-based system may be divided into two categories: software debugging and hardware debugging. Both debug processes are usually carried out separately from each other because software debugging can be carried out on an emulator without having the final system hardware.

a. Software Development Tools. The usual software development tools provided with the development system are:

Single-step facility.
Breakpoint facility.
Register dump program.
Memory dump program.
Simulator program.

Single-step facility. A single-stepper simply allows the user to execute the program being debugged one instruction at a time. A single-stepper allows the user to follow program logic one step at a time, examining all processor information before allowing the next instruction to be executed. During debugging it is usually helpful to examine the state of the data bus, the address bus, the status flags, and the control lines. By examining the state of the processor during each step, the debugger can detect such program faults as incorrect jumps, incorrect addressing, erroneous op codes, and so on.

When single-steppers are used for hardware debugging, they are unable to detect timing errors, incorrect interrupts, or DMA errors.

Since the single-stepper does a large amount of processing on each instruction that is executed for the target processor, the single-stepper is much slower than real-time program execution. For this reason, single-stepping is usually limited to debugging small sections of the program and is not used to step through an entire program.

Breakpoints. Single-stepping allows the user to stop the program execution after each instruction is executed, but as pointed out, this procedure is slow and is useless when the program must be executed at full speed. It is desirable to be able to execute a program at full speed and then be able to halt the program for examination at a specific instruction. A breakpoint program allows the user to insert a special instruction, called the breakpoint, at the point that the user wishes the program to halt. When the breakpoint instruction is executed, control will be returned to the monitor routine and the user may examine the processor status to see how the program is operating.

There are two types of breakpoint systems, hardware and software. The hardware breakpoint uses hardware to monitor the system address bus and detect when the program is executing the desired breakpoint location. When the breakpoint is detected, the hardware uses the processor control lines to either halt the processor for inspection or cause the processor to execute an interrupt to a breakpoint routine. Hardware breakpoints can be used to debug both ROM- and RAM-based programs. Software breakpoint routines may only operate on a system with the program in RAM because the breakpoint instruction must be inserted into the program that is to be executed.

Breakpoint routines are extremely useful for debugging programs because they allow the user to execute a large portion of the program before stopping execution. An entire subroutine may be executed and then halted to examine the processor registers to see if the subroutine executed properly. When the breakpoint is no longer needed, it may be removed and the program will execute normally.

Most debuggers combine single-steppers and breakpoint routine to provide a complete package. The user may insert a breakpoint (either manually or automatically, depending on the system) at the desired point and let the program execute up until that point. When the program stops at the breakpoint the user may use a single-stepper to then examine the program one instruction at a time.

Register dump. Register dump routines allow the user to examine the register contents of the processor via the CRT. The routine will display the hex value of a register next to the register name. The user is then able to alter the register value and continue program execution with the new register data.

Memory dump. A memory dump is similar to a register dump and the user may examine any portion of memory as well as alter it if the memory is RAM. Memory dumps are convenient for examining entire blocks of memory rather than single locations.

Simulator. A simulator is a program that allows the execution of a program to be simulated while keeping track of all parameters (address, data, flags, etc.) of the target processor. The processor that executes the simulator does not need to be of the same type as the target processor because the program to be debugged is not actually executed by the development system processor. The simulator operates by taking one instruction at a time and then simulating all actions that the target processor would perform for that instruction.

Simulators are usually very large programs which will include all the software debugging tools (single-stepper, breakpoints, register dumps, etc.) necessary in a complete software development program.

b. Hardware Debugging Tools. There are two main hardware debugging tools: the logic analyzer and the in-circuit emulator.

Logic analyzer. Logic analyzers are usually used to debug hardware faults in a system. The logic analyzer is the digital version of an oscilloscope because it allows the user to view logic levels in the hardware.

Logic analyzers consist of several parallel inputs (usually 16 to 32) that are attached via probes to the hardware under test. The logic threshold of the signal may be preset on the analyzer to allow for the different logic families used in microprocessors. The analyzer uses a clock signal (internal or external) to reference the inputs. Once every clock pulse the parallel inputs are sampled and the logic levels (0 or 1) stored in the analyzer memory. The memory contents may then be displayed on a CRT as either 1's and 0's or in logic levels. By using an analyzer, the user may observe the relationships between many signals in the hardware and therefore detect signals that do not behave as expected. Most logic analyzers are fast enough to observe noise signals that are causing the hardware to malfunction.

Because the logic analyzer contains limited memory, the analyzer may only operate for a limited amount of time. For this reason, the analyzer must not operate at all times but must be started at a specific point in the hardware execution. The technique of starting the analyzer at a specific point is called *triggering* and two basic methods are used. The first method uses edge triggering. One of the parallel inputs is selected as the trigger signal and the logic level desired is selected. The hardware is started and when the desired trigger occurs (a transition from low to high, for example)

Software Development Aids 351

with the development system are: an editor, an assembler, linkers, compilers, loaders, debuggers, monitors, and the operating system. This section will cover these programs in detail.

9.2.1 Editors

The editor is usually the first program used in developing the software for the systems being developed. The editor allows the user to enter the source code (either assembly language or some high-level language) into the development system. The editor includes commands that facilitate changing (additions or deletions) the source code whenever necessary.

Editors have been developed along with the microprocessor. Older main frame computers used punched cards and card readers to enter their programs. When a change had to made in a program on punched cards, the new cards could be inserted where necessary or erroneous cards removed and retyped. Card readers are too expensive for microprocessors and other methods were developed for program entry. Early microprocessors used paper tape or audio cassette tape to enter the program, but no means was available to easily edit a program already on a paper or audio tape. Editors were developed so a program could be read into the system via tape, be corrected, and then be stored on a new tape. Current editors perform the same function but the storage is usually disk (floppy disk or hard disk) instead of tape. Figure 9.2 shows a simplified block diagram of the editor.

The editor functions start by loading a segment of the input file into the development system RAM. The program segment is displayed to the user in some manner and the user edits the segment to make any needed

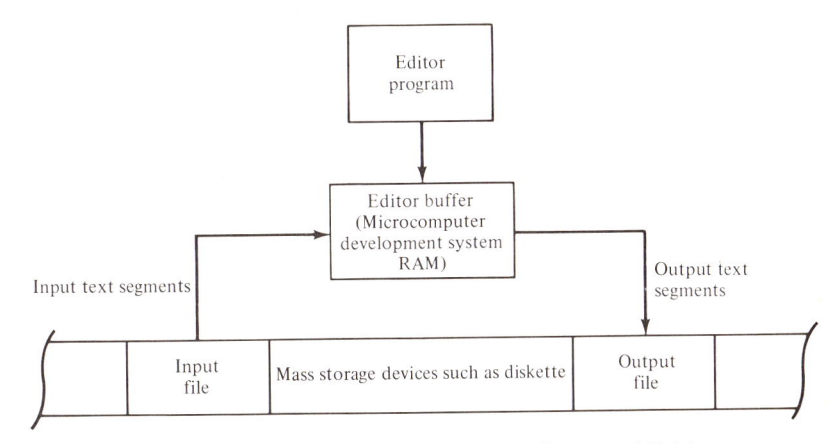

Figure 9.2 Editor information flow. Source: Camp, Smay, and Triska, *Microcomputer Systems Principles Featuring the 6502/KIM*, copyright © 1978, Matrix Publishers.

changes. When the changes for a segment are complete, the segment is stored back on disk and the next segment loaded into RAM.

There are two types of editors currently in use, the line-oriented editor and the character-oriented editor.

1. Line-Oriented Editor

The first editors developed were line-oriented editors. Line editors have fewer features than character editors and are therefore less expensive. Line editors are limited mostly to home computer systems and are rarely found on modern development systems. The main difference between line editors and character editors is that line editors do not display any changes in the file until the user prints the file whereas character editors will display the change when the user makes the change.

Some line editors allow the user to enter a line number with the line so that it may be stored in numerical order. When the line needs to be edited, the user enters a new line with the same number and it replaces the old line. In order to allow for insertion of extra lines in between other lines, lines are usually numbered in increments of 5 or 10. With line numbers such as 10, 20, 30, and so on, a new line may be entered between 10 and 20 by giving it a line number of 17.

A line-number-based editor is very tedious to use because even the smallest change requires that the entire line be retyped. As an advantage, the line-number-based editor requires little program space for the editor and allows more available RAM for the text. The program simplicity is what contributes to the low cost of the line-number-based editor.

A second type of line-oriented editor allows the user to enter lines without line numbers. The user enters lines by positioning a *pointer* to the location in the program where the new line is desired and the new line is typed into RAM. The user may also position the pointer to locations within a line, thus allowing characters to be added or deleted without retyping the entire line. This type of line editor supports more advanced features than the line-number-based line editor but is still inferior to the character-oriented editor.

2. Character-Oriented Editors

Almost all current microprocessor development systems use the character-oriented editor, more commonly referred to as the screen editor. The editor is called a screen editor because the text is dynamically displayed on the screen and the display automatically updates any edits made by the user.

The screen editor uses the pointer concept to point to the character(s) that need editing. The pointer in a screen editor is called the cursor and special commands allow the user to position the cursor to any location displayed on the screen. Other commands allow the user to scroll the display forward or backward to allow display of any segment of the file. When the cursor is positioned, the user may insert characters, delete characters, or simply type over the existing characters.

A screen editor is not possible without a high-speed CRT terminal to display the text. In a typical screen editor, the text is stored in RAM and all edits are made to the text stored in RAM. The cursor positioning determines which portions of the text are to be displayed. The editor displays the current text on the screen and whenever a change is made to the text in RAM, the screen is updated to reflect the change in RAM. When the CRT is able to communicate with the precursor at speeds of 9,600 baud and higher, the screen update is almost impossible to see.

The following features are standard on most screen editors and some of the features are available on line editors. The editor's user manual will give exact details on how to use the specific editor features.

Complete lines may be added or deleted using special editor commands. By placing the editor in the *insert* mode, any text typed will be inserted at the cursor position when the cursor is positioned between two existing lines. If the cursor is positioned on a line to be deleted, a single command will remove the entire line from the file.

Search commands allow the user to search the file for occurrences of specific characters of text called *strings*. The user can specify a string of text and the editor will compare the file text for any matches with the string and then display the segment of text that holds the matched string. A similar function of *find and replace* is also available where the user can specify one string that is to be found and another string that is to replace the first string. This feature is extremely valuable for correcting misspelled words or phrases.

Other useful commands allow portions of other files to be merged into the current file, move segments to other positions in the file, delete old files, copy files, and perform many other functions that speed up the process of writing and debugging source code.

Screen editors implement the editor commands in different fashions. Some editors use dedicated keys to provide some cursor movements. The cursor keys are usually marked with arrows to show the direction of cursor movement. Other special editor functions are accomplished with the use of *control keys*. A control key is activated by pressing a special key (usually labeled control or CTRL) simultaneously with a normal key. This combination of key strokes creates a new character that is sent to the editor program.

More advanced editors (such as the HP-64000) use *soft keys*. A soft key is an unmarked key located on the keyboard directly below the bottom of the CRT screen. The mode of the editor decides what functions the keys are to perform. The function of each key is displayed on the screen directly above the appropriate key. The soft key approach is valuable because it frees the user from the problem of memorizing many different special control keys. The soft key approach also allows the editor to reassign a key to a new function when necessary.

As development systems continue to become more sophisticated, more and more features are added which allow the user to develop the source code more quickly and easily.

The fastest, and therefore most convenient, editors are on development systems using *directly refreshed* CRTs. A directly refreshed CRT does not communicate with the system processor via a serial data path, but rather is a part of the system hardware. The memory that the CRT uses to display on the screen is directly accessible by the system processor and can therefore be updated at the same rate as any other system memory component. This technique can lead to character transfer rates of up to 200,000 characters per second (compared to 960 characters per second with serial data paths).

An editor designed to complement the directly refreshed CRT operates at extremely high speeds and can reduce editing time by 30 to 50% when used by an experienced operator.

9.2.2 Assemblers

The source code generated on the editor is stored as ASCII characters and can not be executed by a microprocessor. Before the code can be executed, it must be converted to a form acceptable by the microprocessor. An assembler is the program used to translate the assembly language source code generated with an editor into object code or machine code which may be executed by a microprocessor.

Assemblers recognize four *fields* on each line of source code. The fields consist of a variable number of characters and are identified by their position in the line. The fields, from left to right on a line, are the label field, the mnemonic op code field, the operand field, and the comment field. Fields are separated by characters called *delimiters* which serve as a flag to the assembler that one field is done and the next one is to start. Typical delimiters and their uses are:

space	used to separate fields
TAB	used to separate fields
,	used between addresses or data in the operand field
;	used before a comment statement
:	used after a label

A few typical lines of 8085 source code are:

LABEL FIELD	OP CODE FIELD	OPERAND FIELD	COMMENT FIELD
	MVI	A,5	; LOAD A 5 INTO A
LOOP:	DCR	A	; DECREMENT THE COUNT
	JNZ	LOOP	; REPEAT LOOP IF COUNT NOT ZERO
	RET		; RETURN TO CALLER WHEN LOOP DONE

As can be seen in the above example, tabs are used instead of spaces to separate the fields to give a more *spread out* line which is easier to read during debugging.

In order for the assembler to differentiate between numbers and labels, specific rules are set up which apply to all assemblers. A label must start with a letter. After the letter, a combination of letters and numbers (called alphanumerics) may be used. For example, when grouping lines of code by function, a common alphabetic string may be used followed by a unique number for the label: L00P01, L00P02, L00P10, and so on.

A numeric quantity must start with a number, even though the number may be in hex (which may start with a letter). Most assemblers assume that a number is expressed in the decimal system and if another base is desired, a special code letter is used immediately following the number. The usual letter codes used are:

B   binary
C   octal
H   hex

To avoid confusion when hex quantities are used, a leading zero is inserted to tell the assembler that the quantity is a number and not a label (for example, the quantity FA in hex would be represented by 0FAH in the source code).

1. Pseudoinstructions

Pseudoinstructions are instructions entered into the source code along with the assembly language. Pseudoinstructions do not get translated into object code but are used as special instructions to the assembler to perform some special functions. The assembler will recognize pseudoinstructions that assign memory space, assign addresses to labels, format the pages of the source code, and so on.

The pseudoinstruction is placed in the op code field. If any labels or data are required by the pseudoinstruction, they are placed in the label or operand field as necessary.

Some common pseudoinstructions will now be discussed in detail.

a. ORIGIN (ORG). The ORG statement is used by the programmer when it is necessary to place the program in a particular location in memory. As the assembler is translating the source code, it keeps an internal counter (similar to the microprocessor program counter) that keeps track of the address for the machine code. The counter is incremented automatically and sequentially by the assembler. If the programmer wishes to alter the locations where the machine code is going to be located, the ORG statement is used.

For example, if it is desired to have a subroutine at a particular location in memory, such as 2000H, the ORG statement would be placed immediately before the subroutine to direct the assembler to alter the internal program counter:

```
          ORG  2000H   ; SET PROGRAM COUNTER TO 2000H
    SUB:  MVI  A,5     ; SUBROUTINE PUTS A 5 IN 'A'
          RET          ; RETURN TO CALLER
```

Most assemblers will assume a starting address of zero if no ORG statement is given in the source code.

b. EQUATE (EQU). The EQU instruction is used to assign the data value or address in the operand field to the label in the label field. The EQU instruction is valuable because it allows the programmer to write the source code in symbolic form and not be concerned with the numeric value needed. In some cases, the programmer is developing a program without knowing what addresses or data may be required by the hardware. The program may be written and debugged in symbolic form and the actual data added at a later time. Using the EQU instruction is also helpful when a data value is used several times in a program. If, for example, a counter value was loaded at ten different locations in the program, a symbolic label (such as COUNT) could be used and the label count defined at the end of the program. By using this technique, if it is found during debugging that the value in COUNT must be changed, it need only be changed at the EQU instruction and not at each of the ten locations where it is used in the program.

As an example of EQU, consider the following 8085 code:

```
    PORTA EQU  00      ; ASSIGN A DUMMY VALUE
    PORTB EQU  00      ; ANOTHER DUMMY VALUE
```

```
       MVI   A, 0FFH  ; DATA TO BE SENT TO OUTPUTS
       OUT   PORTA    ; INITIALIZE PORT A
       OUT   PORTB    ; AND PORT B TOO
```

In the example, the programmer does not know the hardware addresses of output ports A and B, but may still write the source code. When the I/O addresses are known, they may be used to replace the 00 in the EQU statement.

Some assemblers require the programmer to assign a value to a label before it is used (as in the above example) but most current assemblers allow the programmer to place the EQU instructions anywhere in the source code.

c. DEFINE BYTE (DEFB or DB). The DB instruction is used to set a memory location to a specific data value. Th DB instruction is usually used to create data tables or to preset a flag value used in a program. As the name implies, the DB instruction is used for creating an 8-bit value.

For example, if a table of four values, 45H, 34H, 25H, and 0D3H, had to be created at address 2000H, the following code could be written:

```
         ORG  2000H                ; SET TABLE ADDRESS
TABLE:   DB   45H,34H,25H,0D3H     ; PRESET TABLE VALUES
```

The commas are necessary for the assembler to be able to differentiate between data values. When the code is assembled, the machine code would appear as follows:

```
    . . .
    2000 45
    2001 34
    2002 25
    2003 D3
    . . .
```

d. DEFINE WORD (DEFW or DW). Similarly to DB, DW defines memory locations to specific values. As the name implies, the memory alloted is in word lengths which are usually 16 bits wide. When assigning a 16-bit value to memory locations, two 8-bit memory locations must be used. By convention, most assemblers store the least significant byte of the 16-bit value in the first memory location and the most significant byte of the 16-bit value to the next memory location. This technique is sometimes referred to as *Intel style,* because the first microprocessors were developed by Intel and this storage method is how the Intel processors store 16-bit words.

Data tables may be created with the DW instruction, but care must be taken to remember the order in which the 16-bit words are stored. For example, consider the following table:

```
        ORG       2500H
DATA:   DW    4000H, 2300H, 4BCAH
```

The machine code generated for this table would appear as follows:

```
. . .
2500 00
2501 40
2502 00
2503 23
2504 CA
2505 4B
. . .
```

e. TITLE. TITLE is a formatting instruction that allows the user to name the program and have the name appear on the source code listing. Consider the following line:

```
TITLE   'MULTIPLICATION ROUTINE'
```

When the assembler generates the program listing, each time it starts a new page the title MULTIPLICATION ROUTINE appears at the top of each page.

f. PAGE (also called EJECT). PAGE is another formatting instruction that causes the assembler to skip to the next page. The PAGE instruction is used to keep subroutines or modules of source code on separate pages which makes the source code easier to read and debug.

g. SPACE. The SPACE instruction simply instructs the assembler to skip a line.

h. END. The END psuedoinstruction signals to the assembler that the source code is complete. Any lines after the END statement will be ignored by the assembler. Some assemblers require an END statement while some assemblers merely assume an END after the last line of the source code has been processed.

i. LIST. The LIST instruction is a direct command to the assembler and will cause the assembler to print the entire source code program.

2. Types of Assemblers

Several types of assemblers are available, the most common of which are the one-pass assembler, the two-pass assembler, the macroassembler, cross assemblers, resident assemblers, and the metaassembler.

a. One-Pass Assembler. The one-pass assembler was the first type to be developed and is therefore the most primitive. Very few systems use a one-pass assembler because of the inherent problem that only *backward references* may be used.

In a one-pass assembler the source code is processed only once. As the source code is processed, any labels encountered are given an address and stored in a table. Therefore, when the label is encountered again, the assembler may look backward to find the address of the label. If the label has not been defined yet (for example, a jump instruction that skips forward), the assembler issues an error message.

Since only one pass is used to translate the source code, a one-pass assembler is very fast, but because of the forward reference problem the one-pass assembler is seldom used.

b. Two-Pass Assembler. The two-pass assembler is similar in operation to the one-pass assembler with one important difference. The first pass made through the source code is specifically for the purpose of assigning an address to all labels. When all labels have been stored in a table with the appropriate addresses, a second pass is made to actually translate the source code into machine code.

The two-pass style assembler is the most popular type of assembler currently in use.

c. Macroassembler. A macroassembler is a type of two-pass assembler that allows the programmer to write the source code in *macros*. A macro is a sequence of instructions that the programmer gives a name. Whenever the programmer wishes to duplicate the sequence of instructions, the macro name is inserted into the source code.

For example, a macro could be devised to shift the accumulator right 1 bit and then clear the most significant bit:

```
SHFT  MACRO        ; SET THE MACRO NAME
      RRC          ; ROTATE THE ACCUMULATOR RIGHT
      ANI    7FH   ; CLEAR THE MOST SIGNIFICANT BIT
      ENDM         ; END OF MACRO
```

A macro called SHFT now exists which may used merely by using its name as follows:

```
LDA  TEMP  ; GET A VALUE FROM STORAGE
SHFT       ; SHIFT IT
```

```
        MOV  C,A   ; STORE THE VALUE
        SHFT       ; SHIFT IT AGAIN
        MOV  B,A   ; AND STORE THAT VALUE TOO
```

When the preceding code is assembled it would be equivalent to the following sequence of code:

```
        LDA  TEMP  ; GET A VALUE FROM STORAGE
        RRC        ; ROTATE THE ACCUMULATOR RIGHT
        ANI  7FH   ; CLEAR THE MOST SIGNIFICANT BIT
        MOV  C,A   ; STORE THE VALUE
        RRC        ; ROTATE THE ACCUMULATOR RIGHT
        ANI  7FH   ; CLEAR THE MOST SIGNIFICANT BIT
        MOV  B,A   ; AND STORE THAT VALUE TOO
```

A macroroutine is *not* the same as a subroutine call in assembly language. An assembly language call is a function of the microprocessor. When the CALL (8085) instruction is encountered in the machine code, the 8085 will save the address of the next sequential instruction to be executed and alter the program counter to the address given in the CALL instruction. When a macro is used, it is a function of the assembler and not the microprocessor. Every time the macro name is encountered in the source file, the macroassembler substitutes the macro sequence in place of the macro name.

The macro technique is useful in cases where subroutines are not practical. Some microprocessors do not support subroutines easily and therefore macros are used. In some situations the programmer does not want to waste the processor time associated with the CALL and RET instructions needed for a subroutine and wishes to directly insert the code to be executed.

When using macros the programmer must be careful to keep in mind the effects of the macro on the processor registers and status flags. If a macro clears a particular flag and the user then attempts to use the flag which he thinks is still set, the program will malfunction.

Conditional assembly is included with most macroassemblers (as well as with most two-pass assemblers) and is very useful under certain conditions. In some cases a program is being written which will execute on two or more hardware systems which are similar, but have minor differences. Instead of writing a customized program for each system, the same program may be used with conditional assembly. A flag is defined in the source code as either true or false depending on which system is going to execute the program. A conditional statement is then inserted at the locations in the program where different actions must be taken depending on the hardware.

The following example illustrates the technique:

```
SYSTEMA EQU    TRUE      ; WE ARE USING SYSTEM A
SYSTEMB EQU    FALSE     ; AND NOT SYSTEM B

        IF     SYSTEMA
        MVI    A,23H
        ENDIF


        IF     SYSTEMB
        MVI    A,45H
        ENDIF
```

In the example, when system A is being used the accumulator will be loaded with a value of 23H, whereas the accumulator will be loaded with a value of 45H if system B is being used.

Typical examples of using macroassemblers are covered in Chapter 11.

d. Cross Assemblers. A cross assembler may be of any of the types already mentioned. The distinguishing feature of a cross assembler is that it is not written in the same language used by the microprocessor that will execute the machine code generated by the assembler.

Cross assemblers are usually written in a high-level language such as FORTRAN which will make them machine independent. For example, an 8085 assembler may be written in FORTRAN and then the assembler may be executed on another machine such as the Motorola 6800. Microprocessors will provide cross assemblers to develop machine code for one of their microprocessors using their own development system that uses another microprocessor.

e. Resident Assembler. A resident assembler is almost the complete opposite of the cross assembler because it is written to run on the same machine that will execute the source code. For example, an 8085 assembler that is written in 8085 assembly language is a resident assembler.

f. Metaassembler. The most powerful assembler is the metaassembler because it will support many different microprocessors. The programmer merely specifies at the start of the source code which microprocessor assembly language will be used and the metaassembler will translate the source code to the correct machine code.

3. Characteristics of Typical Development System Assemblers

When selecting an assembler for use on a microprocessor development system, there are several factors to keep in mind. Two-pass assemblers are almost universally used on modern development systems but the assemblers differ in their ability to handle macros, generate relocatable code (code that is not dependent on address), and process the various psuedoinstructions.

Before selecting an assembler, consider the time savings that an advanced assembler may afford. Many of the advanced features of advanced assemblers allow the programmer to more efficiently generate source code. As the programmer's labor cost increases, the efficiency of an assembler can translate into many dollars saved.

Some assemblers allow complex mathematical and logical expressions in the operand field which will save time in defining a value. The ease with which data tables and character strings may be generated should also be considered.

The capabilities of the assembler may even affect the structure of the program. A good macroassembler will facilitate the creation of a library of macros which may be used by several programmers to simplify their program generation. As a large library of macros is developed, the ease of generating assembly language can approach that of some high-level languages.

The speed at which an assembler translates the source code can be a major point to consider in some cases. During the development of a program, reassembly may have to be performed dozens of times. If much time is spent waiting for the assembler to finish its task, many dollars are wasted. On a typical 8K program, assembly times run anywhere from 4 to 40 min. Multiply that by a factor of 10 or 20 and it becomes apparent how much time can be wasted by a slow assembler.

9.2.3 Disassembly

Disassembly is the reverse process of assembly and is generally used during debugging to verify that the hex machine code being executed actually matches the assembly language that the user thinks is being executed. Most emulators and debuggers have a disassembler built into the program. A typical disassembly of a section of machine code may appear as follows:

```
0100 21 00 05   LXI  H,0500
0103 06 05      MVI  B,05
0105 AF         XRA  A
```

By using the disassembly feature of a debugger, some bugs may be found without actually referring to the source code listing because the code may be displayed in assembly language form on the CRT.

EXAMPLE 9.1

For the following 8085 assembly language program, find the contents of location 200AH and 200BH.

```
        ORG  2009H
DATA    EQU  7
        MOV  A,M
        MVI  B,DATA
        RET
```

SOLUTION

The first line sets the internal program counter to 2009H. The EQU statement defines the label DATA as a 7. The first machine code byte is 7EH (MOV A,M) which would be stored at the first available program counter value (2009H). The next instruction (MVI B,DATA) loads the B register with the 8-bit value held in DATA. MVI B,DATA translates into two machine code bytes, one for MVI B (06) and one for the data. The data value was defined in the EQU statement and is 07. The machine code for MVI B,DATA is stored at the next program counter location available after the MOV A,M which is 200AH. The actual machine code would appear as follows:

```
2009 7E
200A 06
200B 07
200C C9
```

EXAMPLE 9.2

Find the contents of location 2005H in the following instruction sequence:

```
        ORG  2002H
TABLE:  DW   2367,3378
```

SOLUTION

Care must be taken in solving this problem because there are two pitfalls: the Intel style of storing the least significant byte of a 16-bit word first and the fact that the data values are given in decimal and not hex. The first step to solution is to convert the data to hex. By examination of the source code, it may be seen that location 2005H will be loaded with the most significant byte of the 16-bit word 3378. The first 16-bit word does not need to be converted because it does not affect the solution.

$$3378_D = 0D32_H$$

When the value of the second word is known, the solution may be found:

2002 3F
2003 09   HEX VALUES FOR 2367 DECIMAL

2004 32
2005 0D   HEX VALUES FOR 3378 DECIMAL

EXAMPLE 9.3

Find the value of location 2000H in the following code:

```
            ORG     2000H
SYSTEMA     EQU     FALSE
SYSTEMB     EQU     TRUE

            IF      SYSTEMA
            MVI     A,75H
            MVI     B,1
            RET
            ENDIF

            IF      SYSTEMB
            XRA     A
            MVI     B,2
            RET
            ENDIF
```

SOLUTION

The ORG statement will set the program counter to 2000H. The machine code value stored at the program counter is what we want to find. The problem deals with conditional assembly so the answer depends on which module is assembled. The EQU statements show that the condition is TRUE for SYSTEMB and FALSE for SYSTEMA. Therefore, the module for SYSTEMB will be assembled. The only code we are concerned with is the first instruction for SYSTEMB which is XRA A. The hex code for XRA A is 0AFH. The value at 2000H is therefore 0FAH.

9.2.4 Linkers

The output file from most development system assemblers is an object file. The object file is usually relocatable code that may be configured to execute at any address. The function of the linker is to convert the object file to an *absolute* file which consists of the actual machine code at the correct address for execution. The absolute files thus created are used for debugging and finally for programming PROMs.

9.2.5 Loaders

The loader program takes the linked object file and actually loads it into the development system memory for execution. The four most common types of loaders are: the bootstrap loader, the absolute loader, the relocating loader, and the linking loader.

1. Bootstrap Loader

A bootstrap loader is a small binary program that is placed at the beginning of the object program by the assembler to perform the task of loading the object program into memory. Sometimes a bootstrap loader is a very primitive program that will load into memory a more advanced loading program which will in turn actually load in the object file.

2. Absolute Loader

An absolute loader is a primitive program that will always load the file into fixed memory locations. The file must already be in absolute machine code form for the absolute loader to operate.

3. Relocating Loader

A relocating loader will take an object file and load it into any memory location. The loader performs the relocation procedures necessary to relocate the file from one address to another.

4. Linking Loader

The linking loader is the most sophisticated of the loaders. It is capable of taking independent program files and linking them together identically to a standard linker. The linking loader can also perform the load function that puts the absolute machine code into memory for execution.

9.2.6 Command Files

A command file is a file that contains a sequence of commands that are to be executed. Instead of the programmer entering an identical sequence of commands over and over while debugging a program, the programmer uses a command file to perform the operations. A typical command file may hold the commands necessary to load a program into an emulator, set the emulator parameters, and execute the program. A command file saves the programmer time while at the same time providing repeatability by removing the possibility of operator error from command entry.

9.2.7 High-Level Language Compilers

A compiler will take the source code written in a high-level language (such as FORTRAN, COBOL, PL/M, PASCAL, etc.) and translate it into assembly language instructions. Each high-level statement may translate to many assembly language instructions and therefore much programming time is saved because the programmer does not have to deal with the many details of assembly language. The main disadvantage of high-level compilers is that they are not as efficient in their code generation as an experienced programmer and therefore the final machine code programs tend to be larger and execute more slowly than pure assembly language. The large memory requirements of high-level languages is becoming less and less of a problem as the cost of memory components continues to drop.

9.2.8 Interpreters

Interpreters are another form of high-level language but they do not convert to assembly language. The interpreter (such as BASIC) is a program that is written for the system and the interpreter directly executes the high-level statements one at a time.

The major advantage of interpreters is their user interaction. The user may write an interpretive program, immediately execute it, edit the statements to correct problems, and then immediately execute the program again. The lengthy process of using a text editor, assembler, linker, and loader is avoided.

The big disadvantage of interpreters is their speed. Since all statements must be interpreted at the high-level stage each time they are encountered, the interpreter program takes longer to perform the desired execution. Program execution speed is not always a concern because some operations, even though they are ten times slower than assembly language, still execute with minute delay.

9.2.9 Monitors

The monitor is the program responsible for supervising the overall operation of the development system. The monitor contains the hardware dependent routines that are necessary to allow programs to communicate with the development system I/O. Programs usually communicate with the I/O through the monitor by passing parameters between subroutines. In this manner a program does not need to know actual I/O addresses to communicate with the printer, but need only put the character to send to the printer in a particular register and then call the printer output subroutine. This modular approach to I/O allows a program to be transported from one system to another with a large degree of I/O independence.

9.2.10 Operating Systems

Operating systems are sometimes referred to as *enhanced monitors* but in reality they are far more than simple monitors. The more advanced operating systems allow multiple users simultaneously. The operating system automatically allocates mass storage space and keeps all files in an organized manner. Some operating systems utilize password protection on a user's files so that no accidental changes may be made by another user.

Most operating systems have built-in utility programs that allow the user to manipulate files. Common utilities include file deletion routines, file creation routines, and file duplication routines.

The real purpose of the operating system is to remove the time consuming job of file and memory management from the user and allow the user to concentrate on the job of efficiently creating programs.

9.3 Operator Consoles for Microcomputer Development Systems*

Microcomputer development systems vary in the types of operator control consoles they use to enter and display data. Table 9.1 shows five types of

Table 9.1 Operator Console Types and Major Function Times

Operator Console	Application Example	Debug Function Time (Overhead)[a]	Edit Function Time[b]
Binary lamps and switches	Front panel; Imsai, Altair	10 min	Not practical
Hex keyboard and display	Intel SDK-85 KIM-1	180 s	Not practical
Printer terminal with PROM debug monitor	Motorola	120 s; printout time is significant	48 s; must list program to check edit
CRT terminal 120–960 characters per second and debug monitor	Tektronix Intel	80 s	240 s; must list program to check edit
Memory-refreshed CRT display	GenRad HP-64000	40 s; minimum operator entry	90 s; context editing

[a] Standard debug example: set breakpoint, execute, examine register and 32 bytes of memory, make a five-instruction patch, reexecute, examine registers, and continue execution.
[b] Standard edit example: change two lines, delete three lines, and insert five lines. Assume that all data are in memory.
*This material is reprinted with permission from B. Gladstone, "Comparing Microcomputer Development System Capabilities," *Computer Design,* Feb. 1979.

operator consoles. The consoles range from the primitive binary lamps and toggle switches to high-speed interactive CRTs. As a carry-over from the beginnings of computers, many minicomputers available today still have a *front panel* consisting of lamps and toggle switches. Primitive debugging can be carried out by manually entering data on the switches and reading the data displayed on the lamps. Some minicomputers such as the Data General Eclipse line still implement the front panel concept but have replaced the manual switches and lamps with a serial terminal. Data are entered in octal as with the first Data General minicomputers, but instead of being toggled in with switches, they are simply typed in on the keyboard of the terminal. The computer's response to the request is in turn displayed via the CRT or printer. Even though this approach is an improvement over the original switches and lamps, debugging in this manner is extremely tedious.

The first improvements in development systems was the addition of a printer with a debugger. Debuggers built around the printer (usually a 10-character per second teletype) were slow and cumbersome because of the slow data exchange rate. The teletypes were soon replaced by other types of consoles: one being a low-cost type (hexadecimal keyboard and display) and the other being a high-speed type (CRT terminal).

The hexadecimal keyboard and display is a low-cost method of implementing the operator's console necessary to develop software and hardware. Information that used to be entered by toggle switches is now entered via the hex keyboard. Instead of toggling from 8 to 16 switches, data are now entered with two or four keystrokes. This reduction in operator input reduces the chance for error, but a hex keyboard provides very limited features for other inputs. In the place of the binary lamp display, seven-segment LED readouts are used. Typically six displays are used, four for address and two for data.

Many development systems using high-speed CRTs are merely sped up versions of the original teletype-style debuggers. The high speed of the CRT allows much faster communications, but many systems still do not have software that takes full advantage of the features of the modern CRTs.

The most advanced development system use a memory-refreshed CRT terminal to provide true high-speed user interaction. Editors and debuggers are designed to use the high-speed screen update features of memory-refreshed CRTs to provide the user with continuously updated data. During debugging, registers and memory may be displayed on the screen without user interaction (such as having to request a register dump). The current state of the art and direction of microprocessor development design indicate that most new development systems will be of the high-speed memory-refreshed type.

9.4 Mass Storage for Microcomputer Development Systems*

Storage facilities for software being developed on a system can be divided into five basic types currently in use: no storage, paper tape, cassette tape, flexible disk, and hard disk.

9.4.1 No Storage

As may be expected, no mass storage is the most primitive level of development. When the developer only has a simple single-board computer with a hex keyboard and display, he must enter the data in machine code form and execute. Changes in the program may be made during debug, but the changes must be documented by hand because the program cannot be saved on a mass storage device.

9.4.2 Paper Tape

Paper tape as a mass storage technique was very popular for many years, and is still being used in some facilities. The low cost and high reliability of paper tape is hard to match by other mass storage media. The most common combination for a paper tape operation is to use a teletype that has the paper tape reader/punch built into the unit. This provides an integrated package of operator's console and mass storage device. A severe limitation of paper tape is the speed. Typical teletype devices operate at 10 characters per second. High-speed paper tape punches and readers are available but the speed is slow compared to other media.

9.4.3 Cassette Tape

A very popular storage media for home-type systems and some low-cost business systems, cassette tape provides a good compromise between storage size and cost. Typical cassette systems operate 3 to 40 times faster than paper tape and the cassettes are easy to store. A development system with good software and a reliable cassette for mass storage can be an extremely powerful development tool.

9.4.4 Flexible Disk

One of the most popular and versatile systems for mass storage consists of a flexible disk (floppy disk) in either the 5¼-in. size or the 8-in. size. Typical storage capabilities for a floppy range from 250K bytes on a single-sided disk to over a million bytes on a double-sided, double-density disk. Data

---

*This material is reprinted with permission from B. Gladstone, "Comparing Microcomputer Development System Capabilities," *Computer Design,* Feb. 1979.

transfer rates between the development system and the disk are typically greater than 1000 characters per second.

A development system consisting of a high-speed screen-oriented editor, assembler, and debugger coupled with two or more 8-in. floppy disk drives for mass storage is most common. A designer is able to create and debug programs very efficiently using floppy disk systems. A drawback of floppy systems is that even a million bytes of mass storage is sometimes insufficient for program development.

9.4.5 Hard Disk

The hard disk mass storage device is the most powerful of all the currently available devices. Most hard disk units have a fixed disk that cannot be removed, but some of the very large systems use a hard disk device that features removable disks that are contained in cartridges resembling a large stack of records.

Even smaller hard disk systems provide 5–20 million bytes of mass storage and data transfer rates much higher than flexible disks. There is enough storage space on a hard disk to support multiple users easily and many systems that use hard disks also provide the capability of supporting several development stations.

9.5 Development System Architectures

Architectures for development systems can be generally divided into two categories, the master/slave configuration and the single-processor configuration.

9.5.1 Master/Slave System

In a master/slave configuration, the master (host) processor controls all development functions such as editing, assembling, and so on. The master processor controls the mass storage device and processes all I/O (CRT, printer, etc).

The software for the development systems is written for the master processor which is usually not the same as the slave (target) processor. The slave microprocessor is typically connected to the user prototype via a 40-pin connector (the number varies with the processor) which links the slave processor to the master processor. Figure 9.3 shows a typical master/slave configuration.

Some development systems such as the HP-64000 completely separate the system bus from the emulation bus and therefore use a separate block of memory for emulation. This separation allows passive monitoring of the

Development System Architectures   371

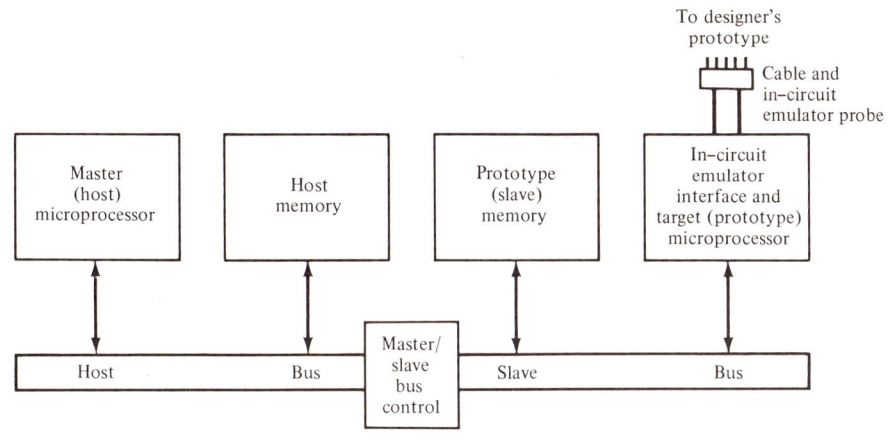

Figure 9.3 Master/slave architecture.

software executing on the target processor without stopping the emulation process. A benefit of the separate emulation facilities allows the master processor to be used for editing, assembling, and so on, while the slave processor continues the emulation. A designer may therefore start an emulation running, exit the emulator program, and at some future time return to the emulation program.

Another advantage of the separate bus architecture is that a software operating system needs to be written only once for the master processor and will be used no matter what type of slave processor is being emulated. When a new slave processor is to be emulated, only the emulator probe needs to be changed.

A disadvantage of the master/slave architecture is that the memory is not continuous because it is in isolated blocks. This separation makes it a little harder to work with in some systems. Under some situations, the higher cost associated with the master/slave architecture is a disadvantage, but in a system capable of simultaneously running two emulators (such as the Intel system), the increased throughput may make the master/slave system cheaper than two individual development systems.

9.5.2 Single-Processor System

As the name implies, only one processor is used for system operation and target emulation. Figure 9.4 shows a block diagram of a single-processor architecture.

The system processor does both jobs of executing system software as well as acting as the target processor. Since there is only one processor involved, the system software must be rewritten for each type of processor that is to

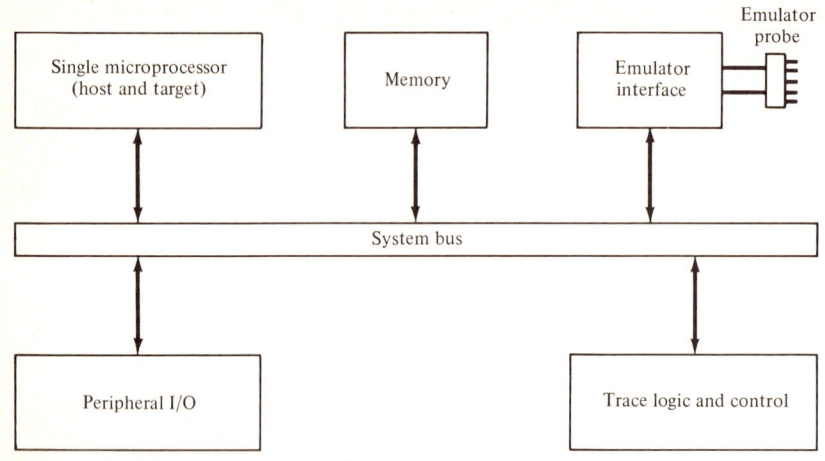

372 Chapter 9 FUNDAMENTALS OF MICROCOMPUTER DEVELOPMENT SYSTEMS

Figure 9.4 Single-processor architecture.

be emulated. Since the system software must reside in the same memory used by the emulator, not all memory will be available to the emulation process, which may be a disadvantage when large prototypes are being developed.

System cost is lower because less hardware is required, but as mentioned in the section on master/slave systems, the cost is a viable factor only if a single development facility is needed.

9.6 Debugging and Integration

In a well-designed microprocessor development system, the three phases of system development, software debugging, hardware debugging, and software-hardware integration, tend to merge together into one combined operation. During this combined *integrated debugging* phase, several capabilities of the development system are needed. The main software function needed is the debugger while the main hardware function needed is the in-circuit emulator.

9.6.1 In-Circuit Emulators

The in-circuit emulator allows the development system to be connected to the prototype system while placing very few restrictions, if any, on the hardware design of the prototype. As far as the prototype hardware is concerned, the emulator acts exactly like the target microprocessor, and therefore the designer does not need to concern himself with the specifications of the development system.

The advantages of the emulator are easy to see. If the actual target microprocessor is installed in the prototype hardware, the designer has almost no control over the execution of the program. If the designer has given the hardware some external switches and displays, then a system monitor may be designed to allow some debugging capabilities in the prototype. This is a very cumbersome and slow process and the emulator removes the need for such an approach. When the emulator is installed in the prototype, the designer has full control over the execution of the software.

Another advantage of the emulator is that it allows work to progress on system development even before the prototype hardware is complete. Most emulators can supply their own clock signal so one is not needed immediately on the prototype. If the prototype does not contain any of its own memory yet, the emulator may use system memory (or sometimes its own memory) to substitute for prototype memory.

9.6.2 Debugger

The debugger provides two main functions: to allow the designer to execute his program under controlled conditions, and to provide a means for the designer to control the emulation of the prototype. In actual practice these two functions are usually accomplished together because the program is debugged on the prototype hardware using the in-circuit emulator.

A very useful feature of most debuggers is *symbolic* debugging. As the name implies, debugging is performed using symbols instead of hex machine code.

To appreciate the value of symbolic debugging, consider the following situation. During prototype debugging the designer often wishes to locate a specific location in the program. When the program was written, symbolic assembly language was used and this is what the designer is accustomed to using. To find the absolute address of a particular symbol, the designer may have to refer to the linker listing as well as the assembler listing. If the designer must go through this process of calculating a symbol address several times, the time wasted becomes very large. A symbolic debugger keeps its own symbol table with the symbol's name and its absolute address. With a symbolic debugger the designer may simply refer to any of the symbols in the program without being aware of the absolute address. For example, if a given program is to be executed and the first instruction to be executed has a name (START, for example) then during debugging the designer could simply command the debugger to start execution at the label START without really knowing where in memory START resides.

9.6.3 Debugging with Emulation

Using an emulator, the debugging of hardware and software may be carried out in a very systematic manner. The basic rule of debugging is to break the process into the smallest possible steps and then debug each step one at a time.

Basic hardware checkout may be performed easily with an emulator. A few simple commands at the development system console can cause an output instruction to be executed on the prototype hardware. The results of the instruction, whether it be to light a display or turn on a relay, may easily be verified either with visual methods or simple test equipment. Similarly, input data can be tested using the emulator by simulating an input instruction on the prototype hardware. If a problem is encountered in the hardware, the emulator may be used to set up simple instruction loops that will allow the designer to see the same instruction executed over and over while tracing the signals through the circuit to find the problem.

After the prototype hardware has been verified, the software may be debugged using the prototype hardware. It is at the software debugging stage that the debugger really proves its worth.

Two main techniques for software debugging are used: single-stepping and tracing. Single-stepping executes one instruction at a time while pausing for operator intervention, while tracing executes instructions one after the other, displaying register and status information on the CRT between each instruction. Neither technique allows the target processor to run in real time and therefore problems that are time dependent (such as timing loops) cannot be detected using these two techniques.

Some debuggers while they are single-stepping require that the designer command the debugger to display registers or status after each instruction. This can be very time consuming and the more advanced debuggers allow the user to preset the data to be displayed (such as registers or memory) and then the user merely uses a single key each time a new step is to be executed. After each step is executed, the CRT screen is automatically updated with the new data. This technique is much more efficient for designers.

Trace mode is like an automated single-stepper. The designer specifies what data are to be displayed after each instruction (usually only the registers and status may be displayed) and then starts the debugger at some specific location. After each instruction is executed, the screen is updated with the new data, and the next instruction is automatically executed. Even through tracing may appear fast, it must be remembered that it is usually at least 500 times slower than real-time execution. A limiting factor is often the speed of the display device. If only a teletype is available, the trace will be extremely slow, whereas a serial-communication CRT is often ten time faster.

When either method is used in conjunction with a memory-refreshed display, the debugging process is sped up considerably because of the time saved in screen updates.

After a software module has been debugged, it would be a waste of time to allow the single-stepper or tracer to execute through these debugged modules. At this time, the breakpoint feature of most debuggers becomes usable. A breakpoint routine allows the designer to preset the program location where he wishes debugging to start. The program may then be executed at full speed and then when the emulator encounters the breakpoint instead of an instruction, control of the execution is returned to the designer who may then single-step or trace through the program. As stated, breakpoints are usually inserted in the program to be executed, but some debuggers allow a breakpoint to be set whenever a read and/or write occurs to a specific memory location. This is extremely valuable in the case of a program that is malfunctioning and the designer does not know why a particular memory location is being altered. A breakpoint is set at the memory location that is being altered to the wrong value and the emulation started. Whenever the memory location is read or written, the emulator will stop and the designer can determine if the program is in the right location. Symbolic debugging during breakpoints is also available on most advanced debuggers, allowing the designer to set breakpoints without calculating the absolute addresses of the program.

During all stages of debugging, it is wise to use the prototype hardware whenever possible. By using the prototype, actual outputs may be seen and actual inputs may be given through the hardware. Most well-designed emulators allow the debugging to be carried out with different levels of hardware. Programs may be emulated with interrupts (or DMA) disabled or enabled, allowing the designer greater flexibility.

9.6.4 Debugging in Real Time

When a microprocessor design is dependent on operation in real time for any reason (such as software timing loops), normal single-stepping and tracing cannot do the complete job of debugging the software. For example, consider a timing loop designed to execute for 10 ms. Taking into account the clock speed, it may be determined that the software must execute 1000 loops to consume 10 ms. A single-stepper or tracer could be used to verify that 1000 loops have occurred, but it would be far simpler to merely let the prototype execute the program in real time and use an oscilloscope to check the timing.

To cope with the problems of real-time debugging, many development systems offer logic analyzers or real-time trace options. These options, which are integrated into the development system, are closely related to general-purpose logic analyzers. The development system options differ from general-purpose analyzers in three respects:

1. The development system analyzers are not as fast as standard analyzers and therefore usually lack the ability to detect subtle hardware timing errors.
2. The development system analyzers are permanently installed in the

376 Chapter 9 Fundamentals of Microcomputer Development Systems

    development system and their inputs are permanently connected to the emulator bus which leaves a limited number of uncommitted inputs for general-purpose testing.

3. The development system analyzers are optimized for detecting hardware/software problems and the development system software can aid the designer in interpreting the data captured by the analyzer.

Functionally, the development system analyzers use very fast memory, organized as up to 64 bits wide by 256 words deep, which is used to capture data from the emulator bus during real-time emulation. Usually included are breakpoint circuits (hardware analogs to the software breakpoints previously described), delay counters (to start tracing a fixed amount of time after a trigger), and timers and circuits to enable storage of only selected bits on the emulator bus. The delay counter can be extremely valuable in debugging looping software. The analyzer can be set to wait until the nth time through a loop before the display begins. Some analyzers allow the presetting of complicated sequences to act as triggers. For example, some software routines may be similar and the designer does not want to start the trace until a particular sequence occurs.

The debugger software used to control the analyzer hardware provides the means for using the analyzer effectively. Since the same debugger is used for single-stepping and tracing, the transition from one mode to another is relatively simple. All debugging displays, including the logic analyzer display, are on the development system CRT which allows the designer to become proficient with the single system rather than using multiple pieces of test equipment to debug a prototype.

When the real-time analyzer is in use, the emulator bus is constantly monitored and the results stored in the analyzer memory. The analyzer continues to run and store data in the memory until the preset breakpoint is encountered. If the memory storage capability should be exceeded, old data are discarded and the new data are stored. Therefore in an analyzer with 256 words of storage, only the last 256 words for data can be captured.

A limitation of the logic analyzer as compared to the trace mode of the debugger is that the logic analyzer can capture external microprocessor information such as addresses and data, but cannot display the contents of microprocessor registers. When the analyzer is used in conjunction with a single-stepper and a tracer, almost any microprocessor bug can be detected and corrected.

While some analyzers do not have external inputs (the HP-64000, for example) others do provide some external inputs (the Intel ICE-85 has 18 external inputs in addition to normal bus inputs).

9.6.5 Getting It All Together

Debugging a design, microprocessor or otherwise, is basically an iterative process of testing, correcting bugs, and testing again. The process continues until testing no longer detects any bugs in the design. In a conventional hardware-only design, the prototype is built and tested. If a bug is found, a fix is devised and patched into the circuit. The designer then incorporates the fix into the circuit documentation and the circuit is tested again.

In a microprocessor-based design, the same process takes place for the hardware portion of the design, and a similar process takes place for the software. After a bug is discovered in the software, a fix is devised. The source code for the program is amended by the editor, the program reassembled and linked, and then emulated again. The iterative procedure of testing and fixing is referred to as the *circle of design.*

Evaluating the performance of a microprocessor development system may be accomplished by analyzing the circle of design. Using a typical 2K assembly language program as an example, an inefficient development system may consume 3–4 hours to complete one circle. The circle time does not include the editing time or the debugging time. With a modern disk-based development system the circle time is closer to 15 min (which includes a hard copy listing). If the debugger used on the advanced development system contains a symbolic debugger, the need for a program listing may be discarded, thereby reducing the circle to as little as 2–3 min. This short time assumes that the development system supports command files which can perform the assembly, linking, and loading functions with a single high-level command.

It is obvious from the above example that an advanced development system can save much time in the design of a microprocessor-based system. What may not be obvious is the fact that by using an advanced system, it is more likely that program documentation will be kept at a high level. When a program is developed with a low-level development system, there is a great temptation on the part of the designer to make small software patches in hex rather than reedit and reassemble the program. It is easy to understand how a designer can fall into this trap if it may take him half a day to make a simple change to the program and get a new listing. On the other hand, if the process of creating new documentation is highly automated and as fast as it is in advanced development systems, it is far more likely that the documentation will be kept current with the prototype.

9.7 High-Level Languages with Microprocessors

The high-level languages typically used by microprocessors are BASIC, FORTRAN, PL/M, PASCAL, and COBOL. Table 9.2 shows the five languages in a chart that rates them to show their comparative advantages and disadvantages. Currently, PASCAL is the most widely accepted high-level language used on microprocessors because of its structured

Table 9.2. Advantages and Disadvantages of Various High-Level Languages

	BASIC	FORTRAN	PL/M	PASCAL	COBOL
Ease of learning 1 = easy 5 = hard	1	2	3	3	5
Ease of programming (small vs large program) 1 = easy (small) 5 = hard (large)	1 3	2 4	2 3	2 3	5 5
Speed of execution 1 = fast 10 = slow	10	3	1	6	3
Amount of memory used	Program and 12K for interpreter	No formatted I/O and 3K program	Program	Program and interpreter	Program

Source: Reprinted by permission of Intel Corporation.

nature, and will therefore be covered in this section in more detail than the other languages.

9.7.1 BASIC*

BASIC is an easy language to learn, but since it usually is implemented in the form of an interpreter, it is an inefficient language. Interpreters require a large amount of memory to implement and are generally very slow in execution. However, interpreters are an interactive language with the user and therefore the programs can be edited and then immediately executed without assembling, linking, and so on. A simple example of BASIC and some interactive commands follows:

```
10 INPUT B
20 FOR A = 1 TO 5
30 PRINT A*B;
40 NEXT A
50 END
RUN              Command to run program
?4               Program requests value for B
4 8 12 16 20     Program prints results
OK               Prompt sign; waiting for command
30 PRINT A*B*2;  Edit line 30
RUN              Execute program again
?4               Give same input for B
8 16 24 32 40    New output is twice first run output
OK               Prompt sign
```

* This section contains material reprinted courtesy of Intel Corporation.

9.7.2 PL/M*

PL/M is a block structured language developed at Intel in 1971 for their new line of microprocessors. PL/M has been used to create all of the Intel written software for their development systems. A compiler language, PL/M generates code that executes much more quickly than an interpretive language like BASIC. Block structure languages are easy to learn, even if it is the user's first computer language. PL/M is especially good for executive routines of large programs, as well as for smaller logic-oriented process control programs or subprograms. The popular operating system, CP/M, was written by Digital Research using PL/M.

Due to the easy readability of PL/M code, it is often better than an assembler, even for small programs. The following is a sample of PL/M code:

```
/* THIS PROGRAM ROTATES THE LIGHTS AND OUTPUTS A TONE ON
THE SDK-85. THE ROTATION AND FREQUENCY OF THE TONE IS
READ FROM THE SWITCHES. THE FLOWCHART FOR THE PROGRAM
IS:
                    INITIALIZATION
        MAIN:       DO FOREVER
                    READ SWITCHES
                    CALL DELAY
                    OUTPUT LIGHTS
                    OUTPUT TONE
        END MAIN;                               */

        PLAY 85:DO;
           DECLARE SPEED BYTE, SPEED VALUE STORED IN 1 BYTE
                   PATTERN BYTE, LIKEWISE
                   TONE BYTE, LIKEWISE
           DECLARE LIGHTS LITERALLY '22H',
                   SPEAKER LITERALLY '23H',
                   SWITCHES LITERALLY '21H',
                   COMMAND LITERALLY '20H',
                   FOREVER LITERALLY 'WHILE 1';
    /* PROGRAM BEGINS HERE */
        /* INITIALIZATION */
            TONE = 0;
            PATTERN = 0FH;
        /* CONFIGURE 8155 TO PROPER INPUT
                OUTPUT STATE */
            OUTPUT (COMMAND) = 0EH;
        /* END OF INITIALIZATION */
```

---
* This section contains material reprinted courtesy of Intel Corporation.

```
            /* NEVER ENDING MAIN LOOP STARTS HERE */
         MAIN: DO FOREVER;
            /* READ THE SWITCHES */
               SPEED = INPUT (SWITCHES);
            /* DELAY FOR AWHILE */
               CALL TIME (SWITCHES);
            /* OUTPUT A LIGHT PATTERN */
               OUTPUT (LIGHTS) = PATTERN;
            /* ROTATE PATTERN FOR NEXT OUTPUT */
               PATTERN = ROL (PATTERN, 1);
            /* OUTPUT ON OR OFF DATA TO SPEAKER */
               OUTPUT (SPEAKER) = TONE;
            /* INVERT DATA FOR SPEAKER OUTPUT TO OCCUR IN
            /* NEXT LOOP */
               TONE = NOT (Tone);
         END MAIN;        /* END OF MAIN LOOP */
   END     PLAY85;        /* END OF PROGRAM */
```

9.7.3 COBOL

Although COBOL is a difficult language to learn, it is one of the most frequently used lanugages because COBOL's real strength is in business applications, and since the early 1960s there has been a high volume of business data processing. COBOL reads almost like English and is divided into paragraphlike sections. COBOL was originally written for main frame computers, then migrated to minicomputers, and finally is available for microprocessors.

9.7.4 PASCAL

PASCAL is a structured language that is currently very popular among microprocessor users because of its structured nature and its ease in debugging.

1. A Typical PASCAL Program

Figure 9.5 shows a typical PASCAL program which converts Fahrenheit temperatures to Celsius and Kelvin temperatures. There are two main sections in the program: a HEADING and a BLOCK. The HEADING assigns a title to the program and includes any predefined variables (INPUT and OUTPUT, for example). The BLOCK portion of the program consists of a declaration section and the main program. The declaration section must appear before the main program. In the block, names and types are assigned to all variables, arrays, functions, and so on.

```
PROGRAM FCNVRT;
(* CONVERTS FAHRENHEIT TO CLESIUS AND KELVIN *)

VAR LP, DISK:FILE OF CHAR;
  FAREN:REAL;
FUNCTION CNVRT(F:REAL):REAL;
(* CONVERTS FAHRENHEIT TO CELSIUS *)
BEGIN CNVRT:=(ROUND( (F-32.)*50./9.))/10.;
END;

BEGIN (* THE PROGRAM STARTS HERE *)
REWRITE (LP,-LP:') (* OPENS LINE PRINTER AS FILE *)
REWRITE (DISK, 'DX1:DATA'); (* OPENS DISK FILE NAMED DATA *)
WRITELN('CONVERSION OF FAHRENHEIT TO CELSIUS AND KELVIN'); (*TO CONSOLE*)
WRITELN(LP,'CONVERSION OF FAHRENEHIT TO CELSIUS AND KELVIN');
WRITELN('TYPE FAHRENHEIT VALUES, SEPARATED BY COMMAS OR BLANKS');
WRITELN('AFTER LAST VALUE, TYPE -1000');
REPEAT
  BEGIN READ (FAREN);
  IF FAREN >-1000 THEN WRITELN(DISK,FAREN);
  END
UNTIL FAREN <=-1000.;
CLOSE (DISK); (* NON-STANDARD PROCEDURE TO CLOSE FILES *)
RESET(DISK,'DX1:DATA');
WRITELN(LP);
WRITELN(LP,'FAHRENHEIT CELSIUS KELVIN');
WHILE NOT EOF(DISK) DO
  BEGIN READLN(DISK,FAREN);
  WRITELN(LP,FAREN;8:1,
    CNVRT(FAREN):12:1,CNVRT(FAREN+273.2):8:1);
  END;
CLOSE(LP);
END.
```
(a)

CONVERSION OF FAHRENHEIT TO CELSIUS AND KELVIN

FAHRENHEIT	CELSIUS	KELVIN
32.0	0.0	273.2
0.0	-17.8	255.4
212.0	100.0	373.2
98.6	37.0	310.2
-40.0	-40.0	233.2

(b)

Figure 9.5 (a) PASCAL program to convert Fahrenheit temperatures to Celsius and Kelvin. (b) Program listing and sample run. Source: D. Hall, *Microprocessors and Digital Systems*, McGraw-Hill, 1982. Reprinted by permission.

For example, if the square root of a variable is defined by a real number, then the function must be defined at the beginning of the BLOCK as

FUNCTION SQRT (A"REAL)"REAL

The main program is bounded by BEGIN and END (END must be followed by a period).

2. PASCAL Declarations

The five types of PASCAL declarations, CONSTANT, VARIABLE, LABEL, TYPE and PROCEDURE/FUNCTION, are now briefly described.

a. VARIABLE. A VARIABLE used in a BLOCK must be declared at the beginning of the BLOCK along with the type. The length of the VARIABLE is usually 8 characters and can be any name. Typical VARIABLE types are INTEGER, REAL, CHARACTER, and BOOLEAN. For example:

TOM:CHAR   [TOM is defined as a character variable.]
TIME:INTEGER [TIME is defined as an integer variable.]

INTEGER variables contain only integer numbers whereas REAL variables contain both integer and fractional parts. CHARACTER variables consist only of alphabetic characters or punctuation symbols.

b. TYPE. New types of variables and their allowable values can be declared using the TYPE command. For example, TYPE START (BEGIN, END) defiens a variable of type START which can have either values of BEGIN or END.

c. Procedures or FUNCTIONS. Subroutines in PASCAL are called procedures or functions. Similar to assembly language, after PASCAL executes the procedure or function, the program will return to the next statement in the main program after the procedure or function statement.

Procedures are general subroutines which are written to do some general job, while functions are subroutines which perform a specific trigonometric or arithmetic function (i.e. cosine, sine, etc.).

Procedures or functions must occur in the program before the BLOCK which actually calls the procedure or function. Table 9.3 shows some predeclared functions in PASCAL.

3. PASCAL Operators

Table 9.4 shows typical PASCAL operators along with their respective priority in execution. When a program statement has many different

Table 9.3. PASCAL Predeclared Functions

	ARITHMETIC FUNCTIONS
abs(x)	Computes the absolute value of x. The type of the result is the same as that of x, which must be either integer or real.
sqr(x)	Computes x*x. The type of the result is the same as that of x, which must be either integer or real.
sin(x)	For the following, the type of x must be either real or integer. The type of the result is always real.
cos(x)	
arctan(x)	
exp(x)	
ln(x)	(Natural logarithm)
sqrt(x)	(Square root)

	TRANSFER FUNCTIONS
trunc(x)	x must be of type real; the result is the greatest integer less than or equal to x for $x >= 0$, and the least integer greater or equal to x for $x < 0$.
round(x)	x must be of type real; the result, of type integer, is the value x rounded. That is, round(x) = trunc(x + 0.5), for $x \geq 0$ trunc(x − 0.5), for $x < 0$
ord(x)	The ordinal number of the argument x in the set of values defined by the type of x.
chr(x)	x must be of type integer, and the result is the character whose ordinal number is x (if it exists).

Source: D. Hall, *Microprocessors and Digital Systems*, McGraw-Hill, 1982. Reprinted by permission.

Table 9.4. PASCAL Arithmetic, Logical, and Relational Operators

PRIORITY	OPERATOR	DESCRIPTION
1	NOT	BOOLEAN NOT
2	*	MULTIPLICATION
2	/	DIVISION (REAL)
2	DIV	INTEGER DIVISION
2	MOD	MODULUS (REMAINDER FROM INTEGER DIVISION)
2	AND	BOOLEAN AND
3	+	ADDITION
3	−	SUBTRACTION
3	OR	BOOLEAN OR
4	=	EQUAL
4	< >	NOT EQUAL
4	<	LESS THAN
4	< =	LESS THAN OR EQUAL TO
4	> =	GREATER THAN OR EQUAL TO
4	>	GREATER THAN
4	IN	IN A SET

Source: D. Hall, *Microprocessors and Digital Systems*, McGraw-Hill, 1982. Reprinted by permission.

operations to perform, the order in which the operations are performed is called the hierarchy, or priority. For example, if a statement contained a Boolean NOT operation and a multiplication, the NOT operation would be performed before the multiplication.

4. PASCAL Statements

After all required declarations have been made, the main program body is written using PASCAL statements. Some typical statements are now discussed.

a. Assignment Statement. The assignment statement is equivalent to the LET statement in BASIC. A colon and an equal sign are used to show that a value or a variable is to be assigned to another variable. For example:

Y:=Y+1   This has the effect of adding 1 to Y.
SQUARE:=Y*Y   This squares the value of Y and stores it in SQUARE.

b. Procedure Statement. A procedure subroutine is called using the subroutine's name. The parameters needed for the subroutine are also passed to it when the subroutine is called. For example, START(5,8) will call the procedure START and pass the two parameters 5 and 8.

c. BEGIN and END. As their names imply, the BEGIN statement is used at the start of the program block and END is used at the end of the program block.

d. WHILE ... DO. Repetitive tasks may be performed using the WHILE ... DO statement. The WHILE portion will set up the condition and the DO portion will specify the operation to repeat. As long as the condition is met, the operation will be repeated. For example, WHILE x < 0 DO X:X + 1 will keep adding 1 to the value of X until the value of X is nonnegative.

e. GO TO. The GO TO statement simply performs an unconditional jump to a label.

f. IF ... THEN ... ELSE. IF ... THEN ... ELSE is used to conditionally perform a particular operation. If the expression following the IF is true, the statement following the THEN will be executed. If the expression following the IF is false, the statement following the ELSE will be executed. For example, IF X = 5 THEN Y:= 5 ELSE Z:= 3 is a typical IF ... THEN ... ELSE statement. If the value of X is indeed 5, the Y will be assigned the value of 5. If the value of X is not 5, then Z will be assigned the value of 3.

g. INPUT/OUTPUT Statements. PASCAL inputs data with a READ or READLN statement and outputs data with a WRITE or WRITELN statement. READ and WRITE statements are used when single-character input or output is desired, while READLN or WRITELN statements are used when character strings are desired.

PROBLEMS AND QUESTIONS

9.1 What is the purpose of a microcomputer development system?

9.2 What are the typical software and hardware development aids provided with a development system? Describe them briefly.

9.3 What is the purpose of the MODEM interface provided with a development system?

9.4 Describe the software and hardware debugging tools provided with a typical microcomputer development system.

9.5 What is an editor? Define "context-based editing."

9.6 What is the difference between a one-pass and a two-pass assembler?

9.7 Write an assembly language instruction sequence using 8085 instructions and/or the typical assembler pseudoinstructions described in this chapter to perform the following:
   (a) Input a byte from port 20.
   (b) Form a table to store five data values, F6H, 31H, 1DH, 09H, EAH, in a sequential order starting at location 2000H.

9.8 What is the difference between DB and DW pseudoinstructions?

9.9 What is a macro?

9.10 What is the difference between a macro and a subroutine? What are the advantages and disadvantages of using either?

9.11 What is a macroassembler?

9.12 What is the definition of emulation?

9.13 What are the basic differences among masters/slave, modified master/slave, and the single-processor development system architectures? Discuss the advantages and disadvantages for each.

9.14 Describe the meaning of the following PASCAL statements:
   (a) A:=A+2
   (b) IF X<1 THEN GO TO 100
       ELSE IF X=1 THEN GO TO 150
       ELSE GO TO 200;

CHAPTER 10

POPULAR MICROCOMPUTER DEVELOPMENT SYSTEMS

In this chapter, we describe some of the popular microcomputer development systems manufactured by Intel, Tektronix, GenRad (formerly Futuredata), and Hewlett-Packard.

> These manufacturers (except Hewlett-Packard) recently announced new models, which are basically modifications to their previous systems. Intel, Tektronix, and GenRad do not intend to make any changes to these systems for the next three years. Even though the HP 64000 is used in this book to develop a number of microcomputer-based applications, the concepts learned can readily be extended in order to understand the Intel, Tektronix, and GenRad systems described in this chapter.

A comparison of useful functions available with various systems is included in Table 10.2.

> Finally, in order to demonstrate the operational and functional differences, one example with each of the development systems (Intel, Tektronix, and GenRad) is included.

This chapter contains material modified with permission from Intel (see Example 10.1), Tektronix (see Example 10.2), GenRad (see Example 10.3), and Hewlett-Packard manuals.

10.1 Hewlett-Packard HP 64000

The HP 64000 is the only development system offered by Hewlett-Packard. The HP 64000 provides a number of interesting development system features and includes both software and hardware development capabilities. We will briefly cover the HP 64000 in this section, since Chapters 11 and 12 will include a thorough discussion on hardware and software development using the HP 64000.

The HP 64000 is universal and utilizes a master/slave architecture. The host processor is HP's own 16-bit microprocessor. The host processor manages the operating system, I/O transactions, and system data transfers on the development station bus. The slave processor is the emulation processor and each emulation card and probe support one particular processor.

The HP 64000 has a new feature which makes it a very unique development system. It has what are called "soft keys." A row of keys on the top of the keyboard are not physically labeled, but on the bottom row of the CRT display what each key represents at a certain time is defined. Based on what mode of operation (edit, assemble, link, or emulate) the user is in, the bottom row of the CRT changes dynamically to define the physically unlabeled soft keys. For example, rather than typing in "assembler," the soft key labeled "assemble" is pushed. The soft keys are then automatically renamed to show the options available in the assemble mode.

The HP 64000 has a context-based editor. The editor text may be scrolled through and revised as desired by moving a "cursor" and making the revisions. As mentioned before, this type of editor is very efficient and easy to use in making the edit function time smaller.

The HP 64000 offers a software package including the editor, assembler, and linker. For debugging, the system has a master/slave emulator with the previously described capabilities such as breakpoints, trace and memory, and register modify and dump. The availability of these features by the directed syntax "soft keys" makes the system easy to use.

Other options available for the HP 64000 include a printer, PROM programmer, expandability of up to six development stations, high-level language compiler (PASCAL), and real-time logic analyzer.

The HP 64000 supports the software and hardware development for 8048, 8049, 8080, 8085, 8086, Z80, 6800, 6802, 6809, 68000, and Z8000.

10.2 Intel Development Systems

Intel offers four different types of development systems, namely, Models 120, 225, 286, and 290. Models 120 and 225 are basically similar to Intel's

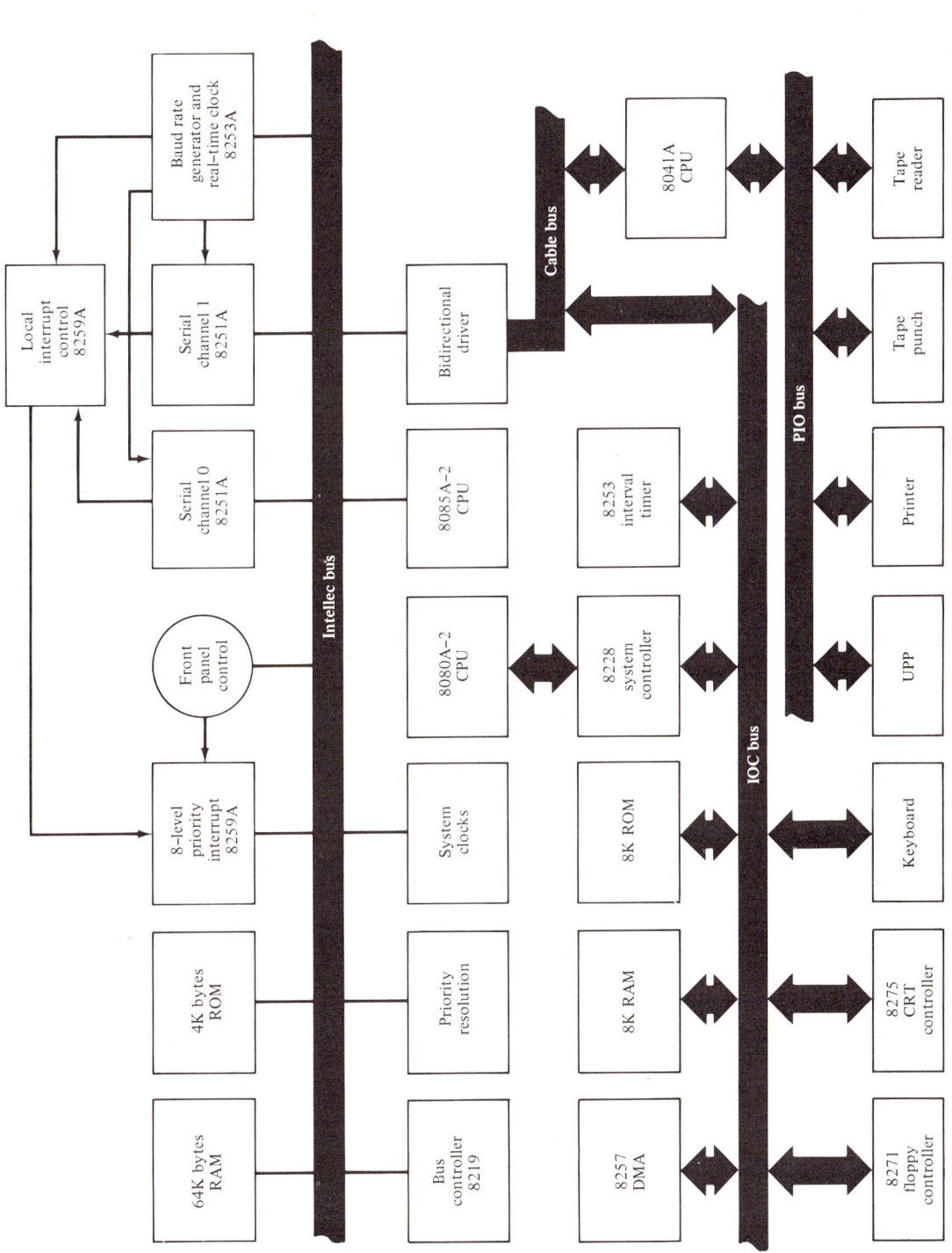

Figure 10.1 Intellec Series II/85 Model 225 microcomputer development system block diagram. Source: Reprinted by permission of Intel Corporation, copyright © 1981.

previous systems, Models 220 and 230, respectively. The main difference between the 120 and 220 is that the 120 is expandable to more memory. On the other hand, the 225 is 8085-based whereas the 230 is 8080-based.

All of Intel's models are nonuniversal and use a modified master/slave architecture. Both the host microprocessor and the emulation microprocessor share one large memory. When both microprocessors attempt to access memory the host microprocessor is given priority. This delay slows the target microprocessor down whenever it must access host memory. This is true for all three of Intel's Microcomputer Development Systems (MDSs) (Models 120, 225, and 286). Intel also offers a multiple-development system MODEM (the Intellec Mainframe Link) and a network development system (Model 290) which helps manage large software projects. Intel uses the industry standard MULTIBUS protocol in its systems.

10.2.1 Intel Models 120 and 225

Intel Models 120 and 225 (Figure 10.1) MDSs are very similar and can be introduced together. Their differences will be pointed out in the process.

Both models have a master CPU card called the Integrated Processor Board (IPB) which contains its own microprocessor, memory, two serial I/O channels, interrupt, and bus interface circuitry. Table 10.1 shows the main differences between the IPBs of Models 120 and 225. Note that the two IPB cards have different CPUs and sizes of RAM. Other than this the two IPB cards are the same. The IPB card will be discussed again shortly.

A second, slave CPU card called the I/O Controller (IOC) handles the I/O for the CRT, the keyboard interface, integral floppy disk, printer, high-speed paper tape reader/punch, and Intel's Universal PROM Programmer. The IOC card is identical on both Models 120/225. It uses an 8080 CPU which controls all I/O operations, as well as supervising communications with the IPB over an 8-bit bidirectional data bus.

Note that the I/O subsystem in the Models 120/225 consists of two parts: the IOC card and two serial channels on the IPB itself. Both channels are RS232 compatible and are implemented using Intel's 8251 USART. One channel contains current loop adapters. The baud rate is controlled using an Intel 8253 interval timer and is under software control. The 8253 also serves as the real-time clock for the entire system. The two interrupt

Table 10.1. Model 120 vs Model 225 IPB Card

Model 120 IPB Card	Model 225 IPB Card
8080 CPU	8085 CPU
32K bytes RAM	64K bytes RAM
4K bytes ROM	4K bytes ROM

Intel Development Systems 391

controllers (8259) are on the IPB. This is an eight-level nested, maskable priority interrupt system.

The IOC also has the following on it:

Chips on IOC:	Function:
8k bytes ROM	I/O control firmware
8K bytes RAM	CRT screen refresh
	Floppy disk buffer
8275	Programmable CRT Controller
8257	DMA controller
8253	Interval timer
8271	Programmable floppy disk controller
8041	Universal peripheral interface (printer, paper tape reader/punch, and Intel's Universal PROM Programmer)
Chips on IPB:	
(2) 8259s	Interrupt controller
8251	USART
8253	Interval timer

One 8259 interrupt controller can be used for programming the interrupt system while the other 8259 permits I/O activity through both serial channels to interrupt the system.

Intel uses a memory-refreshed CRT display which is a very fast, high-quality display. With this type of display it is possible to provide a context-based debugger and editor. The IPB CPU transfers each character for display to IOC RAM. The CRT controller reads one line at a time through the DMA and then feeds one character at a time to the character generator to produce the video signal. An Intel 8253 interval timer is used to time the CRT control. The screen displays 25 rows of 80 characters. Both upper and lower ASCII characters are displayed. Both Models 120/225 use the same CRT, and full ASCII keyboard (with cursor controls and detachable connections).

Both Models 120/225 have self-test diagnostic capability. The expansion capabilities (hardware) for both 120/225 Models is as follows:

1. 2.25 megabytes of floppy disk storage.
2. 7.3 megabytes of hard disk storage.
3. RAM to 64K (Model 120 has 32K) or possibly beyond.
4. ICE-49, 85, 80, 22, and HSE-49.

Both Models 120/225 come with 250K bytes of floppy disk storage, as well as the ISIS II disk operating software. This is the system software for editing, assembling, linking, and debugging Intel's microprocessors. The MDS Model 120 has software to support the MCS-48 and MCS 80/85.

The MDS Model 225 can also support the MCS-86 as well as the MCS-48 and MCS 80/85. The Model 120 MDS provides optional emulation capabilities for the MCS-48, and MCS 80/85. The Model 225 MDS has the same options as the above but also includes the MCS-86.

The various microprocessor assemblers have symbolic reference, conditional assembly, and macroassembly capability. The Model 120 does not support any high-level languages in the basic system but is able to use all of Intel's high-level languages and design aids. The Model 225 supports PL/M, FORTRAN, BASIC, PASCAL, and COBOL.

10.2.2 Intel MDS Model 286

The Model 286 (Figure 10.2) has three microprocessors (instead of two). Instead of one main CPU card called IPB there are two cards. The 8086 microprocessor (16-bit) resides on the resident processor board (RPB-86) and the 8085 microprocessor resides on the integrated processor card (IPC-85). Both CPU cards also have memory, I/O, interrupt, and bus interface circuitry. The advantage of this dual host processor system is that it can develop any and all microprocessors in the Intel product line as well as all the single-chip microcontrollers and the 2920 analog signal processor.

The third microprocessor is on the IOC. The IOC interface, CRT, keyboard, and 250K-byte floppy disk are the same as on the Models 120/225.

A new feature (optional) that the Model 286 offers is the Intellec Series III double-density diskette system (not single density). An intelligent controller and two diskette drives provide direct access bulk storage. Each drive contains $\frac{1}{2}$ megabyte at a data rate of 500,000 bits per second. The controller interfaces directly with the Model 286 and allows expansion to more than 2 million bytes (four diskette drives).

Another new option is the Intellec Series III hard disk system (which has an intelligent controller and one removable cartridge). Each cartridge provides roughly 2.65 million bytes of memory at a data rate of 2.5 megabits per second.

The RPB-86 has 64K bytes of RAM and 16K bytes of ROM. All 16-bit programs are executed and debugged on the host 8086 microprocessor. The ROM contains a debugger program for the 8086/8088.

The IPC-85 has 64K bytes of RAM and 4K bytes of ROM. The ROM contains the Intellec System Monitor and a system bootstrap "self-test" diagnostics program. The 8-bit 8085 microprocessor executes all 8-bit software, and also serves as an I/O slave processor for the 8086.

The MDS Model 286 has an interesting software package. The screen-oriented text editor, credit, has two operating modes: SCREEN and COMMAND. In the SCREEN mode the editor displays a movable cursor

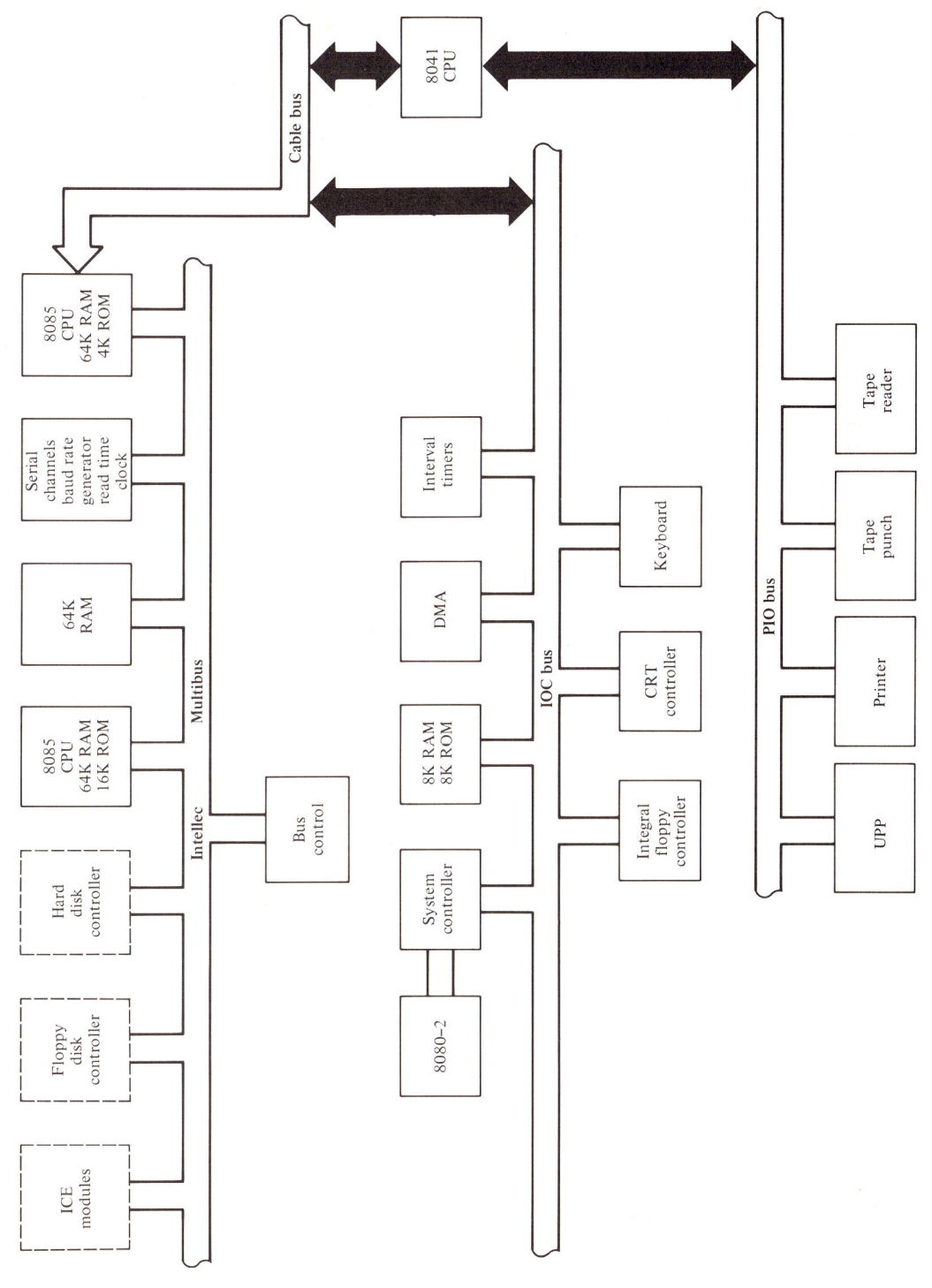

Figure 10.2 Intellec Series III block diagram (Model 286). Source: Reprinted by permission of Intel Corporation, copyright © 1981.

on the screen and has such features as type over and character or line insertion or deletion. In the COMMAND mode the editor provides string search and replace capabilities, formatting, and other edit commands. The editor can search through the source code and replace a specified incorrect entry everywhere it occurs with the correct text (as specified by the programmer). More than one high-level language can be used on the same project because the object modules produced are linkable and relocatable.

Intel's family of 16-bit software languages includes an 8086/8088 macroassembler, a new PASCAL 86/88 compiler, a FORTRAN 86/88 compiler, and a PL/M 86/88 compiler.

Intel's family of 8-bit software language includes a PL/M compiler, a FORTRAN compiler, a BASIC interpreter, a PASCAL 86/88 compiler/interpreter, as well as macroassemblers. There is a macroassembler available for each member of the single-chip microcontroller family, plus an assembler for the 2920 signal processor.

The first true compiler available on any development system is the PASCAL 86/88. There is a strong trend in industry away from nonstructured languages such as FORTRAN and in favor of structured languages such as PASCAL. PASCAL 86/88 has certain special modifications suitable for microcomputer programming (which include interrupt handling, direct port I/O, and separate compilations).

Intel designed PL/M 86/88 as a high-level language that is suited for microprocessor control. A new feature with the Model 286 is a PL/M syntax checking mode that does not generate object code. This feature is similar to FORTRAN in the quick mode.

10.2.3 Intel Network Development System I (NDS 1)—Model 290

For large software projects there are advantages to interconnecting separate Intellec development systems through a shared hard disk storage system. The NDS-I (Figures 10.3 and 10.4) manages file access and printer control for up to eight Intel MDSs.

Two identical Intellec Model 740 hard disk subsystems provide a combined 15 megabytes of on-line storage divided evenly between a fixed disk and removable cartridge.

Even if the Intellec MDSs are not used together on a combined project the shared disk storage still has the advantage of providing hard disk speed and storage capabilities to all the Intellec MDSs at a fraction of the usual cost. If each MDS had its own hard disk it would be far more expensive. Each work station (MDS) can be up to 120 ft away from the NDS-I and 20 ft away from another work station.

An especially nice feature of the NDS-I is the way in which it acts to prevent older and more limited Intellec MDSs from becoming obsolete. Each of the eight work stations can be any model of the Intel development

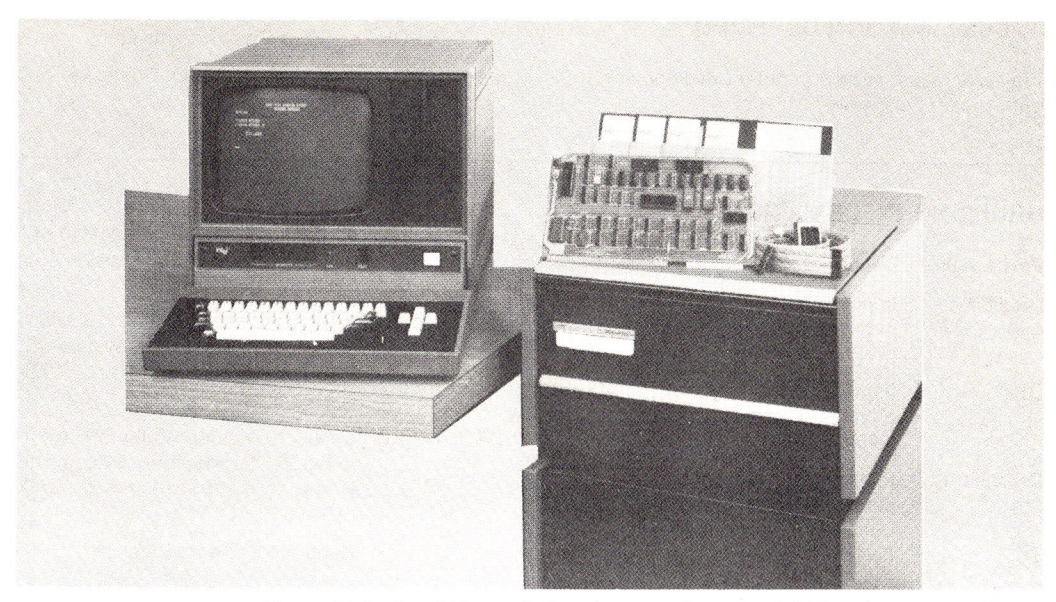

Figure 10.3 Intel Network Development System—I (NDS-I)—Model 290. Source: Reprinted by permission of Intel Corporation, copyright © 1981.

system. When an older model MDS does not have a needed function it can still be used to do all of the preliminary work at which point a newer model work station would take over.

The NDS-I Network Manager (Figure 10.5) consists of a CRT chassis with six-slot card cage, a power supply, fans, cables, a single floppy diskette

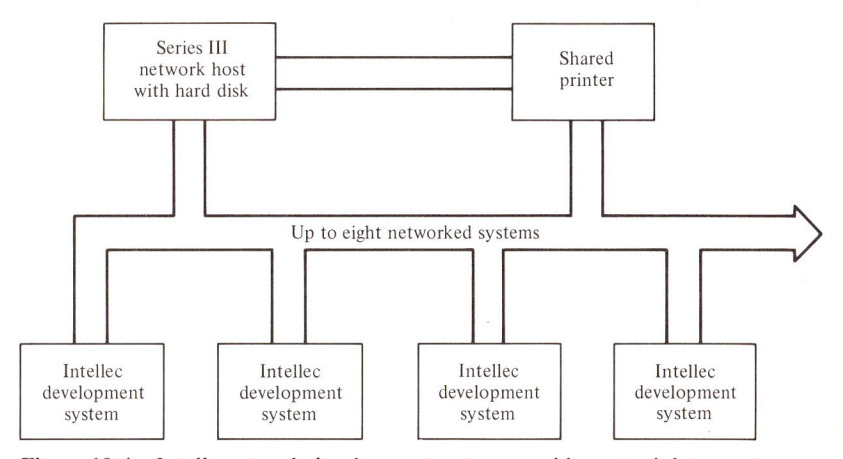

Figure 10.4 Intel's network development systems enable up to eight users to simultaneously have files on one or two hard disk drives. Source: Courtesy Intel Preview Magazine.

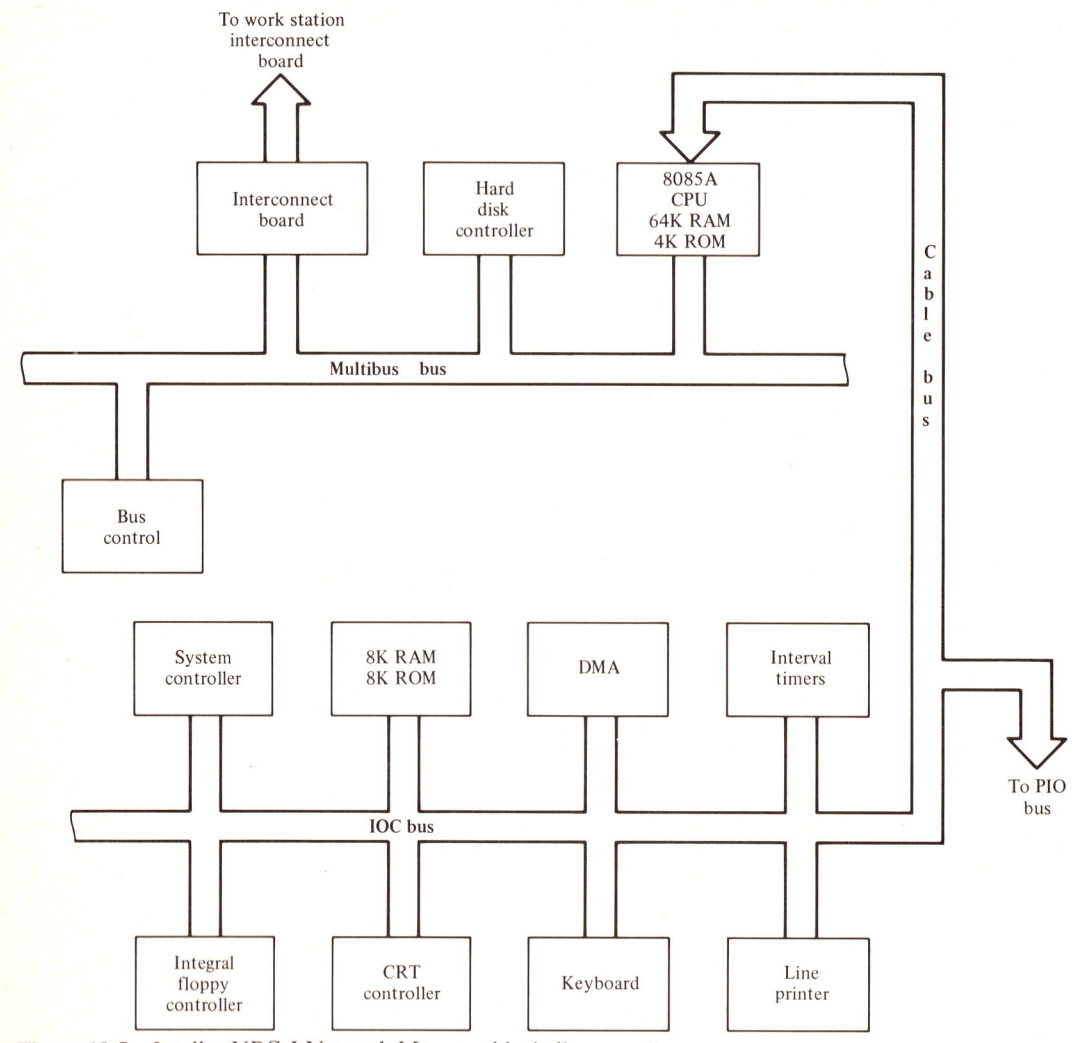

396 Chapter 10 POPULAR MICROCOMPUTER DEVELOPMENT SYSTEMS

Figure 10.5 Intellec NDS-I Network Manager block diagram. Source: Reprinted by permission of Intel Corporation, copyright © 1981.

drive, a detachable full ASCII keyboard, and five printed circuit cards. A free-standing pedestal houses the hard disk drive along with power supply, fans, and cables for connection to the main chassis.

The master CPU card is called the Integrated Processor Card (IPC). It occupies the first slot in the card cage. The IPC card uses the 8085 microprocessor, has 64K RAM, I/O, and interrupt and bus interface circuitry. The input/output controller card is a slave CPU card to the IPC card. This card was discussed in previous sections.

The hard disk controller can support one or two hard disk drives. It has two boards: the channel board receives, decodes, and responds to channel commands from the 8085 on the IPC. The channel board is the DMA that enables the disk controller to access Intellec system memory. It also acknowledges I/O commands as required by the Intellec bus. The disk controller is interfaced with the disk drives and with the Intellec system bus by means of the interface board. The interface board generates a cyclical redundancy check polynomial and validates data during reads using a CRC polynomial.

The InterConnect Board (ICB) interfaces the Network Manager to the work stations. The ICB is a multibus bus compatible board with an 8085 microprocessor, 1.25K bytes of RAM, 4K bytes of ROM, and seven I/O ports. This interrupt-driven interface allows the master CPU to keep busy while the ICB is processing a command from the master CPU. The ICB then sets a flag which generates a MULTIBUS bus interrupt. The data transfer rate is 40K bytes per second (over a wire up to 120 ft long).

The CRT is a 12-in. raster-scan type monitor with a 50/60-Hz vertical scan rate and a 15.5-kHz horizontal scan rate. An Intel 8275 single-chip programmable CRT controller interfaces the CRT to the NDS-I. The 8085 on the IPC transfers a character for display to the IOC, where it is stored in RAM. The CRT controller reads a line at a time into its line buffer through an Intel 8257 DMA controller and then feeds one character at a time to the character generator to produce the video signal. Timing for the CRT control is provided by an Intel 8253 interval timer. The screen display is formatted as 25 rows of 80 characters. The full set of ASCII characters is displayed. The keyboard uses an Intel UPI-41 Universal Peripheral Interface and interfaces directly to the IOC processor via an 8-bit data bus. The floppy disk controller uses the 8271 and 8257 as previously discussed.

SOFTWARE COMPONENTS

Network manager operating system
Disk I/O
Communications
File management
Public/private file control (of hard disk)

10.2.4 The Intellec Mainframe Link (IML)

The Intellec Mainframe Link (Figure 10.6) provides the following features:

1. To gain the main frame facilities of source code entry and editing, program storage and management, back-up, source control, and high-speed printing.

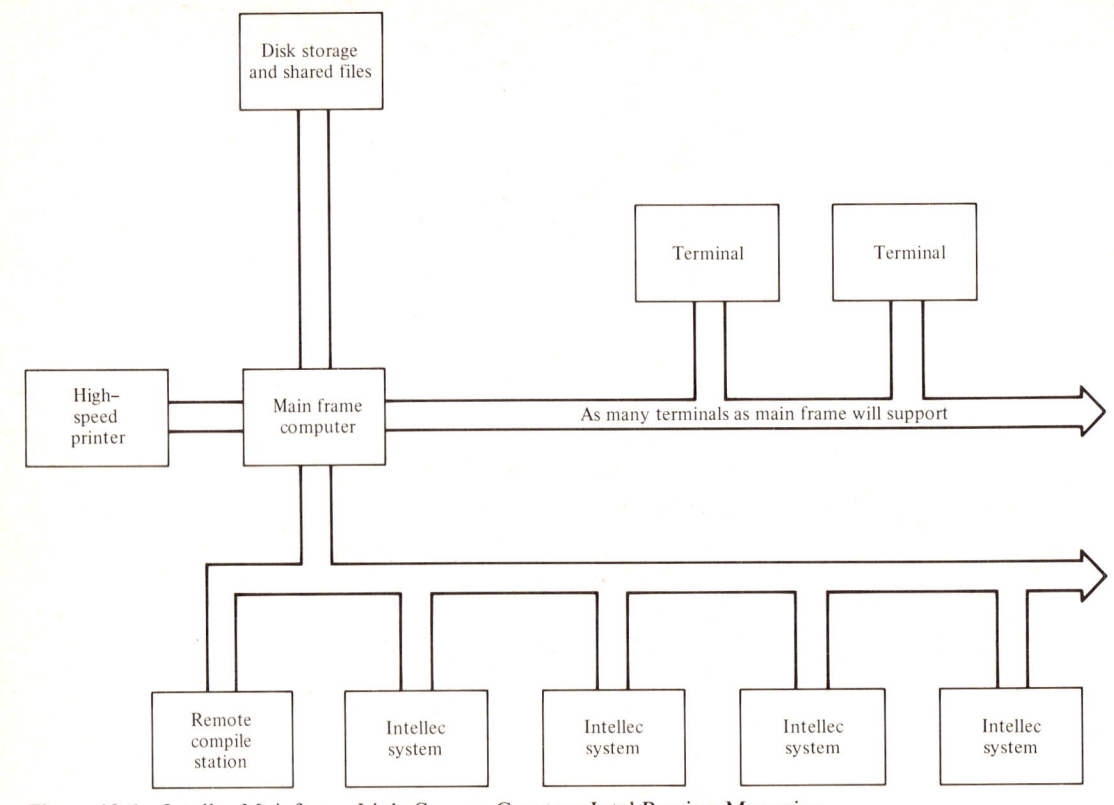

398 Chapter 10 POPULAR MICROCOMPUTER DEVELOPMENT SYSTEMS

Figure 10.6 Intellec Mainframe Link. Source: Courtesy Intel Preview Magazine.

2. To share an Intellec hard disk with assorted Intellec programmers via the mainframe.

The IML uses IBM's 2780/3780 bisync communications protocol for file transfers.

EXAMPLE 10.1

Assuming an 8085 assembly language program, demonstrate the editing, assembling, linking, and emulating features on the Intellec Series II/85 Model 2250.

SOLUTION

1. Editing
To demonstrate some of the features of the Intellec text editor in operation, let us enter an 8085 program and then make some changes to it. The dialog of the session is shown on the program with explanatory

Intel Development Systems 399

comments keyed to numbers in the margin. Note that the program sends the letter X to the system console once every second. Editing steps are given below:

1. I initialize the system by turning on power and pressing the reset key on the Intellec front panel. The system responds with the ISIS identification and the ISIS hyphen prompt. Note that ISIS (Intel System Implementation Supervisor) is a collection of programs that facilitate the development of microcomputer software.
2. I enter the ISIS EDIT command, specifying a file on diskette unit 1 named ONESEC which has an extension of SRC (for source).
3. The text editor identifies itself and notes that since there is no file with this name on diskette 1 this is a new file.
4. The editor prompts with an asterisk. Using the I (Insert) command, I enter a simple assembly language program. The I command continues until I hit ESC twice, as shown by the two dollar signs after the END, which is identified as step 7. In entering the program text I make free use of the tab feature; anytime I simultaneously press control and the letter I, the system responds as a typewriter would to the tab key, with automatic tab stops every eight positions.
5. I type DEALY where I meant DELAY. Noticing the mistake before going on, I press the rubout key three times; the three wrong characters are echoed back as they are erased. I then type the correct characters. To be sure I have made the correction properly, before hitting carriage return to enter the line I press the control key and R together, which repeats the line as corrected. Since it appears to be correct, I press carriage return and continue entering the program.
6. I get a line so badly messed up that I decide to start over. Pressing control and X causes the entire line to be erased; the crosshatch (#) indicates that this was done.
7. I press ESC twice, once to terminate the input string and a second time to terminate the I command.
8. Now there are errors to correct. Using the B command I move the pointer to the beginning of the text, then use the S (substitute) command to correct the spelling of ASSEMBLY. The OLT combination prints the modified line, which is now correct.
9. I use the F (find) command to locate the label L2, which I entered without the colon. The T (type) command types from where the pointer is positioned after the F; this is to assure myself that I am where I want to be.
10. I insert the colon, then type the entire line.
11. I notice that I have entered an instruction twice, so I use the F to find it.
12. The K (kill) command removes the entire line; to be doubly sure that I removed what I wanted to, I type the three lines before and the three lines after the current position of the pointer.

1 ISIS-II, V2.2
2 -EDIT :F1:ONESEC.SRC

3 ISIS-II TEXT EDITOR, V1.6
NEW FILE
4 ::I   ; AN ASSEMLBY LANGUAGE PROGRAM TO SEND THE LETTER 'X'
         ; TO THE CONSOLE OUTPUT DEVICE, ONCE EACH SECOND
         ;
```
    CO      EQU     0F809H  ; PROVIDE ADDRESS OF CO ROUTINE IN MONITOR
            CSEG            ; MAKE THE SEGMENT RELOCATABLE
            STKLN   2       ; SET STACK LENGTH
    START:  LXI     SP,STACK ; INITIALIZE STACK POINTER
    L1:     MVI     D,50    ; WILL CALL DELAY SUBROUTINE 50 TIMES
    L2      MVI     A,200   ; SUBROUTINE PARAMETER
```
5
```
            CALL    DEALYYLALAY     ; INVOKE SUBROUTINE
            CALL    DELAY   ; INVOKE SUBROUTINE
            DCR     D
            DCR     D
            JNZ     L2      ; 50 TIMES AROUND THIS LOOP = 1 SEC
            ;
            MVI     C,'X'   ; SEND 'X' TO CONSOLE OUTPUT DEVICE
```
6
```
    CALL    CO              ; MONTIRO CONSOLE#
            CALL    CO      ; MONITOR CONSOLE OUTPUT ROUTINE
            JMP     L1      ; AROIUND THE LOOP INDEFINITELY
            ;
            ; THE DELAY SUBROUTINE
            ;
    DELAY:  MVI     B,12
    L3:     MOV     C,B
            JNZ     L4
            DCR     A
            JNZ     L3
            RET
            ;
            END     START   ; PROGRAM EXECUTION BEGINS WITH SYMBOL 'START'
```
7 $$
8 ::BSLBYBLYOLT$$
         ; AN ASSEMBLY LANGUAGE PROGRAM TO SEND THE LETTER 'X'
9 ::FL2$T$$
```
            MVI     A,200   ; SUBROUTINE PARAMETER
```
10 ::I:$OLT$$
```
    L2:     MVI     A,200   ; SUBROUTINE PARAMETER
```
11 ::FDCR$OLT$$
```
            DCR     D
```
12 ::K-3T3T$$
```
    L1:     MVI     D,50    ; WILL CALL DELAY SUBROUTINE 50 TIMES
    L2:     MVI     A,200   ; SUBROUTINE PARAMETER
            CALL    DELAY   ; INVOKE SUBROUTINE
            DCR     D
            JNZ     L2      ; 50 TIMES AROUND THIS LOOP = 1 SEC
            ;
```
13 ::FJNZ$OLT$$
```
            JNZ     L2      ; 50 TIMES AROUND THIS LOOP = 1 SEC
```
14 ::LFJNZ$OLT$$
```
            JNZ     L4
```

```
15  IL4:       DCR     C
    $$
16  ⁎BSAROIU$AROU$0LT$$
               JMP     L1      ; AROUND THE LOOP INDEFINITELY
17  ⁎B50T$$
               ; AN ASSEMBLY LANGUAGE PROGRAM TO SEND THE LETTER 'X'
               ; TO THE CONSOLE OUTPUT DEVICE, ONCE EACH SECOND
               ;
    CO         EQU     0F809H  ; PROVIDE ADDRESS OF CO ROUTINE IN MONITOR
               CSEG            ; MAKE THE SEGMENT RELOCATABLE
               STKLN   2       ; SET STACK LENGTH
    START:     LXI     SP,STACK ; INITIALIZE STACK POINTER
    L1:        MVI     D,50    ; WILL CALL DELAY SUBROUTINE 50 TIMES
    L2:        MVI     A,200   ; SUBROUTINE PARAMETER
               CALL    DELAY   ; INVOKE SUBROUTINE
               DCR     D
               JNZ     L2      ; 50 TIMES AROUND THIS LOOP = 1 SEC
               ;
               MVI     C,'X'   ; SEND 'X' TO CONSOLE OUTPUT DEVICE
               CALL    CO      ; MONITOR CONSOLE OUTPUT ROUTINE
               JMP     L1      ; AROUND THE LOOP INDEFINITELY
               ;
               ; THE DELAY SUBROUTINE
               ;
    DELAY:     MVI     B,12
    L3:        MOV     C,B
    L4:        DCR     C
               JNZ     L4
               DCR     A
               JNZ     L3
               RET
               ;
               END     START   ; PROGRAM EXECUTION BEGINS WITH SYMBOL 'START'
18  ⁎E$$
```

13. I notice that there is an instruction missing in the subroutine; the missing line should be immediately after the one having the label L3, which means that the pointer must be positioned at the start of the following line, so I use the F command to find the operation code of the following instruction. But there was another JNZ before the one I wanted.
14. I use the L (line) command to move the pointer past the JNZ that I do not want, and use F again. This time the desired instruction is found.
15. I insert the entire line, including a carriage return, then hit ESC twice.
16. Now I notice an error earlier in the program. I could use L with a negative argument to back up, but the program is short enough that there is no time penalty in simply going back to the beginning and then using an S. (I am reasonably sure that the combination AROIU does not occur elsewhere in the program).
17. Now I move the pointer to the beginning again and ask for 50 lines to be typed. I do not really know how many lines there are, but there are certainly less than 50, so I get the entire program.
18. All seems to be in order, so I use the E (exit) command to store the program on diskette (under the name used with the ISIS EDIT command at the beginning), and return to ISIS.

2. Assembling

A listing of the program is shown in Figure 10.7 which shows a listing produced by the assembler, which contains the assembled machine language instructions and line numbers, as well as everything that was in the source program as we entered it. We shall study the program from this listing version; it will be more meaningful to discuss the assembly process after that.

The headings above the program are as follows: LOC is the location where the assembled instruction would be loaded if the program started at location zero; OBJ is the assembled object program instruction; SEQ is the sequence number, which we more commonly call the line number; SOURCE STATEMENT is what we wrote, reproduced exactly from the source program.

On every line, anything after a semicolon is taken as a comment. It is carried along to the listing, but has no effect on the assembly. Thus, any line that begins with a semicolon is entirely a comment. We see that no code is ever generated for such a line.

Line 4, the first one that has any effect on the assembler, establishes a meaning for the symbol CO, which is the entry point for the console output routine in the monitor. With the symbol CO equated to the hex address 0F809, any appearance of that symbol in the program will be replaced with the numerical address. We see that this has been done in the CALL instruction on line 15.

Line 5 says that this entire program is to be a code segment (CSEG) which means that it can be relocated. In brief, it will be possible, using the LOCATE command, to put the assembled program anywhere in memory that we please. This is very useful in product development, when we may not know as the program is being written where the different segments will fit or, indeed, even how much memory there will be.

Line 6 is a final preliminary instruction to the assembler, this time giving the maximum length of the 8080 stack so that appropriate memory space can be allocated. In this extremely simple program, the stack is never more than 2 bytes in length, so we specify that stack length.

Line 7 is the first instruction. In its label field we see START; we will be able later (line 28) to refer to this location symbolically without having any idea now what the actual memory location of the instruction may turn out to be. The operation code LXI means load register pair immediate, and in the operand field we see that the stack pointer is being loaded with the stack origin address using the reserved word STACK. Following the semicolon, a comment explains the purpose of the instruction.

The instructions on lines 8 and 9 also have labels since we need to refer to them from elsewhere in the program, but the CALL instruction in line 10 does not. The CALL invokes the subroutine named DELAY, which starts in line 20, transferring control to that location after placing on the stack the

ISIS-II 8080/8085 MACRO ASSEMBLER, V2.0   MODULE   PAGE   1

```
LOC     OBJ        SEQ           SOURCE STATEMENT

                    1           ;AN ASSEMBLY LANGUAGE PROGRAM TO SEND THE LETTER 'X'
                    2           ;TO THE CONSOLE OUTPUT DEVICE, ONCE EACH SECOND
                    3           ;
F809                4      CO    EQU     0F809H    ; PROVIDE ADDRESS OF CO ROUTINE IN MONITOR
                    5            CSEG              ; MAKE THE SEGMENT RELOCATABLE
                    6            STKLN   2         ; SET STACK LENGTH
0000  310000  S     7  START: LXI     SP,STACK  ; INITIALIZE STACK POINTER
0003  1632          8  L1:    MVI     D,50      ; WILL CALL DELAY SUBROUTINE 50 TIMES
0005  3EC8          9  L2:    MVI     A,200     ; SUBROUTINE PARAMETER
0007  CD1600  C    10         CALL    DELAY     ; INVOKE SUBROUTINE
000A  15           11         DCR     D
000B  C20500  C    12         JNZ     L2        ; 50 TIMES AROUND THIS LOOP = 1 SEC
                   13         ;
000E  0E58         14         MVI     C,'X'     ; SEND 'X' TO CONSOLE OUTPUT DEVICE
0010  CD09F8       15         CALL    CO        ; MONITOR CONSOLE OUTPUT ROUTINE
0013  C30300  C    16         JMP     L1        ; AROUND THE LOOP INDEFINITELY
                   17         ;
                   18         ;THE DELAY SUBROUTINE
                   19         ;
0016  060C         20  DELAY: MVI     B,12
0018  48           21  L3:    MOV     C,B
0019  0D           22  L4:    DCR     C
001A  C21900  C    23         JNZ     L4
001D  3D           24         DCR     A
001E  C21800  C    25         JNZ     L3
0021  C9           26         RET
                   27         ;
0000          C    28         END     START; PROGRAM EXECUTION BEGINS WITH SYMBOL 'START'
```

PUBLIC SYMBOLS

EXTERNAL SYMBOLS

USER SYMBOLS
CO A F809 DELAY C 0016 L1 C 0003 L2 C 0005 L3 C 0018 L4 C 0019 START C 0000

ASSEMBLY COMPLETE, NO ERRORS

Figure 10.7   Assembled 8085 program.

information necessary for the RET (return) instruction at the end of the subroutine to get back to the instruction after the CALL. The rest of the program follows similar patterns.

The last line of the program is an END, which must always be present to inform the assembler that nothing else follows. The START in its operand field causes program execution to begin with the instruction having that label, when the program is loaded.

The Assembly Process

When we began editing the program, we gave it the name :F1:ONESEC.SRC. The :F1: specifies diskette unit 1: ONESEC is the name of the file; and SRC is the extension, which stands for source. When we want to assemble the program, we use the ISIS command for the assembler we want, ASM80, ASM48, and so on, depending on the microprocessor on which the program will run. We might use the command

    ASM80:F1:ONESEC.SRC

There are two output files from this process, both on the same diskette as the source program, and both having the same name, but different extensions. The file :F1:ONESEC.LST is the listing file, which is what was shown in Figure 10.7. On the left side of this listing are the machine instructions assembled from the source program, in relocatable form since we made a CSEG (code segment) of the program. The instructions that will have to be modified when the program is relocated are marked with a C.

Relocation

The second file that results from assembly is :F1:ONESEC.OBJ which contains the object program instructions—essentially what we see on the left side of the listing, formatted to be acceptable by the LOCATE program (and the LINK program, as we shall consider later). In other words, the output of assembly is called an object program, but it is not quite ready for execution.

Converting the relocatable object program into an absolute version ready to be executed is the function of the ISIS program called LOCATE. In our case we might enter the ISIS command

    LOCATE:F1:ONESEC.OBJ CODE (4000H)

This identifies the file to be processed, and specifies that the program is to be prepared for loading into absolute memory location 4000 hexadecimal. If needed, we could also specify the absolute location of the stack, the data (of which we have none in this program), and the free memory area

Intel Development Systems   405

(ditto). The output of this command is a final file, identified as

:F1:ONESEC

that is, it has no extension. This file is now ready to be executed simply by entering its name, which makes it, in effect, a command.

If you entered the program while studying the text editor section, all you need do is enter the commands just described.

3. Linking
Since we have only one program, the ISIS LINKER is not required here.

4. Emulating
We will use the program of Figure 10.8 which is a modified version of Figure 10.7 and contains a coding error. The paragraphs of Figure 10.9 are numbered and are explained below.

1. Prior to the operation shown here, I execute the ISIS command ICE85. ICE85 responds with a prompting asterisk. I execute the ICE85 command

    LIST:F1:ONESEC.ICE

    which causes all subsequent terminal material, whether typed by me or produced by ICE85, to be sent to the listing file named. I later print this file. I use the MAP command to specify that the block starting at the logical address 2000 (hex assumed by default) is to be placed in Intellec memory starting at 7000. Since I do not specify otherwise, this is a 2K block. I also map a block of specified length, F000 to FFFF, into the same address in Intellec memory, since my program uses the monitor, and likewise map the block starting at zero. ICE85 warns me that I am mapping over the system, but since it is precisely the system I am trying to get at anyway, I am not worried. The I/O ports that are used by the C0 routine that my program calls are mapped to the Intellec; I have no option to map these into any other port numbers. Note that anything following a semicolon is treated as a comment, just as with the assembler.

2. I use the LOAD command to bring my program (ONESEC) in from the diskette on drive 1.

3. I use the SYMBOLS command to see the symbols (and their corresponding values, memory addresses in this case) that were brought in with the program when it was loaded. These symbols are available because I used the DEBUG option when I assembled the program. The line MODULE ..MODULE means that the name of the object program

406 Chapter 10 POPULAR MICROCOMPUTER DEVELOPMENT SYSTEMS

```
ISIS-II 8080/8085 MACRO ASSEMBLER, V2.0          MODULE    PAGE   1

LOC   OBJ            SEQ      SOURCE STATEMENT

                      1       ; AN ASSEMBLY LANGUAGE PROGRAM TO SEND THE LETTER 'X'
                      2       ; TO THE CONSOLE OUTPUT DEVICE, ONCE EACH SECOND
                      3       ;
F809                  4   CO       EQU     0F809H    ; PROVIDE ADDRESS OF CO ROUTINE IN MONITOR
                      5            CSEG              ; MAKE THE SEGMENT RELOCATABLE
                      6            STKLN   2         ; SET STACK LENGTH
0000 310000      S    7   START:   LXI     SP,STACK  ; INITIALIZE STACK POINTER
0003 1632             8   L1:      MVI     D,50      ; WILL CALL DELAY SUBROUTINE 50 TIMES
0005 3EC8             9            MVI     A,200     ; SUBROUTINE PARAMETER
0007 CD1600      C   10            CALL    DELAY     ; INVOKE SUBROUTINE
000A 15              11            DCR     D
000B C20500      C   12            JNZ     L2        ; 50 TIMES AROUND THIS LOOP = 1 SEC
                     13       ;
000E 0E58            14            MVI     C,'X'     ; SEND 'X' TO CONSOLE OUTPUT DEVICE
0010 CD09F8      C   15            CALL    CO        ; MONITOR CONSOLE OUTPUT ROUTINE
0013 C30300      C   16            JMP     L1        ; AROUND THE LOOP INDEFINITELY
                     17       ;
                     18       ; THE DELAY SUBROUTINE
                     19       ;
0016 060C            20   DELAY:   MVI     B,12
0018 48              21   L3:      MOV     C,B
0019 0D              22            DCR     C
001A C21900      C   23            JNZ     L4
001D 3D              24            DCR     A
001E C21800      C   25            JNZ     L3
0021 C9              26            RET
                     27       ;
0000             C   28            END     START     ; PROGRAM EXECUTION BEGINS WITH SYMBOL 'START'

PUBLIC SYMBOLS

EXTERNAL SYMBOLS

USER SYMBOLS
CO    A F809        DELAY  C 0016    L1   C 0003   L2  C 0005   L3  C 0018   L4  C 0019   START  C 0000

ASSEMBLY COMPLETE,  NO ERRORS
```

Figure 10.8

```
 1  ::MAP 2000 = INTELLEC 7000  ; LOWEST INTELLEC ADDRESS ALLOWED
    ::MAP F000 TO FFFF = INTELLEC F000 ; MONITOR
    ::MAP 0 = INTELLEC 0 ; MONITOR NEEDS THIS
    WARN C1:MAPPING OVER SYSTEM
    ::MAP IO F0 TO FF = INTELLEC
 2  ::LOAD :F1:ONESEC
 3  ::SYMBOLS
    MODULE ..MODULE
    .C0=F809H
    .DELAY=2016H
    .L1=2003H
    .L2=2005H
    .L3=2018H
    .L4=2019H
    .START=2000H
 4  ::PC  ; LOADED FROM FILE?
    2000H
 5  ::GO
    EMULATION BEGUN
 6  EMULATION TERMINATED, PC=2019H
    PROCESSING ABORTED
 7  ::REGISTERS
    P=2019H S=202EH A=07H F=14H B=0CH C=0AH D=27H E=00H H=00H L=00H I=00H
 8  ::DEFINE .L2A = .DELAY - 8
    ::; THAT'S A LABEL ON "MVI C,'X'"
 9  ::SYMBOLS
    .L2A=200EH
    MODULE ..MODULE
    .C0=F809H
    .DELAY=2016H
    .L1=2003H
    .L2=2005H
    .L3=2018H
    .L4=2019H
    .START=2000H
10  ::BYTE .L2A LENGTH 2 ; DISPLAY INSTRUCTION AT THAT ADDRESS
    200EH=0EH 58H
11  ::GO FROM .START TILL .L2A EXECUTED
    EMULATION BEGUN
12  EMULATION TERMINATED, PC=2010H
13  ::RC ; SHOULD HAVE JUST LOADED 'X'
    58H
14  ::BASE = ASCII ; LET'S SEE IT IN ASCII
15  ::RC
    X
16  ::BASE = H
17  ::PRINT -20 ; LOOK AT TRACE
        ADDR INSTRUCTION ADDR-S-DA ADDR-S-DA ADDR-S-DA ADDR-S-DA
    0947: 2019 DCR C
    0949: 201A JNZ  2019
    0955: 2019 DCR C
    0957: 201A JNZ  2019
    0963: 2019 DCR C
    0965: 201A JNZ  2019
    0971: 2019 DCR C
    0973: 201A JNZ  2019
    0979: 2019 DCR C
    0981: 201A JNZ  2019
    0987: 2019 DCR C
    0989: 201A JNZ  2019
    0995: 2019 DCR C
```

Figure 10.9

408   Chapter 10   POPULAR MICROCOMPUTER DEVELOPMENT SYSTEMS

```
        0997: 201A JNZ
        1001: 201D DCR A
        1003: 201E JNZ
        1007: 2021 RET            202E-R-0A 202F-R-20
        1013: 200A DCR D
        1015: 200B JNZ
        1019: 200E MVI C, 58
18    ✻GO FROM .START TILL .DELAY EXECUTED
      EMULATION BEGUN
19    EMULATION TERMINATED, PC=2018H
20    ✻WORD SP    ; WORD AT TOP OF STACK
      202EH=200AH
      ✻; 200AH IS RETURN ADDRESS OF 'DELAY'
21    ✻RD = 50T
22    ✻ENABLE DUMP CALL RETURN
23    ✻BYTE (.L2+1) = 2 ; CHANGE DELAY PARAMETER
24    ✻STEP FROM .START TILL RD < 47T
      EMULATION BEGUN
        2007-E-CD 2008-R-16 2009-R-20 202F-W-20 202E-W-0A
      P=2016H S=202EH A=02H F=54H B=0CH C=58H D=32H E=00H H=00H L=00H I=00H
        2021-E-C9 202E-R-0A 202F-R-20
      P=200AH S=2030H A=00H F=54H B=0CH C=00H D=32H E=00H H=00H L=00H I=00H
        2007-E-CD 2008-R-16 2009-R-20 202F-W-20 202E-W-0A
      P=2016H S=202EH A=02H F=10H B=0CH C=00H D=31H E=00H H=00H L=00H I=00H
        2021-E-C9 202E-R-0A 202F-R-20
      P=200AH S=2030H A=00H F=54H B=0CH C=00H D=31H E=00H H=00H L=00H I=00H
        2007-E-CD 2008-R-16 2009-R-20 202F-W-20 202E-W-0A
      P=2016H S=202EH A=02H F=14H B=0CH C=00H D=30H E=00H H=00H L=00H I=00H
        2021-E-C9 202E-R-0A 202F-R-20
      P=200AH S=2030H A=00H F=54H B=0CH C=00H D=30H E=00H H=00H L=00H I=00H
        2007-E-CD 2008-R-16 2009-R-20 202F-W-20 202E-W-0A
      P=2016H S=202EH A=02H F=00H B=0CH C=00H D=2FH E=00H H=00H L=00H I=00H
        2021-E-C9 202E-R-0A 202F-R-20
      P=200AH S=2030H A=00H F=54H B=0CH C=00H D=2FH E=00H H=00H L=00H I=00H
      EMULATION TERMINATED, PC=200BH
25    ✻MAP
      SHARED
      0000=I 0000       0800=G         1000=G         1800=G
      2000=I 7000       2800=G         3000=G         3800=G
      4000=G            4800=G         5000=G         5800=G
      6000=G            6800=G         7000=G         7800=G
      8000=G            8800=G         9000=G         9800=G
      A000=G            A800=G         B000=G         B800=G
      C000=G            C800=G         D000=G         D800=G
      E000=G            E800=G         F000=I F000    F800=I F800
      ✻
26    ✻RESET HARDWARE ; WE CHANGED ICE HARDWARE CONFIGURATION, NOW USING SDK-85
27    ✻MAP 2000 = USER
28    ✻BYTE 2000 = IBYTE 7000 TO 7023 ; MOVE PROGRAM FROM INTELLEC TO SDK MEMORY
29    ✻MAP
      SHARED
      0000=I 0000       0800=G         1000=G         1800=G
      2000=U            2800=G         3000=G         3800=G
      4000=G            4800=G         5000=G         5800=G
      6000=G            6800=G         7000=G         7800=G
      8000=G            8800=G         9000=G         9800=G
      A000=G            A800=G         B000=G         B800=G
      C000=G            C800=G         D000=G         D800=G
      E000=G            E800=G         F000=I F000    F800=I F800
      ✻;STILL BORROWING INTELLEC MEMORY FOR MONITOR
```

Figure 10.9   Continued

Intel Development Systems 409

```
30 *BYTE 2000 TO 2023 ; VERIFY MOVE WORKED
   2000H=31H 30H 20H 16H 32H 3EH 02H CDH 16H 20H 15H C2H 05H 20H 0EH 58H
   2010H=CDH 09H F8H C3H 03H 20H 06H 0CH 48H 0DH C2H 19H 20H 3DH C2H 18H
   2020H=20H C9H 0AH 72H
   *GO FROM .START
   EMULATION BEGUN
31 EMULATION TERMINATED, PC=0024H
   *GO FROM .START FOREVER
   EMULATION BEGUN
32 EMULATION TERMINATED, PC=2018H
33 *GO FROM .START FOREVER
   EMULATION BEGUN
34 EMULATION TERMINATED, PC=2019H
   PROCESSING ABORTED
35 *BYTE (.L2+1) = 200T ;RESTORE DELAY PARAMETER
36 *GO FROM .START
   EMULATION BEGUN
37 EMULATION TERMINATED, PC=2019H
   PROCESSING ABORTED
38 *EXIT
39 *MAP 4000 = INTELLEC 7000
   *MAP F000 TO FFFF = INTELLEC F000
   *MAP 0 = INTELLEC 0
   WARN C1:MAPPING OVER SYSTEM
   *MAP IO F0 TO FF = INTELLEC
40 *LOAD :F1:ONEERR
41 *SYMBOLS
   MODULE ..MODULE
   .CO=F809H
   .CHAR=4028H
   .DELAY=401CH
   .L1=4006H
   .L2=4008H
   .L3=401EH
   .L4=401FH
   .START=4000H
42 *GO
   EMULATION BEGUN
43 EMULATION TERMINATED, PC=4020H
   PROCESSING ABORTED
   *; CHARACTERS CAME OUT, BUT ALL WRONG
44 *GO FROM .START TILL .CO EXECUTED
   EMULATION BEGUN
45 EMULATION TERMINATED, PC=FD1DH
46 *PRINT -3
         ADDR INSTRUCTION ADDR-S-DA ADDR-S-DA ADDR-S-DA ADDR-S-DA
   1003: 4011 MOV C,M      4028-R-41
   1007: 4012 CALL   F809  4036-W-40 4035-W-15
   1017: F809 JMP    FD1D
47 *GO ; SAME BREAK CONDITION AS BEFORE
   EMULATION BEGUN
   EMULATION TERMINATED, PC=FD1DH
48 *PRINT -3
         ADDR INSTRUCTION ADDR-S-DA ADDR-S-DA ADDR-S-DA ADDR-S-DA
   1003: 4011 MOV C,M      4029-R-00
   1007: 4012 CALL   F809  4036-W-40 4035-W-15
   1017: F809 JMP    FD1D
49 *GO ; SAME BREAK CONDITION AS BEFORE
   EMULATION BEGUN
   EMULATION TERMINATED, PC=FD1DH
```

Figure 10.9 Continued

Chapter 10 POPULAR MICROCOMPUTER DEVELOPMENT SYSTEMS

```
50 *PRINT -3
        ADDR  INSTRUCTION  ADDR-S-DA  ADDR-S-DA  ADDR-S-DA  ADDR-S-DA
   1003: 4011 MOV C,M      4029-R-00
   1007: 4012 CALL  F809   4036-W-40  4035-W-15
   1017: F809 JMP   FD1D
   *GO
   EMULATION BEGUN
   EMULATION TERMINATED, PC=FD1DH
   *PRINT -3
        ADDR  INSTRUCTION  ADDR-S-DA  ADDR-S-DA  ADDR-S-DA  ADDR-S-DA
   1003: 4011 MOV C,M      402A-R-00
   1007: 4012 CALL  F809   4036-W-40  4035-W-15
   1017: F809 JMP   FD1D
51 *STEP TILL RHL = 402B
   EMULATION BEGUN
   EMULATION TERMINATED, PC=4019H
52 *PRINT -5
        ADDR  INSTRUCTION  ADDR-S-DA  ADDR-S-DA  ADDR-S-DA  ADDR-S-DA
   0999: FD43 MOV A,C
   1001: FD44 OUT   F6     F6F6-O-00
   1007: FD46 RET          4035-R-15  4036-R-40
   1013: 4015 LXI B, 0001
   1019: 4018 DAD B
53 *BYTE 4015 = C6,01,77,00   ; PATCH THE FIX
54 *GO FROM .START FOREVER
   EMULATION BEGUN
55 EMULATION TERMINATED, PC=401FH
   PROCESSING ABORTED
56 *EXIT
```

Figure 10.9 Continued

module is "MODULE"; this was assigned as a default name because I did not specify otherwise in the LOCATE operation.

4. I ask to see the value of the Program Counter (PC). It should have been loaded with the value of the symbol START, because I put that symbol on the END operation in my program. It has indeed been loaded as desired.
5. I say GO, which is the simplest possible emulation command. My program runs as expected, at full speed, producing X's on the CRT (which is the console output device on the microcomputer development system I am using). Since this is program output rather than ICE85 dialog, it does not show on the listing.
6. I press the ESC (escape) key on the console. ICE85 responds with the address (in the PC) of the next instruction that would have been executed if I had not interrupted the program.
7. I ask to see the registers as they stand at this point. The program counter is as noted; the stack pointer is two less than its starting value, which is right since there had been one PUSH in connection with the CALL; the A register has been decremented from its starting value; the flags I do not care about; the B register contains the 12 (decimal) placed in it at the beginning of the DELAY subroutine; the E, H, and L

registers have not been used; the interrupt register I do not care about.
8. I define a new symbol, L2A, to be an address in the program at which I would like to terminate a later emulation. Note that a period must appear before every symbol, and that expressions may be used in defining symbols.
9. Now when I ask to see my symbols the new one is there. It is shown at the beginning of the listing to indicate that it is not among the symbols brought in with the module.
10. I ask for a display of the bytes beginning with the byte at the symbol just defined, with a length of two bytes. The purpose is to be sure that I defined the symbol properly, and that it does point to the instruction I intended. All is in order.
11. Now I begin emulation again, telling ICE85 to begin execution with the instruction at START rather than picking up where the program was interrupted earlier, and to stop when the instruction beginning at L2A has been executed.
12. When emulation is terminated, the program counter is pointing at the instruction after the one at L2A.
13. The command RC displays the contents of the C register, which should just have been loaded with the letter X. ICE85 responds with the hex value.
14. I could look this up, but instead I change the base to ASCII, so that the character will be printed out in its external form.
15. Now when I ask for the contents of the C register, I get the letter X as such.
16. I restore the base to hex.
17. I ask for the 20 instructions most recently executed to be printed. (I could also have asked for the last 20 machine cycles, or machine states; instructions is the default.) ICE85 responds with the instructions, oldest listed first, in "disassembled" form, that is, with mnemonic operation codes and register names rather than just hex bytes. The numbers at the extreme left are the trace buffer addresses, which do not concern us. The locations of the instructions and their mnemonic operation codes are shown. When a jump condition was satisfied the jump address appears, and otherwise not. For any instruction having a memory reference, the address and contents are shown, together with an indication whether the memory reference was a read (R), input (I), output (O) or write (W). The only memory references in this trace are to the stack, in the RET at 2021; we see that the return address (200A) was retrieved from the stack (202E and 202F).
18. I ask to begin again at the beginning, and stop after the instruction at DELAY is executed.
19. Emulation stops as requested.

20. I ask to see the stack pointer and the word at the top of the stack. That word is pointing to the instruction after the CALL or DELAY, as it should.
21. To prepare for what I want to do next, I set the contents of D register to 50 decimal (T for base ten).
22. I enable the DUMP operation, specifying that I want to dump the state of the machine after each CALL and RETURN.
23. In order to permit the testing and displaying that are required in the DUMP operation, the program will have to be able to run one STEP at a time. Such execution is much slower than real time. To speed up the program, I change the parameter in the DELAY call. Note the use of an expression in naming a byte to be changed, with enclosing parentheses.
24. For every CALL and RETURN executed until the contents of the D register have been reduced below 47, DUMP gives me the information shown. Note that the contents of the D register start at 32H = 50 decimal, and work down to 2FH = 47 decimal, as desired.
25. Now I want to transfer my program to prototype memory. I decide to check the memory mapping. All blocks are guarded (not defined) except the four blocks I mapped to Intellec memory.
26. I plug the ICE85 umbilical cable into an SDK-85 board, which contains enough memory for my program. This can be thought of as a prototype system. Connecting the cable requires resetting the hardware, which means to let ICE85 reinitialize its description of the hardware configuration.
27. I map the 2K block at 2000 to user memory.
28. I transfer the program from Intellec memory (actual physical location) to my "user memory" on the SDK-85 board, in actual locations 2000 and following, which is where this version of the program was LOCATEd to run.
29. The memory mapping now shows that the block at 2000 is user memory. The memory corresponding to the Intellec monitor is still being borrowed from the Intellec memory, and the input and output facilities are still borrowed.
30. Not quite convinced, I ask to see the contents of the memory locations where my program should be. It is there.
31. I start the program, which is now executing from a combination of user and Intellec memory.
32. The program stops under the same condition as given in step 24, which ICE85 remembers, to save me the trouble of repeating the condition if I want it to apply again.
33. But I do not, so I give the GO command with a FOREVER to wipe out the previous stopping condition.

Intel Development Systems 413

34. The program works just fine, except that the X's are sent out much too rapidly. I use the ESC key to abort emulation.
35. The problem is the DELAY parameter that I changed in step 23. I put it back to its original value.
36. Starting at the beginning now gives the expected behavior of one X per second.
37. I am done, so I interrupt the program.
38. And exit from ICE85.
39. I do the necessary memory mapping, taking into account that this program was LOCATEd to run in 4000.
40. I load the program.
41. I ask for the program symbols.
42. I start the program.
43. The program works, after a fashion: the letter A is followed by random characters having no obvious relation to one another.
44. Detective work is required. I decide to stop emulation at the nearest convenient point after the loading of the character into the C register on line 18; execution of C0 will do.
45. Execution terminates with the program counter in high memory, which is the monitor where C0 is located.
46. I ask to see the three most recently executed instructions. The interesting one is the MOV, which read (R) from 4028 and obtained 41 hex, which is an A. All seems to be in order.
47. I say GO, without naming a break condition; the previous one (TILL.C0 EXECUTED) is still in effect.
48. The MOV instruction now is highly suspicious: It obtains a character from 2049, whereas my intention in writing the program was that it should obtain a modified character from 2048. What is going on?
49. Try again.
50. The MOV address is still being modified.
51. If the program is really doing this, the H and L registers should contain 402B the next time around this loop. Let us STEP through the program until the combined registers contain this address.
52. There it is! Time for a hard look at the program. Sure enough, I have written it to modify the contents of the HL register instead of the contents of the address pointed to by the HL register. The old programming 101 confusion between address and contents!
53. To see if this really is the trouble, I program a 4-byte fix in hex and enter the change in absolute. Naturally, I will later go back and correct the source program and reassemble.
54. I start the corrected program.
55. Everything works as intended. I interrupt emulation.
56. And exit from ICE85.

10.3 Tektronix Development Systems

All of Tektronix's MDSs are universal and together they provide developmental support for 26 microprocessors and microcomputers including 8086, Z8000, and 68000. These systems all use master/slave architecture. The Tektronix 8001, 8002A, 8540, 8550, and 8560 will now be described.

10.3.1 Tektronix 8001 Microprocessor Development Lab (MDL)

The 8001 MDL (Figure 10.10) is designed to be the logical choice for those who have a host computer which is only capable of microcomputer software development, but who want to add in-circuit emulation. The 8001 comes with its own software command set that enables the unit to accept software downloaded from another computer, and then to execute this software using one of three emulation modes. The 8001 uses two RS232 links for serial data transfer to and from the local CRT terminal as well as the host computer. We now describe the three emulation modes.

Emulation Mode 0 (Figure 10.11)

This mode does not use any external prototype hardware. The host computer downloads the machine program into the 8001 and it is executed within the 8001 on the emulator processor. Since this mode does not use any prototype hardware all I/O takes place using system peripherals.

Emulation Mode 1 (Figure 10.12)

This mode includes the prototype hardware in the emulation process. The prototype's microprocessor is unplugged from its socket and the 8001's prototype control probe is plugged in. The prototype hardware provides the clock and I/O but the 8001's emulator processor executes the code. The

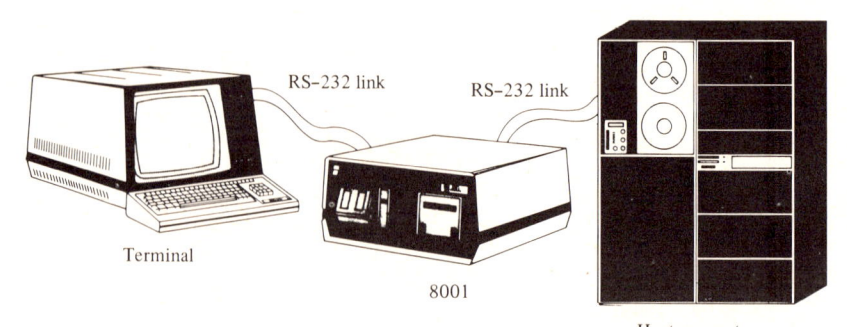

Figure 10.10 Standard 8001 host computer setup. Source: Courtesy Tektronix, Inc., © 1980.

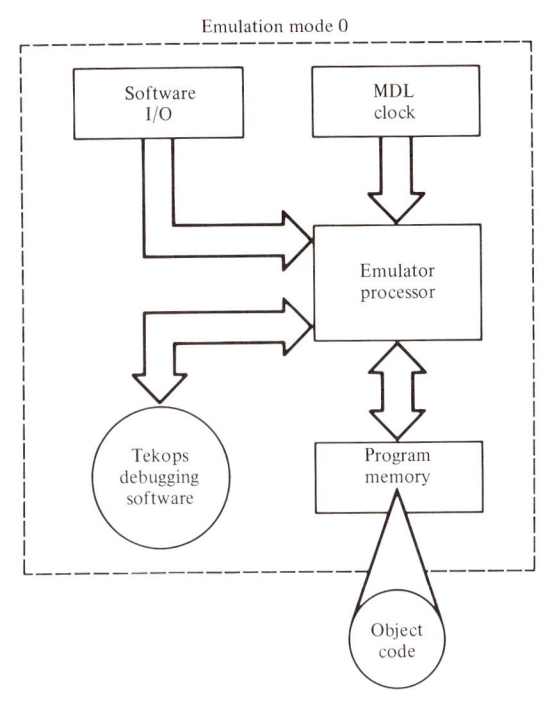

Figure 10.11

Figure 10.11 8001 MDL (mode 0) (does not require prototype). Source: Courtesy Tektronix, Inc., © 1980.

program can be in either emulation RAM (in 128-byte blocks) or in prototype RAM.

Emulation Mode 2 (Figure 10.13)

This mode is the same as mode 1 except that no emulator RAM or I/O is used. All program data and I/O functions are contained in the prototype.

The advantage of emulation is that program control is always under software control of the 8001, which has the following debugging features: Breakpoints may be set, program flow may be traced, and register contents can be monitored and changed at will.

As an optional feature (modes 1 and 2) a Real-Time Prototype Analyzer (RTPZ) with 36 internal and 8 external channels is available.

The Downloading Process

The software in the 8001 allows for the CRT terminal to be used in two different modes. In the first mode the CRT terminal communicates directly with the host computer and appears to be the same as any other computer terminal. This allows the person operating the 8001 to use all of

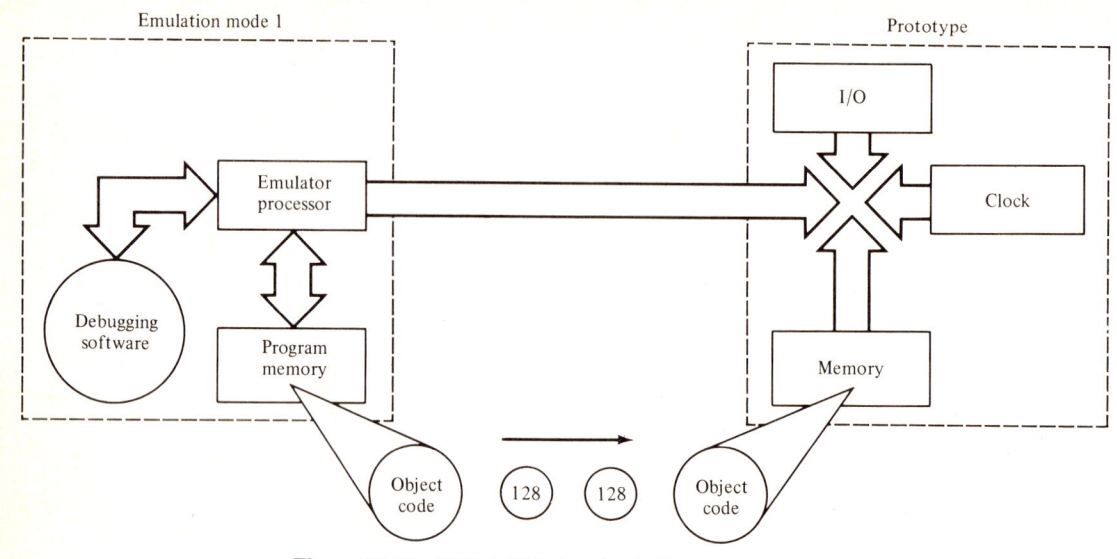

416 CHAPTER 10 POPULAR MICROCOMPUTER DEVELOPMENT SYSTEMS

Figure 10.12 8001 MDL (mode 1). Source: Courtesy Tektronix, Inc., © 1980.

the software development programs that are on the host computer as if they were part of the 8001. To do this the 8001 must be given the COMM command. Then the programmer can develop his software just as if he had a stand-alone MDS.

In this mode the 8001 acts as the interface between the CRT terminal

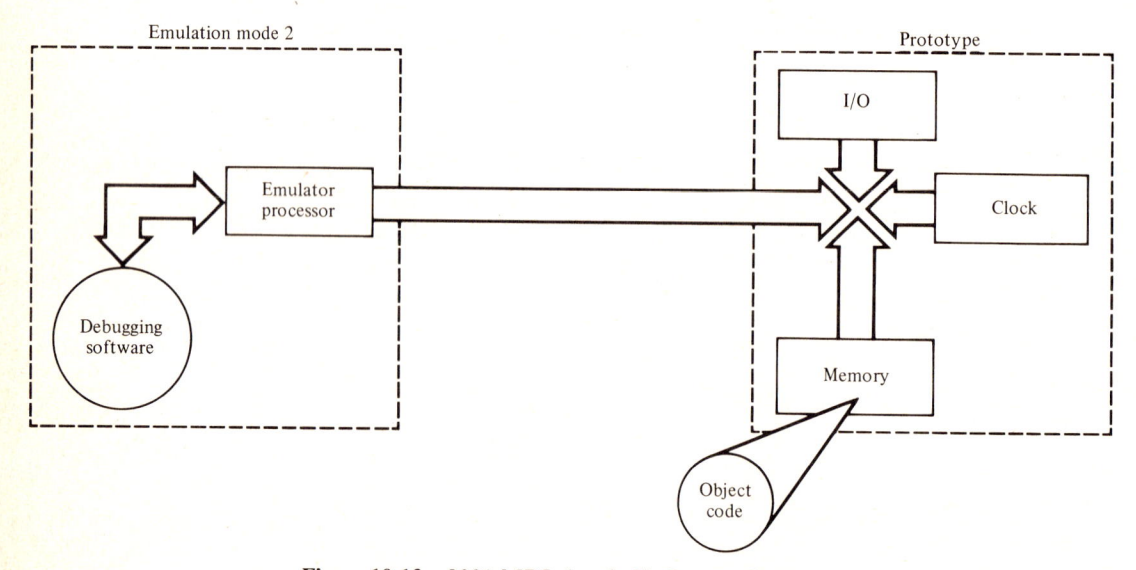

Figure 10.13 8001 MDL (mode 2). Source: Courtesy Tektronix, Inc., © 1980.

and the host computer. The 8001 must have flexible hardware and software interface capabilities in order to be able to interface to a variety of host computers. The 8001 communications module uses a RS232C compatible serial data port, and can select between all standard baud rates from 110 to 2400 bits per second by means of a jumper. The 8001 can also be adapted to the host computer's software requirements for peripheral communication. The 8001's COMM command has a set of user-specified parameters which include echo (local or remote), line feed (included or omitted), prompt sequence (up to six characters), turnaround time (0 to 25.5 s), and parity (8 different combinations).

The programmer develops the object code file, and downloads it from the host computer to the 8001. Since the 8001 and the host computer may be communicating over a long wire the host computer encodes each data block in a format that allows the 8001 to detect errors. This format is called TEKHEX. The host computer must have a program which converts the pure object code file into the TEKHEX format.

The 8001 uses handshake I/O and the host computer must also have a handshake program. The 8001 decodes each incoming data block and stores the pure object code in the 8001 program memory. Before the code can be executed the CRT terminal must be taken out of the COMM mode through a (NULL) (ESC) command. The 8001 software now uses the CRT to monitor the debugging process. The uploading process is very similar to the downloading process.

The 8001 is especially cost effective when the equivalent power of a series of dedicated stand-alone MDSs is needed. For example, the host computer's central disk unit can cost-effectively replace the many, independent floppy disk units required by multiple stand-alone MDSs. Also, a single high-speed printer is more cost effective than multiple medium-speed printers.

Another very important consideration in favor of the host approach is increased labor efficiency. Each nonuniversal MDS has a unique command language the user must learn. This represents a financial loss for the employer because it takes time for the engineers to learn each new system. As a host 8001 user changes from one microprocessor to another, he needs to learn only the new processor's instruction set. All 8001 and host commands stay the same.

10.3.2 Tektronix 8002A

The 8002A (Figure 10.14) Microprocessor Lab is a universal microprocessor software development system and can support 26 microprocessors. Separate assembler software and emulators must be brought for each different microprocessor. The 8002A main frame can hold up to 20 cards. The 8002A system comes with 32K of program memory and a dual floppy

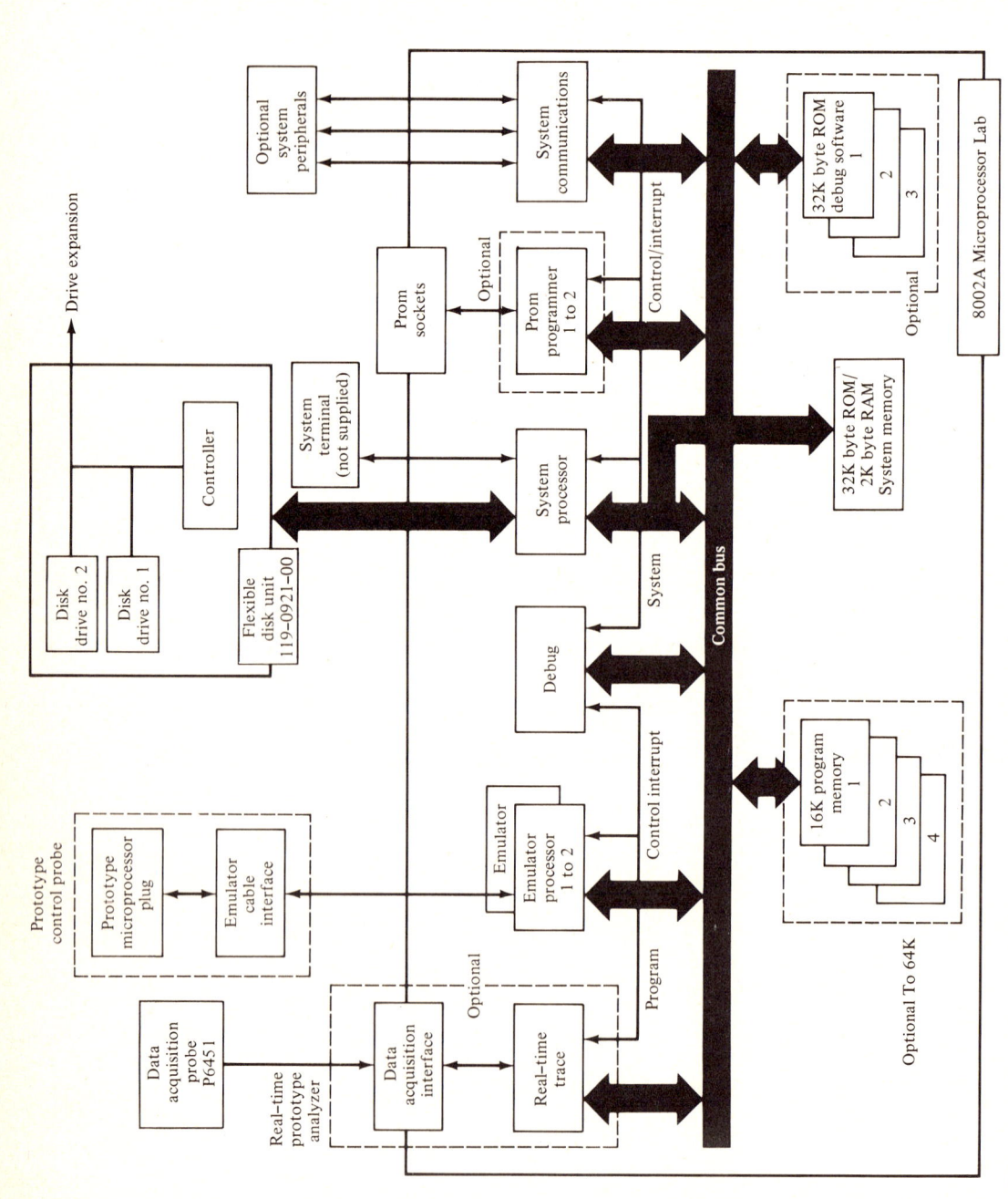

Figure 10.14 8002A simplified block diagram. Source: Courtesy Tektronix, Inc., © 1980.

disk unit. The LP8200 Line Printer and the 4024/4025 Computer Display Terminal are optional peripherals.

The 8002A operating system software is superior to most and includes a powerful text editor, macrorelocatable assembler, debugging programs; three levels of emulation for software debugging, and a real-time analyzer option. (The latter two features are the same as for the 8001).

Tekdos is the disk-operating system for the 8002 and contains floppy disk and file utility functions, data transfer functions, and system/peripheral device control functions. Tekdos also supervises the text editor, assembler, and linker programs, and the optional emulation support, debugging system, and PROM programming routines.

Even though the text editor is line oriented (not character oriented) it does offer several convenient features for program modification. Macros are allowed. Tekdos has a single command to merge all program files.

The new assembly software for each type of microprocessor is installed with a change to the appropriate floppy disk. Tekdos must be modified for each new microprocessor (the linker and relocating assembler with macros are changed). The 8002A and 8001 both have emulator modes 0, 1, and 2, as well as the RTPA option.

The 8002A system includes the following modules: a system processor, debug card, system memory, program memory, system communications, and assembler processor card. Optional modules include an emulator processor and prototype control probe, real-time analyzer, two 16K-byte program memory cards, and an EPROM programmer module for the 2704/2708.

The system processor is controlled by the user inputs from the console and functions as the control for the 8002A. It has its own I/O port to the keyboard and controls the systems communications module to perform all peripheral I/P functions. It also controls the debug module which, in turn, controls the emulator processors through the system bus.

The debug module interfaces between the system processor and the emulator processor and also supports all software debug features.

The system processor has its own private system memory which contains 256K bytes of ROM (system bootstrap), and 16K of RAM.

Program memory (32K bytes of RAM) is shared by the system and emulator processors and may be expanded to 64K using 16K modules.

The systems communications module has three RS232 compatible ports for interface with the Tektronix LP8200 Line Printer, CRT display, and a modem. Baud rates of 110, 300, 600, 1200, or 2400 can be selected for each port. This module has a memory mapping feature which allows the user to direct memory functions to prototype memory or 8002A program memory when in mode 1.

The assembler processor module works with all of the available emulators and serves to translate assembler code into machine code.

The debug and front-panel I/O module separate the system bus from the program bus. Both buses share the same architecture so that if a board works in one bus it will work in the other.

10.3.3 Tektronix 8500 Series MDL

So far there are three systems in the 8500 series: the 8550, 8560, and 8540 systems. The Tek 8500 series offers multivendor chip support: 26 chips in all (including some new 16-bit processors). All three systems are capable of Tek emulation modes 0, 1, and 2 but the 8540 has a self-contained peripheral station to accomplish mode 2 emulation.

The 8500 series uses an emulator processor functionally identical to the one targeted for the prototype system. This is called Real-Time Emulation (RTE) and all the normal debugging features are available.

For 8-bit systems the standard optional Real-Time Prototype Analyzer (RTPA) is offered and for 16-bit systems the Trigger Trace Analyzer (TTA) is offered as an option.

Tektronix offers a complete line of software support for all 26 chips that includes high-level language (selected chips only) and assembly support. The same software is compatible on all the 8500 systems. This includes relocatable assemblers with conditional macros, interactive linkers, and a library generator.

Tek offers two high-level languages, PASCAL and MDL/μ, with special features for microprocessor control.

The 8550 series DOS/50 operating system has several convenience features for program modification. A more advanced screen-oriented editor is offered as an option.

The 8550 Single-User System

The 8550 offers the single-user support for 26 different chips, and consists of two hardware units. The CRT terminal and line printer are optional. The system CPU, optional PROM programmer, and all debugging features are contained in the central control unit or 8301 Microcomputer Development Unit. The other hardware unit houses dual floppy disks and oversees an advanced filing system. This is the 8501 Data Management Unit (DMU).

As already mentioned, two high-level languages (PASCAL and MDL/μ) and two analyzers (RTPA and TTA) are available for all series 8500 systems. Also, all 8500 systems use Tek emulation modes 0, 1, and 2.

The 8550 single-user system can be connected with other Tek MDLs in two ways: (1) via a host computer, and (2) by merging the 8550 components into a Tek 8650 multiuser system.

The 8500 system offers a choice of assembler packages for 29 different chips. The standard assembler features have already been outlined for all 8500 series systems.

Even though each assembler package supports a different chip, the assembler software operations are fundamentally the same for every microprocessor assembler. This makes it easier for the programmer to change from one microprocessor to another. The programmer must know each new microprocessor instruction set but from the 8550 system viewpoint the assembler commands stay the same.

The 8550 offers extended logical, numeric, and string language functions. Data constants may be in binary, octal, decimal, or hexadecimal, or as strings of ASCII characters enclosed in quotes.

The library generator program can be used to create up to 100 object module files. These files can be replaced or modified by inserting or deleting object modules. A command file of common library operations can be made and thereafter used to save time later on.

In addition to its standard functions the linker does the following: (1) a linker memory map which notes conflicting address ranges; (2) a listing of linker activity (commands executed, global and internal symbols used); and linker statistics (number of errors, undefined symbols, modules, sections, and any transfer addresses).

The CT8500 terminal is an optional peripheral and has already been mentioned with reference to the Tek 8001 MDL.

The 8560 Multi-User Development Lab (M-UDL)

The 8560 (Figure 10.15) includes the following:

1. Time-shared software development using low-cost RS232 terminals.
2. Distributed hardware/software integration.
3. 8502 central processing unit.
    a. Hardware—Dec LSI 11/23.
        i. 128K words dynamic memory.
        ii. Up to eight work stations via RS232 or high-speed interface.
        iii. 35 megabytes, 8-in. Winchester disk.
        iv. 1-megabyte floppy disk.
    b. Software—UNIX V7 Time Share Operating System.
        i. Advanced screen-oriented editor.
        ii. PASCAL compilers.
        iii. Relocatable macroassemblers.
        iv. 8550 MDL assembler and source code compatible.

The 8560 can be used to interconnect the 8550 single-user MDL with other Tek MDLs. Various MDLs are interconnected through the portion of

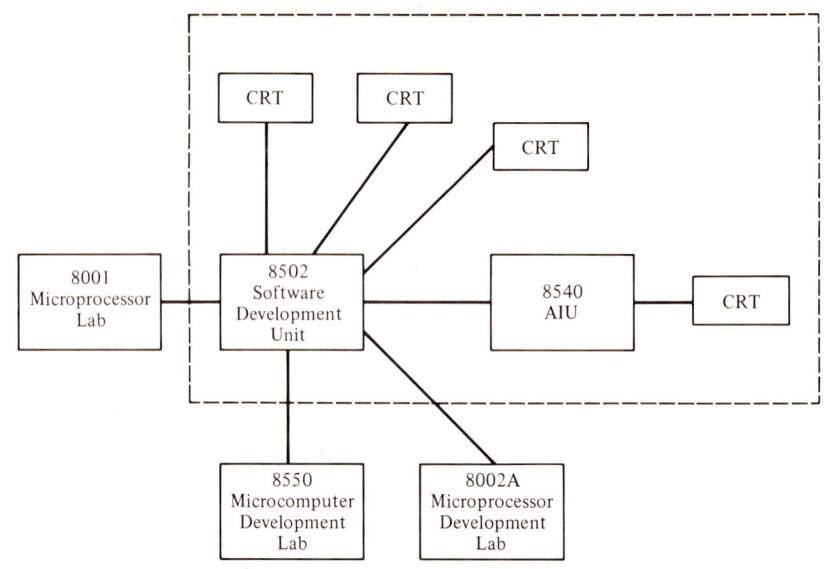

422 Chapter 10 Popular Microcomputer Development Systems

Figure 10.15 The 8560 simplified block diagram along with other MDLs.
Source: Courtesy Tektronix, Inc., © 1980.

the 8560 called the 8502 Software Development Unit, (which will support up to eight work stations). A work station can be either a complete MDL or just a CRT terminal (RS232 compatible) for software development purposes. MDL work stations can be any Tek MDL (8550, 8001, 8002A).

The 8540 Advanced Integration Unit

The 8540 (Figure 10.16) includes the following:

1. Versatile configuration.
   a. Host.
   b. Multiuser.
   c. 8002A expansion.
2. Distributed hardware/software integration unit.
3. ROM-based operating system.
4. Split bus architecture.
5. 24-bit address bus.
6. Supports nine 8- and 16-bit emulators.
7. PROM programmer.
8. Supports Tek trigger trace analyzer.
9. Sophisticated communication package.
   a. RS232 up to 9600 baud (3).
   b. High-speed interface for 8560 configuration.
10. Resident diagnostics.
11. Symbolic debug for assembly code.

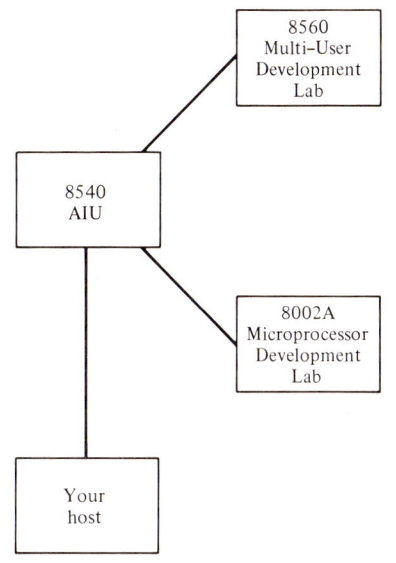

Figure 10.16 The 8540 block diagram along with other MDLs. Source: Courtesy Tektronix, Inc., © 1980.

12. 32K byte/16K word fast static memory module.
13. Compatible with RS232 terminals.
14. Easily configurable communications parameters.
15. Debug features include:
    a. Trace.
    b. Disassembly.
    c. Breakpoints.
    d. Examine and modify registers or memory.
    e. Memory mapping.
    f. Memory write protect (ROM simulation).
    g. Simulated I/O supported in modes 0 and 1 for selected emulators.

Host computers (PDP11, IBM, etc.) can gain emulation capability using the 8540 Advanced Integration Unit (AIU). With the optional trigger trace analyzer installed, the 8540 AIU becomes the most powerful integration tool now available to host system owners. The 8540 AIU is also useful to owners of existing Tek MDLs because it provides expansion capability.

EXAMPLE 10.2

This example shows how to edit, assemble, link, and emulate an 8085 assembly language program (shown below) on the Tektronix 8550 containing a DOS/50 system disk.

Chapter 10 Popular Microcomputer Development Systems

```
              TITLE    "8085  DEMONSTRATION RUN PROGRAM"
              ORG      100H        ;START PROGRAM CODE AT ADDRESS 100
     DEMO     LXI      H,500H      ;SET TABLE POINTER
              MVI      B,5         ;SET PASS COUNTER
              XRA      A           ;CLEAR ACCUMULATOR
     LOOP     ADD      M           ;ADD BYTE FROM TABLE
              INX      H           ;POINT TO NEXT BYTE
              DCR      B           ;DECREMENT PASS COUNTER
              JNZ      LOOP        ;LOOP IF NOT FIVE PASSES YET
              OUT      0F7H        ;OTHERWISE CALL EXIT SVC
              NOP                  ;   TO END PROGRAM EXECUTION
     ;SRB  POINTER
              ORG      40H         ;STORE SRB POINTER AT ADDRESS 40
              BYTE     00,42H      ;POINT TO SRB FOR EXIT SVC
     ;SRB  FOR EXIT  SVC
              BYTE     1AH         ;1AH = FUNCTION CODE FOR EXIT SVC
              END      DEMO        ;END OF SOURCE CODE
```

SOLUTION

The source file ASM contains the source code for this example program. Commands and text that are entered by the user are underlined. System responses to user commands are not underlined.

Enter assembly language program using the editor with the following commands.

```
> EDIT ASM
* EDIT VERSION |·|
* INPUT
```

The assembly language program can now be entered. Editor features such as SUBSTITUTE, SEARCH, ADD, and DELETE lines can also be demonstrated. The reader should consult appropriate manuals for details.

Now use the DATE command to set the current date and time. For example, if it is 8:30 AM on October 31, 1980, enter the following command line:

```
> DATE 31-OCT-80/8:30:00 <CR>
```

Use the SELECT command to tell DOS/50 to use the assembler and emulator software designed for the 8085:

```
> SELECT 8085 <CR>
```

The following paragraphs outline the functions of the Tektronix assembler directives, shown in the assembly language program above:

TITLE "8085 EXAMPLE PROGRAM"

The TITLE directive helps the programmer identify the source code. The title appears in the source file and also in the listing produced by the assembler.

ORG 100H

This directive tells the assembler where in memory to locate the object code for the next instruction. In this case, the object code for the 8085 instruction LXI H, 500H will be stored at memory location 100.

ORG 40H

This directive specifies that the information for the exit service call is to be stored at address 40. A service call (SVC) is a request for DOS/50 to perform a special service for an executing program. An EXIT SVC ends program execution and returns control to the operating system.

An SVC always has at least three parts:

An I/O instruction that initiates the SVC.
A Service Request Block (SRB) that contains the parameters of the SVC to be performed.
A SRB pointer that tells where in memory the SRB is located.

In this program, the instruction OUT 0F7H directs DOS/50 to perform the SVC whose parameters are pointed to by the address in locations 40 and 41.

BYTE 00, 42H

This directive specifies that the SRB pointer (the address of the SRB for the EXIT SVC) is 0042.

BYTE 1AH

This SRB contains only one parameter: the SVC function code (1A = EXIT). No other parameters are needed.

END DEMO

The END directive signals the end of the source code and specifies that DEMO is the transfer address: the address of the first instruction to be executed when you start the program with a GO command. Since DEMO is the label of the LXI instruction, that instruction will be executed first.

Semicolon (;)

Text following a semicolon in a source line is treated as a comment by the assembler.

What the Example Program Does

The example program adds five numbers from a table stored in locations 500 through 504 in program memory and leaves the sum in the accumulator. You will place values in the table later in this example. The steps of the program are illustrated in the flowchart in Figure 10.17.

Set Table Pointer

The first instruction in the program LXI H, 500H loads the address of the table into the H-L register pair. As a result, the H-L register pair contains the address 500, the location of the first element of the table. The label DEMO represents the address of this instruction. DEMO is used by the END directive to specify that the LXI instruction is the first to be executed.

Set Pass Counter

Register B is used as the pass counter. The MVI B, 5 instruction moves the value 5 into register B. This step sets the number of passes to 5. Each time a number is taken from the table and added into the accumulator, register B is decremented.

Clear Accumulator

The XRA A instruction sets the accumulator to zero by performing an exclusive OR on itself. We want the accumulator to be cleared when we start adding numbers in the table.

Add Byte from Table

The ADD M instruction adds the data addressed by the H-L register pair into the accumulator. The label LOOP represents the address of this instruction; this label is used by the JNZ instruction.

Point to Next Byte

The INX H instruction increments the address contained by the H-L register pair; the H-L register pair then points to the next byte in the table. For example, the H-L register pair is initialized to contain address 500. When the INX H instruction is first executed, the H-L register pair will contain address 501, the address of the second element of the table.

Decrement Pass Counter

The DCR B instruction decrements register B, the pass counter. In this program, because the DCR B instruction follows the ADD M instruction, the

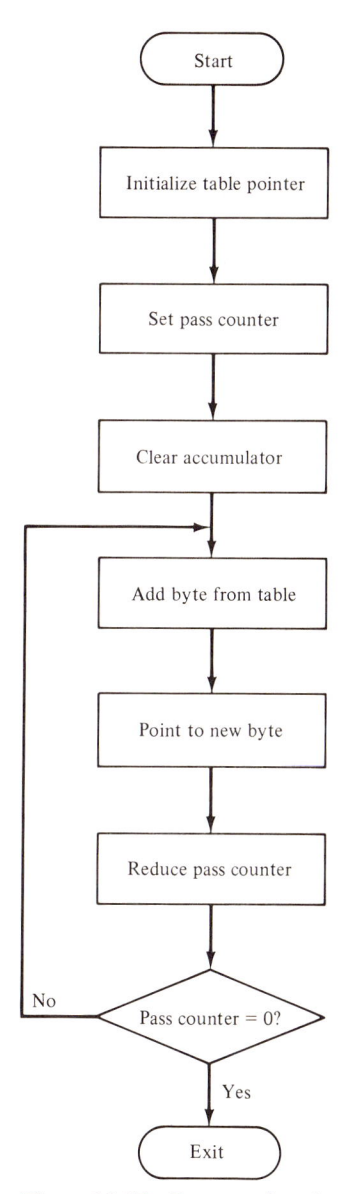

Figure 10.17 Program flowchart example. Source: Courtesy Tektronix, Inc., © 1980.

pass counter is decremented each time a number is added to the accumulator.

Loop if Not Five Passes Yet

The JNZ instruction effectively checks the contents of register B and jumps to the loop label if the register does not contain zero. If register B contains zero, the program proceeds to the OUT 0F7H instruction.

Exit

The OUT 0F7H instruction followed by the NOP is a call to the EXIT SVC. This SVC invokes the operating system to handle termination of the program. A NOP always follows an SVC invocation to allow the system time to execute the SVC.

Run the Example Program

Running the program involves several steps:

1. Converting the assembly language source code into executable machine language.
2. Loading the executable code into program memory.
3. Setting initial conditions before executing the code.
4. Entering the command that starts program execution.

Assemble the Source Code

The ASM (assemble) command converts assembly language (source code) into binary machine language (object code). In some cases, object code must undergo linking before it can be properly executed. The object code for this program, however, can be executed without being linked.

The ASM command also creates an assembler listing which can be used to correlate the object code with the source code. Enter the following command line to assemble the source code in the file named ASM and create the resulting listing and object files ASML and OBJ:

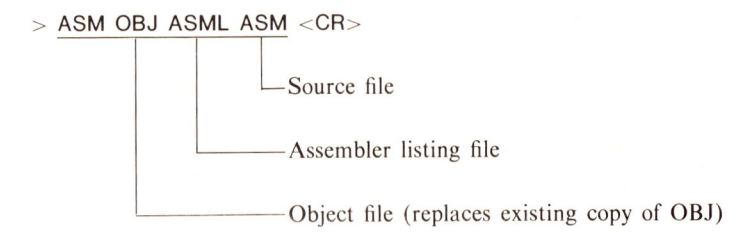

```
> ASM OBJ ASML ASM <CR>
            │    │    └─ Source file
            │    └────── Assembler listing file
            └─────────── Object file (replaces existing copy of OBJ)
```

Tektronix 8080/8085 ASM Vx.x
****Pass 2
    17 Source Lines   17 Assembled Lines 47417 Bytes Available
       >>>No assembly errors detected<<<

The files generated by the above ASM command should now be on your disk. Enter the following command line to list the files in your current directory:

> <u>LDIR</u> <CR>

Filename

ASM
OBJ
ASML

Files used 97
Free files 159
Free blocks 730
Bad blocks 0

Notice that there are now three files listed in this directory: ASM, and the two files that were just created, OBJ and ASML. OBJ contains the object code you will load into program memory and ASML contains the assembler listing.

The following command copies the assembler listing onto the line printer.

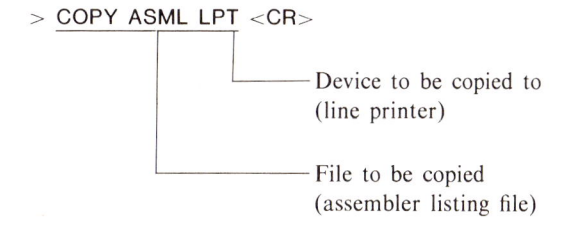

> <u>COPY ASML LPT</u> <CR>
             │   └──── Device to be copied to
             │   (line printer)
             │
             └──── File to be copied
                    (assembler listing file)

This listing is shown in Figure 10.18.

Load the Program into Memory

The object code generated by the ASM command must be loaded into program memory before it can be executed. The following command lines load the program into memory and show the memory contents before and after loading.

Zero out Memory

Use the FILL command to fill program memory with zeros before you load any code. Later, when you examine memory, the zeros make it easy to identify the beginning and end of your code. (Zeroing out memory has no

Chapter 10 Popular Microcomputer Development Systems

```
Tektronix   8080/8085 ASM Vx.x   8085 DEMONSTRATION RUN PROGRAM   Page    1

00002          0100      >           ORG     100H     ;START PROGRAM CODE AT ADDRESS 100
00003 0100 210005        DEMO        LXI     H,500H   ;SET TABLE POINTER
00004 0103 0605                      MVI     B,5      ;SET PASS COUNTER
00005 0105 AF                        XRA     A        ;CLEAR ACCUMULATOR
00006 0106 86            LOOP        ADD     M        ;ADD BYTE FROM TABLE
00007 0107 23                        INX     H        ;POINT TO NEXT BYTE
00008 0108 05                        DCR     B        ;DECREMENT PASS COUNTER
00009 0109 C20601 >                  JNZ     LOOP     ;LOOP IF NOT FIVE PASSES YET
00010 010C D3F7                      OUT     0F7H     ;OTHERWISE CALL EXIT SVC
00011 010E 00                        NOP              ;   TO END PROGRAM EXECUTION
00012                    ;SRB  POINTER
00013          0040                  ORG     40H      ;STORE SRB POINTER AT ADDRESS 40
00014 0040 0042                      BYTE    00,42H   ;POINT TO SRB FOR EXIT SVC
00015                    ;SRB FOR EXIT SVC
00016 0042 1A                        BYTE    1AH      ;1AH = FUNCTION CODE FOR EXIT SVC
00017          0100      >           END     DEMO     ;END OF SOURCE CODE


                  Tektronix   8080/8085 ASM Vx.x   Symbol Table        Page    2

                  Scalars

                         A ----- 0007  B ----- 0000  C ----- 0001  D ----- 0002  E ------ 0003
                         H ----- 0004  L ----- 0005  M ----- 0006  PSW --- 0006  SP ---- 0006

                  %OBJ (default) Section (010F)

                         DEMO --- 0100        LOOP --- 0106

                         17 Source Lines      17 Assembled Lines     47417 Bytes available

                              >>>No assembly errors detected<<<
```

Figure 10.18 Assembler listing of the example program.

effect on how the program is loaded.) Fill memory from address 0 through address 13F with zeros with the following command line.

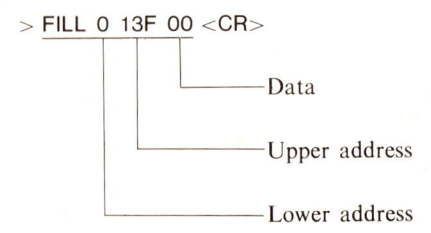

```
> FILL 0 13F 00 <CR>
           │  │   └─ Data
           │  └───── Upper address
           └──────── Lower address
```

Check That Memory Was Filled with Zeros

Check the contents of memory with the DUMP command. The DUMP display shows the data in program memory, the data addresses, and the ASCII characters corresponding to the data. Examine the contents of the memory addresses 0 through 13F with the following command line:

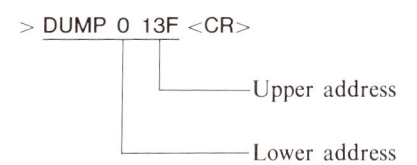

> DUMP 0 13F <CR>
             │   └────── Upper address
             └────────── Lower address

```
       0  1  2  3  4  5  6  7  8  9  A  B  C  D  E  F
0000  00 00 00 00 00 00 00 00 00 00 00 00 00 00 00 00  ................
0010  00 00 00 00 00 00 00 00 00 00 00 00 00 00 00 00  ................
0020  00 00 00 00 00 00 00 00 00 00 00 00 00 00 00 00  ................
0030  00 00 00 00 00 00 00 00 00 00 00 00 00 00 00 00  ................
0040  00 00 00 00 00 00 00 00 00 00 00 00 00 00 00 00  ................
0050  00 00 00 00 00 00 00 00 00 00 00 00 00 00 00 00  ................
0060  00 00 00 00 00 00 00 00 00 00 00 00 00 00 00 00  ................
0070  00 00 00 00 00 00 00 00 00 00 00 00 00 00 00 00  ................
0080  00 00 00 00 00 00 00 00 00 00 00 00 00 00 00 00  ................
0090  00 00 00 00 00 00 00 00 00 00 00 00 00 00 00 00  ................
00A0  00 00 00 00 00 00 00 00 00 00 00 00 00 00 00 00  ................
00B0  00 00 00 00 00 00 00 00 00 00 00 00 00 00 00 00  ................
00C0  00 00 00 00 00 00 00 00 00 00 00 00 00 00 00 00  ................
00D0  00 00 00 00 00 00 00 00 00 00 00 00 00 00 00 00  ................
00E0  00 00 00 00 00 00 00 00 00 00 00 00 00 00 00 00  ................
00F0  00 00 00 00 00 00 00 00 00 00 00 00 00 00 00 00  ................
0100  00 00 00 00 00 00 00 00 00 00 00 00 00 00 00 00  ................
0110  00 00 00 00 00 00 00 00 00 00 00 00 00 00 00 00  ................
0120  00 00 00 00 00 00 00 00 00 00 00 00 00 00 00 00  ................
0130  00 00 00 00 00 00 00 00 00 00 00 00 00 00 00 00  ................
```

Address of first byte in block   Values of bytes in block   ASCII characters corresponding to data

Load the Object Code into Memory

The following command line loads the object code for the example program into program memory:

> LOAD OBJ <CR>
          └────── Object file

The object code is loaded in two different blocks:

The 8085 machine instructions are loaded at address 100 (specified by the first ORG directive in the source code).

The information for the EXIT SVC is loaded at address 40 (specified by the second ORG directive).

Check Memory Contents Again

Now that you have loaded the object code into program memory, look at the same memory area again, with the following command line:

> DUMP 0 13F <CR>

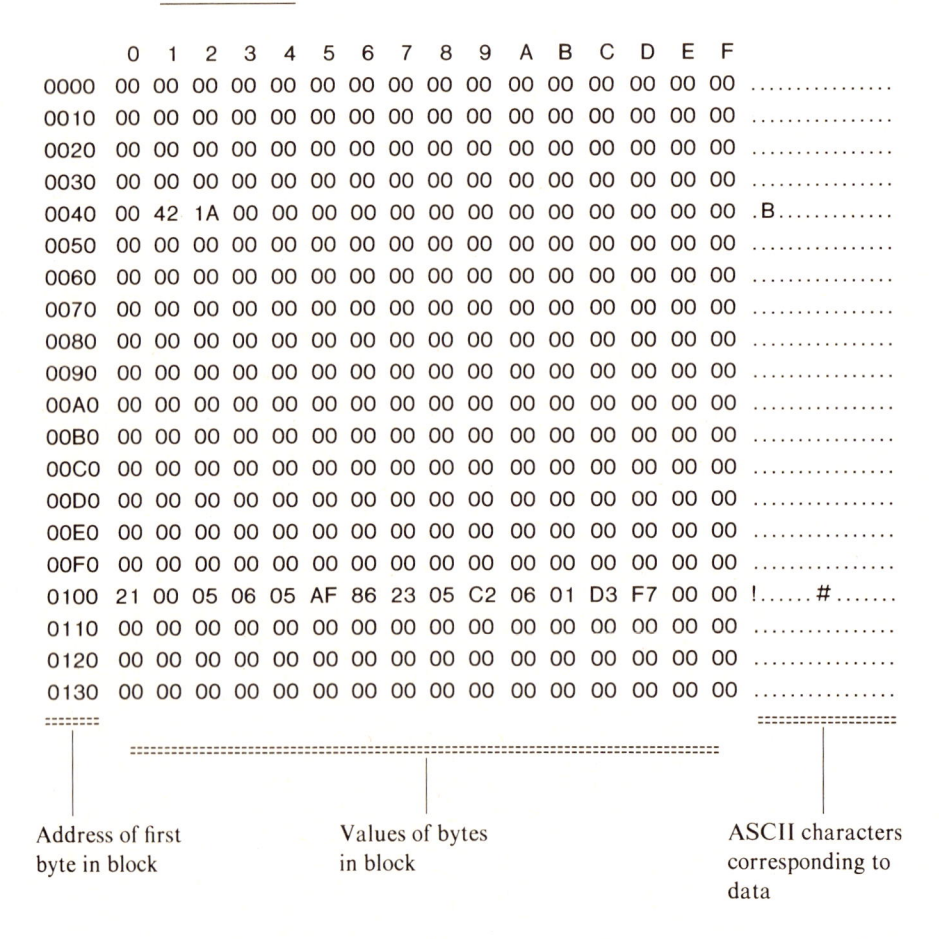

```
        0  1  2  3  4  5  6  7  8  9  A  B  C  D  E  F
0000   00 00 00 00 00 00 00 00 00 00 00 00 00 00 00 00   ................
0010   00 00 00 00 00 00 00 00 00 00 00 00 00 00 00 00   ................
0020   00 00 00 00 00 00 00 00 00 00 00 00 00 00 00 00   ................
0030   00 00 00 00 00 00 00 00 00 00 00 00 00 00 00 00   ................
0040   00 42 1A 00 00 00 00 00 00 00 00 00 00 00 00 00   .B..............
0050   00 00 00 00 00 00 00 00 00 00 00 00 00 00 00 00   ................
0060   00 00 00 00 00 00 00 00 00 00 00 00 00 00 00 00   ................
0070   00 00 00 00 00 00 00 00 00 00 00 00 00 00 00 00   ................
0080   00 00 00 00 00 00 00 00 00 00 00 00 00 00 00 00   ................
0090   00 00 00 00 00 00 00 00 00 00 00 00 00 00 00 00   ................
00A0   00 00 00 00 00 00 00 00 00 00 00 00 00 00 00 00   ................
00B0   00 00 00 00 00 00 00 00 00 00 00 00 00 00 00 00   ................
00C0   00 00 00 00 00 00 00 00 00 00 00 00 00 00 00 00   ................
00D0   00 00 00 00 00 00 00 00 00 00 00 00 00 00 00 00   ................
00E0   00 00 00 00 00 00 00 00 00 00 00 00 00 00 00 00   ................
00F0   00 00 00 00 00 00 00 00 00 00 00 00 00 00 00 00   ................
0100   21 00 05 06 05 AF 86 23 05 C2 06 01 D3 F7 00 00   !......#........
0110   00 00 00 00 00 00 00 00 00 00 00 00 00 00 00 00   ................
0120   00 00 00 00 00 00 00 00 00 00 00 00 00 00 00 00   ................
0130   00 00 00 00 00 00 00 00 00 00 00 00 00 00 00 00   ................
```

Address of first byte in block

Values of bytes in block

ASCII characters corresponding to data

Dump to the Line Printer

The DUMP command also allows you to obtain a hard copy of memory contents. (IF you do not have a line printer, skip this command.) To display the contents of memory on the line printer, make sure your line printer is on, then enter the following command.

> DUMP 40 10F LPT <CR>

```
       0  1  2  3  4  5  6  7  8  9  A  B  C  D  E  F
0040  00 42 1A 00 00 00 00 00 00 00 00 00 00 00 00 00  .B..............
0050  00 00 00 00 00 00 00 00 00 00 00 00 00 00 00 00  ................
0060  00 00 00 00 00 00 00 00 00 00 00 00 00 00 00 00  ................
0070  00 00 00 00 00 00 00 00 00 00 00 00 00 00 00 00  ................
0080  00 00 00 00 00 00 00 00 00 00 00 00 00 00 00 00  ................
0090  00 00 00 00 00 00 00 00 00 00 00 00 00 00 00 00  ................
00A0  00 00 00 00 00 00 00 00 00 00 00 00 00 00 00 00  ................
00B0  00 00 00 00 00 00 00 00 00 00 00 00 00 00 00 00  ................
00C0  00 00 00 00 00 00 00 00 00 00 00 00 00 00 00 00  ................
00D0  00 00 00 00 00 00 00 00 00 00 00 00 00 00 00 00  ................
00E0  00 00 00 00 00 00 00 00 00 00 00 00 00 00 00 00  ................
00F0  00 00 00 00 00 00 00 00 00 00 00 00 00 00 00 00  ................
0100  21 00 05 06 05 AF 86 23 05 C2 06 01 D3 F7 00 00  !......#.......
```

Disassemble Object Code

The DISM command displays memory contents both in hexadecimal notation and in assembly language mnemonics. You can use the DISM command to make sure that the object code corresponds to the source code. The following command line disassembles the object code in memory:

> DISM 100 10E <CR>

```
LOC    INST    MNEM   OPER
0100   210005  LXI    H,0500
0103   0605    MVI    B,05
0105   AF      XRA    A
0106   86      ADD    M
0107   23      INX    H
0108   05      DCR    B
0109   C20601  JNZ    0106
010C   D3F7    OUT    F7
010E   00      NOP
```

Now the object code is properly loaded, and you have verified that the object code matches your source code. You are ready to set initial conditions and execute the program.

Set Initial Conditions
Before you execute the program, you need to:

1. Set the emulation mode.
2. Put values into the table in memory, for the program to add together.
3. Set a breakpoint to suspend program execution after the last number has been added. (The breakpoint display will show you the sum in the accumulator.)

When these three conditions are set, you will be ready to execute the program.

Set the Emulation Mode
The following command line selects emulation mode 0:

> **EMULATE 0** <CR>

Put Values into the Table in Memory
This program sums the numbers found in the memory table at addresses 500 through 504. The EXAM command shows you what is already in those locations, and lets you put the five numbers into the memory table. The following command line puts the numbers 1, 2, 3, 4, and 5 into the table:

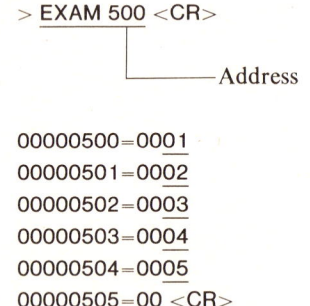

> **EXAM 500** <CR>
             └──────── Address

```
00000500=0001
00000501=0002
00000502=0003
00000503=0004
00000504=0005
00000505=00 <CR>
```

When 00000500 = 00 appears, the user types 0102030405. The system fills in the rest. The carriage return terminates the EXAM command. Notice that addresses 500 through 504 contained random data left over from previous system operations.

Set a Breakpoint to Suspend Execution After the Last Addition
Use the BKPT command to set a program breakpoint. When the breakpoint is encountered during a program execution, information about the emulator will be displayed on the system terminal. Set the breakpoint with

the following command line:

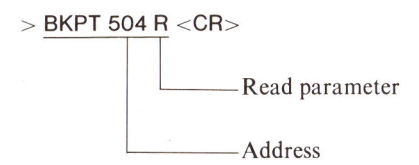

> BKPT 504 R <CR>

      └── Read parameter

    └── Address

The R parameter means that the program will be suspended after the emulator reads from memory address 504. (The 8085A ADD M instruction reads from memory and adds the data read into the accumulator; the program will break after the last number in the table has been read and added.) By setting the breakpoint to suspend program execution after the last number is added into the accumulator, you can see the final sum in the accumulator.

  The emulation mode has been set, the table contains the five numbers to be added, and the breakpoint has been set. You are now ready to start program execution.

Start Program Execution

  The GO command starts program execution at location 100, the transfer address specified by the END directive in the source code:

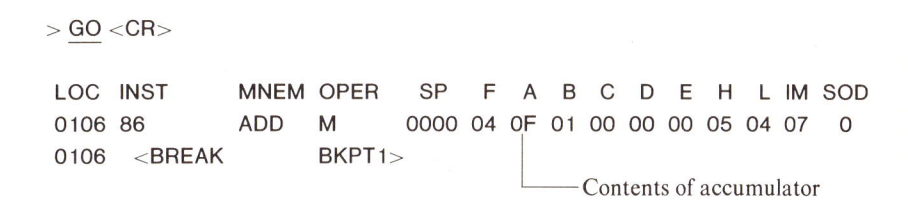

> GO <CR>

```
LOC   INST      MNEM OPER    SP   F  A  B  C  D  E  H  L  IM SOD
0106  86        ADD  M       0000 04 0F 01 00 00 00 05 04 07 0
0106  <BREAK         BKPT1>
```

             └── Contents of accumulator

The program breaks at address 106, the ADD M instruction, which adds the last value from the memory table into the accumulator. The display line is a result of the BKPT command you entered. The accumulator contains the sum of the numbers in the memory table: 1 + 2 + 3 + 4 + 5 = 0F.

  Notice that the breakpoint suspends program execution just before the program reaches the 8085A OUT instruction (which initiates the EXIT SVC). The SVC, when executed, terminates program execution and returns control to the system. Throughout this example, the breakpoint will continue to break the program's execution just before the EXIT SVC. At the end of the example, we will allow the program to execute complete and return control to the system.

Monitor Program Execution

The following command lines are used to monitor program execution. You can watch the changes in the emulator's registers and observe the effect of each instruction as the program proceeds.

Trace All Instructions

The TRACE command lets you observe the changes in the 8085A registers as the program proceeds. When you enter the TRACE command and then start execution with the GO command, display lines are sent to the system terminal. As each instruction executes, the display line shows the instruction, its address in memory, and the contents of the registers after that instruction has executed. The following command line traces all of the program's instructions:

> TRACE ALL <CR>

The GO command will begin program execution.

> GO 100 <CR>

As the program executes, the following trace is displayed.

LOC	INST	MNEM	OPER	SP	F	A	B	C	D	E	H	L	IM	SOD
0100	210005	LXI	H,0500	0000	54	0F	01	00	00	00	05	00	07	0
0103	0605	MVI	B,05	0000	54	0F	05	00	00	00	05	00	07	0
0105	AF	XRA	A	0000	44	00	05	00	00	00	05	00	07	0
0106	86	ADD	M	0000	00	01	05	00	00	00	05	00	07	0
0107	23	INX	H	0000	00	01	05	00	00	00	05	01	07	0
0108	05	DCR	B	0000	10	01	04	00	00	00	05	01	07	0
0109	C20601	JNZ	0106	0000	10	01	04	00	00	00	05	01	07	0
0106	86	ADD	M	0000	04	03	04	00	00	00	05	01	07	0
0107	23	INX	H	0000	04	03	04	00	00	00	05	02	07	0
0108	05	DCR	B	0000	14	03	03	00	00	00	05	02	07	0
0109	C20601	JNZ	0106	0000	14	03	03	00	00	00	05	02	07	0
0106	86	ADD	M	0000	04	06	03	00	00	00	05	02	07	0
0107	23	INX	H	0000	04	06	03	00	00	00	05	03	07	0
0108	05	DCR	B	0000	10	06	02	00	00	00	05	03	07	0
0109	C20601	JNZ	0106	0000	10	06	02	00	00	00	05	03	07	0
0106	86	ADD	M	0000	04	0A	02	00	00	00	05	03	07	0
0107	23	INX	H	0000	04	0A	02	00	00	00	05	04	07	0
0108	05	DCR	B	0000	10	0A	01	00	00	00	05	04	07	0

```
LOC   INST     MNEM  OPER   SP      F  A  B  C  D  E  H  L  IM SOD
0109  C20601   JNZ   0106   0000   10 0A 01 00 00 00 05 04 07  0
0106  86       ADD   M      0000   04 0F 01 00 00 00 05 04 07  0
0106  <BREAK         TRACE, BKPT1  — —                 ‾‾‾‾‾
```

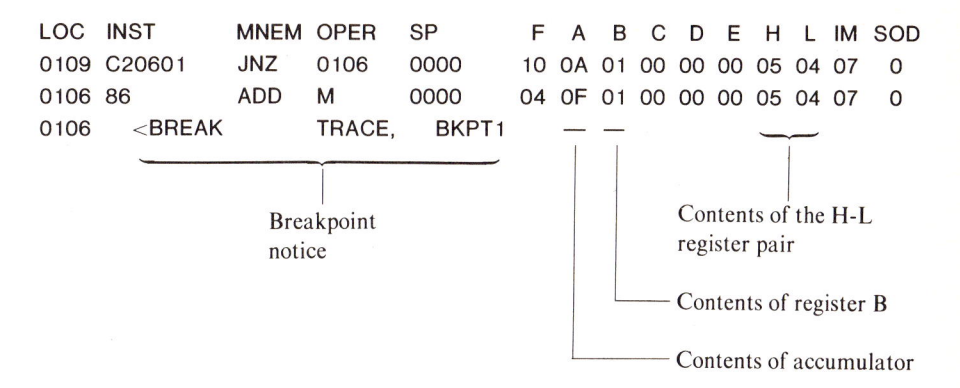

- Breakpoint notice (under MNEM/OPER/SP columns)
- Contents of the H-L register pair
- Contents of register B
- Contents of accumulator

After the accumulator is cleared, it begins to store the sum of the numbers being added. The 8085A ADD M instruction adds a number from the table into the accumulator. At the end of the program, the accumulator contains the sum of the numbers you put into the table, or 1 + 2 + 3 + 4 + 5 = 0F.

Register B, the pass counter, is set to contain 5 at the beginning of the program. It decreases by one (because of the DCR B instruction) each time a number is added into the accumulator. The program ends after register B reaches zero.

The H-L register pair, set to contain 500 at the start of the program, increases by one (because of the INX H instruction) each time a number is added to the accumulator. At the end of the program, the register pair has been incremented four times and contains 504.

Set a Breakpoint After a Specific Instruction

Now that you have seen how the program adds the numbers together, here is a new task: to add only the third and fourth numbers from the table. To perform this task, you want the pass counter to contain 2, and the table pointer to contain 502 (the address of the third number in the table). You can accomplish these changes without altering the object code in memory. First, suspend program execution after the pass counter and the table pointer have been set. Next, while the program is suspended, enter new values for the pass counter and the table pointer. When execution resumes, the program will treat the new values as if they were the original programmed values. Enter the following command line to trace all of the instructions as the program executes:

> TRACE ALL <CR>

Check the trace status again with the following command line:

> TRACE <CR>
TRACE ALL 0000,FFFF

438 Chapter 10 POPULAR MICROCOMPUTER DEVELOPMENT SYSTEMS

The TRACE selections we set earlier are made obsolete by the TRACE ALL command just entered. Enter the following command line to set a breakpoint:

> BKPT 103 <CR>

Use the GO command to start program execution:

> GO 100 <CR>

```
LOC   INST      MNEM  OPER    SP      F  A  B  C  D  E  H  L  IM SOD
0100  210005    LXI   H,0500  0000    04 0F 01 00 00 00 05 00 07  0
0103  0605      MVI   B,05    0000    04 0F 05 00 00 00 05 00 07  0
0103            <BREAK       TRACE,  BKPT2>
```

The TRACE ALL command enabled display of all the instructions up to and including the instruction at the breakpoint.

Set New Values in Pass Counter and Table Pointer; Check Results

Now that you have reached the breakpoint, you can change the contents of the registers while execution is suspended. The BKPT display line shows that the pass counter contains 5, and that the H-L register pair (the table pointer) points to address 500. Set the number of passes to 2, and set the table pointer to 502 with the following command line:

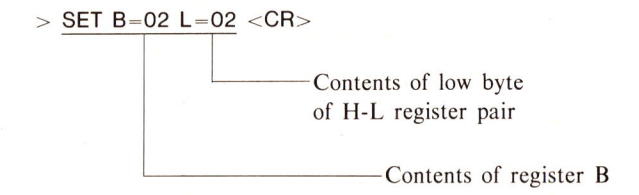

> SET B=02 L=02 <CR>
         │   └──── Contents of low byte
         │   of H-L register pair
         └────────── Contents of register B

The SET command does not produce a display, but you can use the DSTAT command to check the values in the registers you changed. DSTAT displays the contents of each emulator register and status flag. Check the result of the previous SET command with the following command line:

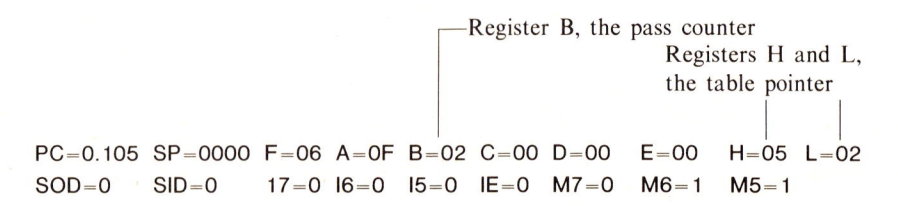

> DSTAT <CR>

                              ┌── Register B, the pass counter
                              │   Registers H and L,
                              │   the table pointer
PC=0.105 SP=0000 F=06 A=0F B=02 C=00 D=00 E=00 H=05 L=02
SOD=0   SID=0   I7=0 I6=0 I5=0 IE=0 M7=0 M6=1 M5=1

The DSTAT display line shows that the pass counter and the table pointer now contain the new values.

Resume Program Execution

If you enter the GO command with no parameters, program execution starts where it left off at the breakpoint. Resume program execution after the breakpoint with the following command line:

> GO <CR>

LOC	INST	MNEM	OPER	SP	F	A	B	C	D	E	H	L	IM	SOD
0105	AF	XRA	A	0000	44	00	02	00	00	00	05	02	07	0
0106	86	ADD	M	0000	04	03	02	00	00	00	05	02	07	0
0107	23	INX	H	0000	04	03	02	00	00	00	05	03	07	0
0108	05	DCR	B	0000	10	03	01	00	00	00	05	03	07	0
0109	C20601	JNZ	0106	0000	10	03	01	00	00	00	05	03	07	0
0106	86	ADD	M	0000	00	07	01	00	00	00	05	03	07	0
0107	23	INX	H	0000	00	07	01	00	00	00	05	04	07	0
0108	05	DCR	B	0000	54	07	00	00	00	00	05	04	07	0
0109	C20601	JNZ	0106	0000	54	07	00	00	00	00	05	04	07	0

Notice that the program performed two passes through the loop, and that the program added the third and fourth numbers in the table (3 + 4 = 7). Also notice that since address 504 was never read from, the break at that address did not occur. Program execution dropped through to the EXIT SVC, which brought the program to a normal stop.

10.4 GenRad Systems

A few years ago, Futuredata offered a popular single processor-based universal development system called the AMDS (Advanced Microcomputer Development Systems). Recently, General Radio bought Futuredata and modified the Futuredata systems to provide a number of new development systems. These are the 2300 series, 2301 systems, and the 2302 slave emulator control unit. The 2300 system is a universal stand-alone software station whereas the 2301 system is a universal multistation hardware/software network supporting up to eight stations. Both of these systems are designed using the Z80-based single-processor architecture. Each 2301 network system can be interfaced to up to eight 2302 slave emulators via RS-422. Therefore, a 2301–2302 configuration can provide both hardware and software development capabilities for a maximum of 64 microprocessors (any combination supported by GenRad).

The GenRad 2300 Series system includes the Models 2300-9100 and 2300-9200 Universal Stand-alone Software Development Systems and the 2301-9100, 2301-9200, 2301-9300, and 2301-9400 Universal Multistation Hardware/Software Development Network Systems. The 2302-9000 Slave Emulator Control Unit is provided to support various 8- and 16-bit microprocessors and microcomputers. With the 2302-9000, emulation is performed transparently at full processor speed to 10 MHz. The slave emulator requires a Z80-based stand-alone system for operation.

10.4.1 2300 Stand-Alone Software

The 2300 system is a universal stand-alone software station and includes a keyboard, CRT, and CPU in one package. The 2300 can develop software for the 8086, 8085, 8080, Z80, 6800, Z8000, 6809, 8048, 1802, 6502, 3870, and SC/MP.

Two models are available: the 2300-9100 (48K bytes) and the 2300-9200 (64K bytes). Both models have 1 megabyte of floppy disk storage.

Both 2300 models have the following software: a relocatable macroassembler, object program linker, screen-based editor, debugger with disassembly, and symbolic debugging and command control language. A basic interpreter is available for the 8080/6800 families. The Z8000, 8086, 6809, 8085, 8080, and Z80 have BASIC and PASCAL compilers.

The GenRad 2301

The 2301 system is a universal multistation hardware/software network that supports up to eight users simultaneously. The 2301 supports the 8086, 8080, 8085, 6800, 6802, and Z80.

The 2301 offers four systems. The 2301-9100 (48K bytes) and the 2301-9200 (64K bytes) are both software development network stations. The 2301-9300 (48K bytes) and the 2301-9400 (64K bytes) are both hardware/software development network stations.

The customer's requirements determine how many of each of the hardware/software stations and of the software stations are bought. The cost per station is lowered by sharing a network control processor, a disk facility, a printer, and a PROM programmer.

Each hardware/software station is a complete development system and has optional plug-in boards to in-circuit emulate five microprocessors (the 8080, 8085, 6800, 6802, and Z80). In order for a hardware/software station to emulate and logic analyze other supported microprocessors (such as the 8086) the GenRad 2302 Slave Emulator Control Unit and Universal Slave Logic Analyzer must be used. Each hardware/software station comes with its own real-time in-circuit emulator, logic analyzer, and high-speed static RAM.

The network control processor oversees the sharing of the floppy disk, printer, and PROM programmer with up to eight stations.

The CRT is a high-speed (over 20K characters per second), high-resolution (24 × 80) display. The system software (NDOS) takes advantage of this speed to offer the display of hexadecimal memory, ASCII data, and disassembled data, combined with symbolic debugging and string search capabilities.

These string search capabilities eliminate the need for linker maps and assembly listings because specific program steps can be located by their label names.

This high-speed CRT permits all editing results to be displayed instantaneously which reduces editing errors. The editor permits scrolling through 2,500 lines of workspace.

GenRad system software (NDOS) includes a relocatable macroassembler, object program linker, powerful screen-based editor, and interaction debugger with assembly and symbolic debugging and command control language. A command file can be used to reduce numerous steps to one simple command.

Two high-level languages are available: BASIC and PASCAL. A BASIC interpreter and compiler is offered for the 8080/6800 families (just as for the 2300). A PASCAL interpreter and compiler is available for the 8080, Z80, and 8086 16-bit processor. Due to its highly structured design PASCAL is easier and thus faster (up to 50% faster) than other nonstructured high-level languages.

During in-circuit emulation RAM is used as ROM so that errors can be easily reprogrammed.

The GenRad Real-Time Logic Analyzer has 256 × 48 bits of storage, three hardware break registers, loop counters, and a delay counter. Complex or simple break conditions can be specified. The utility of the Logic Analyzer (LA) is greatly expanded because the user can eliminate the storage of extraneous data by qualifying the data to be stored.

Even difficult hardware and software problems can be solved by the combined use of real-time emulation and real-time logic analysis.

GenRad 2302 Slave Emulator

In order to develop modern multiply processor systems the emulator needs to be separate from the development system's master CPU controller. Accordingly, the 2302 (Figure 10.19) has its own emulation processor, emulation memory, and emulator bus, as well as a 64-channel logic analyzer.

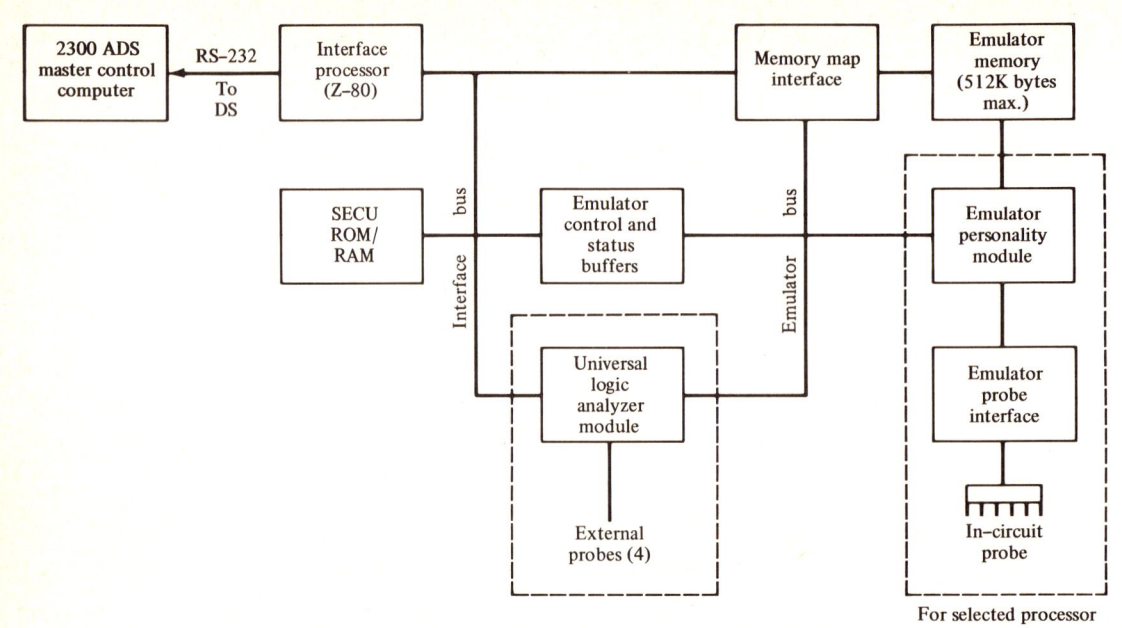

442   Chapter 10   POPULAR MICROCOMPUTER DEVELOPMENT SYSTEMS

Figure 10.19   Slave emulator block diagram. Source: GenRad Corp., Development Systems Division, Culver City CA 90230.

The slave emulator is controlled by the 2300 Advanced Development System (ADS) Computer, (which supplies the necessary emulator-control and software development programs). With the addition of a disc and printer the user's development system is complete.

The 2300 ADS has multiemulator debugger software which allows a single user to control and debug a single system with up to eight microprocessors running simultaneously. Multiple slave emulators are linked together via a high-speed RS232 daisy chain. The user can debug any one microprocessor at a time via the CRT terminal and debug program. This is shown in Figure 10.20.

Each debug command to the slave emulator only briefly interrupts the emulation processor since the emulation hardware is completely separate from the development system's hardware. This is a very significant feature because the target system does not have to come to a complete halt whenever debugging occurs. In the case of a microprocessor-based engine control this means that the engine will not be stopped whenever debugging occurs.

A unique application of the slave emulator is as follows: The system under test can be stimulated while it is running normally. Variables can be forced out of range and I/O ports can be manipulated.

The above feature can also be combined with the command file

GenRad Systems   443

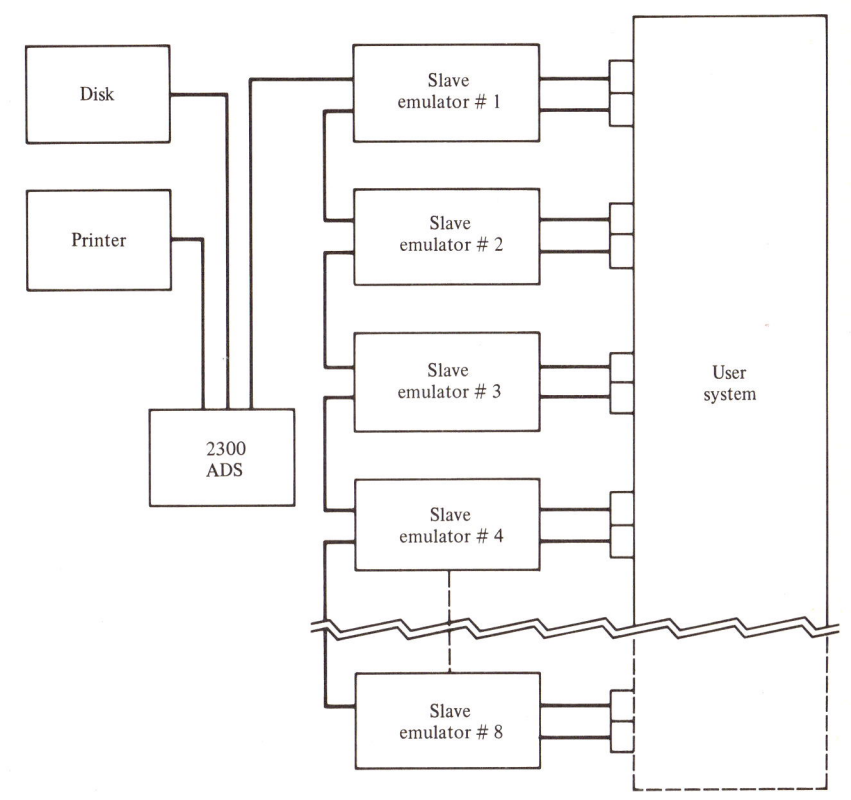

Figure 10.20 System diagram multiple slave emulators. Source: GenRad Corp., Development Systems Division, Culver City, CA 90230.

processing function of the debugger program to do automated testing of single- or multiple-processor systems.

The slave emulator uses high-speed 10-MHz RAM. Up to 128K bytes static RAM or 512K bytes dynamic RAM can be mapped in 4K or 16K blocks to any address locations within a total 1 mega byte address space. Mapping of memory references to internal or external memory is done in 256-byte sections. For ROM simulation any portion of RAM can be write-protected in 256-byte blocks. All I/O is mapped externally.

EXAMPLE 10.3

Using the GenRad 2301 System, edit, assemble, link, and emulate the following Z80 assembly language program. The program polls a keyboard for a key actuation and outputs the key closed by means of row and column numbers.

```
*
* Pro-Log Keyboard/Display Demo Program          VER 1.0
*       Z80 CODE (Also 8080/85 Compatible)
*
            RSEG    PROLOG
MAIN        CALL    KEYBD               Poll keyboard
            INC     A
            LD      HL,MSGTBL-8
            LD      DE,8
MLOOP       ADD     HL,DE               Point to appropriate message
            DEC     A
            JP      NZ,MLOOP
            CALL    DISPLAY             Display message
            JP      MAIN
            SPC
* Subroutine to poll the keyboard
            SPC
KEYBD       LD      B,X'01'             Set up column select mask
KLOOP       LD      A,B
            OUT     (X'D0'),A           Output column select mask
            IN      A,(X'D0')
            AND     X'3F'
            JP      NZ,KEY              Check for key
            LD      A,B
            RLCA                        Rotate column select mask
            LD      B,A
            SUB     X'10'
            JP      Z,KRET
            JP      KLOOP
KEY         LD      HL,-4               Calculate key position
            LD      DE,4
KLP1        ADD     HL,DE
            RRCA
            JP      NC,KLP1
            LD      A,B
KLP2        INC     L
            RRCA
            JP      NC,KLP2
            LD      A,L
KRET        RET
            SPC
* Subroutine to display message on PROLOG display
            SPC
DISPLAY     LD      B,8                 Set character position pointer
DLOOP       LD      A,(HL)              Get character
            INC     HL
            OR      X'80'
            OUT     (X'D0'),A           Output character
            LD      A,B
            DEC     A
            AND     X'F7'
            OUT     (X'D1'),A           Strobe character to display
            OR      X'08'
            OUT     (X'D1'),A
            AND     X'F7'
            OUT     (X'D1'),A
            DEC     B
            JP      NZ,DLOOP
            RET
            SPC
```

```
* Table of key messages
          SPC
MSGTBL    DC        '         '
          DC        'ROW5COL1'
          DC        'ROW5COL2'
          DC        'ROW5COL3'
          DC        'ROW5COL4'
          DC        'ROW4COL1'
          DC        'ROW4COL2'
          DC        'ROW4COL3'
          DC        'ROW4COL4'
          DC        'ROW3COL1'
          DC        'ROW3COL2'
          DC        'ROW3COL3'
          DC        'ROW3COL4'
          DC        'ROW2COL1'
          DC        'ROW2COL2'
          DC        'ROW2COL3'
          DC        'ROW2COL4'
          DC        'ROW5COL5'
          DC        'ROW4COL5'
          DC        'ROW3COL5'
          DC        'ROW2COL5'
          DC        'ROW1COL1'
          DC        'ROW1COL2'
          DC        'ROW1COL3'
          DC        'ROW1COL4'
          SPC
          END       MAIN
```

SOLUTION

The development process involved can be represented by means of a circular path as follows:

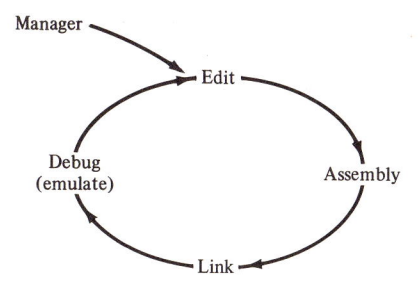

Note that GenRad uses the term debug for emulation.

Inside the 2301, there are six software modules. The names of these packages and the associated commands to get to them are given in the following:

Program Name	Command	Description
MANAGER	JM	Jump to manager
EDITOR	JE	Jump to editor
ASSY	JA	Jump to assembler
LINKER	JL	Jump to linker
DEBUG	JD	Jump to debug
COM FILE PROCESSOR	JA FILE NAME	Jump to command file

In MANAGER, one would basically create files and assign attributes. Through the process of creating files, one or more file names are defined to which programs are assigned during the development phase. The process of assigning attributes is to assign an identification tag to the file. The identification tag might be S for source program (editor input), R for relocatable program (linker input), and so on. In this example, we create the following files:

PROLOG.N   New Source file
PROLOG.R   Relocatable file
PROFLOG   Object file

In order to create the relocatable file PROLOG.R, one should do the following:

    Enter > CPROLOG
        Return
Display will show V02
Enter (R)PROLOG R

The PROLOG R will be specified as relocatable. Similarly, the other files can be defined. Now let us proceed with the edit, link, and emulate sessions as follows:

    Enter JE
        >I Return

Now, enter the assembly language program. Note that in the 2301, there are two dashed lines around the center of the screen:

Any text to be entered or modified must be moved within these two lines using appropriate commands on the keyboard. Therefore, in order to edit the assembly language program, one must enter each line within the two dashed lines using appropriate keys.

    To end the edit session, enter A E PROLOG Return
    For assembling, the user enters JA Return
CRT DISPLAY SELECT OPTION
    User enters >TS where 'T' represents truncated list (truncates 80 characters)
    'S' represents include symbol table

Note that there are many other options. TS is selected arbitrarily.

```
CRT DISPLAY SOURCE FILE
User Enters >1:PROLOG, N
            Return
CRT DISPLAY MACRO FILE
User         >Return
CRT DISPLAY OUTPUT FILE
User         >1:PROLOG.R
            Return
CRT DISPLAY LISTING FILE
User         >Return
```

Assembler output will appear on the display as follows:

For linking,

```
User Enters   : JL
CRT DISPLAY   : SELECT OPTIONS
USER          : >SL Return
```

Note that S includes the symbol table with absolute addresses and L lists tables on CRT.

```
CRT DISPLAY : SPECIFY INPUT FILE
User        : >1:PROLOG.R
CRT DISPLAY : SPECIFY OUTPUT FILE
User        : >1:PROLOG
              Return
CRT DISPLAY : LINKER INPUT
User        : >#ORG 0100H
              Return
```

448 Chapter 10 Popular Microcomputer Development Systems

```
-------- Z80 ASSEMBLER V02.1 ------------------------------    PAGE    1
                                                               FUTUREDATA --------

                    *
                    * Pro-Log Keyboard/Display Demo Program           VER 1.0
                    *       Z80 CODE (Also 8080/85 Compatible)
                    *
0000                        RSEG    PROLOG
0000 CD1500         MAIN    CALL    KEYBD               Poll Keyboard
0003 3C                     INC     A
0004 215200                 LD      HL,MSGTBL-8
0007 110800                 LD      DE,8
000A 19             MLOOP   ADD     HL,DE               Point to appropriate message
000B 3D                     DEC     A
000C C20A00                 JP      NZ,MLOOP
000F CD3F00                 CALL    DISPLAY             Display message
0012 C30000                 JP      MAIN

                    * Subroutine to poll the keyboard

0015 0601           KEYBD   LD      B,X'01'             Set up column select mask
0017 78             KLOOP   LD      A,B
0018 D3D0                   OUT     (X'D0'),A           Output column select mask
001A DBD0                   IN      A,(X'D0')
001C E63F                   AND     X'3F'
001E C22C00                 JP      NZ,KEY              Check for key
0021 78                     LD      A,B
0022 07                     RLCA                        Rotate column select mask
0023 47                     LD      B,A
0024 D610                   SUB     X'10'
0026 CA3E00                 JP      Z,KRET
0029 C31700                 JP      KLOOP
002C 21FCFF         KEY     LD      HL,-4               Calculate key position
002F 110400                 LD      DE,4
0032 19             KLP1    ADD     HL,DE
0033 0F                     RRCA
0034 D23200                 JP      NC,KLP1
0037 78                     LD      A,B
0038 2C             KLP2    INC     L
0039 0F                     RRCA
003A D23800                 JP      NC,KLP2
003D 7D                     LD      A,L
003E C9             KRET    RET

                    * Subroutine to display message on PROLOG display

003F 0608           DISPLAY LD      B,8                 Set character position pointer
0041 7E             DLOOP   LD      A,(HL)              Get character
0042 23                     INC     HL
0043 F680                   OR      X'80'
0045 D3D0                   OUT     (X'D0'),A           Output character
0047 78                     LD      A,B
0048 3D                     DEC     A
0049 E6F7                   AND     X'F7'
004B D3D1                   OUT     (X'D1'),A           Strobe character to display
004D F608                   OR      X'08'
004F D3D1                   OUT     (X'D1'),A
0051 E6F7                   AND     X'F7'
```

```
-------- Z80 ASSEMBLER V02.1 ------------------------------ FUTUREDATA --------                        PAGE    2

 0053 D3D1                OUT      (X'D1'),A
 0055 05                  DEC      B
 0056 C24100              JP       NZ,DLOOP
 0059 C9                  RET

                 * Table of key messages

 005A 20        MSGTBL    DC
 0062 52                  DC       'ROW5COL1'
 006A 52                  DC       'ROW5COL2'
 0072 52                  DC       'ROW5COL3'
 007A 52                  DC       'ROW5COL4'
 0082 52                  DC       'ROW4COL1'
 008A 52                  DC       'ROW4COL2'
 0092 52                  DC       'ROW4COL3'
 009A 52                  DC       'ROW4COL4'
 00A2 52                  DC       'ROW3COL1'
 00AA 52                  DC       'ROW3COL2'
 00B2 52                  DC       'ROW3COL3'
 00BA 52                  DC       'ROW3COL4'
 00C2 52                  DC       'ROW2COL1'
 00CA 52                  DC       'ROW2COL2'
 00D2 52                  DC       'ROW2COL3'
 00DA 52                  DC       'ROW2COL4'
 00E2 52                  DC       'ROW5COL5'
 00EA 52                  DC       'ROW4COL5'
 00F2 52                  DC       'ROW3COL5'
 00FA 52                  DC       'ROW2COL5'
 0102 52                  DC       'ROW1COL1'
 010A 52                  DC       'ROW1COL2'
 0112 52                  DC       'ROW1COL3'
 011A 52                  DC       'ROW1COL4'

 0122                     END      MAIN


-------- Z80 ASSEMBLER V02.1 ------------------------------ FUTUREDATA --------                        PAGE    3

 DISPLAY    003F      DLOOP      0041      KEY        002C      KEYBD      0015
 KLOOP      0017      KLP1       0032      KLP2       0038      KRET       003E
 MAIN       0000      MLOOP      000A      MSGTBL     005A      PROLOG   G 0000
 NO ERRORS
```

The CRT display will be as follows:

```
--------LINKER V02.1----------------------------------------FUTUREDATA                        PAGE   1
         ADDR   RSEG    FILE       LENGTH
         0100   PROLOG  PLZ80.R    0122
```

         User   : ># END
The display will be as follows:

```
                                                                    PAGE    2
             --------LINKER VO2.1 ----------------------------------------- FUTUREDATA
             FILE      RSEG       ADDR  LENGTH
             PLZ80.R  PROLOG     0100   0122

                       GLOBALS
                       PROLOG   0100

             ENTRY POINT 0100
```

In order to enter the emulation or debug mode do the following:

User : >JD

In the debug mode, the following functions using the appropriate commands can be carried out:

FUNCTION	COMMANDS
Display memory	C
Store memory	S
Find string	F
Set register	Z
Breakpoint set, reset, display	BS,BR,BD
Trace program	TR
Execute	E
Single-step	SINGLE STEP

Typical debug displays are shown below:

```
PC    A   B C   D E   H L   IX     SZHVNC V    SP    A´  B´C´  D´E´  H´L´  IY    SZHVNC  I
0100  00  0000  0000  0000  0000   000000 00   6E00  00  0000  0000  0000  0000  000000  00

0100 >CD1501     CALL    X'0115'         00B8  B5 59 86 58   B9 59 86 58   .Y.X.Y.X
                                         00C0  49 59 44 59   A9 51 49 59   IYDY.QIY
0103  3C         INC     A               00C8  44 59 37 58   18 5B D8 5A   DY7X.[.Z
                                         00D0  30 00 4A 0A   24 69 99 28   0..J.$i.(
0104  215201     LD      HL,338          00D8  92 28 0D 0D   4A 0A 38 21   .(..J.8!
                                         00E0  F4 03 7F 01   F3 31 E4 00   .. ..1..
0107  110800     LD      DE,8            00E8  AF D3 1F D3   3F D3 5F D3   ....?._.
                                         00F0  7F D3 9F D3   BF D3 DF CD   ........
010A  19         ADD     HL,DE           00F8  8F 6A 22 E5   2A C3 23 01   .j"*.#.
                                         0100 >CD 15 01 3C   21 52 01 11   ...<!R..
010B  3D         DEC     A               0108  08 00 19 3D   C2 0A 01 CD   ...=....
                                         0110  3F 01 C3 00   01 06 01 78   ?......x
010C  C20A01     JP      NZ,X'010A'      0118  D3 D0 DB D0   E6 3F C2 2C   .....?.,
                                         0120  01 78 07 47   D6 10 CA 3E   .x.G...>
010F  CD3F01     CALL    X'013F'         0128  01 C3 17 01   21 FC FF 11   ....!...
                                         0130  04 00 19 0F   D2 32 01 78   .....2.x
0112  C30001     JP      X'0100'         0138  2C 0F D2 38   01 7D C9 06   ,..8.}..
                                         0140  08 7E 23 F6   80 D3 D0 78   .~#....x
0115  0601       LD      B,1             0148  3D E6 F7 D3   D1 F6 08 D3   =.......
                                         0150  D1 E6 F7 D3   D1 05 C2 41   .......A
>JS
```

GenRad Systems   451

Note that in the above, the last few columns are the ASCII representation of the contents of each of the memory locations in the memory map. This feature is useful if the contents of memory displayed are alphabetic data. If a byte does not contain a printable ASCII character, a "." is displayed. A display with useful ASCII display is shown below:

```
PC    A   B C   D E   H L   IX    SZHVNC  V    SP    A´  B´C´  D´E´  H´L´  IY    SZHVNC  I
0000  00  0000  0000  0000  0000  000000  00   6E00  00  0000  0000  0000  0000  000000  00

015A >2020       JR    NZ,X´017C´         0110  3F 01 C3 00   01 06 01 78    ?......x
                                          0118  D3 D0 DB D0   E6 3F C2 2C    .....?.,
015C  2020       JR    NZ,X´017E´         0120  01 78 07 47   D6 10 CA 3E    .x.G...>
                                          0128  01 C3 17 01   21 FC FF 11    ....!...
015E  2020       JR    NZ,X´0180´         0130  04 00 19 0F   D2 32 01 78    .....2.x
                                          0138  2C 0F D2 38   01 7D C9 06    ,..8.}..
0160  2020       JR    NZ,X´0182´         0140  08 7E 23 F6   80 D3 D0 78    .~#....x
                                          0148  3D E6 F7 D3   D1 F6 08 D3    =.......
0162  52         LD    D,D                0150  D1 E6 F7 D3   D1 05 C2 41    .......A
                                          0158  01 C9>20 20   20 20 20 20    ..
0163  4F         LD    C,A                0160  20 20 52 4F   57 35 43 4F       ROW5CO
                                          0168  4C 31 52 4F   57 35 43 4F    L1ROW5CO
0164  57         LD    D,A                0170  4C 32 52 4F   57 35 43 4F    L2ROW5CO
                                          0178  4C 33 52 4F   57 35 43 4F    L3ROW5CO
0165  35         DEC   (HL)               0180  4C 34 52 4F   57 34 43 4F    L4ROW4CO
                                          0188  4C 31 52 4F   57 34 43 4F    L1ROW4CO
0166  43         LD    B,E                0190  4C 32 52 4F   57 34 43 4F    L2ROW4CO
                                          0198  4C 33 52 4F   57 34 43 4F    L3ROW4CO
0167  4F         LD    C,A                01A0  4C 34 52 4F   57 33 43 4F    L4ROW3CO
                                          01A8  4C 31 52 4F   57 33 43 4F    L1ROW3CO
>JS
```

Table 10.2 gives an overall comparison of the three different types of popular systems, namely, Intel and GenRad, Tektronix, Hewlett-Packard, and others.

Table 10.2. Development System Emulator Architecture and Associated Hardware/Software Devices

Manufacturer	Characteristics	Microprocessors	Memory and Peripherals	Software	CRT Display
Hewlett-Packard 64000	Master/slave multistation with (up to 6) complete separations of host processor from the emulation system. This allows the host processor to run the emulation support software independently of the emulator Universal Soft key features Provides both hardware and software development capabilities	8080 8085 8086 6800 6802 68000 8048 8049 6809 8040 8035 8039 8050	HP 16-bit host microprocessor with 128K of 16-bit host and 64K bytes of emulation memory Hard disk of up to 960 megabytes Line printers Universal PROM programmers Logic analysis Cassette interface	Editor Assembler Macroassembler Linker PASCAL compiler	Memory refreshed (smart terminal)
Intel 120	Basically similar to Intel's previous model 220 Modified master/slave single memory Nonuniversal In-circuit emulator is provided as an option	8080/8085 8048/8049 May expand to support other Intel microprocessors	8080 microprocessor host with 32K bytes of RAM and 4K bytes of ROM 250K byte floppy disk Universal PROM programmers High-speed paper tape reader/punch Single station Line printer	Editor Assembler Macroassembler Debugger Linker No high-level language compilers of interpreters in the basic system	Memory refreshed (smart terminal)
Intel 225	Similar to previous Model 230. The main difference is 230 was 8080 based whereas 225 is 8085 based. Modified master/slave Nonuniversal Standard emulation capabilities	8080/8085 8048/8049 8086	8085 host microprocessor with 64K bytes of RAM and 4K bytes ROM 250K bytes floppy disk plus 7.3 megabytes hard disk Single station PROM programmer Line printer Tape reader/punch	Editor Assembler Macroassembler Debugger Linker PL/M compiler FORTRAN compiler PASCAL compiler COBOL compiler	Memory refreshed (smart terminal)

Intel 286	A new system with two host processors (8085 and 8086). 8086 host supports development of 8080/8085 and 8048. Nonuniversal Modified master/slave Standard emulation capabilities	8086/8088 8080/8085 8048	Two host processors with 96K bytes of user RAM 250K bytes floppy disc and 7.3 megabytes of hard disk Single Station Paper tape reader/punch PROM programmer Line printer	Editor Assembler Macroassembler Debugger Linker Supports PL/M 88/86 PASCAL 88/86 FORTRAN 88/86	Memory refreshed (smart terminal)
Intel 290	A new network with 8085 host and supporting up to 8 stations Nonuniversal Modified master/slave Supports all Intel development systems as work stations	8080/8085 8048/8049 8086/8088	8085 host with up to 8 stations 64K RAM, 4K ROM Maximum 15 megabytes of hard and floppy disks Line printer PROM programmer	Editor Assembler Macroassembler Debugger Linker Supports PL/M 88/86 PASCAL 88/86 FORTRAN 88/86	Memory refreshed (smart terminal)
Tektronix 8001	Offered to those who already have the software development capability using a host. The 8001 basically provides full debugging and software/hardware integration. Provides three modes of emulation Master/slave with split memory Universal	For hardware emulation 8080/8085 6800 Z80 9900 68000 8086 Z8000 Software development depends on the availability of cross assemblers on the host.	Single-station CRT terminal for control and display Logic analyzer	System development software depends on the host computer. The 8001 uses a format called the TEKHEX for transferring the object code from host to the 8001.	RS-232C (dumb terminal)

Table 10.2. (continued)

Manufacturer	Characteristics	Microprocessors	Memory and Peripherals	Software	CRT Display
Tektronix 8002A	Master/slave with split memory. Provides both hardware and software development capabilities. Three emulation modes. Universal	Supports 29 microprocessors such as: 8086, 68000, Z8000, 8080/8085, 6800, 6802 1802 and many more	16K byte of host and up to 64K byte of target. Floppy disk. PROM programmer. Logic analyzer. Printer. Single station	Editor. Assembler. Debugger. Macroassembler. Linker	RS-232C (dumb terminal)
Tektronix 8550	Single-user system. Universal. Master/slave. Can be interfaced to multiuser systems	29 microprocessors	Two hardware units plus optional CRT terminal and line printer. Dual floppy disk. Logic analyzer	Editor. Assembler. Debugger. Linker. Macroassembler. MDL/μ and PASCAL compilers	RS-232C (dumb terminal)
Tektronix 8560	Time-shared software development. Multiuser up to 8 stations. Uses DEC LSI II/23. 8001, 8002A, and 8550 can be added to provide hardware development stations. Universal	29 microprocessors	128K words dynamic RAM. 35 megabytes hard disk. 1 megabyte floppy disk. Line printer. PROM programmer	Editor. Assembler. Debugger. Linker. Macroassembler. PASCAL compilers	RS-232C (dumb terminal)
Tektronix 8540	Provides multiuser capabilities via a host. Similar to 8560 with emulation capabilities. Master/slave. Expandable using 8002A. Universal. Developed basically for host system owners	29 microprocessors	32K byte RAM. PROM programmer. Logic analyzer. Depends on host	Debugger. System development software depends on host	RS-232C (dumb terminal)

GenRad (formerly Futuredata) 2300	Universal stand-alone software station Single processor	Software development for 8086 8080/8085 8048 Z80 6800 6801 Z8000 6809 1802 6502 many more	Up to 64K bytes 1 megabyte floppy disk CRT and keyboard	Editor Assembler Debugger BASIC and PASCAL compilers	Memory refreshed (smart terminal)
GenRad (formerly Futuredata) 2301	Universal multistation (up to 8) Single processor	8080/8085 6800 6802 Z80	Up to 64K bytes CRT and keyboard Logic analyzer PROM programmer Disk Line printer	Editor Assembler Debugger Linker BASIC and PASCAL compilers	Memory refreshed (smart terminal)
GenRad (formerly Futuredata) 2302	Universal Slave emulator The master computer is the 2300 system. Separates emulation memory bus and control Master/slave	Up to a maximum of 64 different combinations of microprocessors	Up to 512K bytes of emulation memory CRT and keyboard Logic analyzer PROM programmer	System development in software depends on the host 2300 ADS	Memory refreshed (smart terminal)

PROBLEMS AND QUESTIONS

10.1 Identify the main differences among the HP 64000, Intel 290, Tektronix 8560, and GenRad 2301 systems.

10.2 What is the maximum number of stations the 64000 can support? Is it possible to configure each station as either software and/or hardware stations?

10.3 What type of development system architectures do the Intel systems use?

10.4 What is meant by IOC and IPB in Intel systems?

10.5 What is the purpose of HSE-49?

10.6 Form a table showing the basic differences between the following Intel development systems: Model 120 versus Model 225; Model 286 versus Model 290.

10.7 Summarize the software and hardware capabilities of Tektronix 8001, 8002A, 8540, 8550, and 8560. What types of debugging tools are available with these?

10.8 What is meant by RTE and RTPA in relation to the Tektronix systems?

10.9 What is the purpose of the library generator on the 8550?

10.10 What are the basic differences among GenRad 2300, 2301, and 2302 systems?

10.11 What is the maximum number of microprocessor hardware and software that can be carried out utilizing eight 2301 and 64 2302 systems?

10.12 What are the advantages of using slave emulators?

CHAPTER 11

THE HEWLETT-PACKARD (HP) 64000

> This chapter provides fundamental concepts associated with a typical microcomputer development system such as the HP 64000. Once its operations are learned, it would be easier to transfer those skills to learning about other systems. Note that the 64000 is used as a typical example.

11.1 System Description

The HP 64000 Microprocessor Logic Development System is a universal development system which provides all of the necessary tools to create, develop, modify, and debug software for microprocessor-based systems. In-circuit emulation provides the capability of performing an in-depth analysis of hardware and software interfacing during the integration phase of the development process.

The HP 64000 Microprocessor Logic Development System is a multi-user development system, allowing up to as many as six users to operate on the system simultaneously. All users of the system share a line printer and a common data base in the form of a 12-megabyte Winchester Technology Disc Drive or a selection of one to eight Multi-Access Controller (MAC) disk drives connected to the system via the HP Interface Bus, commonly referred to as HP-IB. Eight disk drives can provide up to 960 megabytes of HP-formatted storage space.

11.2 Development Station Description

Figure 11.1 shows the front view of the HP 64000 Development Station. The keyboard (Figure 11.2) is divided into four areas: (1) an ASCII-encoded typewriter-type keyboard; (2) a group of edit keys, which facilitate movement of text or cursor when in the edit mode; (3) special function keys, for system reset or pause or to access a command recall buffer; (4) the all important system "soft keys," eight unobtrusive large key pads just beneath the bezel which surrounds the display.

The soft keys provide a quick and easy means to invoke system commands, virtually eliminating the typographical errors one usually has to contend with when having to enter commands character by character. The definition of each soft key is written on the display just above the bezel. The soft key syntax changes depending on the mode of operation and the

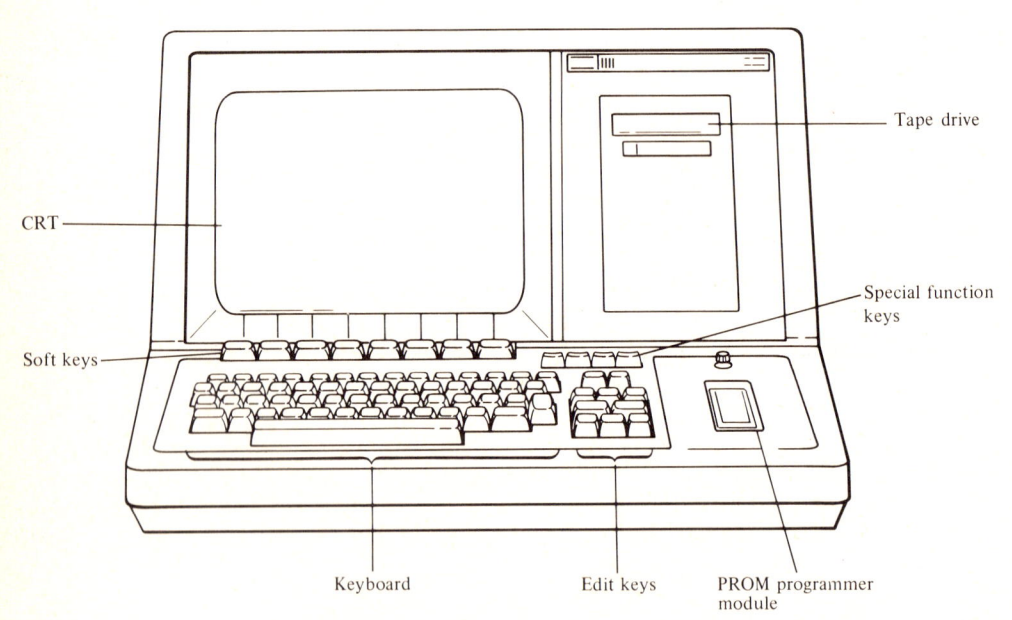

Figure 11.1 Front view of the HP 64000 Development Station (Model 64100A). Front Panel: The seven major areas of the front panel are shown. Each area provides the interface necessary to operate and control the system. CRT Display: The CRT is a large-screen, raster-scan magnetic display. Screen capacity is 25 rows and 80 columns of characters. The standard 128-character (upper and lower case) ASCII set can be displayed. A blinking underline cursor is present as the prompt. Video enhancements are inverse video, blinking, and underline. Soft Keys: Just below the CRT are eight unlabeled keys. These keys are defined as the "soft keys." Each key ties to the soft key label line at the bottom of the CRT. During operation, the soft keys are labeled on the CRT screen. Source: Courtesy of Hewlett-Packard.

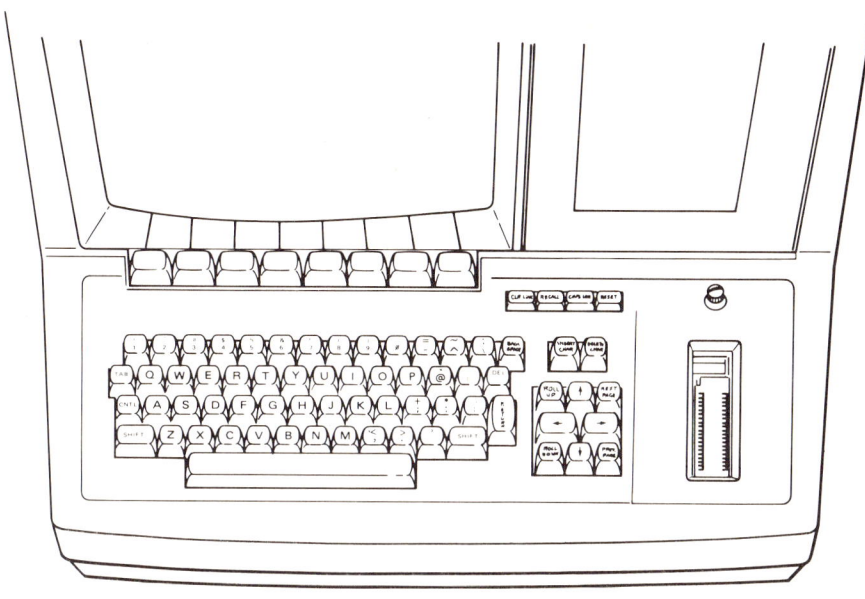

Figure 11.2 Model 64100A keyboard. Source: Courtesy of Hewlett-Packard.

position of the cursor. This greatly enhances the ease of use of the system since it provides a list of alternatives available and guides the operator to use the system. In cases where the form of the input required is unknown, brackets surrounding a key word, a syntactical variable will prompt the user with the correct form of input the system expects.

The system display is a Raster Scan CRT which provides a display of 18 lines of text entry, a status line which always displays the system's status and date and time, three lines for command entry, and the soft key label line which indicates the function of each key. The display is 80 columns wide, but with the edit keys the display can be relocated to show text or data out to 240 columns. This is convenient for adding comments and really enhances the program documentation.

Other external station hardware includes RS232 ports for communication with either Data Communications Equipment (DCE) or Data Terminal Equipment (DTE). The RS232 port has a selectable baud rate up to 9,600 and uses the X-ON X-OFF convention for handshaking at baud rates 2,400 and above. There is a 20-mA current loop for TTY interfacing and two ports for triggering of external devices such as an oscilloscope during a logic trace. As system options, the front panel hosts a PROM programmer (Figure 11.1) to the immediate right of the keyboard and a tape drive for file back-up. The tape drive performs a high-speed read and write and each cassette holds 250K bytes of data.

11.3 Getting Started

11.3.1 Powering up

When first powering up the development station, there are a couple of considerations. The first consideration is that the address of the station is set accordingly and the operating mode of the system is also set. On the back of the station, there is a 5-bit dip switch which performs two functions. While facing this set of switches, the right 3 bits determine the address of the station. In multiuser systems, each station has its own unique address as determined by these 3 bits. This address is a value between two and seven. The disk is at address zero and the printer is at address one. These addresses are fixed and cannot be changed by the user. The left two bits of this switch determine the operating mode of the system. The normal mode when operating with a disk is the "system bus" mode. Ensure that the switches are set accordingly.

To power up the system, it is good practice to turn on the disk first, then the printer, and then the development station last. All of the power switches are located next to the power cord of each element of the system and are easily located.

Upon completion of power-up, you will hear two beeps from the station indicating the completion of an internal self-verification and successful power-up. The display will then show the I/O bus configuration. After power-up, the display should look as follows:

```
I/O BUS CONFIGURATION

ADRS   DEVICE
  0    13037 DISC CONTROLLER
       UNIT  0  7906 DISC MEMORY   LU=0   NA32
  4    THIS 64100, MASTER CONTROLLER
```

Each device that is a part of the system will be named along with its corresponding address. This will provide a quick check of the system, letting the user know that all the elements are on-line.

11.3.2 Loading System Software

The operating system software or system manager is contained on one or two cassettes depending upon the revision of software. The operating software and other proprietary software products by Hewlett-Packard are loaded by first setting the two left-most switches (Figure 11.1) located on the back of the station to the position of "LOCAL MASS STORAGE." Then initiate a "RESET" by depressing the reset key located among the special function keys. The CRT will then display a message "WAITING FOR CARTRIDGE." Next insert the tape into the tape drive. There will be a number of queries for the operator to answer.

Formatting the disk creates a link list of 2K blocks of storage space and will obliterate any data currently residing on the disk. The user is given the option of formatting what should be done the first time the system is powered up during installation. Later one would generally only want to load the system software and overlay any previous versions. This can be done without formatting the disk. Merely by answering NO to the formatting questions, one can select the proper operation from the soft key labels displayed at the bottom of the CRT.

Upon completion of any necessary preliminary disk operations, the user can then begin the work session by first looking over the alternatives presented by the soft key syntax displayed at the bottom of the CRT.

11.3.3 Soft Keys

Upon powering up the station the soft keys will display a variety of definitions. Initially the left-most soft key label will be "edit." Note that there are eight keys and the right-most key label will read "etc." Depressing this key twice will display two more groups of eight soft key definitions. The left-most key now reads "userid" surrounded by the keys labeled "time" and "date."

Let us start our session by entering the time and date using the appropriate soft keys. First depress the soft key "time." Notice how the syntax changed. You will now see a key labeled "(time)." Whenever this type of bracket is displayed it is a prompt to the user that this key will provide a definition of the form of the syntactical variable required. Depress the "time" soft key and the status line now shows the form of the required time entry "HH:MM." This is a 24-hour clock so enter the appropriate digits, then "RETURN." The time will be displayed on the far right of the status line and will be continuously updated as long as power is applied to the system.

Now depress the date key and enter in the correct form of the date. Note that you are once again provided with the correct form that the system expects. This type of prompting is a lot faster than thumbing through a manual to find the correct form and saves frustration of trial and error. The date will then be displayed on the status line. The date will no longer be displayed once the system status changes but if one forgets, then merely depress the date key and then return. The date will appear on the status line.

The date and time entry of the system is only one of a number of interesting features. The file manager allows access to files by date. This is a useful tool if you wish to pull from the archives a file you created or worked on six months ago, but you cannot remember the name, just a rough estimate of the date. You can request a directory of all files modified or accessed on or before a certain date.

The userid is a user identification which the system uses to differentiate one user from another. This allows users to keep their own files separate from those of other users. The advantage of the userid is obvious to those using a shared data base. A description of the system monitor soft keys is provided in Appendix D. Note that the new HP operating system combines the date and time functions. HP recently made a minor update to the 64000 operating system. For details, consult the HP 64000 new manuals.

11.3.4 Special Function Keys

The special function keys located at the top right of the keyboard (Figure 11.3) provide the user with some added functions. The function of the "CLEARLINE" and "CAPS LOCK" keys is somewhat obvious. The "RECALL" key and the "RESET" key deserve some special attention.

The RECALL key allows the user to recall the last command to be entered on the command line and executed. This is of great help since one often wishes to reexecute commands without reentering the whole line of command syntax. The RESET key has two functions. Depressing the key once causes the system to pause. When the system is paused, it will continue when any other key on the keyboard is depressed. If the reset is depressed twice in succession, the system will reset by clearing the CRT return to the system monitor. Depressing the SHIFT key and the RESET key simultaneously will cause the system to do a complete reboot. Depressing the CNTL key and the RESET key simultaneously will cause the system to initiate performance verification.

Table 11.1 provides a summary of the special function keys.

11.4 Editor

The editor provides a means to create or generate new programs and to revise existing programs. The editor of the HP 64000 is a context-based editor. It allows entry of text or data over a range of 240 columns of which only 80 are visible immediately. The remaining 160 columns can be viewed by depressing simultaneously the shift key and the left arrow key residing among the edit keys.

There are three basic modes of operation for the editor in the HP 64000. These modes are the command mode, the insert mode, and the revise mode. The insert mode allows entry of text or data as a newly created source file or as new text in a previously existing file. The revise mode allows for the modification of previously existing files by adding or deleting characters or

Editor 463

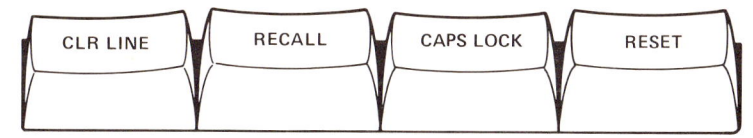

Figure 11.3 Special function keys. Source: Courtesy of Hewlett-Packard.

Table 11.1. Summary of Special Functions Keys

Key	Description
[CLR LINE]	Press to clear the current line containing cursor on the CRT.
[RECALL]	Used to recall, to the command line, previous commands from a stack. The commands are displayed one at a time for each time the [RECALL] key is pressed. The number of recallable commands is variable. Only valid commands are pushed into the stack. If the [RECALL] key is pressed and the buffer is empty the system responds with "Recall buffer is empty" message.
[CAPS LOCK]	Used to lock keyboard in all uppercase letters. A message is presented on the CRT indicating "CAPS LOCK on" or "CAPS LOCK off." At the next key stroke, the message is erased, but the mode remains in effect.
[RESET]	Pressing [RESET] once initiates a pause in system operation. A flashing "PAUSED" message, in inverse video, is presented on the status line. To continue operation, press any key except [RESET].
	Pressing the [RESET] key the second time will clear the CRT and return the system to the system monitor.
[SHIFT] [RESET]	Holding the [SHIFT] key down and pressing [RESET] initiates a complete system reboot. This function should be regarded as a last resort when the system does not respond.
[CNTL] [RESET]	Holding [CNTL] key down and pressing [RESET] initiates system performance verification.

Source: Courtesy of Hewlett-Packard.

lines. The command mode allows the setting of tabs, renumbering of lines of source, the extracting or the retrieving of text, and the merging of files.

11.4.1 Using the Editor

Before starting to edit, we will review a few conventions used for assembly language programming using the editor.

1. There are four dedicated fields for assembly language programming.

    LABEL   OPCODE   OPERAND   COMMENTS

    The label field always starts in column one. If the first column is a ";" or an "*" the rest of the line is treated as a comment. The comment field should be preceded by a ";". When you type in your assembly language program it is recommended to use the "TAB" key to keep everything spaced properly.

    LABEL "TAB"   OPCODE "TAB"   OPERAND "TAB"   COMMENTS "TAB"

2. The very first line in your program must contain the processor type that you are currently using. In this case it is the 8085. This is called the "assembler directive" and must start in column one.
3. You may wish to define the starting address of your program with the pseudo op "ORG." This will set the program counter to the absolute address used as the operand in the instruction.

    ```
    LABEL    OPCODE   OPERAND   COMMENTS
    "8085"
             ORG      1000H     ;Program starts at 1000 H
    ```

4. If you desire to write your program symbolically and not use absolute address information this can be accomplished through the use of the "EQU" pseudo op.

    ```
    LABEL    OPCODE   OPERAND   COMMENTS
    PORTA    EQU      10H       ;Address for port A is 10H
    ```

   The advantage to this method is that you do not have to remember the actual physical addresses of the ports or memory locations associated with the program. If a value must be changed in the future it is merely necessary to update the single EQU instruction rather than all the occurrences of the absolute value if it had been used. A typical 8085 assembly language program is given below:

LABEL	OPCODE	OPERAND	COMMENTS
"8085"			
	ORG	1000H	
PORTA	EQU	10H	;Port A is at address 10H
PORTB	EQU	20H	;Port B is at address 20H
	NOP		
START	MVI	A,00H	;Load A with 00H
	OUT	PORTA	;Output to address 10H
	OUT	PORTB	;Output to address 20H
	END		

Now that we have covered some of the more basic aspects, we are ready to enter a program.

1. Press the soft key "edit."
2. Press "RETURN." The screen should display: Editing new file. The editor should be in the "insert" mode, which allows you to enter in new text. Notice that the labels on the soft keys changed to "insert," "revise," and "delete," . . . and so on.

Some hints for those who have not used the editor before:

1. When the editor is in the insert mode a "RETURN" must be pressed to insert the line and go to the following line.
2. If you make a mistake, press the "revise" soft key and move the cursor to the appropriate location using the edit keys, that is, "roll up," "roll down," and "insert char" or the "delete char." These edit keys allow you to position the text or the cursor or both out to columns 240.
3. To continue adding to the file after a correction, press the "insert" key once again and begin adding text after the last line in your program.
4. To end the edit session press the "end" soft key and enter the name you wish to give the file.
5. To edit an existing file depress the soft key "edit" followed by the file name of the existing file you wish to edit. The file will then be displayed on the screen ready for editing.

The 64000 editor commands are listed in Appendix D.

11.5 The HP 64000 Assembler

The assembler for the HP 64000 is referred to as a two-pass relocatable macroassembler. It is so named because the 64000 assembly goes through the assembly language program twice, it has macrohandling capability, and will assemble a source file and generate a relocatable object code. This relocatable code does not have absolute address assignments until completion of the linking process. It is during the linking process that the object code receives specific address assignments and only then can it be located into designated memory locations for execution.

11.5.1 Assembler Commands

Once the source program has been completed and properly edited, we are then ready to convert the program into a form that the processor will understand. The first step in this process is the assembly process in which the source program gets converted into a relocatable object code.

To use the assembler perform the following:

1. Depress the soft key "assemble."
2. Enter the name of the course file to be assembled.
3. Depress the soft key "listfile." This tells the assembler there is to be an output.
4. Depress one of the following soft keys.
   a. "Printer."
   b. "Display."
   c. Or enter in a file name to be used as the destination for the assembler output listing.
5. Depress the soft key "option." This tells the assembler that an option is selected.
6. Depress the soft key "x_ref." This will cause the assembler to generate a cross-reference listing of the symbols defined within the source program. The command line should now look like the following: "assemble FILENAME listfile printer options x_ref."
7. Depress "RETURN." This will cause the system to execute the command syntax just entered.

An example of an assembled program listing is shown below. Note the headings above each column, the line number, the code, and the source program. Also note the date and time supplied with the listing. At the end of the program listing, you will find the number of errors and the definition of any error codes displayed within the body of the listing.

Following the listing, one finds the cross-reference table which lists the line number of any labels or symbols, the symbol, the type of symbol, and

The HP 64000 Assembler **467**

any line numbers which reference that symbol. This is a time saver when having to debug programs.

The listings of the assembler soft keys, pseudoinstructions, and error codes are given in Appendix D.

```
FILE: VALVE:STUDN   HEWLETT-PACKARD: INTEL 8085 ASSEMBLER     Wed, 19 Mar 1980, 0:48   PAGE
LINE LOC  CODE ADDR  SOURCE STATEMENT

   1                    *0085*
   2                    *
   3                    *THE FOLLOWING PROGRAM CONTROLS B VALVES OF A CHEMICAL PLANT
   4                    *
   5 0000                      ORG   0000H           ;DEFINE STARTING ADDRESS OF PROGRAM
   6        0000 PORTA         EQU   00H             ;DEFINE ADDRESS OF PORT(A) DATA
   7        0002 ADIREC        EQU   02H             ;DEFINE ADDRESS OF DIRECTION REGISTER FOR PORT(A)
   8        0001 VALVE1        EQU   01H             ;DEFINE BIT TO CONTROL VALVE #1 (BIT 0)
   9        0002 VALVE2        EQU   02H             ;DEFINE BIT TO CONTROL VALVE #2 (BIT 1)
  10        0004 VALVE3        EQU   04H             ;DEFINE BIT TO CONTROL VALVE #3 (BIT 2)
  11        000B VALVE4        EQU   00H             ;DEFINE BIT TO CONTROL VALVE #4 (BIT 3)
  12        0010 VALVE5        EQU   10H             ;DEFINE BIT TO CONTROL VALVE #5 (BIT 4)
  13        0020 VALVE6        EQU   20H             ;DEFINE BIT TO CONTROL VALVE #6 (BIT 5)
  14        0040 VALVE7        EQU   40H             ;DEFINE BIT TO CONTROL VALVE #7 (BIT 6)
  15        0080 VALVE8        EQU   D0H             ;DEFINE BIT TO CONTROL VALVE #8 (BIT 7)
  16 0000 00                   NOP

  47 0049 CD 004F              CALL  DELAY           ;WAIT FOR 2 SECONDS
  48 004C C3 0005              JMP   START           ;REPEAT PROGRAM ALL OVER AGAIN
  49 004F 00           DELAY   NOP                   ;THIS SUBROUTINE WAITS FOR APROX. 2 SECONDS
  50 0050 21 0FFF              LXI   H,0FFFH         ;LOAD REGISTER PAIR (HL) WITH 0FFF HEX
  51 0053 2B           LOOP    DCX   H               ;DECREMENT (HL)
  52 0054 C2 0053              JNZ   LOOP            ;LOOP UNTIL (HL) = 0
  53 0057 C9                   RET                   ;RETURN FROM SUBROUTINE
  54                           END

Errors= 0

                     FILE: VALVE:STUDN   CROSS REFERENCE TABLE     PAGE 2
                     LINE#  SYMBOL   TYPE   REFERENCES

                            A        A      17,19,22,25,28,31,34,37,40
                       7    ADIREC   A      18
                      49    DELAY    A      21,24,27,30,33,36,39,42,43,44,45,46,47
                            H        A      50,51
                      51    LOOP     A      52
                       6    PORTA    A      20,23,26,29,32,35,38,41
```

19	START	A	48
8	VALVE1	A	19
9	VALVE2	A	22
10	VALVE3	A	25
11	VALVE4	A	28
12	VALVE5	A	31
13	VALVE6	A	34
14	VALVE7	A	37
15	VALVE8	A	40

Upon completion of the assembly, we can look at a directory listing and see the addition of two files to the list. The relocatable file is referred to as reloc and the assembler symbol file is called asmb_sym.

Directory List   File:VALVE: Disc: 0   Wed, 19 Mar 1980,   0:44   Page 1

NAME	TYPE	SIZE	LAST MODIFY	LAST ACCESS
VALVE:STUDN	asmb_sym	1	19 Mar 1980, 0:32	19 Mar 1980, 0:32
VALVE:STUDN	reloc	1	19 Mar 1980, 0:32	19 Mar 1980, 0:32
VALVE:STUDN	source	1	19 Mar 1980, 0:34	19 Mar 1980, 0:32

**** Files listed   3,   0.34% disc space used   ****
**** 22.53% disc space available   ****

11.5.2 64000 Macros

As mentioned before, using macros can make programming in assembly language easier by reducing the amount of code the programmer has to actually write. This is accomplished by letting the assembler produce those redundant pieces of program that are used routinely in various places in the program. Basically a macro is a set of instructions used repeatedly throughout the program. When the macro is written, it is assigned a name. Rather than rewrite the same sequence of instructions each time they are needed, the name of the macro is inserted in their place. During assembly wherever the name of the macro is encountered the assembler will insert the sequence of instructions that this name represents.

The macro is in some ways similar to a subroutine, in that the usage is repeated. The subroutine may be more efficient in some applications but not in others. If a macro is used extensively it will generate more code than if the same code was used in a subroutine. There are a number of factors to be considered in the application of macros and subroutines. There is no doubt however, that macros facilitate the entry of code and make program entry less work for the programmer.

The HP 64000 provides the capability of conditional macroassembly. Note that conditional assembly means that the portions of the macro will be assembled depending on certain conditions determined by the relational operators.

Typical 64000 macro pseudoinstructions are given below:

.IF Allows the user to include a condition for conditional macroassembly.
.SET Assigns the value in the operand field to the name or expression specified in the label field.
.GOTO Unconditional jump.
.NOP No operation. Typically used with .IF or .GOTO for branching to instructions that are not labeled.
MEND End of macro.

Examples 11.1 and 11.2 illustrate the implementation of a macro. Example 11.1 is of a simple macro with no parameter passing. The assembled version is shown with and without expansion of the code within the macro. If the macro is not expanded during the assembly process, the assembler output listing will not show the macro code where it is called. Example 11.2 indicates usage of parameter passing. Note that parameter passing is the ability to pass a variable from one program to another. This example is also followed by the nonexpanded and expanded versions of the assembler listing. The treatment of macros here is limited and it is recommended that the appropriate manuals be studied for a greater understanding of the implementation of macros.

EXAMPLE 11.1

```
"8085"
        Title  "SIMPLE MACRO"
        EXT VALUE, TEMP, NOW
NAME    MACRO                   ;The macro starts at "MACRO" and ends at "MEND"
        LDA NOW                 ;Whenever the Macro is called by using the
        STA TEMP                ;name of the Macro "NAME" the section of
        LXI H,VALUE             ;code in the Macro will be substituted.
        MOV A,M                 ;This can be observed in the assembly process
        MEND                    ;if the assembler is invoked using the expand
        STA VALUE               ;command.
                "assemble FILENAME listfile FILENAME options expand."
        NAME                    :Macro call
        END
```

In the above, the instruction sequence starting with NAME MACRO and ending with MEND is the macro program. This macro program utilizes the

470 Chapter 11 THE HEWLETT-PACKARD (HP) 64000

operands VALUE, TEMP, and NOW which are defined in another program. The EXT pseudoinstruction lets the user accomplish this. STA VALUE is an arbitrary instruction. NAME is used to call the macroprogram.

The following is the nonexpanded version of the assembly listing.

```
FILE: MACRO:YOURID    HEWLETT-PACKARD: SIMPLE MACRO
LOCATION  OBJECT CODE  LINE      SOURCE LINE
                       1  "8085"
                       2             Title "SIMPLE MACRO WITHOUT EXPANSION"
                       3
                       4             EXT VALUE, TEMP,NOW
                       5  NAME       MACRO
                       6             LDA NOW      ;The macro consists of lines
                       7             STA TEMP     ;5 thru 10
                       8             LXI H,VALUE
                       9             MOV A,M
                       10            MEND         ;End of the macro
  000     320000       11            STA VALUE
  0003                 12            NAME         ;Here the macro was called
                       13            END          ;But it was not expanded
Errors= 0
```

The next listing is of the expanded macro.

```
FILE: MACRO:YOURID    HEWLETT-PACKARD: SIMPLE MACRO
LOCATION  OBJECT CODE  LINE      SOURCE LINE
                       1  "8085"
                       2             Title        "SIMPLE MACRO EXPANDED"
                       3
                       4             EXT VALUE, TEMP,NOW
                       5  NAME       MACRO
                       6             LDA NOW
                       7             STA TEMP
                       8             LXI H,VALUE
                       9             MOV A,M
                       10            MEND
  0000    320000       11            STA VALUE
  0003                 12            NAME         ;This is the macro call
  0003    3A0000       +             LDA NOW      ;Note that this section of
  0006    320000       +             STA TEMP     ;code is the same as the
  0009    210000       +             LXI H,VALUE  ;macro listed above
  000C    7E           +             MOV A,M
                       13            END
Errors= 0
```

EXAMPLE 11.2

The following source listing is an example of passing parameters within the macro.

```
"8085"
         TITLE "MACRO EXAMPLE   WITH PARAMETERS"
ONCE     EQU 0
TWICE    EQU 1
VALUE    EQU 400H
REPEAT   MACRO &VAL1,&VAL2       ;The parameters are passed using
         .IF &VAL1 .EQ. 1 TRADE  ;dummy variables preceded by "&".
         .IF &VAL2 .EQ. 1 MOVE   ;This example indicated two parameters
TRADE    LXI H,VALUE             ;being passed.
         .GOTO END               ;Note the use of the relational operators.
MOVE     MOV A,M
END      MEND
         STA VALUE
         REPEAT ONCE,TWICE       ;Here is the macro call and the actual
         END                     ;parameters being passed. "ONCE" is the
                                 ;first parameter and "TWICE" is the second.
```

In the above program, the first three EQU pseudoinstructions assign the values 0, 1, and 400H, repetively, to ONCE, TWICE, and VALUE. REPEAT MACRO &VAL1, &VAL2 gives the name REPEAT to the macro and contains the dummy variables &VAL1, &VAL2 used for passing parameters. The next two instructions contain relational operators which determine which instructions within the macro will be assembled. For example, if &VAL1 .EQ. 1 is true, then the instruction sequence with the label TRADE i.e., LXI H,VALUE will be assembled; otherwise, the program will go the the next statement IF &VAL1 .EQ. 1 MOVE. In this case, if &VAL is equal to 1, then the instruction sequence MOV A,M with the label MOVE will be assembled. MEND indicates end of macro. STA VALUE is an arbitrary instruction. REPEAT ONCE, TWICE calls the macro REPEAT with ONCE and TWICE as parameters. &VAL1 and &VAL2 are equated to ONCE and TWICE which have values 0 and 1, repsectively. Therefore, the condition &VAL2 is equal to 1 and the instruction sequence MOV A,M with label MOVE is assembled. The assembled listing for the macro REPEAT with expanded version can be used to verify this.

Next is the assembled listing of the macro without expansion.

472 Chapter 11 The Hewlett-Packard (HP) 64000

```
FILE: MACROVAR:YOURID    HEWLETT-PACKARD: MACRO EXAMPLE
                         WITH PARAMETERS

LOCATION OBJECT CODE LINE
                        1  "8085"
                        3
                        4
            (0000)      5  ONCE    EQU 0
            (0001)      6  TWICE   EQU 1
            (0400)      7  VALUE   EQU 400H
                        8  REPEAT  MACRO &VAL1,&VAL2
                        9          .IF &VAL1 .EQ. 1 TRADE
                       10          .1F &VALW .EQ. 1 MOVE
                       11  TRADE   LXI H,VALUE
                       12          .GOTO END
                       13  MOVE    MOV A,M
                       14  END     MEND
     0000   320400     15          STA VALUE
     0003              16          REPEAT ONCE,TWICE
                       17          END

          Errors=  0
```

Now for the expanded version.

```
FILE: MACROVAR:YOURID    HEWLETT-PACKARD: MCAROEXAMPLE WITH PARAMETERS

LOCATION OBJECT CODE LINE       SOURCE LINE
                        1  "8085"
                        3
                        4
          (0000)        5  ONCE    EQU 0
          (0001)        6  TWICE   EQU 1
          (0400)        7  VALUE   EQU 400H
                        8  REPEAT  MACRO &VAL1,&VAL2
                        9          .IF &VAL1 .EQ. 1 TRADE    ;The relational operators
                       10          .IF &VAL2 .EQ. 1 MOVE     ;allow conditional
                       11  TRADE   LXI H,VALUE               ;assembly as illustrated
                       12          .GOTO END                 ;in line 16+. The macro
                       13  MOVE    MOV A,M                   ;was expanded according to
                       14  END     MEND                      ;the results of the
   0000   320400       15          STA VALUE                 ;relational operations.
   0003                16          REPEAT ONCE, TWICE
   0003   7E         + MOVE        MOV A,M
                       17          END

Errors=  0
```

In order to demonstrate an application of conditional macro, consider rotating the contents of the accumulator twice either to the left or right many times in a program. This can be accomplished using macro in two ways:

1. By defining two separate macros as unconditional for rotating either right or left.
2. By defining one conditional macro by setting the conditions based on whether the rotation is to the right or left.

The conditional macro program for accomplishing the above is given below:

CONDITIONAL MACROPROGRAM FOR ROTATING THE CONTENTS OF THE ACCUMULATOR EITHER TO THE RIGHT OR LEFT

```
          "8085"
RIGHT     EQU 1
LEFT      EQU 0
ROTATE1   MACRO &DIRECT
          .IF &DIRECT .EQ. 1 ROTATE-RT
          RAL
          RAL
          .GOTO END
ROTATE-RT RAR
          RAR
END       MEND
              .
              .
              .
          ROTATE1 RIGHT
          NOP
          ROTATE1 LEFT
              .
              .
              .
```

In the above, the two EQU pseudoinstructions assign 1 to RIGHT and 0 to LEFT, respectively. ROTATE1 MACRO &DIRECT defines ROTATE1 as macro with &DIRECT as the dummy variable. .IF &DIRECT .EQ. 1 ROTATE-RT checks whether &DIRECT has a value of 1 and if it is true, then the program jumps to ROTATE-RT and rotates accumulator to the right twice. On the other hand, if &DIRECT is not equal to 1, then the accumulator is rotated twice to the left and then .GOTO END takes the

474 Chapter 11 THE HEWLETT-PACKARD (HP) 64000

program to MEND. ROTATE1 RIGHT and ROTATE1 LEFT are used for calling the macro for the right or left shifts, respectively. NOP is used as an arbitrary instruction.

11.5.3 Using Assembler Pseudos

The programs ADD1, ADD2, and PSEUDO85 given below will be used to demonstrate the use of the assembler pseudos. A close inspection of the source listing and a comparison with the assembler output listing and the linker listing files will show the result of using these pseudos.

Displays of memory contents are also provided so that a correlation between memory contents and the various pseudos can be made. For example, the program section labeled PROG is linked starting at address 2000H. One can look at those sequential address locations and observe the assembled code for that module. The pseudo ASC is located following the COMMON section. If we look at the address location 2200H where this section is linked we will see the corresponding hexadecimal values for the ASCII string. The reader will be pleased to observe that the string has already been decoded under the column labeled ASCII. This is an easy way to verify that memory has been loaded with the correct ASCII information.

Program Listings

In the following listings, the reader will find all of the 64000 assembler pseudos used at least once.

PROGRAM NAME "ADD_1"

```
"8085"
        TITLE    "EXAMPLE OF THE USE OF ASSEMBLER PSEUDO OPS"
*        THIS PROGRAM STARTS AT 0 AND ADDS LOCATION 100H TO
*        LOCATION 101H AND STORES THE RESULT IN LOCATION 102H.
*
*        PROG, COMN, DATA PSEUDOINSTRUCTIONS ARE ASSIGNED THE
*        LOCATIONS 2000, 2100, AND 2200, RESPECTIVELY, DURING THE
*        LINK PROCESS AS DICTATED BY THE LOAD ADDRESSES.

        PROG                        ;PROGRAM ORIGIN WILL BE AT HEXADECIMAL
                                    ;ADDRESS 2000. THIS IS ACCOMPLISHED THRU
                                    ;THE LINKER AND SPECIFICATION OF PROG STARTING
                                    ;AT 2000H. USE OF COMMON AND DATA SECTIONS
                                    ;IS SIMILAR.
        NAME    "ADD WORKSHOP I"
                                    ;
                                    ;
        SPC     2
```

The HP 64000 Assembler

```
          GLB     VALUE,HERE           ;THE OPERAND LISTED HERE IS DEFINED IN
                                       ;THIS MODULE BUT REFERENCED IN ANOTHER.
          EXT     AWAY                 ;THE SYMBOL "AWAY" IS REFERENCED BY THIS
                                       ;MODULE BUT DEFINED IN ANOTHER.
          SPC     3
VALUE     EQU     17H                  ;EXAMPLE OF THE USE OF THE EQUATE PSUEDO.
TEMP      EQU     800H
          SPC     2
Macro1    MACRO                        ;THIS IS AN EXAMPLE OF A SIMPLE MACRO.
          LDA     VALUE                ;THE MACRO IS CALLED USING THE NAME Macro1
          STA     TEMP                 ;IN THE REMAINDER OF THE PROGRAM, WHEN THE
          MEND                         ;PROGRAM IS ASSEMBLED THE CODE CAN BE LISTED
                                       ;FOR EACH MACRO USAGE BY USING THE
                                       ;"EXPAND" INSTRUCTION.
          SPC     3
START     LXI     H,100H               ;LOAD HL PAIR WITH 100 HEX
          MOV     A,M                  ;MOVE NUMBER IN LOCATION 100 INTO THE ACC.
          INX     H                    ;INCREMENT H AND L PAIR.
          COMN                         ;COMMON SECTION BEGINS AT 2100H AS PER LINKER
                                       ;USE OF THE COMN SECTION IS SIMILAR TO
          SPC     3                    ;THE USE OF PROG.
          ASC     "THIS IS AN ASCII MEMORY EXAMPLE."
          ASC     "THE FOLLOWING ARE CONSTANTS ENTERED THROUGH USE OF"
          NOLIST
          SPC     5                    ;THIS WILL CAUSE THE ASSEMBLER TO SKIP 5 LINES.
                                       ;IN THE OUTPUT LISTING.
          LIST
          ASC     "DEC, OCT, HEX       PSEUDOS."
          DATA                         ;THE DATA SECTION WILL BEGIN AT 2200H AS
                                       :DICTATED BY THE LINKER ASSIGNMENT.
          DEC     1,2,3,4,5,6,7,8,9
          BIN     10110011
          HEX     0A,0B,0C,0FF
          SPC     3
          ADD     M                    ;ADD LOCATION 101 TO ACCUMULATOR.
          INX     H                    ;INCREMENT HL PAIR.
          MOV     M,A                  ;STORE ACC. IN LOCATION 102H
          JMP     START                ;JUMP TO START
          SPC     2
HERE      LDA     VALUE                ;EXAMPLE OF USE OF SYMBOLIC DATA MOVEMENT.
                                       ;VALUE WAS ASSIGNED THE VALUE OF 17H by USING
                                       ;THE EQU STATEMENT.
          SPC 3
          NOLIST
```

```
*         THIS SECTION OF COMMENTS WILL NOT APPEAR IN THE OUTPUT LISTING BECAUSE
*         OF THE NOLIST INSTRUCTION.
          SPC 2
          LIST
*         THIS SECTION OF COMMENTS WILL APPEAR BECAUSE OF RESUMPTION OF THE LISTING
*         USING THE LIST COMMAND.
          SPC 2
          Macro1
          EXAPND              ;THIS PSEUDO WILL CAUSE ANY MACRO NAMES
                              ;WHICH FOLLOW TO BE EXPANDED TO SHOW THE
                              ;CODE FOR THAT MACRO.
          SPC 2
          Macro1              ;THIS IS THE EXPANDED CODE FOR THE MACRO.
                              ;NOTE THAT THE PREVIOUS CALL BEFORE "EXPAND"
                              ;WAS NOT EXPANDED.
          SPC 3
          JMP AWAY            ;THE SYMBOL IS DECLARED EXTERNAL TO THIS
                              ;MODULE BUT GLOBAL IN MODULE ADD_2.
                              ;THE END STATEMENT IS THE LOGICAL TERMINATOR
                              ;OF THE PROGRAM.
          END
```

PROGRAM NAME "ADD_2"
"8085"
```
          TITLE "CONTINUATION OF PSEUDO EXAMPLES"
          NAME "ADD_2: TO SATISFY EXTERNALS"
          SPC 2
*     THIS MODULE DOES NOT PERFORM ANY FUNCTION OTHER THAN TO
*     PROVIDE EXAMPLES OF THE USE OF THE ASSEMBLER PSEUDO OPS
*     AND TO SATISFY THE EXTERNAL DECLARED BY MODULE "ADD_1"
          SPC 2
          ORG 2300H    ;THIS ASSIGNS STARTING ADDRESS OF THIS
                       ;MODULE AS 2300H. (ABSOLUTE)
          GLB AWAY     ;THIS GLOBAL ASSIGNMENT MEANS THAT THE
                       ;SYMBOL "AWAY" IS DEFINED IN THIS MODULE.
                       ;IT IS REFERENCED BY THE MODULE CALLED
                       ;ADD_1.

          EXT HERE

AWAY      EQU 3000H
          LXI H,AWAY
          NOP
          NOP
          JMP HERE
```

The HP 64000 Assembler 477

```
PROGRAM NAME "PSEUDO_85"
"8085"
                TITLE   "8085 PSEUDO EXAMPLES."
                ORG     800H
                NOP
RESERVE_ONE     DB      08H         ;STORES THE VALUE OF 08H AT THE CURRENT
                                    ; SETTING OF THE PROG COUNTER.
RESERVE_STRING  DB      "STRING"    ;THE HEX VALUE FOR THE ASCII CHARACTERS
                                    ; IN THE WORD "STRING" WILL BE STORED IN
                                    ; SEQUENTIAL LOCATIONS IN MEMORY STARTING
                                    ; AT THE CURRENT SETTING OF THE PROGRAM
                                    ; COUNTER.
RESERVE_BLOCK   DS      10          ; THE DEFINE STORAGE PSEUDO WILL RESERVE
                                    ; 10 SEQUENTIAL LOCATIONS IN MEMORY STARTING
                                    ; AT THE CURRENT SETTING OF THE PROGRAM
                                    ; COUNTER. THIS IS ACCOMPLISHED BY INCREMENTING
                                    ; THE PROGRAM COUNTER BY THE VALUE IN THE
                                    ; OPERAND FIELD.
DEFINE_WORD     DW      0102H       ; THIS WILL STORE THE TWO BYTES IN MEMORY AS
                                    ; AN ADDRESS.

                END
```

11.5.4 Examples of Some Common Errors and Their Results

ERROR CODE "CL" CONDITIONAL LABEL (CL—CONDITIONAL LABEL, SYNTAX REQUIRES A CONDITIONAL LABEL AND IT WAS NOT FOUND.)

FILE: AECCL:YOURID   HEWLETT-PACKARD: ERROR CODE: CONDITIONAL LABEL

```
LOCATION  OBJECT     CODE LINE  SOURCE LINE
                         1 "8085"
                         3
                         4
          <0000>         5 ONCE    EQU 0
          <0001>         6 TWICE   EQU 1
          <0400>         7 VALUE   EQU 400H
                         8 REPEAT  MACRO &VAL1,&VAL2
                         9         .IF &VAL1 .EQ. 1 TRADE
                        10         .IF &VAL2 .EQ. 1         ;MISSING CONDITIONAL
                        11 TRADE   LXI H,VALUE              ;LABEL.
                        12 MOVE    MOV A,M
                        13         MEND
  0000    320400        14         STA VALUE
```

478   Chapter 11   THE HEWLETT-PACKARD (HP) 64000

```
    0003              15        REPEAT ONCE, TWICE
                       +        .IF TWICE .EQ. 1
ERROR-CL                                           ∧
                      16        END
```

Errors= 1, previous error at line   15

ERROR CODE "DS" DUPLICATED SYMBOL (DS—DUPLICATE SYMBOL, THE INDICATED SYMBOL IS DEFINED MORE THAN ONCE IN THE PROGRAM MODULE.)

FILE: AECDS:YOURID   HEWLETT-PACKARD: ASSEMB. ERROR CODE: DUPLICATE SYMBOL (DS).

```
LOCATION   OBJECT      CODE LINE   SOURCE LINE
                        1 "8085"
   0000    00           3 START    NOP
   0001    3A0040       4 HERE     LDA VALUE
ERROR-DS                     ∧
   0004    C30001       5          JMP HERE
           <0040>       6 VALUE    EQU 040H
   0007    210040       7          LXI H,VALUE
           <5000>       8 HERE     EQU 5000H
ERROR-DS, see line   4     ∧
   000A    77           9          MOV M,A
                       10          END
```

Errors= 2, previous error at line   8

ERROR CODE "IC" ILLEGAL CONSTANT (IC—ILLEGAL CONSTANT, ILLEGAL CHARACTER FOUND IN CONSTANT.)

FILE: AECIC:YOURID   HEWLETT-PACKARD: ASSEMBLER ERROR CODE: ILLEGAL CONSTANT

```
LOCATION  OBJECT   CODE LINE   SOURCE LINE
                    1 "8085"
   0000    00       3 START    NOP
   0001    3A0000              LDA OFFB     ;THIS IS A HEX VALUE WITH
ERROR-IC                  ∧                 ;WITH A OCTAL DESIGNATOR.
                    5          END
```

Errors= 1, previous error at line   4

ERROR CODE "IO" INVALID OPERAND (IO—INVALID OPERAND, INVALID OR UNEXPECTED OPERAND ENCOUNTERED OR OPERAND IS MISSING.)

FILE: AECIC:YOURID   HEWLETT-PACKARD: ASSEMBLER ERROR CODE: INVALID OPERAND

```
LOCATION  OBJECT    CODE LINE   SOURCE LINE
                     1 "8085"
   0000    00        3 START    NOP
           <0040>    4 VALUE    EQU 040H
```

The HP 64000 Assembler   479

```
       0001    320040      5           STA VALUE
       0004    03          6           INX C          ;INX REFERS TO A REGISTER PAIR
ERROR-IO                               ^              ;SUCH AS B,C. NOT C ONLY.
       0005    C30000      7           JMP START
                           8           END
```

Errors=   1, previous error at line   6

ERROR CODE "IP" ILLEGAL PARAMETER (IP—ILLEGAL PARAMETER, INVALID PARAMETER ON MACRO HEADER.)

FILE: AECIP:YOURID   HEWLETT-PACKARD: ERROR CODE: ILLEGAL PARAMETER

```
LOCATION  OBJECT        CODE LINE  SOURCE LINE
                          1 "8085"
                          3
                          4
              <0000>      5 ONCE     EQU 0
              <0001>      6 TWICE    EQU 1
              <0400>      7 VALUE    EQU 400H
                          8 REPEAT   MACRO &VAL1,&VAL2,VAL3
ERROR-IP                                                  ^
                          9          .IF &VAL1 .EQ. 1 TRADE
                         10          .IF &VAL2 .EQ. 1 MOVE
                         11 TRADE    LXI H,VALUE
                         12 MOVE     MOV A,M
                         13          MEND
       0000   320400     14          STA VALUE
       0003              15          REPEAT ONCE, TWICE, VALUE
                         16          END
```

Errors=   1, previous error at line   8

ERROR CODE "MC" MACRO CONDITION (MC—MACRO CONDITION, INVALID MACRO CONDITIONAL RELATIONAL OPERATOR.)

FILE: AECMC:YOURID   HEWLETT-PACKARD: ERROR CODE: MACRO CONDITION

```
LOCATION  OBJECT        CODE LINE  SOURCE LINE
                          1 "8085"
                          3
                          4
              <0000>      5 ONCE     EQU 0
              <0001>      6 TWICE    EQU 1
              <0400>      7 VALUE    EQU 400H
                          8 REPEAT   MACRO &VAL1,&VAL2
                          9          .IF &VAL1 .EQ. 1 TRADE   ;MISSING PERIOD
                         10          .IF &VAL1 .EQ   REPEAT   ;AND VALUE.
                         11 TRADE    LXI H,VALUE
```

Chapter 11 The Hewlett-Packard (HP) 64000

```
                            12 MOVE    MOV A,M
                            13         MEND
   0000    320400           14         STA VALUE
   0003                     15         REPEAT ONCE, TWICE
                  +                    .IF ONCE .EQ   REPEAT
ERROR-MC                                      ∧
                            16         END
```

Errors=   1, previous error at line   15

ERROR CODE "MD" MACRO DEFINITION (MD—MACRO DEFINITION, THE MACRO IS CALLED BEFORE IT IS DEFINED IN THE SOURCE FILE, DEFINITION MUST PRECEDE CALL.)

FILE: AECMD:YOURID   HEWLETT-PACKARD: ERROR CODE: CONDITIONAL LABEL

```
LOCATION   OBJECT    CODE LINE  SOURCE LINE
                            1  "8085"
                            3
                            4
            <0000>          5  ONCE     EQU 0
            <0001>          6  TWICE    EQU 1
            <0400>          7  VALUE    EQU 400H
   0000                     8           REPEAT
ERROR-MD                                   ∧
                            9  REPEAT   MACRO &VAL1,&VAL2
                           10           .IF &VAL1 .EQ. 1TRADE
                           11           .IF &VAL2 .EQ. 1 MOVE
                           12  MOVE     JMP THERE
                           13  TRADE    LXI H,VALUE
                           14           MOV A,M
                           15           MEND
   0000    320400          16  THERE    STA VALUE
   0003                    17           REPEAT ONCE, TWICE
                           18           END
```

Errors=   1, previous error at line   8

ERROR CODE "ML" MACRO LABEL (ML—MACRO LABEL, LABEL NOT FOUND WITHIN MACRO BODY.)

FILE: AECCL:YOURID   HEWLETT-PACKARD: ERROR CODE: MACRO LABEL (ML)

```
LOCATION   OBJECT    CODE LINE  SOURCE LINE
                            1  "8085"
                            3
                            4
            <0000>          5  ONCE     EQU 0
```

```
              <0001>    6 TWICE    EQU 1
              <0400>    7 VALUE    EQU 400H
                        8 REPEAT   MACRO &VAL1,&VAL2
                        9            .IF &VAL1 .EQ. 1 TRDE
                       10            .IF &VAL2 .EQ. 1 MOVE
                       11 TRADE    LXI H,VALUE
                       12          MOV A,M
                       13          MEND
 0000   320400         14          STA VALUE
 0003                  15          REPEAT ONCE,TWICE
                       15          .IF TWICE .EQ. 1 MOVE
ERROR-ML                                    ∧
                       16          END

Errors=  1, previous error at line  15
```

ERROR CODE "MM" MISSING MACRO END (MEND) (MM—MISSING MEND, A MEND PSEUDO MUST TERMINATE MACRO, NOT FOUND.)

FILE: AECMM:YOURID   HEWLETT-PACKARD: ERROR CODE: CONDITIONAL LABEL

```
LOCATION  OBJECT     CODE LINE  SOURCE LINE
                       1 "8085"
                       3
                       4
              <0000>   5 ONCE     EQU 0
              <0001>   6 TWICE    EQU 1
              <0400>   7 VALUE    EQU 400H
                       8 REPEAT   MACRO &VAL1,&VAL2
                       9            .IF &VAL1 .EQ. 1 TRADE
                      10            .IF &VAL2 .EQ. 1 MOVE
                      11 MOVE     JMP THERE
                      12 TRADE    LXI H,VALUE    ;THE MACRO MEND STATEMENT
                      13 THERE    MOV A,M        ;SHOULD BE BEFORE "STA VALUE".
                      14          STA VALUE
                      15          REPEAT ONCE,TWICE
                      16          END
         ERROR-MM              ∧

Errors=  1, previous error at line  17
```

ERROR CODE "MP" MISSING PARENTHESIS (MP—MISMATCHED PARENTHESIS, MISSING RIGHT OR LEFT PARENTHESIS.)

FILE: AECMP:YOURID   HEWLETT-PACKARD: ASSEMBLER ERROR CODE: MISSING PARENTHESIS

```
LOCATION  OBJECT     CODE LINE  SOURCE LINE
                       1 "8085"
 0000     00           3 START    NOP
```

482 Chapter 11 The Hewlett-Packard (HP) 64000

```
              <0040>  4  VALUE    EQU 040H
              <5000>  5  HERE     EQU 5000H
   0001   3A5000     6           LDA (VALUE+HERE    ;MISSING RIGHT PARENTHESIS
ERROR-MP                                       ∧
   0004   210040     7           LXI H,VALUE
   007    77         8           MOV M,A
                     9           END
```

Errors= 1, previous error at line 6

ERROR CODE "NM" NESTED MACRO (NI—NESTED INCLUDE, THE INCLUDE PSEUDO CANNOT BE NESTED.)

FILE: AECNM:YOURID   HEWLETT-PACKARD: ERROR CODE: NESTED MACRO

```
LOCATION  OBJECT     CODE LINE  SOURCE LINE
                     1  "8085"
                     3
                     4
          <0000>     5  ONCE     EQU 0
          <0001>     6  TWICE    EQU 1
          <0400>     7  VALUE    EQU 400H
                     8  REPEAT   MACRO           ; TWO NESTED MACROS ENCOUNTERED
                     9           LDA VALUE       ; BEFORE THE MEND, NESTED MACROS
                    10           STA TWICE       ; NOT ALLOWED.
                    11  AGAIN    MACRO
                    12           LXI H,VALUE
                    13           MOV M,A
                    14           MEND
  0000   320400     15           STA VALUE
  0003              16           REPEAT
                   + AGAIN       MACRO
ERROR-NI                                ∧
                    17           END
```

Errors= 1, previous error at line 16

ERROR CODE "RC" REPEAT CALL (RC—REPEAT CALL, REPEAT CANNOT PRECEDE A MACRO CALL.)

FILE: AECRC:YOURID   HEWLETT-PACKARD: ERROR CODE: REPEAT CALL

```
LOCATION  OBJECT  CODE LINE  SOURCE LINE
                  1  "8085"
  0003           +            REPEAT ONCE,TWICE
ERROR-RC                             ∧
```

Errors= 1, previous error at line 16

The HP 64000 Assembler   483

ERROR CODE "RM" REPEAT MACRO (RM—REPEAT MACRO, THE REPEAT PSEUDO CANNOT PRECEDE A MACRO DEFINITION.)

FILE: AECRM:YOURID   HEWLETT-PACKARD: ERROR CODE: REPEAT MACRO

```
LOCATION  OBJECT CODE LINE SOURCE LINE
                       1 "8085"
                       9 REPEAT    MACRO &VAL1,&VAL2
ERROR-RM                              ∧
```

Errors= 1, previous error at line 9

ERROR CODE "UO" UNDEFINED OP CODE (UO—UNIDENTIFIED OP CODE, OP CODE ENCOUNTERED IS NOT DEFINED FOR THIS MICROPROCESSOR.)

FILE: AECUD:YOURID   HEWLETT-PACKARD: ASSEMBLER ERROR CODE: UNDEFINED OP CODE

```
LOCATION  OBJECT   CODE LINE SOURCE LINE
                       1 "8085"
  0000    00           3 START   NOP
          <0040>       4 VALUE   EQU 040H
          <5000>       5 HERE    EQU 5000H
                       6         LDI A,VALUE  ;OP CODE NOT DEFINED FOR
ERROR-UO                              ∧             ;THIS PROCESSOR
  0001    C35000       7         JMP HERE
  0004    210040       8         LXI H,VALUE
  0007    77           9         MOV M,A
                      10         END
```

Errors= 1, previous error at line 6

ERROR CODE "UP" UNDEFINED PARAMETER (UP—UNDEFINED PARAMETER, THE PARAMETER FOUND IN MACRO WAS NOT INCLUDED IN THE MACRO HEADER.)

FILE: AECUP:YOURID   HEWLETT-PACKARD: ERROR CODE: UNDEFINED PARAMETER

```
LOCATION  OBJECT   CODE LINE SOURCE LINE
                       1 "8085"
                       3
                       4
          <0000>       5 ONCE    EQU 0
          <0001>       6 TWICE   EQU 1
          <0400>       7 VALUE   EQU 400H
                       8 REPEAT  MACRO &VAL1,&VAL2
                       9         LXI &REG,VALUE
                      10         .IF &VAL1 .EQ. 1 TRADE
                      11         .IF &VAL2 .EQ. 1 MOVE
```

484   Chapter 11   THE HEWLETT-PACKARD (HP) 64000

```
                        12 TRADE   LXI H,VALUE
                        13 MOVE    MOV A,M
                        14         MEND
    0000   320400       15         STA VALUE
    0003                16         REPEAT ONCE,TWICE
                         +         LXI &REG,VALUE
ERROR-UP                           ∧
                        17         END
```

Errors=   1, previous error at line   16

            ERROR CODE "US" UNDEFINED SYMBOL (US—UNDEFINED SYMBOL, THE INDICATED SYMBOL IS NOT DEFINED AS A LABEL OR DECLARED AS AN EXTERNAL.)

FILE: AECUS:YOURID   HEWLETT-PACKARD: ASSEMBLER ERROR CODE: UNDEFINED SYMBOL

```
LOCATION  OBJECT     CODE LINE  SOURCE LINE
                       1  "8085"
  0000    00           3  START  NOP
          <0040>       4  VALUE  EQU 040H
          <5000>       5  HERE   EQU 5000H
  0001    3A0040       6         LDA VALUE
  0004    C35000       7         JMP HERE
  0007    210000       8         LXI H,F7H  ;THE VALUE MUST BE PRECEEDED
ERROR-US                          ∧         ;BY A ZERO TO DISTINGUISH
  000A    77           9         MOV M,A    ;A VARIABLE AND A VALUE.
                      10         END
```

Errors=   1, previous error at line   8

11.6 HP 64000 Linker

As mentioned before, the purpose of the linker is to generate absolute code with absolute address assignments from the relocatable modules produced by the assembler. The linker provides greater flexibility in the design process by linking together multiple relocatable program modules into a single absolute program. In addition, each program can be relinked and loaded into a different portion of memory. Programs do not have to be rewritten for different memory assignments in different system configurations.

The linker will provide as output error messages relating to errors that have occurred in the link process and an optional linker load map indicating where various relocatable modules have been linked. In addition, a cross-reference table can be generated which will show each symbol or label where it is defined and which statements reference each symbol.

11.6.1 Linker Initialization

To initialize the linker, perform the following steps:

1. Press the soft key "link" followed by "RETURN." The system will respond as follows:
   a. Object files?
      Enter the name of any relocatable modules to be linked.
   b. Library files?
      Enter the name assigned to a previously defined group of relocatable modules.
   c. Load addresses? PROG, DATA, COMN=0000H, 0000H, 0000H
      Enter the starting address desired for the program modules. Relocatable modules can be grouped under headings of PROG, DATA, COMN. Then depress "RETURN."
   d. More files?
      Enter the appropriate soft key, then depress "RETURN."
   e. Absolute file name?
      Enter the desired linker command file name. Since the file manager qualifies files by file type as well as by file name, we can use the same name as given the relocatable file. Then press "RETURN."

   Each time there is a need to modify the source programs, it is a simple matter to reassemble the programs and then relink them using the linker command file name.

2. Press the soft keys "link (FILENAME)," then depress "RETURN." This file name will be the name of the executable absolute file. The following directory listing of the file "SAMENAME" shows the addition of the link_sym file, the link_com file, and the absolute file, each having the same name "SAMENAME."

Directory List   File:SAMENAME: Disc: 0   Mon, 9 Feb 1981,   4:04   Page

NAME	TYPE	SIZE	LAST MODIFY	LAST ACCESS
SAMENAME:	source	1	9 Feb 1981, 2:37	9 Feb 1981, 2:37
SAMENAME:	asmb_sym	1	9 Feb 1981, 2:37	9 Feb 1981, 2:37
SAMENAME:	link_com	1	6 Jun 1981, 0:35	6 Jun 1981, 0:35
SAMENAME:	listing	1	9 Feb 1981, 2:37	9 Feb 1981, 2:37
SAMENAME:	absolute	1	6 Jun 1981, 0:35	6 Jun 1981, 0:35

```
    SAMENAME:   reloc       1      9 Feb 1981, 2:37    9 Feb 1981, 2:37
    SAMENAME:   link_sym    1      6 Jun 1981, 0:36    6 Jun 1981, 0:36
**** Files listed   8,  0.34% disc space used    ****
**** 23.41% disc space available    ****
```

The link_sym file is a symbolic file generated by the linker. The link_com file is a command file which contains all of the linker configuration information. Each time it is desired to relink files using the same configuration information it is only necessary to specify the name of the linker command file rather than answering the same questions again. A listing of the 64000 linker commands is given in Appendix D.

11.7 HP 64000 Emulator

Hardware emulation in a microprocessor-based system is the replacement of the microprocessor and/or associated memory with hardware that appears to be the same as that which is being replaced. It is performed by replacing the processor in a microprocessor-based system with another processor that resides in the emulation probe and is linked to the host system; this allows us to control the operation and examine the necessary signals of the target system. It is this control over the emulation processor in conjunction with powerful analysis capability available in the HP 64000 which provides designers with the tools necessary to debug complex hardware and software related problems in the design process.

A listing of the 64000 emulation soft keys is given in Appendix D.

11.7.1 Emulation Equipment

The HP 64000 should be equipped with the appropriate emulation system with additional emulation memory and memory control card. The internal analysis card is also recommended since this provides additional analysis capability by having a powerful logic analyzer fully integrated into the HP 64000.

11.7.2. Analysis

With the addition of the logic analyzer into the HP 64000 a new dimension is added to software analysis. The designer has a means to time events in time relative to other events or in absolute time which provides a measure of how long an event occurred. This allows the designer to measure the efficiency of his software by determining how much time is actually spent in various routines. This may also point out areas which can be streamlined with more efficient code. The analyzer allows sequential triggering on address or data information which must be found in a specific order before the analyzer triggers. It also allows selective capturing of address or data information.

11.7.3 Symbolic Debug

For programs that have been linked on the 64000 a linker symbol file is automatically created. The existence of this file is what allows the user to perform software debug and analysis symbolically. When using the logic analyzer in emulation, predefined points in the program can be referred to by the symbols or labels used to define them rather than by the absolute address locations which are assigned when the program is linked. The emulator will also allow specification of a start address for program execution in a symbolic form. If a label called "START" is used at the beginning of the program for the first executable instruction in emulation, one can use the command "run from START" and program execution will begin from the symbolic address.

11.7.4 64000 Emulator Architecture

Emulation in the HP 64000 is accomplished using a two-processor (master/slave) system and a separate bus for emulation only. One of the processors is the host processor which directs the systems activities and allows the user to interact with the emulation system. The other processor is the emulation processor located in the emulation probe. This processor executes the instructions in the designer's software. This two-processor system and the separate emulation bus allow the emulation system to run at the rated speed of the microprocessor even while the host processor is completing its housekeeping system functions or while the user wishes to revise some software by using the editor. The emulation mode can be exited while the processor continues to execute the user's program. This is a valuable characteristic of the dual bus structure since there may be a software bug that only occurs once in a while and it is necessary to leave the system emulating and allow the analyzer to babysit the user's system. Once the emulation mode is exited the user can modify software in the edit mode or link and assemble programs, then reenter the emulation mode without interrupting the emulation processor (Figure 11.4).

11.7.5 Emulation with a Different Processor

Since emulation memory and the emulation processor are not shared by the host processor it is a simple matter to change the emulation system to emulate another 8-bit processor. To modify the system merely requires the changing of the emulation probe, which contains the emulation processor, and the emulation control card.

488 Chapter 11 THE HEWLETT-PACKARD (HP) 64000

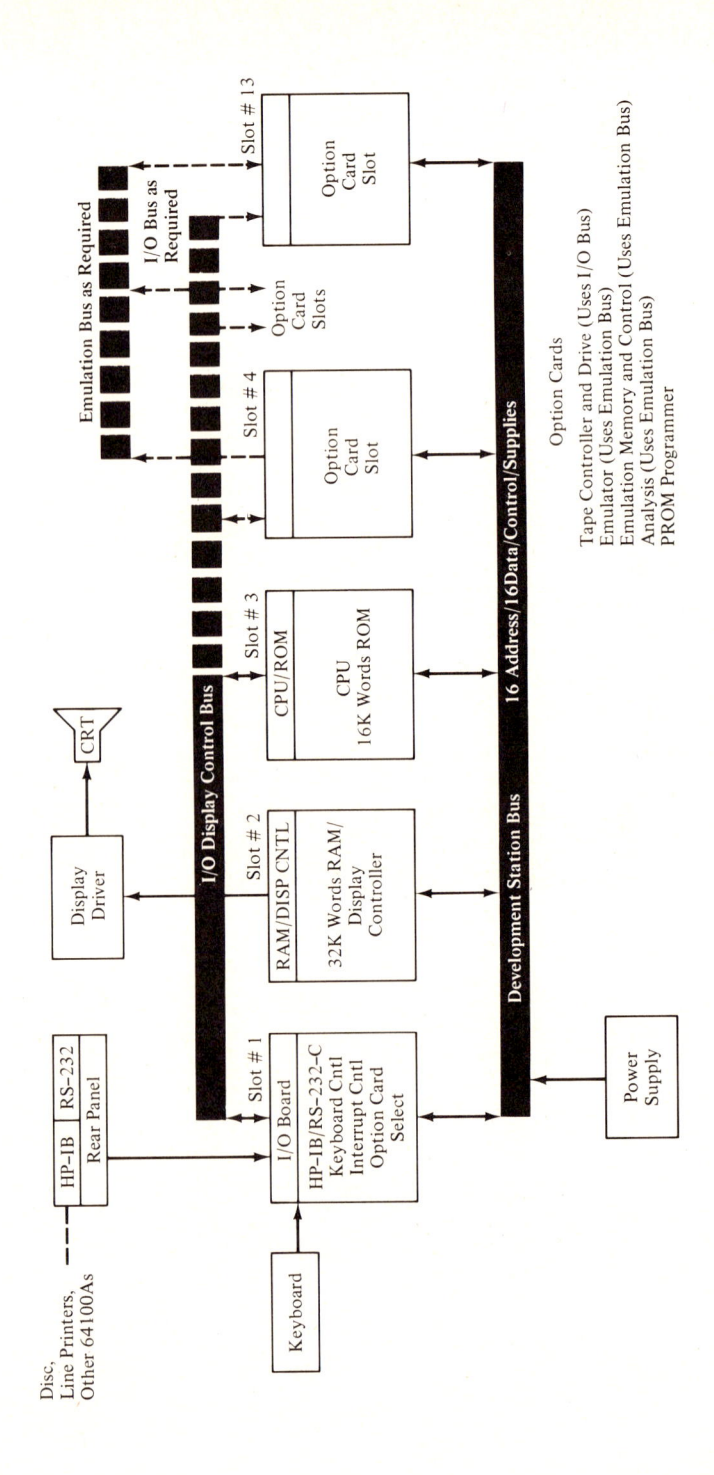

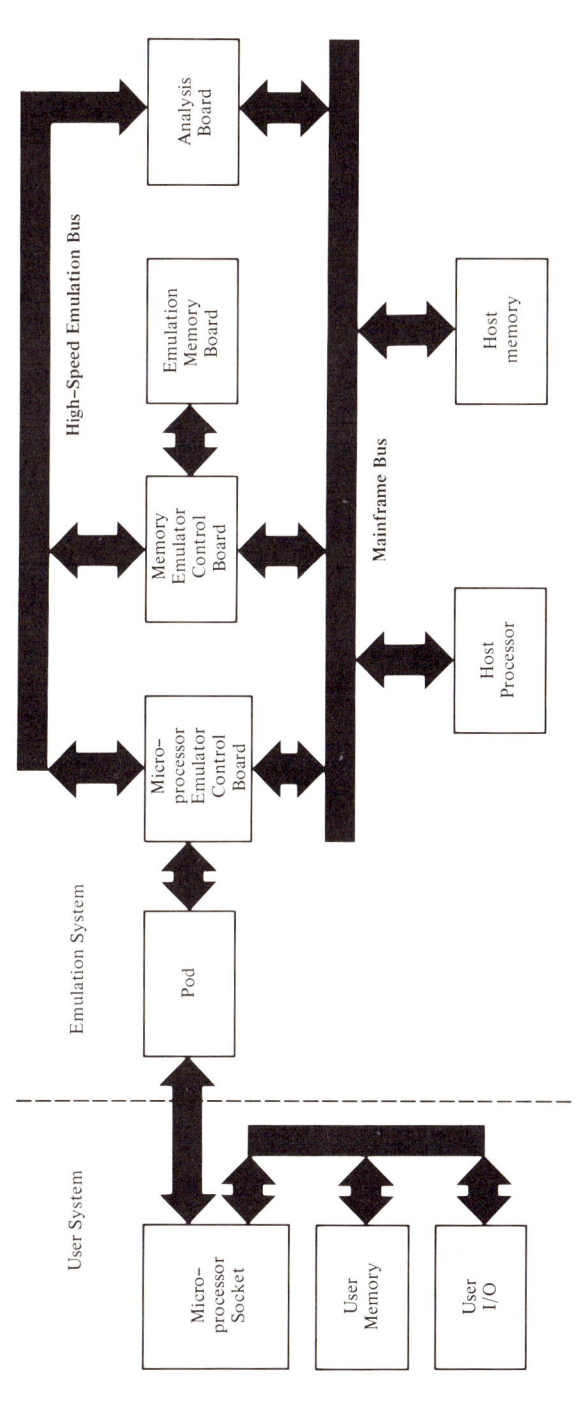

Figure 11.4 (a) The host processor and the microprocessor being emulated have independent buses and can run simultaneously. Thus software development can be concurrent with emulation. (b) the 64000 emulator subsystem consists of a microprocessor emulator, a memory emulator, a logic analyzer, and a software support package. Source: Courtesy of Hewlett-Packard.

11.7.6. Beginning the Emulation Session

Before using the emulator it is important to mention the following:

1. Never insert or remove the emulation probe from a target system while the power to that system is on.
2. All programs must be assembled and linked before they can be loaded into emulation memory or be used by the PROM programmer.
3. The HP 64000 emulator does not supply power to the target system. The target system requires its own power supply.

The first time the emulator is initialized to run a particular program, a command file is established by the system based upon the answers to a number of queries. These answers supplied by the designer determine the configuration of the emulation system. To use the emulator:

1. Press soft key "emulate" then "RETURN." The system will respond:

   a. Processor Clock:
      internal   external

Depress the appropriate soft key response followed by "RETURN." Internal clock is chosen in the absence of external hardware.

   b. Restrict processor to real time runs?
      yes   no

Depress the appropriate soft key response followed by "RETURN." Answering yes will not allow the user to invoke commands which will cause the processor to drop out of real-time execution. Using the comand "display registers dynamic" causes interruption of the processor so that register information can be obtained.

   c. Stop processor on illegal opcodes?
      yes   no

Depress the appropriate soft key response followed by "RETURN." Before continuing with the rest of the queries let us define some terms.

Emulation RAM: This read/write memory located in the 64000 is used for program memory only.

HP 64000 Emulator

    Emulation ROM: This allows the user to declare emulation RAM as read-only memory. This provides protection for code or programs which the user does not want altered while in emulation.
    User RAM: This is RAM located in the target system.
    User ROM: This is ROM located in the target system.

    d. Emulation RAM address range?
       (address)

Enter the ending address for a range of memory followed by "thru" then enter the ending address for a range of memory. If no emulation is available or desired then depress return. Sections of memory are allocated in 1K byte blocks. The system will continue to ask for emulation RAM until no input is provided and "RETURN" is depressed.

    e. Emulation ROM address range?
       (address)

If ROM is desired then enter any ROM address range as before. If no emulation ROM then no entry is required. Depress "RETURN."

    f. User RAM address range?
       (address)

Proceed as before.

    g. User ROM address range?
       (address)

Proceed as before.

    h. Illegal memory address range?
       (address)

If the program is to remain within known boundaries then an illegal range of addresses can be designated. If the program executes out of its range the processor will be halted and the last address of the memory fetch will be displayed.

    i. Simulate I/O?
       yes   no

Depress the appropriate soft key response followed by "RETURN." Unless you are familiar with the simulated I/O section in the emulator/analyzer manual, the answer to the above should be no.

    j. Command file name?
       (file)

Input a name for this emulator command file. It can be used whenever this same emulation configuration is needed.

The system will respond by clearing the screen and printing "Program Loaded." The emulation soft key syntax options will be displayed across the bottom of the CRT. Since the system file manager classes files by file type as well as by file name this emulation command file can assume the same name as the program that is being executed. This reduces the need to remember several different file names.

The next time this emulation configuration is desired, merely perform the following;

    k. Enter "emulate" (Filename) "load" (Filename)

The system will set up the emulator according to the previously defined configuration and load the program to be executed. The system will respond by clearing the screen and printing "Program Loaded." The emulation soft key syntax options will be displayed across the bottom of the CRT.

  2. To verify that the program was loaded properly press soft keys "display memory (address) mnemonic" then "RETURN." The screen should show the program in the assembly language mnemonics of the processor being used. Use the roll keys to scroll the screen up or down.

  3. To run the program press soft keys "run from (address)" then "RETURN." Note that (address) may be in the form of a constant or an expression.

  4. To verify register contents press soft keys "display registers dynamic" then "RETURN."

  5. To single-step from any address press soft keys "step from (address)" then "RETURN." This presets the program counter to (address) and sets the single-step mode. Press soft keys "step" then "RETURN." Press "RETURN." Press "RETURN." Press "RETURN." Notice that every time "RETURN" is pressed the program will single-step, and the contents of the various registers will be displayed in addition to the op code mnemonics.

The display should look like this:

REGISTER(Hex)

pc	opcode		a	b	c	d	e	h	l	szxac	xpxcy	sp	next_p
0000	**		C9	80	00	00	00	07	0E	00	0 1 0	00FF	0000
0000	**		C9	80	00	00	00	07	0E	00	0 1 0	00FF	0700
0700	3E MVI A,	01H	01	80	00	00	00	07	0E	00	0 1 0	00FF	0702
0702	32 STA	0901H	01	80	00	00	00	07	0E	00	0 1 0	00FF	0705
0705	32 STA	0920H	01	80	00	00	00	07	0E	00	0 1 0	00FF	0708
0708	32 STA	0902H	01	80	00	00	00	07	0E	00	0 1 0	00FF	070B
070B	32 STA	0921H	01	80	00	00	00	07	0E	00	0 1 0	00FF	070E
070E	3E MVI A,	80H	80	80	00	00	00	07	0E	00	0 1 0	00FF	0710

6. To stop the program press soft keys "stop run" then "RETURN."

7. To run until a specific address or symbol, press soft keys "run from (address) until (address)." Then "RETURN."

8. To end emulation press soft keys "end" then "RETURN."

11.8 Command Files

Another useful tool supported by the HP 64000 is the implementation of command files. Command files provide a means to accomplish routine tasks in the shortest time possible. The linker and emulator command files accomplish this by storing the information relating to the memory configuration and linker load maps along with other information relating to the hardware setup. Once the appropriate file is established the linker or emulator can be invoked by using the link or emulate command along with the name of the command file. The setup is performed by the linker or the emulator once it is provided with the name of the command file.

So far we have mentioned the linker and emulator command files but the HP 64000 also supports a general-purpose command file. This type of command file is written by the user and can perform additional routine functions tailored to the user's wishes. The task of modifying software then reassembling, relinking, and reentering the emulator takes considerable time. If the designer were free of this routine task then his time could be used in a more productive way.

An example of the use of the command file would be as follows. After editing a source file to correct a coding error, a command file name is entered in via the keyboard. This could be a single character such as "Q." The command file would perform the following functions. It would reassemble the file, provide the appropriate listing, and if no errors were present, it would then link the relocatable file. If no errors occurred in the link process it would then enter the emulator and begin program execution at some predetermined symbolic address. All of this procedure could be accomplished with one keystroke.

The command file can be established in two ways. The first is by the use of the log soft key which will record consecutive key strokes of valid system commands into a file name provided by the user. Another way is to use the editor and enter the command sequence line by line as they would be executed. Commands used in the file are any valid system command as it would appear above the soft key.

Parameters can be passed to a command file which allows the command file to be used for other files. As an example, a file name would be a parameter to be passed to the file. When the file was invoked it would request from the user a file name and begin executing its routine on that file.

11.8.1 Simple Command File Example

A simple example of a command file established by use of the editor would appear as follows:

```
assemble KEY_DISP listfile KEY_DISP
```

This command file was established for a particular file name by using the editor. The file was named "A". Depressing the "A" key on the keyboard would cause the file named KEY_DISP to be assembled and provide an assembler output listing to the listing file named KEY—DISP.

11.8.2 Another Command File Example

This command file was also established through the use of the editor.

```
assemble KEY_DISP listfile KEY_DISP
link KEY_DISP listfile KEY_DISP
emulate KEY_DISP load KEY_DISP
```

This command file will assemble KEY_DISP with the appropriate output listing and then link according to the predefined linker command file called KEY_DISP with the output to the file KEY_DISP. The emulator will be invoked according to the emulator command file

KEY_DISP and the absolute file KEY_DISP will be loaded into memory.

11.8.3 Command File Example: Passing Parameters

This command file was established through the use of the editor. The term "PARMS" indicates that a parameter is to be passed. This parameter must be listed on the same line and be preceded by a "&." More than one parameter may be passed.

```
PARMS &FILENAME
assemble &FILENAME listfile &FILENAME
link &FILENAME listfile &FILENAME
emulate &FILENAME load &FILENAME
run from START
```

This file will assemble, link, emulate, and run from a symbolic addressed called "START."

11.9 Simulated I/O

It is advantageous to be able to integrate hardware and software as early as possible in the design phase. This early integration allows close monitoring of development and the early detection of problems through analysis before modifications become more expensive later on. Early in the integration phase, however, all of the hardware for the target system may not be present. For a more conventional design which requires the use of such devices as a printer, a display, a disk, a keyboard for data entry, or maybe even an RS232 port, the HP 64000 has a facility called simulated I/O which allows the user's software to hook into the system's I/O devices.

This allows the user to use the keyboard of the HP 64000 or the display for user interface. The designer has an optional printer and even the RS232 port available for communications. As many as five disk files can be open for simulation at the same time.

An example of a program that uses the simulated I/O capability of the HP 64000 is illustrated in Chapter 10. This program is simple in that it takes a keyboard input and outputs that character to the display. This program could potentially be part of a system monitor.

Simulated I/O has many applications from allowing the user to simulate his external hardware to allowing the user to design an operating system based on the processor currently used for emulation. Regardless of the application the use of simulated I/O is one more tool added to the many tools provided in the HP 64000 development system. It is the use of these tools provided within one unique system which provides for the rapid development and analysis of microprocessor-based products.

11.10 64000 Examples Demonstrating the Software and Hardware Development on Typical Systems

This section consists of a series of examples which are designed to guide the HP 64000 user through the steps necessary to learn the basic features of the HP 64000. An in-depth knowledge of the use of the various facets of the 64000 system can be obtained by studying the appropriate manuals concurrently or upon completion of the examples.

The examples that follow begin by powering up the system step by step. This systematic approach is also applied to the use of the editor, the assembler, the linker, and the emulator. Upon completion of the examples there will be additional programs which will show the implementation of simulated I/O and hardware emulation using the HP 5036 microcomputer. Note that the HP 5036 is an 8085-based microcomputer and a description is given in Appendix C.

Note that the concepts associated with these examples will help the reader to learn the other systems.

11.10.1 64000 Boot up

The objective is to boot up the development system.

Step 1: Turn on the power to all disk drives connected to the system bus. Switches are located next to the power cords.
Step 2: Turn on the power to the printer. Make sure the "on-line" LED is on. If not, then depress the adjacent button.
Step 3: Turn on the power to any slave stations on the system bus.
Step 4: Turn on the power to the station designated the master controller. The master must be powered up for the system to operate.
Step 5: Verify that all powered-up devices appear on the I/O bus configuration on the screen similar to that shown below.

I/O BUS CONFIGURATION

```
ADRS DEVICE
  0   13037 DISC CONTROLLER
      UNIT  0   7906 DISC MEMORY   LU=0   NA32
  1   2631 PRINTER
  2   64100
```

64000 Examples Demonstrating Development on Systems

```
            3    64100
            4    64100
            5    64100
            6    64100
            7    THIS 64100, MASTER CONTROLLER
```

STATUS: Awaiting command   userid: ------------- 00:00
edit   compile   assemble   link   emulate   prom_prog <CMDFILE>
---ETC---

Common Problems

If a device is turned on after power-up or does not appear on the I/O bus configuration reset all the stations on the bus by depressing a "SHIFT" and "RESET" simultaneously. If the device still does not appear on the bus configuration check the bus cabling.

Powering up the system by first turning on the master may result in some devices not appearing on the bus configuration. One common example is the printer which may not be recognized when attempting to list a file. If the error "print file not found" is obtained then reset the master controller with a shift and reset, ensuring that the printer power is on beforehand.

EXAMPLE 11.3

Using the 6400 editor, enter the following program and create a new file by following the steps listed below.

Program Listing: Add

```
"8085"
*           THIS PROGRAM STARTS AT 0 AND ADDS LOCATION 100H TO
*           LOCATION 101H AND STORES THE RESULT IN LOCATION 102H
*
*
        NAME  "ADD:WORKSHOP I"
        ORG   2000H             ;PROGRAM ORIGIN WILL BE AT HEXADECIMAL
                                ;2000
START   LXI   H,100H            ;LOAD HL PAIR WITH 100 HEX
        MOV   A,M               ;MOVE NUMBER IN LOCATION 100 INTO THE ACC.
        INX   H                 ;INCREMENT H AND L PAIR.
        ADD   M                 ;ADD LOCATION 101 TO ACCUMULATOR.
        INX   H                 ;INCREMENT HL PAIR.
        MOV   M,A               ;STORE ACC. IN LOCATION 102H
        JMP   START
```

Procedure

Step 1: Press soft key userid, type in YOURID (the first character must be an upper case alpha character, maximum up to six characters) and set the correct time and date. Note that it is a good idea not to use the same userid on more than one station. If it is used, the message "I/O bus wait" may be displayed on those stations.

    userid YOURID (RETURN)
    time HH:MM (RETURN)
    date DD/MM/YY (RETURN)

HP currently offers time and date functions in one operation.

Step 2: Enter the edit mode and name your new file "ADD."

    edit into ADD (RETURN)

Step 3: The first line of your program must be the assembler directive starting in column 1. Enter the directive.

    "8085" (RETURN)

Step 4: Enter comment lines beginning with "*".

    *This program starts at 0 and . . . .

Comment lines can begin with a "*" in column 1 or a ";" elsewhere on the line.

Step 5: Enter "NAME" if needed, this name will be referred to when linking multiple modules together.

    "TAB" NAME "TAB" "ADD_WORKSHOP_I" (RETURN)

Step 6: Enter ORG statement.

    (TAB) ORG (TAB) 2000H (TAB) * COMMENTS (RETURN)

Step 7: Enter "START" in the label field beginning at column 1.

    START (TAB) LXI (TAB) H,100H (TAB) * COMMENTS (RETURN)

Step 8: Since there are no labels use the autotab function to save time. Depress the "autotab" soft key then (RETURN). The system will respond with "autotab is now on." When the carriage return is depressed the cursor will return to the column position of the first character in the preceding line.

64000 Examples Demonstrating Development on Systems   499

Step 9: Enter the rest of the program, referring to the printout found in Section 9.3.1.

(TAB) MOV (TAB) A,M (TAB) * COMMENTS (RETURN)
INX (TAB) H (TAB) * COMMENTS (RETURN)

Step 10: List files as follows, making sure the printer is on-line.

list printer all (RETURN)

Step 11: Close file, if file has been named then close as follows.

end (RETURN)

If the file was started with an edit (RETURN) then name as follows.

end ADD (RETURN)

Step 12: The file is now stored on the disk. Now let us get a directory of the files under our userid.

directory (RETURN)

The result should be as follows:

Directory List User:YOURID Disc: 0 Mon, 9 Feb 1981, 2:53 Page

```
NAME    TYPE    SIZE    LAST MODIFY         LAST ACCESS
-------------------------------------------------------------
ADD     source   1      9 Feb 1981, 2:53    9 Feb 1981, 2:53
****  Files listed  2,  0.08% disc space used   ****
****  18.30% disc space available   ****
```

This directory lists all the programs under your userid. Note the type of file.

Step 13: Recall your program for editing by using the following commands.

edit ADD (RETURN)

Note that disk number may be specified as edit ADD:0 for disk 0 or edit ADD:1 for disk 1. If the disk number is not specified with the file number, then it defaults to disk 0.

Step 14: Let us insert a "NOP" after line 9. Proceed as follows.

    9 (RETURN)
    insert (TAB) NOP (TAB) (TAB) ; NO OPERATION (RETURN)

Step 15: Now we can renumber the lines for easier editing.

    renumber (RETURN)

Step 16: In programs larger than this it is more difficult and time consuming to search for a string or variable interest. We can locate a string or variable by using the "find" command. Find the instruction "NOP" by doing the following.

    find "NOP" all (RETURN)

The cursor will stop at the line number of the first occurrence of the string "NOP" and indicate the column in which it occurs.

Step 17: To insert text, enter the following command and position the cursor up, down, and sideways using the edit keys.

    insert

Step 18: To revise text, enter the following command and position the cursor up, down, and sideways using the edit keys.

    revise

Step 19: To move the display to allow viewing of all 240 columns depress the shift and left arrow keys simultaneously.

Step 20: To insert or delete characters when revising text simply depress the "INSERT CHAR" or "DELETE CHAR" keys after positioning the cursor to the appropriate column.

Step 21: Using the "delete" soft key delete part of the file. The original file is still safe on the disk as long as you do not end the edit session.

Step 22: Portions of the file can be duplicated by performing the following. Position the cursor to any chosen line number.

    extract (RETURN)
    retrieve 5 (RETURN)

The chosen line will be retrieved the indicated number of times.

64000 Examples Demonstrating Development on Systems

Step 23: Do not end the edit session by depressing "end" but rather depress the reset key twice. This will preserve the original file on the disk by not having it replaced by the current version being edited. Continue to experiment with the following keys;

replace, find, copy, extract, retrieve, list, merge

EXAMPLE 11.4

Using the 64000 assembler, enter in the source file "ADD" and assemble it using the assembler soft keys. This procedure will create a relocatable "reloc" program module.

Procedure

Step 1: Enter the userid and set the correct time and date.

    userid YOURID (RETURN)
    time HH:MM (RETURN)
    date DD/MM/YY (RETURN)

Step 2: Enter the assembler mode, existing source file name, and list file options. Upon depressing the return key the process of assembling the source file begins. The output of the assembler is directed to the device selected by the user. This can be the display, the printer, or another file. Type in the following commands.

assemble ADD listfile printer options xref (RETURN)

The following program listing will be obtained.

```
FILE: ADD:YOURID    HEWLETT-PACKARD: 8085 Assembler   Mon, 9 Feb 1981,  3:45

    LOC. OBJ.      CODE LINE  SOURCE LINE
                    1 "8085"
                    2 *             THIS PROGRAM STARTS AT 0 AND ADDS LOCATION 100H
                    3 *             LOCATION 101H AND STORES THE RESULT IN LOCATION
                    4 *
                    5 *
                    6          NAME  "ADD WORKSHOP I"
                    7          ORG   2000H  ;PROGRAM ORIGIN WILL BE AT HEXADECIMAL
                    8                       ;2000
    2000 210100     9 START   LXI   H,100H ;LOAD HL PAIR WITH 100 HEX
    2003 7E        10         MOV   A,M    ;MOVE NUMBER IN LOCATION 100 INTO THE
    2004 23        11         INX   H      ;INCREMENT H AND L PAIR.
```

```
2005 86      12        ADD   M       ;ADD LOCATION 101 TO ACCUMULATOR.
2006 23      13        INX   H       ;INCREMENT HL PAIR.
2007 77      14        MOV   M,A     ;STORE ACC. IN LOCATION 102H
2008 C32000  15        JMP   START   ;JUMP TO START
```

Errors=0

FILE: ADD:YOURID   CROSS REFERENCE TABLE   PAGE 2

LINE#   SYMBOL   TYPE   REFERENCES

  9   START   A   15

The cross-reference table which follows the assembler listing shows the line number which defines a symbol, the type of symbol, and any other line numbers which reference that symbol. This is helpful if one wishes to locate all occurrences of a particular symbol.

There are several symbol-type codes which may occur and these are listed below.

Symbol-Type Codes

Code	Type	Code	Type
A	Absolute	M	Multiply defined
E	External	R	Predefined register
D	Data	C	Common
P	Program	U	Undefined

Step 3: To further illustrate the features of the assembler add an error to the source program by entering the following.

    edit ADD (RETURN)
    11 (RETURN)
    insert (TAB) MVI (TAB) D,FFH (RETURN)
    end (RETURN)

Step 4: Now assemble the modified program by typing the commands below.

    assemble ADD listfile printer options xref (RETURN)

Following is a listing of the program; note that the assembler recognized the "FFH" as a symbol. Since the symbol was undefined an error message was generated.

FILE: ADD:YOURID HEWLETT-PACKARD: 8085 Assembler   Mon, 9 Feb 1981,   5:54

```
LOC. OBJ. CODE  LINE  SOURCE LINE
                  1   "8085"
                  2   *
                  3*      THIS PROGRAM STARTS AT 0 AND ADDS
                  4*      LOCATION 100H TO LOCATION 101H AND
                  5*      STORES THE RESULT IN LOCATION 102H
                  6              NAME    "ADD WORKSHOP I"
                  7              ORG     2000H       ;PROGRAM ORIGIN
                                                     WILL BE AT HEXADECI-
                                                     MAL
                  8                                  ;2000
2000  210100      9   START  LXI     H,100H       ;LOAD HL PAIR WITH
                                                     100 HEX
2003  7E         10          MOV     A,M          ;MOVE NUMBER IN LOCA-
                                                     TION 100 INTO THE ACC.
2004  23         11          INX     H            ;INCREMENT H AND L
                                                     PAIR.
2005  86         12          ADD     M            ;ADD LOCATION 101
                                                     TO ACCUMULATOR.
2006  23         13          INX     H            ;INCREMENT HL PAIR.
2007  77         14          MOV     M,A          ;STORE ACC. IN LOCA-
                                                     TION 102H
2008  3E00       15          MVI     A,FFH
ERROR-US
200A  C32000     16          JMP     START        ;JUMP TO START
```

Errors= 1, previous error at line 15
US — Undefined Symbol, The indicated symbol is not defined as a label or declared as an external.

FILE: ADD:YOURID   CROSS REFERENCE TABLE   PAGE 2

LINE* SYMBOL   TYPE   REFERENCES
 *** FFH   U   15
   9 START   A   16

Note that the error also appears in the cross-reference table.

Step 5: Whenever the assembler sees an alpha character in the operand field it interprets this character as a symbol. Numerical hex values must therefore be preceded by a 0. This will distinguish them as literal values. Correct the error by entering the following commands.

edit ADD (RETURN)
12 (RETURN)
revise (TAB) (TAB) D,OFFH (RETURN)
end

Step 6: Now assemble the program again, this time listing the program to the display.

assemble ADD listfile display options xref (RETURN)

The program will begin to scroll passed on the display. To stop the scroll depress "RESET" only once. To continue scrolling depress any other key on the keyboard.

Step 7: Your assembled file is now stored on the disk. Take a look at a directory of the files in "YOURID."

directory all_files listfile display (RETURN)

Directory List   User:YOURID   Disc: 0   Mon, 9 Feb 1981,   6:25   Page 1

NAME	TYPE	SIZE	LAST MODIFY	LAST ACCESS
ADD	source	1	9 Feb 1981, 5:54	9 Feb 1981, 6:24
ADD	reloc	1	9 Feb 1981, 6:24	9 Feb 1981, 6:24
ADD	asmb_sym	1	9 Feb 1981, 6:24	9 Feb 1981, 6:24

**** Files listed 3, 0.25% disc space used ****
**** 18.05% disc space available ****

Note that assembling the source file created a "reloc," relocatable object code file, and an assembler symbol file.

EXAMPLE 11.5

Using the 64000 linker, link the relocatable file called "ADD" thereby producing the absolute file "ADD" with absolute address assignments. This file will be executable in either user memory or emulation memory and is in the correct form to be used by the PROM programmer.

Procedure

Step 1: Initialize the linker and declare list file options by performing the following:

   link listfile display (RETURN)
   "Object files ?"

Step 2: Enter the name of any file or files to be linked.

   ADD (RETURN)
   "Library files ?"

Step 3: For this program there are no library routines; therefore continue by using the default with no entry.

   (RETURN)
   "Load addresses: PROG,DATA,COMN = 0000H,0000H,0000H"

Step 4: This command allows the user to specify separate, relocatable memory areas for the program, data, and common modules. No memory assignment is needed here since we used the ORG statement in the beginning of the program. Declare the default by making no selection.

   (RETURN)
   "More files ?"

Step 5: There is only the one file so respond with the appropriate soft key.

   no

Step 6: At this point the linker will ask if you wish to link any more object files. Default by depressing return.

   (RETURN)
   "LIST, XREF = on off"

Step 7: The linker is prompting the user to specify the output and declaring the default for the output listing. The default here is that the linker will produce an output listing with no cross-reference listing.

   (RETURN)
   "Absolute file name ?"

Step 8: The linker is now asking for the name to be assigned to the absolute file and to the linker command file. The command file is a file that contains the responses to the queries thus far presented and a record of which files were linked and how they were linked.

ADD (RETURN)
"HP 64000S linker: Pass1"
"HP 64000S linker: Pass2"
"HP 64000S linker: End of link"

Step 9: The linker output will appear on the display and be similar to that shown below.

HP 64000 LINKER 2.0   Mon, 9 Feb 1981,   7:22

FILE/PROG NAME PROG DATA COMN ABSOLUTE DATE
                                                                       TIME   COMMENTS

ADD:YOURID   2000-200A Mon, 9 Feb 1981, 7:21 ADD WORKSHOP
next address

XFER address= 0000   Defined by DEFAULT
absolute & link_com file name=ADD:YOURID
Total# of bytes loaded= 000B

Please make the following observations about the linker listing.

1. The name of the file and userid in the upper left corner.
2. The absolute and command file name listed in the lower left. Notice that the file names are the same. This is advantageous and permissible since the file manager classifies files by type as well as by name.
3. The absolute address assignments which were assigned through the use of the "ORG" statement.
4. The comments field which contains information resulting from the use of the assembler pseudo op "NAME."

Step 10: The link process established files which are now stored on the disk. Let us look at the directory of these files.

directory (RETURN)

64000 Examples Demonstrating Development on Systems

Directory List   User:YOURID   Disc: 0   Mon, 9 Feb 1981, 7:36   Page 1

NAME	TYPE	SIZE	LAST MODIFY	LAST ACCESS
ADD	source	1	9 Feb 1981, 7:21	9 Feb 1981, 7:21
ADD	link_sym	1	9 Feb 1981, 7:22	9 Feb 1981, 7:22
ADD	link_com	1	9 Feb 1981, 7:14	9 Feb 1981, 7:22
ADD	absolute	1	9 Feb 1981, 7:22	9 Feb 1981, 7:22
ADD	reloc	1	9 Feb 1981, 7:21	9 Feb 1981, 7:22
ADD	asmb_sym	1	9 Feb 1981, 7:21	9 Feb 1981, 7:21

****   Files listed   6,   0.38% disc space used   ****
****   17.88% disc space available   ****

Two files of special interest are the linker command file and the absolute file. The command file will be demonstrated in the next step. The absolute file is the correct form of the program for use in the emulator or the PROM programmer.

Step 11: The process of software development requires the redundant processes of modifying source files, reassembling, relinking, and reentering the emulator. To speed up the process HP has implemented the feature called the command file. The linker command file retains the link information necessary to relink previously linked files without having to reinitialize the linker. To illustrate this perform the following.

link ADD listfile ADD_L (RETURN)

This will relink "ADD" using the previous link setup and will output a linker listing to a file called ADD_L.

EXAMPLE 11.6

Using the 64000 emulator, emulate the absolute file "ADD" without external hardware, allocating internal emulation memory space for the program. During emulation the following functions will be executed:

LOAD, DISPLAY MEMORY, RUN, STEP, BREAK POINTS, DISPLAY REGISTERS, STOP RUN, and END EMULATION.

To obtain a listing of the display contents during emulation use the following commands.

list display to printer (RETURN)

Procedure

Step 1: Type in the source program "ADD" which is listed in Example 11.3. Then assemble and link as performed in Examples 11.4 and 11.5. This is the same program used in Examples 11.3, 11.4, and 11.5 so if this has already been done continue with step 2.

Step 2: Enter the emulation mode and load the absolute file.

emulate load ADD (RETURN)
"Processor clock ?"

Step 3: The first question asks if the source of the processor clock is internal or external to the development station. Since we have no external hardware, select internal.

internal (RETURN)
"Restrict processor to real-time runs ?"

Step 4: To restrict the processor to real-time runs limits the analysis functions that can be performed. An example of this would be asking the system to "display registers dynamic." This analysis command requires that the host interrupt the processor to fetch the register contents. Therefore the processor is no longer running in real time. Answer no to the above question.

no (RETURN)
"Stop processor on illegal opcodes ?"

Step 5: Specify "yes" to this prompt. By so doing, emulation will stop if an illegal op code is detected.

yes (RETURN)
"Emulation RAM address range ?"

Step 6: Define the memory space to meet the specific needs of this program. Since all memory is internal there will be no user external memory. Address 100H to 103H is used for storing the variables used in the program so define RAM for these locations. In order to protect the user program memory, one should declare the user program memory space as ROM. Therefore, define ROM for your program located at 2000H through 200CH. Note that if one tries to write into a ROM location, an error message will be generated.
100H thru 103H
(RETURN)
"Emulation RAM address range ?"

64000 Examples Demonstrating Development on Systems

(RETURN)
"Emulation ROM address range ?"
2000H thru 20FFH
(RETURN)
"Emulation ROM address range ?"
(RETURN)
"User RAM address range ?"
(RETURN)
"User ROM address range?"
(RETURN)
Note that in the above as long as entries for address range are made, responses will be given "Emulation (or user) RAM or (ROM) Address range?" This is because memory can be mapped non-contiguously.
"Illegal memory address range?"

Step 7: Any address value or range of values entered here will produce an error message if referenced by the processor during emulation. In more critical applications this is a good technique to use to flag the user that the program has escaped its anticipated boundaries.

(RETURN)
Step 8: "SIMULATED I/O?"
"NO"

(RETURN) A memory map will appear.
"Command file name ?"

Step 9: The next query requires an entry of a valid file name under which the command file will be stored. This file appears on the directory as a "emul_com", emulation command, file.

ADD (RETURN)

Step 10: All conditions for emulation have now been set up. The absolute file must now be loaded into emulation memory.

load_memory ADD (RETURN)
"STATUS: 8085----Program loaded"

If you want to modify the program, you have to repeat edit, assemble, and link as before. Then, for emulation, use command file. That is, type in emulate ADD load ADD (RETURN). This will perform all the steps from 1 through 10.

Step 11: Select the memory display function to show your program loaded in memory.

display memory 2000H   mnemonic   (RETURN)

Your display should appear similar to that below. Note that the 64000 displays one whole page at a time. Therefore, disregard information on the page which is unnecessary.

MEMORY

```
2000H  LXI  H, 0100H
2003H  MOV  A,M
2004H  INX  H
2005H  ADD  M
2006H  INX  H
2007H  MOV  M,A
2008H  JMP  2000H
         -
         -
         -
```

Step 12: Now let us modify the two locations "ADD" will add together and display the modification on the CRT.

modify memory 100H thru 102H to 02H   (RETURN)
display memory 100H   dynamic   (RETURN)

The display should appear similar to that below. Note that only the first three locations 100H through 102H are of interest here. Disregard the others.

MEMORY__DYNAMIC

Adr	--------------------Data (hex)----------------------							---(ASCII)---
0100	02	02	04	B7	80	D4	2F	B5	7 T / 5
0108	19	01	0E	56	CC	0A	13	BE	V L >
0110	C3	0B	9C	1C	D3	41	1A	AE	C S A .
0118	6F	40	1F	19	0F	2A	DD	B8	o⊞ *] 8
0120	BF	7B	03	7B	FF	02	42	06	? { { # B
0128	C8	38	54	00	74	F9	44	49	H 8 T t y D I
0130	79	81	C4	C7	EE	AA	05	8B	y D G n *
0138	9A	76	0B	22	B6	42	E7	C6	v '' 6 B g F
0140	EF	C4	1F	D4	83	92	9E	8B	o D T
0148	9E	41	7A	D6	38	42	75	12	A z V 8 B u

64000 Examples Demonstrating Development on Systems 511

```
0150  45  0C  CA  0A  D4  40     DB  DD    E  J   T⊞ [ ]
0158  3C  B2  38  DD  76  10     CB  90    < 2 8 ]  v  K
0160  B8  0B  20  84  E4  64     43  7B    8       d d C {
0168  FB  9A  18  A5  C9  FF     19  95    {    %  I #
0170  AB  E0  8B  D5  7D  ED     DE  DC    +  `  U } m ` \
0178  7F  63  44  55  E5  25     20  CD    # c D U  e %  M
```

The column of ASCII characters above are the ASCII equivalent of the hex values in the data field.

Step 13: Leaving the memory dynamic display mode on, run "ADD" and observe the sum being placed in location 0102H.

run from 2000H (RETURN)
    or
run from START (RETURN)
"STATUS: 8085----Running"

then modify location 0100H and note the sum (location 0102H) changing. modify memory 100H to 0FH (RETURN).

Step 14: Single-stepping is one of the several analysis tools available on the 64000. To single-step "ADD" while displaying registers follow the steps below.

stop run (RETURN)
"STATUS: 8085----Stopped"
display registers   dynamic (RETURN)
step from START   or   step from 2000H (RETURN)
step (RETURN)
(RETURN)

Every time the return key is depressed the program is single cycled. The display should show the program counter changing and the various register contents.

REGISTER (Hex)

pc	opcode		a	b	c	d	e	h	l	szxac	xpxcy	sp	next_p
2000	21	LXI H, 0100H	01	00	00	00	00	01	00	00 0	1 0	00FF	2003
2003	7E	MOV A,M	01	00	00	00	00	01	00	00 0	1 0	00FF	2004
2004	23	INX H	01	00	00	00	00	01	01	00 0	1 0	00FF	2005
2005	86	ADD M	03	00	00	00	00	01	01	00 0	1 0	00FF	2006
2006	23	INX H	03	00	00	00	00	01	02	00 0	1 0	00FF	2007
2007	77	MOV M,A	03	00	00	00	00	01	02	00 0	1 0	00FF	2008
2008	C3	JMP 2000H	03	00	00	00	00	01	02	00 0	1 0	00FF	2000
2000	21	LXI H, 0100H	03	00	00	00	00	01	00	00 0	1 0	00FF	2003
2003	7E	MOV A,M	01	00	00	00	00	01	00	00 0	1 0	00FF	2004

512 Chapter 11 THE HEWLETT-PACKARD (HP) 64000

Step 15: Study the single-step printout and the "ADD" source listing below. For the above listing the location 0100H was loaded with 01H and location 101H was loaded with 02H and the sum appears in location 103H. One can insert a breakpoint by typing run from 2000H until 2006H (RETURN). On the display one would be interested in the contents of all the registers up to execution of the instruction at 2006H. Disregard any other information.

Source Statement

FILE: ADD:YOURID   HEWLETT-PACKARD: 8085 Assembler   Mon, 9 Feb 1981,   3:45

LOC. OBJ.	CODE LINE		SOURCE LINE		
	1		"8085"		
	2	*			THIS PROGRAM STARTS AT 0
	3	*			AND
	4	*			ADDS LOCATION 100H
	5	*			LOCATION 101H AND STORES THE
					RESULT IN LOCATION
	6		NAME		"ADD WORKSHOP I"
	7		ORG	2000H	;PROGRAM ORIGIN WILL BE AT HEXADECIMAL
	8				;2000
2000 210100	9 START		LXI	H,100H	;LOAD HL PAIR WITH 100 HEX
2003 7E	10		MOV	A,M	;MOVE NUMBER IN LOCATION 100 INTO THE
2004 23	11		INX	H	;INCREMENT H AND L PAIR.
2005 86	12		ADD	M	;ADD LOCATION 101 TO ACCUMULATOR.
2006 23	13		INX	H	;INCREMENT HL PAIR.
2007 77	14		MOV	M,A	;STORE ACC. IN LOCATION 102H
2008 C32000	15		JMP	START	;JUMP TO START

Errors= 0

Step 16: Another powerful analysis feature is setting breakpoints and checking register contents, flag status, and so on after the breakpoint. Looking at the program listing, the command

"ADD M" is found on line #9 at address 2005H. To set up a breakpoint for this address follow the steps below.

    run from START until address = 2005H (RETURN)

Step 17: Here is one more example of using breakpoints. Follow the steps below to halt the program after a memory write has been executed.

    run from 2000H until status = memory_write (RETURN)

The program will stop after the "MOV M,A" instruction is executed.

Step 18: To end the emulation session, execute the following command.

    end (RETURN)

Step 19: If you wish to emulate this program or any other program with the same emulation configuration (i.e., memory map, internal clock, etc.) simply invoke the emulator command file and load the program.

    emulate ADD load ADD (RETURN)

To change the emulation configuration during emulation use the "edit-cnfg" soft key.

    edit-cnfg (RETURN)

Note that the HP 64000 system can perform in-circuit emulation with or without target system hardware, allowing the user to specify a memory map and fault options. Logic analysis can also be performed allowing monitoring of the bus and various registers for the purpose of software development and troubleshooting.

EXAMPLE 11.7

The following example demonstrates hardware emulation by using the HP 5036 microprocessor laboratory as the target system. The software contains three software modules "EXEC," "DISP," and "KYBRD." These modules are given in Appendix E. The "EXEC" program controls the interface between the service routines. "DISP" controls the seven-segment display and "KYBRD" services the keyboard.

Objective

Copy the software modules "EXEC," "DISP," and "KYBRD" into your userid then assemble and link these modules into an absolute program called "SYS."

Procedure

Step 1: Type in the source program listings into your userid. If the files currently exist in another userid they can be transferred as shown below.

    userid YOURID
    copy EXEC:OTHERID :source to EXEC (RETURN)
    copy DISP:OTHERID :source to DISP (RETURN)
    copy KYBRD:OTHERID :source to KYBRD (RETURN)

    The three source programs should now appear on your directory.

Step 2: Now assemble the source files to create the relocatable modules.

    assemble EXEC (RETURN)
    assemble DISP (RETURN)
    assemble KYBRD (RETURN)

    The three "reloc" programs should now appear on your directory.

Step 3: Link the three relocatable modules into one absolute program called "SYS." As part of the linking process establish the linker command file and list the link map to the printer.

    link listfile printer (RETURN)
    "object files ?"

Step 4: Type in the names of the object files separated by a comma.

    EXEC, DISP, KYBRD, (RETURN)
    "Library files"
    (RETURN)
    "Load addresses: PROG, DATA, COMN = 0000H, 0000H, 0000H"
    (RETURN)
    "More files ?"
    (RETURN)
    "LIST, XREF = on off
    (RETURN)
    "Absolute file name = "

Step 5: Type in the name of the absolute file and link command file.

SYS (RETURN)

The printout should appear similar to that below.

HP 64000 LINKER 2.0   Mon, 9 Feb 1981, 1:16

FILE/PROG NAME PROG. DATA COMN. ABSOLUTE DATE   TIME COMMENTS

EXEC:CHAP_9   0810-0848 Mon, 9 Feb 1981, 4:18
DISP:CHAP_9   0A00-0A46 Mon, 9 Feb 1981, 5:24
KYBRD:CHAP_9   0900-0962 Mon, 9 Feb 1981, 4:52
next address

XFER address= 0000 Defined by DEFAULT
absolute & link_com file name=SYS
Total# of bytes loaded= 00E3

Step 6: Get a directory of the files under your userid. The directory should appear similar to that below.

Directory List User:YOURID Disc: 0 Mon, 9 Feb 1981, 1:43 Page 1

NAME	TYPE	SIZE	LAST MODIFY	LAST ACCESS
ADD	emul_com	1	9 Feb 1981, 0:40	9 Feb 1981, 1:05
ADD	link_sym	1	9 Feb 1981, 7:22	9 Feb 1981, 1:05
ADD	link_com	1	9 Feb 1981, 7:14	9 Feb 1981, 7:22
ADD	source	1	9 Feb 1981, 7:21	9 Feb 1981, 1:27
ADD	reloc	1	9 Feb 1981, 1:27	9 Feb 1981, 1:27
ADD	asmb_sym	1	9 Feb 1981, 1:27	9 Feb 1981, 1:27
ADD	absolute	1	9 Feb 1981, 7:22	9 Feb 1981, 1:05
ADD	listing	1	9 Feb 1981, 7:21	9 Feb 1981, 7:21
DISP	asmb_sym	1	9 Feb 1981, 1:39	9 Feb 1981, 1:39
DISP	reloc	1	9 Feb 1981, 1:38	9 Feb 1981, 1:38
DISP	source	1	9 Feb 1981, 1:34	9 Feb 1981, 1:34
EXEC	asmb_sym	1	9 Feb 1981, 1:41	9 Feb 1981, 1:41
EXEC	reloc	1	9 Feb 1981, 1:40	9 Feb 1981, 1:40
EXEC	source	1	9 Feb 1981, 1:34	9 Feb 1981, 1:34
KYBRD	asmb_sym	1	9 Feb 1981, 1:37	9 Feb 1981, 1:37

KYBRD	reloc	1	9 Feb 1981, 1:37	9 Feb 1981, 1:37
KYBRD	source	2	9 Feb 1981, 1:37	9 Feb 1981, 1:37
SYS	link_sym	1	9 Feb 1981, 1:36	9 Feb 1981, 1:36
SYS	link_com	1	9 Feb 1981, 1:36	9 Feb 1981, 1:36
SYS	absolute	1	9 Feb 1981, 1:35	9 Feb 1981, 1:35

**** Files listed   19,   1.13% disc space used   ****
****   16.71% disc space available   ****

Summary

The three modules have now been relocated and linked together into one module called "SYS." The various analysis tools and the symbolic debug capability of the HP 64000 provide the capability to debug each software module as it is completed. Once the modules are complete they can be linked together and any final modifications made.

EXAMPLE 11.8

Objective

Using the HP 5036 microprocessor lab as the target system perform in-circuit emulation with the file called SYS. It should be noted that the emulation probe may be damaged if not installed correctly with the target system power turned off.

Procedure

Step 1: Carefully remove the 8085 microprocessor from its socket and place on a piece of conductive foam or some static protection material. Be sure to discharge yourself of excess static before handling the microprocessor.

Step 2: Insert the emulation probe into the socket of the microprocessor being careful to observe the correct orientation of pin 1.

Step 3: Power up the target system.

Step 4: Enter the emulation mode and load the absolute file name.

emulate load SYS (RETURN)
"Processor clock"

Step 5: The first question asks if you would like the processor clock to be provided by the target system or the 64000 in the absence of external hardware.

external (RETURN)
"is clock speed greater than 4.48 MHz?"

64000 Examples Demonstrating Development on Systems

Step 6: Since the 8085 divides the incoming clock by two and the crystal frequency is 4 MHz the clock speed is only 2 MHz.

   no (RETURN)
   "Restrict processor to real time runs?"

Step 7: To restrict the processor to "REAL TIME RUNS" limits the analysis tools available. For example, trying to trace register contents during program execution results in dropping out of real-time program execution to fetch the register contents.

   no (RETURN)
   "Stop processor on illegal opcodes?"

Step 8: Specify yes to this prompt. The processor will halt if an illegal op code is encountered. If the wrong absolute file is loaded this will act as a flag to the user.

   yes (RETURN)
   "Emulation RAM address range?"

Step 9: This prompt asks you to define the memory space needed for proper execution during emulation. Memory may be mapped internally or externally or a combination of both depending on the needs of the user. On the 5036 the following addresses are already defined.

   0000-07FFH ROM Monitor
   0800-0BFFH RAM Memory
   1800H Keyboard Register
   2800H Scan Register
   3800H Display Register
   0FFF0H-0FFFFH Top Defined Addresses

   The program modules are defined at the following addresses.

   0810H-0848H EXEC Program Module
   0A00H-0A46H DISP Program Module
   0900H-0962H KYBRD Program Module

   For the memory map we wish to define the monitor and target registers as user memory, and define the RAM space 0800-0BFFH

518   Chapter 11   THE HEWLETT-PACKARD (HP) 64000

as emulation memory. It could have been mapped as user memory. Now enter the memory map.

"Emulation RAM address range ?"
0800H thru 0BFFH (RETURN)
"Emulation RAM address range?" (RETURN)
"Emulation ROM address range ?"

(RETURN)
"User RAM address range?"
1800H thru 3800H (RETURN)

"User RAM address range ?"

OFFF0H thru 0FFFFH (RETURN)
"User RAM address range?" (RETURN)
"User ROM address range ?"

0 thru 7FFH (RETURN)

"User ROM address range?

(RETURN)

Your memory map should look exactly like the map below. If you have any problems with the map continue through the query process. When the emulation command file is complete it can be edited and corrections made at that time. Note that in the listing below, the first ROM is mapped from 0000H through 03FFH, the second ROM from 0400H through 07FFH, and so on.

Configuring I8085 processor in slot #9, Memory slot #7. Analysis slot #8.

Emulation and User Memory assignments

	-000	-400	-800	-C00		-000	-400	-800	-C00
0---	ROM	ROM	RAM		8---				
1---			RAM	RAM	9---				
2---	RAM	RAM	RAM	RAM	A---				
3---	RAM	RAM	RAM		B---				
4---					C---				
5---					D---				
6---					E---				
7---					F---				RAM

STATUS: Memory assignments --------------- 12:12

"Illegal memory address range?"

64000 Examples Demonstrating Development on Systems

Step 10: We are allowed to specify a range of addresses that will be considered out of bounds for the processor. If this range is penetrated the processor will halt and the last program counter will be displayed. For this application answer no.

no (RETURN)
"Simulated I/O ?"

Step 11: This prompt is asking if we wish to use the simulated input or output capability of the HP 64000 during emulation. In the event we were doing development of a project that required a printer, a display device, as many as five disk files, a keyboard, or the RS232 port and these I/O devices were not yet available on the target system, we could continue to do the development work by simulating them using the I/O devices of the HP 64000. For this application we do not use simulated I/O.

no (RETURN)
"Command file name ?"

Step 12: The last query requires an entry of a valid file name under which the command file will be stored. Name the file "SYS." This duplication of file names is permissible since files are classified by type as well as file name.

SYS (RETURN)

The display should now appear similar to that below. The register contents are arbitrary.

REGISTER (Hex)
pc	opcode	a	b	c	d	e	h	l	szxac	xpxcy	sp	next_pc
0000	**	00	00	00	00	00	00	00	00 0	0 0	0000	0000

STATUS: 8085---program loaded   ---13:00

Step 13: Reset the 5036A microprocessor lab by beginning program execution from address zero. This will cause a power on reset changing the contents of all RAM addresses to 00H. A beep should be heard and the display of the 5036 should appear as "uLAB UP."

run from 0 (RETURN)

See ⏐U⏐L⏐A⏐b⏐ ⏐U⏐P⏐ on the HP 5036 display.

Chapter 11 THE HEWLETT-PACKARD (HP) 64000

Step 14: Run the demonstration program "ROCT." This is a demonstration program stored in ROM of the HP5036.

    run from 05F9H (RETURN)

A countdown will be displayed on the target system display along with the beep sound.

Step 15: Run the demonstration program "WTM" located at address 053EH in HP 5036 ROM.

    run from 053EH (RETURN)

The microprocessor lab will produce tones which are the product of a pseudorandom tone generator.

Step 16: End emulation mode to demonstrate the advantage of the dual bus configuration. The processor of the emulation probe will continue to execute the programs in user memory without being interrupted from the host system. This allows software development while performing emulation.

    end_emulation (RETURN)

The target system will continue to generate tones.

Step 17: Enter emulation once again by using the emulation command file name and the option selection. We can regain control of the emulation process without interrupting the current programs activity.

    emulate SYS options continue (RETURN)

Step 18: Stop program execution thereby ending the tone generation.

    stop run (RETURN)

Step 19: Display memory contents starting from location 810H. In this way we can check to see if our program has been loaded properly.

    display memory 810H (RETURN)

Note that SYS is loaded from 0810H through 0848H. The other locations are arbitrary. The display will appear similar to that below.

64000 Examples Demonstrating Development on Systems

MEMORY

Adr				Data (hex)				-(ASCII)-
0810	31	00	0C	21	05	08	3E	F7	1 ! >w
0818	77	2D	F2	18	08	CD	00	09	w-r M
0820	D2	2B	08	AF	2F	32	06	08	R+ / /2
0828	C3	43	08	21	26	03	BE	CA	CC ! & >J
0830	43	08	77	F5	21	05	08	11	C wu !
0838	04	08	1A	77	1D	2D	C2	3A	w -B :
0840	08	F1	77	CD	00	0A	C3	1D	qwM C
0848	08	B7	86	45	23	A7	74	9C	7 E # ′ †
0850	96	F7	F0	5A	FF	30	5A	E6	wpZ #0Zf
0858	8A	A6	8B	EA	A4	34	A5	BE	& j $4%>
0860	C3	3B	56	D5	F8	21	11	FD	C;VU x! }
0868	F5	80	A0	9D	E0	37	17	05	u m7
0870	A1	47	33	59	F2	D4	12	AC	!G3Y rT ,
0878	F1	2C	6D	3F	F8	9D	10	B4	q,m? × 4
0880	42	20	2C	35	C2	C3	01	91	B ,5 BC
0888	09	0B	BE	3E	EA	01	21	FC	≫ j !	

During reset or power-up of the HP 5036, the above display might be zero.

Step 20: To run from a location until a certain command is executed use the following instructions. First do a software reset which will put the processor through its power-up sequence and reset the program counter. Other registers are not affected.

display registers dynamic
restart (RETURN)

"STATUS: 8085 READY"

run from 0810H until address = 0A00H status = read (RETURN)

The display will appear similar to that below.

REGISTER (Hex)

pc	opcode		a	b	c	d	e	h	l	szxac	xpxcy	sp	next_pc
0810	31	LXI SP, 0C00H	00	00	00	00	00	00	00	00 0	0 0	0C00	0813
0813	21	LXI H, 0805H	00	00	00	00	00	08	05	00 0	0 0	0C00	0816
0816	3E	MVI A, F7H	F7	00	00	00	00	08	05	00 0	0 0	0C00	0818
0818	77	MOV M,A	F7	00	00	00	00	08	05	00 0	0 0	0C00	0819
0A00	**		C9	00	00	00	00	08	18	01 0	1 0	00FF	0000
0A00	E5	PUSH H	FF	00	00	00	00	08	FF	01 0	1 0	0BFC	0A01

STATUS: 8085---stopped

522 Chapter 11 The Hewlett-Packard (HP) 64000

Step 21: The target system can be instructed to run from an address until it is commanded to stop a "stop run" command. For example to run the program from 0810H enter the following commands.

run from 0810 (RETURN)

Step 22: Now display the memory again and modify it while the program is running.

display memory 800H mode dynamic (RETURN)

The display will appear similar to that below. If it does not then try reloading the program.

```
MEMORY---DYNAMIC
 Adr      ----------------------Data (hex)---------------------   -(ASCII)-
 0800   F7   F7   F7   F7   F7   F7   FF   00      wwww ww#
 0808   00   00   00   00   00   00   00   00
 0810   31   00   0C   21   05   08   3E   F7      1   !    >w
 0818   77   2D   F2   18   08   CD   00   09      w-r     M
 0820   D2   2B   08   AF   2F   32   06   08      R+  / /2
 0828   C3   43   08   21   06   08   BE   CA      CC !    >J
 0830   43   08   77   F5   21   05   08   11      C wu !
 0838   04   08   1A   77   1D   2D   C2   3A          w   -B:
 0840   08   F1   77   CD   00   0A   C3   1D      qwM     C
 0848   08   00   00   00   00   00   00   00
 0850   00   00   00   00   00   00   00   00
 0858   00   00   00   00   00   00   00   00
 0860   00   00   00   00   00   00   00   00
 0868   00   00   00   00   00   00   00   00
 0870   00   00   00   00   00   00   00   00
 0878   00   00   00   00   00   00   00   00
```

To modify address 0800 through 0805 to another value enter the following commands.

modify memory 0800H thru 0805H to 0FFH

The display will appear similar to that below.

```
MEMORY---DYNAMIC
 Adr      ----------------------Data (hex)---------------------   -(ASCII)-
 0800   FF   FF   FF   FF   FF   FF   00   00      #### ###
 0808   00   00   00   00   00   00   00   00
 0810   31   00   0C   21   05   08   3E   F7      1   !    >w
```

64000 Examples Demonstrating Development on Systems

```
0818  77  2D  F2  18  08  CD  00  09    w-r    M
0820  D2  2B  08  AF  2F  32  06  08    R+  / /2
0828  C3  43  08  21  06  08  BE  CA    CC !    >J
0830  43  08  77  F5  21  05  08  11    C wu !
0838  04  08  1A  77  1D  2D  C2  3A       w  -B:
0840  08  F1  77  CD  00  0A  C3  1D    qwM    C
0848  08  00  00  00  00  00  00  00
0850  00  00  00  00  00  00  00  00
0858  00  00  00  00  00  00  00  00
0860  00  00  00  00  00  00  00  00
0868  00  00  00  00  00  00  00  00
0870  00  00  00  00  00  00  00  00
0878  00  00  00  00  00  00  00  00
```

Step 23: To stop execution at any time use the stop command.

    stop run (RETURN)
    "STATUS: 8085----Stopped"

Step 24: Every time a source file is assembled a symbol cross-reference table is generated. Two tables are created. One table contains the local symbols used only within the module being assembled and a global symbol file. Global symbols are symbols defined in the current module and referenced in other modules. To display local symbols in the file "EXEC" use the following commands.

    display local "symbols in" EXEC (RETURN)

The symbols and values are displayed similarly to that shown below.

    LOCAL SYMBOLS IN EXEC: CHAP_9

Symbol	Address	Value
EXEC	0810H	31H
GO1	083AH	1AH
LIGHT	0843H	CDH
LP1	0818H	77H
LP2	081DH	CDH
XX	082BH	21H

Step 25: To display your program in memory to verify proper loading, simply display the memory address in the mnemonic mode.

    display memory 810H mode mnemonic (RETURN)

Chapter 11 The Hewlett-Packard (HP) 64000

The display will appear similar to that shown below (the display will not be updated dynamically unless the program is running and a dynamic display was specified).

MEMORY

```
0810H  LXI   SP, 0C00H
0813H  LXI   H, 0805H
0816H  MVI   A, F7H
0818H  MOV   M,A
0819H  DCR   L
081AH  JF    0818H
081DH  CALL  0900H
0820H  JNC   082BH
0823H  XRA   A
0824H  CMA
0825H  STA   0806H
0828H  JMP   0843H
082BH  LXI   H, 0326H
082EH  CMP   M
082FH  JZ    0843H
0832H  MOV   M,A
```

Step 26: Now run the program from 0810H and watch the memory address 0800H through 085H change as numbers are entered from the target keyboard.

run from 0810H (RETURN)
display memory 0800H mode dynamic (RETURN)

The display will appear similar to that below before numbers are entered from the keyboard.

MEMORY---DYNAMIC

Adr	---------Data (hex)---------						-(ASCII)-
0800	F7	F7	F7	F7	F7	F7	FF	00	wwww ww#
0808	00	00	00	00	00	00	00	00	
0810	31	00	0C	21	05	08	3E	F7	1 ! >w
0818	77	2D	F2	18	08	CD	00	09	w-r M
0820	D2	2B	08	AF	2F	32	06	08	R+ / /2
0828	C3	43	08	21	06	08	BE	CA	CC ! >J
0830	43	08	77	F5	21	05	08	11	C wu !
0838	04	08	1A	77	1D	2D	C2	3A	w -B:
0840	08	F1	77	CD	00	0A	C3	1D	qwM C
0848	08	00	00	00	00	00	00	00	

STATUS: 8085---Running

64000 Examples Demonstrating Development on Systems

Depress the 1, 2, 3 keys in sequence on the target system keyboard. The memory will change dynamically as the keys are depressed. The display will look as follows.

MEMORY---DYNAMIC

Adr	----------Data (hex)----------							-(ADCII)-
0800	03	02	01	F7	F7	F7	FF	00	wwww ww#
0808	00	00	00	00	00	00	00	00
0810	31	00	0C	21	05	08	3E	F7	1 ! >w
0818	77	2D	F2	18	08	CD	00	09	w-r M
0820	D2	2B	08	AF	2F	32	06	08	R+ / /2
0828	C3	43	08	21	06	08	BE	CA	CC ! >J
0830	43	08	77	F5	21	05	08	11	C wu !
0838	04	08	1A	77	1D	2D	C2	3A	w -B:
0840	08	F1	77	CD	00	0A	C3	1D	qwM C
0848	08	00	00	00	00	00	00	00
0850	00	00	00	00	00	00	00	00

Step 27: Valuable information about program flow can be gained by watching the registers in the dynamic mode. The following commands will allow you to watch them during a pseudorun.

display registers mode dynamic (RETURN)

Pause the display by depressing the reset once, twice to reset the system to the monitor mode, and any other key to resume program operation. When paused the display will look similar to that below.

REGISTER (Hex)

pc	opcode		a	b	c	d	e	h	l	szxac	xpxcy	sp	next_pc
0A33	6F	MOV L,A	38	16	10	08	FF	0A	38	00 0	0 0	0BF4	0A34

Step 28: To display the current run specifications execute the following commands.

display run spec (RETURN)

The display will appear similar to that below.

CURRENT RUN SPECIFICATION

run from 0810H

STATUS: 8085---Stopped   ---14:29

526 Chapter 11 THE HEWLETT-PACKARD (HP) 64000

Step 29: This example shows how to determine how often the keyboard is scanned on the target system. Each time the keyboard is scanned "EXEC" calls "KYBRD" at location 900H.

trace only address = 900H (RETURN)

Your display will be similar to that below. The actual times may differ however.

TRACE			COUNT TIME ABSOLUTE	
ADDRESS,DATA,STATUS				
AFTER	0A15H DCR A		+ 0.	µS
+001	0900H PUSH H	sp-1 **** h1 ****	+ 8.390	MS
+002	0900H PUSH H	sp-1 **** h1 ****	+ 23.756	MS
+003	0900H PUSH H	sp-1 **** h1 ****	+ 39.121	MS
+004	0900H PUSH H	sp-1 **** h1 ****	+ 54.487	MS
+005	0900H PUSH H	sp-1 **** h1 ****	+ 69.852	MS
+006	0900H PUSH H	sp-1 **** h1 ****	+ 85.218	MS
+007	0900H PUSH H	sp-1 **** h1 ****	+100.583	MS
+008	0900H PUSH H	sp-1 **** h1 ****	+115.949	MS
+009	0900H PUSH H	sp-1 **** h1 ****	+131.315	MS
+010	0900H PUSH H	sp-1 **** h1 ****	+146.680	MS
+011	0900H PUSH H	sp-1 **** h1 ****	+162.046	MS
+012	0900H PUSH H	sp-1 **** h1 ****	+177.411	MS
+013	0900H PUSH H	sp-1 **** h1 ****	+192.777	MS
+014	0900H PUSH H	sp-1 **** h1 ****	+208.142	MS
+015	0900H PUSH H	sp-1 **** h1 ****	+223.508	MS

STATUS: 8085----Running   Trace complete ---14:39

Step 30: The trace command defaults to counting time elapsed once the trigger word is detected. To determine the time interval between calls use the count relative mode.

display count relative (RETURN)

The display will appear similar to that below.

TRACE			COUNT TIME RELATIVE	
ADDRESS,DATA,STATUS				
AFTER	0A16H JNZ ****			
+001	0900H PUSH H	sp-1 **** h1 ****	3.269	MS
+002	0900H PUSH H	sp-1 **** h1 ****	15.371	MS
+003	0900H PUSH H	sp-1 **** h1 ****	15.371	MS

64000 Examples Demonstrating Development on Systems   527

+004	0900H PUSH H	sp-1 **** h1 ****	15.371	MS
+005	0900H PUSH H	sp-1 **** h1 ****	15.371	MS
+006	0900H PUSH H	sp-1 **** h1 ****	15.371	MS
+007	0900H PUSH H	sp-1 **** h1 ****	15.371	MS
+008	0900H PUSH H	sp-1 **** h1 ****	15.371	MS
+009	0900H PUSH H	sp-1 **** h1 ****	15.371	MS
+010	0900H PUSH H	sp-1 **** h1 ****	15.371	MS
+011	0900H PUSH H	sp-1 **** h1 ****	15.372	MS
+012	0900H PUSH H	sp-1 **** h1 ****	15.371	MS
+013	0900H PUSH H	sp-1 **** h1 ****	15.371	MS
+014	0900H PUSH H	sp-1 **** h1 ****	15.371	MS
+015	0900H PUSH H	sp-1 **** h1 ****	15.371	MS

STATUS: 8085 ---Running   trace complete ---14:46

Step 31: To trace about an event of interest is a powerful debug tool. To trace the program that shifts data through the display buffer use the following commands.

trace about address = 805H status = write (RETURN)

Now enter data from the target system to complete the trace. After the data are entered the display will appear similar to that below.

TRACE   COUNT TIME RELATIVE
    ADDRESS,DATA,STATUS

−008	082EH CMP M	h1 0806H (h1) FFH	5.	μS
−007	082FH JZ ****		3.	μS
−006	0832H MOV M,A	h1 0806H (h1) 01H	3.	μS
−005	0833H PUSH PSW	sp-1 0BFFH a 01H flag 01H	3.	μS
−004	0834H LXI H, 0805H		6.	μS
−003	0837H LXI D, 0804H		4.	μS
−002	083AH LDAX D	de 0804H a 02H	5.	μS
−001	083BH MOV M,A	h1 **** (h1) **	3.	μS
ABOUT	0805H 02H 15H		1.	μS
+001	083CH DCR E		1.	μS
+002	083DH DCR L		1.	μS
+003	083EH JNZ 083AH		1.	μS
+004	083AH LDAX D	de 0803H a 03H	5.	μS
+005	083BH MOV M,A	h1 0804H (h1) 03H	3.	μS
+006	083CH DCR E		3.	μS
+007	083DH DCR L		1.	μS

STATUS: 8085---Running   Trace complete ---14:51

Chapter 11 The Hewlett-Packard (HP) 64000

Step 32: Not only are you able to trace about an event, you can also trace after an event. This example shows how you can determine the number of times the display buffer locations are modified when new data are entered from the keyboard.

trace after address = 82BH (RETURN)

Depress a key on the target system to fill the text buffer. The trace will then appear similar to that below.

TRACE	ADDRESS,DATA,STATUS		COUNT	TIME	RELATIVE
AFTER	082BH LXI H, 0806H				
+001	082EH CMP M	h1 0806H (h1) FFH		5.	µS
+002	082FH JZ ****			3.	µS
+003	0832H MOV M,A	h1 0808H (h1) 01H		3.	µS
+004	0833H PUSH PSW	sp-1 0BFFH a 01H flag 01H		3.	µS
+005	0834H LXI H, 0805H			5.	µS
+006	0837H LXI D, 0804H			5.	µS
+007	083AH LDAX D	de 0804H a 03H		5.	µS
+008	083BH MOV M,A	h1 0805H (h1) 03H		3.	µS
+009	083CH DCR E			3.	µS
+010	083DH DCR L			1.	µS
+011	083EH JNZ 083AH			1.	µS
+012	083AH LDAX D	de 0803H a 01H		5.	µS
+013	083BH MOV M,A	h1 0804H (h1) 01H		3.	µS
+014	083CH DCR E			3.	µS
+015	083DH DCR L			1.	µS

STATUS: 8085---Running   Trace complete ---14:54

Step 33: Another useful debugging trace is counting states. To count the relative states as data are entered from the keyboard, use the following commands.

count address = 80XH status = write (RETURN)

After you depress a key on the target system the display will appear similar to that below.

TRACE	ADDRESS,DATA,STATUS		COUNT	STATES	RELATIVE
AFTER	082BH LXI H, 0806H				
+001	082EH CMP M	h1 0806H (h1) FFH		0	
+002	082FH JZ ****			0	

64000 Examples Demonstrating Development on Systems

+003	0832H MOV M,A	h1 0806H (h1) 01H	0
+004	0833H PUSH PSW	sp-1 0BFFH a 01H flag 01H	1
+005	0834H LXI H, 0805H		0
+006	0837H LXI D, 0804H		0
+007	083AH LDAX D	de 0804H a 01H	0
+008	083BH MOV M,A	h1 0805H (h1) 01H	0
+009	083CH DCR E		1
+010	083DH DCR L		0
+011	083EH JNZ 083AH		0
+012	083AH LDAX D	de 0803H a 02H	0
+013	083BH MOV M,A	h1 0804H (h1) 02H	0
+014	083CH DCR E		1
+015	083DH DCR L		0

STATUS: 8085---Running   Trace complete ---15:00

Step 34: Now stop run and end emulation.

        stop run (RETURN)
        end_emulation (RETURN)

Step 35: Power down the target system. Once the power is removed carefully remove the emulation probe and insert the 8085 microprocessor back into the socket of the target system. Note that anytime the display shows "8085 slow clock" during emulation, press soft key restart (RETURN). If the "8085 slow clock" is still displayed, check to make sure: (1) the target system clock operates properly; (2) low hold request line; (3) HIGH reset line; (4) low interrupt lines.

Summary

The HP 64000 is a powerful development tool. The preceding workshops have shown some of the debug and trace analysis capability available in the HP 64000. The application of these analysis tools to the development process allows rapid development of microprocessor-based products.

EXAMPLE 11.9

Objective

Become familiar with the PROM programmer by reading a PROM to a list file then modifying the PROM list file and reprogramming the PROM. It is not necessary to have a PROM to go through the following procedure. It is, however, necessary to have the PROM programmer option with one or more PROM modules.

Procedure

Step 1: Enter in your userid and set the date and time correctly, then enter the PROM programmer mode as follows.

prom_prog (RETURN)
"Prom_type?"
2716 (RETURN)
"ENTER: Command"

Step 2: Insert, if available, an Intel 2716A EPROM. This is not necessary if a PROM is not available. Press down the locking lever on the socket.

Step 3: Now we will copy the contents of an unknown PROM to a list file. We can then edit the list file and reprogram the PROM or create an absolute file by editing and reassembling the list file in order that the absolute file can be linked and loaded into emulation memory. This would allow us to perform a mnemonic disassembly if the ROM contents were written for the type of processor you are currently using for emulation. In this case it would be the 8085 microprocessor.

list_rom to PROM (RETURN)
end (RETURN)

Step 4: Now let us look at the contents of the listing file called "PROM."

edit PROM:listing

The display should look like the following except there will be different amounts of data, depending on the PROM used and the data therein. These data are the result of reading an empty socket of the 2716 PROM programmer.

```
<0000>  FF FF FF FF FF FF FF FF FF FF FF FF FF FF FF FF
<0010>  FF FF FF FF FF FF FF FF FF FF FF FF FF FF FF FF
<0020>  FF FF FF FF FF FF FF FF FF FF FF FF FF FF FF FF
<0030>  FF FF FF FF FF FF FF FF FF FF FF FF FF FF FF FF
<0040>  FF FF FF FF FF FF FF FF FF FF FF FF FF FF FF FF
<0050>  FF FF FF FF FF FF FF FF FF FF FF FF FF FF FF FF
<0060>  FF FF FF FF FF FF FF FF FF FF FF FF FF FF FF FF
           .
           .
           .
```

64000 Examples Demonstrating Development on Systems

```
<07C0>  FF FF FF FF FF FF FF FF FF FF FF FF FF FF FF FF
<07D0>  FF FF FF FF FF FF FF FF FF FF FF FF FF FF FF FF
<07E0>  FF FF FF FF FF FF FF FF FF FF FF FF FF FF FF FF
<07F0>  FF FF FF FF FF FF FF FF FF FF FF FF FF FF FF FF
```

Step 5: We can now edit this listing file and change the contents of the PROM, then reprogram the EPROM. In this case we will pretend that we have already changed a location and are ready to reprogram. If we did change the data the PROM programmer would not complete the programming cycle since the programmer cannot store a zero in a blank PROM socket. Let us end the edit session and reprogram the PROM.

end (RETURN)
prom_prog (RETURN)
program from PROM: listing (RETURN)
end (RETURN)

The display will then show the history of the commands that has been given to the programmer and indicate the total number of bytes that have been programmed.

Step 6: By editing the listing file "PROM" we can convert this to the form that can be assembled and linked. This can then be loaded into memory and disassembled mnemonically using the procedures covered in the linker and emulator workshops.

edit PROM: listing into PROM (RETURN)

Use the editor to put the listing file into the following form.

```
"8085"
     HEX    FF,FF,FF,FF,FF,FF,FF,FF,FF,FF,FF,FF,FF,FF,FF,FF
     HEX    FF,FF,FF,FF,FF,FF,FF,FF,FF,FF,FF,FF,FF,FF,FF,FF
     HEX    FF,FF,FF,FF,FF,FF,FF,FF,FF,FF,FF,FF,FF,FF,FF,FF
     HEX    FF,FF,FF,FF,FF,FF,FF,FF,FF,FF,FF,FF,FF,FF,FF,FF
     HEX    FF,FF,FF,FF,FF,FF,FF,FF,FF,FF,FF,FF,FF,FF,FF,FF
     HEX    FF,FF,FF,FF,FF,FF,FF,FF,FF,FF,FF,FF,FF,FF,FF,FF
      .
      .
      .
     HEX    FF,FF,FF,FF,FF,FF,FF,FF,FF,FF,FF,FF,FF,FF,FF,FF
     HEX    FF,FF,FF,FF,FF,FF,FF,FF,FF,FF,FF,FF,FF,FF,FF,FF
     HEX    FF,FF,FF,FF,FF,FF,FF,FF,FF,FF,FF,FF,FF,FF,FF,FF
```

This is accomplished by inserting the assembler directive in column one, replacing the spaces between the data bytes with commas, and replacing the address values with the word HEX.

The result of assembling and linking the above file would be an absolute file which could be loaded into memory. Once in memory we can perform a "display memory ADDRESS mnemonic." This would give us the mnemonic disassembly of the PROM file. By implementing a command file to do the editing of a PROM listing file it would be a simple matter to identify any unknown PROMs, providing the code contained in the PROM was for the processor currently being emulated.

Summary

The PROM programmer allows us to very quickly read a PROM to a listing file which can be readily edited for changing data in a hex format and then reprogramming the PROM from the listing file. It also provides the tool necessary to download from memory the results of all our programming effort into a ROM for the target system.

The use of a command file provides us with a fast means of identifying unknown PROM contents and performing a mnemonic disassembly of PROM contents written for the processor currently being emulated.

Note that all locations in a new EPROM before programming contain FF. Also, an EPROM must be erased by exposing to ultraviolet light before reprogramming.

EXAMPLE 11.10

Objective

This module consists of a keyboard self-test routine that is made of six software modules. These are not very long modules and serve very well to demonstrate the linking and emulation of external hardware. When these files are entered into the system they will be used in workshop number 9. When the files have been assembled, linked, and loaded into memory by using the emulator, the command is given to run from "START." The result will be that a number will appear on the display of the 5036. This is a prompt to the user to enter that value in through the keyboard of the microprocessor lab. The key is then compared to the displayed character to determine if the depressed key was the correct one. If so then a "GO" is displayed on the LED display of the target system. If not then the message "ER" is displayed and the same prompt is repeated. This procedure is repeated until all of the keys of the keyboard have been sequenced through. When the cycle is complete a "PASSED" message will be displayed.

64000 Examples Demonstrating Development on Systems

Procedure

Step 1: Enter via the editor the following programs listed in Appendix E.

    KYTST,SEQKY,KSCAN,VALID,MSGRQ,DBASE

Step 2: Assemble each file.

Step 3: Link the files as follows.

    link listfile KYTST (RETURN)
    Object files? KYTST,SEQKY,KSCAN,VALID,MSGRQ,DBASE (RETURN)
    Library? (RETURN)
    load_addresses PROG,DATA,COMN-0800H,0900H,0000H (RETURN)
    more files? no (RETURN)
    Absolute filename? KYTST (RETURN)

Step 4: Set up the emulation hardware for emulation. Ensure that the power of the 5036 is off and insert the emulation probe into the socket of the 8085 microprocessor. Be careful to observe the correct orientation of the probe.

Step 5: Set the emulator command file as follows.

    Emulate load KYTST (RETURN)
    Processor clock: external (RETURN)
    Is clock speed greater than 4.48 MHz? no (RETURN)
    Restrict processor to real time runs? no (RETURN)
    Stop processor on illegal opcodes? yes (RETURN)
    Emulation RAM address range? (RETURN)
    Emulation ROM address range? (RETURN)
    User RAM address range? 0 thru 0FFFFH (RETURN)
    User ROM address range? (RETURN)
    Illegal address range? (RETURN)
    Simulate I/O? no (RETURN)
    Command filename? KYTST (RETURN)
    run from START

The keyboard self-test routine will display a 0 on the display of the target system. Depress the corresponding keys and see the results. Once you have entered the files correctly and this procedure works then go on to Example 11.11.

534   Chapter 11   THE Hewlett-Packard (HP) 64000

EXAMPLE 11.11

Objective

Show that in the absence of various pieces of external hardware that emulation can still take place. In this instance we are going to substitute the keyboard and display of the HP 64000 for the keyboard and display of the 5036 microprocessor lab. Keyboard entry will be through the system's keyboard and the messages will be flashed to the display of the HP 64000. We will be using the same files that were entered in Example 11.10. Two of the modules however had to be rewritten to incorporate the links necessary to simulate the display and the keyboard. These two modules will be input in this workshop.

Procedure

Step 1: Remove power from the 5036 and remove the probe. The 5036 will not be used in this workshop.
Step 2: Using the editor input the following files into yourid.

   SIMDS,SIMKD,REALTOSIM,SIMTOREAL

These files are listed in Appendix E.
Step 3: Assemble SIMDS and SIMKD.
Step 4: Link the files according to the following command file setup.

   Link listfile SIMIO (RETURN)
   Object files? KYTST,SEQKY,SIMDS,SIMKD,VALID,DBASE (RETURN)
   Library files? (RETURN)
   Load addresses? PROG,DATA,COMN=0800H,09D0H,0000H (RETURN)
   More files? no (RETURN)
   List,Xref on   on (RETURN)
   Absolute filename? SIMIO (RETURN)

The linker map should look as follows:

HP 64000 LINKER 2.0   Mon, 9 Feb 1981, 23:1

FILE/PROG NAME	PROGRAM	DATA	COMN	ABS	DATE	TIME	COMMENTS
KYTST:YOURID	0800				Mon, 9 Feb 1981,	22:31	KYTST
SEQKY:YOURID	0824				Mon, 9 Feb 1981,	22:31	SEQKY
SIMDS:YOURID	0848	09D0					
SIMKD:YOURID	08D8	0A27					

64000 Examples Demonstrating Development on Systems   535

```
VALID:YOURID      099E                    Mon, 9 Feb 1981, 22:31   VALID
DBASE:YOURID                 0A28
next address      09C9       0AB5

XFER address = 084B      Defined by SIMDS
absolute & link_com file name = SIMIO:YOURID
Total # of bytes loaded = 02AE
SYMBOL    R VALUE   DEF BY         REFERENCES
----------------------------------------------------------------------------------------------------

BUFR      D 0A28    DBASE:YOURID
KEYCT     D 0AB4    DBASE:YOURID   VALID:YOURID   SEQKY:YOURID
KYTST     P 080B    KYTST:YOURID
MATRX     D 0A9C    DBASE:YOURID
SEQKY     P 0824    SEQKY:YOURID   KYTST:YOURID
SIMDS     P 084B    SIMDS:YOURID   VALID:YOURID   SEQKY:YOURID   KYTST:YOURID
SIMKD     P 08D8    SIMKD:YOURID   SEQKY:YOURID
VALID     P 099E    VALID:YOURID   SEQKY:YOURID
```

Step 5: Invoke the command file "REALTOSIM."

REALTOSIM (RETURN)

This command file will make the required changes in the modules used in Example 11.10. When necessary to make the changes back again for purposes of hardware emulation, merely invoke the commane file "SIMTOREAL."

Step 6: Create the emulator command file as follows.

Emulate load SIMIO
Processor clock? internal (RETURN)
Is clock speed greater than 4.48 MHz? no (RETURN)
Restrict processor to real time runs? no (RETURN)
Stop processor on illegal opcodes? yes (RETURN)
Emulation RAM address range? 0800H to 0BFFH (RETURN)
User RAM address range? 0FC00H to 0FFFFH (RETURN)
Simulate 1O? yes (RETURN)
Simulate display? yes (RETURN)
Control address? 0AC0H (RETURN)
Simulate printer? no (RETURN)
Simulate rs232? no (RETURN)
Simulate keyboard? yes (RETURN)
Control address? 00B4H (RETURN)
Simulate disc files? no (RETURN)

>   Command file name? SIMIO (RETURN)
>   Run from START (RETURN)

The system will now display the prompt on the display of the HP 64000 and the keyboard input will be via the keyboard of the HP 64000.

Summary

The use of simulated I/O provides the opportunity to perform analysis of software before the actual hardware is available. This is a great boon since early problems may be detected and resolved, resulting in a shortened development time.

EXAMPLE 11.12

Procedure

Step 1: Invoke the edit mode and enter in the program listing "KEY_DISP" found in Table 11.2.

>   edit into KEY_DISP (RETURN)

Step 2: Assemble the program "KEY_DISP."

>   assembly KEY_DISP listfile KEY_DISP (RETURN)

The assembled listing should appear as in the listing of Section 10.12.4

Step 3: Invoke the linker and link the file called "KEY_DISP."

>   link (RETURN)
>   Object files? KEY_DISP (RETURN)
>   Library files? (RETURN)
>   Load addresses:PROG,DATA,COMN=0700H,0000H,0000H (RE-
>   TURN)
>   More files? no (RETURN)
>   LIST,XREF on on (RETURN)
>
>   Absolute file name = KEY_DISP (RETURN)

If a program change is made to the source listing then the program must be reassembled and relinked. When the linker is invoked again it is only necessary to specify the linker command file name such as

link KEY_DISP (RETURN)

The output of the linker should appear as follows:

```
HP 64000 LINKER 2.0                                         Mon, 9 Feb 1981, 2:17

FILE/PROG NAME    PROG    DATA    COMN    ABS    DATE        TIME    COMMENTS
---------------------------------------------------------------------------------
KEY_DISP:KWG      0700                            Mon, 9 Feb 1981, 2:17 KEY_DISP
next address      078E

XFER address = 0000   Defined by   DEFAULT
absolute & link_com file name = KEY_DISP:KWG
Total # of bytes loaded = 008E
```

Step 4: Establish the emulator configuration and command file.

Emulate (RETURN)
Processor clock: internal (RETURN)
Restrict processor to real time runs? no (RETURN)
Stop processor on illegal op_codes? yes (RETURN)
Emulation RAM address range? 0000H thru 017FFH (RETURN)
Emulation ROM address range? (RETURN)
User RAM address range? (RETURN)
User ROM address range? (RETURN)
Illegal memory address range? (RETURN)
Simulate I/O? yes (RETURN)
Simulate display? yes (RETURN)
Control address? 0900H (RETURN)
Simulate printer? no (RETURN)
Simulate rs232? no (RETURN)
Simulate keyboard? yes (RETURN)
Control address? 0800H (RETURN)
Simulate disc files? no (RETURN)
Command file name? KEY_DISP (RETURN)

Once the command file is established it is only necessary to specify the command file name when reentering the emulator.

emulate KEY_DISP (RETURN)

Step 5: Begin emulation.

run from START

538 Chapter 11 THE HEWLETT-PACKARD (HP) 64000

Now it is only necessary to type in characters via the keyboard and watch them come up on the display of the 64000. It should be understood that this program is running on the 8085 located in the emulation probe. The program requests usage of the display and the keyboard from the host which then allows transfer of data to and from the keyboard and display.

Summary

This illustration of simulated I/O has shown the steps necessary to simulate a keyboard or display of a target system in the instance when such devices are not yet available on the target system.

TABLE 11.2. Source Program Listing: KEY_DISP

```
FILE: KEY_DISP:CHAP10    HEWLETT-PACKARD: 8085 Assembler    Mon, 9 Feb 1981, 2:41    PAGE 1

LOCATION OBJECT CODE LINE    SOURCE LINE

                   1  "8085"
                   2
                   3 **
                   4 **       FUNCTION:           THE PURPOSE OF THIS PROGRAM IS TO SERVE AS
                   5 **                           AN EXAMPLE OF USING SIMULATED I/O. THE PROGRAM
                   6 **                           TAKES KEYBOARD INPUTS AND DISPLAYS THESE INPUTS
                   7 **                           ON THE CRT. THIS PROGRAM MAY TYPICALLY BE USED
                   8 **                           AS PART OF A SYSTEM MONITOR.
                   9 **
                  10 **
                  11               NAME "KEY_DISP"
                  12 **
                  13 **
                  14 **       ***************************************************
                  15 **       **    THE FOLLOWING SECTION OF EQUATES DEFINE     *
                  16 **       **    NUMERICAL VALUES TO BE FOUND IN THE         *
                  17 **       **    LOCATION CALLED KEY_CMD WHEN ONE OF THESE   *
                  18 **       **    KEYS IS DEPRESSED.                          *
                  19 **       ***************************************************
                  20 **
                  21 **
                  22          ;    THE SYMBOLS WHICH ARE LISTED HERE AND
                  23          ;EQUATED TO VALUES ARE PROVIDED TO ALLOW
                  24          ;RAPID PROGRAM ENHANCEMENT. CURRENTLY ONLY
                  25          ;THE CONTROL CHARACTER FOR CARRIAGE RETURN
                  26          ;IS USED. WHEN A CARRIAGE RETURN IS DETECTED
                  27          ;THE PROGRAM WILL RESET THE COLUMN NUMBER TO
                  28          ;COLUMN 1 AND INCREMENT THE LINE NUMBER. BY
                  29          ;CHECKING ALSO FOR THE VALUES LISTED HERE
                  30
                  31
```

Table 11.2. (*Continued*)

```
         (0008)    32 INSERT_KEY    EQU 8H     ;THESE OTHER KEY DEPRESSIONS CAN BE DETERMINED
         (0009)    33 TAB_KEY       EQU 9H     ;AND A BRANCH MADE TO THE APPROPRIATE ROUTINE
         (000A)    34 DOWN_KEY      EQU 0AH    ;WRITTEN BY THE USER. THIS IS A GOOD EXERCISE
         (000B)    35 UP_KEY        EQU 0BH    ;IN LEARNING TO USE THE SIMULATED I/O CAPABILITY
         (0010)    36 DELETE_KEY    EQU 10H    ;OF THE HP 64000.
         (0011)    37 SHIFT_KEY     EQU 11H    ;
         (0013)    38 ROLL_DOWN     EQU 19     ;
         (0014)    39 ROLL_UP       EQU 20     ;
         (0015)    40 SHIFT_RIGHT   EQU 21     ;
         (0016)    41 SHIFT_LEFT    EQU 22     ;
                   42 *


FILE: KEY_DISP:CHAP10    HEWLETT-PACKARD: 8085 Assembler   Mon, 9 Feb 1981, 2:41     PAGE   2

LOCATION OBJECT CODE LINE      SOURCE LINE

                   43 *
                   44 **        ****************************************
                   45 **        **   THE FOLLOWING SECTION OF EQUATES DEFINES   *
                   46 **        **   NUMERICAL VALUES USED IN THE DISPLAY       *
                   47 **        **   AND KEYBOARD ROUTINES WHICH FOLLOW.        *
                   48 **        **                                              *
                   49 **        ****************************************
                   50 **
                   51 **
         (000D)    52 CAR_RET       EQU 0DH
         (0800)    53 KEY_CONT      EQU 800H
         (0801)    54 KEY_CMD       EQU 801H
         (0802)    55 K_REC_LEN     EQU 802H
         (0804)    56 KEY_CHAR      EQU 804H
         (0080)    57 OPEN_KYBD     EQU 80H
         (0080)    58 OPEN_DISP     EQU 80H
         (0083)    59 SAV_BUFF      EQU 83H
         (0900)    60 DISP_CONT     EQU 0900H
         (0901)    61 D_REC_LEN     EQU 0901H
         (0901)    62 LINE          EQU 0901H
         (0902)    63 COLUMN        EQU 0902H
         (0902)    64 DISP_CHAR     EQU 0902H
         (0920)    65 TEMP_LINE     EQU 0920H
         (0921)    66 TEMP_COL      EQU 0921H
         (1000)    67 STACK         EQU 1000H
                   68 *
                   69 *
0000 311000        70              LXI SP,STACK     ;INITIALIZE THE STACK POINTER.
                   71 *
                   72 *
```

Table 11.2. (*Continued*)

```
73    ************************************************************
74    ****  THIS SECTION SETS UP THE REQUIRED DISPLAY  ******
75    ****  PARAMETERS BEFORE THE DISPLAY IS OPENED.   ******
76    ****  THE DISPLAY IS THEN OPENED.                ******
77    ************************************************************
78 *
79 *
80    ************************************************************
81 *****    SET THE INITIAL LINE NUMBER             ******
82    ************************************************************
```

FILE: KEY_DISP:CHAP10   HEWLETT-PACKARD: 8085 Assembler   Mon, 9 Feb 1981, 2:41   PAGE   3

LOCATION OBJECT CODE LINE   SOURCE LINE

```
  0003 3E01         83 START       MVI A,1
  0005 320901       84             STA LINE
  0008 320920       85             STA TEMP_LINE
                    86    ************************************************************
                    87 *****    SET THE INITIAL COLUMN NUMBER           ******
                    88    ************************************************************
  000B 320902       89             STA COLUMN
  000E 320921       90             STA TEMP_COL
                    91    ************************************************************
                    92 *****    OPEN THE DISPLAY                         ******
                    93    ************************************************************
  0011 3E80         94             MVI A,OPEN_DISP    ;80H IS PLACED IN THE DISPLAY
  0013 320900       95             STA DISP_CONT      ;CONTROL ADDRESS.
                    96    ************************************************************
                    97 *****    WAIT FOR A RESPONSE                      ******
                    98    ************************************************************
  0016 210900       99             LXI H,DISP_CONT
  0019 CD0087      100             CALL WAIT          ;CALL THE WAIT ROUTINE.
                   101    ************************************************************
                   102 *****    SAVE INITIAL LINE AND COL. INFO IN THE   ******
                   103 *****    64000 BUFFER.                            ******
                   104    ************************************************************
  001C 3E83        105 NEXT_LINECOL  MVI A,SAV_BUFF
  001E 320900      106             STA DISP_CONT
                   107    ************************************************************
                   108 *****    WAIT FOR A RESPONSE                      ******
                   109    ************************************************************
  0021 210900      110             LXI H,DISP_CONT
  0024 CD0087      111             CALL WAIT
                   112    ************************************************************
                   113        *****    THIS SECTION SETS UP THE KEYBOARD    ******
                   114        *****    BEFORE OPENING, THEN OPENS THE       ******
                   115        *****    KEYBOARD.                            ******
                   116    ************************************************************
```

Table 11.2. (*Continued*)

```
0027 210801      117              LXI H,KEY_CMD
002A 36FE        118              MVI M,-2            ;SETUP KEYBOARD COMMAND.
002C 210802      119              LXI H,KEY_CONT+2    ;SET POINTER TO RECORD LENGTH.
002F 3601        120              MVI M,1             ;DEFINE MAX RECORD LENGTH OF 1.


FILE: KEY_DISP:CHAP10    HEWLETT-PACKARD: 8085 Assembler   Mon, 9 Feb 1981, 2:41    PAGE  4

LOCATION OBJECT CODE LINE    SOURCE LINE

                 121 ************************************************************
                 122 *****     THIS SECTION OPENS THE KEYBOARD    *********
                 123 *****     AND WAITS FOR A RESPONSE.          *********
                 124 ************************************************************
0031 210800      125              LXI H,KEY_CONT      ;SET MEMORY POINTER TO CONTROL ADDRESS.
0034 3680        126              MVI M,OPEN_KYBD     ;OPEN THE KEYBOARD
0036 CD0087      127              CALL WAIT
                 128 ************************************************************
                 129 *****     CHECK THE KB OUTPUT COMMAND WORD TO *********
                 130 *****     DETERMINE CARRIAGE RETURN.          *********
                 131 ************************************************************
0039 3A0801      132              LDA KEY_CMD
003C FE0D        133              CPI CAR_RET
003E CA005F      134              JZ  NEXT_LINE
                 135 ************************************************************
                 136 *****     STORE THE CHARACTER TO BE DISPLAYED *********
                 137 *****     AT CONTROL ADDR + 2: 0902H          *********
                 138 ************************************************************
0041 3A0804      139              LDA KEY_CHAR
0044 320902      140              STA DISP_CHAR
                 141 ************************************************************
                 142 *****     STORE THE RECORD LENGTH TO BE DISPLAYED******
                 143 *****     AT CONTROL ADDR +1                  ******
                 144 ************************************************************
0047 3E01        145              MVI A,1
0049 320901      146              STA D_REC_LEN
                 147 ************************************************************
                 148 *****     HAVE THE DESIGNATED CHARACTER WRITTEN ******
                 149 *****     TO THE DISPLAY                      ******
                 150 ************************************************************
004C 3E84        151              MVI A,84H
004E 320900      152              STA DISP_CONT
                 153 ************************************************************
                 154 *****     WAIT FOR A RESPONSE                 ******
                 155 ************************************************************
0051 210900      156              LXI H,DISP_CONT
0054 CD0087      157              CALL WAIT
                 158 ************************************************************
                 159 *******   THE FOLLOWING SECTION CHECKS THE    ******
```

Table 11.2. (*Continued*)

```
                    160 ******  COLUMN AND LINE NUMBER TO SEE IF     *******
                    161 ******  COL 80 IS REACHED. IF COL 80 IS      *******
                    162 ******  REACHED THE LINE NUMBER IS INCREMENTED *******
                    163 ******  AND THE COLUMN IS SET TO 1.          *******
                    164 ********************************************************
0057 3A0921         165           LDA TEMP_COL        ;GET COLUMN NUMBER.
005A FE50           166           CPI 80              ;IS IT COL 80?
```

FILE: KEY_DISP:CHAP10   HEWLETT-PACKARD: 8085 Assembler   Mon, 9 Feb 1981, 2:41   PAGE 5

LOCATION OBJECT CODE LINE   SOURCE LINE

```
005C C20074         167           JNZ NEXT_COL        ;INCREMENT TO NEXT COL IF NOT EQUAL TO 80.
005F 3E01           168 NEXT_LINE MVI A,1             ;OTHERWISE RESET TO FIRST COL.
0061 320902         169           STA COLUMN          ;AT LOC 902H
0064 320921         170           STA TEMP_COL
0067 3A0920         171           LDA TEMP_LINE
006A 3C             172           INR A               ;BY INCREMENTING THE ACCUMULATOR.(LINE #)
006B 320901         173           STA LINE
006E 320920         174           STA TEMP_LINE
0071 C3001C         175           JMP NEXT_LINECOL    ;AFTER SETTING THE NEW LINE AND COL
                    176                               ;REINITIALIZE THE NEXT COL&LINE.
0074 3A0921         177 NEXT_COL  LDA TEMP_COL
0077 3C             178           INR A               ;INCREMENT THE COL NO.
0078 320902         179           STA COLUMN          ;RESTORE THE COL NO AT 0902H
007B 320921         180           STA TEMP_COL
007E 3A0920         181           LDA TEMP_LINE
0081 320901         182           STA LINE
0084 C3001C         183           JMP NEXT_LINECOL    ;RETURN TO GET THE NEXT KEY CHARACTER.
0087 7E             184 WAIT      MOV A,M
0088 FE00           185           CPI 0
008A C20087         186           JNZ WAIT
008D C9             187           RET
                    188           END
```

Errors= 0

PROBLEMS AND QUESTIONS

11.1 Describe briefly the hardware and software development tools provided with the HP 64000.

11.2 In a multiuser system, what elements of the HP 64000 are shared?

11.3 How many disk drives can be put on the HP 64000 at one time?

11.4 Define the 64000 soft keys.

11.5 What are the advantages of the HP 64000 soft keys?

Problems and Questions 543

11.6 What aspects of the development system contribute to reducing the cost of development?
11.7 (a) In the HP 64000 with six development stations, how many CPUs are in the system?
(b) Can you think of any advantages or disadvantages of this type of arrangement?
11.8 What is the meaning of the 64000 display of the "I/O bus configuration?"
11.9 What are the means by which the software operating system is introduced into the HP 64000?
11.10 (a) What is the 64000 userid?
(b) Can you think of some advantages to this feature?
11.11 What is a library file?
11.12 What is the benefit of using libraries?
11.13 How many display columns are available with the HP 64000 while using the editor?
11.14 What are the different modes of the 64000 editor?
11.15 (a) Is it possible to merge 64000 files?
(b) If so, can you merge files from another userid to your own?
11.16 When using the 64000 editor to enter an assembly language program what is the first item that must be at the top of the program?
11.17 What is the purpose of the 64000 range key?
11.18 What is the difference between the 64000 copy command and the extract command?
11.19 Describe the form of the output of the 64000 assembler.
11.20 What is the meaning of the word "LISTFILE" on the 64000 display?
11.21 When changing the 64000 userid, what is meant by the following words "listfile default"?
11.22 If you use the 64000 command "assembly filename" return, where does the output listing of the assembler go?
11.23 In Example 11.2, why was only part of the macro expanded?
11.24 What is the significance of column 1 of the 64000 assembler source listing?
11.25 The following instruction is an 8085 mnemonic to load the accumulator with the contents of address location FF hex. What is wrong with the way the following instruction is entered into the HP 64000?

LDA FFH

11.26 What is the purpose of the 64000 linker?
11.27 What is the product of the 64000 linker?
11.28 (a) What are the designations of "PROG," "DATA," "COMN," in the 64000?
(b) What are the advantages of having them?

Chapter 11 The Hewlett-Packard (HP) 64000

11.29 What is a load address?
11.30 What is a transfer address?
11.31 What is a linker command file?
11.32 What is the advantage of the command file?
11.33 How can different files have the same name?
11.34 How is one file differentiated from the other?
11.35 What is a link map?
11.36 What is a syntactical variable?
11.37 What is meant by "SYMBOLIC DEBUG?"
11.38 What is meant by "REAL TIME EMULATION?"
11.39 What is the 64000 emulation configuration?
11.40 What is the emulator command file?
11.41 What is the advantage of the emulator command file?
11.42 When you use the 64000 command "end emulation" what happens to the emulation process?
11.43 What is the advantage of using command files?
11.44 Can you write a simple command file that would be useful in developing a project?
11.45 What is simulated I/O?
11.46 (a) What is the advantage of simulated I/O?
(b) Can you think of how this feature might be useful in the development process?
(c) Perhaps you can think of some innovative applications for using simulated I/O.
11.47 Using the 8085 assembly language, write a conditional macroprogram to add two numbers at locations 2000H and 2001H if the contents of the accumulator are odd and subtract the two numbers if the contents of the accumulator are even.
11.48 What does it mean if the address of an I/O device does not appear on the I/O bus configuration display after turning on the power?
11.49 What happens if you press reset twice during editing?
11.50 Can you recover a purged file?
11.51 (a) How many clocks are available for emulation?
(b) When performing emulation without a prototype, what clock do you use?
11.52 Edit, assemble, link, and emulate without using a command file the following programs used in the examples before:
(a) KYTST, SEQKY, MSGRQ, VALID, KSCAN and DBASE
(b) Write a command file to perform the same function.
11.53 Do you need to link if there is only one program module?
11.54 Given two program modules PROG1 and PROG2 of lengths 100 bytes and 50 bytes, respectively, if PROG1 is linked at 2000H and PROG2 is linked at 2032H, what will happen?

CHAPTER 12

DESIGN PROBLEMS

This chapter includes a number of design problems that utilize external hardware. The systems are based on a typical microprocessor such as the 8085. The HP 64000 is used for software and hardware development. The design examples presented here can readily be developed by using another development system. The 64000 is used to demonstrate the basic features of a typical system.

12.1 Design Problem No. 1

12.1.1 Problem Statement

A chemical plant needs some type of intelligent system that will turn on and off eight valves in a specific sequence in intervals of 2 s. These valves must function in the following sequence:

TIME	VALVE1	VALVE2	VALVE3	VALVE4	VALVE5	VALVE6	VALVE7	VALVE8
0	OFF	OFF	OFF	OFF	OFF	OFF	OFF	OFF
2	ON	OFF	OFF	OFF	OFF	OFF	OFF	OFF
4	OFF	ON	OFF	OFF	OFF	OFF	OFF	OFF
6	OFF	OFF	ON	OFF	OFF	OFF	OFF	OFF
8	OFF	OFF	OFF	ON	OFF	OFF	OFF	OFF
10	OFF	OFF	OFF	OFF	ON	OFF	OFF	OFF
12	OFF	OFF	OFF	OFF	OFF	ON	OFF	OFF
14	OFF	OFF	OFF	OFF	OFF	OFF	ON	OFF
16	OFF	OFF	OFF	OFF	OFF	OFF	OFF	ON

In other words, first all valves are off, then we turn valve number 1 on, wait for 2 s, turn valve number 1 off and turn valve number 2 on, then turn valve number 2 off and number 3 on, and so forth. After going through the complete sequence, valve number 8 must be on for 12 s. After the 12 s we repeat the entire sequence, beginning again with valve number 1.

12.1.2 Solution to Design Problem No. 1

This problem can be easily solved with a microprocessor system with a dedicated program to control the valves. The advantages of a microprocessor system over a regular discrete logic design is for one, "FLEXIBILITY." For example, if the chemical plant decides to change the sequence of operation for the valve, all it would take using a microprocessor system would be a small change to the program. Another advantage that can be mentioned is that this design presents itself for future expansion. Or in other words, if new valves needed control, all we would need to do would be to add new ports and modify the program.

Figure 12.1 shows an 8085/8755/8155-based valve control circuit. The development procedure using the HP 64000 is covered in detail for this design problem. This is done for the convenience of the reader.

Hardware Design and Configuration

For this project we will use the following*:

One 8085A CPU
    One 8755 I/O (two ports) plus 2K bytes EPROM
    One 8155 (3 ports) plus 256 bytes RAM
One 4-MHz crystal
Eight LEDs
One momentary switch

Development Procedure

i. Editing Session. Before we start editing let us review certain conventions used for assembly language:

1. As mentioned before, there are four dedicated fields for assembly language programming:

    LABEL OPCODE OPERAND COMMENTS

---

* Note that in a typical application, the stack is usually needed. Therefore, the microcomputer must have RAM.

Design Problem No. 1

When you type in your assembly language program it is recommended to use the (TAB) key to keep everything spaced properly.

LABEL (TAB)   OPCODE (TAB)   OPERAND (TAB)   COMMENTS

2. The very first line in your program must contain the processor type that you are using "8085."
3. After you define the processor type, you must define the starting address of your program with the pseudoinstruction ORG.

LABEL	OPCODE	OPERAND	COMMENTS
"8085"			
	ORG	1000H	;Program starts at 1000H

4. If you desire to define addresses with labels, you may use the pseudoinstruction EQU.

LABEL	OPCODE	OPERAND	COMMENTS
PORTA	EQU	10H	;Address for port A= 10H

The advantage of this method is that you do not have to remember the physical addresses of the ports or memory locations while you are programming.

Example

LABEL	OPCODE	OPERAND	COMMENTS
"8085"			
	ORG	1000H	
PORTA	EQU	10H	;Port A is at address 10H
PORTB	EQU	20H	;Port B is at address 20H
	NOP		
START	MVI	A,00H	;Load A with 00H
	OUT	PORTA	;Output to address 10H
	OUT	PORTB	;Output to address 20H
	END		

The pseudoinstruction EQU can be used to equate addresses as well as any other label which is not an address. This is a little bit confusing, but the way to remember how to use EQU is that EQU is used to establish a relationship between a label and a value, where a value could be an address or any other expression.

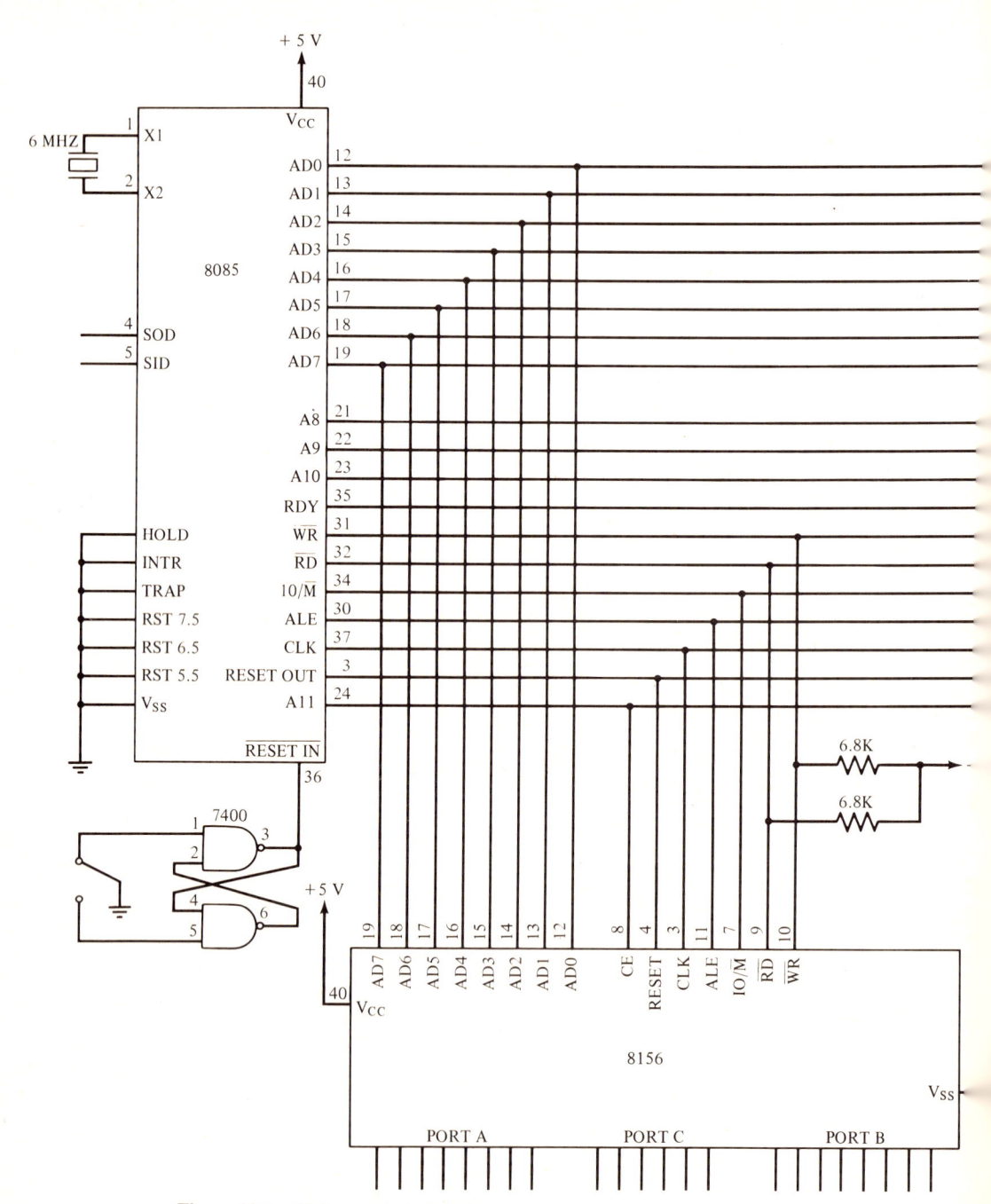

Figure 12.1 Valve control circuit.

Design Problem No. 1

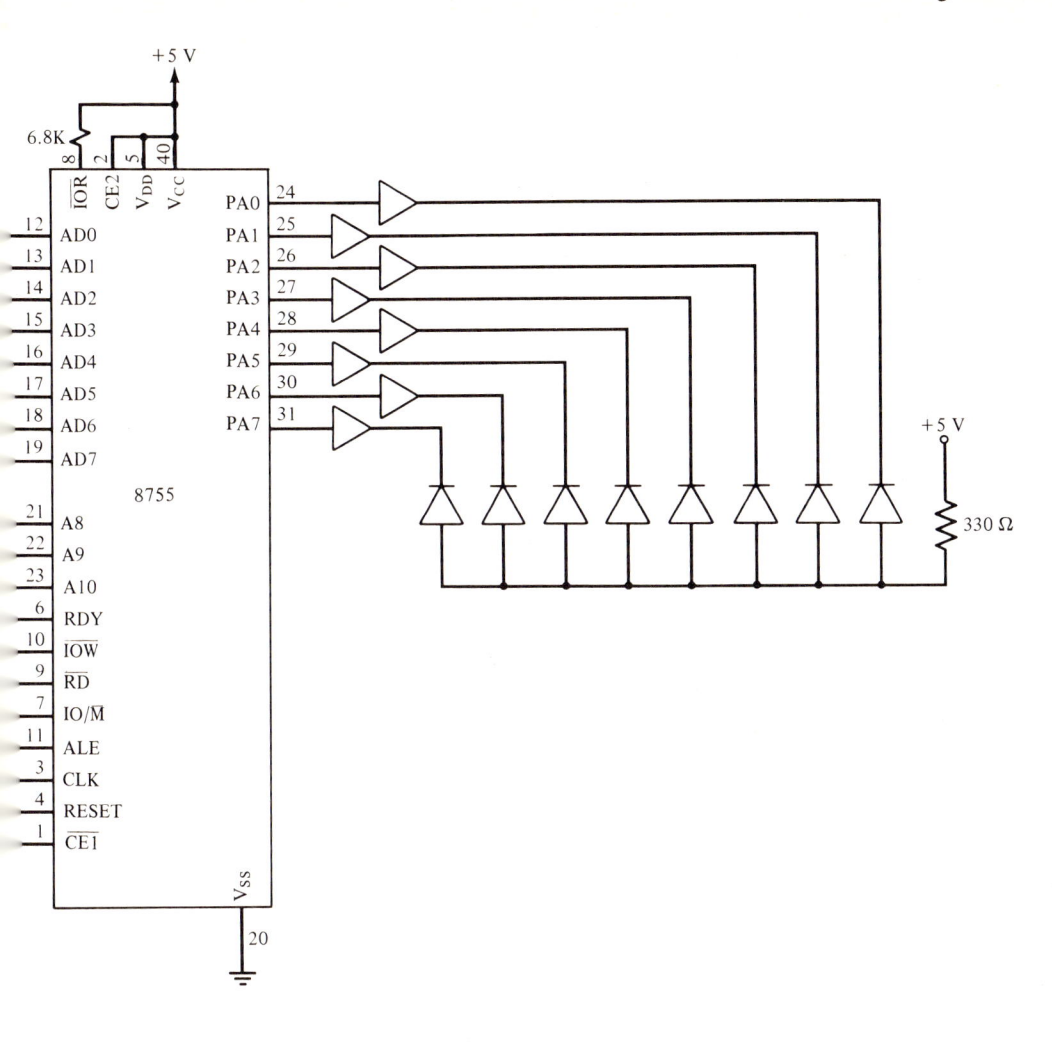

Example

LABEL	OPCODE	OPERAND	COMMENTS
"8085"			
	ORG	1000H	
PORTA	EQU	10H	
OFF	EQU	00H	
	NOP		
START	MVI	A,OFF	
	OUT	PORTA	
	END		

Now that we have covered some basic ideas, let us type in our assembly language using the EDITOR.

Press soft key [EDIT]
Press (RETURN)

The screen should say: Editing new file. The editor should be in the [INSERT] mode, which allows you to type in your program. Notice that the labels on your soft keys changed to [INSERT], [REVISE], [DELETE], and so on.

All these are commands within the editor which allow you to do several things like replace a word, renumber a whole file, find a specific word in a file, and so on.

SOME HINTS FOR THE BEGINNER

1. When the editor is in the INSERT mode, a [RETURN] must be pressed to "insert" the line, and to go to the following line.
2. If you make a mistake, press the soft key [REVISE] and move the cursor with one of these [∧], [<], [>] keys to place the cursor where you want to make a correction. Then use the [INSERT CHAR] or [DEL CHAR] to modify that character.
3. To continue adding to the file, take the cursor all the way down to the last line you typed, and press the soft key [INSERT]. Again you are ready to add new lines to your file.
4. To end the editing session, you must give a name to the file you typed in. For example:

Press soft key [EDIT]
Type FILENAME
Press [RETURN]

Note that you only do this for the creation of a brand new file. The editor will save your file on the disk as a "source" file.

Design Problem No. 1

5. If you already have a file stored on the disk, and you desire to edit it, simply

Press soft key [EDIT]
Type FILENAME
Press [RETURN]

The file will be shown on the screen, ready for any manipulation. After getting acquainted with the editor, edit the following program and name it "VALVE."

SOFTWARE

```
"8085"
*
*       THE FOLLOWING PROGRAM CONTROLS EIGHT VALVES OF A CHEMICAL PLANT
*
        ORG     0000H           ;DEFINE STARTING ADDRESS OF PROGRAM
PORTA   EQU     00H             ;DEFINE ADDRESS OF PORT(A) DATA
ADIREC  EQU     02H             ;DEFINE ADDRESS OF DIRECTION REGISTER FOR PORT(A)
VALVE1  EQU     01H             ;DEFINE BIT TO CONTROL VALVE #1 (BIT 0).
VALVE2  EQU     02H             ;DEFINE BIT TO CONTROL VALVE #2 (BIT 1).
VALVE3  EQU     04H             ;DEFINE BIT TO CONTROL VALVE #3 (BIT 2).
VALVE4  EQU     08H             ;DEFINE BIT TO CONTROL VALVE #4 (BIT 3).
VALVE5  EQU     10H             ;DEFINE BIT TO CONTROL VALVE #5 (BIT 4).
VALVE6  EQU     20H             ;DEFINE BIT TO CONTROL VALVE #6 (BIT 5).
VALVE7  EQU     40H             ;DEFINE BIT TO CONTROL VALVE #7 (BIT 6).
VALVE8  EQU     80H             ;DEFINE BIT TO CONTROL VALVE #8 (BIT 7).
        NOP
        LXI     SP,20FFH        ;SET STACK POINTER
        MVI     A,0FFH          ;DEFINE ALL BITS OF PORT(A)
        OUT     ADIREC          ;AS OUTPUTS
START   MVI     A,VALVE1
        OUT     PORTA           ;TURN VALVE 1 ON, THE REST OFF
        CALL    DELAY           ;WAIT FOR 2 SECONDS
        MVI     A,VALVE2
        OUT     PORTA           ;TURN VALVE 2 ON, THE REST OFF
        CALL    DELAY           ;WAIT FOR 2 SECONDS
        MVI     A,VALVE3
        OUT     PORTA           ;TURN VALVE 3 ON, THE REST OFF
        CALL    DELAY           ;WAIT FOR 2 SECONDS
        MVI     A,VALVE4
        OUT     PORTA           ;TURN VALVE 4 ON, THE REST OFF
        CALL    DELAY           ;WAIT FOR 2 SECONDS
```

552 Chapter 12 DESIGN PROBLEMS

```
            MVI     A,VALVE5
            OUT     PORTA       ;TURN VALVE 5 ON, THE REST OFF
            CALL    DELAY       ;WAIT FOR 2 SECONDS
            MVI     A,VALVE6
            OUT     PORTA       ;TURN VALVE 6 ON, THE REST OFF
            CALL    DELAY       ;WAIT FOR 2 SECONDS
            MVI     A,VALVE7
            OUT     PORTA       ;TURN VALVE 7 ON, THE REST OFF
            CALL    DELAY       ;WAIT FOR 2 SECONDS
            MVI     A,VALVE8
            OUT     PORTA       ;TURN VALVE 8 ON, THE REST OFF
            CALL    DELAY       ;WAIT FOR 2 SECONDS
            CALL    DELAY       ;WAIT FOR 2 SECONDS
            CALL    DELAY       ;WAIT FOR 2 SECONDS
            CALL    DELAY       ;WAIT FOR 2 SECONDS
            CALL    DELAY       ;WAIT FOR 2 SECONDS
            CALL    DELAY       ;WAIT FOR 2 SECONDS
            JMP     START       ;REPEAT PROGRAM OVER AGAIN
DELAY       NOP                 ;THIS SUBROUTINE WAITS FOR APPROX 2 SECONDS.
            LXI     H,0FFFH     ;LOAD REG PAIR (HL) WITH 0FFF HEXADECIMAL.
LOOP        DCX     H           ;DECREMENT (HL)
            MOV     A,H
            ORA     L
            JNZ     LOOP        ;LOOP UNTIL (HL)=0
            RET                 ;RETURN FROM SUBROUTINE
            END
```

ii. Assembly Session.   Now that we have edited our program in assembly language into a file called (VALVE, Source) we are ready to convert it into binary form so the computer can understand it for practical purposes.

To convert this source file into binary we must use the assembler. For example:

Press soft key: [ASSEMBLE]
Type: VALVE
Press soft keys: [LISTFILE], [PRINTER], [OPTIONS], [XREF]
Press [RETURN]

The screen will show:

assemble VALVE listfile printer options x_ref

After getting the printout make sure you have no errors. If you do, go back to the editor and fix your program. If you have no errors, you may continue to the following section.

Design Problem No. 1   553

Note that the assembler generates a file with all the assembly language mnemonics translated to binary. This file is called a relocatable file. If you look at a DIRECTORY at this point the screen will show

Directory List   User:STUDN   Disc: 0   Wed, 19 Mar 1980, 0:44   Page 1

NAME	TYPE	SIZE	LAST MODIFY	LAST ACCESS
VALVE	reloc	1	19 Mar 1980, 0:43	19 Mar 1980, 0:43
VALVE	source	1	19 Mar 1980, 0:38	19 Mar 1980, 0:43

****   Files listed   2,   0.07% disc space used   ****
****   67.00% disc space available   ****

The printout of the assembly results should look like this:

FILE: VALVE:STUDN   HEWLETT-PACKARD: INTEL 8085 ASSEMBLER   Wed, 19 Mar 1980, 0:48   PAGE

```
LINE LOC   CODE            SOURCE STATEMENT
           ADDR
 1                         "8085"
 2                         *
 3                         *THE FOLLOWING PROGRAM CONTROLS 8 VALVES OF A CHEMICAL PLANT
 4                         *
 5  0000                   ORG    0000H           ;DEFINE STARTING ADDRESS OF PROGRAM
 6          0000  PORTA    EQU    00H             ;DEFINE ADDRESS OF PORT(A) DATA
 7          0002  ADIREC   EQU    02H             ;DEFINE ADDRESS OF DIRECTION REGISTER FOR
                                                     PORT(A)
 8          0001  VALVE1   EQU    01H             ;DEFINE BIT TO CONTROL VALVE #1 (BIT 0)
 9          0002  VALVE2   EQU    02H             ;DEFINE BIT TO CONTROL VALVE #2 (BIT 1)
10          0004  VALVE3   EQU    04H             ;DEFINE BIT TO CONTROL VALVE #3 (BIT 2)
11          0008  VALVE4   EQU    08H             ;DEFINE BIT TO CONTROL VALVE #4 (BIT 3)
12          0010  VALVE5   EQU    10H             ;DEFINE BIT TO CONTROL VALVE #5 (BIT 4)
13          0020  VALVE6   EQU    20H             ;DEFINE BIT TO CONTROL VALVE #6 (BIT 5)
14          0040  VALVE7   EQU    40H             ;DEFINE BIT TO CONTROL VALVE #7 (BIT 6)
15          0080  VALVE8   EQU    80H             ;DEFINE BIT TO CONTROL VALVE #8 (BIT 7)
16  0000 00                MOP
17  0001 3E    FF          MVI    A,0FFH          ;DEFINE ALL BITS OF PORT(A)
18  0003 D3    02          OUT    ADIREC          ;AS OUTPUTS
19  0005 3E    01   START  MVI    A,VALVE1
20  0007 D3    00          OUT    PORTA           ;TURN VALVE 1 ON , REST OFF
21  0009 CD    004F        CALL   DELAY           ;WAIT FOR 2 SECONDS
22  000C 3E    02          MVI    A,VALVE2
23  000E D3    00          OUT    PORTA           ;TURN VALVE 2 ON , REST OFF
24  0010 CD    004F        CALL   DELAY
25  0013 3E    04          MVI    A,VALVE3,
```

554 Chapter 12 Design Problems

```
26 0015 D3   00              OUT    PORTA       ;TURN VALVE 3 ON , REST OFF
27 0017 CD   004F            CALL   DELAY
28 001A 3E   08              MVI    A,VALVE4
29 001C D3   00              OUT    PORTA       ;TURN VALVE 4 ON , REST OFF
30 001E CD   004F            CALL   DELAY       ;WAIT FOR 2 SECONDS
31 0021 3E   10              MVI    A,VALVE5
32 0023 D3   00              OUT    PORTA       ;TURN VALVE 5 ON , REST OFF
33 0025 CD   004F            CALL   DELAY       ;WAIT FOR 2 SECONDS
34 0028 3E   20              MVI    A,VALVE6
35 002A D3   00              OUT    PORTA       ;TURN VALVE 6 ON , REST OFF
36 002C CD   004F            CALL   DELAY       ;WAIT FOR 2 SECONDS
37 002F 3E   40              MVI    A,VALVE7
38 0031 D3   00              OUT    PORTA       ;TURN VALVE 7 ON , REST OFF
39 0033 CD   004F            CALL   DELAY       ;WAIT FOR 2 SECONDS
40 0036 3E   80              MVI    A,VALVE8
41 0038 D3   00              OUT    PORTA       ;TURN VALVE 8 ON , REST OFF
42 003A CD   004F            CALL   DELAY       ;WAIT FOR 2 SECONDS
43 003D CD   004F            CALL   DELAY       ;WAIT FOR 2 SECONDS
44 0040 CD   004F            CALL   DELAY       ;WAIT FOR 2 SECONDS
45 0043 CD   004F            CALL   DELAY       ;WAIT FOR 2 SECONDS
46 0046 CD   004F            CALL   DELAY       ;WAIT FOR 2 SECONDS
47 0049 CD   004F            CALL   DELAY       ;WAIT FOR 2 SECONDS
48 004C C3   0005            JMP    START       ;REPEAT PROGRAM ALL OVER AGAIN
49 004F 00         DELAY     MDP                ;THIS SUBROUTINE WAITS FOR APPROX. 2 SEC-
                                                  ONDS
50 0050 21   0FFF            LXI    H,0FFFH     ;LOAD REGISTER PAIR (HL) WITH 0FFF HEX
51 0053 2B         LOOP      DCX    H           ;DECREMENT (HL)
52 0054 C2   0053            JNZ    LOOP        ;LOOP UNTIL (HL)=0
53 0057      C9              RET                ;RETURN FROM SUBROUTINE
54                           END
```

Errors= 0

```
                    FILE: VALVE:STUDN    CROSS REFERENCE TABLE    PAGE  2
                    LINE#    SYMBOL      TYPE          REFERENCES
                             A           A      17,19,22,25,28,31,34,37,40
                      7      ADIREC      A      18
                     49      DELAY       A      21,24,27,30,33,36,39,42,43,44,45,46,47
                             H           A      50,51
                     51      LOOP        A      52
                      6      PORTA       A      20,23,26,29,32,35,38,41
                     19      START       A      48
                      8      VALVE1      A      19
                      9      VALVE2      A      22
```

10	VALVE3	A	25
11	VALVE4	A	28
12	VALVE5	A	31
13	VALVE6	A	34
14	VALVE7	A	37
15	VALVE8	A	40

iii. Linking Session. As mentioned before, the main purpose of the linker is to combine several relocatable programs into one "absolute" module which can be executed by the HP 64000 Emulation System.

The advantage to this is that a big software project can be written simultaneously by several programmers, and at the end all the individual modules can be linked together as one executable unit.

In our case, with the program VALVE we only have one relocatable (VALVE,Reloc). You might think that if you only have one relocatable, there is no need for linking, because there are no more programs to link it with. But this is not true, even if you only have one relocatable, there is a need for linking, because after linking, an "absolute" file is created which is the *only* kind of file that can be executed on the emulator or programmed on a PROM.

For example:

```
Press soft key [LINK]
Press [RETURN]
```

The system will ask:

1. Object files? VALVE [RETURN]

   In this case VALVE is the relocatable file.

2. Library files? [RETURN]

   No library files to be linked with our program.

3. Load addresses? PROG, DATA, COMN=0000H,0000H,0000H

   For our case we just press [RETURN] because our program starts at 0000H, and we do not care about the location of DATA or COMN space during link. If our program started at 1000H then we would change the first field to 1000H.

   Load addresses? PROG,DATA,COMN=0000H,0000H,0000H
4. More files? no [RETURN]

5. List, xref? no [RETURN]
6. Absolute file name? VALVE85 [RETURN]

This will be the name of the executable absolute file; for this example we picked the name VALVE85. With this file, we can emulate the target system and if we get the results we expected, we can burn this file on a PROM because this is 8085 executable code.

Note that if you take a directory after a linking session, three new files will be added as a result of the linker:

NAME	TYPE	SIZE	LAST MODIFY	LAST ACCESS
VALVE	asmb_sym	1	10 Dec 1980, 12:55	10 Dec 1980, 12:55
VALVE	reloc	1	19 Mar 1980, 0:48	10 Dec 1980, 12:55
VALVE	source	1	19 Mar 1980, 0:38	19 Mar 1980, 0:48
VALVE85	absolute	1	10 Dec 1980, 12:55	10 Dec 1980, 12:55
VALVE85	link_sym	1	10 Dec 1980, 12:55	10 Dec 1980, 12:55
VALVE85	link_com	1	10 Dec 1980, 12:55	10 Dec 1980, 12:55

****   Files listed   6,   0.20% disc space used   ****
****   66.79% disc space available   ****

VALVE85 link_sym   Is a symbolic file generated by the linker.

VALVE85 link_com   Is a command file where all the answers you give to the linker get recorded. The advantage to this is that if you are debugging your programs and you are always linking in the same manner, then there is no need to repeat the question/answer section of the linker every single time. All you have to do is call the COMMAND file when you start the linking session and all the questions will be answered automatically.

For example:

Press soft key [LINK] Command file name [RETURN]

If you wish to change some of the answers in the command file use the soft keys [OPTIONS] [EDIT].

For example:

[LINK] VALVE85 [OPTIONS] [EDIT] [RETURN]

Now that you linked your program, we are ready to emulate the target system (your board).

iv. Emulation Session. The purpose of this section is to troubleshoot your hardware and software by simulating the CPU with the HP 64000. This simulation is called ICE (In-Circuit Emulation). Before we start emulating, let us mention a few important things:

1. Do not plug the emulator probe into anything with the power on.
2. You must have an absolute file to emulate the target system (your board). The emulator will not work with source files or relocatable files.
3. All files must be linked before using the emulator or the PROM programmer.
4. The HP 64000 does *not* supply power to the target system. You need a separate power supply for the target system.

The advantage of using an emulator is that all the troubleshooting tools are included in one package. In other words, you can single-step, look into registers (HL, DE, PC, SP, . . . , etc.) and look into memory while you are single-stepping. Also you can modify the contents of memory and registers without having to reedit the program.

You can set breakpoints to stop the program in specific places to check registers and other parameters. Last but not least, the analyzer allows you to store 256 continuous events after a certain triggering point (a condition) that you specify.

Let us start by connecting the target system to the HP 64000. Make sure that when you do this *power is off*. Apply power to both systems. To use the EMULATOR:

Press soft keys [EMULATE] [LOAD] VALVE85 (absolute filename)

The system will respond:

1. Processor clock:[EXTERNAL] [RETURN]

Answer "external" because the clock is on the target system.

2. Is processor clock speed greater than 4.48 MHz? [NO] [RETURN]
3. Restrict Processor to Real time runs: [NO] [RETURN]

Answer NO because YES will not allow any program code that interrupts the emulation system to be executed.

4. Stop Processor on Illegal Opcodes: [YES] [RETURN]

Answer YES so the processor will stop on an invalid op code.

Before we continue with the rest of the questions, let us describe some terms:

Emulation RAM: Is read/write memory located in the HP 64000 and is used for emulation
Emulation ROM: Is read-only memory located in the HP 64000 and is used for emulation
User RAM: Is the RAM located in the target system
User ROM: Is the ROM located in the target system

You may execute out of any of these four types of memory. The reason for mapping it this way is that the system will warn you if accidentally (in your program) there is an attempt to write to ROM.

Now let us finish answering the questions for the emulator so we can describe some emulator commands.

5. Emulation RAM address range? [RETURN]
6. Emulation ROM address range? [RETURN]
7. User RAM address range? [RETURN]
8. User ROM address range? [RETURN]
9. Illegal memory address range? [RETURN]

Use this if you want to protect a certain section of memory.

10. Command file Name? VALVECOM [RETURN]

This is the same type of command file as the link command file we described before, but this one records all the answers to the emulation set up for future use.

The system will clear the screen and print:

Program Loaded

1. To check if the program is loaded press soft keys [DISPLAY] [MEMORY] 0000H [MODE] [MNEMONIC] [RETURN]. The screen should show the program in assembly and hex values. To look at the complete program use the [ROLL UP] and [ROLL DOWN] keys to scroll the screen.

2. To check registers press soft keys [DISPLAY] [REGISTERS] [MODE] [DYNAMIC] [RETURN]. Now that all registers are displayed we can observe the program single-stepping.

Design Problem No. 1   **559**

3. To single-step press soft keys [STEP] [FROM] 0000H [RETURN]. This presets the PC to 0000H, and sets the single-step mode

    Press soft key : [STEP] [RETURN]
    Press key : [RETURN]
    Press key : [RETURN]
    Press key : [RETURN]
    Press key : [RETURN]
    Press key : [RETURN]

    Notice that every time you press [RETURN] the program will single-step, and the contents of some registers like the PC will change.
4. To RUN program press soft keys [RUN] [FROM] 0000H [RETURN].
5. To STOP program press soft keys [STOP] [RUN] [RETURN].
6. To RUN up to a specific address press soft keys [RUN] [FROM] 0000H [UNTIL] [REGISTERS] [ETC_] [PC] [=] (Address).
7. To END emulation press soft keys [END] [RETURN].

v. PROM Programmer Session. After we make sure that every detail in our program works properly, we should be ready to take the absolute file and program it on the PROM.

To program the PROM do the following:

    Press soft key: [PROM PROGRMR] [RETURN]

The system will respond with the PROM card configuration, and will ask

    Socket Type?

For this question you must answer [8755]. If you are using a 2716 then the personality card must be installed, and the answer will be the soft key [2716].

To program press:

    [PROGRAM] [RETURN]

The system will reply:

    Program from?

You should answer

> VALVE85 (absolute file) [RETURN]

If you need to look at concepts of the PROM,

> Press soft keys: [LIST PROM] [TO] [DISPLAY] [RETURN]

To end the programming session

> Press [END] [RETURN]

12.2 Design Problem No. 2

12.2.1 Problem Statement

The primary objective of this project was the complete development of a stand-alone microcomputer-based system which would measure, compute, and display the Root-Mean-Square (RMS) value of a sinusoidal voltage. Secondary objectives included familiarization with microprocessor development systems in general and the Hewlett-Packard 64000 Development System in particular.

The complete system is required to:
1. Sample a 60-Hz sinusoidal voltage 128 times.
2. Digitize the sampled value through a microprocessor-controlled analog-to-digital converter.
3. Input the digitized value to the 8085—a microprocessor through the RST6.5 interrupt.
4. Compute the RMS value of the waveform using the equation RMS value = 1.11 (average value).
5. Display the RMS value to the operator.

12.2.2 Solution to Design Problem No. 2

Hardware

The microcomputer used in this project incorporates the Intel 8085 microprocessor, the 8156 RAM-I/O, and the 8755 EPROM-I/O Chips. These three devices constitute the core of a bus-oriented microcomputer.

Figure 12.2 depicts the microcomputer circuit. The following tristated

Design Problem No. 2   561

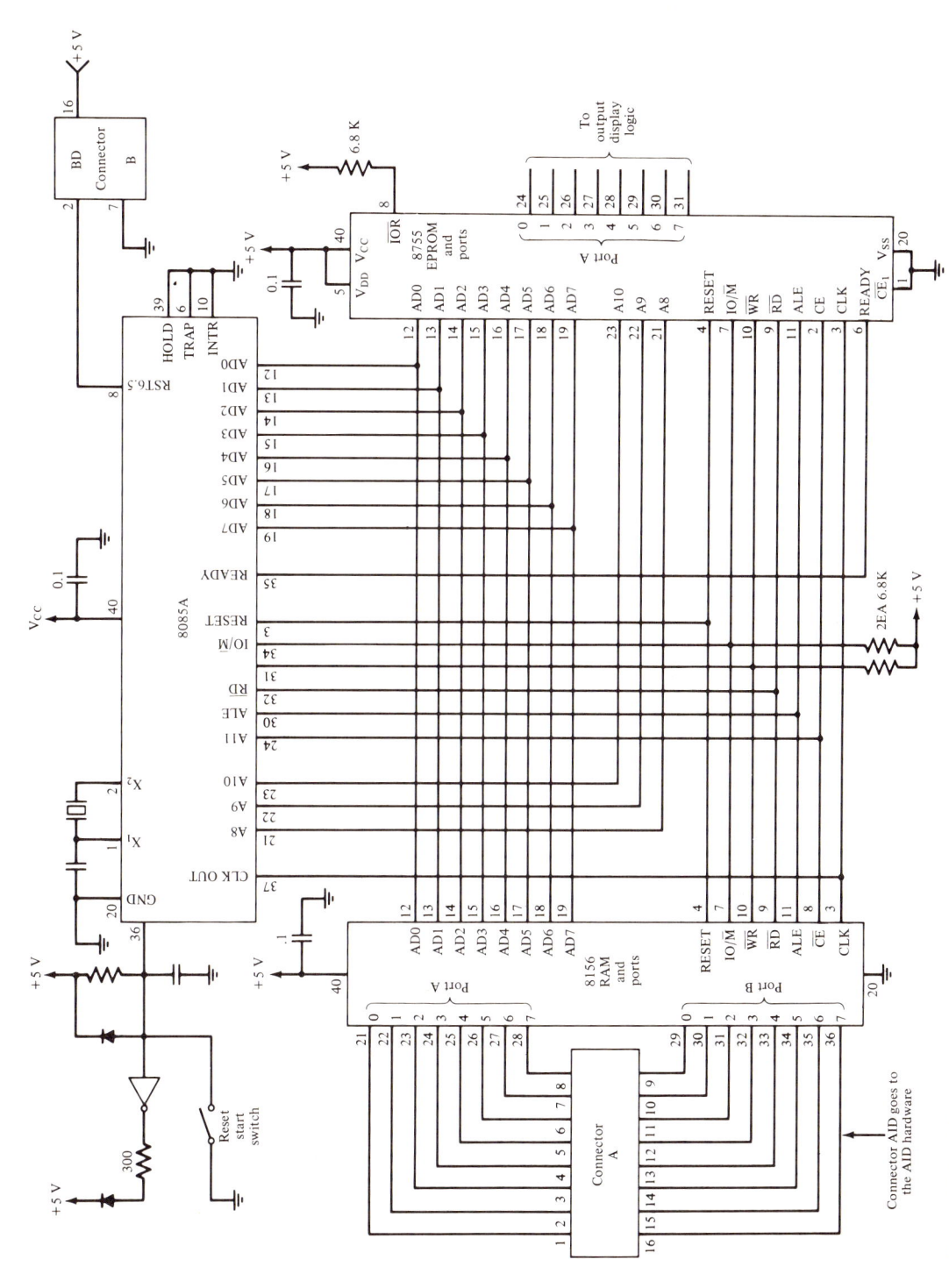

Figure 12.2 Microcomputer system schematic.

control lines are connected to all three devices:

ALE	(ADDRESS LATCH ENABLE, LATCHES ADDRESS LINES)
$\overline{RD}$	(USED TO READ FROM A DEVICE)
$\overline{WR}$	(USED TO WRITE TO A DEVICE)
IO/$\overline{M}$	(USED TO DESIGNATE EITHER MEMORY OPERATION OR I/O PORT OPERATION)
READY	(CYCLE DELAY, TIED LOW TO DISABLE)
CLK	(CLOCK OUTPUT OF 8085)
RESET	(GENERATED BY THE 8085 IN RESPONSE TO EXTERNAL HARDWARE, WILL RESET ALL I/O PORTS TO INPUT)

Additionally, the following control signals of the 8085 are connected to fixed voltages or external hardware:

HOLD	(USED TO HALT THE PROCESSOR FOR DMA, CONNECTED TO GROUND TO DISABLE)
INTR	(RST 0-7 INTERRUPT, CONNECTED TO GROUND TO DISABLE)
RST5.5	(INTERRUPT, CONNECTED TO GROUND TO DISABLE)
RST6.5	(VECTORED INTERRUPT, CONNECTED TO APPLICATIONS HARDWARE, VECTOR LOCATION = 0034H)
RST7.5	(INTERRUPT, CONNECTED TO GROUND TO DISABLE)
$\overline{\text{RESET IN}}$	(WILL GENERATE RESET SIGNAL AND FORCE PROGRAM COUNTER TO 0000, CONNECTED TO EXTERNAL HARDWARE TO INITIATE PROGRAM)

The eight data and address lines (AD0–AD7) are bussed between the three devices. They are used to transmit the eight data bits and the eight low-order address bits between the processor and memory devices. Address lines A8–A10 are connected between the 8085 and the 8755. Since the 8156 RAM possesses only 256 bytes of memory, it does not require these additional address bits.

RAM (8156) and ROM (8755) are mapped by address bit A11. The 8755 program resides in memory location 0000H through 07FFH (the extent of its 2K byte memory), and the chip is selected with A11 is low. Hence, the A11 line is connected to the $\overline{CE}$ pin of the 8755. In contrast, the 8156 RAM chip is selected when A11 is high, thus giving it the memory range 0800H through 08FFH (256 bytes).

Output ports A and B of the 8156 interface to the external hardware. Port A is designated as an output from the 8085 and issues control bits to the conversion hardware. Port B is designated as an input and receives the 8-bit data word from the analog-to-digital converter.

Input/output is performed by standard I/O; when executing an in or out instruction, the 8085 deselects memory and selects I/O ports by bringing IO/$\overline{M}$ high and transmitting the 8-bit port address on address lines

Design Problem No. 2 563

DA0–DA7 and A8–A15. Since the 8156 is enabled when A11 is high, the software designer must be certain to enable that bit in the port address.

On the 8156 chip, bits AD0–AD3 control the specific port accessed:

AD2	AD1	AD0	COMMENTS
0	0	0	(COMMAND/STATUS REGISTER)
0	0	1	(PORT A)
0	1	0	(PORT B)
0	1	1	(PORT C)
1	0	0	(LOW-ORDER TIMER)
1	0	1	(HIGH-ORDER TIMER)

For this project, we wish to use the command/status register and ports A and B. Therefore, AD2 will be low, and AD0–AD1 will be either high or low, depending on the port accessed.

Address bit A11 translates to address bit A3 in the port address. Therefore, A3 will be high for all 8156 I/O port address:

PORT ADDR.	AD3	AD2	AD1	AD0	COMMENTS
08H	1	0	0	0	(COMMAND/STATUS REG.)
09H	1	0	0	1	(PORT A)
0AH	1	0	1	0	(PORT B)

Data to the seven-segment LED displays are output from the 8085 processor through port A of the 8755 ROM/I/O Device. The output data word consists of a 4-bit hexadecimal number (lower four bits) and a 4-bit display address (upper four bits). A combination latch/hex, seven-segment decoder becomes high. Each display/latch reads its data in turn.

Each bit of the 8755 port A must be defined as an output by a data direction register (DDRA). Also, writing into either port A or DDRA demands that the 8755 device be enabled. Therefore, A11 (corresponding to AD3 in an out operation) must be low. The resulting port addresses for the 8755 are

AD3	AD2	AD1	AD0	PORT ADDRESS
0	0	0	0	00H (PORT A)
0	0	1	0	02H (DDRA)

Besides the three Intel devices, the microcomputer includes a 1-MHz crystal oscillator to provide a master clock, a reset switch to reset the system, and latched LED displays to output the RMS value to the operator.

The analog-to-digital conversion hardware is composed of three circuits: absolute value, sample and hold, and analog-to-digital converter.

The absolute value circuit used rectifies the input voltage within the feedback loop of an operational amplifier (Figure 12.3). When the input voltage E1 becomes negative, the output of op amp no. 1 becomes positive by one diode drop and turns off the upper diode. No effective current flows from op amp no. 1 and becomes ($-$E1 0.7N). The output of op amp no. 2 then becomes $[-(-2E1 + E1)] = E1$. In either case, the output voltage of op amp no. 2 is the absolute value of the input sine wave, and no diode drop error is introduced.

After the input voltage is rectified it is sampled by the sample and hold circuit: a "SAMPLE" signal of 650 μs duration is transmitted from I/O port A or the 8156 and inverted by a 4049 CMOS buffer. When "SAMPLE" is high the output of the buffer is low, and the 2N2222 transistor is turned off. Since it is not conducting, its collector voltage remains = 15 V, and the 4066 analog switch is closed. To open the switch, sample is set low, the 2N2222 transistor saturates, and the gate voltage of the analog switch is effectively set to 0 V. When this analog switch is closed a capacitor charges to the sample voltage.

Finally, the sampled and rectified voltage is converted to an 8-bit digital word by the 8703 analog-to-digital converter. The 8703 is biased to provided a 0–10 V scale range (i.e., 00H is equivalent to 0 V, FFH to 10 V, see Figure 12.3). All signals to the I/O ports of the microcomputer are buffered to isolate the expensive CMOS ADC.

The eight digital output bits are connected to port A of the 8156 and are read during the interrupt service routine. Conversion is begun by a programmed "START CONVERSION" pulse transmitted from the 8085 through port B of the 8156. After the ADC has completed conversion of the input voltager, the status line "BUSY" goes low. When enabled by the software-controlled "ENABLE" bit, the inverted signal "$\overline{\text{BUSY}}$" triggers the RST6.5 interrupt, and the interrupt service routine reads the now-valid data.

Since the "BUSY" output from the 8703 remains low ("$\overline{\text{BUSY}}$" remains high) between conversions, a software latch must be used to prevent further interrupts. Therefore, "BUSY" is "ANDED" with "EN-ABLE" to provide an RST6.5 interrupt only when the microcomputer is ready to accept it. During the interrupt service routine "ENABLE" is set low and remains in that state until the next sample is taken and the next A/D conversion begins. Figure 12.4 depicts the timing of the control signals.

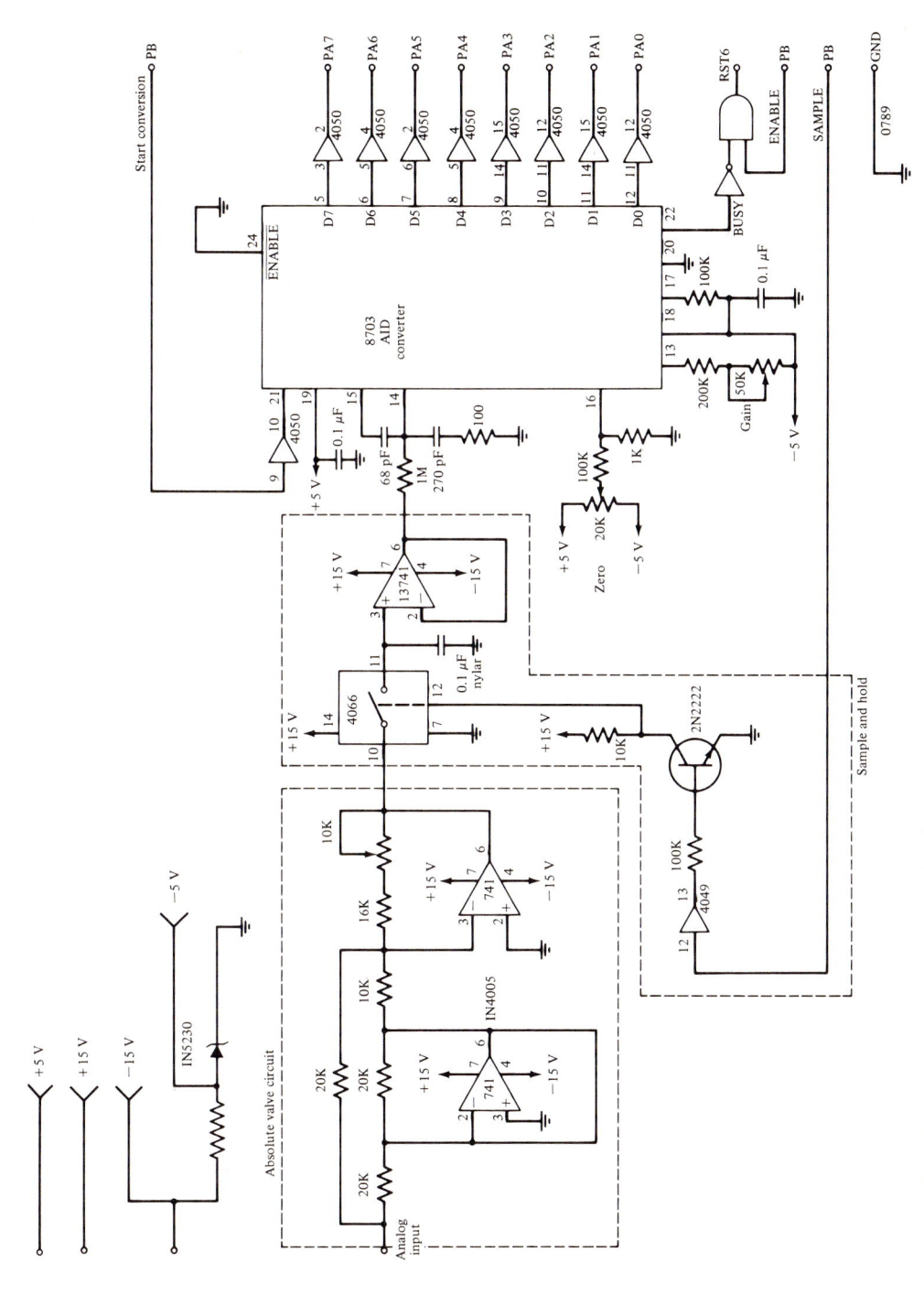

Figure 12.3 RMS voltage of a sine wave hardware.

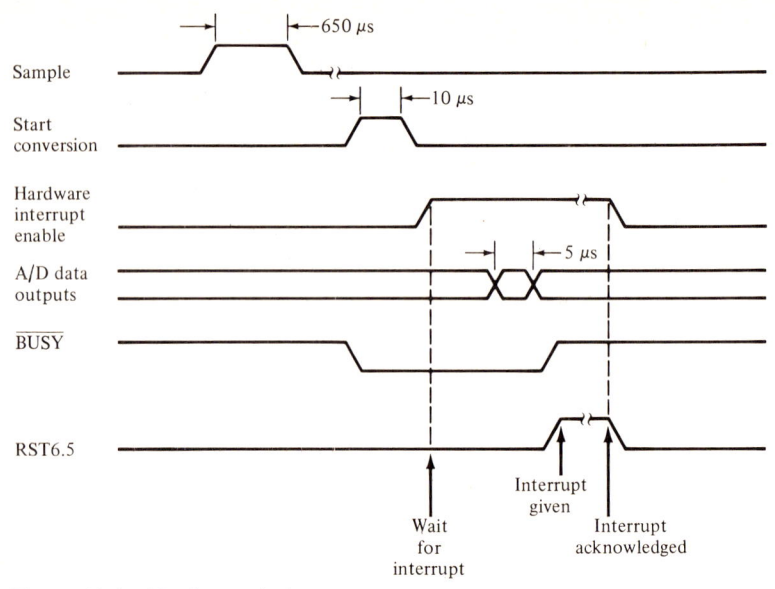

Figure 12.4 Hardware timing.

Software

The software used in this project exists as a single program, edited and assembled as an integral unit. It performs three primary functions: sampling of data, servicing interrupts, and computing the RMS value. Each function may be considered separately. The flowcharts for the software are shown in Figure 12.5.

When the system is reset by manually enabling the "RESET" line of the 8085, the program counter is automatically forced to 0000H. A JMP instruction at this address sends the processor to the beginning of the sampling and acquisition sequence (0037H). This portion of the program enables the RST6.5 interrupt, initializes the "B" register to 128 to count the samples, defines the 8156 I/O ports (PORT A=INPUT, PORT B=OUTPUT) and clears registers "C," "D," "E."

Next the program turns on the sample bit (bit 1 of the 8156 port "B") for 650 μs by using a timing loop. It then disables "SAMPLE" and issues a "START CONVERSION" command (bit 2), after which is the software interrupt latch (bit 0). Finally it reaches a "HLT" instruction and waits for the interrupt. Upon return from the interrupt, the program will decrement the B register, and branch back to the sampling sequence if 128 samples have not been taken. If the proper number of samples has been taken, the processor falls through to the RMS-calculation portion of the program.

The interrupt service routine (008E) first enables the output of the 8703 analog-to-digital converter. It then reads the 8-bit data word through port A of the 8156 (address 09) and adds it to a continuing sum in registers C,

Design Problem No. 2

Initialization

```
START
  ↓
Set DDR for ports:
  A = output
  B = input
  ↓
Set interrupt mask
enable only RST6.5
  ↓
Initialize registers
  CDE = 0
  B   = 128 (loop counter)
  SPR = 08F0
```

Sample and Hold Routine

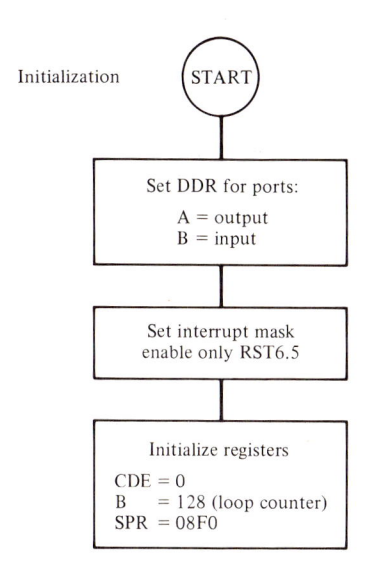

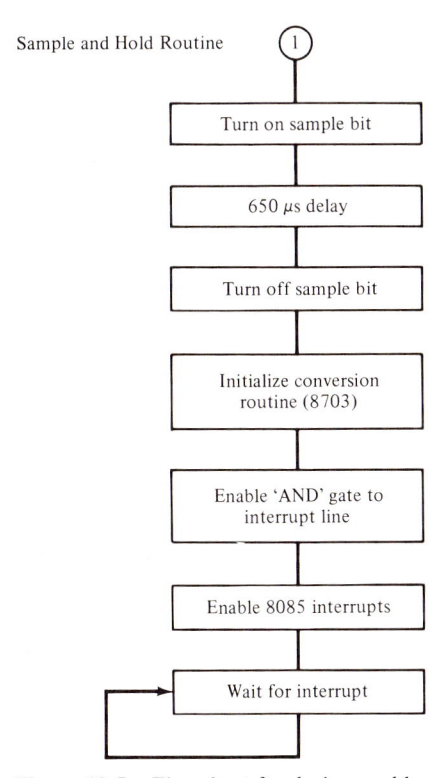

```
(1)
  ↓
Turn on sample bit
  ↓
650 μs delay
  ↓
Turn off sample bit
  ↓
Initialize conversion
routine (8703)
  ↓
Enable 'AND' gate to
interrupt line
  ↓
Enable 8085 interrupts
  ↓
Wait for interrupt ⟲
```

Figure 12.5 Flowchart for design problem no. 2.

Chapter 12 DESIGN PROBLEMS

Interrupt Routine

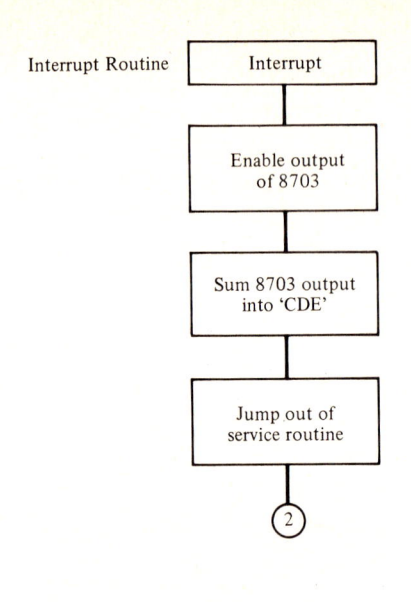

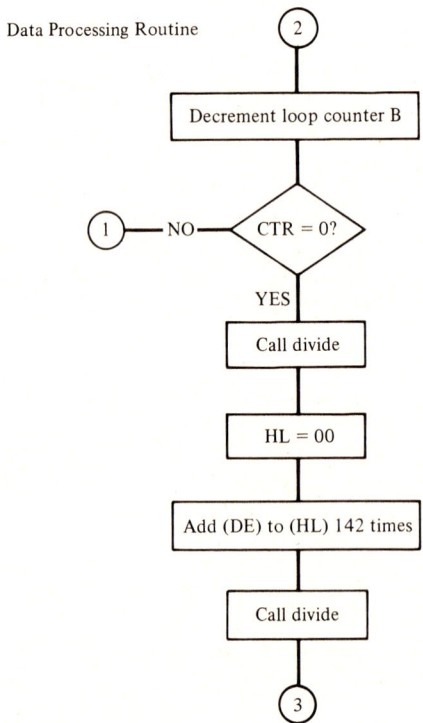

- Interrupt
- Enable output of 8703
- Sum 8703 output into 'CDE'
- Jump out of service routine
- (2)

Data Processing Routine

(2)
- Decrement loop counter B
- CTR = 0? — NO → (1)
- YES
- Call divide
- HL = 00
- Add (DE) to (HL) 142 times
- Call divide
- (3)

Figure 12.5 (*Continued*)

Design Problem No. 2   569

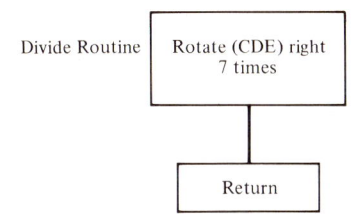

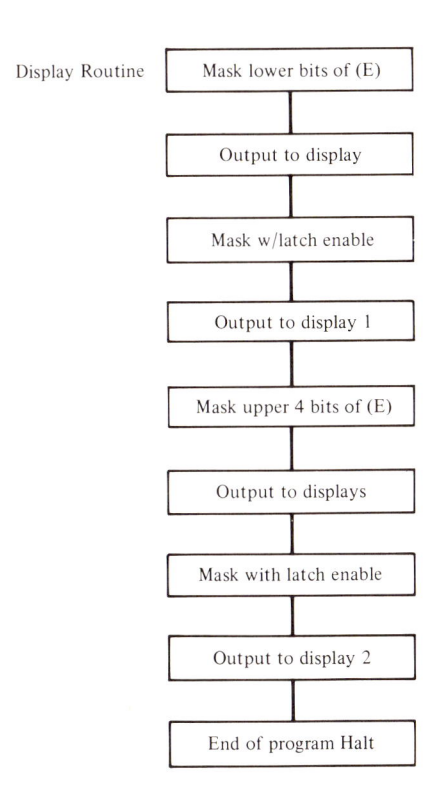

Divide Routine → Rotate (CDE) right 7 times → Return

Display Routine → Mask lower bits of (E) → Output to display → Mask w/latch enable → Output to display 1 → Mask upper 4 bits of (E) → Output to displays → Mask with latch enable → Output to display 2 → End of program Halt

Figure 12.5   (*Continued*)

570 Chapter 12 DESIGN PROBLEMS

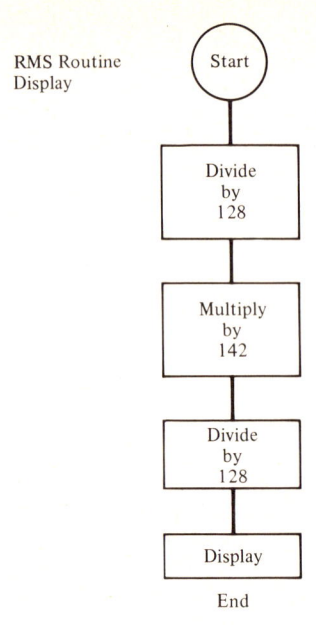

RMS Routine Display

```
Start
  │
┌─────┐
│Divide│
│ by  │
│ 128 │
└─────┘
  │
┌─────┐
│Multiply│
│  by   │
│  142  │
└─────┘
  │
┌─────┐
│Divide│
│ by  │
│ 128 │
└─────┘
  │
┌─────┐
│Display│
└─────┘
  │
 End
```

Figure 12.5 (*Continued*)

D, and E. Maintaining such a summing register avoids the problems of 128 entry data table. Immediately after this step, the loop counter is decremented and a jump is made back to the main program—the sample and hold routine. An interrupt instruction pushes a 2-byte address onto the stack. By jumping instead of returning, this address is not popped. To avoid a stack of 256 address locations, the contents of the stack are popped into unused registers H and L after the service routine.

Finally, the program computes the RMS value of the sine wave by dividing the cumulative sum in C, D, and E by 128 for an average. The average is then multiplied by 142 with a short multiplication routine. This result is divided with the same divide-by-128 routine previously used. This yields the RMS value:

$$\text{NOTE:} \quad \frac{142}{128} = 1.11$$

Average value $\times$ 1.11 = RMS

Division of the sum of registers C, D, and E is accomplished by shifting seven times to the right the contents of this register group.

Multiplication is accomplished by rotating the sum of products and the multiplicand in steps. If the carry bit is set after rotation of the multiplicand left, the multiplier (142) is added to the shifted sum of products.

Once the RMS value has been calculated, all that remains is to display the result to the operator. The display routine masks the hexadecimal data from register E in groups of 4 bits each. The masked data are sent out through port A of the 8755 so the data will be present before display registers are clocked. Once the data are stable, the masked data are "OR'ed" with control bits to clock the display registers. Two 9356 latch/decoders are used for the display. The complete word is now outputted to the latch and the display is latched to new data. The four upper bits of the register are then rotated into the four lower bits and the same routine is followed.

12.2.3 Methodology

The project was conducted in a straightforward manner: hardware and software were designed as discussed in the technical discussion. Disk files of the software were created and debugged until error-free assemblies were achieved. The hardware was fabricated and emulation was begun.

During emulation, problems such as miswired hardware and hardware and software mismatch were discovered and resolved. Checkout and emulation of the system required approximately 90 man-hours.

After emulation from emulation memory was successful the program was programmed into the 8755 EPROM. The system operation was also successful with the program running in user memory space. Finally the emulation probe was replaced by the 8085A microprocessor chip and the target system operated in a stand-alone mode. Again the system successfully sampled the waveform, computed, and displayed the RMS value to the operator. This completed the development phase of the project.

12.2.4 Results

In a stand-alone mode, the microcomputer system measured an input voltage and displayed the following results:

Case 1: dc measurement*
        5.0 dc, displayed RMS 8E
Case 2: 7.5 V ac unregulated*
        7.5 V ac, displayed RMS A5–C0
Case 3: 7.5 V ac regulated line voltage*
7.5 V ac, displayed RMS Be-Bd

The fluctuation in case 2 is attributable to wide variation over the sampling period of the line voltage. The accuracy of the 5.0-V dc test remained

---

* Measured with a Beckman 310 VOM.

constant due to the efficiency of the constant voltage regulation. When the regulated 120-V line was used, calculated, and measured, values agreed within 1 bit.

12.2.5 Conclusion

It was found that developing and debugging of software and hardware components was greatly enhanced by the Hewlett Packard 64000 Development System. The excellent results obtained in this experiment (within 1 bit accuracy) are proof of the system's effectiveness. Both objectives of the experiment were achieved—familiarization with a software/hardware development system and the actual construction of a device to measure the RMS value of a sinusoidal waveform.

FILE: ADCONV:GROUP9   HEWLETT-PACKARD: INTEL 8085 ASSEMBLER

Wed, 10 Dec 1980, 14:48   PAGE 1

LINE	LOC	CODE	ADDR		SOURCE	STATEMENT	
1					"8085"		
2	0000				ORG	0000H	!PROGRAM COUNTER WILL BEGIN EXECUTION AT LOCATION $0000
3	0000	C3	0037		JMP	START	!JUMP TO BEGINNING OF PROGRAM. . RST INTERRUPT VECTOR AT $0034
4	0034				ORG	0034H	!RST INTERRUPT VECTOR POINTS TO LOCATION $0034
5	0034	C3	008D		JMP	SVC	
6	0037	00		START	NOP		
7	0038	3E	0D		MVI	A,0DH	
8	003A	30			SIM		!SET MASK . . . ENABLE ONLY RST6.5 INTERRUPT
9	003B	3E	02		MVI	A,02H	
10	003D	D3	08		OUT	08H	!COMM, STATUS REG.; A=INPUT, B=OUTPUT
11	003F	01	8000		LXI	B,8000H	!B=LOOP COUNTER FOR 128 SAMPLES
12	0042	11	0000		LXI	D,0000H	! C,D AND E WILL STORE CUMULATIVE SUM OF SAMPLES
13	0045	31	08F0		LXI	SP,08F0H	!INITIALIZE STACK POINTER FOR RESTART
14	0048	3E	01	SAMPLE	MVI	A,01H	
15	004A	D3	0A		OUT	0AH	!TURN ON SAMPLE BIT
16	004C	21	004F		LXI	H,004FH	!BEGIN 650 MICROSECOND DELAY
17	004F	2B		LOOP1	DCX	H	!
18	0050	7D			MOV	A,L	!
19	0051	B4			ORA	H	!
20	0052	C2	004F		JNZ	LOOP1	!END 650 MICROSECOND DELAY

Design Problem No. 2

21	0055	D3	0A		OUT	0AH	!TURN OFF SAMPLE BIT, ANALOG VOLTAGE STORED IN CAPACITOR
22	0057	00			NOP	
23	0058	3E	04	CONV	MVI	A,04H
24	005A	D3	0A		OUT	0AH	!INITIALIZE A/D CONVERSION ... PORT 0A-2 = 1 (LATCHED BIT)
25	005C	3E	00		MVI	A,00H
26	005E	D3	0A		OUT	0AH	!TURN OFF INIT. CONV. PIN ... PORT 0A-2 = 0
27	0060	3E	02		MVI	A,02H
28	0062	D3	0A		OUT	0AH	!ENABLE 'AND' GATE ... PORT 0A-2
29	0064	FB			EI		!ENABLE RST6.5 INTERRUPT
30	0065	C3	0065	WAIT	JMP	WAIT	!WAIT FOR INTERRUPT
31	0068	00			NOP	
32	0069	E1		BACK	POP	H
33	006A	05			DCR	B	!DECREMENT LOOP COUNTER (FOR TOTAL OF 128 SAMPLES)
34	006B	C2	0048		JNZ	SAMPLE	!IF COUNTER DOES NOT EQUAL '0', RETURN TO SAMPLE ROUTINE
35	006E	00			NOP	
36	006F	CD	007A		CALL	DIVIDE	!CUMULATIVE SUM OF SAMPLES (CDE) IS DIVIDED BY 128) =AVERAGE
37	0072	00			NOP		!RESULTS IN REGISTERS D AND E
38	0073	00			NOP		!MOVE DE TO HL
39	0074	00			NOP		!STORE HL IN MEMORY LOCATION $0800 (FOR MULT. ROUTINE)
40	0075	C3	00A2		JMP	MULT	!
41	0078	00			NOP	
42	0079	00			NOP	
43	007A	06	07	DIVIDE	MVI	B,07H	!B=COUNTER FOR SHIFTER... (DE) WILL BE SHIFTED RIGHT 7 TIMES
44	007C	AF		LOOP2	XRA	A	!CLR CARRY BIT FOR SHIFTING
45	007D	79			MOV	A,C
46	007E	1F			RAR	
47	007F	4F			MOV	C,A
48	0080	7A			MOV	A,D
49	0081	1F			RAR	
50	0082	57			MOV	D,A
51	0083	7B			MOV	A,E
52	0084	1F			RAR	
53	0085	5F			MOV	E,A
54	0086	05			DCR	B	!DECREMENT LOOP COUNTER
55	0087	C2	007C		JNZ	LOOP2	!IF COUNTER DOES NOT EQUAL '0', JUMP BACK TO SHIFT
56	008A	C9			RET		!RETURN FROM DIVIDE SUBROUTINE
57	008B	00			NOP	

574 Chapter 12 DESIGN PROBLEMS

FILE: ADCONV:GROUP9   HEWLETT-PACKARD: INTEL 8085 ASSEMBLER

Wed, 10 Dec 1980, 14:48   PAGE 2

```
LINE LOC    CODE  ADDR          SOURCE STATEMENT
 58  008C   00                  NOP
 59  008D   3E    08     SVC    MVI    A,08H           !SERVICE ROUTINE
 60  008F   D3    0A            OUT    0AH             !ENABLE 8703 OUTPUT (8 BITS OF DATA) PORT
                                                           0A-3
 61  0091   AF                  XRA    A               !CLEAR CARRY BIT
 62  0092   DB    09            IN     09H             !INPUT DATA FROM A/D CONVERTER TO PORT
                                                           09
 63  0094   83                  ADD    E               !*******************************************
 64  0095   5F                  MOV    E,A              *
 65  0096   7A                  MOV    A,D              *
 66  0097   C3    00            ACI    00H              * SUM OUTPUT FROM 8703 INTO REGISTERS
                                                                  C,D AND E
 67  0099   57                  MOV    D,A              *
 68  009A   79                  MOV    A,C              *       (E IS THE LOWEST ORDER BYTE)
 69  009B   CE    00            ACI    00H              *
 70  009D   4F                  MOV    C,A             !*******************************************
 71  009E   C3    0069          JMP    BACK            ! END OF SERVICE ROUTINE
 72  00A1   00                  NOP                    !*******************************************
 73  00A2   00           MULT   NOP                    !*MULTIPLICATION SUBROUTINE
 74  00A3   21    0000          LXI    H,0000H         !*
 75  00A6   06    8D            MVI    B,08DH          !*      ADD (D)(E) TO (H)(L) 141 TIMES
 76  00A8   19           LOOP4  DAD    D               !*
 77  00A9   05                  DCR    B               !*
 78  00AA   C2    00A8          JNZ    LOOP4           !*******************************************
 79  00AD   00                  NOP
 80  00AE   54                  MOV    D,H             !MOVE DATA IN REGISTERS H AND L TO D AND
                                                           E FOR DIVIDE
 81  00AF   5D                  MOV    E,L             !
 82  00B0   00                  NOP
 83  00B1   0E    00            MVI    C,00H
 84  00B3   CD    007A          CALL   DIVIDE          !DIVIDE DATA IN C,D AND E BY 128
 85  00B6   00                  NOP
 86  00B7   CD    00BC          CALL   UPDAD           !CALL DISPLAY ROUTINE
 87  00BA   00                  NOP
 88  00BB   76                  HLT                    !END OF PROGRAM
 89  00BC   00           UPDAD  NOP                    !DISPLAY ROUTINE
 90  00BD   3E    FF            MVI    A,0FFH
 91  00BF   D3    02            OUT    02H             !SET DDR FOR PORT A
 92  00C1   AF                  XRA    A               !CLEAR ACCUMULATOR
 93  00C2   7B                  MOV    A,E
 94  00C3   E6    0F            ANI    0FH             !MASK - 0000 DDDD
 95  00C5   D3    00            OUT    00H             !SET DATA LINES D3-D0
```

```
 96 00C7 F6  1F      ORI   1FH       !MASK - 0001 DDDD
 97 00C9 D3  00      OUT   00H       !LATCH DIGIT 0
 98 00CB AF          XRA   A         !CLEAR CARRY
 99 00CC 7B          MOV   A,E
100 00CD 1F          RAR             !
101 00CE 1F          RAR             !ROTATE 4 MSB'S INTO
102 00CF 1F          RAR             !4 LSB POSITIONS
103 00D0 1F          RAR             !
104 00D1 E6  1F      ANI   1FH       !MASK - 0001 DDDD
105 00D3 F6  10      ORI   10H       !MASK - 0001 DDDD
106 00D5 D3  00      OUT   00H       !SET DATA D7-D4
107 00D7 F6  30      ORI   30H       !MASK - 0011 DDDD
108 00D9 D3  00      OUT   00H       !LATCH DIGIT 1
109 00DB AF          XRA   A         !CLEAR ACC., CARRY
110 00DC F6  30      ORI   03H       !MASK - 0011 0000
111 00DE D3  00      OUT   00H       !SET DATA D15-D8
112 00E0 F6  F0      ORI   0F0H      !MASK - 1111 0000
113 00E2 D3  00      OUT   00H       !SET DIGIT 2 & 2
114 00E4 76          HLT             !END OF PROGRAM
```

Errors= 0

12.3 Design Problem No. 3

12.3.1 Problem Statement

Design an 8085-based RMS meter similar to the Design Problem No. 2 but using the algorithm,

$$\text{RMS value} = \sqrt{\frac{\Sigma x_i^2}{N}}$$

where x_i's are the samples and N is the total number of samples

12.3.2 Solution to Design Problem No. 3

In this project, it is intended to develop a microprocessor system that will measure and display the RMS value of a given sinusoidal waveform. The system is constructed using an Intel 8085 microprocessor chip, Intel 8156 RAM/timer chip, Intel 8755 EPROM, and a Teledyne A/D converter.

The sine wave is passed through the A/D converter. The RMS value of this waveform is computed from its samples. This value is then displayed on a pair of seven-segment displays.

Figure 12.6 shows the system block diagram for the RMS meter.

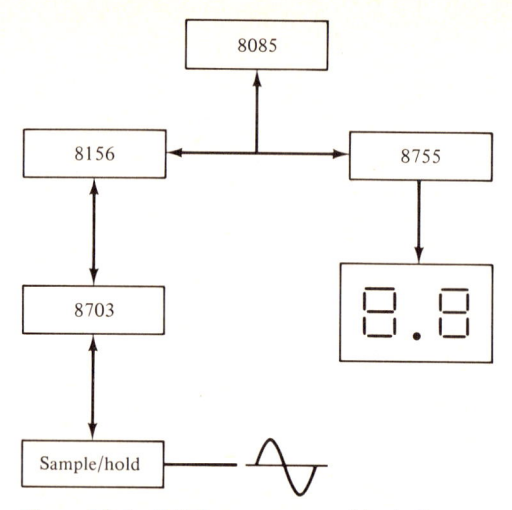

Figure 12.6 RMS meter system block diagram.

12.3.3 System Hardware Description

A microprocessor-based RMS voltmeter was designed and built by utilizing the Intel 8085 microcomputer family. The Intel 8085 8-bit microprocessor was used in conjunction with the Intel 8156 RAM-I/O timer chip and the Intel 8755 PROM-I/O chip. Analog-to-digital conversion was performed by the Teledyne 8703 converter and an associated sample and hold circuit. Figure 12.7 depicts the hardware schematic.

A summary of each chip and its system function is as follows:

8085 Microprocessor

All of the systems arithmetic and control functions are performed by the 8085 microprocessor. Many features of the 8085 are not required or utilized in this application. INTR, RST5.5, and TRAP are not used.

On power-up, the system is initialized by the RESET IN which is tied to an RC network which maintains a low voltage on the pin for approximately 20 ms. The 8085 has a reset out pin which provides a clock-synchronized signal used to initialize the other system chips.

The microprocessors low-order bits AD0–AD7 serve the dual function of multiplexed data and address bus. In this application memory-mapped I/O is used and the high-order address bits AD8–AD15 provide the chip select function and the I/O-memory select function. The peripheral devices and functions are selected according to the scheme shown on page 577.

The 8085 provides internal clock generation and the only requirement is an external crystal (4 MHz in this application) which is connected to the X1 and X2 input pins.

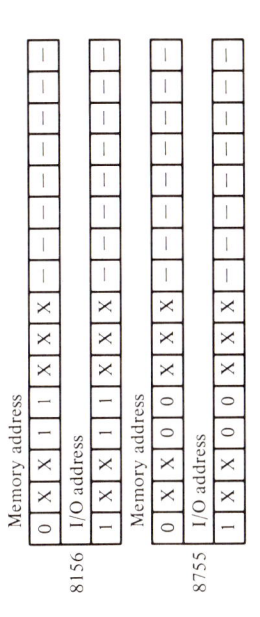

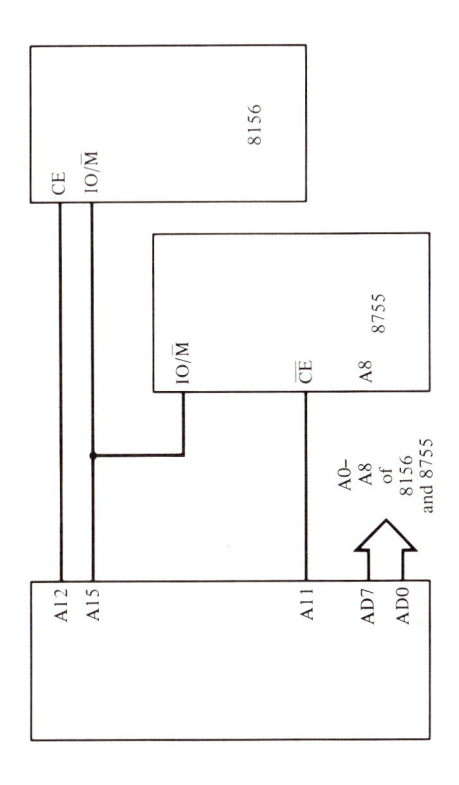

Design Problem No. 3

0	X	X	1	1	X	X	X	—	—	—	—	—	—	—	—

Memory address

1	X	X	1	1	X	X	X

8156 I/O address

0	X	X	0	0	X	X	X	—	—	—	—	—	—	—	—

Memory address

1	X	0	X	X	X	X	X

8755 I/O address

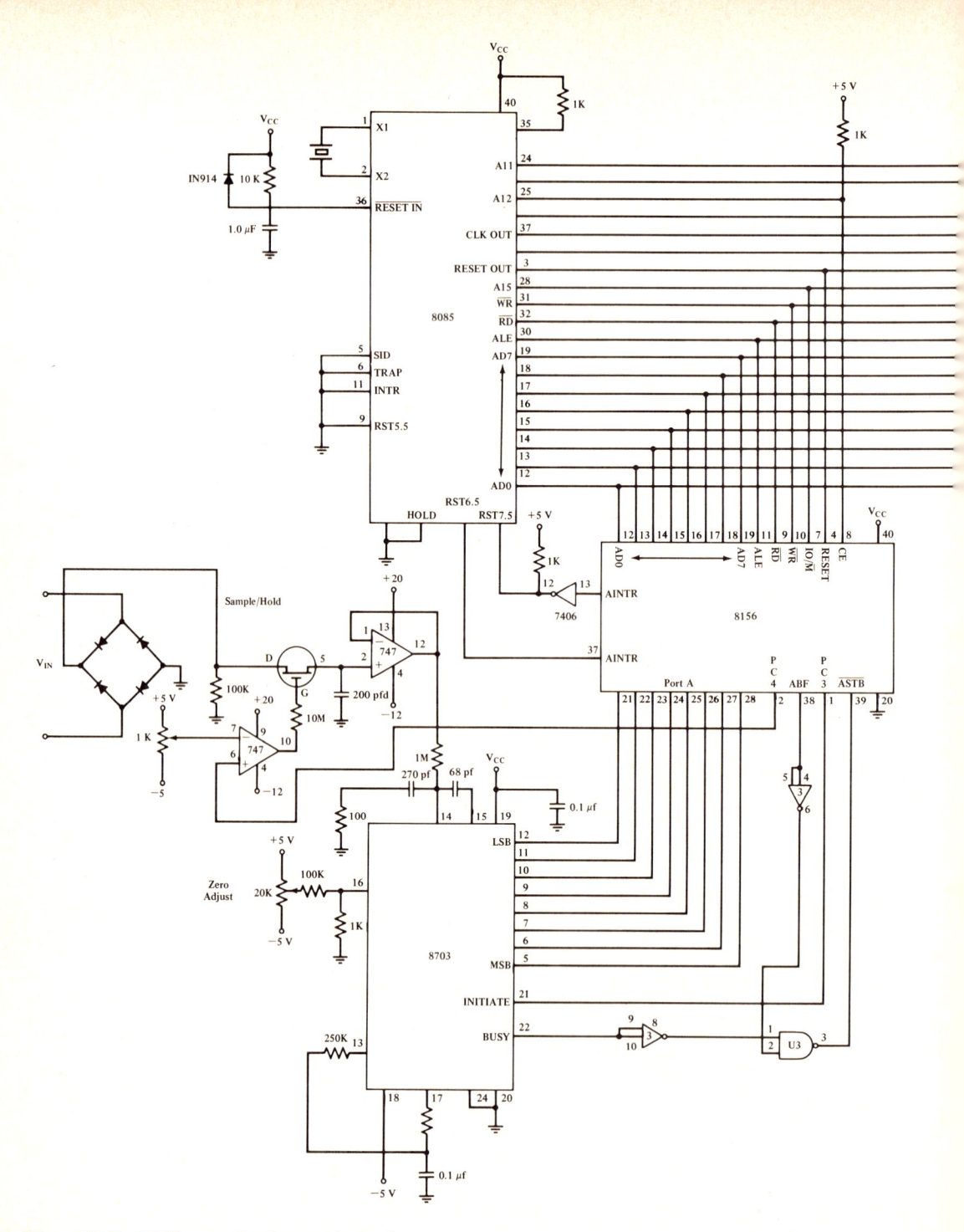

Figure 12.7 RMS meter hardware schematic.

Design Problem No. 3

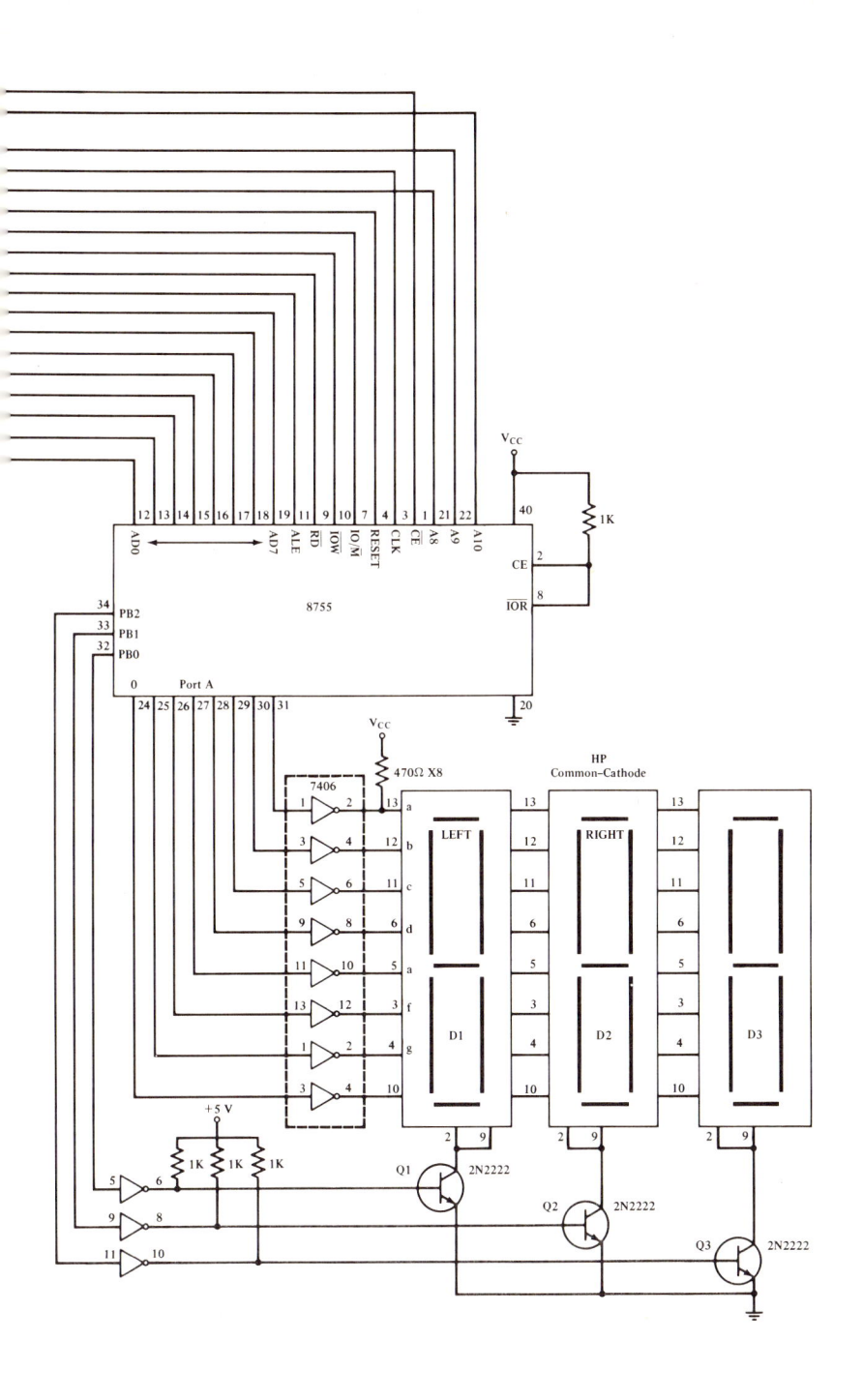

8156 RAM-I/O and Timer

The 8156 provides the communication between the 8085 and the Sample/Hold (S/H) circuit, software controlled timing, and 256 bytes of random access memory. Port A is used to provide interface with the S/H circuit and port C manages the handshaking procedure.

The 8156 contains a command register which will be set up to provide the necessary I/O functions for this application. The register is set as follows:

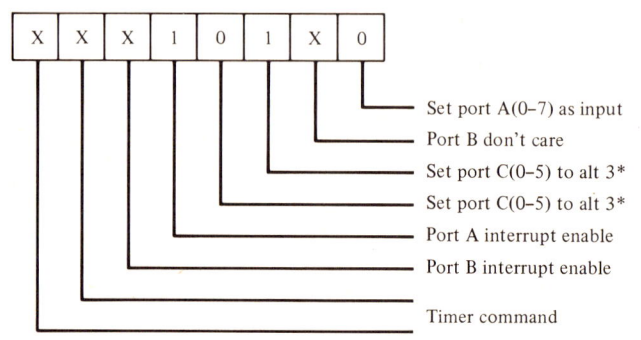

```
| X | X | X | 1 | 0 | 1 | X | 0 |
              │   │   │   │   │   └── Set port A(0–7) as input
              │   │   │   │   └────── Port B don't care
              │   │   │   └────────── Set port C(0–5) to alt 3*
              │   │   └────────────── Set port C(0–5) to alt 3*
              │   └────────────────── Port A interrupt enable
              └────────────────────── Port B interrupt enable
                                      Timer command
```

Command register. (*Alt 3 sets up port C according to the following: PC0—A port interrupt; PC1—A port buffer full; PC2—A port strobe; PC3—Output; PC4—Output; PC5—Output.)

The status register provides I/O and the timer status information (flags) when pulled. The individual bits of the registers provide the following information:

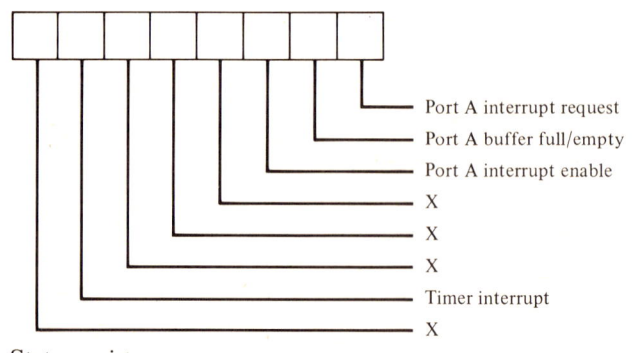

```
└── Port A interrupt request
└── Port A buffer full/empty
└── Port A interrupt enable
└── X
└── X
└── X
└── Timer interrupt
└── X
```

Status register.

The timer is used in the single pulse/terminal count mode. The timer is controlled by the command register and the count length register. The count length register's MSBs 6 and 7 set the timer mode and the remaining 12 bits specify the count length.

Analog-to-Digital Conversion Circuit

Transformation of the ac input voltage into usable digital information is performed by the sample and hold circuit and an 8703 A/D converter chip.

The ac input is first converted into a full-wave rectified dc waveform by a bridge circuit consisting of four 1N4002 diodes. The rectified voltage across a 100K resistor is sampled by an N-channel FET. A 747 op amp wired as a comparator provides the software controlled FET gating pulse. The comparator input is connected to the C port output bit #4. A 200-pF mylar capacitor is connected to the input of another 747 op amp which is wired as a voltage follower. The output of this op amp feeds a voltage divider on the input of the 8703 A/D converter. The A/D output is directly proportional to the input current, determined by the divider on the input, and the reference voltage. The 8-bit A/D output is connected to the port A input of the 8156 chip.

The handshaking procedure (Figure 12.8) begins with a logic high on the PC4 output pin. This in turn gates the FET to collect a voltage sample. The initiate conversion pulse is then provided to the 8703 input from PC3. At this time A/D converter will put out a busy signal which indicates to the

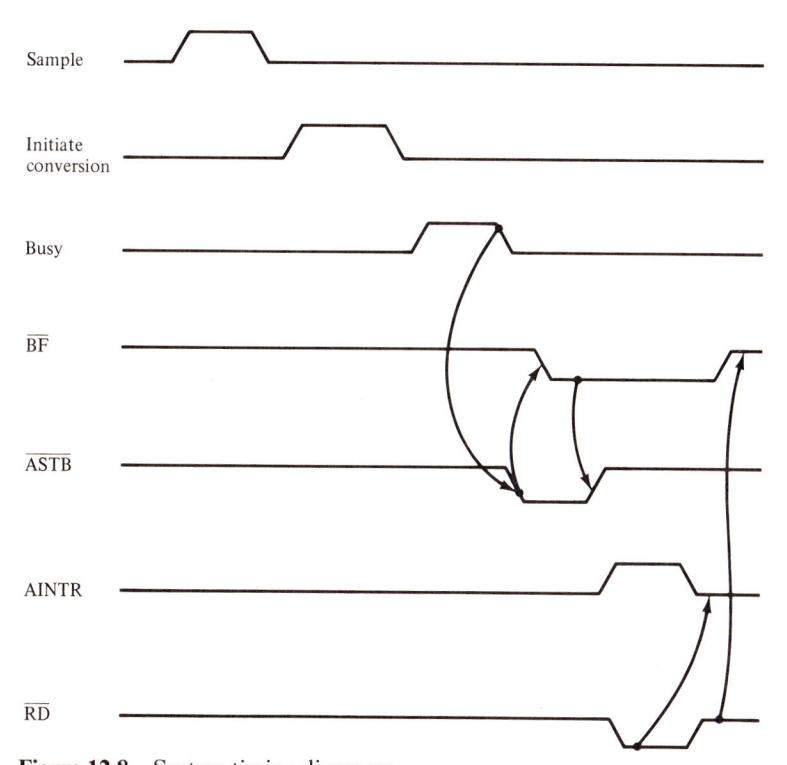

Figure 12.8 System timing diagrams.

processor that the conversion is taking place. The busy output is inverted by external logic and is fed into the PC2 input of the 8156 via a NAND gate which will permit the busy signal and the buffer full (PC1) to control the strobe input (PC2).

When the port A buffer is full the strobe will be permitted to go high and will initiate an INTR signal which will trigger the 8085 RST6.5 interrupt. This will interrupt the processor and cause the processor to enter into an interrupt service routine. This service routine loads the data into the RAM system. It loads 128 samples from the A/D converter into the RAM. After this, the arithmetic operations are performed.

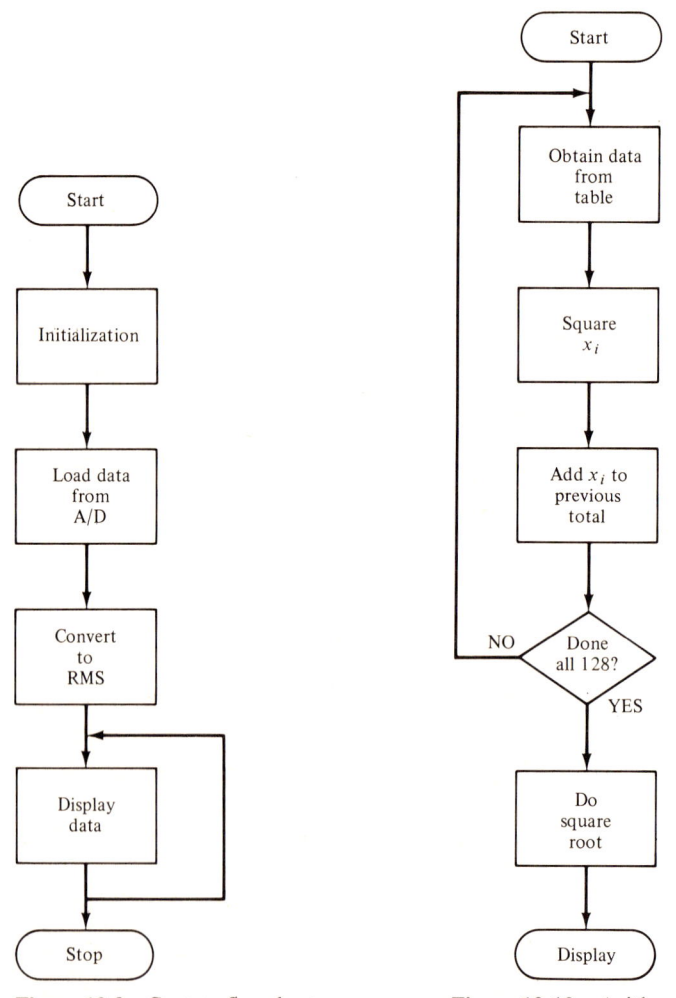

Figure 12.9 System flowchart.

Figure 12.10 Arithmetic operations.

Design Problem No. 3   583

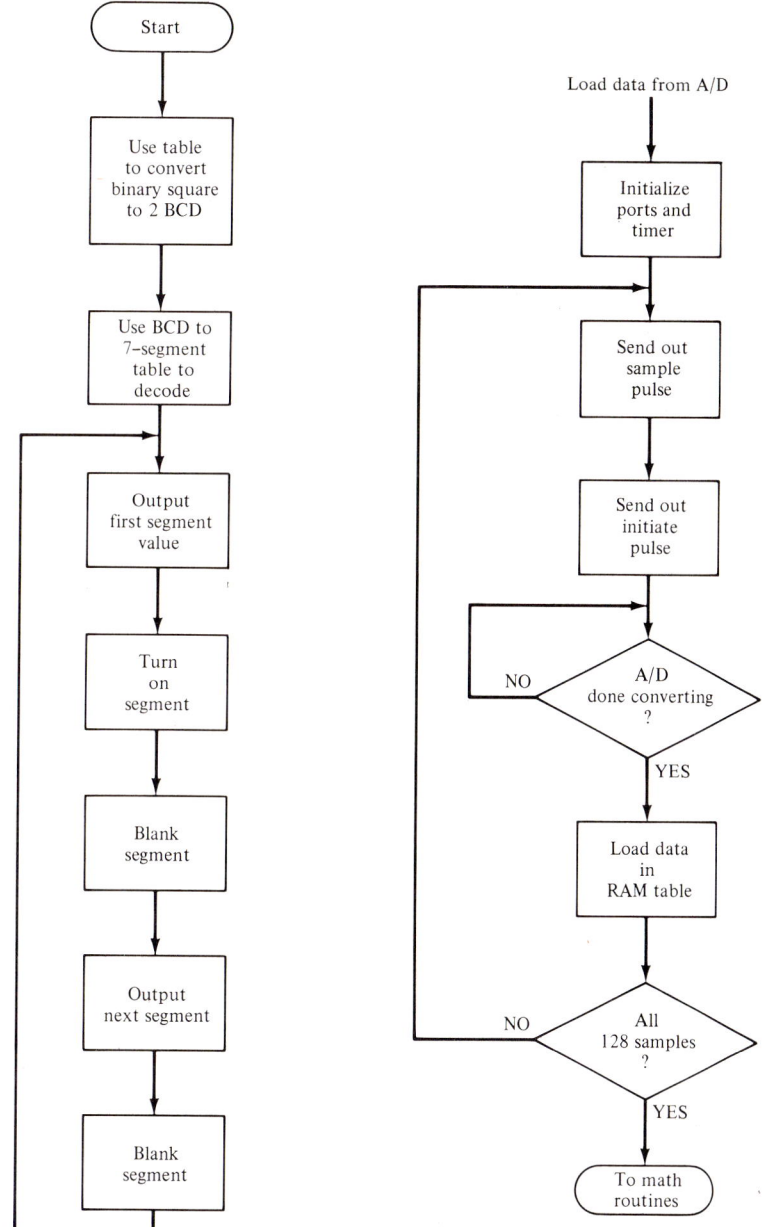

Figure 12.11 Multiplexed display.

Figure 12.12 Analog-to-digital converter operation.

12.3.4 System Software Description

After the data (x_i) is obtained from the conversion, it is squared and added to the previous total. This routine is done until all the 128 samples are finished. Then this sum is divided by the number of samples which is 128. The square root of this result is then obtained. The obtained result is in a binary code so by the use of a look-up table, this result is converted to decimal and displayed out of the I/O ports of the 8755.

Square root algorithm is done by successive approximation. If B is the value from which the square root will be taken and A is the guess value, B is stored in the 16-bit register. And then A is squared and compared to the B value. If A^2 is greater than B then A is decreased but if A^2 is less than B then A is increased. This procedure is done until approximately A^2 equals B. When A^2 is equal to B, A is the result of the square root. This result then is obtained from the look-up table and then displayed.

Figures 12.9 through 12.12 provide the flowcharts for the software.

```
FILE: RMS:DJ   HEWLETT-PACKARD: INTEL 8085 ASSEMBLER       Thu, 4 Jun 1981, 12:10   PAGE 1

LINE LOC   CODE ADDR      SOURCE STATEMENT
   1                      "8085"
   2                      *RMS VOLTMETER BY MICROPROCESSOR CONTROL
   3                      *432 LAB PROJECT
   4                      *
   5                      *
   6                      *INITIALIZATION ROUTINE
   7         1890  LDIGIT   EQU    1890H        ;LOWER DIGIT
   8         1891  HDIGIT   EQU    1891H        ;HIGHER DIGIT
   9 0100                   ORG    0100H        ;START AT 100H
  10 0100 31 18FF  START    LXI    SP,18FFH     ;STACK POINTER TO TOP OF RAM MEMORY
  11 0103 0E 80             MVI    C,80H        ;128 TO ADC SAMPLE COUNTER
  12 0105 3E FF             MVI    A,0FFH       ;SET UP 8755 PORTS
  13 0107 32 8002           STA    8002H        ;PORT A = OUTPUT
  14 010A 32 8003           STA    8003H        ;PORT B = OUTPUT
  15 010D 3E D4             MVI    A,0D4H       ;SET UP 8156 PORTS
  16 010F 32 9800           STA    9800H        ;PORT A = INPUT, PORT C = OUTPUT/HAND-
                                                    SHAKE
  17 0112 3E 10             MVI    A,10H        ;TURN OFF SAMPLE
  18 0114 32 9803           STA    9803H
  19 0117 21 1800           LXI    H,1800H      ;SET RAM POINTER TO TABLE TOP
  20                      *START LOADING RAM WITH A/D CONVERTER INPUT
  21 011A 31 18FF  LOAD     LXI    SP,18FFH     ;KEEP SP AT TOP RAM
  22 011D 3E 1B             MVI    A,1BH        ;SIM SET UP VALUE
  23 011F 30               SIM                  ;ENABLE RST 7.5
```

Design Problem No. 3

```
24 0120 3E  00              MVI   A,00H       ;SEND OUT SAMPLE PULSE
25 0122 32  9803            STA   9803H       ;ENABLE SAMPLE
26 0125 3E  83              MVI   A,83H       ;SET TIMER
27 0127 32  9805            STA   9805H
28 012A 3E  FF              MVI   A,0FFH      ;FOR 650 USEC
29 012C 32  9804            STA   9804H
30 012F 3E  D4              MVI   A,0D4H      ;START TIMER
31 0131 32  9800            STA   9800H
32 0134 FB                  EI                ;ENABLE INTERRUPTS
33 0135 C3  0135  WAIT1     JMP   WAIT1       ;WAIT UNTIL TIME OUT
34                 *INTERRUPT ROUTINE WILL STOP TIMER AND TURN OFF SAMPLE PULSE
                    THEN RETURNS HERE
35                 *A/D STARTS CONVERTING NOW
36 0138 3E  1B    ADSTRT    MVI   A,18H       ;INITIATE CONVERSION
37 013A 32  9803            STA   9803H
38 013D 00                  NOP
39 013E 00                  NOP
40 013F 3E  10              MVI   A,10H       ;TURN OFF PULSE
41 0141 32  9803            STA   9803H
42 0144 3E  1D              MVI   A,1DH       ;SIM SET UP
43 0146 30                  SIM               ;ENABLE RST 6.5
44 0147 FB                  EI                ;ENABLE INTERRUPTS
45 0148 C3  014B  WAIT2     JMP   WAIT2       ;WAIT FOR A/D CONVERTER TO FINISH
46                 *
47                 *
48                 *
49                 *INTERRUPT SERVICE ROUTINES
50 0000                     ORG   0000H       ;RESET JUMP TO PROGRAM START
51 0000 C3  0100            JMP   0100H
52                 *
53                 *
54                 *
55                 *
56 003C                     ORG   03CH        ;RESTART 7.5
57 003C 3E  10              MVI   A,10H       ;TURN OFF SAMPLE PULSE
```

FILE: RMS:DJ   HEWLETT-PACKARD: INTEL 8085 ASSEMBLER   Thu, 4 Jun 1981, 12:10   PAGE 2

```
LINE LOC   CODE ADDR        SOURCE STATEMENT
58 003E 32  9803            STA   9803H
59 0041 3E  54              MVI   A,54H       ;STOP TIMER
60 0043 32  9800            STA   9800H
61 0046 C3  0138            JMP   ADSTRT
62                 *
63                 *
```

586 Chapter 12 Design Problems

```
64                      *
65  0034                ORG     034H            ;RESTART 6.5
66  0034 C3 0005        JMP     RST65
67  0005                ORG     05H
68  0005 34 9801 RST65  LDA     9801H           ;INPUT A/D DATA
69  0008 77             MOV     M,A             ;STORE IN RAM SAMPLE TABLE
70  0009 23             INX     H               ;INCREMENT RAM TABLE POINTER
71  000A 0D             DCR     C               ;DECREMENT COUNTER
72  000B CA 0300        JZ      MAIN            ;
73  000E C3 011A        JMP     LOAD            ;CONTINUE LOADING
74                      *
75                      *
76                      *
77                      *OBTAIN THE SUM OF THE XI SQUARED TERMS.
78                      *ROUTINE FIRST SQUARES XI
79                      *THEN ADDS EACH SUCCESSIVE TERM TO THE PREVIOUS SUM.
80                      *ROUTINE THEN DIVIDES BY 128 AND LEAVES THE RESULT IN RP D E.
81                      *FROM HERE GO TO SQUARE ROOT ROUTINE
82  0300                ORG     0300H
83  0300 31 18FF MAIN   LXI     SP,18FFH        ;SP TO TOP RAM
84  0303 3E 00          MVI     A,00H
85  0305 11 0000 MULT   LXI     D,00H           ;SET UP SUM = 0.
86  0308 F5             PUSH    PSW
87  0309 D5             PUSH    D               ;STORE SUM
88  030A 21 1800        LXI     H,1800H         ;TOP OF DATA TABLE
89  030D 1E 08   MULT1  MVI     E,08H           ;MULTIPLY COUNT
90  030F 46             MOV     B,M             ;GET DATA
91  0310 0E 00          MVI     C,00H           ;SET UP FOR MULTIPLY ALGORITHM
92  0312 B7     SHIFT   ORA     A               ;CLEAR CARRY
93  0313 79             MOV     A,C             ;SHIFT 16 BITS LEFT
94  0314 17             RAL
95  0315 4F             MOV     C,A
96  0316 78             MOV     A,B
97  0317 17             RAL
98  0318 47             MOV     B,A
99  0319 D2 0323        JNC     MULT2
100 031C 7E             MOV     A,M             ;GET DATA
101 031D 81             ADD     C               ;ADD LOWER BYTE PRODUCT
102 031E 4F             MOV     C,A
103 031F 78             MOV     A,B             ;ADD CARRY TO UPPER BYTE PRODUCT
104 0320 CE 00          ACI     00H
105 0322 47             MOV     B,A
106 0323 1D     MULT2   DCR     E               ;CHECK IF 8 BITS DONE
```

Design Problem No. 3   587

```
107 0324 C2  0312           JNZ   SHIFT
108 0327 D1         ADD1    POP   D
109 0328 F1                 POP   PSW     ;GET XI SQUARED SUM
110 0329 81                 ADD   C
111 032A F5                 PUSH  PSW
112 032B 78                 MOV   A,B     ;NOW AND UPPER BYTE
113 032C 8B                 ADC   E       ;WITH CARRY
114 032D 5F                 MOV   E,A     ;DONE
```

FILE: RMS:DJ   HEWLETT-PACKARD: INTEL 8085 ASSEMBLER   Thu, 4 Jun 1981, 12:11   PAGE 3

```
LINE LOC   CODE ADDR        SOURCE STATEMENT
115 032E 7A                 MOV   A,D
116 032F CE  00             ACI   00H
117 0331 57                 MDV   D,A
118 0332 D5                 PUSH  D
119 0333 23                 INX   H
120 0334 7D                 MOV   A,L     ;CHECK IF 128 SAMPLES DONE
121 0335 EE  80             XRI   80H     ;AT THE BOTTOM OF THE LIST?
122 0337 C2  030D           JNZ   MULT1   ;GET NEXT DATA
123 033A D1                 POP   D       ;DATA IN RP D_E
124 033B F1                 POP   PSW     ;AND IN ACC
125 033C B7                 ORA   A       ;CLEAR CARRY
126 033D 17                 RAL           ;GET LSB AFTER DIVIDE
127 033E 7B                 MOV   A,E
128 033F 17                 RAL
129 0340 5F                 MOV   E,A
130 0341 7A                 MOV   A,D
131 0342 17                 RAL
132 0343 57                 MOV   D,A     ;XI SQUARED DIVIDED BY 128 NOW IN RP D_E
133 0344 C3  0347           JMP   SQRT    ;GO DO SQUARE ROOT
134                 *
135                 *
136                 *
137                 *SQUARE ROOT ROUTINE
138                 *
139                 *
140 0347 26  80     SQRT    MVI   H,80H   ;SET MSB OF SHIFT COUNTER
141 0349 2E  00             MVI   L,0     ;CLEAR THE BINARY VALUE
142 034B 7D         SQRT1   MDV   A,L     ;GET BINARY VALUE
143 034C B4                 ORA   H       ;SET A BIT IN L
144 034D 6F                 MOV   L,A
145 034E 47                 MOV   B,A     ;SQUARE BINARY VALUE
```

588 Chapter 12 Design Problems

```
146 034F CD  037A          CALL  SQRB
147 0352 7A                MOV   A,D        ;IS B>D? YES, RESET BIT
148 0353 B8                CMP   B          ;NO, LEAVE BIT
149 0354 DA  035F          JC    RSTBIT
150 0357 C2  0362          JNZ   SHFTCTR    ;IS B=D? NO, LEAVE BIT SET
151 035A 7B                MOV   A,E        ;YES, COMPARE LO BYTE
152 035B B9                CMP   C          ;IS C>E? YES, RESET BIT
153 035C D2  0362          JNC   SHFTCTR    ;NO, LEAVE BIT SET
154 035F 7D     RSTBIT     MOV   A,L        ;GET THE BIT SET LAST
155 0360 AC                XRA   H          ;RESET THAT BIT IN BINARY VALUE
156 0361 6F                MOV   L,A
157 0362 7C     SHFTCTR MOV   A,H        ;GET THE COUNTER
158 0363 1F                RAR              ;SHIFT RIGHT
159 0364 67                MOV   H,A        ;HAS IT BEEN SHIFTED 8 TIMES?
160 0365 D2  034B          JNC   SQRT1      ;YES, FALL THRU
161 0368 45                MOV   B,L        ;SQUARE L
162 0369 CD  037A          CALL  SQRB
163 036C 7B                MOV   A,E        ;GET LO BYTE OF HL
164 036D 91                SUB   C          ;SUBTRACT LO BYTE L**2
165 036E BD                CMP   L          ;IS DIFFERENCE < L OR = L
166 036F DA  0376          JC    DONE       ;YES, L**2 IS CLOSER
167 0372 CA  0376          JZ    DONE
168 0375 2C                INR   L          ;NO, (L+1)**2 IS CLOSER
169 0376 4D     DONE       MOV   C,L        ;SQUARE ROOT TO REG C
170 0377 C3  0397          JMP   CDATA      ;GO DISPLAY
171                         *
```

FILE: RMS:DJ   HEWLETT-PACKARD: INTEL 8085 ASSEMBLER   Thu, 4 Jun 1981, 12:11   PAGE 4

LINE LOC   CODE ADDR   SOURCE STATEMENT

```
172                         *
173                         *
174                         *SUBROUTINE FOR SQUARING REGISTER B
175                         *RESULT IN RP B_C
176                         *
177 037A D5     SQRB       PUSH  D
178 037B 1E  08            MVI   E,08H      ;MULTIPLY COUNT
179 037D 0E  00            MVI   C,00H
180 037F 50                MOV   D,B
181 0380 B7     SHIFT1     ORA   A          ;CLEAR CARRY
182 0381 79                MOV   A,C        ;SHIFT 16 BITS LEFT
183 0382 17                RAL
184 0383 4F                MOV   C,A
185 0384 78                MOV   A,B
```

Design Problem No. 3

```
186 0385 17                      RAL
187 0386 47                      MOV    B,A
188 0387 D2   0391               JNC    SQRB1
189 038A 7A                      MOV    A,D          ;GET DATA
190 038B 81                      ADD    C
191 038C 4F                      MOV    C,A
192 038D 78                      MOV    A,B
193 038E CE   00                 ACI    00H
194 0390 47                      MOV    B,A
195 0391 1D        SQRB1         DCR    E            ;CHECK IF DONE
196 0392 C2   0380               JNZ    SHIFT1
197 0395 D1                      POP    D
198 0396 C9                      RET                 ;DONE
199                  *
200                  *
201                  *GENERATE THE DISPLAYABLE CHARACTERS
202                  *PUT UPPER AND LOWER DIGITS IN HDIGIT AND LDIGIT
203                  *ROUTINE USES 256 BYTE LOOKUP TABLE FOR VALUES
204                  *AND USES SEPARATE LOOKUP TABLE FOR SEGMENTS DISPLAYED
205                  *TRANSFER WITH RMS RESULT IN REGISTER C
206                  *
207                  *
208 0397 21   0500   CDATA        LXI    H,0500H      ;DATA LOOKUP
209 039A 69                       MOV    L,C
210 039B 7F                       MOV    A,M          ;GET UPPER DIGIT FIRST
211 039C 1F                       RAR                 ;ROTATE FOUR TIMES
212 039D 1F                       RAR                 ;TO MASK BCD DIGIT
213 039E 1F                       RAR
214 039F 1F                       RAR
215 03A0 E6   0F                  ANI    0FH          ;MASK BCD DIGIT
216 03A2 21   0600                LXI    H,0600H      ;LOOK AT SEGMENT VALUE TABLE
217 03A5 6F                       MOV    L,A          ;POINTER VALUE
218 03A6 7E                       MOV    A,M          ;GET SEGMENT VALUE
219 03A7 32   1891                STA    HDIGIT       ;STORE FOR FUTURE USE
220 03AA 21   0500                LXI    H,0500H      ;DATA LOOKUP
221 03AD 69                       MOV    L,C
222 03AE 7E                       MOV    A,M          ;NOW GET LOWER DIGIT
223 03AF E6   0F                  ANI    0FH          ;MASK BCD DIGIT
224 03B1 21   0610                LXI    H,0610H      ;LOWER SEGMENT LOOKUP
225 03B4 85                       ADD    L
226 03B5 6F                       MOV    L,A          ;POINTER LOOKUP VALUE
227 03B6 7E                       MOV    A,M          ;GET SEGMENT VALUE
228 03B7 32   1890                STA    LDIGIT       ;STORE FOR FUTURE USE
```

590 Chapter 12 DESIGN PROBLEMS

FILE: RMS:DJ   HEWLETT-PACKARD: INTEL 8085 ASSEMBLER   Thu, 4 Jun 1981, 12:12   PAGE 5

```
LINE LOC  CODE ADDR     SOURCE STATEMENT
229  03BA C3 0200          JMP    DISPLY      ;GO DISPLAY THE RESULT
230                     *
231                     *DISPLAY ROUTINE
232                     *ENTER WITH VALUES TO BE DISPLAYED IN LDIGIT AND HDIGIT
233                     *LDIGIT = LOWER . . . . . . . HDIGIT = HIGHER
234                     *
235                     *
236  0200                  ORG    0200H
237  0200 21  8002 DISPLY  LXI    H,8002H     ;SET UP DISPLAY PORTS
238  0203 36  FF           MVI    M,0FFH      ;A = OUTPUT
239  0205 23               INX    H
240  0206 36  FF           MVI    M,0FFH      ;B = OUTPUT
241  0208 3A  1891         LDA    HDIGIT      ;GET HIGH DIGIT
242  020B 21  8000         LXI    H,8000H     ;OUTPUT TO DISPLAY
243  020E 77               MOV    M,A
244  020F 23               INX    H
245  0210 36  FD           MVI    M,0FDH      ;DISPLAY ON
246  0212 3A  1890         LDA    LDIGIT      ;GET LOW DIGIT
247  0215 36  FF           MVI    M,0FFH      ;DISPLAY OFF
248  0217 2B               DCX    H
249  0218 77               MOV    M,A         ;OUTPUT TO DISPLAY
250  0219 23               INX    H
251  021A 36  FB           MVI    M,0FBH      ;DISPLAY ON
252  021C 00               NOP
253  021D 00               NOP
254  021E 36  FF           MVI    M,0FFH      ;DISPLAY OFF
255  0220 C3  0200         JMP    DISPLY      ;REPEAT
256                     *
257                     *
258                     *
259                     *
260                     *SEVEN SEGMENT LOOKUP TABLE
261  0600                  ORG    0600H
262  0600 20               HEX    20,F1,05,41,D0,48,08,E1,00,C0
263  0610                  ORG    0610H
264  0610 22               HEX    22,F3,07,43,D2,4A,0A,E3,02,C2
265                     *
266                     *
267                     *
268                     *
269                     *LOOKUP TABLE FOR THE RMS VALUE GENERATED
```

Design Problem No. 3   591

```
270                     *CONTAINS THE FINAL VALUE IN BCD
271                     *BINARY CONVERSION TO BCD VALUE
272                     *
273                     *
274 0500                ORG     0500H
275 0500 00             HEX     00,00,01,01,02,02,02,03,03,04,04,04,05,05,06,06
276 0510 06             HEX     06,07,07,08,08,08,09,09,10,10,10,11,11,12,12,12
277 0520 13             HEX     13,13,14,14,14,15,15,16,16,16,17,17,18,18,18,19
278 0530 19             HEX     19,20,20,20,21,21,22,22,22,23,23,24,24,24,25,25
279 0540 26             HEX     26,26,26,27,27,28,28,28,29,29,30,30,30,31,31,32
280 0550 32             HEX     32,32,33,33,34,34,34,35,35,36,36,36,37,37,38,38
281 0560 38             HEX     38,39,39,40,40,40,41,41,42,42,42,43,43,44,44,44
282 0570 45             HEX     45,45,46,46,46,47,47,48,48,48,49,49,50,50,50,51
283 0580 51             HEX     51,52,52,52,53,53,54,54,54,55,55,56,56,56,57,57
284 0590 58             HEX     58,58,58,59,59,60,60,60,61,61,62,62,62,63,63,64
285 05A0 64             HEX     64,64,65,65,66,66,66,67,67,68,68,68,69,69,70,70
```

FILE: RMS:DJ   HEWLETT-PACKARD: INTEL 8085 ASSEMBLER   Thu, 4 Jun 1981, 12:12   PAGE 4

```
LINE LOC   CODE ADDR        SOURCE STATEMENT
286 05B0 70             HEX     70,71,71,72,72,72,73,73,74,74,74,75,75,76,76,76
287 05C0 77             HEX     77,77,78,78,78,79,79,80,80,80,81,81,82,82,82,83
288 05D0 83             HEX     83,84,84,84,85,85,86,86,86,87,87,88,88,88,89,89
289 05E0 90             HEX     90,90,90,91,91,92,92,92,93,93,94,94,94,95,95,96
290 05F0 96             HEX     96,96,97,97,98,98,98,99,99,99,99,99,99,99,99,99
291                     *
292                     *
293                     *
294                     END
```

Errors = 0

FILE: RMS:DJ   CROSS REFERENCE TABLE   PAGE 7

LINE#	SYMBOL	TYPE	REFERENCES
	A	A	12,15,17,22,24,26,28,30,36,40,42,57, 59,69,84,93,95,96,98,100,102,103,105, 112,114,115,117,120,127,129,130,132, 142,144,145,147,151,154,156,157,159, 163,182,184,185,187,189,191,192,194, 210,217,218,222,226,227,243,249
108	ADD1	A	

36	ADSTRT	A	61
	B	A	90,96,98,103,105,112,145,161,180,185, 187,192,194
	C	A	11,71,91,93,95,102,169,179,182,184, 191,209,221
208	CDATA	A	170
	D	A	85,87,108,115,117,118,123,130,132, 147,177,180,189,197
237	DISPLY	A	229,255
169	DONE	A	166,167
	E	A	89,106,114,127,129,151,163,178,195
	H	A	19,70,88,119,140,157,159,208,216,220, 224,237,239,242,244,248,250
8	HDIGIT	A	219,241
	L	A	120,141,142,144,154,156,161,168,169, 209,217,221,226
7	LDIGIT	A	228,246
21	LOAD	A	73
	M	A	69,90,100,210,218,222,227,238,240, 243,245,247,249,251,254
83	MAIN	A	72
85	MULT	A	
89	MULT1	A	122
106	MULT2	A	99
	PSW	A	86,109,111,124
68	RS765	A	66
154	RSTBIT	A	149
157	SHFTCTR	A	150,153
92	SHIFT	A	107
181	SHIFT1	A	196
	SP	A	10,21,83
177	SQRD	A	146,162
195	SQRB1	A	188
140	SQRT	A	133
142	SQRT1	A	160
10	START	A	
33	WAIT1	A	33
45	WAIT2	A	45

PROBLEMS AND QUESTIONS

Design and develop the software and hardware for the following using a particular microprocessor and its support chips with a microcomputer development system of your choice.

Problems and Questions

12.1 Capacitance meter. Consider the RC network in Figure 12.13. The voltage across the capacitor is $V_0(t) = ke^{-t/RC}$. In one-time constant RC, this voltage is discharged to the value k/e. By counting the time span τ, the value of the capacitor, $C = \tau/R$ can be determined if R is known. Design the software and hardware for a microprocessor-based system that generates a pulse to charge the

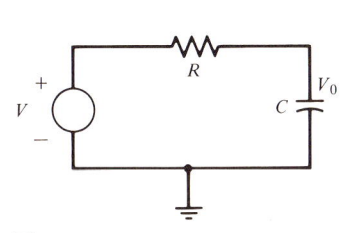

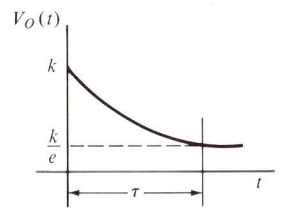

Figure 12.13

capacitor up to 10 V peak voltage through an amplifier and then stops charging the capacitor. The circuit measures the discharge time of the capacitor for one-time constant and then computes the value of the capacitor.

12.2 Design and develop the hardware and software for a microprocessor-based system to drive a 2-digit seven-segment display for displaying a number of 00 to FF.

12.3 Design a microprocessor-based digital clock. The clock will display time in hours, minutes, and seconds.

12.4 It is desired to sense the temperature of a thermistor using a microprocessor of your choice. The thermistor controls the timing pulse duration of a monostable multivibrator. You may use a counter to convert the timing pulse to a decimal count that is software mapped into a temperature and displays in degrees Celsius. Design and develop the hardware and software.

12.5 Design a microprocessor-based system to test five different types of IC, namely, OR, NOR, AND, NAND, and XOR. The system will apply inputs to each chip and read the output. It will then compare the output with the truth table stored inside the memory. If the comparison passes, a red LED will be turned OFF. If the comparison fails, the red LED will be turned ON.

12.6 Design a microprocessor-based system that reads a thermistor via an A/D converter and then displays the temperature in degrees Celsius on two seven-segment displays.

12.7 Design a microprocessor-based system to measure the power absorbed by the 1K resistor. The system will input the voltage V across the 1K resistor and then compute the power using V^2/R.

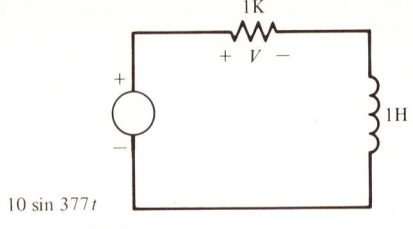

Figure 12.14

12.8   It is desired to design a priority vectored interrupt system using a daisy-chain structure for a microcomputer. Assume that the system includes eight interrupt devices DEV0, DEV1, ..., DEV7, which, during the interrupt sequence, places the respective instructions RST0, RST1, ..., RST7 on the data bus. Also assume that DEV0, ..., DEV7 are Teledyne 8703 A/D converters (DEV7 highest, DEV0 lowest priority) or equivalent.
   (a) Flowchart the problem to provide service routines for inputting the A/D converters' outputs.
   (b) Design and develop the hardware and software.

12.9   It is desired to drive an 8-digit display through eight output lines of a microcomputer system. Use eight Texas Instruments TIL 311, 14-pin MSI hexadecimal displays or equivalent:
   (a) Design the interface with minimum hardware.
   (b) Flowchart the software.
   (c) Convert the flowchart to the assembly language program.
   (d) Implement the hardware and software.

12.10   Design a microcomputer-based combinational lock which has a combination of four digits. The four digits are entered from a hexadecimal keyboard and they are to be entered within 16 s. If the right combination is entered within the same limit, the lock will open. If after 16 s, either all four digits are not entered or a wrong combination is entered, then the display will show an error signal by displaying "E." The system will allow 6 s for the first digit to be entered the second time. If after this time, the digit is not entered, the system will turn ON the alarm. If the second try fails, the alarm is also turned ON. When the alarm is ON, in order to reset the system, power has to be turned OFF.

12.11   Design a microcomputer-based stopwatch. The stopwatch will operate in the following way: The operator enters three digits (two digits for minutes and one digit for tenths of minutes) from a keyboard and then presses the GO key. The system counts down the remaining time on three seven-segment LED displays.

12.12   Design an 8085-based system as follows:

Problems and Questions 595

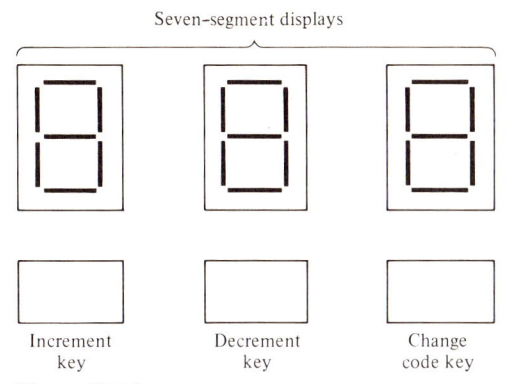

Figure 12.15

Seven-segment displays / Increment key / Decrement key / Change code key

The system drives three seven-segment digits and monitors three key switches. The system starts displaying 000. If the increment key is pressed, it will increment the display by one. Similarly, if the decrement key is pressed, the display will be decremented by one. The display goes from 00–FF in the hex mode and from 0–256 in the decimal mode. The system will count correctly in either mode. The change mode key will cause the display to change from hex to decimal or vice versa, depending on its present mode.

12.13 Design an 8085-based system as follows:

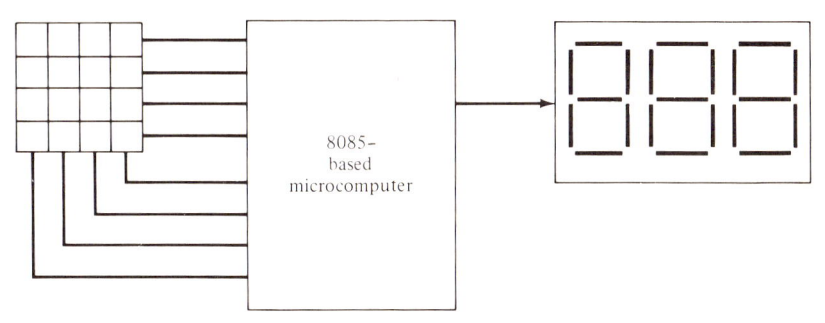

Figure 12.16

The system scans a 16-key keyboard and drives three seven-segment displays. The keyboard is scanned in a 4 × 4 X–Y matrix. The system will take each key pressed and scroll them in from the right side of the display and keep scrolling as each key is pressed. The left-most digit is just discarded. The system continues indefinitely.

APPENDIX A
8085 INSTRUCTION SET*

* Reprinted by permission of Intel Corporation, copyright © 1976.

5.1 WHAT THE INSTRUCTION SET IS

A computer, no matter how sophisticated, can do only what it is instructed to do. A program is a sequence of instructions, each of which is recognized by the computer and causes it to perform an operation. Once a program is placed in memory space that is accessible to your CPU, you may run that same sequence of instructions as often as you wish to solve the same problem or to do the same function. The set of instructions to which the 8085A CPU will respond is permanently fixed in the design of the chip.

Each computer instruction allows you to initiate the performance of a specific operation. The 8085A implements a group of instructions that move data between registers, between a register and memory, and between a register and an I/O port. It also has arithmetic and logic instructions, conditional and unconditional branch instructions, and machine control instructions. The CPU recognizes these instructions only when they are coded in binary form.

5.2 SYMBOLS AND ABBREVIATIONS:

The following symbols and abbreviations are used in the subsequent description of the 8085A instructions:

SYMBOLS	MEANING
accumulator	Register A
addr	16-bit address quantity
data	8-bit quantity
data 16	16-bit data quantity
byte 2	The second byte of the instruction
byte 3	The third byte of the instruction
port	8-bit address of an I/O device
r,r1,r2	One of the registers A,B,C, D,E,H,L

*All mnemonics copyrighted © Intel Corporation 1976.

DDD,SSS The bit pattern designating one of the registers A,B,C,D, E,H,L (DDD = destination, SSS = source):

DDD or SSS	REGISTER NAME
111	A
000	B
001	C
010	D
011	E
100	H
101	L

rp One of the register pairs:

B represents the B,C pair with B as the high-order register and C as the low-order register;

D represents the D,E pair with D as the high-order register and E as the low-order register;

H represents the H,L pair with H as the high-order register and L as the low-order register;

SP represents the 16-bit stack pointer register.

RP The bit pattern designating one of the register pairs B,D,H,SP:

RP	REGISTER PAIR
00	B-C
01	D-E
10	H-L
11	SP

rh The first (high-order) register of a designated register pair.

rl The second (low-order) register of a designated register pair.

THE INSTRUCTION SET

PC	16-bit program counter register (PCH and PCL are used to refer to the high-order and low-order 8 bits respectively).
SP	16-bit stack pointer register (SPH and SPL are used to refer to the high-order and low-order 8 bits respectively).
r_m	Bit m of the register r (bits are number 7 through 0 from left to right).
LABEL	16-bit address of subroutine.
	The condition flags:
Z	Zero
S	Sign
P	Parity
CY	Carry
AC	Auxiliary Carry
( )	The contents of the memory location or registers enclosed in the parentheses.
←	"Is transferred to"
∧	Logical AND
⊻	Exclusive OR
∨	Inclusive OR
+	Addition
−	Two's complement subtraction
*	Multiplication
↔	"Is exchanged with"
‾	The one's complement (e.g., $\overline{(A)}$).
n	The restart number 0 through 7
NNN	The binary representation 000 through 111 for restart number 0 through 7 respectively.

The instruction set encyclopedia is a detailed description of the 8085A instruction set. Each instruction is described in the following manner:

1. The MCS-85 macro assembler format, consisting of the instruction mnemonic and operand fields, is printed in **BOLDFACE** on the first line.
2. The name of the instruction is enclosed in parentheses following the mnemonic.
3. The next lines contain a symbolic description of what the instruction does.
4. This is followed by a narrative description of the operation of the instruction.

*All mnemonics copyrighted © Intel Corporation 1976.

5. The boxes describe the binary codes that comprise the machine instruction.
6. The last four lines contain information about the execution of the instruction. The number of machine cycles and states required to execute the instruction are listed first. If the instruction has two possible execution times, as in a conditional jump, both times are listed, separated by a slash. Next, data addressing modes are listed if applicable. The last line lists any of the five flags that are affected by the execution of the instruction.

5.3 INSTRUCTION AND DATA FORMATS

Memory used in the MCS-85 system is organized in 8-bit bytes. Each byte has a unique location in physical memory. That location is described by one of a sequence of 16-bit binary addresses. The 8085A can address up to 64K (K = 1024, or 2^{10}; hence, 64K represents the decimal number 65,536) bytes of memory, which may consist of both random-access, read-write memory (RAM) and read-only memory (ROM), which is also random-access.

Data in the 8085A is stored in the form of 8-bit binary integers:

DATA WORD

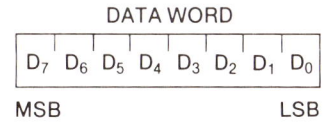

| D_7 | D_6 | D_5 | D_4 | D_3 | D_2 | D_1 | D_0 |

MSB   LSB

When a register or data word contains a binary number, it is necessary to establish the order in which the bits of the number are written. In the Intel 8085A, BIT 0 is referred to as the **Least Significant Bit (LSB)**, and BIT 7 (of an 8-bit number) is referred to as the **Most Significant Bit (MSB)**.

An 8085A program instruction may be one, two or three bytes in length. Multiple-byte instructions must be stored in successive memory locations; the address of the first byte is always used as the address of the instruction. The exact instruction format will depend on the particular operation to be executed.

Single Byte Instructions

| D_7 | | | | | | | D_0 | Op Code

Two-Byte Instructions

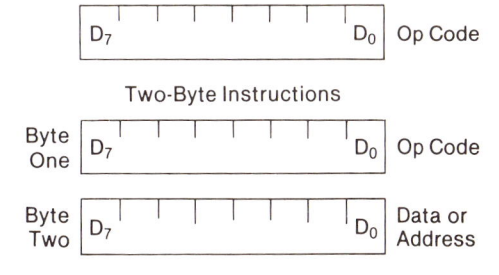

Byte One | D_7 | | | | | | | D_0 | Op Code

Byte Two | D_7 | | | | | | | D_0 | Data or Address

THE INSTRUCTION SET

Three-Byte Instructions

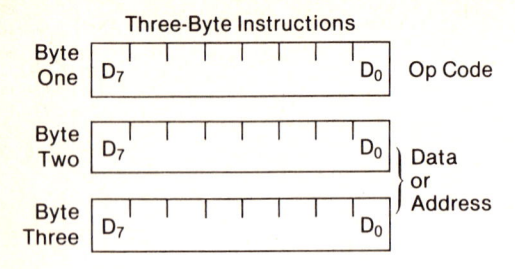

Byte One: D₇ — D₀ Op Code
Byte Two: D₇ — D₀ ⎫ Data
Byte Three: D₇ — D₀ ⎬ or Address

5.4 ADDRESSING MODES:

Often the data that is to be operated on is stored in memory. When multi-byte numeric data is used, the data, like instructions, is stored in successive memory locations, with the least significant byte first, followed by increasingly significant bytes. The 8085A has four different modes for addressing data stored in memory or in registers:

- Direct — Bytes 2 and 3 of the instruction contain the exact memory address of the data item (the low-order bits of the address are in byte 2, the high-order bits in byte 3).

- Register — The instruction specifies the register or register pair in which the data is located.

- Register Indirect — The instruction specifies a register pair which contains the memory address where the data is located (the high-order bits of the address are in the first register of the pair the low-order bits in the second).

- Immediate — The instruction contains the data itself. This is either an 8-bit quantity or a 16-bit quantity (least significant byte first, most significant byte second).

Unless directed by an interrupt or branch institution, the execution of instructions proceeds through consecutively increasing memory locations. A branch instruction can specify the address of the next instruction to be executed in one of two ways:

- Direct — The branch instruction contains the address of the next instruction to be executed. (Except for the 'RST' instruction, byte 2 contains the low-order address and byte 3 the high-order address.)

- Register Indirect — The branch instruction indicates a register-pair which contains the address of the next instruction to be executed. (The high-order bits of the address are in the first register of the pair, the low-order bits in the second.)

The RST instruction is a special one-byte call instruction (usually used during interrupt sequences). RST includes a three-bit field; program control is transferred to the instruction whose address is eight times the contents of this three-bit field.

5.5 CONDITION FLAGS:

There are five condition flags associated with the execution of instructions on the 8085A. They are Zero, Sign, Parity, Carry, and Auxiliary Carry. Each is represented by a 1-bit register (or flip-flop) in the CPU. A flag is set by forcing the bit to 1; it is reset by forcing the bit to 0.

Unless indicated otherwise, when an instruction affects a flag, it affects it in the following manner:

Zero: If the result of an instruction has the value 0, this flag is set; otherwise it is reset.

Sign: If the most significant bit of the result of the operation has the value 1, this flag is set; otherwise it is reset.

Parity: If the modulo 2 sum of the bits of the result of the operation is 0, (i.e., if the result has even parity), this flag is set; otherwise it is reset (i.e., if the result has odd parity).

Carry: If the instruction resulted in a carry (from addition), or a borrow (from subtraction or a comparison) out of the high-order bit, this flag is set; otherwise it is reset.

Auxiliary Carry: If the instruction caused a carry out of bit 3 and into bit 4 of the resulting value, the auxiliary carry is set; otherwise it is reset. This flag is affected by single-precision additions, subtractions, increments, decrements, comparisons, and logical operations, but is principally used with additions and increments preceding a DAA (Decimal Adjust Accumulator) instruction.

*All mnemonics copyrighted ©Intel Corporation 1976.

THE INSTRUCTION SET

5.6 INSTRUCTION SET ENCYCLOPEDIA

In the ensuing dozen pages, the complete 8085A instruction set is described, grouped in order under five different functional headings, as follows:

1. **Data Transfer Group** — Moves data between registers or between memory locations and registers. Includes moves, loads, stores, and exchanges. (See below.)
2. **Arithmetic Group** — Adds, subtracts, increments, or decrements data in registers or memory. (See page 5-13.)
3. **Logic Group** — ANDs, ORs, XORs, compares, rotates, or complements data in registers or between memory and a register. (See page 5-16.)
4. **Branch Group** — Initiates conditional or unconditional jumps, calls, returns, and restarts. (See page 5-20.)
5. **Stack, I/O, and Machine Control Group** — Includes instructions for maintaining the stack, reading from input ports, writing to output ports, setting and reading interrupt masks, and setting and clearing flags. (See page 5-22.)

The formats described in the encyclopedia reflect the assembly language processed by Intel-supplied assembler, used with the Intellec® development systems.

5.6.1 Data Transfer Group

This group of instructions transfers data to and from registers and memory. **Condition flags are not affected by any instruction in this group.**

MOV r1, r2 (Move Register)
(r1) ← (r2)
The content of register r2 is moved to register r1.

0	1	D	D	D	S	S	S

Cycles: 1
States: 4 (8085), 5 (8080)
Addressing: register
Flags: none

*All mnemonics copyrighted © Intel Corporation 1976.

MOV r, M (Move from memory)
(r) ← ((H) (L))
The content of the memory location, whose address is in registers H and L, is moved to register r.

0	1	D	D	D	1	1	0

Cycles: 2
States: 7
Addressing: reg. indirect
Flags: none

MOV M, r (Move to memory)
((H) (L)) ← (r)
The content of register r is moved to the memory location whose address is in registers H and L.

0	1	1	1	0	S	S	S

Cycles: 2
States: 7
Addressing: reg. indirect
Flags: none

MVI r, data (Move Immediate)
(r) ← (byte 2)
The content of byte 2 of the instruction is moved to register r.

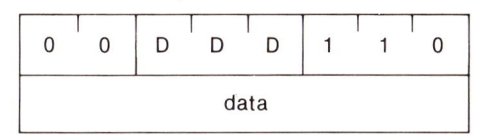

0	0	D	D	D	1	1	0
data								

Cycles: 2
States: 7
Addressing: immediate
Flags: none

MVI M, data (Move to memory immediate)
((H) (L)) ← (byte 2)
The content of byte 2 of the instruction is moved to the memory location whose address is in registers H and L.

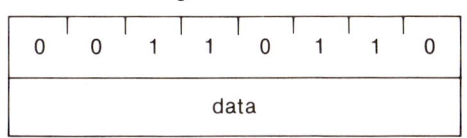

0	0	1	1	0	1	1	0
data								

Cycles: 3
States: 10
Addressing: immed./reg. indirect
Flags: none

THE INSTRUCTION SET

LXI rp, data 16 (Load register pair immediate)
(rh) ← (byte 3),
(rl) ← (byte 2)
Byte 3 of the instruction is moved into the high-order register (rh) of the register pair rp. Byte 2 of the instruction is moved into the low-order register (rl) of the register pair rp.

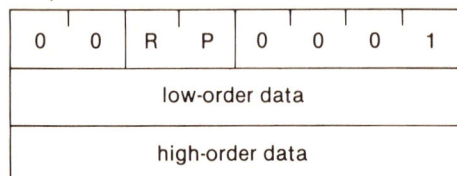

0	0	R	P	0	0	0	1
low-order data							
high-order data							

      Cycles: 3
      States: 10
Addressing: immediate
      Flags: none

LDA addr (Load Accumulator direct)
(A) ← ((byte 3)(byte 2))
The content of the memory location, whose address is specified in byte 2 and byte 3 of the instruction, is moved to register A.

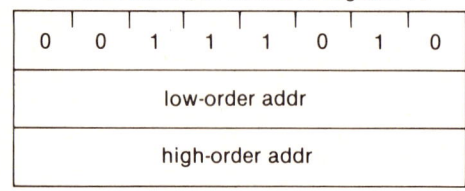

0	0	1	1	1	0	1	0
low-order addr							
high-order addr							

      Cycles: 4
      States: 13
Addressing: direct
      Flags: none

STA addr (Store Accumulator direct)
((byte 3)(byte 2)) ← (A)
The content of the accumulator is moved to the memory location whose address is specified in byte 2 and byte 3 of the instruction.

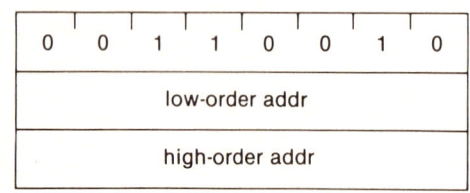

0	0	1	1	0	0	1	0
low-order addr							
high-order addr							

      Cycles: 4
      States: 13
Addressing: direct
      Flags: none

LHLD addr (Load H and L direct)
(L) ← ((byte 3)(byte 2))
(H) ← ((byte 3)(byte 2) + 1)
The content of the memory location, whose address is specified in byte 2 and byte 3 of the instruction, is moved to register L. The content of the memory location at the succeeding address is moved to register H.

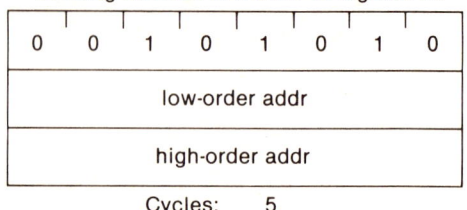

0	0	1	0	1	0	1	0
low-order addr							
high-order addr							

      Cycles: 5
      States: 16
Addressing: direct
      Flags: none

SHLD addr (Store H and L direct)
((byte 3)(byte 2)) ← (L)
((byte 3)(byte 2) + 1) ← (H)
The content of register L is moved to the memory location whose address is specified in byte 2 and byte 3. The content of register H is moved to the succeeding memory location.

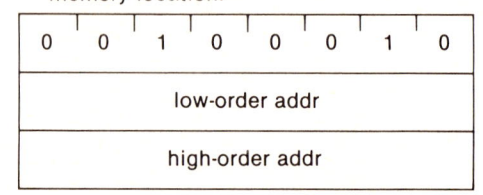

0	0	1	0	0	0	1	0
low-order addr							
high-order addr							

      Cycles: 5
      States: 16
Addressing: direct
      Flags: none

LDAX rp (Load accumulator indirect)
(A) ← ((rp))
The content of the memory location, whose address is in the register pair rp, is moved to register A. Note: only register pairs rp = B (registers B and C) or rp = D (registers D and E) may be specified.

0	0	R	P	1	0	1	0

      Cycles: 2
      States: 7
Addressing: reg. indirect
      Flags: none

*All mnemonics copyrighted © Intel Corporation 1976.

THE INSTRUCTION SET

STAX rp   (Store accumulator indirect)
((rp)) ← (A)
The content of register A is moved to the memory location whose address is in the register pair rp. Note: only register pairs rp = B (registers B and C) or rp = D (registers D and E) may be specified.

| 0 | 0 | R | P | 0 | 0 | 1 | 0 |

Cycles: 2
States: 7
Addressing: reg. indirect
Flags: none

XCHG   (Exchange H and L with D and E)
(H) ↔ (D)
(L) ↔ (E)
The contents of registers H and L are exchanged with the contents of registers D and E.

| 1 | 1 | 1 | 0 | 1 | 0 | 1 | 1 |

Cycles: 1
States: 4
Addressing: register
Flags: none

5.6.2 Arithmetic Group

This group of instructions performs arithmetic operations on data in registers and memory.

Unless indicated otherwise, all instructions in this group affect the Zero, Sign, Parity, Carry, and Auxiliary Carry flags according to the standard rules.

All subtraction operations are performed via two's complement arithmetic and set the carry flag to one to indicate a borrow and clear it to indicate no borrow.

ADD r   (Add Register)
(A) ← (A) + (r)
The content of register r is added to the content of the accumulator. The result is placed in the accumulator.

| 1 | 0 | 0 | 0 | 0 | S | S | S |

Cycles: 1
States: 4
Addressing: register
Flags: Z,S,P,CY,AC

ADD M   (Add memory)
(A) ← (A) + ((H) (L))
The content of the memory location whose address is contained in the H and L registers is added to the content of the accumulator. The result is placed in the accumulator.

| 1 | 0 | 0 | 0 | 0 | 1 | 1 | 0 |

Cycles: 2
States: 7
Addressing: reg. indirect
Flags: Z,S,P,CY,AC

ADI data   (Add immediate)
(A) ← (A) + (byte 2)
The content of the second byte of the instruction is added to the content of the accumulator. The result is placed in the accumulator.

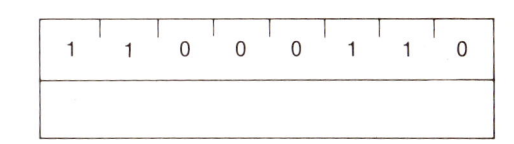

| 1 | 1 | 0 | 0 | 0 | 1 | 1 | 0 |
| | | | | | | | |

Cycles: 2
States: 7
Addressing: immediate
Flags: Z,S,P,CY,AC

ADC r   (Add Register with carry)
(A) ← (A) + (r) + (CY)
The content of register r and the content of the carry bit are added to the content of the accumulator. The result is placed in the accumulator.

| 1 | 0 | 0 | 0 | 1 | S | S | S |

Cycles: 1
States: 4
Addressing: register
Flags: Z,S,P,CY,AC

*All mnemonics copyrighted © Intel Corporation 1976.

THE INSTRUCTION SET

ADC M (Add memory with carry)
(A) ← (A) + ((H) (L)) + (CY)
The content of the memory location whose address is contained in the H and L registers and the content of the CY flag are added to the accumulator. The result is placed in the accumulator.

1	0	0	0	1	1	1	0

Cycles: 2
States: 7
Addressing: reg. indirect
Flags: Z,S,P,CY,AC

SUB M (Subtract memory)
(A) ← (A) − ((H) (L))
The content of the memory location whose address is contained in the H and L registers is subtracted from the content of the accumulator. The result is placed in the accumulator.

1	0	0	1	0	1	1	0

Cycles: 2
States: 7
Addressing: reg. indirect
Flags: Z,S,P,CY,AC

ACI data (Add immediate with carry)
(A) ← (A) + (byte 2) + (CY)
The content of the second byte of the instruction and the content of the CY flag are added to the contents of the accumulator. The result is placed in the accumulator.

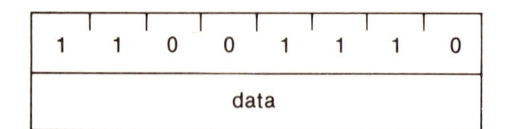

1	1	0	0	1	1	1	0
data

Cycles: 2
States: 7
Addressing: immediate
Flags: Z,S,P,CY,AC

SUI data (Subtract immediate)
(A) ← (A) − (byte 2)
The content of the second byte of the instruction is subtracted from the content of the accumulator. The result is placed in the accumulator.

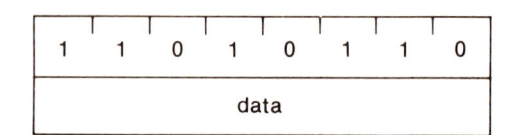

1	1	0	1	0	1	1	0
data

Cycles: 2
States: 7
Addressing: immediate
Flags: Z,S,P,CY,AC

SUB r (Subtract Register)
(A) ← (A) − (r)
The content of register r is subtracted from the content of the accumulator. The result is placed in the accumulator.

1	0	0	1	0	S	S	S

Cycles: 1
States: 4
Addressing: register
Flags: Z,S,P,CY,AC

SBB r (Subtract Register with borrow)
(A) ← (A) − (r) − (CY)
The content of register r and the content of the CY flag are both subtracted from the accumulator. The result is placed in the accumulator.

1	0	0	1	1	S	S	S

Cycles: 1
States: 4
Addressing: register
Flags: Z,S,P,CY,AC

*All mnemonics copyrighted ©Intel Corporation 1976.

THE INSTRUCTION SET

SBB M (Subtract memory with borrow)
(A) ← (A) − ((H) (L)) − (CY)
The content of the memory location whose address is contained in the H and L registers and the content of the CY flag are both subtracted from the accumulator. The result is placed in the accumulator.

| 1 | 0 | 0 | 1 | 1 | 1 | 1 | 0 |

      Cycles: 2
      States: 7
  Addressing: reg. indirect
       Flags: Z,S,P,CY,AC

SBI data (Subtract immediate with borrow)
(A) ← (A) − (byte 2) − (CY)
The contents of the second byte of the instruction and the contents of the CY flag are both subtracted from the accumulator. The result is placed in the accumulator.

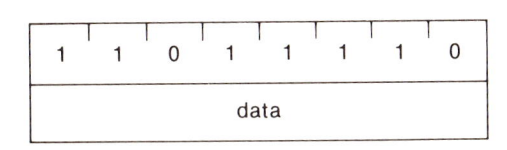

| 1 | 1 | 0 | 1 | 1 | 1 | 1 | 0 |
| data |

      Cycles: 2
      States: 7
  Addressing: immediate
       Flags: Z,S,P,CY,AC

INR r (Increment Register)
(r) ← (r) + 1
The content of register r is incremented by one. Note: All condition flags **except CY** are affected.

| 0 | 0 | D | D | D | 1 | 0 | 0 |

      Cycles: 1
      States: 4 (8085), 5 (8080)
  Addressing: register
       Flags: Z,S,P,AC

INR M (Increment memory)
((H) (L) ← ((H) (L)) + 1
The content of the memory location whose address is contained in the H and L registers is incremented by one. Note: All condition flags **except CY** are affected.

| 0 | 0 | 1 | 1 | 0 | 1 | 0 | 0 |

      Cycles: 3
      States: 10
  Addressing: reg. indirect
       Flags: Z,S,P,AC

DCR r (Decrement Register)
(r) ← (r) − 1
The content of register r is decremented by one. Note: All condition flags **except CY** are affected.

| 0 | 0 | D | D | D | 1 | 0 | 1 |

      Cycles: 1
      States: 4 (8085), 5 (8080)
  Addressing: register
       Flags: Z,S,P,AC

DCR M (Decrement memory)
((H) (L)) ← ((H) (L)) − 1
The content of the memory location whose address is contained in the H and L registers is decremented by one. Note: All condition flags **except CY** are affected.

| 0 | 0 | 1 | 1 | 0 | 1 | 0 | 1 |

      Cycles: 3
      States: 10
  Addressing: reg. indirect
       Flags: Z,S,P,AC

*All mnemonics copyrighted © Intel Corporation 1976.

THE INSTRUCTION SET

INX rp (Increment register pair)
(rh) (rl) ← (rh) (rl) + 1
The content of the register pair rp is incremented by one. Note: **No condition flags are affected.**

| 0 | 0 | R | P | 0 | 0 | 1 | 1 |

Cycles: 1
States: 6 (8085), 5 (8080)
Addressing: register
Flags: none

DCX rp (Decrement register pair)
(rh) (rl) ← (rh) (rl) − 1
The content of the register pair rp is decremented by one. Note: **No condition flags are affected.**

| 0 | 0 | R | P | 1 | 0 | 1 | 1 |

Cycles: 1
States: 6 (8085), 5 (8080)
Addressing: register
Flags: none

DAD rp (Add register pair to H and L)
(H) (L) ← (H) (L) + (rh) (rl)
The content of the register pair rp is added to the content of the register pair H and L. The result is placed in the register pair H and L. Note: **Only the CY flag is affected.** It is set if there is a carry out of the double precision add; otherwise it is reset.

| 0 | 0 | R | P | 1 | 0 | 0 | 1 |

Cycles: 3
States: 10
Addressing: register
Flags: CY

*All mnemonics copyrighted ©Intel Corporation 1976.

DAA (Decimal Adjust Accumulator)
The eight-bit number in the accumulator is adjusted to form two four-bit Binary-Coded-Decimal digits by the following process:

1. If the value of the lease significant 4 bits of the accumulator is greater than 9 **or** if the AC flag is set, 6 is added to the accumulator.
2. If the value of the most significant 4 bits of the accumulator is now greater than 9, **or** if the CY flag is set, 6 is added to the most significant 4 bits of the accumulator.

NOTE: All flags are affected.

| 0 | 0 | 1 | 0 | 0 | 1 | 1 | 1 |

Cycles: 1
States: 4
Flags: Z,S,P,CY,AC

5.6.3 Logical Group

This group of instructions performs logical (Boolean) operations on data in registers and memory and on condition flags.

Unless indicated otherwise, all instructions in this group affect the Zero, Sign, Parity, Auxiliary Carry, and Carry flags according to the standard rules.

ANA r (AND Register)
(A) ← (A) ∧ (r)
The content of register r is logically ANDed with the content of the accumulator. The result is placed in the accumulator. **The CY flag is cleared and AC is set (8085). The CY flag is cleared and AC is set to the OR'ing of bits 3 of the operands (8080).**

| 1 | 0 | 1 | 0 | 0 | S | S | S |

Cycles: 1
States: 4
Addressing: register
Flags: Z,S,P,CY,AC

THE INSTRUCTION SET

ANA M (AND memory)
(A) ← (A) ∧ ((H) (L))
The contents of the memory location whose address is contained in the H and L registers is logically ANDed with the content of the accumulator. The result is placed in the accumulator. **The CY flag is cleared and AC is set (8085). The CY flag is cleared and AC is set to the OR'ing of bits 3 of the operands (8080).**

1	0	1	0	0	1	1	0

   Cycles: 2
   States: 7
  Addressing: reg. indirect
   Flags: Z,S,P,CY,AC

ANI data (AND immediate)
(A) ← (A) ∧ (byte 2)
The content of the second byte of the instruction is logically ANDed with the contents of the accumulator. The result is placed in the accumulator. **The CY flag is cleared and AC is set (8085). The CY flag is cleared and AC is set to the OR'ing of bits 3 of the operands (8080).**

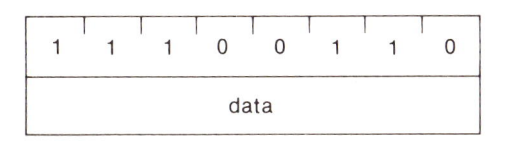

1	1	1	0	0	1	1	0
			data				

   Cycles: 2
   States: 7
  Addressing: immediate
   Flags: Z,S,P,CY,AC

XRA r (Exclusive OR Register)
(A) ← (A) ∀ (r)
The content of register r is exclusive-OR'd with the content of the accumulator. The result is placed in the accumulator. **The CY and AC flags are cleared.**

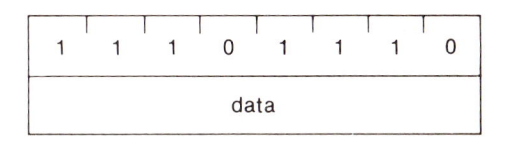

1	0	1	0	1	S	S	S

   Cycles: 1
   States: 4
  Addressing: register
   Flags: Z,S,P,CY,AC

XRA M (Exclusive OR Memory)
(A) ← (A) ∀ ((H) (L))
The content of the memory location whose address is contained in the H and L registers is exclusive-OR'd with the content of the accumulator. The result is placed in the accumulator. **The CY and AC flags are cleared.**

1	0	1	0	1	1	1	0

   Cycles: 2
   States: 7
  Addressing: reg. indirect
   Flags: Z,S,P,CY,AC

XRI data (Exclusive OR immediate)
(A) ← (A) ∀ (byte 2)
The content of the second byte of the instruction is exclusive-OR'd with the content of the accumulator. The result is placed in the accumulator. **The CY and AC flags are cleared.**

1	1	1	0	1	1	1	0
			data				

   Cycles: 2
   States: 7
  Addressing: immediate
   Flags: Z,S,P,CY,AC

ORA r (OR Register)
(A) ← (A) V (r)
The content of register r is inclusive-OR'd with the content of the accumulator. The result is placed in the accumulator. **The CY and AC flags are cleared.**

1	0	1	1	0	S	S	S

   Cycles: 1
   States: 4
  Addressing: register
   Flags: Z,S,P,CY,AC

*All mnemonics copyrighted © Intel Corporation 1976.

THE INSTRUCTION SET

ORA M (OR memory)
(A) ← (A) V ((H) (L))
The content of the memory location whose address is contained in the H and L registers is inclusive-OR'd with the content of the accumulator. The result is placed in the accumulator. **The CY and AC flags are cleared.**

1	0	1	1	0	1	1	0

Cycles: 2
States: 7
Addressing: reg. indirect
Flags: Z,S,P,CY,AC

ORI data (OR Immediate)
(A) ← (A) V (byte 2)
The content of the second byte of the instruction is inclusive-OR'd with the content of the accumulator. The result is placed in the accumulator. **The CY and AC flags are cleared..**

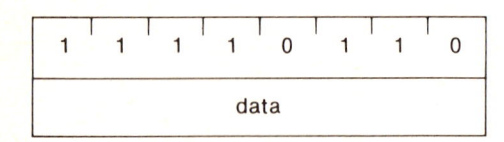

1	1	1	1	0	1	1	0
			data				

Cycles: 2
States: 7
Addressing: immediate
Flags: Z,S,P,CY,AC

CMP r (Compare Register)
(A) − (r)
The content of register r is subtracted from the accumulator. The accumulator remains unchanged. The condition flags are set as a result of the subtraction. **The Z flag is set to 1 if (A) = (r). The CY flag is set to 1 if (A) < (r).**

1	0	1	1	1	S	S	S

Cycles: 1
States: 4
Addressing: register
Flags: Z,S,P,CY,AC

CMP M (Compare memory)
(A) − ((H) (L))
The content of the memory location whose address is contained in the H and L registers is subtracted from the accumulator. The accumulator remains unchanged. The condition flags are set as a result of the subtraction. **The Z flag is set to 1 if (A) = ((H) (L)). The CY flag is set to 1 if (A) < ((H) (L)).**

1	0	1	1	1	1	1	0

Cycles: 2
States: 7
Addressing: reg. indirect
Flags: Z,S,P,CY,AC

CPI data (Compare immediate)
(A) − (byte 2)
The content of the second byte of the instruction is subtracted from the accumulator. The condition flags are set by the result of the subtraction. **The Z flag is set to 1 if (A) = (byte 2). The CY flag is set to 1 if (A) < (byte 2).**

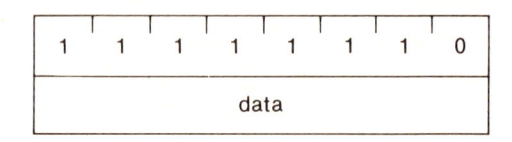

1	1	1	1	1	1	1	0
			data				

Cycles: 2
States: 7
Addressing: immediate
Flags: Z,S,P,CY,AC

RLC (Rotate left)
(A_{n+1}) ← (A_n) ; (A_0) ← (A_7)
(CY) ← (A_7)
The content of the accumulator is rotated left one position. The low order bit and the CY flag are both set to the value shifted out of the high order bit position. **Only the CY flag is affected.**

0	0	0	0	0	1	1	1

Cycles: 1
States: 4
Flags: CY

*All mnemonics copyrighted ©Intel Corporation 1976.

THE INSTRUCTION SET

RRC (Rotate right)
$(A_n) \leftarrow (A_{n+1}); (A_7) \leftarrow (A_0)$
$(CY) \leftarrow (A_0)$
The content of the accumulator is rotated right one position. The high order bit and the CY flag are both set to the value shifted out of the low order bit position. **Only the CY flag is affected.**

| 0 | 0 | 0 | 0 | 1 | 1 | 1 | 1 |

    Cycles: 1
    States: 4
    Flags: CY

RAL (Rotate left through carry)
$(A_{n+1}) \leftarrow (A_n); (CY) \leftarrow (A_7)$
$(A_0) \leftarrow (CY)$
The content of the accumulator is rotated left one position through the CY flag. The low order bit is set equal to the CY flag and the CY flag is set to the value shifted out of the high order bit. **Only the CY flag is affected.**

| 0 | 0 | 0 | 1 | 0 | 1 | 1 | 1 |

    Cycles: 1
    States: 4
    Flags: CY

RAR (Rotate right through carry)
$(A_n) \leftarrow (A_{n+1}); (CY) \leftarrow (A_0)$
$(A_7) \leftarrow (CY)$
The content of the accumulator is rotated right one position through the CY flag. The high order bit is set to the CY flag and the CY flag is set to the value shifted out of the low order bit. **Only the CY flag is affected.**

| 0 | 0 | 0 | 1 | 1 | 1 | 1 | 1 |

    Cycles: 1
    States: 4
    Flags: CY

*All mnemonics copyrighted © Intel Corporation 1976.

CMA (Complement accumulator)
$(A) \leftarrow (\overline{A})$
The contents of the accumulator are complemented (zero bits become 1, one bits become 0). **No flags are affected.**

| 0 | 0 | 1 | 0 | 1 | 1 | 1 | 1 |

    Cycles: 1
    States: 4
    Flags: none

CMC (Complement carry)
$(CY) \leftarrow (\overline{CY})$
The CY flag is complemented. **No other flags are affected.**

| 0 | 0 | 1 | 1 | 1 | 1 | 1 | 1 |

    Cycles: 1
    States: 4
    Flags: CY

STC (Set carry)
$(CY) \leftarrow 1$
The CY flag is set to 1. **No other flags are affected.**

| 0 | 0 | 1 | 1 | 0 | 1 | 1 | 1 |

    Cycles: 1
    States: 4
    Flags: CY

THE INSTRUCTION SET

5.6.4 Branch Group

This group of instructions alter normal sequential program flow.

Condition flags are not affected by any instruction in this group.

The two types of branch instructions are unconditional and conditional. Unconditional transfers simply perform the specified operation on register PC (the program counter). Conditional transfers examine the status of one of the four processor flags to determine if the specified branch is to be executed. The conditions that may be specified are as follows:

CONDITION		CCC
NZ —	not zero (Z = 0)	000
Z —	zero (Z = 1)	001
NC —	no carry (CY = 0)	010
C —	carry (CY = 1)	011
PO —	parity odd (P = 0)	100
PE —	parity even (P = 1)	101
P —	plus (S = 0)	110
M —	minus (S = 1)	111

JMP addr (Jump)
(PC) ← (byte 3) (byte 2)
Control is transferred to the instruction whose address is specified in byte 3 and byte 2 of the current instruction.

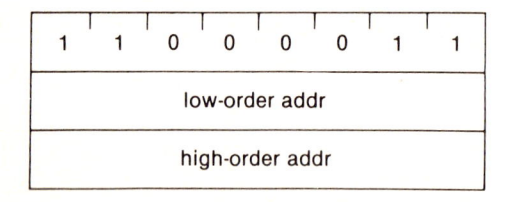

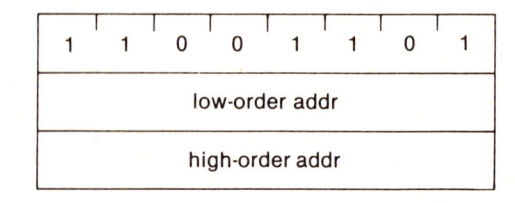

1	1	0	0	0	0	1	1
low-order addr								
high-order addr								

Cycles: 3
States: 10
Addressing: immediate
Flags: none

Jcondition addr (Conditional jump)
If (CCC),
(PC) ← (byte 3) (byte 2)
If the specified condition is true, control is transferred to the instruction whose address is specified in byte 3 and byte 2 of the current instruciton; otherwise, control continues sequentially.

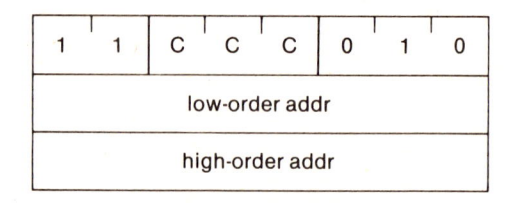

1	1	C	C	C	0	1	0
low-order addr								
high-order addr								

Cycles: 2/3 (8085), 3 (8080)
States: 7/10 (8085), 10 (8080)
Addressing: immediate
Flags: none

CALL addr (Call)
((SP) − 1) ← (PCH)
((SP) − 2) ← (PCL)
(SP) ← (SP) − 2
(PC) ← (byte 3) (byte 2)
The high-order eight bits of the next instruction address are moved to the memory location whose address is one less than the content of register SP. The low-order eight bits of the next instruction address are moved to the memory location whose address is two less than the content of register SP. The content of register SP is decremented by 2. Control is transferred to the instruction whose address is specified in byte 3 and byte 2 of the current instruction.

1	1	0	0	1	1	0	1
low-order addr								
high-order addr								

Cycles: 5
States: 18 (8085), 17 (8080)
Addressing: immediate/reg. indirect
Flags: none

*All mnemonics copyrighted © Intel Corporation 1976.

THE INSTRUCTION SET

Ccondition addr   (Condition call)
If   (CCC),
   ((SP) − 1) ← (PCH)
   ((SP) − 2) ← (PCL)
   (SP) ← (SP) − 2
   (PC) ← (byte 3) (byte 2)
If the specified condition is true, the actions specified in the CALL instruction (see above) are performed; otherwise, control continues sequentially.

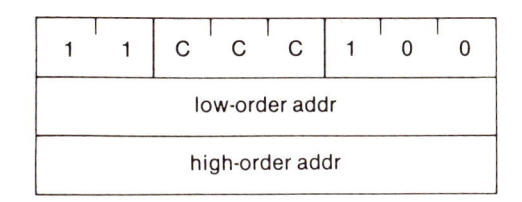

1	1	C	C	C	1	0	0
low-order addr							
high-order addr							

   Cycles: 2/5 (8085), 3/5 (8080)
   States: 9/18 (8085), 11/17 (8080)
Addressing: immediate/ reg. indirect
    Flags: none

RET   (Return)
(PCL) ← ((SP));
(PCH) ← ((SP) + 1);
(SP) ← (SP) + 2;
The content of the memory location whose address is specified in register SP is moved to the low-order eight bits of register PC. The content of the memory location whose address is one more than the content of register SP is moved to the high-order eight bits of register PC. The content of register SP is incremented by 2.

1	1	0	0	1	0	0	1

   Cycles: 3
   States: 10
Addressing: reg. indirect
    Flags: none

Rcondition   (Conditional return)
If   (CCC),
   (PCL) ← ((SP))
   (PCH) ← ((SP) + 1)
   (SP) ← (SP) + 2
If the specified condition is true, the actions specified in the RET instruction (see above) are performed; otherwise, control continues sequentially.

1	1	C	C	C	0	0	0

   Cycles: 1/3
   States: 6/12 (8085), 5/11 (8080)
Addressing: reg. indirect
    Flags: none

RST n   (Restart)
((SP) − 1) ← (PCH)
((SP) − 2) ← (PCL)
(SP) ← (SP) − 2
(PC) ← 8 * (NNN)
The high-order eight bits of the next instruction address are moved to the memory location whose address is one less than the content of register SP. The low-order eight bits of the next instruction address are moved to the memory location whose address is two less than the content of register SP. The content of register SP is decremented by two. Control is transferred to the instruction whose address is eight times the content of NNN.

1	1	N	N	N	1	1	1

   Cycles: 3
   States: 12 (8085), 11 (8080)
Addressing: reg. indirect
    Flags: none

15	14	13	12	11	10	9	8	7	6	5	4	3	2	1	0
0	0	0	0	0	0	0	0	0	0	N	N	N	0	0	0

Program Counter After Restart

---

*All mnemonics copyrighted © Intel Corporation 1976.

THE INSTRUCTION SET

PCHL (Jump H and L indirect — move H and L to PC)
(PCH) ← (H)
(PCL) ← (L)
The content of register H is moved to the high-order eight bits of register PC. The content of register L is moved to the low-order eight bits of register PC.

1	1	1	0	1	0	0	1

Cycles: 1
States: 6 (8085), 5 (8080)
Addressing: register
Flags: none

5.6.5 Stack, I/O, and Machine Control Group

This group of instructions performs I/O, manipulates the Stack, and alters internal control flags.

Unless otherwise specified, **condition flags are not affected by any instructions in this group.**

PUSH rp (Push)
((SP) − 1) ← (rh)
((SP) − 2) ← (rl)
(SP) ← (SP) − 2

The content of the high-order register of register pair rp is moved to the memory location whose address is one less than the content of register SP. The content of the low-order register of register pair rp is moved to the memory location whose address is two less than the content of register SP. The content of register SP is decremented by 2. **Note: Register pair rp = SP may not be specified.**

1	1	R	P	0	1	0	1

Cycles: 3
States: 12 (8085), 11 (8080)
Addressing: reg. indirect
Flags: none

PUSH PSW (Push processor status word)
((SP) − 1) ← (A)
((SP) − 2)$_0$ ← (CY), ((SP) − 2)$_1$ ← X
((SP) − 2)$_2$ ← (P), ((SP) − 2)$_3$ ← X
((SP) − 2)$_4$ ← (AC), ((SP) − 2)$_5$ ← X
((SP) − 2)$_6$ ← (Z), ((SP) − 2)$_7$ ← (S)
(SP) ← (SP) − 2   X: Undefined.

The content of register A is moved to the memory location whose address is one less than register SP. The contents of the condition flags are assembled into a processor status word and the word is moved to the memory location whose address is two less than the content of register SP. The content of register SP is decremented by two.

1	1	1	1	0	1	0	1

Cycles: 3
States: 12 (8085), 11 (8080)
Addressing: reg. indirect
Flags: none

FLAG WORD

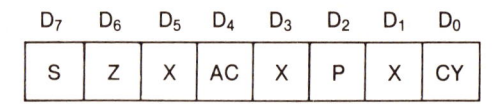

D$_7$	D$_6$	D$_5$	D$_4$	D$_3$	D$_2$	D$_1$	D$_0$
S	Z	X	AC	X	P	X	CY

X: undefined

POP rp (Pop)
(rl) ← ((SP))
(rh) ← ((SP) + 1)
(SP) ← (SP) + 2

The content of the memory location, whose address is specified by the content of register SP, is moved to the low-order register of register pair rp. The content of the memory location, whose address is one more than the content of register SP, is moved to the high-order register of register rp. The content of register SP is incremented by 2. **Note: Register pair rp = SP may not be specified.**

1	1	R	P	0	0	0	1

Cycles: 3
States: 10
Addressing: reg.indirect
Flags: none

*All mnemonics copyrighted © Intel Corporation 1976.

THE INSTRUCTION SET

POP PSW   (Pop processor status word)
(CY) ← ((SP))$_0$
(P) ← ((SP))$_2$
(AC) ← ((SP))$_4$
(Z) ← ((SP))$_6$
(S) ← ((SP))$_7$
(A) ← ((SP) + 1)
(SP) ← (SP) + 2

The content of the memory location whose address is specified by the content of register SP is used to restore the condition flags. The content of the memory location whose address is one more than the content of register SP is moved to register A. The content of register SP is incremented by 2.

| 1 | 1 | 1 | 1 | 0 | 0 | 0 | 1 |

      Cycles: 3
      States: 10
Addressing: reg. indirect
       Flags: Z,S,P,CY,AC

XTHL   (Exchange stack top with H and L)
(L) ↔ ((SP))
(H) ↔ ((SP) + 1)

The content of the L register is exchanged with the content of the memory location whose address is specified by the content of register SP. The content of the H register is exchanged with the content of the memory location whose address is one more than the content of register SP.

| 1 | 1 | 1 | 0 | 0 | 0 | 1 | 1 |

      Cycles: 5
      States: 16 (8085), 18 (8080)
Addressing: reg. indirect
       Flags: none

SPHL   (Move HL to SP)
(SP) ← (H) (L)
The contents of registers H and L (16 bits) are moved to register SP.

| 1 | 1 | 1 | 1 | 1 | 0 | 0 | 1 |

      Cycles: 1
      States: 6 (8085), 5 (8080)
Addressing: register
       Flags: none

IN port   (Input)
(A) ← (data)
The data placed on the eight bit bi-directional data bus by the specified port is moved to register A.

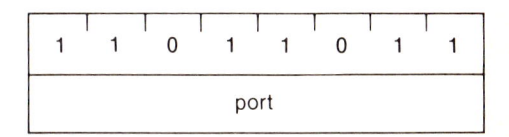

| 1 | 1 | 0 | 1 | 1 | 0 | 1 | 1 |
| port |

      Cycles: 3
      States: 10
Addressing: direct
       Flags: none

OUT port   (Output)
(data) ← (A)
The content of register A is placed on the eight bit bi-directional data bus for transmission to the specified port.

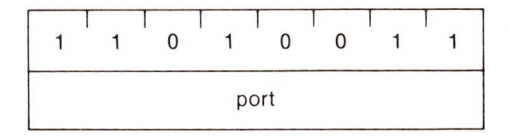

| 1 | 1 | 0 | 1 | 0 | 0 | 1 | 1 |
| port |

      Cycles: 3
      States: 10
Addressing: direct
       Flags: none

*All mnemonics copyrighted © Intel Corporation 1976.

THE INSTRUCTION SET

EI (Enable interrupts)
The interrupt system is enabled **following the execution of the next instruction.** Interrupts are not recognized during the EI instruction.

1	1	1	1	1	0	1	1

    Cycles: 1
    States: 4
    Flags: none

NOTE: Placing an EI instruction on the bus in response to INTA during an INA cycle is prohibited. (8085)

DI (Disable interrupts)
The interrupt system is disabled **immediately following the execution of the DI instruction.** Interrupts are not recognized during the DI instruction.

1	1	1	1	0	0	1	1

    Cycles: 1
    States: 4
    Flags: none

NOTE: Placing a DI instruction on the bus in response to INTA during an INA cycle is prohibited. (8085)

HLT (Halt)
The processor is stopped. The registers and flags are unaffected. (8080) A second ALE is generated during the execution of HLT to strobe out the Halt cycle status information. (8085)

0	1	1	1	0	1	1	0

    Cycles: 1+ (8085), 1 (8080)
    States: 5 (8085), 7 (8080)
    Flags: none

NOP (No op)
No operation is performed. The registers and flags are unaffected.

0	0	0	0	0	0	0	0

    Cycles: 1
    States: 4
    Flags: none

RIM (Read Interrupt Masks) (8085 only)
The RIM instruction loads data into the accumulator relating to interrupts and the serial input. This data contains the following information:

- Current interrupt mask status for the RST 5.5, 6.5, and 7.5 hardware interrupts (1 = mask disabled)
- Current interrupt enable flag status (1 = interrupts enabled) except immediately following a TRAP interrupt. (See below.)
- Hardware interrupts pending (i.e., signal received but not yet serviced), on the RST 5.5, 6.5, and 7.5 lines.
- Serial input data.

Immediately following a TRAP interrupt, the RIM instruction must be executed as a part of the service routine if you need to retrieve current interrupt status later. Bit 3 of the accumulator is (in this special case only) loaded with the interrupt enable (IE) flag status that existed prior to the TRAP interrupt. Following an RST 5.5, 6.5, 7.5, or INTR interrupt, the interrupt flag flip-flop reflects the current interrupt enable status. Bit 6 of the accumulator (I7.5) is loaded with the status of the RST 7.5 flip-flop, which is always set (edge-triggered) by an input on the RST 7.5 input line, even when that interrupt has been previously masked. (See SIM Instruction.)

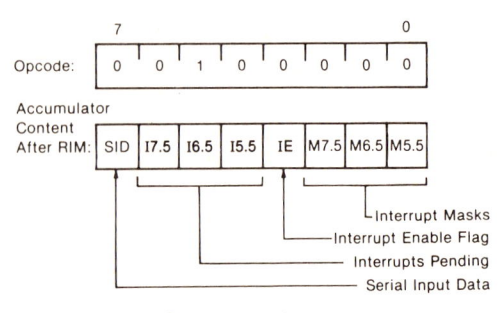

Opcode:

7							0
0	0	1	0	0	0	0	0

Accumulator Content After RIM:

SID	I7.5	I6.5	I5.5	IE	M7.5	M6.5	M5.5

                                   └─ Interrupt Masks
                                ── Interrupt Enable Flag
                           ── Interrupts Pending
                 ── Serial Input Data

    Cycles: 1
    States: 4
    Flags: none

*All mnemonics copyrighted © Intel Corporation 1976.

THE INSTRUCTION SET

SIM   (Set Interrupt Masks) (8085 only)

The execution of the SIM instruction uses the contents of the accumulator (which must be previously loaded) to perform the following functions:

- Program the interrupt mask for the RST 5.5, 6.5, and 7.5 hardware interrupts.
- Reset the edge-triggered RST 7.5 input latch.
- Load the SOD output latch.

To program the interrupt masks, first set accumulator bit 3 to 1 and set to 1 any bits 0, 1, and 2, which disable interrupts RST 5.5, 6.5, and 7.5, respectively. Then do a SIM instruction. If accumulator bit 3 is 0 when the SIM instruction is executed, the interrupt mask register will not change. If accumulator bit 4 is 1 when the SIM instruction is executed, the RST 7.5 latch is then reset. RST 7.5 is distinguished by the fact that its latch is always set by a rising edge on the RST 7.5 input pin, even if the jump to service routine is inhibited by masking. This latch remains high until cleared by a RESET IN, by a SIM Instruction with accumulator bit 4 high, or by an internal processor acknowledge to an RST 7.5 interrupt subsequent to the removal of the mask (by a SIM instruction). The RESET IN signal always sets all three RST mask bits.

If accumulator bit 6 is at the 1 level when the SIM instruction is executed, the state of accumulator bit 7 is loaded into the SOD latch and thus becomes available for interface to an external device. The SOD latch is unaffected by the SIM instruction if bit 6 is 0. SOD is always reset by the RESET IN signal.

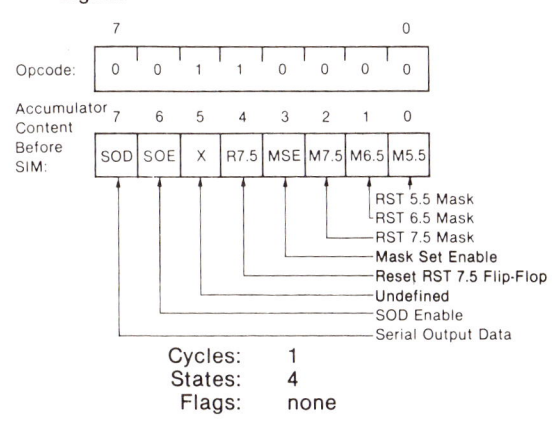

```
                    7                       0
Opcode:           | 0 | 0 | 1 | 1 | 0 | 0 | 0 | 0 |

Accumulator       7   6   5   4   3   2   1   0
Content
Before            |SOD|SOE| X |R7.5|MSE|M7.5|M6.5|M5.5|
SIM:
                                           └─ RST 5.5 Mask
                                       └───── RST 6.5 Mask
                                   └───────── RST 7.5 Mask
                               └───────────── Mask Set Enable
                           └───────────────── Reset RST 7.5 Flip-Flop
                       └───────────────────── Undefined
                   └───────────────────────── SOD Enable
               └───────────────────────────── Serial Output Data
```

    Cycles: 1
    States: 4
    Flags: none

---

*All mnemonics copyrighted © Intel Corporation 1976.

8085A

8080A/8085A INSTRUCTION SET INDEX
Table 5-1

Instruction		Code	Bytes	T States 8085A	T States 8080A	Machine Cycles
ACI	DATA	CE data	2	7	7	F R
ADC	REG	1000 1SSS	1	4	4	F
ADC	M	8E	1	7	7	F R
ADD	REG	1000 0SSS	1	4	4	F
ADD	M	86	1	7	7	F R
ADI	DATA	C6 data	2	7	7	F R
ANA	REG	1010 0SSS	1	4	4	F
ANA	M	A6	1	7	7	F R
ANI	DATA	E6 data	2	7	7	F R
CALL	LABEL	CD addr	3	18	17	S R R W W*
CC	LABEL	DC addr	3	9/18	11/17	S R•/S R R W W*
CM	LABEL	FC addr	3	9/18	11/17	S R•/S R R W W*
CMA		2F	1	4	4	F
CMC		3F	1	4	4	F
CMP	REG	1011 1SSS	1	4	4	F
CMP	M	BE	1	7	7	F R
CNC	LABEL	D4 addr	3	9/18	11/17	S R•/S R R W W*
CNZ	LABEL	C4 addr	3	9/18	11/17	S R•/S R R W W*
CP	LABEL	F4 addr	3	9/18	11/17	S R•/S R R W W*
CPE	LABEL	EC addr	3	9/18	11/17	S R•/S R R W W*
CPI	DATA	FE data	2	7	7	F R
CPO	LABEL	E4 addr	3	9/18	11/17	S R•/S R R W W*
CZ	LABEL	CC addr	3	9/18	11/17	S R•/S R R W W*
DAA		27	1	4	4	F
DAD	RP	00RP 1001	1	10	10	F B B
DCR	REG	00SS S101	1	4	5	F*
DCR	M	35	1	10	10	F R W
DCX	RP	00RP 1011	1	6	5	S*
DI		F3	1	4	4	F
EI		FB	1	4	4	F
HLT		76	1	5	7	F B
IN	PORT	DB data	2	10	10	F R I
INR	REG	00SS S100	1	4	5	F*
INR	M	34	1	10	10	F R W
INX	RP	00RP 0011	1	6	5	S*
JC	LABEL	DA addr	3	7/10	10	F R/F R R†
JM	LABEL	FA addr	3	7/10	10	F R/F R R†
JMP	LABEL	C3 addr	3	10	10	F R R
JNC	LABEL	D2 addr	3	7/10	10	F R/F R R†
JNZ	LABEL	C2 addr	3	7/10	10	F R/F R R†
JP	LABEL	F2 addr	3	7/10	10	F R/F R R†
JPE	LABEL	EA addr	3	7/10	10	F R/F R R†
JPO	LABEL	E2 addr	3	7/10	10	F R/F R R†
JZ	LABEL	CA addr	3	7/10	10	F R/F R R†
LDA	ADDR	3A addr	3	13	13	F R R R
LDAX	RP	000X 1010	1	7	7	F R
LHLD	ADDR	2A addr	3	16	16	F R R R R

Instruction		Code	Bytes	T States 8085A	T States 8080A	Machine Cycles
LXI	RP,DATA16	00RP 0001 data16	3	10	10	F R R
MOV	REG,REG	01DD DSSS	1	4	5	F*
MOV	M,REG	0111 0SSS	1	7	7	F W
MOV	REG,M	01DD D110	1	7	7	F R
MVI	REG,DATA	00DD D110 data	2	7	7	F R
MVI	M,DATA	36 data	2	10	10	F R W
NOP		00	1	4	4	F
ORA	REG	1011 0SSS	1	4	4	F
ORA	M	B6	1	7	7	F R
ORI	DATA	F6 data	2	7	7	F R
OUT	PORT	D3 data	2	10	10	F R O
PCHL		E9	1	6	5	S*
POP	RP	11RP 0001	1	10	10	F R R
PUSH	RP	11RP 0101	1	12	11	S W W*
RAL		17	1	4	4	F
RAR		1F	1	4	4	F
RC		D8	1	6/12	5/11	S/S R R*
RET		C9	1	10	10	F R R
RIM (8085A only)		20	1	4	—	F
RLC		07	1	4	4	F
RM		F8	1	6/12	5/11	S/S R R*
RNC		D0	1	6/12	5/11	S/S R R*
RNZ		C0	1	6/12	5/11	S/S R R*
RP		F0	1	6/12	5/11	S/S R R*
RPE		E8	1	6/12	5/11	S/S R R*
RPO		E0	1	6/12	5/11	S/S R R*
RRC		0F	1	4	4	F
RST	N	11XX X111	1	12	11	S W W*
RZ		C8	1	6/12	5/11	S/S R R*
SBB	REG	1001 1SSS	1	4	4	F
SBB	M	9E	1	7	7	F R
SBI	DATA	DE data	2	7	7	F R
SHLD	ADDR	22 addr	3	16	16	F R R W W
SIM (8085A only)		30	1	4	—	F
SPHL		F9	1	6	5	S*
STA	ADDR	32 addr	3	13	13	F R R W
STAX	RP	000X 0010	1	7	7	F W
STC		37	1	4	4	F
SUB	REG	1001 0SSS	1	4	4	F
SUB	M	96	1	7	7	F R
SUI	DATA	D6 data	2	7	7	F R
XCHG		EB	1	4	4	F
XRA	REG	1010 1SSS	1	4	4	F
XRA	M	AE	1	7	7	F R
XRI	DATA	EE data	2	7	7	F R
XTHL		E3	1	16	18	F R R W W

Machine cycle types:
- F Four clock period instr fetch
- S Six clock period instr fetch
- R Memory read
- I I/O read
- W Memory write
- O I/O write
- B Bus idle
- X Variable or optional binary digit
- DDD Binary digits identifying a destination register   B = 000, C = 001, D = 010 Memory = 110
- SSS Binary digits identifying a source register   E = 011, H = 100, L = 101 A = 111
- RP Register Pair   BC = 00, HL = 10
                     DE = 01, SP = 11

*Five clock period instruction fetch with 8080A.
†The longer machine cycle sequence applies regardless of condition evaluation with 8080A.
•An extra READ cycle (R) will occur for this condition with 8080A.

*All mnemonics copyrighted © Intel Corporation 1976.

8085A CPU INSTRUCTIONS IN OPERATION CODE SEQUENCE
Table 5-2

OP CODE	MNEMONIC	OP CODE	MNEMONIC	OP CODE	MNEMONIC	OP CODE	MNEMONIC	OP CODE	MNEMONIC	OP CODE	MNEMONIC
00	NOP	2B	DCX H	56	MOV D,M	81	ADD C	AC	XRA H	D7	RST 2
01	LXI B,D16	2C	INR L	57	MOV D,A	82	ADD D	AD	XRA L	D8	RC
02	STAX B	2D	DCR L	58	MOV E,B	83	ADD E	AE	XRA M	D9	–
03	INX B	2E	MVI L,D8	59	MOV E,C	84	ADD H	AF	XRA A	DA	JC Adr
04	INR B	2F	CMA	5A	MOV E,D	85	ADD L	B0	ORA B	DB	IN D8
05	DCR B	30	SIM	5B	MOV E,E	86	ADD M	B1	ORA C	DC	CC Adr
06	MVI B,D8	31	LXI SP,D16	5C	MOV E,H	87	ADD A	B2	ORA D	DD	–
07	RLC	32	STA Adr	5D	MOV E,L	88	ADC B	B3	ORA E	DE	SBI D8
08	–	33	INX SP	5E	MOV E,M	89	ADC C	B4	ORA H	DF	RST 3
09	DAD B	34	INR M	5F	MOV E,A	8A	ADC D	B5	ORA L	E0	RPO
0A	LDAX B	35	DCR M	60	MOV H,B	8B	ADC E	B6	ORA M	E1	POP H
0B	DCX B	36	MVI M,D8	61	MOV H,C	8C	ADC H	B7	ORA A	E2	JPO Adr
0C	INR C	37	STC	62	MOV H,D	8D	ADC L	B8	CMP B	E3	XTHL
0D	DCR C	38	–	63	MOV H,E	8E	ADC M	B9	CMP C	E4	CPO Adr
0E	MVI C,D8	39	DAD SP	64	MOV H,H	8F	ADC A	BA	CMP D	E5	PUSH H
0F	RRC	3A	LDA Adr	65	MOV H,L	90	SUB B	BB	CMP E	E6	ANI D8
10	–	3B	DCX SP	66	MOV H,M	91	SUB C	BC	CMP H	E7	RST 4
11	LXI D,D16	3C	INR A	67	MOV H,A	92	SUB D	BD	CMP L	E8	RPE
12	STAX D	3D	DCR A	68	MOV L,B	93	SUB E	BE	CMP M	E9	PCHL
13	INX D	3E	MVI A,D8	69	MOV L,C	94	SUB H	BF	CMP A	EA	JPE Adr
14	INR D	3F	CMC	6A	MOV L,D	95	SUB L	C0	RNZ	EB	XCHG
15	DCR D	40	MOV B,B	6B	MOV L,E	96	SUB M	C1	POP B	EC	CPE Adr
16	MVI D,D8	41	MOV B,C	6C	MOV L,H	97	SUB A	C2	JNZ Adr	ED	–
17	RAL	42	MOV B,D	6D	MOV L,L	98	SBB B	C3	JMP Adr	EE	XRI D8
18	–	43	MOV B,E	6E	MOV L,M	99	SBB C	C4	CNZ Adr	EF	RST 5
19	DAD D	44	MOV B,H	6F	MOV L,A	9A	SBB D	C5	PUSH B	F0	RP
1A	LDAX D	45	MOV B,L	70	MOV M,B	9B	SBB E	C6	ADI D8	F1	POP PSW
1B	DCX D	46	MOV B,M	71	MOV M,C	9C	SBB H	C7	RST 0	F2	JP Adr
1C	INR E	47	MOV B,A	72	MOV M,D	9D	SBB L	C8	RZ	F3	DI
1D	DCR E	48	MOV C,B	73	MOV M,E	9E	SBB M	C9	RET Adr	F4	CP Adr
1E	MVI E,D8	49	MOV C,C	74	MOV M,H	9F	SBB A	CA	JZ	F5	PUSH PSW
1F	RAR	4A	MOV C,D	75	MOV M,L	A0	ANA B	CB	–	F6	ORI D8
20	RIM	4B	MOV C,E	76	HLT	A1	ANA C	CC	CZ Adr	F7	RST 6
21	LXI H,D16	4C	MOV C,H	77	MOV M,A	A2	ANA D	CD	CALL Adr	F8	RM
22	SHLD Adr	4D	MOV C,L	78	MOV A,B	A3	ANA E	CE	ACI D8	F9	SPHL
23	INX H	4E	MOV C,M	79	MOV A,C	A4	ANA H	CF	RST 1	FA	JM Adr
24	INR H	4F	MOV C,A	7A	MOV A,D	A5	ANA L	D0	RNC	FB	EI
25	DCR H	50	MOV D,B	7B	MOV A,E	A6	ANA M	D1	POP D	FC	CM Adr
26	MVI H,D8	51	MOV D,C	7C	MOV A,H	A7	ANA A	D2	JNC Adr	FD	–
27	DAA	52	MOV D,D	7D	MOV A,L	A8	XRA B	D3	OUT D8	FE	CPI D8
28	–	53	MOV D,E	7E	MOV A,M	A9	XRA C	D4	CNC Adr	FF	RST 7
29	DAD H	54	MOV D,H	7F	MOV A,A	AA	XRA D	D5	PUSH D		
2A	LHLD Adr	55	MOV D,L	80	ADD B	AB	XRA E	D6	SUI D8		

D8 = constant, or logical/arithmetic expression that evaluates to an 8-bit data quantity.

Adr = 16-bit address.

D16 = constant, or logical/arithmetic expression that evaluates to a 16-bit data quantity.

*All mnemonics copyrighted © Intel Corporation 1976.

8085A

8085A INSTRUCTION SET SUMMARY BY FUNCTIONAL GROUPING
Table 5-3

Mnemonic	Description	D7	D6	D5	D4	D3	D2	D1	D0	Page
MOVE, LOAD, AND STORE										
MOV r1,r2	Move register to register	0	1	D	D	D	S	S	S	5-4
MOV M,r	Move register to memory	0	1	1	1	0	S	S	S	5-4
MOV r,M	Move memory to register	0	1	D	D	D	1	1	0	5-4
MVI r	Move immediate register	0	0	D	D	D	1	1	0	5-4
MVI M	Move immediate memory	0	0	1	1	0	1	1	0	5-4
LXI B	Load immediate register Pair B & C	0	0	0	0	0	0	0	1	5-5
LXI D	Load immediate register Pair D & E	0	0	0	1	0	0	0	1	5-5
LXI H	Load immediate register Pair H & L	0	0	1	0	0	0	0	1	5-5
STAX B	Store A indirect	0	0	0	0	0	0	1	0	5-6
STAX D	Store A indirect	0	0	0	1	0	0	1	0	5-6
LDAX B	Load A indirect	0	0	0	0	1	0	1	0	5-5
LDAX D	Load A indirect	0	0	0	1	1	0	1	0	5-5
STA	Store A direct	0	0	1	1	0	0	1	0	5-5
LDA	Load A direct	0	0	1	1	1	0	1	0	5-5
SHLD	Store H & L direct	0	0	1	0	0	0	1	0	5-5
LHLD	Load H & L direct	0	0	1	0	1	0	1	0	5-5
XCHG	Exchange D & E, H & L Registers	1	1	1	0	1	0	1	1	5-6
STACK OPS										
PUSH B	Push register Pair B & C on stack	1	1	0	0	0	1	0	1	5-15
PUSH D	Push register Pair D & E on stack	1	1	0	1	0	1	0	1	5-15
PUSH H	Push register Pair H & L on stack	1	1	1	0	0	1	0	1	5-15
PUSH PSW	Push A and Flags on stack	1	1	1	1	0	1	0	1	5-15
POP B	Pop register Pair B & C off stack	1	1	0	0	0	0	0	1	5-15
POP D	Pop register Pair D & E off stack	1	1	0	1	0	0	0	1	5-15
POP H	Pop register Pair H & L off stack	1	1	1	0	0	0	0	1	5-15
POP PSW	Pop A and Flags off stack	1	1	1	1	0	0	0	1	5-15
XTHL	Exchange top of stack, H & L	1	1	1	0	0	0	1	1	5-16
SPHL	H & L to stack pointer	1	1	1	1	1	0	0	1	5-16
LXI SP	Load immediate stack pointer	0	0	1	1	0	0	0	1	5-5
INX SP	Increment stack pointer	0	0	1	1	0	0	1	1	5-9
DCX SP	Decrement stack pointer	0	0	1	1	1	0	1	1	5-9
JUMP										
JMP	Jump unconditional	1	1	0	0	0	0	1	1	5-13
JC	Jump on carry	1	1	0	1	1	0	1	0	5-13
JNC	Jump on no carry	1	1	0	1	0	0	1	0	5-13
JZ	Jump on zero	1	1	0	0	1	0	1	0	5-13
JNZ	Jump on no zero	1	1	0	0	0	0	1	0	5-13
JP	Jump on positive	1	1	1	1	0	0	1	0	5-13
JM	Jump on minus	1	1	1	1	1	0	1	0	5-13
JPE	Jump on parity even	1	1	1	0	1	0	1	0	5-13
JPO	Jump on parity odd	1	1	1	0	0	0	1	0	5-13
PCHL	H & L to program counter	1	1	1	0	1	0	0	1	5-15
CALL										
CALL	Call unconditional	1	1	0	0	1	1	0	1	5-13
CC	Call on carry	1	1	0	1	1	1	0	0	5-14
CNC	Call on no carry	1	1	0	1	0	1	0	0	5-14

Mnemonic	Description	D7	D6	D5	D4	D3	D2	D1	D0	Page
CZ	Call on zero	1	1	0	0	1	1	0	0	5-14
CNZ	Call on no zero	1	1	0	0	0	1	0	0	5-14
CP	Call on positive	1	1	1	1	0	1	0	0	5-14
CM	Call on minus	1	1	1	1	1	1	0	0	5-14
CPE	Call on parity even	1	1	1	0	1	1	0	0	5-14
CPO	Call on parity odd	1	1	1	0	0	1	0	0	5-14
RETURN										
RET	Return	1	1	0	0	1	0	0	1	5-14
RC	Return on carry	1	1	0	1	1	0	0	0	5-14
RNC	Return on no carry	1	1	0	1	0	0	0	0	5-14
RZ	Return on zero	1	1	0	0	1	0	0	0	5-14
RNZ	Return on no zero	1	1	0	0	0	0	0	0	5-14
RP	Return on positive	1	1	1	1	0	0	0	0	5-14
RM	Return on minus	1	1	1	1	1	0	0	0	5-14
RPE	Return on parity even	1	1	1	0	1	0	0	0	5-14
RPO	Return on parity odd	1	1	1	0	0	0	0	0	5-14
RESTART										
RST	Restart	1	1	A	A	A	1	1	1	5-14
INPUT/OUTPUT										
IN	Input	1	1	0	1	1	0	1	1	5-16
OUT	Output	1	1	0	1	0	0	1	1	5-16
INCREMENT AND DECREMENT										
INR r	Increment register	0	0	D	D	D	1	0	0	5-8
DCR r	Decrement register	0	0	D	D	D	1	0	1	5-8
INR M	Increment memory	0	0	1	1	0	1	0	0	5-8
DCR M	Decrement memory	0	0	1	1	0	1	0	1	5-8
INX B	Increment B & C registers	0	0	0	0	0	0	1	1	5-9
INX D	Increment D & E registers	0	0	0	1	0	0	1	1	5-9
INX H	Increment H & L registers	0	0	1	0	0	0	1	1	5-9
DCX B	Decrement B & C	0	0	0	0	1	0	1	1	5-9
DCX D	Decrement D & E	0	0	0	1	1	0	1	1	5-9
DCX H	Decrement H & L	0	0	1	0	1	0	1	1	5-9
ADD										
ADD r	Add register to A	1	0	0	0	0	S	S	S	5-6
ADC r	Add register to A with carry	1	0	0	0	1	S	S	S	5-6
ADD M	Add memory to A	1	0	0	0	0	1	1	0	5-6
ADC M	Add memory to A with carry	1	0	0	0	1	1	1	0	5-7
ADI	Add immediate to A	1	1	0	0	0	1	1	0	5-6
ACI	Add immediate to A with carry	1	1	0	0	1	1	1	0	5-7
DAD B	Add B & C to H & L	0	0	0	0	1	0	0	1	5-9
DAD D	Add D & E to H & L	0	0	0	1	1	0	0	1	5-9
DAD H	Add H & L to H & L	0	0	1	0	1	0	0	1	5-9
DAD SP	Add stack pointer to H & L	0	0	1	1	1	0	0	1	5-9
SUBTRACT										
SUB r	Subtract register from A	1	0	0	1	0	S	S	S	5-7
SBB r	Subtract register from A with borrow	1	0	0	1	1	S	S	S	5-7
SUB M	Subtract memory from A	1	0	0	1	0	1	1	0	5-7
SBB M	Subtract memory from A with borrow	1	0	0	1	1	1	1	0	5-8
SUI	Subtract immediate from A	1	1	0	1	0	1	1	0	5-7

*All mnemonics copyrighted © Intel Corporation 1976.

8085A INSTRUCTION SET SUMMARY (Cont'd)
Table 5-3

Mnemonic	Description	D7	D6	D5	D4	D3	D2	D1	D0	Page
SBI	Subtract immediate from A with borrow	1	1	0	1	1	1	1	0	5-8
LOGICAL										
ANA r	And register with A	1	0	1	0	0	S	S	S	5-9
XRA r	Exclusive OR register with A	1	0	1	0	1	S	S	S	5-10
ORA r	OR register with A	1	0	1	1	0	S	S	S	5-10
CMP r	Compare register with A	1	0	1	1	1	S	S	S	5-11
ANA M	And memory with A	1	0	1	0	0	1	1	0	5-10
XRA M	Exclusive OR memory with A	1	0	1	0	1	1	1	0	5-10
ORA M	OR memory with A	1	0	1	1	0	1	1	0	5-11
CMP M	Compare memory with A	1	0	1	1	1	1	1	0	5-11
ANI	And immediate with A	1	1	1	0	0	1	1	0	5-10
XRI	Exclusive OR immediate with A	1	1	1	0	1	1	1	0	5-10
ORI	OR immediate with A	1	1	1	1	0	1	1	0	5-11
CPI	Compare immediate with A	1	1	1	1	1	1	1	0	5-11
ROTATE										
RLC	Rotate A left	0	0	0	0	0	1	1	1	5-11

Mnemonic	Description	D7	D6	D5	D4	D3	D2	D1	D0	Page
RRC	Rotate A right	0	0	0	0	1	1	1	1	5-12
RAL	Rotate A left through carry	0	0	0	1	0	1	1	1	5-12
RAR	Rotate A right through carry	0	0	0	1	1	1	1	1	5-12
SPECIALS										
CMA	Complement A	0	0	1	0	1	1	1	1	5-12
STC	Set carry	0	0	1	1	0	1	1	1	5-12
CMC	Complement carry	0	0	1	1	1	1	1	1	5-12
DAA	Decimal adjust A	0	0	1	0	0	1	1	1	5-9
CONTROL										
EI	Enable Interrupts	1	1	1	1	1	0	1	1	5-17
DI	Disable Interrupt	1	1	1	1	0	0	1	1	5-17
NOP	No-operation	0	0	0	0	0	0	0	0	5-17
HLT	Halt	0	1	1	1	0	1	1	0	5-17
NEW 8085A INSTRUCTIONS										
RIM	Read Interrupt Mask	0	0	1	0	0	0	0	0	5-17
SIM	Set Interrupt Mask	0	0	1	1	0	0	0	0	5-18

NOTES: 1. DDS or SSS: B 000, C 001, D 010, E 011, H 100, L 101, Memory 110, A 111.
2. Two possible cycle times. (6/12) indicate instruction cycles dependent on condition flags.

*All mnemonics copyrighted © Intel Corporation 1976.

APPENDIX B
THE INTEL 8279*

* Reprinted by permission of Intel Corporation, copyright © 1976.

intel

8279/8279-5
PROGRAMMABLE KEYBOARD/DISPLAY INTERFACE

- MCS-85™ Compatible 8279-5
- Simultaneous Keyboard Display Operations
- Scanned Keyboard Mode
- Scanned Sensor Mode
- Strobed Input Entry Mode
- 8-Character Keyboard FIFO
- 2-Key Lockout or N-Key Rollover with Contact Debounce

- Dual 8- or 16-Numerical Display
- Single 16-Character Display
- Right or Left Entry 16-Byte Display RAM
- Mode Programmable from CPU
- Programmable Scan Timing
- Interrupt Output on Key Entry

The Intel® 8279 is a general purpose programmable keyboard and display I/O interface device designed for use with Intel® microprocessors. The keyboard portion can provide a scanned interface to a 64-contact key matrix. The keyboard portion will also interface to an array of sensors or a strobed interface keyboard, such as the hall effect and ferrite variety. Key depressions can be 2-key lockout or N-key rollover. Keyboard entries are debounced and strobed in an 8-character FIFO. If more than 8 characters are entered, overrun status is set. Key entries set the interrupt output line to the CPU.

The display portion provides a scanned display interface for LED, incandescent, and other popular display technologies. Both numeric and alphanumeric segment displays may be used as well as simple indicators. The 8279 has 16x8 display RAM which can be organized into dual 16x4. The RAM can be loaded or interrogated by the CPU. Both right entry, calculator and left entry typewriter display formats are possible. Both read and write of the display RAM can be done with auto-increment of the display RAM address.

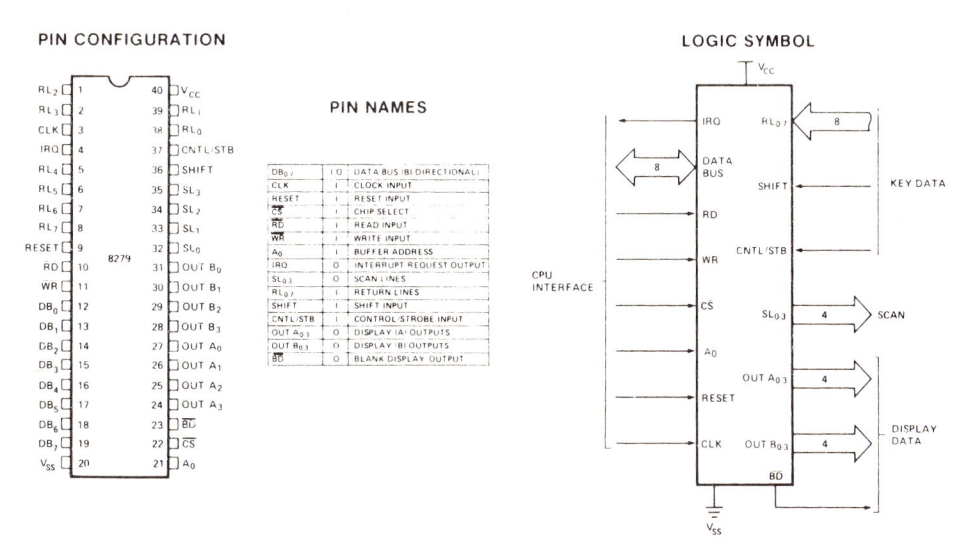

8279/8279-5

HARDWARE DESCRIPTION

The 8279 is packaged in a 40 pin DIP. The following is a functional description of each pin.

No. Of Pins	Designation	Function
8	DB$_0$-DB$_7$	Bi-directional data bus. All data and commands between the CPU and the 8279 are transmitted on these lines.
1	CLK	Clock from system used to generate internal timing.
1	RESET	A high signal on this pin resets the 8279. After being reset the 8279 is placed in the following mode: 1) 16 8-bit character display —left entry. 2) Encoded scan keyboard—2 key lockout. Along with this the program clock prescaler is set to 31.
1	$\overline{CS}$	Chip Select. A low on this pin enables the interface functions to receive or transmit.
1	A$_0$	Buffer Address. A high on this line indicates the signals in or out are interpreted as a command or status. A low indicates that they are data.
2	$\overline{RD}$, $\overline{WR}$	Input/Output read and write. These signals enable the data buffers to either send data to the external bus or receive it from the external bus.
1	IRQ	Interrupt Request. In a keyboard mode, the interrupt line is high when there is data in the FIFO/Sensor RAM. The interrupt line goes low with each FIFO/Sensor RAM read and returns high if there is still information in the RAM. In a sensor mode, the interrupt line goes high whenever a change in a sensor is detected.
2	V$_{SS}$, V$_{CC}$	Ground and power supply pins.
4	SL$_0$-SL$_3$	Scan Lines which are used to scan the key switch or sensor matrix and the display digits. These lines can be either encoded (1 of 16) or decoded (1 of 4).
8	RL$_0$-RL$_7$	Return line inputs which are connected to the scan lines through the keys or sensor switches. They have active internal pullups to keep them high until a switch closure pulls one low. They also serve as an 8-bit input in the Strobed Input mode.
1	SHIFT	The shift input status is stored along with the key position on key closure in the Scanned

No. Of Pins	Designation	Function
		Keyboard modes. It has an active internal pullup to keep it high until a switch closure pulls it low.
1	CNTL/STB	For keyboard modes this line is used as a control input and stored like status on a key closure. The line is also the strobe line that enters the data into the FIFO in the Strobed Input mode. (Rising Edge). It has an active internal pullup to keep it high until a switch closure pulls it low.
4	OUT A$_0$-OUT A$_3$	These two ports are the outputs for the 16 x 4 display refresh registers. The data from these outputs is synchronized to the scan lines (SL$_0$-SL$_3$) for multiplexed digit displays. The two 4 bit ports may be blanked independently. These two ports may also be considered as one 8 bit port.
4	OUT B$_0$-OUT B$_3$	
1	$\overline{BD}$	Blank Display. This output is used to blank the display during digit switching or by a display blanking command.

PRINCIPLES OF OPERATION

The following is a description of the major elements of the 8279 Programmable Keyboard/Display interface device. Refer to the block diagram in Figure 1.

I/O Control and Data Buffers

The I/O control section uses the $\overline{CS}$, A$_0$, $\overline{RD}$ and $\overline{WR}$ lines to control data flow to and from the various internal registers and buffers. All data flow to and from the 8279 is enabled by $\overline{CS}$. The character of the information, given or desired by the CPU, is identified by A$_0$. A logic one means the information is a command or status. A logic zero means the information is data. $\overline{RD}$ and $\overline{WR}$ determine the direction of data flow through the Data Buffers. The Data Buffers are bi-directional buffers that connect the internal bus to the external bus. When the chip is not selected ($\overline{CS}$ = 1), the devices are in a high impedance state. The drivers input during $\overline{WR} \cdot \overline{CS}$ and output during $\overline{RD} \cdot \overline{CS}$.

Control and Timing Registers and Timing Control

These registers store the keyboard and display modes and other operating conditions programmed by the CPU. The modes are programmed by presenting the proper command on the data lines with A$_0$ = 1 and then sending a $\overline{WR}$. The command is latched on the rising edge of $\overline{WR}$.

8279/8279-5

FUNCTIONAL DESCRIPTION

Since data input and display are an integral part of many microprocessor designs, the system designer needs an interface that can control these functions without placing a large load on the CPU. The 8279 provides this function for 8-bit microprocessors.

The 8279 has two sections: keyboard and display. The keyboard section can interface to regular typewriter style keyboards or random toggle or thumb switches. The display section drives alphanumeric displays or a bank of indicator lights. Thus the CPU is relieved from scanning the keyboard or refreshing the display.

The 8279 is designed to directly connect to the microprocessor bus. The CPU can program all operating modes for the 8279. These modes include:

Input Modes

- Scanned Keyboard — with encoded (8 x 8 key keyboard) or decoded (4 x 8 key keyboard) scan lines. A key depression generates a 6-bit encoding of key position. Position and shift and control status are stored in the FIFO. Keys are automatically debounced with 2-key lockout or N-key rollover.

- Scanned Sensor Matrix — with encoded (8 x 8 matrix switches) or decoded (4 x 8 matrix switches) scan lines. Key status (open or closed) stored in RAM addressable by CPU.

- Strobed Input — Data on return lines during control line strobe is transferred to FIFO.

Output Modes

- 8 or 16 character multiplexed displays that can be organized as dual 4-bit or single 8-bit ($B_0 = D_0$, $A_3 = D_7$).
- Right entry or left entry display formats.

Other features of the 8279 include:

- Mode programming from the CPU.
- Clock Prescaler
- Interrupt output to signal CPU when there is keyboard or sensor data available.
- An 8 byte FIFO to store keyboard information.
- 16 byte internal Display RAM for display refresh. This RAM can also be read by the CPU.

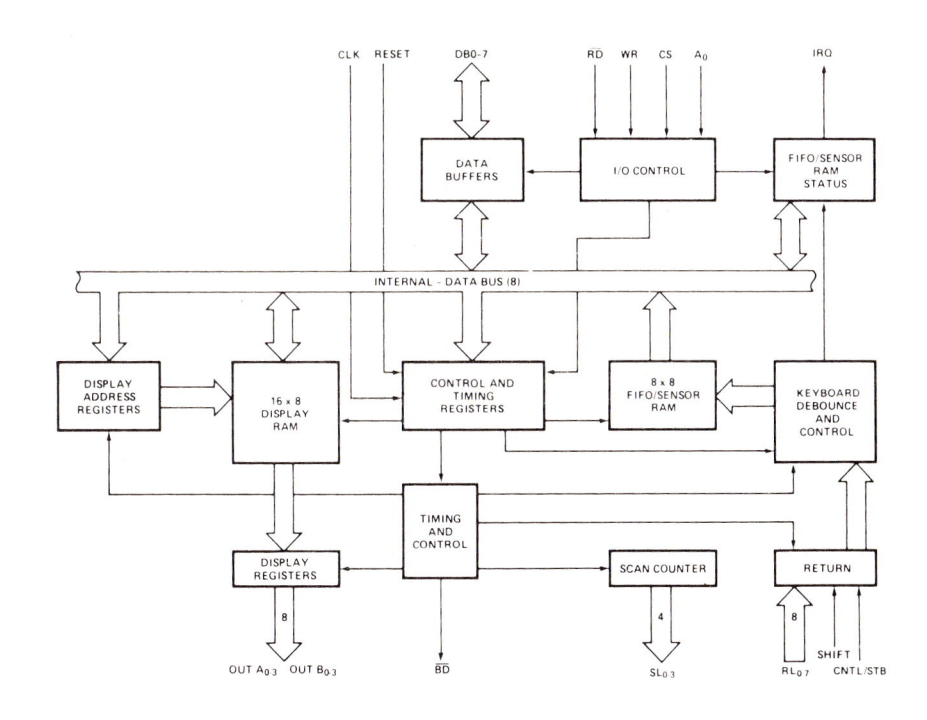

8279/8279-5

The command is then decoded and the appropriate function is set. The timing control contains the basic timing counter chain. The first counter is a ÷ N prescaler that can be programmed to yield an internal frequency of 100 kHz which gives a 5.1 ms keyboard scan time and a 10.3 ms debounce time. The other counters divide down the basic internal frequency to provide the proper key scan, row scan, keyboard matrix scan, and display scan times.

Scan Counter

The scan counter has two modes. In the encoded mode, the counter provides a binary count that must be externally decoded to provide the scan lines for the keyboard and display. In the decoded mode, the scan counter decodes the least significant 2 bits and provides a decoded 1 of 4 scan. Note than when the keyboard is in decoded scan, so is the display. This means that only the first 4 characters in the Display RAM are displayed.

In the encoded mode, the scan lines are active high outputs. In the decoded mode, the scan lines are active low outputs.

Return Buffers and Keyboard Debounce and Control

The 8 return lines are buffered and latched by the Return Buffers. In the keyboard mode, these lines are scanned, looking for key closures in that row. If the debounce circuit detects a closed switch, it waits about 10 msec to check if the switch remains closed. If it does, the address of the switch in the matrix plus the status of SHIFT and CONTROL are transferred to the FIFO. In the scanned Sensor Matrix modes, the contents of the return lines is directly transferred to the corresponding row of the Sensor RAM (FIFO) each key scan time. In Strobed Input mode, the contents of the return lines are transferred to the FIFO on the rising edge of the CNTL/STB line pulse.

FIFO/Sensor RAM and Status

This block is a dual function 8 x 8 RAM. In Keyboard or Strobed Input modes, it is a FIFO. Each new entry is written into successive RAM positions and each is then read in order of entry. FIFO status keeps track of the number of characters in the FIFO and whether it is full or empty. Too many reads or writes will be recognized as an error. The status can be read by an $\overline{RD}$ with $\overline{CS}$ low and A_0 high. The status logic also provides an IRQ signal when the FIFO is not empty. In Scanned Sensor Matrix mode, the memory is a Sensor RAM. Each row of the Sensor RAM is loaded with the status of the corresponding row of sensor in the sensor matrix. In this mode, IRQ is high if a change in a sensor is detected.

Display Address Registers and Display RAM

The Display Address Registers hold the address of the word currently being written or read by the CPU and the two 4-bit nibbles being displayed. The read/write addresses are programmed by CPU command. They also can be set to auto increment after each read or write. The Display RAM can be directly read by the CPU after the correct mode and address is set. The addresses for the A and B nibbles are automatically updated by the 8279 to match data entry by the CPU. The A and B nibbles can be entered independently or as one word, according to the mode that is set by the CPU. Data entry to the display can be set to either left or right entry. See Interface Considerations for details.

SOFTWARE OPERATION

8279 commands

The following commands program the 8279 operating modes. The commands are sent on the Data Bus with $\overline{CS}$ low and A_0 high and are loaded to the 8279 on the rising edge of $\overline{WR}$.

Keyboard/Display Mode Set

Code:

MSB							LSB
0	0	0	D	D	K	K	K

Where DD is the Display Mode and KKK is the Keyboard Mode.

DD

0 0 8 8-bit character display — Left entry
0 1 16 8-bit character display — Left entry*
1 0 8 8-bit character display — Right entry
1 1 16 8-bit character display — Right entry

For description of right and left entry, see Interface Considerations. Note that when decoded scan is set in keyboard mode, the display is reduced to 4 characters independent of display mode set.

KKK

0 0 0 Encoded Scan Keyboard — 2 Key Lockout*
0 0 1 Decoded Scan Keyboard — 2-Key Lockout
0 1 0 Encoded Scan Keyboard — N-Key Rollover
0 1 1 Decoded Scan Keyboard — N-Key Rollover
1 0 0 Encoded Scan Sensor Matrix
1 0 1 Decoded Scan Sensor Matrix
1 1 0 Strobed Input, Encoded Display Scan
1 1 1 Strobed Input, Decoded Display Scan

Program Clock

Code:

0	0	1	P	P	P	P	P

All timing and multiplexing signals for the 8279 are generated by an internal prescaler. This prescaler divides the external clock (pin 3) by a programmable integer. Bits PPPPP determine the value of this integer which ranges from 2 to 31. Choosing a divisor that yields 100 kHz will give the specified scan and debounce times. For instance, if Pin 3 of the 8279 is being clocked by a 2 MHz signal, PPPPP should be set to 10100 to divide the clock by 20 to yield the proper 100 kHz operating frequency.

Read FIFO/Sensor RAM

Code:

0	1	0	AI	X	A	A	A

X = Don't Care

The CPU sets up the 8279 for a read of the FIFO/Sensor RAM by first writing this command. In the Scan Key-

*Default after reset.

board Mode, the Auto-Increment flag (AI) and the RAM address bits (AAA) are irrelevant. The 8279 will automatically drive the data bus for each subsequent read ($A_0 = 0$) in the same sequence in which the data first entered the FIFO. All subsequent reads will be from the FIFO until another command is issued.

In the Sensor Matrix Mode, the RAM address bits AAA select one of the 8 rows of the Sensor RAM. If the AI flag is set (AI = 1), each successive read will be from the subsequent row of the sensor RAM.

Read Display RAM

Code: | 0 | 1 | 1 | AI | A | A | A | A |

The CPU sets up the 8279 for a read of the Display RAM by first writing this command. The address bits AAAA select one of the 16 rows of the Display RAM. If the AI flag is set (AI = 1), this row address will be incremented after each following read *or write* to the Display RAM. Since the same counter is used for both reading and writing, this command sets the next read *or write* address and the sense of the Auto-Increment mode for both operations.

Write Display RAM

Code: | 1 | 0 | 0 | AI | A | A | A | A |

The CPU sets up the 8279 for a write to the Display RAM by first writing this command. After writing the command with $A_0 = 1$, all subsequent writes with $A_0 = 0$ will be to the Display RAM. The addressing and Auto-Increment functions are identical to those for the Read Display RAM. However, this command does not affect the source of subsequent Data Reads; the CPU will read from whichever RAM (Display or FIFO/Sensor) which was last specified. If, indeed, the Display RAM was last specified, the Write Display RAM will, nevertheless, change the next Read location.

Display Write Inhibit/Blanking

The IW Bits can be used to mask nibble A and nibble B in applications requiring separate 4-bit display ports. By setting the IW flag (IW = 1) for one of the ports, the port becomes marked so that entries to the Display RAM from the CPU do not affect that port. Thus, if each nibble is input to a BCD decoder, the CPU may write a digit to the Display RAM without affecting the other digit being displayed. It is important to note that bit B_0 corresponds to bit D_0 on the CPU bus, and that bit A_3 corresponds to bit D_7.

If the user wishes to blank the display, the BL flags are available for each nibble. The last Clear command issued determines the code to be used as a "blank." This code defaults to all zeros after a reset. Note that both BL flags must be set to blank a display formatted with a single 8-bit port.

Clear

The C_D bits are available in this command to clear all rows of the Display RAM to a selectable blanking code as follows:

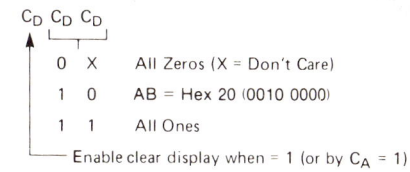

C_D C_D C_D

0 X   All Zeros (X = Don't Care)
1 0   AB = Hex 20 (0010 0000)
1 1   All Ones

Enable clear display when = 1 (or by C_A = 1)

During the time the Display RAM is being cleared (~160 μs), it may not be written to. The most significant bit of the FIFO status word is set during this time. When the Display RAM becomes available again, it automatically resets.

If the C_F bit is asserted ($C_F = 1$), the FIFO status is cleared and the interrupt output line is reset. Also, the Sensor RAM pointer is set to row 0.

C_A, the Clear All bit, has the combined effect of C_D and C_F; it uses the C_D clearing code on the Display RAM and also clears FIFO status. Furthermore, it resynchronizes the internal timing chain.

End Interrupt/Error Mode Set

Code: | 1 | 1 | 1 | E | X | X | X | X | X = Don't care.

For the sensor matrix modes this command lowers the IRQ line and enables further writing into RAM. (The IRQ line would have been raised upon the detection of a change in a sensor value. This would have also inhibited further writing into the RAM until reset).

For the N-key rollover mode — if the E bit is programmed to "1" the chip will operate in the special Error mode. (For further details, see Interface Considerations Section.)

Status Word

The status word contains the FIFO status, error, and display unavailable signals. This word is read by the CPU when A_0 is high and $\overline{CS}$ and $\overline{RD}$ are low. See Interface Considerations for more detail on status word.

Data Read

Data is read when A_0, $\overline{CS}$ and $\overline{RD}$ are all low. The source of the data is specified by the Read FIFO or Read Display commands. The trailing edge of $\overline{RD}$ will cause the address of the RAM being read to be incremented if the Auto-Increment flag is set. FIFO reads always increment (if no error occurs) independent of AI.

Data Write

Data that is written with A_0, $\overline{CS}$ and $\overline{WR}$ low is always written to the Display RAM. The address is specified by the latest Read Display or Write Display command. Auto-Incrementing on the rising edge of $\overline{WR}$ occurs if AI set by the latest display command.

8279/8279-5

INTERFACE CONSIDERATIONS

Scanned Keyboard Mode, 2-Key Lockout

There are three possible combinations of conditions that can occur during debounce scanning. When a key is depressed, the debounce logic is set. Other depressed keys are looked for during the next two scans. If none are encountered, it is a single key depression and the key position is entered into the FIFO along with the status of CNTL and SHIFT lines. If the FIFO was empty, IRQ will be set to signal the CPU that there is an entry in the FIFO. If the FIFO was full, the key will not be entered and the error flag will be set. If another closed switch is encountered, no entry to the FIFO can occur. If all other keys are released before this one, then it will be entered to the FIFO. If this key is released before any other, it will be entirely ignored. A key is entered to the FIFO only once per depression, no matter how many keys were pressed along with it or in what order they were released. If two keys are depressed within the debounce cycle, it is a simultaneous depression. Neither key will be recognized until one key remains depressed alone. The last key will be treated as a single key depression.

Scanned Keyboard Mode, N-Key Rollover

With N-key Rollover each key depression is treated independently from all others. When a key is depressed, the debounce circuit waits 2 keyboard scans and then checks to see if the key is still down. If it is, the key is entered into the FIFO. Any number of keys can be depressed and another can be recognized and entered into the FIFO. If a simultaneous depression occurs, the keys are recognized and entered according to the order the keyboard scan found them.

Scanned Keyboard — Special Error Modes

For N-key rollover mode the user can program a special error mode. This is done by the "End Interrupt/Error Mode Set" command. The debounce cycle and key-validity check are as in normal N-key mode. If during a single debounce cycle, two keys are found depressed, this is considered a simultaneous multiple depression, and sets an error flag. This flag will prevent any further writing into the FIFO and will set interrupt (if not yet set). The error flag could be read in this mode by reading the FIFO STATUS word. (See "FIFO STATUS" for further details.) The error flag is reset by sending the normal CLEAR command with $C_F = 1$.

Sensor Matrix Mode

In Sensor Matrix mode, the debounce logic is inhibited. The status of the sensor switch is inputted directly to the Sensor RAM. In this way the Sensor RAM keeps an image of the state of the switches in the sensor matrix. Although debouncing is not provided, this mode has the advantage that the CPU knows how long the sensor was closed and when it was released. A keyboard mode can only indicate a validated closure. To make the software easier, the designer should functionally group the sensors by row since this is the format in which the CPU will read them.

The IRQ line goes high if any sensor value change is detected at the end of a sensor matrix scan. The IRQ line is cleared by the first data read operation if the Auto-Increment flag is set to zero, or by the End Interrupt command if the Auto-Increment flag is set to one.

Note: Multiple changes in the matrix Addressed by ($SL_{0-3} = 0$) may cause multiple interrupts. ($SL_0 = 0$ in the Decoded Mode). Reset may cause the 8279 to see multiple changes.

Data Format

In the Scanned Keyboard mode, the character entered into the FIFO corresponds to the position of the switch in the keyboard plus the status of the CNTL and SHIFT lines (non-inverted). CNTL is the MSB of the character and SHIFT is the next most significant bit. The next three bits are from the scan counter and indicate the row the key was found in. The last three bits are from the column counter and indicate to which return line the key was connected.

MSB			LSB
CNTL	SHIFT	SCAN	RETURN

SCANNED KEYBOARD DATA FORMAT

In Sensor Matrix mode, the data on the return lines is entered directly in the row of the Sensor RAM that corresponds to the row in the matrix being scanned. Therefore, each switch position maps directly to a Sensor RAM position. The SHIFT and CNTL inputs are ignored in this mode. Note that switches are not necessarily the only thing that can be connected to the return lines in this mode. Any logic that can be triggered by the scan lines can enter data to the return line inputs. Eight multiplexed input ports could be tied to the return lines and scanned by the 8279.

MSB							LSB
RL_7	RL_6	RL_5	RL_4	RL_3	RL_2	RL_1	RL_0

In Strobed Input mode, the data is also entered to the FIFO from the return lines. The data is entered by the rising edge of a CNTL/STB line pulse. Data can come from another encoded keyboard or simple switch matrix. The return lines can also be used as a general purpose strobed input.

MSB							LSB
RL_7	RL_6	RL_5	RL_4	RL_3	RL_2	RL_1	RL_0

Display

Left Entry

Left Entry mode is the simplest display format in that each display position directly corresponds to a byte (or nibble) in the Display RAM. Address 0 in the RAM is the left-most display character and address 15 (or address 7 in 8 character display) is the right most display character. Entering characters from position zero causes the display to fill from the left. The 17th (9th) character is entered back in the left most position and filling again proceeds from there.

8279/8279-5

```
           0  1              14 15  ← Display
1st entry [ 1 |  |- - - - - |  |  ]   RAM Address

           0  1              14 15
2nd entry [ 1 | 2|- - - - - |  |  ]

           0  1              14 15
16th entry[ 1 | 2|- - - - - |15|16]

           0  1              14 15
17th entry[17| 2|- - - - - |15|16]

           0  1              14 15
18th entry[17|18|- - - - - |15|16]

       LEFT ENTRY MODE
       (AUTO INCREMENT)
```

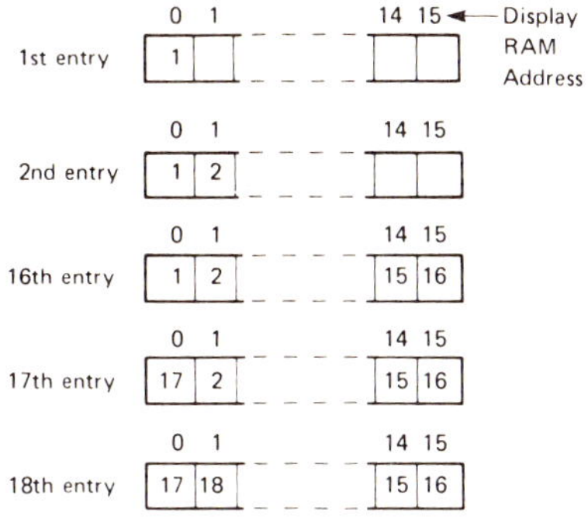

Right Entry

Right entry is the method used by most electronic calculators. The first entry is placed in the right most display character. The next entry is also placed in the right most character after the display is shifted left one character. The left most character is shifted off the end and is lost.

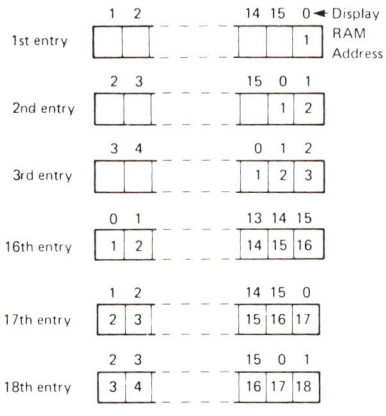

```
           1  2              14 15  0 ← Display
1st entry [  |  |- - - - - |  |  | 1]   RAM Address

           2  3              15  0  1
2nd entry [  |  |- - - - - |  | 1| 2]

           3  4               0  1  2
3rd entry [  |  |- - - - - | 1| 2| 3]

           0  1              13 14 15
16th entry[ 1| 2|- - - - - |14|15|16]

           1  2              14 15  0
17th entry[ 2| 3|- - - - - |15|16|17]

           2  3              15  0  1
18th entry[ 3| 4|- - - - - |16|17|18]

       RIGHT ENTRY MODE
       (AUTO INCREMENT)
```

Note that now the display position and register address do not correspond. Consequently, entering a character to an arbitrary position in the Auto Increment mode may have unexpected results. Entry starting at Display RAM address 0 with sequential entry is recommended.

Auto Increment

In the Left Entry mode, Auto Incrementing causes the address where the CPU will next write to be incremented by one and the character appears in the next location. With non-Auto Incrementing the entry is both to the same RAM address and display position. Entry to an arbitrary address in the Auto Increment mode has no undesirable side effects and the result is predictable:

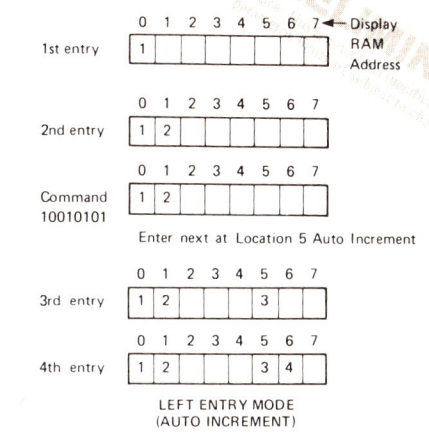

```
           0  1  2  3  4  5  6  7 ← Display
1st entry [ 1|  |  |  |  |  |  |  ]  RAM Address

           0  1  2  3  4  5  6  7
2nd entry [ 1| 2|  |  |  |  |  |  ]

Command    0  1  2  3  4  5  6  7
10010101  [ 1| 2|  |  |  |  |  |  ]
Enter next at Location 5 Auto Increment

           0  1  2  3  4  5  6  7
3rd entry [ 1| 2|  |  |  | 3|  |  ]

           0  1  2  3  4  5  6  7
4th entry [ 1| 2|  |  |  | 3| 4|  ]

       LEFT ENTRY MODE
       (AUTO INCREMENT)
```

In the Right Entry mode, Auto Incrementing and non Incrementing have the same effect as in the Left Entry except if the address sequence is interrupted:

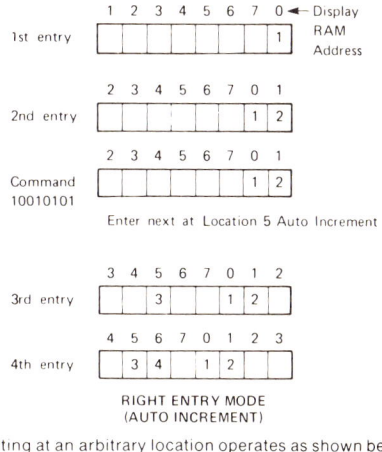

```
           1  2  3  4  5  6  7  0 ← Display
1st entry [  |  |  |  |  |  |  | 1]  RAM Address

           2  3  4  5  6  7  0  1
2nd entry [  |  |  |  |  |  | 1| 2]

Command    2  3  4  5  6  7  0  1
10010101  [  |  |  |  |  |  | 1| 2]
Enter next at Location 5 Auto Increment

           3  4  5  6  7  0  1  2
3rd entry [  |  | 3|  |  |  | 1| 2]

           4  5  6  7  0  1  2  3
4th entry [  | 3| 4|  |  | 1| 2|  ]

       RIGHT ENTRY MODE
       (AUTO INCREMENT)
```

Starting at an arbitrary location operates as shown below:

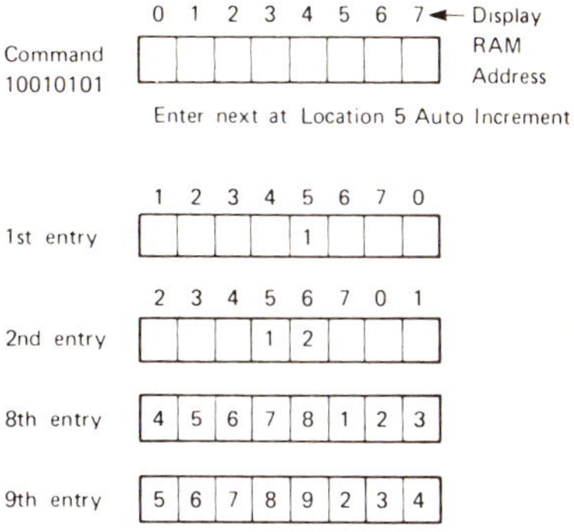

```
Command    0  1  2  3  4  5  6  7 ← Display
10010101  [  |  |  |  |  |  |  |  ]  RAM Address
Enter next at Location 5 Auto Increment

           1  2  3  4  5  6  7  0
1st entry [  |  |  |  | 1|  |  |  ]

           2  3  4  5  6  7  0  1
2nd entry [  |  |  | 1| 2|  |  |  ]

           
8th entry [ 4| 5| 6| 7| 8| 1| 2| 3]

           
9th entry [ 5| 6| 7| 8| 9| 2| 3| 4]

       RIGHT ENTRY MODE
       (AUTO INCREMENT)
```

8279/8279-5

Entry appears to be from the initial entry point.

8/16 Character Display Formats

If the display mode is set to an 8 character display, the on duty-cycle is double what it would be for a 16 character display (e.g., 5.1 ms scan time for 8 characters vs. 10.3 ms for 16 characters with 100 kHz internal frequency).

G. FIFO Status

FIFO status is used in the Keyboard and Strobed Input modes to indicate the number of characters in the FIFO and to indicate whether an error has occurred. There are two types of errors possible: overrun and underrun. Overrun occurs when the entry of another character into a full FIFO is attempted. Underrun occurs when the CPU tries to read an empty FIFO.

The FIFO status word also has a bit to indicate that the Display RAM was unavailable because a Clear Display or Clear All command had not completed its clearing operation.

In a Sensor Matrix mode, a bit is set in the FIFO status word to indicate that at least one sensor closure indication is contained in the Sensor RAM.

In Special Error Mode the S/E bit is showing the error flip and serves as an indication to whether a simultaneous multiple closure error has occurred.

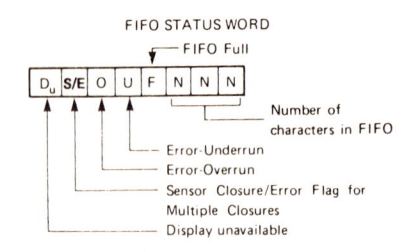

FIFO STATUS WORD

| D_u | S/E | O | U | F | N | N | N |

- FIFO Full
- Number of characters in FIFO
- Error-Underrun
- Error-Overrun
- Sensor Closure/Error Flag for Multiple Closures
- Display unavailable

APPLICATIONS

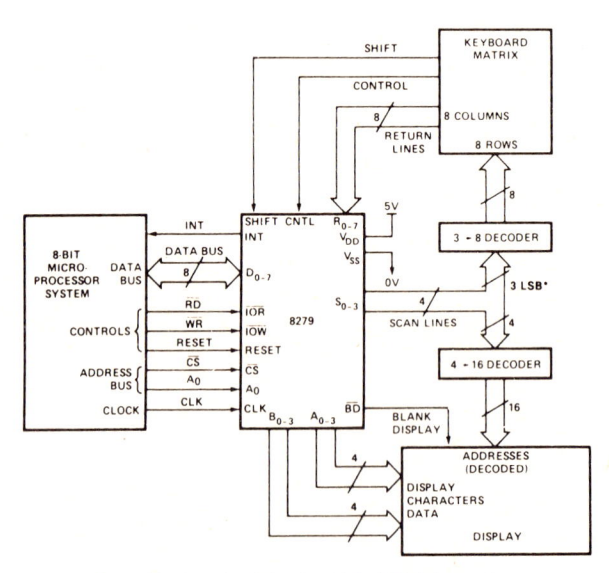

*Do not drive the keyboard decoder with the MSB of the scan lines.

8279/8279-5

ABSOLUTE MAXIMUM RATINGS*

Ambient Temperature .... 0°C to 70°C
Storage Temperature .... -65°C to 125°C
Voltage on any Pin with
  Respect to Ground .... -0.5V to +7V
Power Dissipation .... 1 Watt

*COMMENT: Stresses above those listed under "Absolute Maximum Ratings" may cause permanent damage to the device. This is a stress rating only and functional operation of the device at these or any other conditions above those indicated in the operational sections of this specification is not implied. Exposure to absolute maximum rating conditions for extended periods may affect device reliability.

D.C. CHARACTERISTICS

$T_A = 0°C$ to $70°C$, $V_{SS} = 0V$, $V_{CC} = +5V \pm 5\%$, $V_{CC} = +5V \pm 10\%$ (8279-5)

Symbol	Parameter	Min.	Max.	Unit	Test Conditions
V_{IL1}	Input Low Voltage for Return Lines	-0.5	1.4	V	
V_{IL2}	Input Low Voltage for All Others	-0.5	0.8	V	
V_{IH1}	Input High Voltage for Return Lines	2.2		V	
V_{IH2}	Input High Voltage for All Others	2.0		V	
V_{OL}	Output Low Voltage		0.45	V	Note 1
V_{OH1}	Output High Voltage on Interrupt Line	3.5		V	Note 2
V_{OH2}	Other Outputs	2.4			
I_{IL1}	Input Current on Shift, Control and Return Lines		+10 -100	µA µA	$V_{IN} = V_{CC}$ $V_{IN} = 0V$
I_{IL2}	Input Leakage Current on All Others		±10	µA	$V_{IN} = V_{CC}$ to 0V
I_{OFL}	Output Float Leakage		±10	µA	$V_{OUT} = V_{CC}$ to 0V
I_{CC}	Power Supply Current		120	mA	

Notes:
8279, $I_{OL} = 1.6mA$; 8279-5, $I_{OL} = 2.2mA$.
8279, $I_{OH} = -100µA$; 8279-5, $I_{OH} = -400µA$.

CAPACITANCE

SYMBOL	TEST	TYP.	MAX.	UNIT	TEST CONDITIONS
C_{in}	Input Capacitance	5	10	pF	$V_{in} = V_{CC}$
C_{out}	Output Capacitance	10	20	pF	$V_{out} = V_{CC}$

8279/8279-5

A.C. CHARACTERISTICS
$T_A = 0°C$ to $70°C$, $V_{SS} = 0V$, (Note 1)

Bus Parameters

Read Cycle:

Symbol	Parameter	8279 Min.	8279 Max.	8279-5 Min.	8279-5 Max.	Unit
t_{AR}	Address Stable Before READ	50		0		ns
t_{RA}	Address Hold Time for READ	5		0		ns
t_{RR}	READ Pulse Width	420		250		ns
t_{RD}[2]	Data Delay from READ		300		150	ns
t_{AD}[2]	Address to Data Valid		450		250	ns
t_{DF}	READ to Data Floating	10	100	10	100	ns
t_{RCY}	Read Cycle Time	1		1		μs

Write Cycle:

Symbol	Parameter	8279 Min.	8279 Max.	8279-5 Min.	8279-5 Max.	Unit
t_{AW}	Address Stable Before WRITE	50		0		ns
t_{WA}	Address Hold Time for WRITE	20		0		ns
t_{WW}	WRITE Pulse Width	400		250		ns
t_{DW}	Data Set Up Time for WRITE	300		150		ns
t_{WD}	Data Hold Time for WRITE	40		0		ns
t_{WCY}	Write Cycle Time	1		1		μs

Notes:
1. 8279, $V_{CC} = +5V \pm 5\%$; 8279-5, $V_{CC} = +5V \pm 10\%$.
2. 8279, $C_L = 100pF$; 8279-5, $C_L = 150pF$.

Other Timings:

Symbol	Parameter	8279 Min.	8279 Max.	8279-5 Min.	8279-5 Max.	Unit
$t_{\phi W}$	Clock Pulse Width	230		120		nsec
t_{CY}	Clock Period	500		320		nsec

Keyboard Scan Time:	5.1 msec	Digit-on Time:	480 μsec
Keyboard Debounce Time:	10.3 msec	Blanking Time:	160 μsec
Key Scan Time:	80 μsec	Internal Clock Cycle:	10 μsec
Display Scan Time:	10.3 msec		

Input Waveforms For A.C. Tests

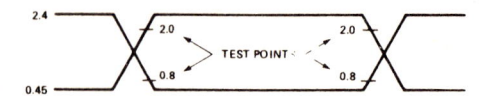

8279/8279-5

WAVEFORMS

Read Operation

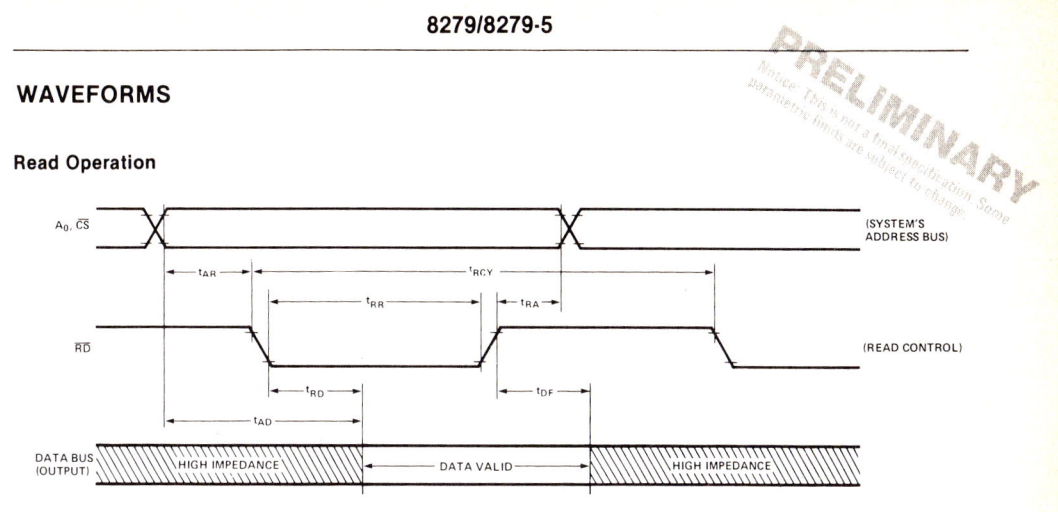

Write Operation

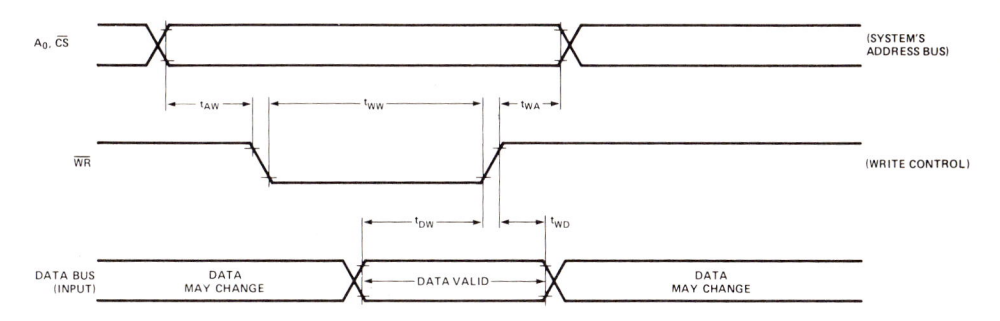

Clock Input

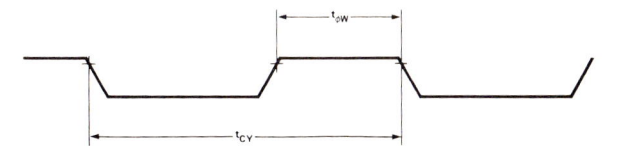

8279 SCAN TIMING

SCAN WAVEFORMS

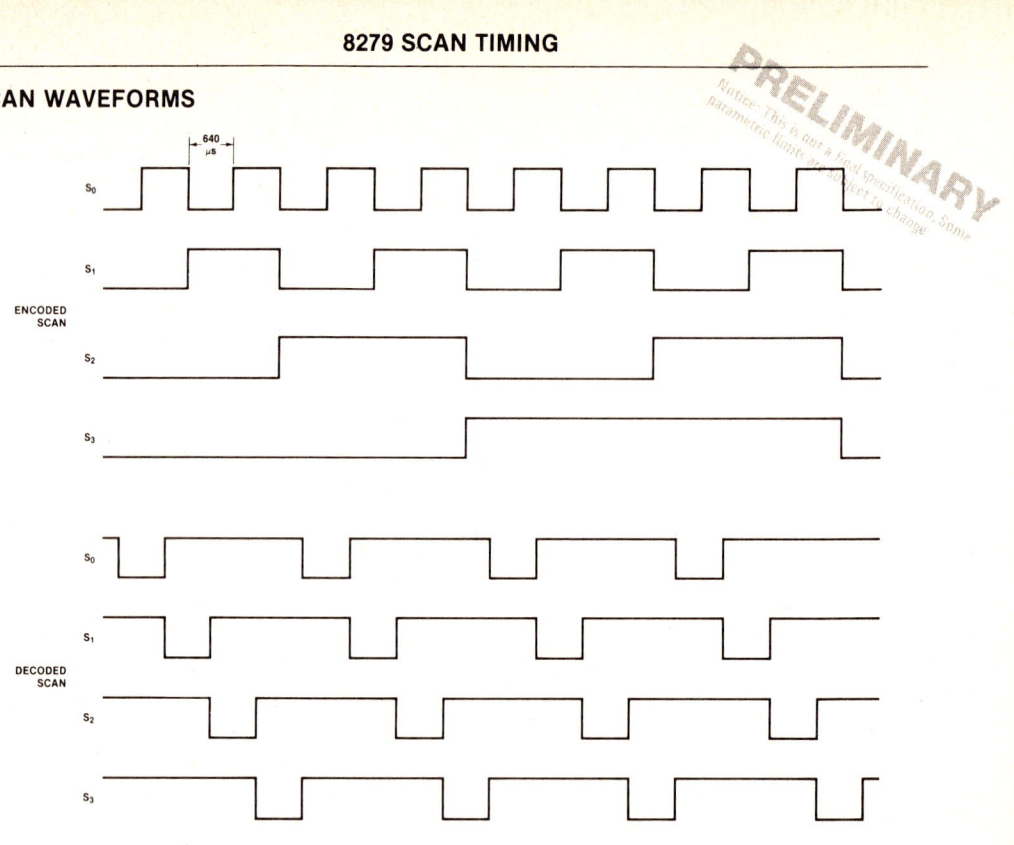

ENCODED SCAN: S_0, S_1, S_2, S_3 (640 μs pulse width on S_0)

DECODED SCAN: S_0, S_1, S_2, S_3

DISPLAY WAVEFORMS

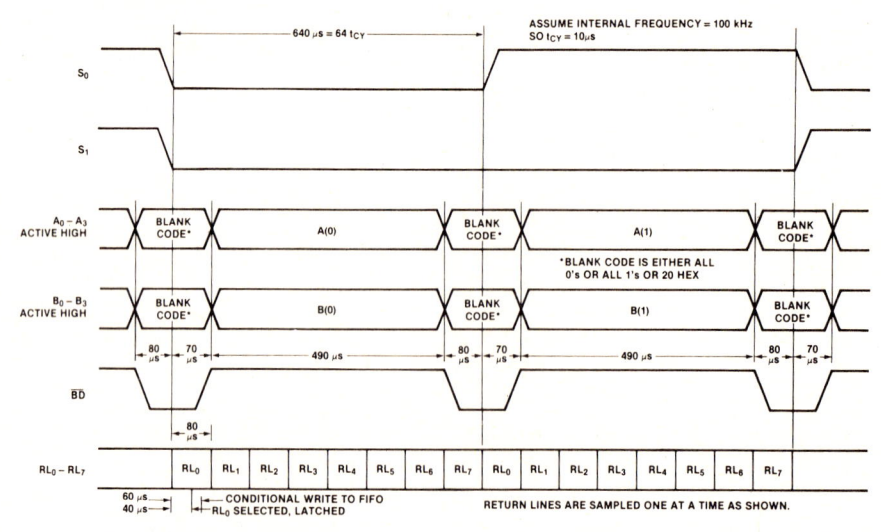

640 μs = 64 t_{CY}

ASSUME INTERNAL FREQUENCY = 100 kHz SO t_{CY} = 10 μs

S_0, S_1

$A_0 - A_3$ ACTIVE HIGH: BLANK CODE*, A(0), BLANK CODE*, A(1), BLANK CODE*

$B_0 - B_3$ ACTIVE HIGH: BLANK CODE*, B(0), BLANK CODE*, B(1), BLANK CODE*

*BLANK CODE IS EITHER ALL 0's OR ALL 1's OR 20 HEX

80 μs — 70 μs — 490 μs — 80 μs — 70 μs — 490 μs — 80 μs — 70 μs

$\overline{BD}$

80 μs

$RL_0 - RL_7$: RL_0, RL_1, RL_2, RL_3, RL_4, RL_5, RL_6, RL_7, RL_0, RL_1, RL_2, RL_3, RL_4, RL_5, RL_6, RL_7

60 μs / 40 μs — CONDITIONAL WRITE TO FIFO RL_0 SELECTED, LATCHED

RETURN LINES ARE SAMPLED ONE AT A TIME AS SHOWN.

NOTE: SHOWN IS ENCODED SCAN LEFT ENTRY
S_2-S_3 ARE NOT SHOWN BUT THEY ARE SIMPLY S_1 DIVIDED BY 2 AND 4

00742A

APPENDIX C

8085-BASED MICROCOMPUTER—THE HP 5036A SCHEMATIC*

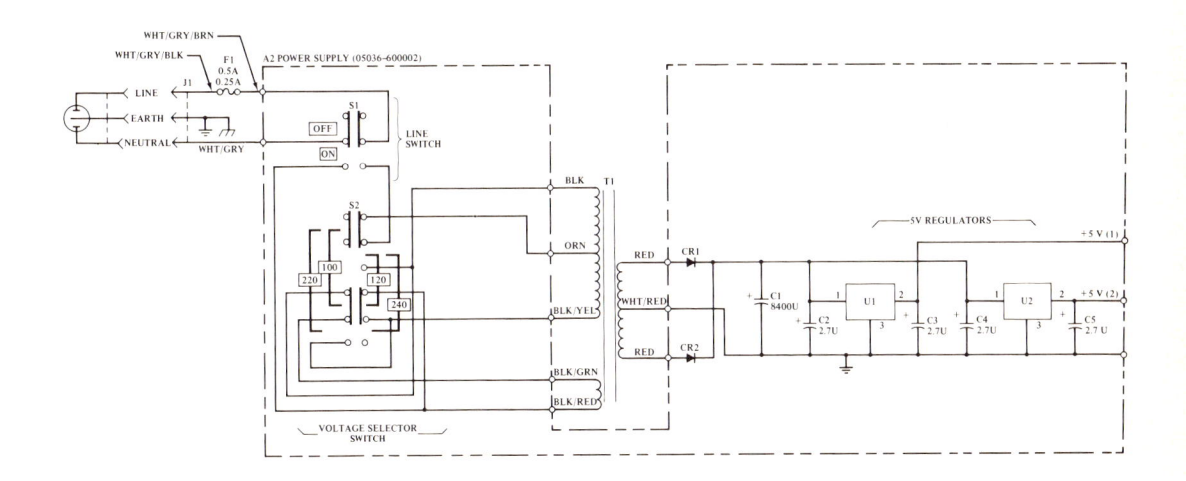

REFERENCE DESIGNATIONS
A1
C1–C16
CR1, CR2
DS1–DS19
LS1
R1–R8
S1–S29
U1–U20
W1–W14
XU4
Y1
A2
C1–C5
CR1, CR2
S1, S2
U1, U2

TABLE OF ACTIVE ELEMENTS

A1

Reference Designation	HP Part Number	Mfg or Industry Part Number
CR1	1901-0518	1901-0518
CR2	1901-0731	1901-0731
DS1–DS6, DS8	1990-0652	HLMP-6220 1X4
DS7A, DS7B	1990-0685	1990-0685
DS9–DS11	1990-0667	1990-0667
DS12, DS16	1990-0673	5082-4690
DS13, DS15, DS17, DS19	1990-0675	5082-4590
DS14, DS18	1990-0674	5082-4990
U1, U13, U14	1820-1794	DM81LS95N
U2	1820-1997	SN74LS374PC
U3	1820-2074	P8085
U4	1818-0773	1818-0773
U5, U6	1818-0438	P2114
U7	1820-1216	SN74LS138N
U8	1820-1195	SN74LS175N
U9	1820-1197	SN74LS00N
U10	1820-1112	SN74LS74N
U11	1820-1208	SN74LS32N
U12	1820-1416	SN74LS14N
U15, U16, U17	1820-1730	SN74LS273N
U18	1820-1759	DM81LS97N
U19	1820-2138	DS8871N
U20	1820-1231	SN75492N
Y1	0410-1142	0410-1142

A2

CR1, CR2	1901-0662	MR751
U1, U2	1826-0122	7805UC

NOTES
1. The trace between the terminals at J1, J2, J3 and J4 must be cut if these lines are to be used with peripherals.
2. S3 switches are shown in closed (LOGIC 0) position.
3. S1 switches are shown in closed (NORM) position. All sections of S1 must be open for freerun mode.
4. Signal mnemonics preceded by the letter "N" indicate low polarity.

* Reprinted by permission of Hewlett-Packard.

633

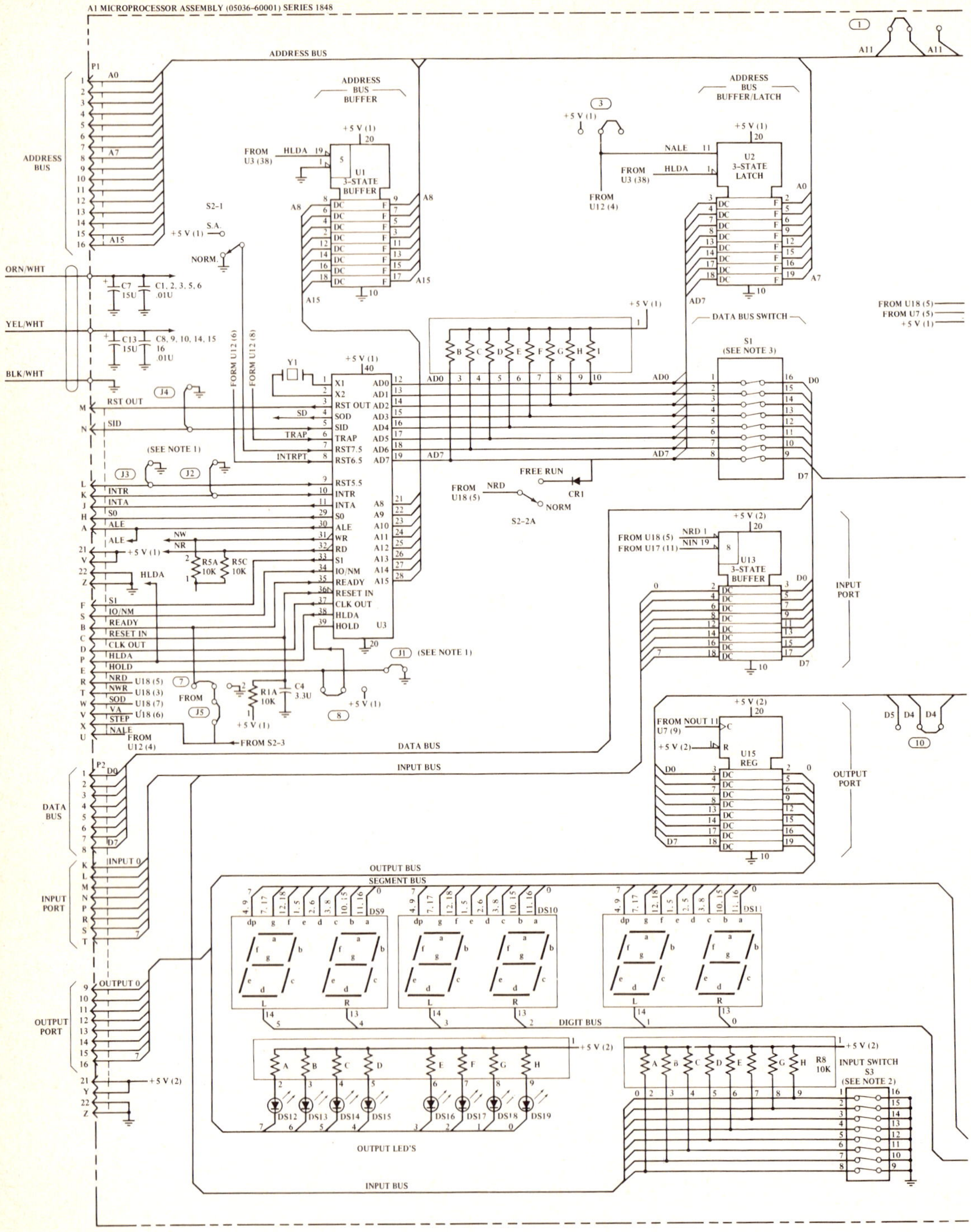
A1 MICROPROCESSOR ASSEMBLY (05036-60001) SERIES 1848
ADDRESS BUS
ADDRESS BUS BUFFER
U1 3-STATE BUFFER
ADDRESS BUS BUFFER/LATCH
U2 3-STATE LATCH
DATA BUS SWITCH
S1 (SEE NOTE 3)
U3
FREE RUN
CR1
S2-2A
S2-1
S.A.
NORM.
(SEE NOTE 1)
ORN/WHT
YEL/WHT
BLK/WHT
RST OUT
SID
U13 3-STATE BUFFER
INPUT PORT
U15 REG
OUTPUT PORT
DATA BUS
INPUT BUS
OUTPUT BUS
SEGMENT BUS
DIGIT BUS
OUTPUT LED'S
INPUT SWITCH S3 (SEE NOTE 2)
R8 10K
FROM S2-3

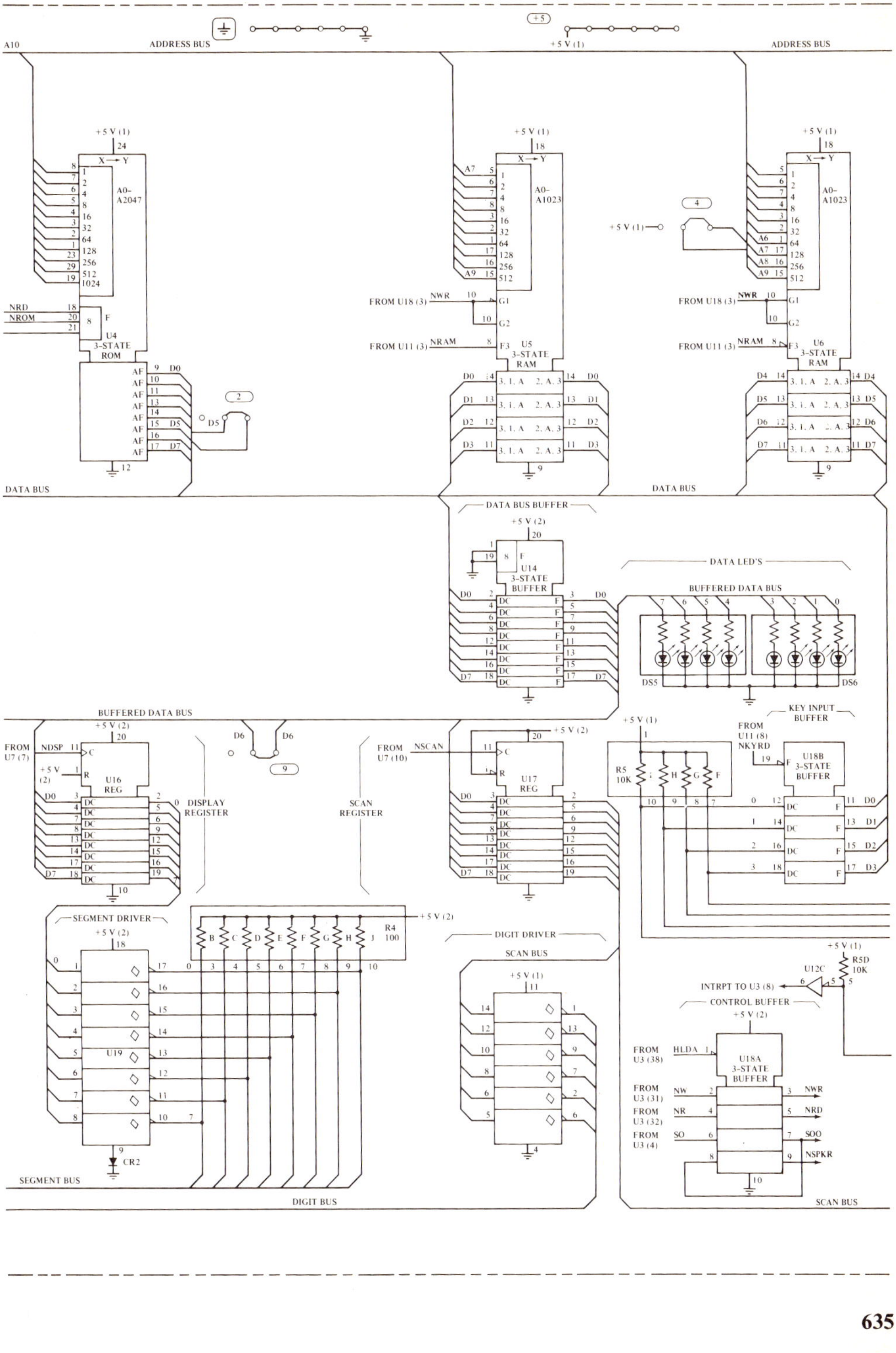
ADDRESS BUS
A10
+5 V (1)
U4
3-STATE
ROM
A0–A2047
NRD
NROM
DATA BUS
D5
A0–A1023
FROM U18 (3)
NWR
FROM U11 (3)
NRAM
U5
3-STATE
RAM
U6
3-STATE
RAM
DATA BUS BUFFER
+5 V (2)
U14
3-STATE
BUFFER
DATA LED'S
BUFFERED DATA BUS
DS5
DS6
BUFFERED DATA BUS
FROM U7 (7)
NDSP
U16
REG
DISPLAY
REGISTER
D6
SCAN
REGISTER
FROM U7 (10)
NSCAN
U17
REG
R5
10K
KEY INPUT
BUFFER
FROM U11 (8)
NKYRD
U18B
3-STATE
BUFFER
SEGMENT DRIVER
U19
CR2
R4
100
DIGIT DRIVER
SCAN BUS
U12C
R5D
10K
INTRPT TO U3 (8)
CONTROL BUFFER
FROM U3 (38)
HLDA
U18A
3-STATE
BUFFER
FROM U3 (31)
NW
FROM U3 (32)
NR
FROM U3 (4)
SO
NWR
NRD
SOO
NSPKR
SEGMENT BUS
DIGIT BUS
SCAN BUS

636

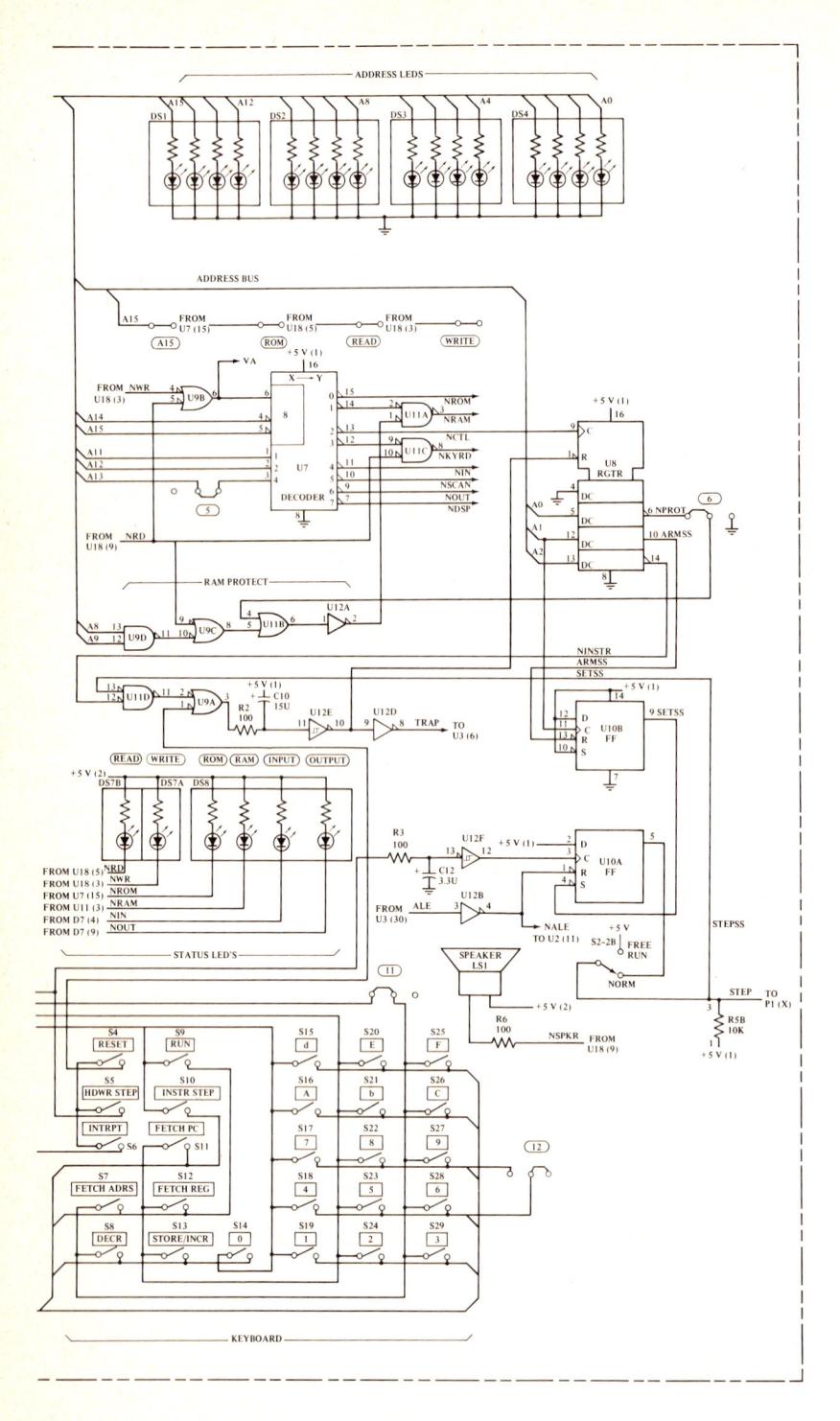

APPENDIX D

HP 64000 MISCELLANEOUS INFORMATION

System Monitor Soft Keys

The following provides a description of the system monitor soft keys:

userid
: The userid or user identification identifies each user as being unique within the system. This facilitates file management in that once the userid command is invoked all future references to files will be to files within that userid unless explicitly stated otherwise. The HP 64000 uses six characters and must begin with an uppercase alpha character.

time
: HH:MM. Allows the user to enter the correct time on the 24-hour clock displayed on the status line. This also facilitates file management since files can be referenced by time and date.

date
: DD/MM/YY. (Day/Month/Year) Allows the user to enter the correct date into the system. This aids the file management system since files can be referenced by date and time.

store
: This command will transfer files from the disk to the tape cartridge. The user specifies the file name and file type or all files. If all files are specified the system will store only the source files, linker command files, and emulator command files. Other file types may be stored but the file type must be specified. Other file types can readily be regenerated. This command will overwrite any previous contents of the tape cartridge.

append	Allows files to be appended to files previously stored on tape.
verify	Verify compares a file on the disk to a file resident on the tape cartridge. The user has the option of specifying a single file or all files on the tape assigned to the current userid.
restore	This command will transfer files from the tape cartridge to the disk. The user can specify file name or names and file type.
purge	This command will remove specified files from the active file list. A purged file can be recovered providing it has not been written over.
recover	Recover is used to recover files which have been purged. Files, if not written over, will be returned to the active file list.
rename	Allows the user to rename files. This is used to rename a file before recovering a previous file with the same name. This command also allows the user to transfer a file from one userid to another userid.
copy	Copy allows a disk file to be copied to, or from, the tape, display, or another file name or the RS232 port. The current display or a file may be copied to the printer.
directory	This command provides a listing of those files on the disk, the tape cartridge, and those recoverable files. The listing information consists of file name, file type, file size, last modified data, and last access date. Options: A directory can be made to include all userids, all types of files, before or after a specified date a file has been accessed or modified, and files on a specified disk unit.
library	This command is used to build libraries of relocatable files for use by the linker. These library files consist of relocatable files to be selectively loaded by the linker.
log	This creates a command file for all legal keystrokes. The log function is either toggled on or off by the "log" soft key.
(CMD_FILE)	This soft key represents a syntactical variable to be supplied by the user. This variable is a file name consisting of system commands which the development system will execute. A command file can be generated through the use of the editor or by using the log soft key.

Editor Commands

The 64000 editor commands are listed below:

revise
: This mode is toggled ON and OFF and allows text to be modified. Modification may include character insertion or deletion. All appropriate command soft keys including "insert" are operational within the "revise" mode.

delete
: This mode allows deletion of one line or a group of lines specified by the limit specified. The syntax "thru" includes deletion of the limit while the syntax "until" is not inclusive of the limit. The limit can be specified as a line #, string within a line, or as a start or end of text.

find
: This command allows the user to search the text for the occurrence of the string. The find parameters include a (string) consisting of a single character or any combination of characters; (limit) allows the user to specify the boundaries of the search.

replace
: This command allows text replacement of a string, a character, partial string with another character, string or partial string. There is an optional (limit) parameter that can specify boundaries of replacement.

(line #)
: This command causes the line to become the current line of text.

end
: This terminates the edit session and directs it to a specific destination. Usually this destination is a new file name. If no new file name is specified, the edit session terminates by purging the original file and replacing it with the edited file.

merge
: Merge allows the user to merge an entire file or portions of it into the file being edited. Any text added to the file being edited will be added after the current line. Delimiters can be specified to determine the amount to be merged.

copy
: Copy places specified text into a temporary storage buffer on disk for future use. The copy command will overwrite any text previously stored in the buffer. This is avoided by selecting the append option. The default value for (limit) is the current line only.

extract
: This command removes the specified lines and places them into temporary storage space. If the append option is not selected, the extracted text will overwrite previously stored text. If (limit) is not specified, the current line will be extracted.

retrieve	This command retrieves the text from temporary storage and inserts into the program following the current line. The user has the option regarding the number of times the text is to be retrieved.
insert	This allows insertion of a combination of ASCII characters, after the current line of text. Insert is executable in the command mode, revise and insert mode.
list	This allows the user to list a file to another file or to a printer in numbered or unnumbered format. The listing will be exactly like the file text. There is also a (limit) option available.
renumber	This command renumbers the edited text starting from line one.
repeat	Repeat allows the user to duplicate the current line of text and add it immediately after the current line. The user can specify the number of times the repeat command is executed.
tabset	This command allows the user to set tabs in the desired column. The user has the choice of all 240 columns. Any character can be used to set tabs in any desired location.
range	Range restricts the columns to which find and replace commands are constrained. Columns 1 through 240 can be specified. The range function is toggled ON and OFF. When ON, the label range displays in inverse video.
autotab	This function provides an automatic tab function that is based on the first nonblank column of the previous line of text. Depressing the shift and the tab keys simultaneously allows tab back from autotab position.

Assembler Soft Key Definitions

The following provides the definitions of the 64000 assembler soft keys.

Key Label	Definition
(FILE)	This indicates the name of the source file that will be assembled.
listfile	This soft key specifies the destination of the assembler's output. The options available are listing the output to a specified file, to the display, to the printer, or to null (no generation of a list). If no list file option is specified, the assembler output listing defaults to the device previously specified by the user when the userid was declared.

options   This soft key provides the user with a selection of five options specifying the type of output listing.

list   This provides a listing of the source program excluding macro or data expansion. All no list pseudoinstructions in the source code are ignored.

nolist   Selection of this soft key provides no listing except error messages. All list pseudoinstructions in the source code are ignored.

expand   This soft key lists all source and macro generated codes. All list pseudoinstructions in the source program are ignored.

nocode   This option causes the source program to be assembled without placing it in a relocatable file.

xref   The selection of this option turns on the symbol cross-reference feature of the assembler and lists this table.

Assembler Pseudoinstructions

Pseudoinstructions are instructions used only by the assembler. They produce no executable code for the processor and normally do not take up any memory locations. They are used by the assembler to make programming easier. The following list contains those pseudo ops and their definitions supported by the HP 64000 assembler.

Op Code	Function
ASC	Stores data in memory in ASCII format.
BIN	Stores data in memory in binary format.
COMN	Assigns common block of data or code to a specific location in memory.
DATA	Assigns data to a specific location in memory.
DEC	Stores data in memory in decimal format.
END	Terminates the logical end of a program module. Operand field can be used to indicate starting address in memory for program execution.
EQU	Defines label field with operand field value. Symbol cannot be redefined.
EXPAND	Causes an output listing of all source and macro generated codes.
EXT	Indicates symbol defined in another program module.
GLB	Defines a global symbol that is used by other modules.
HEX	Stores data in memory in hexadecimal format.
LIST	Used to modify output listing of program.

MASK	Performs and/or logical operations on designated ASCII string.
NAME	Permits user to add comments for reference in the linker list.
NOLIST	Suppresses output listings (except error messages).
ORG	Sets program counter to specific memory address for absolute programming.
PROG	Assigns source statements to a specific location in memory. Assembler default condition is "PROG" storage area.
REPT	Enables user to repeat a source statement any given number of times.
SKIP	Enables user to skip to a new page to continue program listing.
SPC	Enables user to generate blank lines within program listing.
TITLE	Enables user to create a text line at the top of each page listing for the source program.

The following pseudo ops are for the 8080 and 8085 assembler.

DB	Stores data in consecutive memory locations starting with the current setting of the program counter.
DS	Reserves the number of bytes of memory as indicated by the value in the operand field.
DW	The define word pseudo stores each 16-bit value in the operand field as an address with the least significant byte stored at the current setting of the program counter. The most significant is byte stored at the next higher location.

Assembler Error Codes

The following provides a description of the 64000 assembler error codes.

Error Code	Definition
AS	ASCII string; the length of the ASCII string was not valid or the string was not terminated properly.
CL	Conditional label: Syntax of a conditional macro source statement requires a conditional label that is missing.
DE	Definition error: Indicated symbol must be defined prior to its being referenced. Symbol may be defined later in the program sequence.

DS   Duplicate Symbol: Indicates that the noted symbol has been previously defined in the program. This occurs when the same symbol is equated to two values (using EQU directive) or when the same symbol labels two instructions.

DZ   Division by zero: Invalid mathematical operation resulting in the assembler trying to divide by zero.

EG   External Global: Externals cannot be defined as globals.

EO   External Overflow: Program module has too may external declarations (512 externals maximum).

ES   Expanded Source: Indicates insufficient input buffer area to perform macro expansion. It could be the result of too many arguments being specified for a parameter substitution, or too many symbols being entered into the macro definition.

ET   Expression Type: The resulting type of expression is invalid. Absolute expression was expected and not found or expression contains an illegal combination of relocatable types (refer to Chapter 2 of the *Assembler Manual* for rules and conventions).

IC   Illegal Constant: Indicates that the assembler encountered a constant that is not valid.

IE   Illegal Expression: Specified expression is either incomplete or an invalid term was found within the expression.

IO   Invalid Operand: Specified operand is either incomplete or inaccurately used for this operation. This occurs when an unexpected operand is encountered or the operand is missing. If the required operand is an expression, the error indicates that the first item in the operand field is illegal.

IP   Illegal Parameter: Illegal parameters in the macro header.

IS   Illegal Symbol: Syntax expected an identifier and encountered an illegal character or token.

LR   Legal Range: Address or displacement causes the location counter to exceed the maximum memory location of the instruction's addressing capability.

MC   Macro Condition: Relational (conditional) operator in macro is invalid.

MD   Macro Definition: Macro is called before being defined in the source file. Macro definition must precede the call.

ML   Macro Label: Label not found within the macro body.

MM   Missing Mend: Indicates that a macro definition with a missing mend directive was included in the program.

MO   Missing Operator: An arithmetic operator was expected but was not found.

MP   Mismatched Parenthesis: Missing right or left parenthesis.

MS   Macro Symbol: A local symbol within a macro body was not found.

NM   Nested Macro: A macro definition is not permitted within another macro.
PC   Parameter Call: Invalid parameter in macro header.
PE   Paremeter Error: An error has been detected in the macro parameter listed in the source statement.
RC   Repeat Call: Repeat cannot precede a macro call.
RM   Repeat Macro: The repeat pseudo operation code cannot precede a macro definition.
SE   Stack Error: Indicates that a statement or expression does not conform to the required syntax.
TR   Text Replacement: Indicates that the specified text replacement string is invalid.
UC   Undefined Conditional: Conditional operation code invalid.
UO   Undefined Operation code: Operation code encountered is not defined for the microprocessor, or the assembler disallows the operation to be processed in its current context. This occurs when the operation code is misspelled or an invalid delimiter follows the label field.
UP   Undefined Parameter: The parameter found in macro body was not included in the macro header.
US   Undefined Symbol: The indicated symbol is not defined as a label or declared an external.

Linker Commands

The 64000 linker commands are defined below:

Key Label	Definition
link	Initiates the link process.
(CMDFILE)	A syntactical variable supplied by the user. This would be the name of linker command file previously established.
listfile	Allows the user to select a destination other than the system default for the linker output listing.
display	Using this command designates the display as the output destination for the linker output listing.
(FILE)	Syntactical variable supplied by the user. This would be the name of a disk file to which the output of the linker would be directed.
null	Using this command suppresses the output listing. Error messages will still be output to the default destination as previously selected by the user.

printer	This designates the printer to be the destination of the linker output listing.
options	Soft key which precedes the selection of a linker option.
edit	Available linker option to edit a previously established linker command file.
nolist	Available linker option to suppress the generation of a linker load map.

Soft Key Definitions

The 64000 emulator soft key definitions are given below:

Label	Description
run	This starts program execution in the emulation processor. Execution begins at the location specified by "from" and ending under the conditions specified by "until." If no limits are specified, emulation will begin at the current address until halted by a "stop run" or by a boundary specified by "until." Syntax: run from (ADDRESS OR SYMBOL) until (ADDRESS OR SYMBOL)
step	This function causes the emulation processor to execute one instruction at a time. Once in the step mode, each depression of the return key will cause another instruction to be executed and displayed. The user can specify the number of steps to be executed each time the return key is pressed and the address from which stepping occurs. If these parameters are not specified, the system defaults to stepping from the current program counter location, executing one instruction each time the return key is pressed. Syntax: step # of (STATES) from (ADDRESS)
trace	This key is used to control the analysis function of the system, allowing the triggering and capturing of data of the emulation data bus. Syntax: trace in_sequence—permits tracing on a sequence of events. trace after—captures and displays data after the trigger qualifier word is satisfied. trace about—captures and displays data before and after the trigger qualifier. trace only—allows explicit definition of the information to be captured in the trace.

                trace continuous—allows continuous monitoring of trace information without reentering the trace command.

display   This command causes the system to display a variety of data types on the development station's screen. Data types can be specified as global symbols, local symbols, and last active trace specification (valid only with the analysis card), the last active run specification, the trace buffer (valid only with analysis card), contents of proper emulation microprocessor registers, absolute or relative time display (valid only with analysis card), or contents of user or emulation memory.

            Syntax: display trace
            Syntax: display register (REGISTER NAME)
            Syntax: display memory (ADDRESS)
           Syntax: display trace specification
            Syntax: display run specification
            Syntax: display count
            Syntax: display global symbols
            Syntax: display local symbols

The mode option for the trace, register, and memory display provides the user with a choice of how the data will be presented on the screen. The following modes are defined:

static	The system will display the current conditions or contents one time only. No update will be shown.
dynamic	The system will continually update the display as data are changed in the emulation system.
absolute	The system displays data in absolute numeric code (i.e., hexadecimal or octal).
mnemonic	The system presents the data in the appropriate assembly language.
offset by	The system displays program modules so that the address values are offset by a specified value.
no offset	The system displays all addresses in program modules with those values assigned by the linking loader.
packed	The system displays opcodes and operands on the same line.
block	The system displays more data on the development station by displaying multiple columns of data.
modify	This command allows the user to change the contents of the emulation memory or processor registers to correspond to data entered from the console keyboard. Syntax: modify (ADDRESS) to (VALUE)

	Syntax: modify memory (ADDRESS) thru (ADDRESS) to (VALUE) Syntax: modify register (REGISTER NAME) to (VALUE)
stop	This command halts the execution of either the run or trace commands. If stop-run is executed, it can be continued by a run command without skipping any of the intervening of the program code. Syntax: stop run Syntax: stop trace
end	Selecting this soft key changes the operating mode of the station, allowing other tasks to be performed. "end" does not stop the emulation process. Emulation continues even as other functions are performed on the system. Syntax: end_emulation
load	load_memory transfers abolute object files from the system's disk into emulation or user RAM memory. Syntax: load memory (FILE)
count	The count command is used in conjunction with a trace command. The count command is used to measure the elapsed time or the number of times certain user-specified events occurred between the start and end times specified by the trace. Syntax: count time count address = (ADDRESS)
copy	This command allows the user to transfer data from one location of emulation or user memory to the system's disk. The content of memory from which the data are taken remains unchanged. Syntax: copy (ADDRESS) thru (ADDRESS) to (FILENAME)
list_to	This command allows the user to make a permanent record of the contents of the stations display by writing it to a file on the disk or to the line printer. Syntax: list display to printer Syntax: list display to (FILE)
restart	Upon initializing the restart command, the microprocessor's program counter is reset to 0000H and the processor is reinitialized. It is important to execute the run command from the appropriate place in emulation memory.
edit_cnfg	(Edit-Configuration). This command recalls the series of queries which allows mapping of memory space and fault selection. When this command is invoked the previous responses can be modified by the user. Syntax: edit_cnfg

Following are the monitor level soft keys which will be in effect after December 1981:

    edit compile assemble link emulate prom_prog run ---etc---
    directory purge rename copy library recover log ---etc---
    uerid date&time opt_test terminal (CMDFILE) --TAPE--- ---etc---

"--TAPE---" Soft Key

After --TAPE--- is returned the following soft keys are available.

    store restore append verify tension directory ---etc---

"date&time" Soft Key

After date&time is depressed the following soft keys are available.

    (DATE) (TIME)

"opt_test" Soft Key

This executes option test, which provides performance verification tests for options that are present.

Terminal Mode

"terminal Soft Key

This puts the station in an RS232 terminal mode which allows it to be a terminal to another system.

Passwords

The capability to have increased file security using passwords has been added. Following is the new syntax for userid.

"userid" Soft Key

After userid is depressed the following soft keys are available.

    (USERID) listfile

After USERID is entered the following soft keys are available.

    listfile password

After password is entered the following soft keys are available.

    (PASSWD)

The user types in his password. This is nonprinting so he will not see on the display what he entered.

"HOST" PASCAL

"HOST" PASCAL consists of a compiler to allow users of the 64000 system to write programs that will execute on the internal host processor. In order to execute these programs the following syntax is used.

"run" Soft Key

After run is depressed the following soft key is available.

    (FILE)

After a file is specified the following soft keys are available.

    input output

After input is depressed the following soft keys are available.

    (FILE) keyboard

After output is depressed the following soft keys are available.

    (FILE) display display1 printer null

APPENDIX E

MISCELLANEOUS PROGRAM LISTINGS: EXEC, DISP, KYBRD, KYTST, SEQKY, KSCAN, VALID, MSGRQ, DBASE, SIMTOREAL, REALTOSIM, SIMKD, SIMDS*

Program Exec

```
"8085"
    Name "EXEC"
```

This program is the "executive" drive for the HP 64000 demonstration target system software. This algorithm reads numeric hex input from the keyboard and displays the data in the seven-segment display. All control keys except reset are ignored. As new data are entered the display shifts left and the new entry is displayed in the least significant digit position.

Two external programs are required for operation.

1. KYBRD—A routine that services the keyboard.
2. DISP—A routine that services the seven-segment display

This program performs the following functions:

1. Initialize the stack pointer.
2. Call the keyboard service routine.
3. Checks for noncharacter between valid input characters.
4. Shift display buffer (800H to 805H).
5. Call the display service routine to display contents of the display buffer.
6. Repeats steps 1 through 5 above.

* Reprinted courtesy of Hewlett-Packard.

```
            ORG      0810H
            EXT      KYBRD, DISP
EXEC        LXI      SP,0C00H            ;LOAD THE STACK POINTER TO 0C00H
            LXI      H,805H              ;INITIALIZE THE H&L REGISTERS
            MVI      A,0F7H              ;INITIALIZE UNDERLINE DISPLAY FOR
*                                        ;FOR BUFFERS
LP1         MOV      M,A                 ;GET DATA
            DCR      L                   ;DECREMENT BUFFER POINTER
            JP       LP1                 ;IS POINTER AT END OF BUFFER? IF NOT
*                                        ;RETURN TO LP1
LP2         CALL     KYBRD               ;IF POINTER AT END THEN, CALL KEYBOARD
*                                        ;ROUTINE
            JNC      XX                  ;DATA INPUT? IF YES GO TO XX.
            XRA      A                   ;NO, CLEAR THE ACCUMULATOR
            CMA                          ;COMPLEMENT THE ACCUMULATOR.
            STA      0806H               ;STORE OFFH IN LAST FOUND DATA LOCATION.
            JMP      LIGHT               ;GO TO LIGHT TO CALL DISPLAY ROUTINE.
XX          LXI      H,0806H             ;LOAD H&L WITH LAST FOUND DATA ADDRESS.
            CMP      M                   ;COMPARE THIS INPUT WITH THE LAST.
            JZ       LIGHT               ;SAME? YES, IGNORE INPUT, GO TO LIGHT.
            MOV      M,A                 ;NO, STORE CURRENT DATA IN LAST FOUND DATA.
            PUSH     PSW                 ;STORE CURRENT INPUT DATA.
            LX1      H,0805H             ;INITIALIZE REGISTERS FOR BUFFER SHIFT.
            LX1      D,0804H             ;
GO1         LDAX     D                   ;SHIFT BUFFER TO THE LEFT, GET DATA
*                                        ;FROM MEMORY.
            MOV      M,A                 ;STORE IN THE NEXT HIGHER ADDRESS LOCATION.
            DCR      E                   ;DECREMENT THE BUFFER POINTER.
            DCR      L                   ;
            JNZ      GO1                 ;DONE? IF NOT THEN RETURN TO GO1.
            POP      PSW                 ;YES, THEN RESTORE INPUT DATA TO ACCUM
            MOV      M,A                 ;AND STORE IN LOWEST BUFFER LOCATION.
LIGHT       CALL     DISP                ;CALL THE DISPLAY SERVICE ROUTINE.
            JMP      LP2                 ;GO TO BEGINNING, LP2.
            END
```

Program DISP

"8085"
Name "DISP"

This program services the seven-segment display for a single scan. It is called by the 64000 target system software "executive" routine. Since this routine scans one time, it must be called continually when data are to be displayed. Data contained in the display buffer (800H to 805H) in hex are converted to seven-segment data and loaded into the display register. If the data in the display buffer are greater than 0AH no conversion is made and the data are displayed as found in the buffer.

This program performs the following functions.

1. Read the display buffer.
2. Convert the data to seven-segment.
3. Load the scan register.
4. Load the display register.
5. Wait during each segment.
6. Do the above for six digits.
7. Conversion from hex to seven-segment which is done by table look-up.

```
            ORG     0A00H
            GLB     DISP
DISP        PUSH    H               ;SAVE REGISTERS.
            PUSH    B
            PUSH    D
            LXI     H,800H          ;INITIALIZE BUFFER POINTER
            MVI     C,1H            ;INITIALIZE SCAN BUFFER.
LP1         MOV     A,M             ;GET DATA.
            CALL    CNVT            ;CONVERT DATA TO SEVEN SEGMENT.
            STA     3800H           ;LOAD DISPLAY BUFFER.
            MOV     A,C
            STA     2800H           ;LOAD SCAN REGISTER.
            MVI     A,0FFH          ;WAIT DECREMENT FROM 256.
A1          DCR     A
            JNZ     A1
            INX     H               ;INCREMENT BUFFER POINTER.
            MOV     A,C
            RLC                     ;ROTATE SCAN BYTE LEFT.
            MOV     C,A             ;
            JNC     LP1             ;SCAN COMPLETE? NO, GO TO LP1.
            XRA     A               ;YES, CLEAR ACCUMULATOR.
            CMA                     ;COMPLEMENT THE ACCUMULATOR.
            STA     3800H           ;LOAD 0FFH INTO THE DISPLAY REGISTER
                                    ;TO TURN OFF THE DISPLAY.
            POP     D               ;RESTORE REGISTERS.
            POP     B
            POP     H
            RET                     ;RETURN TO CALLING SUBROUTINE.
```

```
CNVT    PUSH    H               ;CONVERSION ROUTINE, SAVE H&L.
        LXI     H,CONV          ;LOAD H,L WITH ADDRESS OF CONVERSION TABLE.
        CPI     10H             ;IS ACCUMULATOR GREATER THAN 0AH?
        JNC     X               ;YES, GO TO X.
        ADD     L               ;NO ADD REGISTER L TO ACCUMULATOR.
        MOV     L,A             ;RETURN THE SUM TO L.
        MOV     A,M             ;GET CONVERSION BYTE.
X       POP     H               ;RESTORE H&L.
        RET                     ;RETURN TO DISP ROUTINE.
CONV    DB      0C0H            ;CONVERSION TABLE FOR 0
        DB      00F9H           ;1
        DB      00A4H           ;2
        DB      00B0H           ;3
        DB      0099H           ;4
        DB      0092H           ;5
        DB      0082H           ;6
        DB      00F8H           ;7
        DB      0080H           ;8
        DB      0098H           ;9
        DB      0088H           ;A
        DB      0083H           ;B
        DB      00C6H           ;C
        DB      00A1H           ;D
        DB      0086H           ;E
        DB      008EH           ;F
        END
```

Program KYBRD

"8085"
Name "KYBRD"

This is a subroutine that is called by the executive of the HP 64000 target system software. "KYBRD" services the keyboard and returns to the executive routine with the input data (in hex) in the accumulator. In the event that no key has been pressed during the keyboard scan, the routine returns to "EXEC" with the carry bit set.

This routine performs the following functions:

1. Load the scan register.
2. Read the keyboard input register.
3. Test for an active key.

4. If a key is activated, debounce the key by requiring the key to read 128 times in succession.
5. If debounce is successful, convert the input data to a hex character.
6. Return to the executive with hex data in the accumulator.
7. If no keystroke is found, return to "EXEC" with the carry bit set.

	ORG	900H	;
	GLB	KYBRD	
KYBRD	PUSH	H	;SAVE REGISTERS
	PUSH	D	
	PUSH	B	
	LXI	B,00FEH	;INTIALIZE B, C TO SCAN BYTES.
READ	MOV	A,C	;LOAD SCAN REGISTER.
	STA	2800H	;
	LDA	1800H	;READ THE KEYBOARD REGISTER.
	CPI	0FFH	;IS KEY ACTIVE? YES, GO TO FOUND.
	CNZ	DBNC	;
	JC	FOUND	;DEBOUNCE SUCCESSFUL? GO TO FOUND.
CONT	INR	B	;NO, OR NO INPUT, INCREMENT SCAN COUNTER.
	MOV	A,C	;ROTATE SCAN BYTE.
	RLC		
	MOV	C,A	;RESTORE SCAN BYTE.
	JC	READ	;SCAN DONE? NO, RETURN TO READ.
	STC		;SET CARRY BIT.
	JMP	QUIT	;JUMP TO QUIT.
FOUND	CPI	0F7H	;CHARACTER FOUND=0F7H? YES, CONTINUE SCAN
	JZ	CONT	;AT CONT.
	CMA		;COMPLEMENT ACCUMULATOR.
	CPI	04H	;ACCUM = 4H? IF NOT THEN SKIP NEXT INST.
	JNZ	FNDA	
	DCR	A	;DECREMENT ACC. 4 BECOMES 3.
FNDA	MOV	D,A	;STORE DATA IN D.
	MOV	A,B	;GET SCAN COUNT.
	ADD	B	;COMPUTE 3 TIMES SCAN COUNT.
	ADD	B	
	ADD	D	;ADD INPUT DATA.
	CPI	0AH	;IS THE RESULT GREATER THAN 0AH? YES,
*			;GO TO HEX.
	JP	HEX	;IF NOT THEN CONTINUE.
	CPI	07H	;IS RESULT = 0? IF YES THEN GO TO ZERO.
	JZ	ZERO	
	JMP	CONT	;DATA IS NOT VALID, CONTINUE SCAN AT COUNT.
ZERO	XRA	A	;DATA IS ZERO, CLEAR ACCUMULATOR.
	ANA	A	;CLEAR CARRY FLAG.

	JMP	QUIT	;GO TO QUIT.
HEX	SUI	9H	;DATA IS HEX SO SUBTRACT 9H TO CONVERT.
	ANA	A	;CLEAR CARRY FLAG.
	JMP	QUIT	;GO TO QUIT.
QUIT	POP	B	;PREPARE TO RETURN TO CALLING ROUTINE.
	POP	D	;RESTORE REGISTERS.
	POP	H	
	RET		
DBNC	PUSH	D	;DEBOUNCE ROUTINE, SAVE THE D REG PAIR.
	MOV	D,A	;STORE KEY FOUND IN D.
	MVI	E,80H	;INITIALIZE E TO 80H.
DBLP	LDA	1800H	;READ INPUT REGISTER.
	CMP	D	;IS IT THE SAME AS D (PREVIOUS DATA)?
	JNZ	BAD	;NO GO TO BAD.
	DCR	E	;YES, DECREMENT ITERATION COUNTER.
	JNZ	DBLP	;COUNTER = 0? IF NOT RETURN TO DBLP
	STC		;YES, SET CARRY FLAG.
DDN	POP	D	;RESTORE D,E REGISTER.
	RET		;RETURN TO DISPLAY ROUTINE.
RAD	ANA	A	;DATA IS NOT THE SAME, KEY BOUNCED.
	JMP	DDN	;CLEAR CARRY FLAG, RETURN TO DDN.
	END		

Program KYTST

"8085"

```
          NAME      "KYTST"
*
*         FUNCTION: MAIN PROGRAM TO EXECUTE THE KEY SEQUENCE ROUTINE
*                   AND THEN ISSUE A 'PASSED' MESSAGE TO THE DISPLAY
*                   PANEL UPON SUCCESSFUL COMPLETION OF THE KEYBOARD
*                   SELF TEST.
*
*         INPUT PARAMETERS : NONE
*
*         OUTPUT PARAMETERS : NONE
COUNT     MACRO
          ASC       "EAGLES BEAK"
          MEND
*
          EXT       SEQKY,MSGRQ
          GLB       KYTST
          COUNT
```

655

```
START       EQU       0800H
*
            PROG
*
*
KYTST       DI                              ;DISABLE INTERRUPTS
            LXI       SP,0BAFH              ;INITIALIZE STACK POINTER.
            CALL      SEQKY                 ;SEQKY
PASS        MVI       A,1AH                 ;SET 'PA' CHARACTER REQUEST.
            CALL      MSGRQ
            MVI       A,1BH                 ;SET 'SS' CHARACTER REQUEST.
            CALL      MSGRQ
            MVI       A,1CH                 ;SET 'ED' CHARACTER REQUEST.
            CALL      MSGRQ
            JMP       PASS                  ;REDISPLAY 'PASSED' MESSAGE
```

Program SEQKY

```
"8085"
            NAME "SEQKY"
*
*           FUNCTION : SEQUENCE THROUGH THE ENTIRE KEYBOARD TEST BY
*                      DISPLAYING A KEY UNDER TEST, READING THE KEYBOARD
*                      FOR AN OPERATOR'S ENTRY, THEN TESTING THE VALIDITY
*                      OF THE ENTRY.
*
*           INPUT PARAMETERS : NONE
*
*           OUTPUT PARAMETERS : NONE
*
            EXT MSGRQ,KSCAN,VALID,KEYCT
            GLB SEQKY
*
*
            PROG
*
SEQKY       XRA       A                     ;SET KEYCT=0
            STA       KEYCT
NEXT        CALL      MSGRQ                 ;DISPLAY KEY UNDER TEST
            CALL      KSCAN                 ;READ KEYBOARD FOR ENTRY
            MOV       B,A                   ;SAVE KEYBOARD ENTRY
            CPI       0FFH                  ;KEYBOARD ENTRY MADE?
            LDA       KEYCT
```

```
        JZ      NEXT
        CALL    VALID               ;YES TEST ENTRY VALIDITY
        ORA     A
        LDA     KEYCT
        JNZ     NEXT                ;VALID ENTRY?
        INR     A
        STA     KEYCT
        CPI     18H
        JNZ     NEXT
        RET
```

Program KSCAN

```
"8085"
*
            NAME        "KSCAN"
*
*           FUNCTION :  TO SCAN THE KEYBOARD MATRIX FOR A DEPRESSED
*                       KEY ON THE KEYBOARD. IF A KEY IS DETECTED,
*                       THE KEY TYPE IS DETERMINED.
*
*
*           INPUT PARAMETERS : NONE
*
*           OUTPUT PARAMETERS :  RESULT OF KEYBOARD SCAN;
*                                WHEN A REG = 0FFH, NO KEY ENTRY
*                                A REG = 0H THUR 17H, KEY TYPE
*
*
            EXT         MATRX
            GLB         KSCAN
*
*
            PROG
*
KSCAN       MVI         B,07FH      ;INITIALIZE SCAN COUNTER
            MOV         A,B
            MVI         D,0FFH
SCAN        RLC                     ;ADJUST SCAN PATTERN
            MOV         B,A
            STA         2800H       ;OUTPUT TO SCAN PORT
            LDA         1800H       ;READ COLUMNS
            INR         D
```

```
           CPI       0FFH                  ;KEY DEPRESSED?
           JZ        LASTC
           SPECIAL CASE : HARDWARE STEP KEY
           CPI       0F7H
           JNZ       NXKEY
           MVI       A,11H
           JMP       KSEND
*
NXKEY      CMA                             ;CALCULATE KEY TYPE
           ORA       A
           RAR
           MOV       C,A
           MOV       A,D
           ADD       D
           ADD       D
           ADD       C
           MOV       C,A

           MVI       B,0
           LXI       H,MATRX               ;GET KEY TYPE FROM DATA BASE
           DAD       B
           MOV       A,M
           JMP       KSEND                 ;RETURN
LASTC      MOV       A,B
           CPI       7FH
           JNZ       SCAN                  ;ALL KYBD KEYS SCANNED?
           MVI       A,0FFH                ;YES, NO KEY ENTRY
KSEND      RET
```

Program VALID

```
"8085"
              NAME      "VALID"
*
*             FUNCTION : TO COMPARE THE KEY UNDER TEST WITH THE OPERATOR'S
*                        KEY ENTRY. A CORRECT 'CO' MESSAGE IS DISPLAYED
*                        FOR A VALID ENTRY WHILE AN ERROR 'ER' MESSAGE
*                        IS DISPLAYED FOR AN INVALID ENTRY. THE RESULT
*                        IS RETURNED TO THE CALLING ROUTINE.
*
*
*             INPUT PARAMETERS : A REG = 0 THUR 17H > KEY TYPE UNDER TEST.
*                                B REG = 0 THUR 17H > KEY TYPE ENTERED.
*
```

```
*
            EXT       MSGRQ,KEYCT
            GLB       VALID
            PROG
*
VALID       CMP       B                      ;IS KEY ENTERED BY OPERATOR CORRECT?
            MVI       D,0                    ;SET VALID FLAG, REG D
            JZ        MATCH
            INR       D                      ;FAILED TEST
MATCH       MVI       C,10H                  ;DELAY COUNTER, REG C
KMSG        LDA       KEYCT                  ;GET KEY TYPE UNDER TEST
            CALL      MSGRQ                  ;OUTPUT KEY REQUEST
            DCR       C
            JZ        TMOUT                  ;DELAY TIMEOUT?
            MOV       A,D
            CPI       0
            JNZ       ERMSG                  ;KEY VALID?
            MVI       A,18H                  ;YES, OUTPUT 'CO'
            CALL      MSGRQ                  ;CORRECT MESSAGE
            JMP       KMSG
ERMSG       MVI       A,19H                  ;FAILED, OUTPUT ERROR 'ER' MESSAGE
            CALL      MSGRQ                  ;ERROR MESSAGE
            JMP       KMSG
TMOUT       MOV       A,D                    ;PUT KEY VALID FLAG INTO REG A.
            RET
```

Program MSGRQ

"8085"
```
*
            NAME      "MSGRQ"
*
*           FUNCTION :  TO DISPLAY TWO CHARACTERS TO TWO DIGITS OF THE
*                       SIX DIGIT LED DISPLAY.
*
*
*           INPUT PARAMETERS :  INTERNAL CODE FOR CHAR PAIR TO BE DISPLAYED.
*                               A REG = 0 THUR 1CH
*
*           OUTPUT PARAMETERS :  NONE
*
*
            EXT       BUFR
            GLB       MSGRQ
```

```
*
*
        PROG
*
MSGRQ   ADD A                       ;CALCULATE LOC. OF DIGIT AND
        ADD     A                   ;SEGMENT DATA FOR DISPLAY
        LXI     H,BUFR
        MOV     L,A
        MVI     A,0FFH              ;TURN OFF PREVIOUS SEGMENTS
        STA     3800H
*
*
        MOV     A,M                 ;SELECT DIGIT FROM
        INX     H                   ;OUTPUT PORT
        STA     2800H
*
*
        MOV     A,M                 ;ENABLE SEGMENTS
        INX     H                   ;FROM OUTPUT PORT
        STA     3800H
*
        MVI     B,5                 ;DELAY WHILE
DELAY1  MVI     A,0FFH              ;SEGMENTS ARE ON
LOOP1   DCR     A
        JNZ     LOOP1
        DCR     B
        JNZ     DELAY1
*
        MVI     A,0FFH              ;TURN OFF PREVIOUS SEGMENTS
        STA     3800H
*
        MOV     A,M                 ;SELECT NEW DIGIT FROM
        INX     H                   ;OUTPUT PORT
        STA     2800H
*
*
        MOC     A,M                 ;ENABLE SEGMENTS
        STA     3800H               ;FROM OUTPUT PORT
*
        MVI     B,5                 ;DELAY WHILE SEGMENTS
DELAY2  MVI     A,0FFH              ;ARE ON
LOOP2   DCR     A
        JNZ     LOOP2
        DCR     B
        JNZ     DELAY2
```

```
*              MVI       A,0FFH              ;TURN OFF PREVIOUS SEGMENTS
               STA       3800H
               RET
```

Program DBASE

```
"8085"
               NAME      "DBASE"
*
*              FUNCTION : CONTAINS DIGIT AND SEGMENT DATA TABLE FOR THE LED
*                         DISPLAYS ALSO THE KEYBOARD DECODER TABLE TO
*                         DETERMINE A KEY TYPE
*
*
*
*              INPUT PARAMETERS : NONE
*
*              OUTPUT PARAMETERS : NONE
*
*
               GLB       BUFR,MATRIX,KEYCT
               DATA
*
BUFR           HEX       08                  ;
               HEX       FF                  ;∧
               HEX       04                  ;
               HEX       C0                  ;0
               HEX       08                  ;
               HEX       FF                  ;∧
               HEX       04                  ;
               HEX       F9                  ;1
               HEX       08                  ;
               HEX       FF                  ;∧
               HEX       04                  ;
               HEX       A4                  ;2
               HEX       08                  ;
               HEX       FF                  ;∧
               HEX       04                  ;
               HEX       B0                  ;3
               HEX       08                  ;
               HEX       FF                  ;∧
               HEX       04                  ;
               HEX       99                  ;4
```

HEX	08	;
HEX	FF	;∧
HEX	04	;
HEX	92	;5
HEX	08	;
HEX	FF	;∧
HEX	04	;
HEX	82	;6
HEX	08	;
HEX	FF	;∧
HEX	04	;
HEX	F8	;7
HEX	08	;
HEX	FF	;∧
HEX	04	;
HEX	80	;8
HEX	08	;
HEX	FF	;∧
HEX	04	;
HEX	98	;9
HEX	08	;
HEX	FF	;∧
HEX	04	;
HEX	88	;A
HEX	08	;
HEX	FF	;∧
HEX	04	;
HEX	83	;B
HEX	08	;
HEX	FF	;∧
HEX	04	;
HEX	C6	;C
HEX	08	;
HEX	FF	;∧
HEX	04	;
HEX	A1	;D
HEX	08	;
HEX	FF	;∧
HEX	04	;
HEX	86	;E
HEX	08	;
HEX	FF	;∧
HEX	04	;
HEX	8E	;F

HEX	08	;
HEX	AF	;R
HEX	04	;
HEX	C1	;U
HEX	08	;
HEX	89	;H
HEX	04	;
HEX	92	;S
HEX	08	;
HEX	CF	;I
HEX	04	;
HEX	92	;S
HEX	08	;
HEX	8E	;F
HEX	04	;
HEX	8C	;P
HEX	08	;
HEX	8E	;F
HEX	04	;
HEX	88	;A
HEX	08	;
HEX	8E	;F
HEX	04	;
HEX	AF	;R
HEX	08	;
HEX	A1	;D
HEX	04	;
HEX	86	;E
HEX	08	;
HEX	92	;S
HEX	04	;
HEX	CF	;I
HEX	02	;
HEX	C6	;C
HEX	01	;
HEX	C0	;O
HEX	02	
HEX	86	;E
HEX	01	
HEX	AF	;R
HEX	20	
HEX	BC	;P
HEX	10	
HEX	88	;A

HEX	08		
HEX	92	;S	
HEX	04		
HEX	92	;S	
HEX	02		
HEX	86	;E	
HEX	01		
HEX	A1	;D	

*
*   MATRIX BUFFER   ;

HEX	08	;
HEX	AF	;R
HEX	04	;
HEX	C1	;U
HEX	08	;
HEX	89	;H
HEX	04	;
HEX	92	;S
HEX	08	;
HEX	CF	;I
HEX	04	;
HEX	92	;S
HEX	08	;
HEX	8E	;F
HEX	04	;
HEX	8C	;P
HEX	08	;
HEX	8E	;F
HEX	04	;
HEX	88	;A
HEX	08	;
HEX	8E	;F
HEX	04	;
HEX	AF	;R
HEX	08	;
HEX	A1	;D
HEX	04	;
HEX	86	;E
HEX	08	;
HEX	92	;S
HEX	04	;
HEX	CF	;I
HEX	02	;
HEX	C6	;C

	HEX	01	;
	HEX	C0	;O
	HEX	02	
	HEX	86	;E
	HEX	01	
	HEX	AF	;R
	HEX	20	
	HEX	8C	;P
	HEX	10	
	HEX	88	;A
	HEX	08	
	HEX	92	;S
	HEX	04	
	HEX	92	;S
	HEX	02	
	HEX	86	;E
	HEX	01	
	HEX	A1	;D
*			;
*	MATRIX BUFFER		;
			;
MATRIX	HEX	12	;IS
	HEX	13	;FP
	HEX	18	;XX
	HEX	10	;RU
	HEX	15	;FR
	HEX	14	;FA
	HEX	0	;O
	HEX	17	;SI
	HEX	16	;DE
	HEX	1	;1
	HEX	2	;2
	HEX	3	;3
	HEX	4	;4
	HEX	5	;5
	HEX	6	;6
	HEX	7	;7
	HEX	8	;8
	HEX	9	;9
	HEX	A	;A
	HEX	B	;B
	HEX	C	;C
	HEX	D	;D
	HEX	E	;E

```
*               HEX     F               ;F
KEYCT           DB      0
```

SIMTOREAL Command File

```
edit KYTST
replace 'SIMKD' with 'KSCAN' all
replace 'SIMDS' with 'MSGRQ' all
end
assemble KYTST
edit SEQKY
replace 'SIMKD' with 'KSCAN' all
replace 'SIMDS' with 'MSGRQ' all
end
assemble SEQKY
edit VALID
replace 'SIMKD' with 'KSCAN' all
replace 'SIMDS' with 'MSGRQ' all
end
assemble VALID
link KYTST
```

REALTOSIM Command File

```
edit KYTST
replace 'KSCAN' with 'SIMKD' all
replace 'MSGRQ' with 'SIMDS' all
end
assemble KYTST
edit SEQKY
replace 'KSCAN' with 'SIMKD' all
replace 'MSGRQ' with 'SIMDS' all
end
assemble SEQKY
edit VALID
replace 'KSCAN' with 'SIMKD' all
replace 'MSGRQ' with 'SIMDS' all
end
assemble VALID
link SIMIO
```

Program SIMKD

```
"8085"
          NAME      "SIMKD"
          GLB       SIMKD
          PROG
*   OPEN DISPLAY AND KEYBOARD
SIMKD     MVI       A,80H              ; OPEN DISPLAY
          STA       K_CMD
NEXT_KEY_DATA
          MVI       A,-2               ;NOW SETUP KEYBOARD FOR CMD=-2
          STA       KEY_BUF+1
          MIV       A,2                ; AND MAX # CHARS.
          STA       KEY_BUF+2
          LDA       K_CMD              ; AND OPEN/READ KEYBOARD
          STA       KEY_BUF
*   WAIT FOR CR(CMD>=0)
WAIT_FOR_CR
          LDA       KEY_BUF
          CPI       0
          JNZ       WAIT_FOR_CR
*
*
          LXI       H,KEY_BUF+3
          MOV       A,M                ;GET # BYTES
          CPI       1
          JNZ       TWOCR
          INX       H
          MOV       A,M
          SBI       40H                ;<A
          JP        ALPHA
          MOV       A,M
          SBI       2FH                ;<0
          JM        ERROR
          JMP       ENDKD
ALPHA     MOV       A,M
          SBI       41H
          JM        ERROR
          SBI       6H
          JP        ERROR
          MOV       A,M
          SBI       36H
          JMP       ENDKD
```

TWOCR	INX	H	
	MOV	A,M	
	CPI	49H	;I
	JNZ	NXT1	
	INX	H	
	MOV	A,M	
	CPI	53H	;S
	JNZ	ERROR	
	MVI	A,12H	
	JMP	ENDKD	
NXT1	CPI	46H	;F
	JNZ	NXT2	
	INX	H	
	MOV	A,M	
	CPI	50H	;P
	JNZ	NXT1A	
	MVI	A,13H	
	JMP	ENDKD	
NXT1A	CPI	52H	;R
	JNZ	NXT1B	
	MVI	A,15H	
	JMP	ENDKD	
NXT1B	CPI	41H	;A
	JNZ	ERROR	
	MVI	A,14H	
	JMP	ENDKD	
NXT2	CPI	52H	;R
	JNZ	NXT3	
	INX	H	
	MOV	A,M	
	CPI	55H	;U
	JNZ	ERROR	
	MVI	A,10H	
	JMP	ENDKD	
NXT3	CPI	53H	;S
	JNZ	NXT4	
	INX	H	
	MOV	A,M	
	CPI	49H	;I
	JNZ	ERROR	
	MVI	A,17H	
	JMP	ENDKD	
NXT4	CPI	44H	;D
	JNZ	NXT5	

```
            INX       H
            MOV       A,M
            CPI       45H              ;E
            JNZ       ERROR
            MVI       A,16H
            JMP       ENDKD
NXT5        CPI       48H              ;H
            JNZ       ERROR
            INX       H
            MOV       A,M
            CPI       53H              ;S
            JNZ       ERROR
            MVI       A,11H
            JMP       ENDKD
ERROR       MVI       A,19H            ;INVALID CHARACTER RETURNED
ENDKD       RET
*
*
            DATA
K_CMD       DB        80H
* KEYBOARD BUFFER
KEY_BUF     EQU       0B40H
            END
```

Program SIMDS

```
"8085"
            NAME      "SIMDS"
*
            GLB       SIMDS
            PROG
SIMDS       PUSH      B
            MOV       C,A
            ADD       C
            ADD       C
            MOV       C,A
            MVI       B,0
            LXI       H,TABLE
            DAD       B
* OPEN DISPLAY
            MVI       A,80H            ; OPEN DISPLAY
            STA       DSP_BUF
WAIT0       LDA       DSP_BUF
            CPI       80H
```

```
            JZ          WAIT0
*
            MVI         A,8
            STA         DSP_BUF+1       ;LINE NUMBER 8
            MOV         A,M
            INX         H
            STA         DSP_BUF+2       ;COLUMN NUMBER
            MVI         A,83H           ;STARTING LINE CMND
            STA         DSP_BUF
*
WAIT1       LDA         DSP_BUF         ;GET STATUS
            CPI         0
            JNZ         WAIT1
*
*WRITE TO DISPLAY
*
            MVI         A,2             ;CHAR COUNT TO BE DISPLAYED
            STA         DSP_BUF+1
            MOV         A,M             ;GET FIRST CHAR
            STA         DSP_BUF+2
            INX         H
            MOV         A,M             ;GET SECOND CHAR
            STA         DSP_BUF+3
            MVI         A,84H           ;WRITE CMND
            STA         DSP_BUF
WAIT2       LDA         DSP_BUF
            CPI         0
            JNZ         WAIT2
*
* ERASE STATUS
*
            MVI         A,8
            STA         DSP_BUF+1       ;LINE NUMBER 8
            DCX         H
            DCX         H
            MOV         A,M
            MOV         B,A
            CPI         28H
            JNZ         ENDMS
            INX         H
            INX         H
            MOV         A,M
            CPI         44H
            JZ          ENDMS
```

```
            MOV     A,B
            STA     DSP_BUF+2       ;COLUMN NUMBER
            MVI     A,83H           ;STARTING LINE CMND
            STA     DSP_BUF
*
WAIT3       LDA     DSP_BUF         ;GET STATUS
            CPI     83H
            JZ      WAIT3
*
            MVI     A,2
            STA     DSP_BUF+1
            MVI     A,20H
            STA     DSP_BUF+2
            STA     DSP_BUF+3
            MVI     A,84H
            STA     DSP_BUF
WAIT4       LDA     DSP_BUF
            CPI     0
            JNZ     WAIT4
ENDMS       POP     B
            RET
* DISPLAY BUFFER
            DATA
DSP_BUF     EQU     0AC0H
TABLE       HEX     24
            HEX     20              ;SP
            HEX     30              ;0
            HEX     24
            HEX     20              ;SP
            HEX     31              ;1
            HEX     24
            HEX     20              ;SP
            HEX     32              ;2
            HEX     24
            HEX     20              ;SP
            HEX     33              ;3
            HEX     24
            HEX     20              ;SP
            HEX     34              ;4
            HEX     24
            HEX     20              ;SP
            HEX     35              ;5
            HEX     24
            HEX     20              ;SP
```

HEX	36	;6
HEX	24	
HEX	20	;SP
HEX	37	;7
HEX	24	
HEX	20	;SP
HEX	38	;8
HEX	24	
HEX	20	;SP
HEX	39	;9
HEX	24	
HEX	20	;SP
HEX	41	;A
HEX	24	
HEX	20	;SP
HEX	42	;B
HEX	24	
HEX	20	;SP
HEX	43	;C
HEX	24	
HEX	20	;SP
HEX	44	;D
HEX	24	
HEX	20	;SP
HEX	45	;E
HEX	24	
HEX	20	;SP
HEX	46	;F
HEX	24	
HEX	52	;R
HEX	55	;U
HEX	24	
HEX	48	;H
HEX	53	;S
HEX	24	
HEX	49	;I
HEX	53	;S
HEX	24	
HEX	46	;F
HEX	50	;P
HEX	24	
HEX	46	;F
HEX	41	;A
HEX	24	

HEX	46	;F
HEX	52	;R
HEX	24	
HEX	44	;D
HEX	45	;E
HEX	24	
HEX	53	;S
HEX	49	;I
HEX	28	
HEX	43	;C
HEX	4F	;O
HEX	28	
HEX	45	;E
HEX	52	;R
HEX	20	
HEX	50	;P
HEX	41	;A
HEX	24	
HEX	53	;S
HEX	53	;S
HEX	28	
HEX	45	;E
HEX	44	;D
END	SIMDS	

BIBLIOGRAPHY

Advanced Micro Devices, Inc., *The Am Z8000 User's Manual,* 1982.

Camp, Smay, and Triska, *Microcomputer Systems Principles Featuring the 6502/KIM,* Matrix Publishers, Inc., 1978.

Electronic Design, *Ideas for Design Algorithm,* Hayden, Rochelle Park, NJ, 1981.

GenRad, Product Bulletins on 2300 Series, 2301 Series, 2302 Slave Emulator, 1980.

G. Gibson and Y. Liu, *Microcomputers for Engineers and Scientists,* Prentice-Hall, Englewood Cliffs, NJ, 1980.

B. Gladstone, "Comparing Microcomputer Development System Capabilities," *Computer Design,* pp. 83–90, Feb. 1979.

D. Hall, *Microprocessors and Digital Systems,* McGraw-Hill, New York, 1980.

Hewlett-Packard, 5036A Microprocessor Lab, 1979.

Hewlett-Packard, *Emulator/Internal Analysis Reference Manual,* 1979.

Hewlett-Packard, *HP 64000 System Overview Manual,* 1980.

Hewlett-Packard, *Hewlett-Packard Journal,* 1980.

Intel, Press Release on Intel 432, 1980.

Intel, "New Dimensions in Microcomputer Development Solutions," *Preview,* Nov./Dec. 1980.

Intel, Product Bulletins on iAPX 43201, iAPX 43202, 432/100, 432/600, 1980.

Intel, *Systems Data Catalog,* 1981.

Intel, *Component Data Catalog,* 1982.

Intel, *8086 Family User's Manual,* 1979.

J. Kane and A. Osborne, *An Introduction to Microcomputers, Vol. 3, Some Real Support Devices,* Osborne/McGraw-Hill, New York, 1978.

L. Leventhal, *8080A/8085 Assembly Language Programming,* Osborne/McGraw-Hill, New York, 1978.

L. Leventhal et al., *Z8000 Assembly Language Programming,* Osborne/McGraw-Hill, New York, 1980.

Motorola, *M68000 Supplement Material (Technical Training),* 1982.

Motorola, *M68000 User's Manual,* 1982.

Motorola, Motorola Product Bulletins on 6800, 6809, 68000, 6850, 1982.

Motorola, *M68000 Course Notes,* 1982.

Motorola, *Article Reprints,* March, 1981.

B. Pettner, *Sample Programs in the MACRO 8000 Assembly Language for the Z8002,* Advanced Micro Devices, Inc., 1981.

M. Rafiquzzaman, *Microcomputer Theory and Applications with the Intel SDK-85,* Wiley, New York, 1982.

R. Rector and G. Alexy, *The 8086 Book,* Osborne/McGraw-Hill, New York, 1980.

K. Short, *Microprocessors and Programmed Logic,* Prentice-Hall, Englewood Cliffs, NJ, 1981.

M. Slater and B. Bronson, *Practical Microprocessors, Hardware, Software, and Troubleshooting,* Hewlett-Packard, 1979.

Tektronix, Product Bulletins on 61AX-4529, AX-4553, AX-4552, AX-4548, AX-4388, 61AX-4562, 61AX-4531, AX-4266-1, and AX-3698-2, 1980.

C. Titus et al., *16-Bit Microprocessors,* Howard W. Sams, and Co., Inc., 1981.

Zilog, Product Bulletins on Z-80 and Z-8000, 1982.

Zilog, *A Small Z-8000 System,* Microprocessor Application Reference Book, Vol. I, 1982.

INDEX

Accumulator, 18
ACIA, 300
Address decoding, 55
   address decoder, 55
   combinational logic decoding, 59
   linear select decoding, 58
   logic comparator decoding, 58
   I/O mapped decoding, 60
ALU, 18
Arithmetic logic unit, 18
Assemblers, 354, 466
   characteristics, 361
   delimiters, 354
   pseudoinstructions, 5, 355
   types, 359
Asynchronous communications interface adapter, 300

Binary and logic operations, 26
Bit, 15
Boolean operations, 24
   AND, 25
   exclusive-OR, 25
   NOT, 25
   OR, 25
Breakpoint, 347
Bus, 14, 43
   address bus, 14
   control bus, 15
   data bus, 14
Byte, 15

Command files, 365, 493
Compilers, 366
Conditional macro, 359, 360
Context editors, 5

Data counter, 18
Debugging techniques, 346, 372
   breakpoint, 347
   memory dump, 348
   register dump, 347
   simulator, 348
   single step, 346
Delimiters, 354
Disassembly, 362
Direct memory access, 63
DMA controller chips, 328

EAROM, 63
Editors, 351, 462
   character-oriented, 352
   line-oriented, 352
   screen, 353
Emulator, 486
EPROM, 62

Flowcharts, 34

GenRad Systems, 439
   2300 series, 440

High-level languages, 377
   BASIC, 378
   COBOL, 380
   Pascal, 380
   PL/M, 379
HMOS, 165
HP 5036, 496
HP 64000, 388, 457, 458
   boot-up, 496
   command files, 493
   examples, 496
   design problems, 545
   development station, 458
   function keys, 462
   loading system software, 460
   powering up, 460
   PROM programmer, 529–532
   simulated I/O, 495
   soft keys, 461
HP 64000 assembler, 466
   commands, 466
   conditional macro, 469
   macros, 468
   typical errors, 477–484
   using assembler pseudos, 474

677

678   Index

HP 64000 editor, 462
   using the editor, 464
HP 64000 emulator, 486
   architecture, 487
   analysis, 486
   beginning the emulation session, 490
   equipment, 486
   symbolic debug, 487
HP 64000 linker, 485
   initialization, 485
HP 6400 special function keys, 462

ICE, 2, 3
In-circuit emulator, 344, 349, 372, 486
Input/output, 63
   Memory-mapped, 60
   Standard, 60
Input ports, 50
Intel Development Systems, 388
   model 120, 390
   model 225, 390
   model 286, 392
   model 290, 394
Intel 432, 250
   applications, 278
   general data processors, 252
   instructions, 257
   interface processor, 268
   operating system, 278
Intel 2716, 282
Intel 8048, 98
   addressing modes, 105
   instruction set, 102
   input/output, 105
   pins and signals, 99
Intel 8085, 66
   flags, 81
   input/output, 145
   instruction cycle and execution, 70
   instruction set, 72
   interfacing to 8279, 312
   mathematical algorithms, 85
   pins and signals, 68
   registers, 76
   subroutine and stack, 83
Intel 8085-based microcomputer, 294
Intel 8085 input/output, 145
   DMA, 160
   interrupt, 150
   programmed, 145
   SID and SOD, 161
Intel 8086, 166
   addressing modes, 173
   architecture, 168
   flags, 171
   input/output, 180
   instruction set, 174
   pins and signals, 183
   stack, 172
Intel 8089 I/O processor, 181
Intel 8155/8156, 286
   command/status register, 288
   handshake, 294
   pins and signals, 288
   ports, 291
   timer, 291
Intel 8257, 331
Intel 8279, 312
   interfacing to 8085, 312
Intel 8355/8755, 284
   I/O, 285
   pins and signals, 285
   prom section, 285
Interpreters, 366

Keyboard/display controller chips, 309

Line editors, 5
Linker, 6, 364, 484
Loaders, 365
Logic analyzers, 344, 348, 375, 376

Macro, 5, 468
Macroassembler, 359
Macro Assembly, 359, 360
Mathematical algorithms, 85
   floating point, 91
   signed division, 89
   signed multiplication, 89
   unsigned division, 87
   unsigned multiplication, 87
   square root, 97
Memory, 60
   EAROM, 63
   EPROM, 62
   PROM, 62
   RAM, 20, 61
   ROM, 20, 61
Memory address register, 18
Microcomputers, 15
Microcomputer development systems, 2, 341
   architecture, 370
   comparisons, 452
   debugging techniques, 346
   hardware, 342
   mass storage, 369
   nonuniversal, 342
   op consoles, 367
   universal, 342
Microcomputer development system architecture, 370
   master/slave, 370
   single processor, 371
Monitors, 366
Microprocessor, 22
Microprocessor interface chips, 281
Microprocessor I/O, 63
   direct memory access, 63
   interrupt I/O, 63
   programmed I/O, 63
Motorola 6800, 127
   addressing modes, 127
   instruction set, 129
   I/O, 129
   pins and signals, 127
Motorola 6809, 133
   addressing modes, 135
   input/output, 139
   instruction set, 136
   pins and signals, 134
Motorola 6850, 300
   interfacing to 68000, 303
Motorola 68000, 215
   addressing modes, 219
   architecture, 216

Index

flags, 218
high-level language, 241
input/output, 216, 238
instruction set, 223
interfacing to 6846, 246
interfacing to 6850, 303
pins and signals, 227
privilege states, 216, 233
system features, 232

N-key rollover, 311
NMOS, 165
Number system, 22
   binary, 22
   hexadecimal, 23
   octal, 23

Operating system, 367
Output ports, 50
Overlay files, 3

Program counter, 18
Programming languages, 35
   assembly, 37

high-level, 37
machine, 39
PROM, 62
Pseudoinstructions, 5, 355

RAM, 20, 61
ROM, 20, 61

Serial interface chips, 299
Simulated I/O, 495
Simulator, 348
Single step, 346
Soft keys, 353
Stack, 83
Subroutines, 83
System bus, 47

Tektronix development systems, 414
   8001, 414
   8002A, 417
   8500 series, 420
Three-state bus, 43
Three-state drivers, 17

Two's complement, 26
Two-key lockout, 311
Two-pass assemblers, 359

UART, 300
Universal asynchronous receiver transmitter, 300
Word, 15

Zilog Z80, 109
   addressing modes, 111
   input/output, 125
   instruction set, 112
   pins and signals, 110
Zilog Z8000, 188
   addressing modes, 192
   CPU organization, 188
   flags, 191
   input/output, 188, 198, 206
   instruction set, 194
   microcomputer, 209
   pins and signals, 206
   register architecture, 190

85 86 87 9 8 7 6 5 4 3